Wolfram von Richthofen

MODERN WAR STUDIES
Theodore A. Wilson
General Editor

Raymond Callahan
J. Garry Clifford
Jacob W. Kipp
Jay Luvaas
Allan R. Millett
Carol Reardon
Dennis Showalter
David R. Stone
Series Editors

Wolfram von Richthofen

*Master of the
German Air War*

James S. Corum

UNIVERSITY PRESS OF KANSAS

Except where otherwise specified, all photographs are courtesy of the von Richthofen family.
© 2008 by the University Press of Kansas
All rights reserved

Published by the University Press of Kansas (Lawrence, Kansas 66045), which was organized by the Kansas Board of Regents and is operated and funded by Emporia State University, Fort Hays State University, Kansas State University, Pittsburg State University, the University of Kansas, and Wichita State University

Library of Congress Cataloging-in-Publication Data

Corum, James S.
   Wolfram von Richthofen : master of the German air war / James S. Corum.
     p.   cm. – (Modern war studies)
   Includes bibliographical references and index.
   ISBN 978-0-7006-1598-8 (cloth : alk. paper)
   1. Richthofen, Wolfram von, 1895–1945. 2. Marshals—Germany—Biography. 3. Germany. Luftwaffe—Biography. 4. World War, 1939–1945—Aerial operations. I. Title.
   DD247.R474C67 2008
   940.54´4943092–dc22
   [B]   2008015523

British Library Cataloguing-in-Publication Data is available.

Printed in the United States of America
10 9 8 7 6 5 4 3 2 1

The paper used in this publication meets the minimum requirements of the American National Standard for Permanence of Paper for Printed Library Materials Z39.48-1992.

CONTENTS

Acknowledgments vii

1 Introduction 1
2 Wolfram von Richthofen's Early Life, 1895–1914 28
3 The Great War 48
4 From Reichswehr to the Wehrmacht, 1919–1936 80
5 The War in Spain, 1936–1939 117
6 The Polish Campaign, 1939 152
7 The Battle for France, 1940 183
8 The Battle of Britain—The Luftwaffe's First Defeat 214
9 The Balkans Campaign, 1941 236
10 The Soviet Campaign Opens, 1941–1942 257
11 The Campaign in the Soviet Union, 1942–1943 284
12 Von Richthofen's Last Campaign—Italy, 1943–1944 318
13 Final Act—Von Richthofen's Last Days 354

Epilogue 373
Notes 375
Index 413

ACKNOWLEDGMENTS

This book would not be possible without the wonderful support I received from the von Richthofen family, most especially the son of the field marshal, Götz Freiherr von Richthofen. The assistance I have received over the several years of research and writing has been invaluable. The von Richthofen family allowed me complete access to photographs, letters, and family papers. Freiherr von Richthofen spent many hours providing me with recollections and bits of information on his father and the von Richthofen family. No historian could have a more helpful source.

Chapter 1

Introduction

"Baron Richthofen was certainly the most outstanding air force leader we had in World War II."
—Field Marshal Erich von Manstein[1]

On hearing the name "von Richthofen" probably ninety-nine of a hundred people will immediately think of World War I's most renowned fighter ace—Rittmeister Baron Manfred von Richthofen. Dozens of books and hundreds of articles have been written about this knight of the air, who managed to shoot down eighty of his opponents. In comparison, Manfred's cousin Wolfram von Richthofen, who was also a baron and also a fighter pilot in World War I, is relatively unknown. It is one of the ironies of history that the lesser-known von Richthofen had, by far, the greater impact on twentieth-century history. The cousin of the Red Knight went from service in the Imperial Air Corps to become one of the central figures in developing a resurgent Luftwaffe in the 1930s, successfully leading the Condor Legion in the Spanish Civil War. In campaign after campaign in World War II he won fame as a brilliant and successful air commander. When Wolfram von Richthofen's career was ended by illness in late 1944, he was one of only five Luftwaffe officers to have reached the rank of field marshal.

As a field marshal and senior air commander Wolfram von Richthofen deserves a proper biography. It is perhaps in the nature of airpower history, which tends to overplay the importance of technology and underplay the human element in warfare, to ignore the role of important air force commanders. If one looks at the military history section of any major library, or in any bibliography of airpower history, one will see that airpower history centers on airplanes. After airplanes come books about fighter aces. In airpower bibliographies one will find more than a hundred books about Rittmeister Manfred von Richthofen, as well as numerous books about British, American, and German fighter aces of World War II. When one thinks of literature about the Luftwaffe, what comes to mind are books about great fighter pilots such as Werner Mölders, Adolf Galland, Johannes Steinhoff, and the Stuka ace Hans-Ulrich Rudel. At the other end of the scale there are books about Hermann Goering, commander in chief of the Luftwaffe, and a biography of Erhard Milch, Goering's deputy and a central figure in the Luftwaffe's administration.[2] But neither Goering nor Milch was a field commander. Of the top Luftwaffe field commanders the only one to merit attention from biographers is Field Marshal Albert Kesselring.[3] Although Kesselring was an important air commander in the early years of World War II, he is of interest to military historians primarily for his role as a commander of ground forces in the Italian campaign—not for leading an air fleet in France or the Soviet Union. In fact, the lesser-known Wolfram von Richthofen was the air commander on the Italian front.

Thus there is very little written about senior Luftwaffe commanders. Compare this with the way the German army has been studied—the contrast is striking. The German army's top field commanders in World War II, including Erich von Manstein, Heinz Guderian, Gerd von Rundstedt, Erwin Rommel, and Walther Model, have all been the subjects of full-length biographies. Other than Kesselring, who was considered more of an army than an air commander, none of the Luftwaffe's equivalent top field commanders—air fleet commanders Hugo Sperrle, Günther Korten, Hans-Jürgen Stumpf, Alexander Löhr, and Wolfram von Richthofen—has been the subject of a serious biography. Part of this imbalance exists because many of the top army generals, such as Manstein and Guderian, wrote memoirs after the war,[4] but senior Luftwaffe field commanders did not. Field Marshal Hugo Sperrle could have written a fascinating memoir. I once interviewed the Luftwaffe's premier bomber expert, Maj. General Dietrich Pelz, who lived for many years after World War II. He had an important story to tell, but unfortunately he declined any offers to publish a memoir. So the picture we have of the Luftwaffe's high command consists of David Irving's very unsatisfactory biographies of Milch and Goering—and neither were field commanders. At best we have the occasional chapter on Luftwaffe commanders. There is an excellent short account of Wolfram von Richthofen written by airpower historian Edward Homze, but it still only scratches the surface.[5]

Thus the popular picture of the Luftwaffe at war consists mostly of books about equipment and the fighter aces. These are indeed important subjects, but they do not tell the reader much about the operational and strategic levels of war and leave readers with a shallow and blurred picture of the Luftwaffe's great campaigns. It is largely to correct this imbalance that I have written this biography of Field Marshal Wolfram von Richthofen. Other senior commanders of the Luftwaffe also deserve detailed biographical treatment, but von Richthofen stands out for several reasons.

As a trained engineer on the army and Luftwaffe general staff in the 1920s and 1930s, von Richthofen played a key role in the buildup of German airpower and in the creation of the Luftwaffe. In the late 1920s he wrote a study of German aircraft production that would form the basis for the Luftwaffe's first rearmament plans. As section chief in the Technical Office in the early 1930s he developed the airplanes that the Luftwaffe would employ so effectively in the first years of World War II. In his first experience as a senior combat commander, as Condor Legion commander and chief of staff in Spain, he earned a reputation for brilliance and ruthlessness. There he developed and refined the air/ground tactics that gave the Germans a major advantage over their opponents in the first half of World War II.

As an air corps and air fleet commander von Richthofen played a key role in several decisive actions of World War II. As commander of an air division in Poland in 1939 he demonstrated to the world what massed armor supported by massed airpower could do—and the results were revolutionary. In May 1940 von Richthofen's VIIIth Air Corps guarded the flanks of General Ewald von Kleist's panzer group and enabled it to drive through France from Sedan to the English Channel. This action separated the Allied armies and won the campaign in a single decisive stroke—and von Richthofen was a key author and player in that strategy. He was also a major player in several other major German victories. In Greece in 1941 his Stukas quickly broke Greek and British resistance. A few weeks later his air support enabled the German paratroop forces to take Crete from the British after a bloody battle. His air corps helped the German army's panzer forces to destroy several Soviet armies and to reach the gates of Moscow and Leningrad in late 1941. There is no doubt that the superb support provided by von Richthofen was a key factor in destroying huge Soviet forces in the first months of the war in the East. As air corps commander, and then air fleet commander, in southern Russia he partnered with the German army's master of operational warfare, Field Marshal Erich von Manstein, to inflict several sharp defeats on the Soviets. Then came the disaster at Stalingrad in late 1942, which destroyed the German Sixth Army and turned the tide of the war in the East. It was a bitter defeat for Manstein and von Richthofen. Yet the two great German field marshals recovered in time to hold the line in Russia after the Stalingrad debacle. Finally, from mid-1943 to late 1944, von Richthofen commanded the Luftwaffe in Italy in a well-fought, but ultimately futile, attempt to stop the Allied landings and subsequent advance up the Italian peninsula. A man with this kind of résumé deserves a thorough biography.

Von Richthofen served as a senior air commander in seven major air campaigns, counting Spain—an astounding record of service. From 1939 to 1944 he was always at the center of the action. In fact, many airpower and military historians regard him as the best tactical air force commander of World War II. This is a fair judgment, and no hyperbole. From 1936 to 1944 von Richthofen pioneered many of the most important elements of air-ground joint warfare to include the use of air forces as flank protection for armored forces and coordination of air support for ground forces by observers on the front lines. Von Richthofen's story is, however, full of ironies. Although he won fame for his tactical and operational employment of the Ju 87 Stuka dive bomber, he would have preferred to focus on strategic air campaigns, which he thought held a much greater promise of decision. He also had a much broader view of airpower in modern warfare than one would guess from a brief look at his résumé. Anyone who fought Spaniards, Poles, French, Belgians, Greeks, Yugoslavs, Britons, Soviets, and Americans—and von Richthofen did indeed fight the armed forces of all of these nations between 1936 and 1944—would tend to have a broad view of aerial warfare. Although an undiplomatic man, he repeatedly argued for better coalition operations and for better industrial cooperation with Germany's allies. Indeed, one of the more interesting ironies about von Richthofen is that he was one of Germany's most effective senior officers in working with coalition allies.

Von Richthofen and the Development of the Luftwaffe

A biography of Wolfram von Richthofen is a useful vehicle for examining the rise and fall of the Luftwaffe and for looking at several aspects of the development of aviation technology in the first half of the twentieth century. Von Richthofen was much more than a gifted field commander; he was also an outstanding engineer and planner. He had an improbable career, from his service as a cavalry officer to his instrumental role in developing Germany's first jets and rockets. He was also the first major commander to employ modern precision munitions in combat. Von Richthofen began his service in the Prussian army's cavalry, the most reactionary branch of the German army. In World War I he became a fighter pilot in his famous cousin's *Jagdgeschwader* (JG) 1. Afterward he was educated as an engineer and attained a Ph.D. in that subject. As part of a tiny cadre of Luftwaffe general staff officers, he played a central role in drawing up the plans for Germany's aerial rearmament. In short, he was an unusual character—a German general who was equally at home in the design shop and on the battlefield. In the career of Wolfram von

Richthofen we see the German military transition from fragile biplanes to jets and rockets. And he had a great deal to do with that transformation. Indeed, if he had never been an operational commander he still would have been an important figure in the evolution of aerial warfare and technology. He was one of the truly "modern" generals who emerged in World War II.

In this full-scale biography of Wolfram von Richthofen I will take a "life and times" approach. To understand von Richthofen one has to look at the context of his life, including an examination of the class of Prussian landed gentry that produced him, officer selection and training in the Prussian army before World War I, the experience of World War I on the ground and in the air, and how the Reichswehr of the Weimar Republic allowed him to develop as a technology expert. Finally, one must look at the relationship of officers such as von Richthofen with German chancellor and Führer Adolf Hitler and the government of the Third Reich.

There is ample material to work with about von Richthofen. Dealing with many of the Luftwaffe commanders and describing the combat operations accurately is difficult because of the destruction of most of the Luftwaffe operational archives in the closing days of World War II. Although there are some Luftwaffe documents, war diaries, and unit records for the campaigns in which von Richthofen played a major role, there are large gaps in the material. Luckily, he kept a detailed diary during his time in Spain, as well as from 1939 to mid-1944. Unlike many men of his generation, von Richthofen had no interest in keeping a diary before his service as a senior commander in wartime. He was not a man to put his personal life and feelings on paper. In late 1936, when he was sent to Spain to serve as the Condor Legion's chief of staff, he began to record his activities in a journal; and he wrote in it again when he was sent to command an air division in the Polish campaign in 1939, continuing to do so until June of 1944. What remains are more than 1,000 pages of detailed entries organized neatly into seven volumes. The content of the diaries betrays their purpose. About 90 percent of the content is a detailed record of military operations. Von Richthofen lays out the tactical and operational problems he encountered, his role in decision making, his discussions and debates with other senior commanders, his assessment of his own and the enemy's operational method, the effectiveness of the equipment, and so on. He often comments on how the war ought to be fought and includes an assessment of mistakes made, including his own. Although he did not admit this to his friends or to his diary, even as a lieutenant colonel in Spain von Richthofen certainly saw himself as a man destined to be one of Germany's top commanders. Thus he would have wanted a detailed record of his wartime activities for a later memoir to ensure that his version of historical events was presented.

The diaries also serve as von Richthofen's record of the tactical and operational lessons that he learned as each campaign unfolded. We know that he regularly briefed the Luftwaffe staff in Berlin on such subjects and that he also sent detailed reports to Berlin as a means of recommending changes in Luftwaffe weapons, aircraft, and doctrine. The diaries undoubtedly served as a useful record to develop his reports and assessments.

Although the diaries are overwhelmingly concerned with war operations, one also sees some glimpses of the inner man. There are numerous if brief personal notes in the diaries. These show him to be a very conventional man, interested in family news, concerned about his son Wolfram's preparation for his high school exams, selecting small souvenirs to be packaged and sent home. Sometimes he expresses exasperation with letters from home chiding him for not writing more—as if the family did not understand that the vagaries of the field post often delayed for weeks his daily letters from the front. Diaries are, of course, biased and unreliable—but this one provides some useful insights into his personality and his views. Von Richthofen was well known for maintaining an outward appearance of calm under stress. But in the evenings he would occasionally pour out some of his feelings and frustrations into his diary. His entries contain numerous acerbic, often harsh, comments about other German officers. Some of his comments are fair, others patently unfair. After the war the von Richthofen diaries remained in the family's possession, and his wife, Baroness Jutta von Richthofen, did not allow them to be released for public use until twenty-five years later because the many caustic comments in them would have been hurtful to too many living people. She was probably right. In the decades immediately after World War II, the offhand comments von Richthofen made throughout his diaries would have generated considerable controversy and bogged down historians in a largely fruitless discussion based on the personality clashes between German generals. Following the death of many major characters noted in the diaries, the von Richthofen family passed them on to the German Military Archives, where they are readily available to historians.

In addition to the diaries are the accounts of Luftwaffe generals written shortly after World War II that analyzed various campaigns. A number of senior Luftwaffe officers became prisoners of the U.S. Army after the war, and many were put to work writing histories and analyses. Because von Richthofen played such a large role in the Luftwaffe, and because so many of the Luftwaffe's senior officers served with him, many of the studies comment on his personality and leadership—and what they tell us is fairly consistent. Authors of historical monographs on the Luftwaffe that contain considerable information on von Richthofen include Luftwaffe generals Wilhelm Speidel,

Hermann Plocher, Paul Deichmann, and Hans-Detlef Hehrhudt von Rohden. All of these officers served under von Richthofen during World War II.[6] Now known as the Karlsruhe Collection, after the German city where the project was initiated, the monograph collection covers almost every campaign and aspect of the German army and Luftwaffe operations during the war. The studies concerning the Luftwaffe, including many that were never published or translated into English, are available at the U.S. Air Force archives at Maxwell Air Force Base, Alabama. A collection of studies written on ground operations is held at the U.S. Army Command and Staff College Library in Ft. Leavenworth, Kansas; many of these studies also provide insights into Luftwaffe operations.

This book also rests on the works of outstanding airpower historians who have written superb accounts of various Luftwaffe campaigns in which von Richthofen played a leading role. Several other works feature various aspects of Luftwaffe development and strategy and also have much to say about von Richthofen's role in those aspects of the Luftwaffe. Foremost of the Luftwaffe historians is Horst Boog, author of *Die deutsche Luftwaffenführung, 1935–1945*.[7] Boog's detailed 700-page book is simply the best single work on Luftwaffe leadership and thinking. It is a necessary starting point for any Luftwaffe scholar. For a detailed overview of the Luftwaffe in various campaigns, the sections on Luftwaffe history written by Colonel Doctor Klaus Meier in the ten volumes of the German official history of World War II (*Das deutsche Reich im Zweiten Weltkrieg*) is another essential starting point. Meier provides an insightful and detailed analysis of the Luftwaffe's part in major blitzkrieg campaigns and should be required reading for anyone studying airpower in World War II. Most of the volumes of the German official history have been translated into English. For the interwar period and the development of the Luftwaffe, Edward Homze's *Arming the Luftwaffe* is an outstanding work of research. Homze provides considerable detail about von Richthofen's role in developing the Luftwaffe's aircraft in the 1930s.[8] Joel Hayward's *Stopped at Stalingrad* thoroughly analyzes von Richthofen's performance as VIIIth Air Corps 4th Air Fleet commander in the 1942–1943 campaigns in the Soviet Union. Hayward has much to say about von Richthofen as a commander, and he describes von Richthofen's great success in the Crimean campaign in 1942 as well as his great failure at Stalingrad a few months later. The book is essential for anyone studying the history of the war on the eastern front.[9] If one wants a broader perspective on the Luftwaffe and the war on the eastern front, Richard Muller's *The German Air War in Russia* is an exceptionally useful work.[10] Each of these scholars has done groundbreaking work and provided important insights into aspects of Wolfram von Richthofen's personality and leadership.

Von Richthofen as a Military Commander

In book one, chapter 3 ("On Military Genius") in his grand treatise *On War*, Carl von Clausewitz outlines some of the qualities required to be a successful senior commander.[11] First are courage, both physical and moral, and a thorough knowledge of one's profession. Wolfram von Richthofen possessed both qualities in abundance. From the time he was a second-lieutenant cavalry platoon commander in World War I up to his service as a colonel general commanding an air fleet, he repeatedly exposed himself to enemy fire as he led his forces from the front. His subordinates often remarked that von Richthofen remained incredibly calm under fire. As commander of the VIIIth Air Corps he carried out his own aerial reconnaissance on the front lines and was hit by enemy (and German) antiaircraft fire on several occasions. Frankly, it is a wonder that he was never wounded in battle. When directing operations from his headquarters, he remained immune from panic as unfavorable information flowed in. He understood that in all the fog and friction of warfare, initial reports and fragmentary pictures of battle operations tended to be exaggerated. And he was usually right. He had a reputation throughout the Luftwaffe as a "cool" character under pressure. The only time he is known to have lost his cool was when he heard of the disastrous decision to support Stalingrad by airlift.

With regard to knowledge of his profession, von Richthofen was an overachiever by any standard. As a combat pilot, and with a Ph.D. in engineering, he was a true master of every aspect of his profession. Aerial warfare demands a thorough understanding of technology, and von Richthofen's thorough knowledge of aviation technology made him one of the great air tacticians and leaders of World War II. Von Richthofen also had a thorough grasp of ground operations, which in combination with his understanding of air operations put him years ahead of almost all of the senior air commanders of the great powers in managing joint operations.

But courage and professional knowledge, though important, do not alone make a great commander. Clausewitz also referred to certain qualities that are not easy to define but are found in the most successful commanders. One is judgment, the ability to size up a situation accurately in all the fog and confusion of warfare. Another is the ability to make decisions. Once he grasps the situation, the commander has to make rapid decisions that may put his force at great risk. He might have to accept heavy casualties. But the commander also has to calculate that by making the correct decisions and having the will to follow them through, he has the chance to achieve decisive results in the battle and campaign. These are the truly rare qualities one can find in a commander, and such qualities separate the great commanders from the good commanders.

By Clausewitz's standard, Wolfram von Richthofen was a great commander. Clausewitz believed that a great commander possesses a special degree of judgment that allows him to quickly evaluate the situation, focus on the decisive point—be it a geographical point or part of the enemy force—and mass his own forces against that point. Such judgment, and the ability to make such decisions, is more a function of character than of training. It also requires a highly intelligent mind that can understand and accept a high degree of risk for a high payoff. When von Richthofen convinced the high command that the VIIIth Air Corps could protect the flanks of Kleist's panzer advance all the way to the English Channel, it was a bold and revolutionary claim. No major force had relied on airpower for flank protection before. Von Richthofen's plan put the main German panzer force at great risk, but von Richthofen knew the capabilities of his air units as well as the cautious nature of the Allied commanders, and he accepted the risk. The result was the envelopment of the Allies' northern army group at Dunkirk and its destruction in short order. France fell soon afterward. Without the bold move by Kleist and von Richthofen that quickly and decisively exploited the Allied weakness, the campaign in France might have dragged on with massive casualties for inconclusive results. For his actions in the spring of 1940 alone, von Richthofen deserves a place in the ranks of World War II's great commanders.

As a leader von Richthofen had an enormous strength of will that drove his men, and himself, to the limits of endurance. When necessary, he would push on to the objective despite heavy casualties. He had a reputation throughout the Wehrmacht as a somewhat cold and ruthless commander—and it was a well-founded assessment. His uncanny ability to act decisively under pressure was apparent during the Spanish Republican offensive at Brunete, which threatened disaster for the Nationalists; von Richthofen pulled the German and Spanish air units out of the battle in the north and quickly redeployed them to strike powerful blows against the Republican Army's best formations. Thanks to the quick intervention of the Condor Legion, the crisis soon passed and Brunete was turned into a Nationalist victory.

Several times during World War II von Richthofen's personal leadership played a major role in the dynamics of the battlefield. In the blitzkrieg campaigns of 1939 to 1942 he helped push the tempo of German operations to a higher level than had been seen before. His brilliant performance in the Polish campaign helped end the fighting within weeks with relatively low German losses. He took much higher losses in France, but his forces played a decisive role in concluding that campaign quickly. It was the same in Greece, where he delivered a stinging defeat to the British forces.

In the Soviet Union from 1941 to 1943 von Richthofen showed what well-coordinated airpower could do in support of ground forces. He proved that airpower that was carefully massed and employed in the right manner could have devastating effects against the enemy forces. In the defensive battles of late 1941 and in early 1943 his forces played a key role in blunting several Soviet offensives. The failure of the airlift at Stalingrad was one of the great defeats of the Luftwaffe in World War II. If the Luftwaffe high command had listened to von Richthofen, the commander on the spot, the disastrous mistake of ordering the Sixth Army to be supplied by air would not have occurred.

One aspect of the commander's genius that Clausewitz discussed was the strength of will needed by a great commander. Von Richthofen certainly had that. He was a relentless taskmaster for his staffs and commanders, but he set the example by the manner in which he drove himself. Through much of World War II he worked to the point of exhaustion. In photographs, he ages visibly through the six years of the war. At the time of the Soviet campaign in 1942, he was three years short of fifty, but he looked a good ten years older. Most men would have taken some time off simply to preserve their health, but von Richthofen was a man driven by his deep sense of duty and, one might add, by an incredible degree of ambition. Whatever the source, von Richthofen's incredible amount of will drove him to constantly push himself and his subordinates to perfect the plans and techniques of aerial warfare.

Wolfram von Richthofen, who continually complained in his diary about the army leadership's ignorance of airpower, is ironically the man who did much to pioneer effective joint operations. Thanks to his depth of technical knowledge, he brought the art of close air support for ground troops to a level not seen before in war. As a tactician and a developer of tactical air doctrine, he again played a major role in the development of military airpower. Historian Joel Hayward, who wrote about von Richthofen in the 1942–1943 campaigns in the Soviet Union, commented on the cooperation achieved by von Richthofen and Field Marshal Manstein: "The partnership of these two men, two of the most talented operational commanders in World War II, was probably unrivalled during that great conflict. They interacted in a highly professional manner, without the jealousy and inter-service rivalry that many observers, including Goering and Hitler, expected. The specter of petty rivalry revealed itself extremely rarely, and even then it appeared only in the pages of their private diaries."[12]

One way to briefly summarize von Richthofen's style of leadership is to compare him with another brilliant air commander, U.S. Air Force General Curtis LeMay. Physically and socioeconomically, the two were opposites. LeMay was short, chubby, had a full head of hair, and came from the American middle class. Wolfram von Richthofen was tall, thin, bald, and born of the German aristocracy. Other than that, they were very much alike. Both were trained engineers and thus had an understanding of the technical side of warfare that far surpassed their contemporaries. Both men were brilliant tactical innovators. And both men were single-minded and ruthless as senior commanders. LeMay firebombed Tokyo and von Richthofen firebombed Warsaw, and neither man ever expressed much sympathy with the civilians on the ground or gave any thought to the broad moral issues of warfare. Both men were hard on their staffs and the men under their command, and the two had few close friends within the military. Neither man was considered likeable, but their staffs respected them and trusted in their judgment. Neither man showed any real talent for the strategic side of war, and together they embodied a new technocratic approach to war. In short, both were characteristic of twentieth-century air war.

Von Richthofen's Personality

All the German generals who wrote about von Richthofen's leadership during World War II describe him as an exceptionally tough, ruthless commander. He was a consummate general in the Prussian tradition; he was very much at home on the battlefield and in the command post. He never had the bonhomie of his sometime superior and colleague Field Marshal Albert Kesselring, who had the nickname "Smiling Albert" for his friendly manner. Von Richthofen's staff in the Condor Legion had a nickname for their boss and his ruthless approach to warfare. It was "The Tartar." Although Kesselring and von Richthofen worked closely together for much of the war, they were never friends. One might think this was because they were so different. In fact, it was because they were so much alike. Beneath Kesselring's friendly exterior was a soul as hard as nails. Like von Richthofen, Kesselring drove his men to their limits and did not hesitate to relieve commanders who he thought were not up to the task. Kesselring had essentially the same approach to war and high command as von Richthofen. And there is something to be said for this style; both men were exceptional commanders.

If von Richthofen was not liked much by his men and staff, he was certainly respected. No one who served with him would ever describe him as being other than coldly rational. Soldiers and officers may not always like their superiors, but they respect and readily follow a man who knows his business and is decisive. Many of his fellow Luftwaffe officers described von Richthofen as vain and ambitious. He was even called a "prima donna" by some because he used his favor with Hitler to obtain additional aircraft and support for his command. Such characteristics tend to come with the rank. On the other hand, one can detect a tone of envy in the remark. What good commander would not be ready to use any influence he had so that his commands received additional reinforcements and a higher supply priority?

However, one does find a tone of arrogance in von Richthofen's diaries. His fellow Luftwaffe officers also found him to be a cold and somewhat arrogant man. Von Richthofen firmly believed that he had a far better understanding of modern air warfare—and sometimes even ground war—than most other generals. In fact, this was probably true. But von Richthofen was rather impolitic in asserting this view of himself as openly as he did. Von Richthofen's views did not make him popular with his fellow officers, but, in his defense, he often found it frustrating to have to explain the basics of air operations to fellow generals. Von Richthofen had nothing of the courtier about him. After the debacle at Stalingrad in 1943 he bluntly told Hitler that the Führer was wrong in micromanaging the war in the East, and he demanded more operational freedom. Hitler, at first taken aback, agreed for the time being. With Hitler, von Richthofen never played the role of court attendant in the manner of Alfred Jodl, Wilhelm Keitel, or Luftwaffe Chief of Staff Hans Jeschonnek. If he had tried, he would have been bad at it. He briefed Hitler and the Luftwaffe staff many times during the war, always careful to portray himself as a field commander visiting from the front so as to distinguish himself from the Berlin staff officers. But as much as he liked being the front line commander, he also wanted to be the chief of staff of the Luftwaffe, and he lobbied hard for the job in 1943. It was a forlorn hope, as Reichsmarschall Hermann Goering would never have allowed such a strong personality in that position. But one wonders how things might have faired if von Richthofen had been Luftwaffe chief of staff instead of the deeply flawed Hans Jeschonnek. Von Richthofen would likely have done very well in the job.

There was something of the pedant about von Richthofen. At staff meetings and planning conferences with the army he would explain the basics of air support to army generals as if they were high school students. Of course, von Richthofen was probably right in his assessment of the average general's understanding of air/ground operations. But as irritating as his manner might have been, from the war in Spain to the battles on the eastern front, von Richthofen made an enormous contribution to the modern concept of joint air/ground operations. Although von Richthofen may have believed that most army generals were stupid, that did not keep him from providing the army with an exceptional level of cooperation and support. In fact, he developed some real friendships with army generals. His partnership with Field Marshal Manstein was based on a meeting of two great operational minds. Indeed, the Manstein and von Richthofen partnership was one of the most effective military partnerships of World War II.

In his personal and family life, Wolfram von Richthofen was an extremely conventional man of his time and class. He was a Prussian nobleman with many of the virtues of that class. He lived well, but not ostentatiously. He was, by all accounts, a loving and devoted husband. As a member of one of the noble families of Silesia, he was well connected with the leading families of that province. The von Richthofen clan, which was a large one, was quite sociable within its own circle. Family events and duties took up a good deal of Wolfram von Richthofen's time, even during the war. He was known to seek out distant cousins and lunch or dine with them on his travels. One of the most common entries in his diary is a notation that he had come across some distant cousin—he would have known the exact relationship—serving as an officer at some divisional headquarters. There were a lot of von Richthofens in the army, and Wolfram did his best to keep in touch with them. Often one finds snippets of news in his diary about some cousin who had won promotion or distinguished himself, illustrating his strong sense of family.

Von Richthofen had a superb mind, but it was a mind oriented toward the practical and technical. He had little interest in literature, religion, or the world of culture and ideas. Given a choice between reading a novel or a book of aircraft data specifications, he would certainly choose the latter. He also was remarkably uninterested in politics or political ideology. His politics consisted of a simple nationalism and belief in the Führer, ideas common to his class.

Yet, in technical matters he was a true visionary. He had a clear idea of the importance of airpower in warfare and understood how airpower could be used with a decisive effect. He had little patience with those who did not share his understanding, and that included most of the German generals. In his work in the 1930s we see some glimpses of a man who was a true scientific visionary. He liked the young engineer Werner von Braun very much and made sure the Luftwaffe provided support for von Braun's research. At a time when the Luftwaffe was being equipped with biplanes, he was supporting research in rocket planes and jet engines. If von Richthofen had not returned to the military life in the 1920s he almost certainly would have won an important place in history as an aircraft engineer and designer.

Colonel General Wolfram von Richthofen, 1942.

Jutta von Richthofen, 1942.

Von Richthofen was a serious man, possessing little in the way of wit or humor. In his diaries we only occasionally catch a glimpse of von Richthofen enjoying a bit of fun, cutting down a tree on a dare or having a bit of horseplay at the lake. Yet he was not all seriousness. He was able to relax with his friends and family, and he loved to hunt with other officers and friends. During the war he would dine with his staff and afterward play cards. One can imagine that he was a formidable bridge player.

His children recall that Wolfram von Richthofen was a good father. Their memories, however, are mostly from their early childhood, because from the time he went to Spain in late 1936 until his death in 1945 he was rarely at home. His only long break from warfare during those nine years came when he commanded a bomber wing in Lüneburg from 1937 to 1938. He took leave at home as often as he could and would stop at his home on the way to and from regular conferences and staff meetings in Berlin. He wrote to his family often, and his diary notes his habit of collecting various souvenirs for his wife and the children on his travels. His absence from home meant that Baroness Jutta was forced to raise their two adolescent sons mostly alone. Despite his reputation as a stern disciplinarian with his troops, Wolfram was a somewhat indulgent father. When he returned home during the war years, Jutta would relate some minor misbehavior of the boys and ask that Wolfram, as their father, discipline them. Wolfram's reply was usually something on the lines of "boys will be boys" and "they're good kids—let's give them a break."

Von Richthofen and the Nazi State

The Weimar Republic was never especially popular with the German officer corps. Officers such as von Richthofen had been raised in the old army and pledged their allegiance to the kaiser as their warlord. Although the officer corps in the wake of World War I had sworn allegiance to the German state, the old desire for hierarchy and strict social order remained. Field Marshal Hindenburg, elected president of the German Reich after the death of Friedrich Ebert in 1925, partially fulfilled the desire of the officer corps for an authoritarian, nationalist leader at the helm of Germany. The economic, social, and political chaos wrought by the Great Depression made Germany's upper and middle classes fear a genuine revolution. With 25 percent of German workers unemployed in 1932 and the communists rising to become a major force in politics, the officer corps and bourgeoisie had every reason to fear a national implosion. Hitler's rise to power and his accession to the chancellorship on 30 January 1933 were welcomed by the majority of the officer corps. Although Hitler had some radical ideas, he was first and foremost a

German nationalist, which appeased the officer corps. Hitler's ruthless suppression of the Storm Trooper leadership, the most radical and revolutionary branch of the Nazi Party, and the chancellor's insistence that the Reichswehr would be the sole armed force of the state, further cemented the alliance between the army and the Führer. Selecting General Werner von Blomberg, a highly talented officer, to be the minister of war also bolstered Hitler's prestige within the armed forces.

After Hindenburg's death Hitler took the opportunity to become president of the Reich and instituted a more dictatorial regime. Because Hitler had ruthlessly suppressed the hated communists, established a state of order, and initiated vast public works programs to put Germans to work, his popularity with the armed forces continued to rise. By 1934 the rearmament of Germany was already underway. The final stroke that cemented the military and Hitler came after the death of President Hindenburg, when Hitler issued an order that required all officers to take a personal oath of loyalty to the person of Adolf Hitler. Indeed, few in the armed forces protested this request, and many welcomed it.[13]

As the Versailles Treaty was renounced and Germany embarked on the path to become a major military power again, the military was more than satisfied with Hitler. The Führer was the strong leader that Germany needed. Von Richthofen was an open admirer of Hitler and was more than willing to cross the old border keeping officers out of politics. Although military officers were expected to be above politics (regular military officers could not become Nazi Party members until after the attempt on Hitler's life in July 1944), von Richthofen was quite willing to speak at various Nazi-sponsored events. A speech he gave at the "Party Day" rally in Lüneburg in the summer of 1938 provides some idea of von Richthofen's sympathies. Von Richthofen, then a colonel but soon to be promoted to major general, extolled the wisdom of the Führer and praised the sound guidance that Hitler provided for Germany. The Nazi Party had created a strong sense of German national unity. Under such leadership, von Richthofen believed, Germany could expect to rise again to its proper status as a great nation.

Although von Richthofen was known to be a staunch admirer of Hitler, he was, as noted earlier, disinterested in the ideology of the Nazi Party—insomuch as it had any coherent ideology beyond following the guidance and person of Adolf Hitler. But there should be no doubt about von Richthofen's sincerity. He did not need to flatter or play political games to get ahead. He could have avoided such speeches, as some officers did, without harm to his career. Why, then, did he speak publicly in support of the Führer? Because he believed that Hitler was the right man for Germany. Throughout the course of the war von Richthofen never wavered in his admiration for Hitler. Indeed, even as the war situation notably deteriorated, von Richthofen blamed Hitler's disastrous decisions on the top generals advising Hitler.

But von Richthofen was not at all unique among Germany's generals. His admiration for Hitler was a mainstream attitude in the German officer corps from the 1930s into the first half of World War II. A great many very talented—even brilliant—officers, such as Werner von Blomberg, Heinz Guderian, Walter Reichenau, and Erhard Milch, were known to be especially staunch admirers of Hitler. Like von Richthofen's, their admiration was evidently sincere.

Von Richthofen truly believed that Adolf Hitler was a leader of genius who had appeared at the right moment to revitalize Germany and lead the nation to a great future. Throughout the war, in his diary and his conversations with fellow officers, von Richthofen never expressed any doubts about Hitler's genius or leadership. After briefing Hitler in the summer of 1943, von Richthofen commented on Hitler's brilliant grasp of strategy and lay all the responsibility for Hitler's bad decisions upon the bad advice he received from "idiotic" army officers such as Jodl, Keitel, and others on the general staff. Of course, von Richthofen could maintain his favorable image of Hitler because he never served closely with the Führer. It helped too that Hitler, who had served four years as a front soldier in World War I, appreciated a true "front fighter" like von Richthofen. In contrast to the general staff officers in Hitler's service, von Richthofen could bring some clear thinking from the front lines to Berlin. Certainly this is how von Richthofen himself saw his role with the Führer. Because he met with Hitler only occasionally, von Richthofen could maintain an idealized image of Hitler as a true prophet who was badly served by his subordinates. Von Richthofen never asked himself the very obvious question—that if the Führer was such a genius, why did he choose to surround himself with yes men such as Jodl and Keitel, and incompetents such as Goering?

Very few German officers questioned the introduction of a new military oath—the "Blood Oath"—in 1934 that required all Wehrmacht soldiers to swear unconditional loyalty to the person of Adolf Hitler and accept the Führer as the inspiration of the German state and people. The German military, traumatized by the Versailles Treaty and the loss of Germany's position as a major military power, was delighted to have a chancellor who promised to overturn the hated Versailles Treaty and to make Germany a first-class military power again. Indeed, Hitler soon delivered on his promises to rebuild Germany's military and to overthrow the Versailles Treaty, acts that solidified the strong support he had from the Wehrmacht's officer corps.

Hitler's relationship with his generals was complex. Intensely aware of his lower-middle-class origins, Hitler had an innate dislike of Germany's nobles—whose instincts were to look down on a man of Hitler's background. Much of Hitler's appeal to the German masses was based on his program for pulling down many of the elites and making Germany more egalitarian. When he came to power Hitler openly distrusted many of the senior officers of the army general staff because such a high percentage of them came from the old landed nobility. Ironically, many of Germany's nobles and most of the officer corps became staunch supporters of the Nazi regime. This apparently improbable occurrence came to be in part because Germany's upper classes yearned for a return to a more authoritarian leadership reminiscent of the empire. Hitler also offered an idealistic vision of a Germany that would again be a first-class world power. Most of the upper classes were solidly nationalistic and even reactionary in their politics and heartily approved of Hitler's destruction of the Weimar system that had brought only materialism, socialism, defeat, and disorder to Germany. Hitler succeeded in rallying the military officer corps and the majority of Germany's nobles to his cause partly because he did not go too far in pushing for a social revolution. For all of his class-war rhetoric, Hitler suppressed his truly revolutionary supporters. Whatever the nature of Hitler's appeal, the support and assent that generals like von Richthofen gave to Hitler was sincere and willing.

Hitler and Corruption of the Officer Corps

Hitler bound the German officer corps to himself through a means of legalized bribery. During the kingdom of Prussia and the German Reich, the king or kaiser had routinely rewarded victorious generals not only with promotions and honors but also with grants of estates, large monetary rewards, and tax-free status. There is, of course, nothing wrong or even unusual for a nation, even a republic like the United States, to grant successful senior officers special rewards for superior service to the nation. Britain rewarded Field Marshal Montgomery with a peerage and, in his retirement, with various sinecure offices with incomes attached in recognition of his brilliant service on the battlefield. In granting the five-star rank to top admirals and generals during World War II the U.S. government enacted a law granting officers such as Admiral Nimitz, General Spaatz, and General MacArthur their full salary for the rest of their lives as well as military aides, transport, and a personal office budget even after they left office. Field Marshal Hindenburg was honored by the Weimar Republic for his wartime service as supreme military commander with the grant of an estate and tax-free status for his holdings, and the

German public approved of such honors. Hitler also had a program to reward his generals for their service, but Hitler's approach was much different and fundamentally corrupt. In Germany before the Third Reich and in Britain and America special rewards for generals were paid for out of the state budget and granted publicly. Rewards and grants to Germany's generals before the Third Reich were published openly in the court circular and through official announcements. Although granted by the king or kaiser, the gifts were understood to be not personal but from a grateful nation. Under Hitler, monetary grants were not made public and were done in great secrecy. Moreover, the rewards system was not openly published as part of state expenses; instead, rewards were considered personal gifts from the Führer to be granted or revoked at his pleasure. Throughout the Third Reich, Hitler granted his top generals large sums as a reward for service. For example, in 1942 Hitler gave Field Marshal Keitel a gift of 250,000 reichsmarks—an amount equal then to nearly US$60,000. In 1944 Keitel received a grant of 739,340 reichsmarks.[14] In 1942 Hitler gave gifts of 192,300 reichsmarks to Col. General Kleist and over a million reichsmarks to Col. General Guderian. In 1944 Field Marshal Manstein received a large estate—tax free—from the Führer.[15]

Hitler granted such large sums to so many senior Nazi party officials and top generals that a small staff worked to organize the payments. Field marshals and colonel generals were given monthly payments in addition to their already considerable salaries and benefits. When he became a field marshal in 1943, von Richthofen was placed on the "List C" payment schedule and received a regular monthly payment of 4,000 reichsmarks (about US$950)—a standard sum for field marshals and grand admirals. Another list, with smaller sums, was prepared for colonel generals.[16] To provide some idea of the scale of Hitler's magnanimity, von Richthofen's monthly payment from the Führer was approximately the yearly pay for a skilled worker in 1943. So that the payments would not be recorded by the German revenue authorities and income tax could be evaded, the checks were made "payable to the bearer."[17]

Von Richthofen, and virtually all of Germany's top generals, played along with this secret rewards program. Because of the personal nature of the gifts from Hitler to his generals, Germany's top generals were even more closely bound to the Führer by means of a personalized economic dependence and even a winked-at program of tax evasion. Von Richthofen certainly earned the promotions and medals publicly granted to him. Even in a democracy he would have been granted special honors and rewards for his brilliant military performance in the campaigns of 1939–1941. So von Richthofen, like most of his fellow senior officers, cheerfully accepted the large sums granted to him by Hitler. This helps to explain the means by which Hitler maintained his control of the military, even to the last days of the war.

The Question of War Crimes

One cannot properly write about the life of a German World War II field marshal without discussing the moral responsibility of the German military leaders for the actions of a criminal regime and to further examine the role that senior military leaders played in ordering or actively participating in war crimes.

Today Wolfram von Richthofen is often regarded as a war criminal, especially in the popular German press, because he was responsible for the bombing of Guernica in April 1937 and Warsaw in September 1939.[18] The tendency to paint von Richthofen as a war criminal for these acts is based on mythology that has grown up around the bombing of Guernica—characterized as the first use of "terror bombing" in history, the destruction of a city with the intention of killing civilians in order to terrorize the enemy into surrender.[19] In fact, as we shall see in Chapter 5, Guernica was a tactical operation carried out for sound tactical military reasons. It was, in fact, just one of many small towns that were bombed during the Spanish Civil War. In this case, the town was targeted because it was a road hub whose destruction would inhibit the retreat of a large part of the Basque army. Inaccurate and sensational press coverage, grossly inflated casualty figures, and a famous painting by Picasso all worked to portray Guernica as a massacre of innocent civilians.[20] The official casualty figures of the bombing raid were given as 1,647 dead. This incredibly high figure and the description of the raid as essentially a terror attack have been endlessly repeated since 1937.[21] In reality, the total death toll at Guernica was approximately 300, and the raid was never intended to be a model for aerial terror attacks.[22]

A similar mythology developed over the bombing of Warsaw by von Richthofen's forces in September 1939. In this case, the aerial attack had all the characteristics of a terror raid.[23] On September 25 von Richthofen's air units dropped 632 tons of high explosive and incendiary bombs on Warsaw, killing perhaps 6,000 civilians and destroying a portion of the city. Since bombers were not available, von Richthofen used Ju 52 transports as bombers. The transports lumbered over the city as airmen literally shoveled thousands of small incendiary bombs out the cargo doors.[24] The bombing of Warsaw received sensational press coverage, and casualty estimates ranged from 20,000 to 40,000 dead.[25] As with Guernica, the casualties and effects of the raid were grossly overestimated. There is no doubt that the bombing of Warsaw was a cruel act of war, but in September 1939 Warsaw was a defended city under siege with at least 150,000 troops manning its defenses. Under the rules of war and international law as they were commonly understood in 1939, the city was a legitimate target for aerial bombardment.[26] Indeed, the Germans had sound military reasons to avoid a street-by-street battle for Warsaw and to prefer aerial bombardment to force the city's surrender. But the sensational coverage of the battle in the world press gave the impression that the Luftwaffe's way of war was about the indiscriminate bombing of civilians. In reality, the Luftwaffe of 1939 had relatively little capability for massive strategic bombardment even if this had been its doctrine.

Hugely inflated casualty figures also accompany the accounts of von Richthofen's bombing of Stalingrad in August 1942. The popular historical figure is 40,000 dead—supposedly more people than were killed by the massive British fire raid on Hamburg in August 1943.[27] It is utterly improbable that von Richthofen's relatively small number of medium bombers and Stukas could inflict more damage and casualties than a massive raid by the Royal Air Force's heaviest bombers. In the Hamburg raid, the RAF dropped approximately seven times the bomb tonnage (6,928 tons of bombs) that von Richthofen dropped at Stalingrad (about 1,000 tons).[28] One can only wonder how Luftwaffe bombs were seven times more lethal than RAF bombs. Indeed, any realistic estimate would have to put the Stalingrad death count at below 10,000.

Some individuals are so eager to make von Richthofen into a ruthless city bomber that for the bombing of Belgrade in April 1941 he is credited by one historian with killing 17,000 people and having "reduced the city to rubble."[29] In fact, the 4th Air Fleet bombed Belgrade in April 1941—not von Richthofen's VIIIth Air Corps.[30] Von Richthofen was busy attacking positions in northern Greece that day, and most of the VIIIth Air Corps aircraft lacked the range to fly to Belgrade from their airfields in Bulgaria. The figure of 17,000 dead in Belgrade was, like the Stalingrad figure, pulled from thin air. One thousand to 3,000 casualties is a more probable range considering the number of aircraft involved and bomb tonnage dropped.

Such emotionally colored and uncritical analysis—coupled with little serious document research—unfortunately tends to be the norm in discussing World War II bombing raids. One can understand how events would be sensationalized at the time with the press eager to print any account of a bombing raid that appeared plausible. But writing decades later, historians can separate the sensational and propagandistic from fact. Wolfram von Richthofen was not a master of "terror bombing" and never made city bombing his primary operational method. When he bombed towns and cities he did it for justifiable tactical and operational reasons. His manner was ruthless, and he never expressed any moral qualms about his actions, nor did he show any sympathy for the people he bombed. His actions were part of a carefully calculated ruthlessness that one accepts in warfare. But in this attitude, von Richthofen was essentially no different than most of the senior Allied air commanders of World War II. As the Allied armies fought their war into Germany in late 1944, German towns and cities behind the lines that contained Wehrmacht reserve forces or served as logistics centers were attacked by British and American bombers with consequent civilian casualties—just like Guernica. In March 1945, American bombers leveled several small German towns that contained rail junctions in an effort to paralyze the German transportation net. Again, civilian casualties were high. Yet there is no record that Allied air commanders ever agonized over the morality of these attacks. These were acts of war that damaged the enemy war-making capability and gave the Allied forces a military advantage.

In the 1930s and during World War II there were some clear international rules dealing with the conduct of war on land and sea, but little specific guidance on the conduct of aerial warfare against an enemy homeland.[31] A few principles were generally recognized. The Hague Convention of 1907 established several rules for protecting civilians in wartime. Specifically, Article 25 forbade the bombardment of an undefended declared "open city."[32] Article 23 judged it unlawful to attack civilian targets except as required by "military necessity." Article 27 listed monuments, churches, and hospitals as specially protected facilities.[33] Yet it was understood that there were huge loopholes in the rules. International negotiators of the interwar period understood that military forces, military installations, armaments factories, storage areas, shipyards, and rail yards were still legitimate targets for an air force and that corresponding civilian casualties would be regrettable, but such casualties would be the result of the military necessity of bombing clearly military targets.[34] The air campaigns of World War I had let the genie out of the bottle. As shocking as it was for civilians, bombing the enemy's cities had become a normal part of war when the Germans bombed London and Paris and the Allied air forces bombed the German cities of the Rhineland. Simply put, cities contained many military and industrial targets whose destruction would make a difference in a nation's ability to wage war. As the airpower doctrine and airpower capability of the major powers evolved in the 1920s and 1930s, no nation was prepared to consider the enemy's cities, or their vital infrastructure, as off limits to aerial bombardment.

The Luftwaffe's operational doctrine for war, Regulation 16 (*Luftkriegführung*) published in 1936, described the primary targets for an air campaign as "the sources of enemy power." These were listed as "all the facilities and installations that serve to supply and support enemy combat forces." Such installations included industrial production, food production, import facilities, power stations, railroads and rail yards, military barracks, and centers of government administration.[35] Given such a target list, fully allowed under normal interpretations of international law, the Luftwaffe could easily justify the bombing of enemy cities. This was not a specifically German doctrine or approach to war. Both the British and American armed forces in the 1930s held similar views on the importance of employing their bombers to destroy vital enemy industrial and economic facilities in wartime.[36]

The British and American airmen who bombed German cities from 1942 to 1945 justified their actions, which included the area bombing campaigns against German cities that were approved at the highest political levels, to be legitimate under the rules that justified the enemy economy as a target of war.[37] The RAF policy to attack the German cities resulted in an estimated 422,000 German civilian dead by 1945.[38] The American bombing campaign against Japanese cities killed 330,000 Japanese before the end of the war.[39] This latter campaign included the single most destructive bombing attack in history, the U.S. firebombing of Tokyo in March 1945, which killed an estimated 100,000 Japanese civilians.[40] Given these facts, neither the British nor the Americans were going to condemn Wolfram von Richthofen, or other senior Luftwaffe generals, for war crimes because of their bombing of cities in the Spanish Civil War and in World War II.

Yet the issue of von Richthofen's behavior, and his personal responsibility for any war crimes, goes beyond a fruitless discussion of the morality of bombing enemy cities. All the senior German military officers understood by 1938–1939 that Hitler's plans for Germany and its armed forces went far beyond revising the hated Versailles Treaty and reestablishing Germany's rightful place as a great power. By 1939, the fundamental irrationality of Hitler's program ought to have been obvious to the well-educated professional officers of the General Staff. Still, highly intelligent and capable officers such as Milch and Jeschonnek were ready and willing to suspend their critical and moral faculties as they loyally supported Hitler and followed his program to conquer, plunder, and enslave whole nations for the glory of the German race.[41] Although their guilt is not in the same degree as some generals who actively participated in operations involving the mass murder of civilians, von Richthofen and most of the senior officers of the German army and Luftwaffe still became willing partners in Hitler's grand program of conquest. It may not have been a crime, per se, but it was a serious moral failing in their duty as officers.

Any discussion of war crimes and personal responsibility by senior Wehrmacht officers should not ignore the manner in which the war was fought on the eastern front. In contrast to the war against the western powers, which the Wehrmacht normally fought in accordance with the rules set out in the Geneva and Hague Conventions, the Wehrmacht's conduct in the Soviet Union consisted of a comprehensive and systematic violation of the laws of war and the norms of civilized behavior. From the start of the campaign, the Wehrmacht operated under a set of Hitler's orders that were clearly illegal under accepted international law. On 6 June 1941, the Wehrmacht High Command issued "Guidelines for the Treatment of Political Commissars," which ordered that captured Red Army officers who served as commissars in Red Army units must be immediately executed.[42] Other grossly illegal orders were issued to senior commanders to take civilian hostages in case of partisan resistance and to intervene "everywhere with the sharpest measures" and kill 50–100 "communists" for every German killed.[43] Such orders were communicated throughout the chain of command, so no senior German officer could be in doubt that Germany was operating outside the rules set by civilized nations.

In the Soviet campaign, the Wehrmacht's record in carrying out the provisions of the Geneva Convention for the Proper Treatment of Prisoners was abysmal. Of the approximately 5.5 million Soviet soldiers taken prisoner by the Germans, an estimated 33 percent to 60 percent died in German custody, with estimates ranging from 1.6 million to 3.3 million dead—mostly killed from starvation, malnutrition, cold, and disease.[44] Although the army was responsible for the care of prisoners, the Luftwaffe cannot escape responsibility for participating in this war crime. This author's interviews with Luftwaffe soldiers who served on the eastern front indicate that Luftwaffe units exhibited the same callous disregard for Soviet prisoners as did the army. In the first days of the invasion of the USSR, von Richthofen's VIIIth Air Corps overran forward Soviet airfields so quickly that Luftwaffe airfield units found Red air force ground crew still at the airfields. One account recalls that Soviet prisoners had been locked up in an empty hangar for a few days without food or water as the Luftwaffe waited for the army to take them off their hands. Von Richthofen, visiting some of his forward units at one recently captured airfield, was told of this callous treatment of the captured Soviets. He heartily approved. Such attitudes were perfectly characteristic behavior for a senior German officer in the eastern front.

In preparation for the spring and summer campaign of 1942, Luftwaffe engineers built and repaired hundreds of airfields in southern Russia using thousands of Soviet prisoners.[45] These prisoners consistently received an insufficient diet, far below the minimum necessary to maintain health.[46] There is no evidence that the Soviets who labored for the Luftwaffe fared any better or worse than those who worked for the army; certainly they were not treated in accord with the standards set by the Geneva Conventions.

In summary, the German behavior toward the Soviet POWs was horrendous and counts as one of the great war crimes of World War II.[47] Although von Richthofen was only marginally involved in disseminating the orders, and the Luftwaffe had only partial responsibility for Soviet POWs, he and the other senior German commanders on the Soviet front knew of Hitler's orders. There were few questions about the policy, and even fewer objections. The army's and Luftwaffe's senior leaders could have done more to see that minimal standards of international law were applied—but they did not. So, in response to the question, "Was von Richthofen a war criminal?" I would have to answer yes. Indeed, *all* the senior German commanders in the Soviet Union in 1941—including such notables as Manstein, Rundstedt, Guderian, Kleist, Kesselring, Leeb, and Bock—were guilty of violating the Geneva Conventions in regards to their handling of POWs and civilians.

On the other hand, von Richthofen was not a war criminal for directing the bombing of Guernica, Warsaw, and Stalingrad. These were harsh acts of war—but not crimes under the international law and norms of the era. If von Richthofen had lived past the end of the war, he would have been arrested and arraigned at the Nuremberg war crimes trials along with Germany's other field marshals. Like Field Marshal Sperrle, the man who directed the bombing of British cities from 1940–1944, von Richthofen likely would have been acquitted of criminal charges related to the wartime actions of the air forces under his command. However, he would have deserved his years spent in prison awaiting trial for his willingness to condone the mistreatment of Soviet POWs in 1941 and 1942.

Final Comment

As I researched the life of Wolfram von Richthofen, it was evident that a study of his life made a good vehicle for a study of the Luftwaffe from World War I to the end of World War II. From his days as a fighter pilot on the western front, serving under his famous cousin Manfred, "The Red Baron"; to the development of a secret Luftwaffe in the 1920s; to the war in Spain; and then to the campaigns of World War II—Wolfram von Richthofen was there, usually playing a central role. Through his life we see the development of German airpower in the years of peace. As chief of staff and commander of the Condor Legion, he played a decisive role in the Nationalist victory in Spain. As an air corps and air fleet commander, he was one of the central figures in making the German style of warfare, the blitzkrieg, famous. By the reckoning of a host of airpower historians, he ranks as one of the greatest tactical air commanders of World War II. When one sees the sheer number of campaigns, there were few that did not involve him, notably the air defense of Germany. Indeed, few commanders served on as many fronts or had the breadth of experience as Wolfram von Richthofen. By examining the life of Wolfram von Richthofen in some detail we can gain considerable insight about the tactics and operations of the Luftwaffe on the major fighting fronts. We can also gain a deeper understanding of the nature of high command in the Third Reich and the relationship of the professional officers of the Wehrmacht with Adolf Hitler and the Nazi regime.

Chapter 2

Wolfram von Richthofen's Early Life, 1895–1914

Wolfram von Richthofen was born 10 October 1895 at the family estate of Barzdorf near the city of Striegau in the Prussian province of Silesia. His father, Freiherr (Baron) Wolfram von Richthofen (1856–1922), and mother, Therese Götz von Olenhusen (1862–1948), were of the old Silesian nobility. When Wolfram was born the family had held noble status for 350 years. With considerable pride, the family could point out that their estate was one of the oldest landed estates in Silesia and predated the conquest of the province by Frederick the Great.

Wolfram was the second child and oldest son of four children. His older sister, Sophie-Therese, was born in 1891 (died 1971). His brother Manfred was born in 1898, and brother Gerhard followed in 1902. Theirs was a world of solid but not ostentatious wealth and also of considerable privilege. The nobility of the Kingdom of Prussia were not only well-off; they held enormous political power relative to their numbers. Under the Prussian constitution that lasted until 1918 the electorate was divided into three estates (nobles, middle class, and working class) for a proportional voting system that ensured that two-thirds of the seats in the Prussian legislature (the Landtag) were elected by one-third of the population (nobles were less than 5 percent of the population, the middle class about 30 percent). However, along with the advantages of birth the Prussian nobility also possessed a stern tradition of duty to the state and steadfast loyalty to their king. Members of the nobility were expected to send their sons to serve in the military, government, church, or another branch of public service such as academia. Although the world was changing rapidly when Wolfram was born, and many of the nobles were embarking on careers in business and industry, the ethic of service to the state was still strong among the noble families of Prussia and Silesia. That Wolfram would enter into a military career, like so many members of his family, is not surprising.

Origins of the Richthofen Family

The founder of the Richthofen family was Paulus Schultheis (1521–1565), from Bernau in Brandenburg, who became a Lutheran preacher and scholar of some renown in the first decades of the Reformation. Paulus was part of the scholastic circle around the great Lutheran theologian Philipp Melanchthon and, as a member of the elector's court at Brandenburg, was granted a patent of nobility and coat of arms. Upon receiving his patent of nobility Paulus Latinized his family name to Pretorius. Because Paulus was childless, a few years before he died he adopted Samuel Faber, the son of a deceased Lutheran minister, as his own son in order to carry the family name. Samuel exceeded his adoptive father in fame and became a noted academic and legal scholar and an important figure in the elector's court.

Samuel's son, Tobias Pretorius, settled the family in Silesia during the Thirty Years' War when Tobias's property was seized by the German emperor because of his close association with General Wallenstein, considered a traitor by the kaiser. Luckily, the Pretorius family had a close friend in Silesia, the Freiherr von Trachenberg, who provided Tobias with a position as chief administrator of his properties. Although the family had lost property, they had at least survived a war that had carried off a third of the German population. Within a generation of the end of the Thirty Years' War the memory of Wallenstein and his followers was rehabilitated and the fortunes of the Pretorius family took a turn for the better. In 1661 Tobias's son, Johann, was officially admitted to the ranks of the Bohemian knights (Silesia was part of the Kingdom of Bohemia at this time) and he Germanized the family name Pretorius (Latin for "judge") to Richthofen (literally, court of law).

The family prospered in Bohemian service, and by the early 1700s various Richthofens held sixteen estates in Lower Silesia. The stature of the family rose, and in 1735 Kaiser Karl IV granted the title of baron (Freiherr) to one of Tobias's descendants. Another Richthofen was made a baron by Frederick the Great shortly after he annexed Silesia in 1740. Fate had come full circle. The first Richthofens had served the Prussian monarchs for three generations before settling in Silesia; now they were again in position to serve Prussia. For his part, Silesia's new ruler (Frederick the Great) wanted the province to remain a quiet and prosperous part of Prussia. The new Prussian rule worked to win over the local nobles by guaranteeing their ranks, privileges, and royal favor in return for loyalty and service to Prussia. Families such as the Richthofens were happy to accept their new rulers under those conditions.

Silesia: The Home Province

Silesia, and especially the region of Lower Silesia where the Richthofens lived, was an especially prosperous and dynamic part of the German empire at the time of Wolfram's birth. Before the mid-nineteenth century, Silesia was something of a backwater province, notable for its scenic hills, woods, and farmland, but well away from the major trading and commerce routes.

Striegau, the town nearest the Richthofen estate, dates back to 1149 when a church was built there.[1] In the thirteenth century the town had been granted a charter as a city along with various rights. Until the sixteenth century the city was essentially Czech in character and under the control of the Kingdom of Bohemia. However, early in that century the city came under Habsburg dominion. Although the area had recently become Protestant, in the aftermath of the Thirty Years' War (1618–1648) the city resumed its Catholic character. Protestants, however, still constituted a significant minority. In 1740, during the War of the Austrian Succession, Silesia was occupied by Frederick the Great of Prussia and the whole region annexed to the Prussian kingdom. Although Prussia was notable for its policy of religious tolerance, Lutheranism was favored as the state religion. By the nineteenth century, Protestants were again the majority in Striegau.

Silesia took off economically with the rapid industrialization of Germany in the nineteenth century. Vast coal deposits were found in Silesia, and between 1850 and 1900 the formerly pastoral region became heavily industrialized. The railroad reached Striegau in 1853, and the town grew quickly. The largest business in Striegau was the nearby granite quarry, which produced the high-quality building stone in great demand throughout Germany. Thanks to the railroad, Silesian stone could now be easily shipped.

By 1905 Striegau was a thriving small city with 13,427 inhabitants and a growing population. With a large ethnically Polish population, Striegau was nonetheless overwhelmingly German (only a handful of the residents in the 1905 census spoke Polish or Czech as their mother tongues) and over 60 percent Lutheran.

Although the large cities of the region, notably Breslau, assumed a very industrial character and plenty of industry was found in the smaller cities, the surrounding countryside still retained a very rural character. One can see this in Germany today, where you can drive just a few miles from the middle of a Ruhr industry city and find yourself in a region of woods and vineyards. As well as industry, Silesia contained great tracts of wooded hills and large farm estates and was a fine region for hunting.

The von Richthofen Family and Estate

There were so many von Richthofens with landed estates living in the Lower Silesian district of Breslau that the area between the towns of Liegnitz and Königzelt was nicknamed Richthofenland by the locals. Wolfram's home estate of Barzdorf lay in the middle of a ring of Richthofen estates. Indeed, the acreage of the twenty-five estates owned by Richthofens in Silesia totaled 140 square kilometers—a territory equivalent to the Duchy of Lichtenstein.

Barzdorf was a fairly typical Silesian estate, with 350 hectares (875 acres) total, of which 269 hectares was cropland and the rest forest. The setting was pleasant and the manor house was an impressive eighteenth-century structure of three stories and included a large tower topped by a cupola at one end. High atop the tower wall, for all to see, was a large plaster relief of the von Richthofen coat of arms. Barns, warehouses, stables, workshops, and outer houses clustered near the manor house, and a lake of several acres fronted the manor; boating and fishing were thus favorite summer pastimes of the von Richthofens and their friends. Because estates normally housed servants and staff and contained small houses for the dozens of tenants who worked the land, Barzdorf and similar estates in the district counted in the country and district records as villages.

Barzdorf is one of the oldest properties of the von Richthofen clan in Silesia and was owned by Wolfram's father. Interestingly, Wolfram, as oldest son, did not inherit the estate from his father. Instead, it eventually passed into the hands of Wolfram's younger brother Manfred. Wolfram, however, was assured the inheritance of a nearby estate through his uncle, General of Cavalry Manfred von Richthofen. Wolfram's uncle was a distinguished career soldier who had served in the Prussian Guards Cavalry and at the court as a military aide to the kaiser. General von Richthofen, who as a young man had the reputation as "the handsomest officer in the army," had no children and wanted to ensure that his property and title remained in the family. In about 1926 the retired general legally adopted Wolfram as his son as a means of passing on his considerable inheritance. Wolfram thus inherited his estate at Bersdorf, which lay in the neighboring *Kreis* (county) of Jauer.[2] "Onkel Manfred" was close to Wolfram and his family and was a regular visitor at Barzdorf. General Manfred von Richthofen outlived his brother, Wolfram's father, by almost two decades (Wolfram's father died in 1922, and the general died in 1939). Through the 1920s and 1930s he continued his tradition of visiting his nephews and niece at Barzdorf and happily played the role of indulgent grandfather with Wolfram's children. Onkel Manfred lived long enough to

Manor house of Wolfram von Richthofen's uncle (and adoptive father) General Baron Manfred von Richthofen at Bersdorf, Silesia, before World War II. Richthofen visited often in his childhood and inherited the manor and estate upon the general's death.

see his adoptive son win fame in Spain and Poland and took great pride in Wolfram's accomplishments during World War I and in the Reichswehr.[3]

By any standards, the Richthofen clan possessed a great deal of intelligence, energy, and talent. As with most of the big Junker families, most of the von Richthofens who achieved fame and high position did so as servants of the Prussian state. Hugo Freiherr von Richthofen (1842–1904) was the chief of the government administration in Cologne. Bernhard Freiherr von Richthofen (1836–1895) became chief of police in Berlin. Oswald von Richthofen (1847–1906) served as Germany's foreign minister. Dieprand Freiherr von Richthofen, a noted jurist, served as vice president of Germany's high court. Many of the von Richthofens achieved high academic positions and some fame. Professor Doktor Ferdinand Freiherr von Richthofen (1833–1905) was one of the best-known geographers of his day. He held professorships at the Bonn, Leipzig, and Berlin universities. Heinz Freiherr von Richthofen

General der Kavallerie and Pour le Merité holder Freiherr Manfred von Richthofen, Wolfram's uncle and adoptive father, in the early 1930s. To the family he was known as "Onkel Manfred." As a young officer he had served as an aide to Kaiser Wilhelm and been called the "handsomest officer in the army." He died in late 1939, in time to see his nephew win fame as an air commander in Poland.

(1889–1986) became a painter and was later the professor at the Dusseldorf Academy of Art. Professor Doktor Karl Freiherr von Richthofen (1811–1888) was a professor of law and wrote several works on early German law. Karl Freiherr von Richthofen was ordained in the Lutheran Church (1832–1876) and served as the rector of the Breslau cathedral. Ludwig Freiherr von Richthofen (1837–1873) was mayor of Gütersloh and elected to the Prussian legislature. And this is only a partial list of the von Richthofens who served in the higher ranks of government and academia.

There was also a strong entrepreneurial, and even rebellious, strain in the family. Walter Freiherr von Richthofen (1850–1898) emigrated to the United States, was one of the founders of the city of Denver, Colorado, and became a wealthy businessman. He built a huge mansion outside Denver, which he named "Richthofen Castle." The best known family rebel was Frieda, Baroness von Richthofen (1879–1956), who scandalized the family by divorcing her husband and taking up with the British author D. H. Lawrence, author of *Lady Chatterley's Lover* and other novels that were highly controversial for the day. She eventually married Lawrence.

As one would expect from a traditional Prussian Junker family, the Richthofens sent a considerable number of their men into the army. In the Franco-Prussian War of 1870, Prussian army records list five Richthofens who were killed or wounded (one second lieutenant killed, one second lieutenant wounded, one first lieutenant wounded, and two captains wounded). Any of the Prussian army officer lists of the nineteenth century will turn up a few von Richthofens. They served in a variety of capacities, from the mundane engineer corps to line infantry regiments 6th West Prussian Grenadier Regiment), to socially distinguished cavalry regiments (16th Uhlans, 5th Hussars), to elite guards regiments (8th Prussian Leib Grenadier Regiment), and to the general staff.[4]

The rise of industry and railroads in Prussia and the enormous growth of the German economy in the latter half of the nineteenth century provided new opportunities for the Prussian nobility in the realms of business, industry, and finance. While the Silesian nobles knew and loved their past, and dutifully honored their ancestors who had served the state on the field of battle or in the councils of government, they were not prisoners of the status quo. Prussian and Silesian nobles were quick to take advantage of the new industrial economy, and the von Richthofen clan was one of the quickest to adapt. In 1860 Wolfram's grandfather, Ulrich Freiherr von Richthofen, along with three brothers (Karl, Ernst, and Bolko), founded a new enterprise, the Gutschdorf Sugar Company, which grew and processed sugar beets and marketed the refined sugar throughout Germany. With large estates to grow the beets and a factory to process them, the entrepreneurial brothers owned every step of the sugar business from the field to the wholesale market. The brothers exhibited uncommon business sense, and in short order the firm prospered and multiplied the family wealth.

The story of the von Richthofens' enthusiastic entry into the world of business and subsequent success was not uncommon in imperial Germany. Although it is hard to find anything good to say about the character of Kaiser Wilhelm II—a ruler renowned for his bigotry, ignorance, arrogance, and general obnoxiousness even by contemporaries—he at least refrained from snubbing the new class of industrialists and businessmen. Indeed, Wilhelm enjoyed the company of the bourgeois businessmen and industrialists who were doing so much to make Germany into Europe's richest and most advanced nation. If his nobles copied the behavior of the bourgeoisie and became wealthy, then they had his imperial blessing. For all their faults, the

German ruling classes refused to adopt the British-style class snobbery directed against those who made their money in "trade."[5]

Wolfram's Childhood

By all accounts Wolfram's childhood was a fairly normal one for the German upper classes of the era. Wolfram's parents were loving but strict. Nicknamed "Ulf" by the family (he kept that nickname for the rest of his life), Wolfram was close to his older sister and two younger brothers. He seems to have been especially close to his brother Manfred, who was nicknamed "Pet." He was somewhat distant to the youngest of the children, Gerhard, who was seven years younger and still in school when Wolfram was winning fame as a cavalry lieutenant and fighter ace. One Richthofen child, Götz, had died as an infant.

Unlike many of the upper class who had private tutors for their children, Wolfram's parents sent the children to elementary school in Striegau, and at age eleven Wolfram progressed on to the local *Gymnasium* (academic high school) in Striegau. Elementary school education then included German language and literature, history, and mathematics. Religious instruction, in Wolfram's case instruction in Lutheranism, also was a normal part of the school curriculum. In addition, students learned Latin and modern foreign languages, the most popular being French and English. Discipline at home and in school tended to be strict.

Wolfram's surviving school grades indicate that Wolfram showed no early inclinations to be a scholar. His scores in mathematics and German were good, whereas his foreign language grades were either a borderline pass or an "unsatisfactory." As the family noted, Wolfram, although clearly a bright child, had no gift for foreign languages. Unlike many from the upper class of his generation who could cite Greek or Latin with ease or carry on a conversation with captured enemy soldiers in fluent French or English, Wolfram always found language study to be painful. Later in life he was especially proud of his effort to learn Italian and become fluent enough so that he could pass the higher-level army translation examinations.

It can be fairly said that in the early decades of the twentieth century Germany had probably the best education system in the world. All but a few German children attended state-run schools, and each German state had a comprehensive system of schools, starting with elementary education and concluding with an extensive system of universities and technical colleges that granted university-level diplomas. All German children attended elementary school until about age twelve, and after that most were tracked into a trade school or apprenticeship program. For the middle and upper classes there was the Gymnasium or *Realschule*. The Gymnasium was an academic prep school in which classical languages and liberal arts were emphasized, and the Realschule was an academic program that emphasized science and mathematics. Both schools prepared pupils for the *Abitur*, or university entrance tests, an examination that the pupil took at the age of eighteen or nineteen. The education process was overseen by a ministry of education in each German state that supervised the schools and set standards—and the standards were high. By the time a German student completed the Gymnasium or Realschule he or she was well-prepared to attend a university or specialist technical college. The Gymnasium at Striegau was a provincial school, certainly not as prestigious as one of the more famous schools found in Berlin or Breslau. Still, under the Prussian system of education, Wolfram was assured a solid education even in a provincial market town and was well-prepared for his later career.

Prior to World War I many of the Prussian nobles sent their boys off to a cadet school at about age twelve where they were prepared for a military life. The cadet schools provided a watered-down version of the Gymnasium course, with marching, drilling, and military discipline emphasized in a clearly Spartan atmosphere. Most students who attended the cadet schools did not take the Abitur but settled instead for a school-leaving certificate. One can draw a few conclusions from the fact that Wolfram lived at home and went to the local Gymnasium. In the Gymnasium he received an education that was much superior to that of a cadet school.[6] Wolfram was clearly not pushed by his family toward a military career. Had that been their intention, Wolfram would certainly have been sent to a cadet school. Of course, he would have to do his duty in the Prussian army. But most noble and middle-class young men of the Wilhelmian era served for a year in the army as "volunteers" with a status above that of a conscript private and below that of a career noncommissioned officer. After the year's service the young man would usually be granted a commission in the army reserves. Germany was a frankly militaristic country in the era of Kaiser Wilhelm II, and an officer's commission, even in the reserves, was a tremendous social advantage. It would have been quite normal for Wolfram to take this route and become a prosperous estate owner and businessman. Clearly the decision to become a professional soldier after the Gymnasium was his own choice.

As leading local gentry, the von Richthofens would have hosted and attended a regular round of social events, from fairs in the town and county to picnics and hunting parties for the relations. With so many von Richthofens living nearby, family events occurred often, and Wolfram and his brothers and sister came to know their many cousins. As the family estate of Manfred and Lothar von Richthofen lay in nearby Schweidnitz, about twenty miles away, Wolfram came to know his cousins (with whom he would fly in the Great War) through various family gatherings. Wolfram became good friends with his cousin Manfred, who was three years older, and his cousin Lothar, who was the same age as he. All the young von Richthofen men were enthusiastic hunters by the time they reached their teens, and they took the opportunity to hunt on each other's family estates during holidays.

Growing up on an estate, Wolfram learned to ride at an early age. Hunting large game, such as stag and wild boar, as well as pheasant and small game was a passion of the German nobility—especially of those who came from landed estates. Hunting was also a social event for the landowners and nobility, who would invite friends and family to shoot game and then host them at the manor house afterward. By his early teens Wolfram was an accomplished hunter, and hunting remained his favorite hobby throughout his life. In his diaries and letters Wolfram, even in the midst of a campaign, would regularly remark on the hunting opportunities afforded by a woods and fields that were then being fought over. He would make personal notes to return and to hunt in a particular forest where the hunting looked especially promising as soon as the battle was done. The variety of game he hunted was impressive. Later in life Wolfram occasionally had the opportunity to hunt exotic species, such as European bison on Hermann Goering's estate. But most of his hunting as a young man would have consisted of small game, deer, and sometimes wild boar. He was also handy with a shotgun and enjoyed hunting for pheasant and duck. By all accounts, he was a first-rate shot.

While at the Gymnasium, Wolfram decided to apply for a commission in the army after his graduation. Many of the Prussian noble families traditionally sent a son or two to the army or government service. In Wolfram's case, pursuing a military career seems to have been a good fit for Wolfram's personality. Although he had a good mind (his Ph.D. in engineering is proof of that), his interests did not lie in an academic career—despite the strong academic strain in a family that produced so many jurists and professors. Though he was not a remarkable sportsman, Wolfram loved the active and outdoor life. He was a competent rider and expressed great pleasure at riding a good horse, and in his thirties he took up skiing in the Swiss Alps with his wife. After the German conquest of France, he found himself stationed in the proximity of several golf courses, so he learned to golf. He noted in his diary that he was an "awful" player, but he seems to have enjoyed the sport all the same. He regularly flew himself about in light aircraft throughout the interwar period and during World War II—almost for the pure enjoyment of it. Given his love of the outdoors, the sporting and outdoors life of a military officer in the early 1900s would have held an undeniable appeal for young Wolfram.

Unlike so many of his ancestors and cousins who excelled in scholarly pursuits, Wolfram's mental powers were invariably geared toward practical problem solving. Even as a child his family noted his orientation toward the practical sciences. According to the family his favorite toys were the mechanical toys that were popular with the middle and upper classes of the era. If the very young Wolfram became cranky or upset, he could be quickly quieted and comforted with a mechanical toy or toy wagon in preference to a stuffed animal.

The Army and the Changing Society of Wilhelmian Germany

Wolfram joined the army at a time of dramatic social and political change in Germany. The rise of the German economy and the rapid modernization of the country required a longer, broader, and more academically tough education in the liberal arts and sciences, and the German army before World War I was likewise trying to adapt. Indeed, one cannot speak of a German army at all, as the German empire was a federation of kingdoms, several of which had their own armies and war ministries—including Bavaria, Saxony, and Württemberg. Of course Prussia, as the largest German state, had by far the largest of the German armies, and when the smaller states joined with Prussia to form the German empire in 1866 and 1870, the Prussian military system became the norm. In some respects Prussia, with a highly developed general staff system, was more progressive than the other German armies. In other respects the Prussian military was much more reactionary than the other states. For example, the Prussian army tended to rely much more on the nobility to provide officers than did other German states.[7] However, the army that Wolfram von Richthofen joined was rapidly changing in its social composition as the officer corps became much more middle class.[8]

With the growth of the German population and economy, the size of the German army also grew. With a larger army there was a need for far more officers. Modern warfare required that officers possess a whole range of new skills and the ability to effectively employ new technologies. The German army of the early twentieth century required a multitude of railroads, as well as officers who could develop complex rail movement and mobilization plans. It was also incorporating motor vehicles into the force and, after 1909, airplanes. Modern rapid-fire and long-range artillery now employed complex firing tables to support troops miles from the guns; the amount of firepower available to a division in 1914 was enormously larger than it had been in 1870. Tactics and operations grew in complexity. Magazine rifles and machine guns required dispersing large forces across the battlefield for survivability, but those forces also needed to be able to concentrate quickly at the decisive point of attack. To ensure command and control, senior commanders now used radios and telephones to maintain contact with their forces. More and more of the army was devoted to "tail," the large number of logistics and specialist troops that were absolutely necessary to keep a modern army functioning. For these reasons, the army needed officers with a much higher education level than earlier warfare had required. The changes in the army came rapidly: in 1890 only 35 percent of the officer corps possessed the Abitur. By 1912, 65 percent of the officers had the Abitur—and this made Wolfram part of a minority of regular officers without the university matriculation certificate.[9] As early as 1872 Bavaria required that every officer cadet applicant hold the Abitur. Although more and more Prussian officer applicants held the Abitur, Prussia was unwilling to raise the educational standards of its officer corps.[10] Kaiser Wilhelm worried incessantly that raising the educational qualifications for the officer corps, which would make the army more middle class, would somehow lead to democratization of the army and a lessening of the traditional Prussian militaristic values. Wilhelm need not have worried. Rather than the nobles becoming more middle class, the middle-class officers tended to take on the traditional values of the nobility. Prussia had long been a highly militarized state, but in the decades before World War I the tradition of Prussian militarism had spread to the other German states and was happily adopted by the rising middle classes. Officers, both active and reserve, enjoyed enormous social prestige. It was common practice for a doctor or professor to include his officer reserve rank on his business card.[11]

While at least middle-class status was necessary to obtain an officer's commission, and noble status was a huge plus in getting into the army—especially in the Prussian Guards and cavalry regiments—once a man was accepted and commissioned into a regiment his background became irrelevant to his future advancement. The German armies, and especially the general staff, were strict meritocracies where only competence counted. One sign of the social changes in the army in the late nineteenth century is the career of Lt. General Wilhelm Groener. Groener came from a fairly humble background; his father had been a warrant officer (paymaster) in the Württemberg army. Groener himself joined the Württemberg army as a lieutenant in 1884. He passed the general staff examinations and performed brilliantly at the Kriegsakademie (1893–1897) and was appointed to the general staff in Berlin, where he served under the famed Count von Schlieffen and became chief of the important railway section of the general staff. By 1914 he had become a colonel and received several promotions, rising to lieutenant general. Groener served directly under Hindenburg and Ludendorff as the senior director of the German war economy. In late 1918 he took over Ludendorff's position as quartermaster general of the army and as second in command of the army. In 1919 he played a central role in leading the army through the postwar revolution and crisis and is largely responsible for building the Reichswehr (post–World War I German army) on a sound foundation.

The ticket to advancement in the German army was to join the general staff corps. About eight years into an officer's career, when he was a senior first lieutenant or captain, he had the option of taking a rigorous examination for selection to the General Staff Academy (*Kriegsschule*—"War School") in Berlin. The examination tested general knowledge, foreign languages, mathematics, and military tactics. Out of the whole officer corps only thirty to forty officers were admitted yearly to the intensive three-year academic program that was designed to develop the brains of the army. Having completed the general staff course, officers were no longer considered as members of the infantry, artillery, engineers, and so on, but were now part of the general staff corps and thereby handled differently from other officers of the same rank. General staff officers wore a special carmine stripe on their trousers and were given preference for battalion and regimental command to ensure that they obtained practical field experience. The German general staff, which had proven its effectiveness in the 1866 and 1870 wars, was widely regarded as the world's best military staff. France, Britain, Russia, and the United States each created general staff schools based on the German model. The German general staff was considered such an important element for success in war that the Allies specifically demanded the dissolution of the German general staff in the post–World War I Versailles Treaty.

First Years of Army Life

In 1913, at age eighteen, Wolfram completed his Gymnasium course and enrolled in the Prussian army officer course at the cadet academy at Gross Lichterfeld in Berlin. This was the best known of the officer academies that provided a one-year course qualifying the cadet for a commission as a lieutenant in the regular army. It was a strict course, similar to the British officer course at Sandhurst, with academic training and plenty of marching, drill, and field exercises. To become an officer in any of the German armies of the time (Prussia, Saxony, Bavaria, and Württemberg all had their own armies and cadet schools) a cadet who sought a commission in a line regiment (cavalry, infantry, or artillery) had to apply to a regiment and be accepted by a vote of the regiment's officers. It was an absolute requirement; even the kaiser could not grant a commission to a line regiment if a cadet had not been voted in.

The regimental system was essentially a means of the army to maintain the social standards of the officer corps. In practical terms it meant that nobles were almost always found acceptable, as were cadets from solid middle-class backgrounds. Young men of exceptional character and academic promise from the lower half of the middle class might have a chance at a commission if they applied to a very undistinguished line regiment or perhaps to one of the non-Prussian German armies. On the social scale, the cavalry ranked the highest, and it contained the highest percentage of nobles. Some elite infantry regiments, especially the Prussian Guards, were overwhelmingly noble in their constitution. However, most infantry regiments were officered by members of the middle class. The artillery ranked somewhat lower on the social scale, and the specialist troops and corps—engineers, railways, communications, and veterinary—attracted few nobles and were overwhelmingly middle class.

Wolfram von Richthofen applied to the 4th Hussars cavalry regiment and was readily accepted with the rank of *Fähnrich*, or "officer cadet." Officer cadets lived apart from the rank-and-file soldiers and dined with the officers. They were put through a round of training and unit duties to prepare them for an officer's commission and command of a platoon of thirty to forty men. Service as a Fähnrich entailed many of the basic duties and responsibilities of an officer, such as commanding the guard mount, leading a platoon on exercises, and preparing a unit for inspections. He would also participate in the social life of the officers. At the end his year as a cadet, something of a probationary year, a Fähnrich who had performed well would then be formally admitted to the officer corps of the regiment by the vote of the officers. At that point he was granted a commission as a lieutenant in the regular army.

The 4th Hussars (official title: Husaren Regiment von Schill Nr. 4) was stationed in the small Silesian city of Ohlau with 9,000 inhabitants per the 1910 census. Ohlau, like Wolfram's home town of Striegau, lay in the district of Breslau.[12] The 4th Hussars belonged to the Twelfth Cavalry Brigade, which came under the command of the Sixth Army Corps headquartered in Breslau. King Frederick the Great founded the 4th Hussars in 1741, just after he had annexed Silesia, and the regiment had an impressive history, having served in the wars against Napoleon and compiled a distinguished combat record in the Franco-Prussian War.

For the most part, German officers joined regiments stationed close to their family homes and thus retained their close bond to family, friends, and

A tall and blond Lt. Wolfram von Richthofen, just commissioned as a lieutenant of the 4th Silesian Hussars on the eve of World War I.

home region. The officer corps of the 4th Hussars was mostly noble, as was typical in the Prussian army cavalry regiments. In the cavalry, most of the young officers came from backgrounds similar to Wolfram's, with fathers who were officers or estate owners. Cavalry officers, especially new lieutenants, were not expected to live on their military officer's pay; rather, the officer's family typically would provide a hefty living allowance to enable the officer to maintain adequate quarters, keep some first-rate horses, socialize, hunt, and play polo. Life for a cavalry officer was considerably more expensive than that of an infantry officer.

When von Richthofen joined the cavalry, its primary mission was to serve as a highly mobile reconnaissance and screening force. The cavalry would most likely operate in small units spread across the countryside, serving as the "eyes" of the army. Cavalry could also be used in larger formations to mount a rapid pursuit of an enemy in retreat or to work behind enemy lines to raid enemy supply bases and rear columns. Finally, it could serve as a mobile reserve for the army, to be quickly deployed to any part of the front that was threatened. In such cases the cavalry would detail some of its troopers to take the horses to the rear while the units would fight as infantry.

The 4th Hussars was nicknamed the "Brown Hussars" for the reddish-brown tunic the cavalrymen wore as their dress uniform.[13] Although the 4th Hussars wore the standard field gray of the German army on campaign and for daily duties, the dress uniform of the cavalry regiments tended to be gaudy. Kaiser Wilhelm II loved military display and colorful uniforms, and the period of his reign saw a revival of Napoleonic fashions in the army. Various Prussian regiments wore red, blue, and green dress uniforms, and, in the case of the 4th Hussars, a fur hat topped off the whole ensemble. As with every cavalry regiment, the 4th Hussars had its own marching music and, in typically German fashion, a regimental drinking song that referred to the admiration of the local girls for the handsome hussars.[14] With its unique traditions and history, the regiment was very much a surrogate family—especially for younger officers like Wolfram. Free time for the unmarried officers revolved around the Kasino, or officers' mess. German cavalry officers behaved pretty much like the officers of other armies of the day. Officers normally ate in the Kasino and, after duty or exercises, would adjourn to the bar. The young lieutenants, almost all unmarried, were a high-spirited group, and there was plenty of drinking, singing, and pranks. The peace of the Kasino, and probably the odd window, would be broken by impromptu games of indoor rugby or soccer, behavior that was tolerated by the older officers.

In a small city such as Ohlau the military garrison and its officers would have been the center of social life. While the life of a young officer or soldier was mostly hard work and care for the horses, there were also a good many local social events and dances to entertain the officers. In Wilhelmian Germany, an overtly militaristic society, a good deal of a cavalry regiment's time was taken up with various sorts of display: ceremonies, parades, and reviews in the local area. The conclusion of the grand army maneuvers, held every fall, featured a huge cavalry charge in which the force commanded by the kaiser would always win. Thousands of cavalry would charge in close formation with lances held high or swords unsheathed and glittering in the sun to provide a satisfying spectacle of military glory for the kaiser. Of course, even the thickest German generals knew that such cavalry charges belonged to a time long past—but they also knew that the kaiser needed a large dose of dramatic and glorious military display.

However, the theatrics that assuaged Kaiser Wilhelm's ego were not the main point of the grand army maneuvers. Corps would execute tactical movements and carry out mock battles (which were more realistic when the kaiser was not looking) to test the latest battle doctrine for ten to twelve days under field conditions. An important part of the regimental training program was the preparation for the annual maneuvers. For most of the time, the cavalry wore their drab gray field uniforms and carried rifles as their primary weapon. The maneuvers, along with regular brigade and division exercises, provided the soldiers and officers the opportunity to operate as part of a much larger force.

When the German army mobilized in 1914 there were 110 regular army cavalry regiments on the army lists, each with four to six squadrons (companies). Backing these up were thirty-three reserve regiments of cavalry, each with only three squadrons. There were a further fifty-six Landwehr cavalry companies composed of older reservists, usually detailed to serve as military police and security troops. The total cavalry force of the German army was 78,622 regular army soldiers and 4,138 officers, in addition to 16,863 reserve soldiers and 891 reserve officers. A 1914-era cavalry division was a much smaller organization than an infantry division. A standard division was composed of a headquarters company and three cavalry brigades, each with two regiments (a regiment consisted of 36 officers, 688 men, 769 horses, and 3 wagons), and each regiment with four squadrons (a squadron consisted of 5 officers, 163 men, 178 horses, and 3 wagons) and a headquarters detachment. For fire support the division had a horse artillery battalion with three batteries of four 75-mm field pieces, a machine-gun company (six machine guns), ammunition for the munitions column, engineer company, signals detachment, and a motor vehicle company.[15]

Coming from the landed nobility, cavalry officers would have already known how to ride well. However, much of their initial training would have been learning how to ride in tight formations and to form columns, wheel, and charge in line. Cavalrymen were equipped with the saber and would have to learn to fight with it on horseback and on foot. As a second lieutenant, von Richthofen was assigned command of a platoon of thirty-six men, mostly conscripts, and was responsible for seeing that they were trained to fight on horseback and as dismounted infantry. Despite the extensive training in mounted combat, the army was realistic enough to know that there would probably be few opportunities for massed cavalry charges in an era when all the major armies were equipped with rapid-firing magazine rifles, capable of accurate fire out to 800 meters. Machine guns were also becoming common in the army, with each cavalry division containing a machine gun company. The infantry were more lavishly equipped with machine guns.

In addition to training his soldiers, von Richthofen was responsible for the horses under his command. To keep a cavalry horse in top condition for military service required a regime of regular exercise, grooming, feeding, shoeing, and veterinary care. In addition, stables had to be kept clean and well maintained. The life of a young cavalry officer was thus a very busy one. However, the German army's development of the professional noncommissioned officer (NCO) system in the early twentieth century greatly simplified officers' duties and ensured that the army ran smoothly.

In the German army, NCOs had a high professional status and considerable authority over soldiers. Unlike other armies of the era in which promotion to NCO was usually on the basis of seniority and time served, promotion to the rank of sergeant and master sergeant in the German army was by written examination. Only soldiers with excellent records, and who were recommended by their commanders, could attain NCO rank. Upon selection as an NCO, the candidates would be sent to the NCO academy in Potsdam for a several-week course that covered the army system, small-unit tactics and, most important, the principles of small-unit leadership. Thus, although Wolfram was officially in command of his cavalry platoon, he acquired several highly competent and experienced NCOs to do the actual work of training the troopers, seeing to the horses and equipment, and checking that the unit ran as an efficient machine. Germany's NCO system ensured that it had the best trained and most efficient army of its day. Second lieutenants were expected to quietly learn their jobs and, if war came, be eager and ready to lead their men from the front. If nothing else, they were expected to be brave when the time came and die in battle if that was necessary to motivate their soldiers under fire.

Officers were not expected to marry before they were thirty years old and had achieved a captain's rank. Before World War I the norm in the German army was to marry considerably later than did civilians. All marriages had to be approved by the regimental commander and the kaiser, and any thought of marriage to a woman of a family or background regarded as unsuitable would have been forbidden. The Prussian army in particular operated under a strict code of honor that regulated the social life and public behavior of the officer. The correct family background for an officer was important, and in the era of Wilhelm II this could be carried to ridiculous lengths. In one Prussian regiment at the turn of the century, someone noted that a noble young officer, Freiherr von Thüngen, had a "stain" on the family tree: his parents (both nobles) apparently had married shortly after his birth. This became an issue of preserving the "honor" of the regiment. Forcing a good officer to resign would have been seen as unfair—but honor still had to be upheld. Finally, a solution was reached. In consideration of his noble birth and his lack of personal guilt in his parents' behavior the young officer was quietly allowed to transfer his commission to the Bavarian army—which was not quite as punctilious about social background and parents' marriage dates. It is no wonder that the more easy-going Bavarian, Württemberg, and Saxon officers often found the Prussians, and their king and mores, somewhat absurd.[16]

There was little in the way of politics or political thinking in the Prussian army. The ideology of the army was a simple monarchism, and it would have been considered unseemly for any officer to take much note of current political debates—other than to support the kaiser's antipathy to social democracy.[17] Religion might be politely discussed; however, most conversation would have centered on girls, sports, social events, and so on. The social life of young officers would not have been much different in other European armies of the era.

What was different was the emphasis on professional study by the officers in the German army. After being commissioned, officers were expected to attend special courses at their branch school, where they would be trained in military administration and instructed in the latest weaponry. The most ambitious officers would take the general staff school examination when they were senior first lieutenants. If they could pass the general staff exams, which were exceptionally tough and required knowledge of mathematics and languages as well as military subjects, they could attend the three-year Kriegsschule in Berlin. If they completed that course they would be part of a select few within the army and become members of the general staff corps. As general staff officers they would receive accelerated promotions and be given positions of responsibility on the army staff. They would also be given greater command opportunities. For the very smart and ambitious officer the general staff course offered the best means of furthering one's career.

Advancement in the army required a program of study. Regiments maintained libraries with a wide range of literature, history, and, most important, books on military history and tactics.[18] Regular army officers were expected to take courses, master their profession, and spend a good deal of their free time keeping up on their professional reading. Officers approaching the examinations for the general staff had to be broadly read and have a thorough grasp of current military literature. Wolfram von Richthofen was commissioned into an army that was intellectually active and expected officers to take their profession seriously. As an ambitious young officer, von Richthofen would have spent a good portion of his free time in the regimental library studying tactics.

Wolfram had little time to experience the peacetime army, however. In August 1914 Germany went to war. The Prussian army that von Richthofen had joined could put more than three million men on the battlefield and included 22,122 active duty officers and 29,230 reserve officers. Man for man, it was a superbly led and well-trained and equipped force. Once the order was given for war, Wolfram could be confident that there was no other force in the world that could equal the German army. In any case, he was as well prepared for war as any young lieutenant could expect to be.

Chapter 3

The Great War

In the early days of World War I, the German cavalry saw considerable action on both the eastern and western fronts. As cavalry units were small organizations compared to their infantry counterparts (a 1914 cavalry division was about 5,000 men, and infantry divisions had 13,000 men) and had little firepower (infantry divisions had seventy-two 77mm guns in contrast to cavalry divisions' twelve), the cavalry served primarily as a support arm for the infantry.[1]

In August 1914 Wolfram von Richthofen's 4th Silesian Hussar Regiment was part of the Twelfth Cavalry Brigade (which consisted of the 4th Hussars and the 6th Hussars—both Silesian units), which in turn belonged to the 5th Cavalry Division, commanded by Lt. General Karl von Ilsemann, and after October by Lt. General Fritz von Unger.[2] Lothar von Richthofen, Wolfram's cousin and brother of the famous ace Manfred, served as a lieutenant in the 4th Silesian Dragoon Regiment in the 5th Cavalry Division. During the initial advance of the German army into Belgium and France the 5th Cavalry Division and the Guards Cavalry Division were organized into the Ist Cavalry Corps under Lt. General Manfred Freiherr von Richthofen, Wolfram's uncle and later his adoptive father. The Ist Cavalry Corps was given the mission of supporting the German Third Army, which lay in the center of the German force advancing into Belgium and northern France. The 5th Calvary Division crossed the border and drove quickly through the Ardennes, then crossed the Meuse River near Dinant—where German armored forces would again cross the Meuse twenty-six years later.[3]

From 14 August 1914, when the 5th Cavalry Division helped force the German army crossing of the Meuse at Dinant, to late October when the unit was transferred to the East, Wolfram's unit saw fairly constant action. Wolfram, as a platoon commander, and his men served as the eyes of the army as they moved to make contact with the French. While searching for the enemy the German cavalry was also expected to drive away the French and British cavalry to prevent them from collecting information on German movements and dispositions. The Ist Cavalry Corps first saw action on 15 August when it collided with the French VIIIth Cavalry Corps, which was serving as a screen for the French army. The 5th Cavalry Division won the opening match and forced the French cavalry to retreat back across the Meuse.[4] The 5th Cavalry Division saw action at Namur on 23–24 August and again at St. Quentin on 29–30 August. The Ist Cavalry Corps was successful in its mission to find French forces and keep the French cavalry away from the Third Army advance. The 5th Cavalry Division continued its drive into northern France until the French counterattack north of Paris in early September stopped the Germans and forced the northern and center German armies to retreat.[5] By 18 September the western front was beginning to harden, and for the next nine days the 5th Cavalry Division was halted in the Champagne region and began to dig in. For both sides, the trench warfare that would dominate the fighting on the western front had already begun. While digging trenches, the cavalry sent their horses to the rear and filled in the line as ordinary infantry. Although it would have been demoralizing for the cavalry to move into trenches, Wolfram could be proud of the fact that he had tasted battle and proven himself as a brave and competent soldier. On 21 September 1914 he was awarded the Iron Cross Second Class in recognition of his bravery and leadership in the fighting of August and early September.

There was little need for cavalry on the western front, which had fully settled down to positional warfare by October 1914. At the end of that month the 5th Cavalry Division was transferred to the eastern front. In the East open warfare would be the norm throughout 1914 and 1915. Although the German army had won a brilliant victory at Tannenberg in East Prussia in August 1914, where it had destroyed the Russian Second Army, the Russians still had an enormous numerical superiority over the Germans, and reinforcements were urgently needed.

At the end of October the 5th Cavalry Division was assigned to General Frommel's Cavalry Corps, which included the 5th and 8th German Cavalry Divisions and the 7th Austrian Cavalry Division. Unlike the infantry corps of the German army, which were very permanent organizations, cavalry corps were elastic formations that were formed for specific operations and included a mix of available cavalry and attached infantry units; as such, they usually were named after the commanding general. After each operation, divisions and brigades would normally be detached to other corps and armies and, as an operational need arose, a news corps tailored for an operation would be formed under a senior cavalry commander.[6]

In November 1914 the Cavalry Corps was ordered to cover the southern flank of the German Ninth Army, which was then defending the southern part of the German front lines in Poland. Wolfram could indeed believe that he was fighting to defend his fatherland because, on 3 November, the 5th Cavalry Division was deployed near the Warthe River, only sixty miles northeast of the city of Breslau and the ancestral region of the von Richthofen clan. General von Hindenburg, recently made commander of the German forces on the eastern front, knew that despite his destruction of a Russian army at Tannenburg, he still faced a dangerous situation. Since the Germans were really too thinly spread to effectively defend, Hindenburg decided to mass his forces and attack. He directed the Ninth Army, under General von Mackensen, to move onto the offense. Frommel's Cavalry Corps, with Wolfram's 5th Cavalry Division, found themselves opposing the Russian 7th Cossack Division advancing to their north and General Nowilow's Russian Cavalry Corps to their south. Frommel decided to strike the Cossack division first. The 5th Cavalry Division advanced on the Russians at Konin, Poland, in two columns. Along with an attached infantry battalion, the Germans advanced to the outskirts of the town under supporting artillery fire. Most of the cavalry fought dismounted, but two cavalry squadrons made a mounted attack and stormed into the northern part of the town while the rest of the force assaulted the south. The Russians' resistance broke, and the main Russian force retreated quickly as the Germans captured 500 prisoners and eight machine guns. General Frommel's corps, having driven off the first threat, discovered that the Russian Cavalry Corps to the south was now advancing. Frommel carried out a successful flank attack on the Russians the next day, again driving the enemy into retreat.[7]

Despite the prewar training of the 4th Hussars en masse cavalry tactics, and probably contrary to the expectations of a young cavalry officer like Wolfram von Richthofen, there were few major cavalry charges by the German army in World War I. Cavalry units usually operated in partnership with attached infantry units and fought as combined arms formations with infantry and artillery. For example, the 1st Battalion of the 32nd Infantry Regiment was assigned to the 5th Cavalry Division from autumn 1914 to February 1915.[8] The small battle at Konin was fairly typical of the cavalry actions on the eastern front in 1914–1915. During German offensive operations in August 1915, the 5th Cavalry Division continued to play a supporting role for the infantry. Attacks against Russian-held towns were carried out by the infantry units of the 5th Cavalry Division, with the mounted troops held in reserve to conduct pursuit operations. During the summer of 1915 the 5th Cavalry Division became more of a combined arms formation as additional infantry and artillery units were attached for operations. The Germans knew enough not to conduct any direct assaults by mounted troops against prepared enemy positions. But it was a lesson that the Russians had not yet learned. On the afternoon of 10 August 1915, a Cossack regiment made a mounted charge against the 5th Cavalry Division's forward outposts. German machine guns and artillery literally massacred the Russian regiment.[9]

During the German offensive to overrun Poland in the fall of 1915, the German cavalry had the mission to cover the relatively open flanks of the German infantry corps and to seek out and defeat Russian cavalry formations conducting reconnaissance. For the cavalry, it was still more a war of small operations and dismounted engagements rather than large battles. During the September offensive that overran the Polish City of Wilna, German cavalry units were able to slip through gaps in the Russian defenses and raid the Russian rail lines and depots a few miles behind the front. On several occasions the German cavalry captured Russian supply columns.

Between offensives the cavalry soldiers were held in the rear as reserves. For long periods they might leave their horses in the rear and fight as dismounted troopers in the front-line trenches. Since troop strength per mile of line was far less on the eastern front, these periods of defense usually consisted of holding a string of forward outposts. Although the winters were bitterly cold, life for the Germans on the eastern front was not nearly as deadly as in the West since the Russians had relatively little artillery, which was the main killer of the war. The Russians, as well as having much less artillery than the Western Allies, also had little spare ammunition to waste on shooting Germans on quiet portions of the front. In most respects, the Russians were a far less capable enemy than the Western Allied soldiers. In the West, the technically proficient British and French soon developed more deadly heavy artillery pieces that fired more lethal ammunition. With modern communications and aircraft spotting, the western Allies were able to employ their guns with far greater effect. Thanks to the huge industrial plants of the British and French, the Allies on the western front soon had a vast number of heavy artillery pieces and machine guns as well as ample ammunition to make life for the Germans positively hellish. In the East the Russians lacked artillery, machine guns, ammunition, and supplies of every sort. Russian leadership tended to be thoroughly mediocre and unable to effectively employ the guns and supplies that were available. From the start of the war, the only thing the Russians had plenty of was men. However, even with an army that numbered in the millions, whose soldiers possessed plenty of stamina and fighting spirit—at least in 1914–1915—Russia could not stand up against the far smaller but better-equipped and better-trained German army.

After driving back the Russians from the borders of German Poland, the 5th Cavalry Division and 4th Hussars were redeployed to the central and southern portion of the eastern front. In early 1915 they were pulled out of the line to serve as the army's reserve for the southern portion of the front. Through 1915 the 4th Hussars, still part of the 5th Cavalry Division, served in Hungary and Bukovina. From March to May 1915 they found themselves holding defensive positions on the Dnjester River and the Bessarabian border. After some advances across the Dnjester, the 5th Cavalry Division again found itself holding defensive positions, this time at Pruth in June and July 1915. In July the division conducted forward reconnaissance and supported the crossing of the Bug River, helping the infantry secure a bridgehead to encircle the Russian fortress of Brest Litowsk.[10] Later that summer the 4th Hussars were transferred to support the First Austrian Army. Autumn 1915 brought more offensive operations and further advances into Poland and Galicia. By late 1915 the era of major cavalry operations on the eastern front was over.[11] Through 1916 the Twelfth Cavalry Brigade served in the vicinity of Pinsk.[12] As the war progressed, the cavalry served more and more of their time as infantry in the trenches, or as military police in the rear of the army. From October 1915 to January 1917 the 5th Cavalry Division's battle summary simply lists "Defensive operations in the Pripet Marshes."[13]

Decline of the Cavalry—Wolfram's Cousins Join the Air Service

From the first days of the war it was obvious that the cavalry was rapidly becoming obsolete as a major arm of battle. Its primary mission, reconnaissance, was being taken over by airplanes. A squadron of airplanes could perform long-range reconnaissance far more quickly and efficiently than a corps of cavalry. During the battle of Tannenberg it was the German airplanes that followed the Russian troop movements and notified headquarters that the Russian First and Second Armies were widely separated and that the Russian troop dispositions left them wide open to a devastating envelopment by the Germans. After the battle, General von Hindenburg, the German Eighth Army commander, commented on the value of the airplane, "Without the airplane, there is no Tannenberg."[14] On the western front it was Allied aircraft that found the gap between the German armies that enabled the French to counterattack successfully and drive the Germans back from Paris. On the eastern front large cavalry operations continued, but even there the airplane soon became the primary means of reconnaissance. The role of the cavalry declined rapidly, and cavalry divisions were broken into ever-smaller detachments and used as military police in the rear or as mobile reserves for the army. For ambitious young career officers, the cavalry was not the place to make one's military reputation.

Wolfram's cousin Manfred was the first of the von Richthofen family to leave the cavalry for the more glamorous, and now much more important, world of aviation. He requested a transfer from the cavalry to the Imperial Air Service and was accepted for training as an aerial observer in May 1915. Completing the course in a few weeks, he was soon back at the Russian front, this time sitting in the rear seat of an Albatros B II biplane as a member of Field Aviation Detachment 69. After a brief tour of duty in the East, Manfred was transferred to the western front to a bomber unit. By late 1915 some German airmen were shooting down the enemy in light and maneuverable single-seat fighter planes. Manfred was eager to try this new form of warfare and was sent on to pilot training, which he completed in early 1916. By the fall of that year he had shot down his first enemy planes and was making a reputation as a superb aerial fighter. In early 1917 he was awarded the coveted Pour le Merité, Germany's highest decoration, and given command of a fighter squadron equipped with the new Albatros D III fighters—superior to anything the French and British had in the air. In April 1917 he would win fame as Germany's "Red Baron" in the sky over Arras when the Luftstreitkräfte (Imperial Air Service) decimated the British Royal Flying Corps.[15]

Shortly after Manfred transferred out of the cavalry, his younger brother Lothar applied for the air service and was accepted for observer training. By the end of 1915 Lothar was flying on the western front. In mid-1916 he was accepted for pilot training, which he completed in early 1917.[16] In March 1917 Lothar was assigned to his brother's squadron, Jasta 11. Since Lothar and Wolfram served as lieutenants in the same division in 1914–1915, and cavalry divisions were small organizations (about 250 officers total), they almost certainly had plenty of chances to get together and talk about the war and their careers. Wolfram knew that his cousins were delighted with the air service and, as members of the World War I generation were inveterate letter writers, the cousins probably corresponded through 1916–1917. In any case, the war was going nowhere in the East as the primary mission of the 4th Hussars was now rear area occupation duty.

Meanwhile, in the fall of 1916 Wolfram was made commander of the horse depot of the Twelfth Cavalry Brigade, an important task for a lieutenant but nothing that would bring him the kind of fame his cousin Manfred was achieving in the air service. He was next promoted to squadron commander, and now had 160 men under his command, but the job of the cavalry had taken on more and more the character of military police troops. With the strong encouragement of his cousins, Wolfram applied for transfer to the Luftstreitkräfte; in June 1917 his transfer was approved.

Rittmeister Manfred von Richthofen, the famous World War I flying ace, and cousin of Wolfram.

The World of Aerial Combat in 1918

During World War I aerial warfare evolved far more rapidly than did ground and naval warfare. Whereas air forces could field dozens of planes in one sector of the front during the 1914–1916 campaigns, the British and Germans deployed hundreds of planes in army sectors during 1917. The greatest aerial campaign of that year occurred during the campaign in the Flanders region of northwest France. From June to November 1917 the Royal Flying Corps, with more than 800 aircraft, confronted the German Imperial Air Service, with 600 aircraft. By using superior numbers the British expected to blast the Germans out of the skies and ensure that British observation and reconnaissance aircraft could support the ground troops relatively unmolested. By controlling the skies the British also intended to deny the Germans the ability to fly reconnaissance and observation missions over British lines. British strategy required a lot of airplanes, and heavy losses were expected. But the British had a clear superiority of men and material throughout the battle, and they expected that superiority to continue as the British aircraft industry reached full production levels.

In late 1916 the Luftstreitkräfte was completely reorganized to reflect the importance of airpower in all facets of combat operations. The new organization placed all the aviation assets of the army, including control of production and procurement, under a single aviation headquarters and general staff. The aviation assets included not only the flying units but observation balloons, flak units, and support services such as communications and training units. The new law established a single commander for the Luftstreitkräfte, the exceptionally capable General of Cavalry Ernst von Hoeppner who, in turn, answered to the high command.[17]

Collecting the experience of more than two years of aerial warfare, in May 1917 the German air staff published a comprehensive manual for operational air war.[18] The Luftstreitkräfte also published a series of other manuals in 1917 in order to standardize air operations and doctrine across the various fighting fronts and to ensure that the most effective tactics and organizational concepts were employed. Before 1917 the Luftstreitkräfte's tactics and organization varied greatly from unit to unit, and units transferred from one sector to another had to learn new command and tactical methods. The new standardized concepts and procedures not only served as a guide for the senior air commanders but also ensured that air units could be transferred from one army to another and from one front to another without having to undergo a time-consuming process of retraining and reorientation. In 1917 additional manuals were published that provided detailed guidance for aerial reconnaissance and artillery spotting units, and also for employing air units in the ground attack role.[19] Under the new organization each field army had an aviation commander and staff to command all air and flak units assigned to support that army.

The Luftstreitkräfte established a forward observer corps of teams that monitored enemy air activity along the front lines. When enemy aircraft crossed the front to observe or strike German positions in the rear, the observer corps, which was tied into an extensive army aviation communications network, would immediately report the activity to the army aviation headquarters and the air defense command center. These command centers would, in turn, notify the flak units of enemy numbers, altitude, and direction. The army aviation commander could then notify his fighter units to intercept the enemy incursion.

Each army aviation commander also maintained a staff and communications net for its observation planes, charged with spotting enemy artillery. Other staff sections dealt with intelligence, air reconnaissance photography, and meteorology. An important new asset on the intelligence side was a signals intelligence section that monitored enemy radio transmissions, broke the tactical codes, and analyzed the enemy communications traffic. Starting in the summer of 1916 the Luftstreitkräfte's signals intelligence service was able to give specific warnings of impending enemy air operations through code breaking and radio traffic analysis.[20]

In 1917 new, specially-designed high-velocity guns appeared that could put an explosive shell into the air at high altitude. The new guns, coupled with fire control directors (early mechanical computers), greatly increased flak's lethality. In 1917 German flak guns shot down 467 Allied planes; they shot down more than 700 the following year.[21] In the whole course of the war British flak on all fronts claimed only 300 airplanes. German flak accounted for 1,588 enemy planes.[22]

Artillery was the big killer of World War I, and success in any major defensive and offensive operation in 1917 depended on effective fire support. Artillery dominance was necessary to first smother the enemy defenders during the initial advance and then to enable the infantry to hold the newly won ground by breaking up any enemy concentrations for counterattack. If artillery dominance was the key to victory, then the airplane was the key to maximizing the effectiveness of the artillery.

The moment of greatest vulnerability for the World War I infantryman came when units were concentrating for the attack or counterattack. Ernst Jünger's classic book of World War I combat, *Storm of Steel*, vividly describes several occasions when whole platoons and companies were wiped out by a few well-placed artillery rounds hitting units poised to go into the attack. Sometimes this deadly effect could be achieved by luck or by a well-constructed artillery fire plan. However, often it was achieved with the assistance of well-trained aerial observers able to spot targets, such as troop concentrations, and bring immediate and accurate fire upon them.

Supporting the artillery was, by far, the most important mission of the World War I air forces. Aircraft conducted aerial surveillance, mapped out enemy positions, and identified targets on the front line and behind the lines so that the artillery could accurately strike those targets. By 1917 the air forces of both sides were processing tens of thousands of aerial photographs per month. When major ground battles erupted, aircraft were needed over the battlefield to identify targets for the artillery such as enemy troop movements and artillery positions.

German versus Allied Air Services

The biggest difference between the respective air forces on the western front, one that gave the Germans a significant advantage, was in pilot training. From the start of the war, German pilot training was far more thorough and systematic than the British, who in 1917 and 1918 were Germany's major opponents in the air. German pilots went through a basic flying course that required sixty-five flight hours before assignment to an air unit at the front. In 1916, when fighter aviation had evolved into a highly specialized branch of aerial warfare, the Germans set up a special fighter school in Valenciennes in France where new pilots detailed to fighter units underwent a three-to-four-week course in fighter tactics taught by pilots with recent experience at the front.[23] In March 1917 the commander of the Luftstreitkräfte's Front Aviation Force ordered that no single-seat fighter pilot was to be posted to a front unit without first going through a special fighter pilot's course.[24]

In contrast to the German approach, the Royal Flying Corps (RFC—which became the Royal Air Force in 1918) pilot training was very informal and haphazard. Indeed, the biggest cause of death for British airmen in World War I was in training accidents. A total of 8,000 British aircrew were killed in training in the U.K.—a record number of casualties per training hours that exceeded the Germans, French, and Americans by several times.[25] In 1917, during the Arras offensive, the RFC threw pilots into the battle with only fifteen hours total flight training.[26] In the summer of 1917 the RFC had only begun to address the training problem, and top fighter pilots such as James McCudden were briefly taken out of the front and sent around to teach fighter tactics in the operational squadrons.[27] However, in the skies over Europe in 1917 and early 1918, the superior German training program paid off handsomely. In the great air battles between the British and Germans over the Flanders sector between June and October 1917, the British lost over 900 aircrew killed in operations, whereas the Germans lost approximately 300 airmen.[28]

By the standards of the day, the flight training program that Wolfram von Richthofen experienced was very thorough; indeed, it was far superior to British training and at least equal to the French and American pilot training of 1917. German flight instruction was carried out in mostly obsolete two-seater aircraft, although specially modified dual-control aircraft were used for the basic flight instruction. In addition to basic flying, the German course included instruction on motors, formation flying, weather, air tactics, night flying, and aircraft recognition. The training was based on a systematic program of passing requirements that included solo flight and progressively longer cross-country flights and landings with and without power, and landings set to precise standards in which the pilot had to land the aircraft within fifty meters of a marker placed on the airfield.[29] German pilots often went through the aerial observer course as part of their flight training, a requirement that made German flight training somewhat longer than the Allied programs. Once the pilot was qualified to fly the two-seater observation planes, those with the best flying aptitude were detailed to be single-seat fighter pilots. During the basic flight instruction, most flying was carried out in the early morning or early evening, when the air was likely to be less turbulent.

When Wolfram left the 4th Hussars at the end of June 1917 he was able to take a long leave at home. In early September he reported to the 14th Flying Replacement Regiment based at Halle, one of the several large flight schools of the German army. Wolfram's basic flight training lasted three and one-half months. From December to early March he was assigned to the 11th Flying Replacement Battalion for advanced training, where he completed the formal flight training course in early March 1918. Von Richthofen must have impressed his instructors with his flying skills and ability to learn, as he was selected to fly single-seat fighters. Because of this, he could take up the invitation of his famous cousin, Manfred, to serve in Manfred's elite unit, Jagdgeschwader (fighter wing) (JG) 1. After a two-week course at the fighter pilot school in Valenciennes, Wolfram reported to JG 1 on 4 April 1918.

Under Manfred von Richthofen's Command

Rittmeister (Captain) Manfred von Richthofen had a highly personal approach to aerial warfare and command of Germany's premier fighter unit. His success as an aerial warrior was based more on his superb shooting skill than on his flying ability. In contrast to the superb aerobatic skills of his younger brother, Lothar (one of the top German aces of the war), or of Ernst Udet (who briefly served in JG 1 and became Germany's second high-scoring ace of the war), Manfred described himself as a somewhat mediocre pilot. He ascribed his success to getting close to the enemy, preferably behind him, and filling him full of lead. Manfred chided his brother for "fancy flying" and forbade his pilots from doing difficult aerobatic maneuvers in unit training.

Manfred put all his new pilots through his own training program before sending them into combat. He made time to fly with all the new pilots to see how they performed and to assess their strengths and weaknesses. Those rated as deficient were sent on to another branch of the Luftstreitkräfte. One exercise was to give each pilot 100 bullets—fifty for each machine gun—and have them shoot at a target. The new pilots might get fifty hits—if they were lucky. The experienced pilots usually got eighty to eighty-five hits. Manfred normally hit the target with ninety or more of his 100 bullets. Sometimes 100 bullet holes could be found in his target. It was an effective way to illustrate the importance of good marksmanship.[30] Lieutenant Carl August von Schoenebeck, who was assigned to Jasta 11 in 1917, described von Richthofen's training regimen for new pilots: "He himself took the training of each one of his pilots in his own hands. . . . On the tenth day I was allowed to go along to the Front. Like a hen, he watched over me, the 'chick.' All of the beginners had to fly very close to him. . . . Every time when he returned he called us together for criticism."[31]

As a highly successful fighter unit leader and ace, Manfred von Richthofen had the credibility to make himself heard in the top circles of the Luftstreitkräfte. Manfred formed a close friendship with aircraft designer and manufacturer Tony Fokker and through 1917 personally lobbied Fokker and the Luftstreitkräfte high command for better fighter planes to meet the challenge of the new British fighters such as the Sopwith Camel, SE 5s, and the fast Bristol two-seater. One aircraft that especially impressed Manfred was the new Sopwith triplane fighter that appeared with the Royal Naval Air Service squadrons flying over the battlefront in Flanders. Anthony Fokker's design team went to work and, within weeks, produced a German version of the triplane that entered service in the fall of 1917 as the Fokker Dr 1.[32] This highly maneuverable rotary-engine aircraft went immediately to Richthofen's JG 1 and then to other fighter wings on the western front.

Although Manfred von Richthofen liked the Dr 1, and for a short time it helped redress the British superiority in matériel, a new fighter plane that encompassed major improvements in speed, maneuverability, and maintainability would be required to help the Germans hold the western front against superior Allied air forces in the expected 1918 battles. One of the great drawbacks of the Fokker Dr 1 was its rotary engine. The rotary engine had reached its maximum potential, and it required castor oil, which was in short supply. The best solution was to use the highly reliable Mercedes Benz 160 and BMW 180 horsepower in-line engines. Manfred again lobbied Anthony Fokker to develop a new fighter and convinced the Luftstreitkräfte high command to hold a fighter competition in January 1918 to determine one or two new fighter designs to be adopted. Five major manufacturers entered twenty-eight aircraft in the competition. Fighter squadrons at the front sent representatives to test-fly the different aircraft and compare their evaluations. Manfred himself flew several of the designs.[33] Fokker's design was the clear winner of the competition according to the German fighter pilots.

Fokker rushed the D 7 into production, and other firms were licensed to produce the plane. Widely regarded as being the best fighter plane of World War I, the Fokker D 7 was the primary reason why the Imperial German Air Service was able to hold its own, even against a huge Allied advantage in numbers, until the very end of the war.

The Fokker D 7 was a biplane fighter that was fast (124 mph) and highly maneuverable. Most important, it had superb handling characteristics.[34] It was essential to design aircraft that were responsive to the controls and easy to fly—especially since new fighter pilots might show up at the front with 100 hours or less total flying time. It was said that the Fokker D 7 could turn a mediocre pilot into an ace because it handled so well. It also had the best climb rate of any major fighter in the war—another major consideration for an effective fighter plane.[35] The D 7 possessed still other advantages. It used a welded tube airframe rather than a wooden frame, which made it easy to mass-produce. The Mercedes 160 and BMW 180 horsepower in-line engines that it was fitted with were more reliable than the aircraft engines produced by the Allies (one of the reasons for the high Allied loss rate was engine failure). The D 7 was also designed to be easily and rapidly dismantled for transport by truck or rail. Upon arrival at an airfield it could be reassembled in a few minutes.[36]

In addition to his role as an adviser to the Luftstreitkräfte high command on selection of fighter aircraft, Manfred took the time to consider tactics and leadership for the squadron and group leaders. Shortly before he was killed in April 1918 he sent the air service high command a brief manual for squadron and wing commanders that outlined the principles for large fighter unit operations. In it, he described his training program for new pilots as well as his rules for conducting target practice and combat flying. He set the tone of a fatherly commander of his pilots but was also a strict disciplinarian: "There is no such thing as a gun jam! When it occurs, I blame only the pilot.... The pilot, not the armorer or mechanic, is responsible for having his machine gun fire faultlessly." He described in detail basic tactical principles and the best battle formations for forces composed of several squadrons. Manfred also outlined the use of large fighter units at the operational level of war. He argued that each army group should be assigned a fighter group to act as a general force for protection of the observation and close support aircraft. He insisted that concentration of forces was the key to success, and he argued against dispersing fighter units across the front.[37] In short, Manfred von Richthofen was much more than a great fighter pilot. He thought clearly and sensibly about the mission of large air forces in the air superiority battle over the front and their role in supporting the other branches of aviation. At the age of twenty-six he demonstrated exceptional potential for command at a high level. Had he survived the war, he certainly would have been selected for higher command and made general's rank.

Spring 1918: Germany on the Offense

With America's entry into the war in April 1917, the German high command embarked on a major expansion of the air service and a major increase of aircraft production in anticipation of major battles to come.[38] By early 1918 the air service had grown to approximately 4,500 aircrew at the front.[39] At the start of the German great spring offensives in March 1918 the Luftstreitkräfte frontline strength in the West was 3,668 planes, a significant increase over the 2,271 planes the air service had in early 1917. While the Germans faced Allied air forces that numbered 4,500 frontline planes, the Imperial Air Service could gain local air superiority by concentrating its aircraft over the main battle sectors.[40] The Germans could only hope that their spring offensives would result in a quick and dramatic victory as the Allies had all the advantages in a war of attrition. The Allied aircraft industries had hit their full stride by 1918, and both the British and French aircraft industries were producing more aircraft than were the Germans. Moreover, the British and French, and now the American, training programs were turning out large numbers of aircrew who were far better trained for combat than the Allied pilots of 1916–1917. Unlike the Germans, the Allies had no shortages of aviation fuel or castor oil to contend with. As the war continued, the Germans could expect constant attrition of aircrew and aircraft. By May 1918 Germany was losing approximately one-seventh of its frontline aircrew strength every month. The German training programs, although they had been expanded in 1917 and early 1918, still could not hope to replace this level of loss. In the long term, the Germans would simply run out of pilots.[41]

In early April when Wolfram arrived in his cousin's unit, he was assigned to the fighter squadron Jasta 11 (Jasta is a shortened form of *Jagdstaffel*, which means "fighter squadron"). Manfred von Richthofen had made his reputation as the commander of Jasta 11 before being promoted to wing commander of JG 1 in June 1917. Jasta 11 was part of Manfred's JG 1, as were Jastas 4, 6, and 10. By early 1917 a German fighter squadron consisted of fourteen planes, usually commanded by a first lieutenant, along with several dozen mechanics and ground support personnel. JG 1 had a total of fifty-two aircraft, usually with several aircraft in reserve to replace damaged or destroyed aircraft.

Then, as now, the primary mission of the fighter plane was to win air superiority. Fighters ensured that one's own artillery spotters and recon planes could do their work effectively. At the same time they would close the sky above and behind their own army to enemy reconnaissance, artillery spotters, and bombers. The Luftstreitkräfte's operational doctrine of 1917 stressed the importance of winning air superiority over the battlefield.[42] German fighters were to be massed in order to defeat enemy fighter forces—and open the way for the free operation of the reconnaissance and bomber forces.[43] A major step toward effective air warfare was taken in June 1917 when the air service began to organize the fighter squadrons into larger groups, starting with the formation of JG 1 under the command of Manfred von Richthofen.[44] The new four-squadron organization would fly and fight as a single unit. By summer 1917 the day of the lone ace seeking knightly aerial combat at dawn had passed. Massed fighter combat became the norm, and new tactics and formations stressed employing several squadrons at once. Through the summer and fall of 1917 the British would commonly fly two to four squadrons of aircraft over the German lines to face an equal number of German squadrons.

Since height provided a major advantage in air combat, the Germans met the British incursions by putting up a squadron at high altitude (14,000–15,000 feet) ready to dive on the enemy. A squadron or two would be positioned to intercept at medium altitude (8,000–10,000 feet), and the wing commander usually kept a squadron to the flank or rear ready to intervene and cut off British stragglers. The new wing organization and tactics proved highly effective in combat, and through the latter half of 1917 the Luftstreitkräfte reorganized other fighter squadrons into wings.

But once battle was joined the careful wing and squadron formations fell apart and aerial combat became a huge melee of individual dogfights where individual skill, good shooting, and a lot of luck were the keys to survival. Cecil Lewis, a British fighter ace with the RFC's famed 56 Squadron, described a few seconds of a typical large dogfight: "A pilot, in the second between his own engagements, might see a Hun diving vertically, an SE 5 on his tail, on the tail of the SE another Hun, and above him another British scout. These four, plunging headlong at two hundred miles an hour, guns crackling, tracers streaming, suddenly break up."[45]

In August, German fighter pilot morale was boosted by the appearance of the Fokker Dr 1 triplane. The British had equipped some squadrons with Sopwith triplanes in the spring of 1917, and the Germans found them to be dangerous opponents. One was captured in April 1917 and sent to Berlin for analysis. Anthony Fokker, at the urging of German aces such as Manfred von Richthofen, created a German version of the machine. The first two Fokker Dr 1 triplanes were sent to von Richthofen's JG 1 in Flanders, where they delighted pilots with their outstanding maneuverability and responsiveness.[46] However, it was soon discovered that the new triplane had major defects due to poor quality control—never a strong point in the Fokker aircraft factory. The top wing of some of the early Dr 1 production models was poorly braced and sometimes collapsed during strenuous flying. Two pilots were killed in accidents in October 1917, and the new Fokkers were grounded for several weeks while modifications were made and the design problems fixed.[47]

The frontline soldiers provided an appreciative audience for fighter combat. German infantryman Gerhard Dose, serving with the 187th Regiment in Flanders, described soldiers relaxing in their trenches, eating their canned meat, and watching the show thousands of feet above them. Soldiers would pass around the officers' binoculars to watch the action and argue about who had shot down whom. The infantrymen, inured to death after a tour in the trenches, saw the aerial war not in terms of a violent life or death struggle but in more poetic terms. Dose recalled, "As they dove and turned they would shine silver in the sun. . . . It looked like they were fish in the water playing with each other until one heard the distant hammering of machine guns."[48] Unless the airplanes were bombing them, soldiers found the spectacle a welcome diversion from the monotony of trench warfare.

Wolfram's First Combat Mission and the Death of Manfred

When Wolfram arrived at JG 1 in the spring of 1918 the unit had been heavily engaged in combat since the start of the "Michael Offensive" that began on 21 March. However, periods of bad weather provided some rest for the fighter pilots. As the German army had made significant advances on the ground between mid-March and mid-April, JG 1 was moved forward twice to occupy former British airfields within a few kilometers of the front. The first move was to the airfield at Lechelle, where the pilots and ground crew occupied British-built corrugated metal huts. It was at this time that Wolfram joined Jasta 11. He shared quarters in the British Nissen huts with Lieutenant Richard Wenzl, who had been a fighter pilot with Jasta 31 since 1917 and already had two kills. As a pilot of some promise, he had been invited to transfer to JG 1.[49] Wenzl described Wolfram as "the young cousin" of Manfred.

Because JG 1 by this time was fully equipped with the Fokker Dr 1 triplanes, Wolfram was issued a plane and was instructed to familiarize himself with it. Due to the limited range of the fighter planes in 1918—most had an endurance of 1–1.5 hours of flying time—airfields were located as close as possible to the front lines, and long-distance navigation skills were not required. The unit's pilots would rarely fly on operational missions outside a thirty-mile radius of their airfield. Under the leadership of Manfred von Richthofen and his carefully chosen subordinate squadron commanders, morale was high. The German army was defeating the British and advancing. Although Allied air forces outnumbered the Germans on the western front, at the main axis of the German advance the Luftstreitkräfte had concentrated superior forces. With an effective fighter plane in the Fokker Dr 1, the Luftstreitkräfte was fighting with good odds.

Although JG 1 and other fighter units had usually made themselves comfortable during the war by commandeering a hotel or manor house near the airfield to serve as the officers' quarters and mess, the spring of 1918 saw a great deal of upheaval as air units were shifted around to support the army where the fighting was heaviest. Considering that the British Royal Flying Corps had a reputation for good living, the aircrew found their captured barracks disappointing. The metal huts became hot by day and were cold at night. Furniture was sparse. Still, for officers like Wolfram who had served in the trenches of the eastern front, even such simple quarters were considerably better than anything experienced by officers in the trenches just a few miles away. The one constant in JG 1 was good food. Manfred insisted on it; and so wherever they were stationed the squadron pilot officers set up an officers' mess (Kasino) where they could eat and relax in the evenings with phonograph records, newspapers from home, and a good bar. Lieutenant Wenzl, who complained of occasional airsickness, reported that he cured his weak stomach in the Jasta 11 Kasino "with ample amounts of red wine and good ham sandwiches. The Staffel 11 Mess was, in general, splendid!"[50]

On 8 April the unit moved to a better airfield site at Cappy, only six kilometers from the front. Until proper barracks could be erected, the aircraft and personnel of JG 1 were sheltered by captured British tents.[51] For his first two weeks in JG 1 Wolfram went through the standard flying and marksmanship training program required by his cousin. On the evening of 20 April the

Fokker Triplane. This was the model of airplane flown by Manfred and Wolfram von Richthofen in the spring of 1918. Unlike his cousin, Wolfram did not score any kills in this aircraft. (U.S. Air Force)

fighter wing celebrated their commander's eightieth confirmed aerial victory of the war. On that day Manfred had shot down two Sopwith Camels of RAF 3 Squadron. There were plenty of drinks in the mess that evening in honor of the renowned fighter commander.

Wolfram's first combat patrol was to be the next day. However, luckily for the pilots who were probably nursing hangovers, the airfield at Cappy was fogged in and no early morning patrols were possible. A candid photograph taken that morning shows Manfred waiting on the edge of the airfield wearing his heavy flying overalls and chatting with his pilots, including Wolfram. Manfred and his seasoned pilots appear bored in the photo; Wolfram, however, clearly looks nervous—certainly the emotion one would expect for a fighter pilot awaiting his first mission.[52] At 10:30 a.m. the fog lifted, and word came that British pilots had crossed the front line. Observation planes of No. 3 Squadron Australian Flying Corps were active over the front, photographing and observing for British artillery. As was the norm, they were covered by RAF fighters, in this case Camels of 209 Squadron. JG 1 planes were to intercept the British and also to provide cover for German observation planes operating in the same sector. Manfred, with his bright red triplane, personally led a flight of Dr 1 fighters from Jasta 11 that included Wolfram and three other planes. They would be joined by Jasta 5 flying D V Albatros fighters. As it was Wolfram's first patrol, he was ordered to stay out of any dogfights and fly on the outside edge of the formation.

The German aircraft spotted the RAF Camels over the Somme River and joined battle. Flying with 209 Squadron was a Canadian novice pilot, Wilfred May, on his first patrol. Like Wolfram, he had been ordered to stay out of the fighting. In the excitement of battle, both he and Wolfram von Richthofen joined in. It is likely that May tried to get on Wolfram's tail. Cousin Manfred, carefully looking out for his new pilots, dived on May, who broke off the engagement and headed for the British lines. At this point, Manfred made several basic mistakes. In his eagerness to get May, who was flying low along the Somme Valley, Manfred also flew low and so became vulnerable to ground fire. Rather than breaking off the chase at this point, Manfred seems to have fixated on the pursuit and crossed over the British lines on his own. This was something the German fighters avoided if possible. (Indeed, if one of Manfred's own pilots had become separated and flown into British territory alone, he would have been soundly rebuked.) Finally, Manfred violated the most basic rule of the fighter pilot—he forgot to continually look behind. Captain Roy Brown, an experienced Canadian pilot and commander of a flight of 209 Squadron, followed Manfred down and fired at him. Whether Manfred was killed by Australian troops on the ground or by a burst from Brown's .303 machine guns is still debated—although Captain Brown was given credit for the victory. In any case, Manfred was killed by a single bullet through the heart, and his plane glided down and landed virtually intact within the Australian lines.[53]

JG 1 after Manfred's Death

Manfred von Richthofen's death was a major blow to the Luftstreitkräfte's morale. Indeed, there was widespread mourning in Germany at the death of one of Germany's most respected combat heroes. Thousands of common citizens and many nobles attended the requiem service for Manfred in Berlin. The German empress, Augusta Viktoria, sat with the von Richthofen family.[54] At the front, the pilots of JG 1 had little time to consider the death of their leader since they were facing a period of unrelenting combat. German air units were engaged in supporting a series of huge army offensives against the center of the Allied lines on the western front from March to July 1918.

After the initial collapse of the British Fifth Army in March 1918, the Allied defenses stiffened, and each successive German attack cost the Germans more casualties for increasingly smaller gains of ground.[55] In the air the Allies massed their aircraft and threw them aggressively against the German forces. The French and British air forces were far more effective than they had been a year before. The British had improved their training system, and new pilots were better prepared for combat.[56] The French trained 5,608 pilots in 1917 and increased that number to 8,000 pilots in 1918.[57] Moreover, the French were helping to train thousands of American pilots, who would soon be ready to support the American divisions landing in France and preparing for combat.[58] The newer Allied fighter planes, such as the French Spad XIII, the SE 5a, and the Sopwith Snipe, were excellent machines and extremely deadly in the hands of capable pilots. The worst part of the equation for the Germans was Allied numbers. At the start of the spring 1918 German offensive the Allies on the Western Front had 4,500 combat aircraft to Germany's 3,668.[59] The French and British aircraft production was in high gear, and the Allies could absorb heavy losses and continue expansion. Moreover, the Americans were training a large air force that would be able to go into battle with a large air force (mostly equipped with French aircraft) by the fall of 1918.

Following Manfred von Richthofen's death, JG 1 and Wolfram's Jasta 11 lost some top fliers. Lieutenant Hans Weiss, with seventeen aircraft to his credit, took over as Jasta 11 commander after Lieutenant Lothar von Richthofen was wounded in March 1918. Weiss survived only until 2 May, when he was killed in a dogfight.[60] Lieutenant Hans Jürgen Wolff, a likeable ex-cavalryman known as "Little Wolff," died in battle with the RAF on 16 May. Nineteen-year-old Edgar Scholz, who had six kills to his credit and had just been promoted to lieutenant, died in May in an aircraft accident. Another of Wolfram's squadron mates, Lieutenant Erich Just, was badly wounded in a fight with a British SE 5a squadron. However, he was able to return to duty before the war ended. In June, Lieutenant Werner Steinhäuser (ten aerial kills) was killed in battle with a French Spad two-seater.[61]

Losses could have been far worse for the German aircrew if not for the order of the Luftstreitkräfte's high command in early 1918 requiring all German aircrew to wear parachutes. During the intense air battles of that year many German pilots, among them Ernst Udet, Germany's top ace after Manfred von Richthofen, were able to bail out of crippled aircraft and live to fight again.[62] Although the Allied powers had also developed efficient parachutes, none of the Allied air forces made parachutes standard equipment. Thus, many Allied pilots fell unnecessarily to their deaths.[63]

Hermann Goering Takes Command of JG 1

Manfred left behind a written note designating Captain Wilhelm Reinhard, the next most senior officer in JG 1, to take command of the unit in the event of his death. A ceremonial cane had been made from the shattered propeller of one of Manfred's victories and became the symbol of command of the wing. The cane was given to Reinhard, a capable pilot with twenty aerial victories to his credit by June 1918. Reinhard tried to lead the fighter wing in the style and spirit of Manfred. In late June he was called back to Germany to evaluate new fighter designs, and on 3 July he was killed when the wings of a Dornier fighter collapsed during trials.[64] The symbolic cane was then passed to First Lieutenant Hermann Goering, an aggressive fighter pilot with twenty aerial victories who had just been awarded the Pour le Merité. By all accounts Goering was a competent commander of JG 1, leading the unit through several moves and through the major combat operations of the fall.[65]

Despite the death of Manfred von Richthofen it wasn't all bad news for Jasta 11 and JG 1 in the spring of 1918. In May and June 1918 the wing turned in its triplanes and was reequipped with the superb Fokker D 7. Flying an aircraft that was superior to their opponents was a big morale booster. Up to May 1918 the British Sopwith Camel, the primary fighter plane of the RAF, was at least the equal of the Fokker triplanes. However, the new Fokker D 7 outclassed the Camel in almost every regard. An American pilot serving with the RAF in 1918 recalled the superiority of the Fokker D 7 against the RAF's Sopwith Camel: "A Camel pilot had to shoot down every German plane in the sky to get home as the Camel could neither outclimb nor outrun a Fokker."[66] The appearance of the Fokker D 7 in large numbers over the front in May 1918 gave Germany the dogfighting advantage, and on 8 May the RAF experienced the heaviest single-day casualties of the war.[67] One of Wolfram von Richthofen's few surviving pictures of World War I shows him in the summer of 1918 in a standard pilot's pose standing in front of his Fokker D 7.

Wolfram Becomes an Ace

Wolfram apparently had little success flying the Fokker triplane. They were relatively slow planes, and in the spring of 1918 the German pilots considered them obsolescent in comparison with the much faster Spad XIII, Sopwith Dolphin, or SE 5a fighters of the Allied fighter squadrons. But when JG 1 was reequipped with the Fokker D 7 in May 1918 Wolfram quickly proved that he had "the right stuff" as a fighter pilot. On 4 June 1918 he shot down a French Spad XII two-seater observation plane near Dammond. Five days

Lt. Wolfram von Richthofen in front of his Fokker D 7 fighter, summer 1918. All eight of his aerial victories were scored in the Fokker D 7, which is regarded as the best fighter plane of World War I.

later he shot down another Spad. In recognition of his aerial bravery he was awarded the Iron Cross First Class (which required an act of bravery in battle and could only be granted after the soldier had won the Iron Cross Second Class). On 21 July he shot down an RAF Sopwith Camel, and on 12 August, just before his unit was taken out of combat, he shot down his second Camel.

During the early part of August 1918, JG 1 was flying in support of the Second Army, which was being hard pressed by the Allied offensives. JG 1 was supported by JG 2, but both wings were greatly outnumbered by the Allied squadrons facing them. German fighters were flying up to five sorties per day in the intensive combat. Typical missions were providing cover for ground attack squadrons and reconnaissance planes. The German reports state that it was very difficult to support German reconnaissance aircraft in the face of Allied air superiority. However, the German fighters managed the job, and the reconnaissance planes covered by fighter pilots such as Wolfram were able to spot major road and rail movements of the French army into the German Second Army sector.[68]

In September Wolfram was back in action with his squadron. There was considerable personnel turnover in Jasta 11, as experienced pilots were wounded or killed. When possible, pilots who had seen extensive action were granted leave from the front. After the death of Lieutenant Weiss in May 1918, command of Jasta 11 passed to Lieutenant Eberhard Mohnicke. When Mohnicke took leave that summer, Wolfram took over as temporary commander of Jasta 11 and led the squadron on patrols.[69] On 6 September, Wolfram shot down one of the RAF's newest fighters, a Sopwith Dolphin, east of St. Quentin. Two days later, Wolfram had his best day as a pilot when he shot down two RAF SE 5a fighters within five minutes on a patrol in the early evening.[70]

Despite attrition and the loss of some top pilots, JG 1 and Jasta 11 continued to shoot down British and French aircraft at an impressive rate. Wolfram also improved his score. By November 1918 Wolfram von Richthofen had eight confirmed aerial victories to his credit—a respectable score for a pilot who had entered action only the preceding April. When he scored his second aerial victory, he seems to have acquired the nickname "Ludewig" among his squadron mates.[71] The origin of the nickname is unknown, but it failed to stick past the war.

The Airman's War: Summer and Fall 1918

In many respects, the pilots of Jasta 11 and JG 1 had a much easier life than their colleagues serving in the infantry and artillery a few miles away at the front. When they flew home from their last sortie of the day they slept in warm barracks with proper beds with sheets. They could bathe with hot water and put on clean uniforms for dinner. Unlike the soldiers at the front, the pilots had excellent food and plenty of good liquor, and could relax in warmth and comfort in the Kasino. The flyers' civilization contrasts with the cold and wet existence in lice-ridden trenches, where the very air was filled with the stench of poison gas and long-dead unburied bodies strewn about no man's land. The front was a place where clean sheets, clean clothes, bathing, and proper hot dinners were almost forgotten memories. Moreover, soldiers in the trenches lived a life of constant danger. The war didn't break off in the evening, and a brief artillery barrage might kill you in your dugout at midnight. Fighter pilots did not fly at night, and periods of bad weather were welcomed as a respite from operations. In the Imperial Air Service, clear weather was known as *Flugwetter*, or "flying weather." Bad weather, including rain, fog, and overcast, was known as *Fliegerwetter*, or "flier's weather," as it meant that the pilots could sleep in and relax for the day.

However, aerial warfare had its own considerable drawbacks. Early in the war most flying was done at comfortable altitudes of 5,000–6,000 feet. As the war progressed and aviation technology made exponential steps forward, aerial combat was carried out at higher and higher altitudes. Height is a major advantage in aerial combat, so by 1918 German and Allied fighter squadrons would routinely climb to as high as 15,000 feet before attempting to intercept a patrol of enemy aircraft. The problem was that above 12,000 feet the lack of oxygen in the atmosphere makes it hard to breathe. Any flying over 14,000 feet carried with it the danger that the pilot might pass out from lack of oxygen. Even if this did not occur, the lack of oxygen to the brain could cause severe headaches and impair the pilot's judgment—and combat flying required first-rate judgment and split-second timing. In the Luftstreitkräfte only the high-altitude, long-range reconnaissance pilots, who operated at altitudes of over 20,000 feet and higher in 1918, carried bottled oxygen.

The normal conditions of flying in 1918 were physically debilitating and would wear down even the fittest young man. Worse than the lack of oxygen encountered at high altitude was the extreme cold that pilots routinely encountered at altitudes above 6,000–7,000 feet. Even in clear and sunny weather it is cold at high altitude, and the World War I fighter pilot flew in open-cockpit aircraft with no heating and no protection from the blast of the wind other than a small windscreen. Routinely flying in the extreme cold meant that the normal clothing for a pilot in 1918 was two sets of underwear, heavy lined overalls, a sweater, and a heavy leather jacket topped off by a leather flying helmet. Pilots wore heavy boots lined with felt and flew with heavy gloves to prevent frostbite.[72] Even with all that clothing, flying was such an exhausting business that the half-frozen pilots would land and have to be helped out of their planes by the ground crews because they did not have the strength to climb out. During the long summer days of 1918, JG 1 pilots normally flew five missions a day, each mission lasting an hour or more. The pilots would land to refuel and rearm and might be on the ground only long enough to grab a sandwich before going aloft again.

A few weeks of such a regimen would break down the best pilots, and many of the top pilots who were killed in 1918 fell to exhaustion as much as enemy bullets. When worn down by constant operations, even the best pilot lost the quick reflexes and snap judgment needed to survive in combat. After months with little break, pilots would make beginner's mistakes that would result in their deaths. In fact, Manfred von Richthofen made several such mistakes the day he was killed in 1918. From the description of his behavior on his last day of battle, Manfred von Richthofen was probably what the Germans termed *abgekämpft*—literally "fought out." By 1918 many of the

German pilots were "fought out." Indeed, it was a common problem in the Allied air forces as well, and several of the top Allied aces died in 1918 to accidents or simple mistakes. An examination of ninety-two French pilots flying for the Second French Army in 1918 found fifteen of them medically unfit for flight operations.[73]

On 8 August 1918, the day the British attack at Amiens broke the German lines wide open, the British and French had managed to mass 1,904 aircraft to cover a twenty-five-mile sector of the front. This total included 988 fighter planes. To oppose the Allies in that sector, the Luftstreitkräfte had only 365 aircraft, of which only 140 were fighters.[74] JG 1 was part of the defending German force that day. Attrition in the spring and summer battles had reduced the wing to only twenty-one serviceable planes, and JG 1 had been pulled out of action for a few weeks to be rebuilt.[75]

Despite heavy attrition and Allied aerial superiority, the Luftstreitkräfte could still hold its own. In September 1918, Jasta Boelcke scored forty-six confirmed victories while losing only two of its pilots. In the fighting from August to November 1918, the Luftstreitkräfte inflicted far heavier losses on its enemies than it experienced. The British, with the largest air force on the western front, took increasingly heavy casualties. During all of 1918 the British recorded 7,000 aircrew killed, wounded, missing, or captured. More than half of the losses, 3,700 aircrew, were from combat operations. The bloodiest month for the RAF was September 1918, when British losses totaled 1,023 personnel. That October, even with the Germans in retreat and the German front collapsing, the RAF lost 941 personnel.[76]

From 12 September to 26 September 1918, JG 1 opposed the numerically far superior American and French air services at St. Mihiel.[77] In October JG 1 again found itself arrayed against the Americans and the French over the Meuse-Argonne sector. Flying out of Marville on 9 October, a patrol of ten Fokker D 7s ran into thirty American Spad XIIIs from the U.S. First Pursuit Group, led by the top American ace, Captain Eddie Rickenbacker. The American commander quickly shot down one D 7, but the pilot was able to bail out and land unharmed within German lines. More German aircraft arrived, and the Germans managed to shoot down five U.S. fighters.[78] In the last months of the war, the Luftstreitkräfte inflicted an especially high toll on the inexperienced American air service units. For example, from March to November 1918 the U.S. 80th Aero Squadron averaged a 75 percent monthly loss of its aircrew.[79]

In mid-October, bad weather over the front and the outbreak of influenza among the German pilots limited flight operations. The fighter wing was back up in the air in late October, but it was clear that JG 1 would have to withdraw soon in order to avoid being overrun by the American advance. Wolfram kept on flying, and on 5 November he would shoot down his eighth and last confirmed enemy plane of the war when he was credited with downing an American DH 4 observation plane south of Montmedy in the Meuse-Argonne.[80] Two days later, JG 1 moved to Tellancourt, where its aircrew awaited the end of the war.

From July 1918 on, the German army on the western front was on the defensive against a series of major offensives by the Allies. Reinforced by American divisions supported by an array of modern weapons such as tanks, and backed up by war industries producing far more matériel than Germany, the Allies turned the tide with a rapidity that surprised both forces. Greatly outnumbered—having taken huge losses in the spring offensive that it could not hope to replace—and weakened by the beginning of the great influenza epidemic of 1918–1919, the ability of the German army to fight even defensive battles collapsed rapidly. When in August 1918 the British made a major breakthrough on their front, the German high command informed the government that the army could no longer hold the front and that the time had come to sue for peace. As major Allied offensives followed in quick succession that autumn, the pace of German retreat became more frantic. The German army still held together and still inflicted heavy casualties on the Allied forces, but complete collapse was only a matter of time as the Germans raced to establish a new government that could negotiate with the Allies. In October the imperial chancellor Georg Michaelis, and General Erich Ludendorff, who had served as virtual military dictator in Germany since 1916, resigned. The way was open to change the imperial constitution, abolish the authoritarian system, and democratize Germany with the hope of obtaining reasonable peace terms from the Allies. The kaiser appointed the popular and liberal Prince Max of Baden as the imperial chancellor, and the kaiser's authority as supreme warlord was revoked. From that moment, the kaiser lost his power as an authoritarian monarch, able to issue direct orders to the army and government without government review, and simply became a constitutional figurehead. The full power to govern now resided in the chancellor's office, and the chancellor was selected by the elected Reichstag.

The Luftstreitkräfte, like the army, was in retreat and hard-pressed by the now overwhelming Allied superiority. By the fall of 1918 the Allied air forces on the western front enjoyed a three-to-one numerical advantage over the Luftstreitkräfte. The Allies possessed excellent equipment and could support their offensives with overwhelming aerial superiority. During the St. Michel offensive in September 1918, the American and French air services put over 1,000 planes in the air. Such aerial power enabled the Allies to conduct

A plaque made to celebrate Wolfram von Richthofen's second air kill, a French aircraft, May 1918. He would shoot down eight Allied aircraft in 1918, earning him an Iron Cross First Class.

An American DH 4 two-seat observation plane. Wolfram von Richthofen's last aerial kill of World War I came on 5 November 1918, when he shot down a DH 4. He had the distinction of shooting down French, British, and American aircraft in World War I. (U.S. Air Force)

reconnaissance, support the artillery, and bomb and strafe German positions at will—the reconnaissance and bomber units covered by dozens of fighter squadrons. Against this armada the Germans could put up only a couple of hundred planes. The losses of the previous spring and summer could not be made up, and Luftstreitkräfte combat strength was declining rapidly. The German aircraft industry still produced first-rate aircraft in large numbers, so airplanes could be easily replaced. The critical problem for German airmen was the shortage of pilots and trained aircrew. The biplanes of 1918 could be produced quickly, but it took months of training to produce an even minimally competent pilot—and the Germans were running out of pilots by the fall of the year. It was estimated that to maintain the strength of 2,551 pilots that the Germans had at the front in May 1918 the air service would have to replace one-seventh of its strength every month. However, the Luftstreitkräfte's training establishment, suffering from fuel shortages, could not hope to meet this figure.[81] Moreover, gasoline and oil shortages were beginning to affect the operations of both the army and the Luftstreitkräfte. If the war continued much longer, senior German air commanders predicted that the Imperial Air Service would simply run out of gas.[82]

Due to the heavy attrition of aircrew and aircraft, the Luftstreitkräfte declined form 3,668 frontline aircraft in March 1918 to 2,709 combat aircraft at the war's end on 11 November 1918. At the end of the war, on the western front, the Luftstreitkräfte numbered 4,500 aircrew organized into 284 units. It was still a balanced and capable force with 1,200 single-seat fighters, 228 CL ground attack planes, 1,000 two-seat reconnaissance and observation planes, and 168 bombers.[83] The Allied air forces, despite massive losses in 1918, fielded 7,200 combat aircraft on the western front for a three-to-one superiority.[84] Yet, despite attrition and heavy casualties, JG 1 maintained its reputation to the end as an elite unit. During the existence of JG 1, from June 1917 until November 1918, the unit was credited with 892 aerial victories. In achieving this remarkable total JG 1 had 58 pilots killed in action, 47 wounded, 11 taken prisoner, 5 killed in accidents, and 4 injured in accidents.[85]

JG 1 flew its last combat missions on 8 November 1918. On the day of the armistice JG 1 was ordered to fly its airplanes to an Allied airfield, but Lieutenant Goering chose not to comply. Instead, he sent only five of his unit's airplanes to the Allies while the rest returned to Germany. The full significance of the kaiser's abdication became apparent when the weapons, vehicles, and equipment of JG 1's ground crew were confiscated by the revolutionary Soldiers' and Workers' Council in Darmstadt. The ground crew were placed under arrest by rebellious soldiers. Informed of the incident, Goering dropped a message to the mutinous soldiers holding the airfield and threatened to conduct an all-out attack with the entire wing unless his personnel and equipment were immediately freed. The rebels saw the better part of valor and complied. A few days later the unit moved a short distance east to Aschaffenburg, a city on the Main River in northern Bavaria. The local residents long remembered the arrival of JG 1's airplanes, still with the red trim made standard by Manfred von Richthofen, as they landed on a large field by the river on a bright and cool November day.

On 17 November, JG 1 had a final dinner for all personnel in the grand hall and restaurant of the Johannisburg Palace in Aschaffenburg. The palace (completed in 1620) is a huge and imposing red sandstone structure and is regarded as one of Germany's grandest Renaissance buildings. It was a fitting site for the last farewell of JG 1—which had been officially renamed the Richthofen Geschwader in honor of its first commander. Goering praised the unit's men and their performance and assured them that despite the disbanding of the famed fighter wing, the spirit of German aviation would live on.[86] The next day the unit's members separated. Most took their discharges from the army and went back home to civilian life. Lieutenant Goering took his discharge and went to southern Germany with the intention of making a living as a civilian aviator. It was a dream that lasted only a short while, for he became enamored of politics and a small political party in Munich led by a recently discharged corporal from a Bavarian regiment. Wolfram, as a prewar regular officer, decided to remain in the army for the time being.

After the Armistice

Wolfram von Richthofen had emerged from the Great War with a very good record. He had served in ground battles for two and one-half years and commanded a cavalry platoon and squadron (company) in battle. He had learned to fly and, by all accounts, had become a very competent aviator. He had served for eight months as a pilot in Germany's most elite fighter unit during the most intense period of the air war and had shot down eight enemy planes. Awarded the Iron Cross Second Class for service as a cavalry officer and the Iron Cross First Class for his bravery in aerial combat, he had demonstrated the courage under fire that is necessary for a leader of men in war. Most important, Wolfram was lucky. He had come through the war in one piece and in good health (his service records indicate no wounds), and this in a branch of the service that was inherently dangerous, as accidents were just as likely to kill pilots as was combat. Wolfram's considerable luck in surviving four years of war is remarkable when one considers the huge cost in blood that German families had paid. No fewer than six young men among the von Richthofen clan died in battle during the war, all cousins of Wolfram. The number of wounded is unknown but would have been higher. And that was just the casualty list among the cousins on his father's side.

Wolfram would have to make a decision whether to remain a career officer in the middle of the chaos of a revolutionary Germany. Unlike many other officers who knew only the army, Wolfram had some civilian career prospects. He could remain in the army or, as with many of his wartime colleagues in the Luftstreikräfte, leave the service and seek out a job in civil aviation—which was poised for a tremendous expansion in the postwar world.

The status of the defeated German armed forces was a matter left to negotiators at Versailles. General Hans von Seeckt, who had served with the Ottoman armies during 1918, was appointed the German army's chief negotiator during treaty negotiations. As was a common practice among the general staff officers, Seeckt had circulated a *Denkschrift* (literally, "thought paper") in February 1918 among the top leaders of the army that argued that the future German army should be based on a relatively small (300,000 man) elite volunteer army. In contrast to the senior Allied military leaders of World War I, Seeckt believed that in the next war mobility and maneuver, not mass and firepower, would be the dominant factors on the battlefield. The army he envisioned would be more mobile and better trained than the mass army of Germany's opponents and could defeat the enemy in a war in which maneuver played the key role. Such an army would have to employ the latest technology, and that meant that the elite professional army would be backed up by a large, independent air force.[87] Seeckt, working with his senior air adviser, Major Helmuth Wilberg, drew up an outline for a proposed peacetime German air force of 1,800 aircraft and 10,000 personnel. The force would be carefully balanced between fighters, reconnaissance aircraft, ground attack aircraft, and bombers.[88]

In November 1918 the old Inspectorate of Aviation was officially disestablished and replaced with the German Air Office. The senior leaders of the wartime Luftstreitkräfte, General von Hoeppner and Colonel Wilhelm Siegert, resigned from their posts as the Luftstreitkräfte front headquarters (Kogenluft) was dissolved in January 1919. The War Ministry Aviation Branch, under Colonel Hermann Lieth-Thomsen, commander of the front aviation forces from 1916–1918, established a program to keep the military aviators employed in civil aviation. The War Ministry decided to form four permanent airlines and a military air mail service employing 500 military aircraft suitable as civilian transports.[89]

In early 1919, its future still uncertain, the wartime Luftstreitkräfte underwent a process of reorganization. The armistice required the Germans to demobilize the Luftstreitkräfte and immediately turn over 2,000 aircraft to the Allies, including hundreds of Fokker D 7 fighters. Those aircraft were held in such high regard that the U.S. Air Service equipped several of its squadrons with them, and Fokker D 7s continued to fly in U.S. service into the 1920s. In addition, the German aircraft industry was required to continue producing combat aircraft to be turned over to the Allied powers.

After the defeat of Germany and the disbanding of units such as JG 1, many of the top young officers of the Luftstreitkräfte asked for their discharges and entered into civilian life. Hermann Goering found himself in Sweden flying airmail until he joined the Nazi party and became a top follower of Hitler. Wolfram's cousin and former squadron commander Lothar von Richthofen, with twenty-four victories to his credit and the reputation of a daredevil aviator, left the service, got married, and became a professional aviator. He died tragically in an air accident on 4 July 1922 while flying a passenger aircraft from Berlin to Hamburg.

Wolfram was assigned to the Luftstreitkräfte's air base at Gotha in November 1918. Gotha was close enough to his family home in Silesia that he was able to return home for regular visits. Luftstreitkräfte officers at Gotha and other large air bases were kept busy with the army's program to set up a commercial air transport and mail service while they were assembling and inventorying German military aviation material to be turned over to the Allies. As with many of the regular officers who remained in the Luftstreitkräfte, Wolfram probably spent the first half of 1919 flying mail around Germany.

On 8 May 1919 the blow came to Germany as the final Allied peace demands were announced. Five articles of the Versailles Treaty abolished all German military and naval aviation. While Germany would be permitted civil aviation, under severe limitations for several years, Allied inspectors would see to the destruction of the Luftstreitkräfte's aircraft and the dismantling of its infrastructure. By early 1920, the whole German air force, which in late 1918 comprised several thousand pilots and aircrew and tens of thousands of ground personnel, would have to be demobilized.[90]

Wolfram, as a prewar regular officer and who had a sterling record as a fighting officer, probably could have remained a cavalry officer in the 100,000-man army allowed the German Weimar Republic under the Versailles Treaty. However, like other officers who had transferred to the Luftstreitkräfte, he had become an aviation enthusiast. Returning to peacetime military duty in a cavalry regiment could not compare with the potential that aviation held. Even though Germany had no air force, the Versailles Treaty allowed the nation to develop its civil aviation potential, and even the most untrained observer could predict a bright future for civil aviation and the aviation industry. Germany had some of the best engineering schools in the world, and a degree in engineering could open the door to a wide range of possibilities, including further work in the exciting field of aviation.

With the announcement that the Versailles Treaty would disband the German air service, Wolfram was officially transferred back to his old regiment, the 4th Hussars. However, with the army in the process of demobilizing and being reorganized into the ten-division Reichswehr, there wasn't much for Wolfram to do in a cavalry regiment. At his own request he was granted extended leave. Although he would be on leave until he was formally discharged from the army on 29 February 1920, Wolfram basically entered civilian life when his leave status began in May 1919. As a final recognition for his wartime service, Wolfram was promoted to first lieutenant upon his discharge from the army.

Wolfram, who even as a young man had a reputation as a serious and deliberate person, had already determined his next step in life. He would get an engineering degree.

Chapter 4

From Reichswehr to the Wehrmacht, 1919–1936

Von Richthofen made an easier transition to civilian life than most of the regular officers discharged in 1919. The Versailles Treaty forced upon Germany in June 1919 stipulated that Germany reduce its army to 100,000 men within two years. Germany was not allowed to have any air force, tanks, or heavy weapons beyond a limited amount of artillery. The requirement to abolish the German air service was a deciding factor in Wolfram's decision to leave the military. Like so many of the young men who had joined the Luftstreitkräfte during the war, he had become enamored of flying and aviation. For a bright and ambitious man in his twenties, aviation, at least in its civilian form (which Germany had not been denied by the Versailles Treaty), offered an exciting and potentially lucrative professional opportunity. Thanks to the rapid and landmark advances in aircraft and engine design made during the Great War, it was clear that civil aviation would soon become a major industry. Von Richthofen, who already had served and proven that he was a competent pilot, saw his opportunities and took them. Coming from a family with considerable means, he had the option of going straight into business—he could have found backing from his family and relatives—or going to engineering school to become qualified to enter the top ranks of industry. He chose engineering school.

With his bent for mathematics and his fascination for technical things it was logical that Wolfram von Richthofen would choose to study engineering. The rapidly growing aviation and motor industries in Germany would need trained engineers, and a degree would open the path to the higher levels of management. Considering the business and entrepreneurial tradition of the von Richthofens, the decision to go into engineering was not an unusual one and was approved of by his family. Indeed, other young noblemen in the 1920s took a similar path—including rocket engineer Werner von Braun and Hans von Ohain, who developed Germany's first jet engine. However, before von Richthofen could be accepted by an engineering school he first had to pass the Abitur—the high school final examinations. He had entered the army in 1913 having completed the Gymnasium and received his school certificate—but had not taken the exams. So the first step to engineering school was to enroll in a short prep course in Breslau to ready himself for the arduous several days of written examinations in the subjects required by the Abitur, with an emphasis on mathematics and science, as good marks in both those subjects were necessary for a place in an engineering school.

Since Breslau was only a short train ride from the family estate, von Richthofen could enter into the local social life. Four years of war and hardship had deprived him of a normal social life and especially of feminine company. In the old peacetime imperial regular army, he probably would have had to wait until he was thirty years of age to marry. But he had just survived four years of war, and he wanted to get on with a normal life and career. So he looked to find a suitable bride. Breslau, as one of the major cities of Germany, offered a varied social life and plenty of opportunities to date and meet young women. His immediate and extended family as well as his local friends would certainly provide him opportunities to meet women from a similar and suitable background. Von Richthofen was young, good looking, a war hero, and from a prominent family. He had also come back from the war in one piece. In short, he was highly eligible. It did not take long for him to meet Jutta von Selchow, the woman who he would marry.

Jutta was tall and dark haired and a couple of years younger than Wolfram. (born March 1896). Like him, she came from the landed nobility of Upper Silesia. Von Richthofen was introduced to Jutta through her older brother, Günther von Selchow, who had served as a naval officer during the war. During the war, like so many of the noblewomen on the home front, she had served as a nurse. Like the von Richthofens, the Selchows were a prominent local family whose roots in the district went back for about three hundred years. Members of the family could be found in business, the military, and government.

The marriage of Wolfram and Jutta was a good match. Although Germany had just become a republic 1919 it was still a very class-conscious nation. Jutta and Wolfram moved in the same circles and had many common interests. Wolfram loved the outdoors and outdoor sports, and Jutta had also grown up on an estate and was comfortable with such things. Like Wolfram, she was a competent horseback rider. When her father and brothers went out hunting she liked to ride along, although she did not take part in the shooting. The surviving von Richthofen family photos usually show the couple together outdoors, skiing together in Switzerland, or swimming with the family at the lake. Not only could Jutta ride, but she apparently skied much better than her husband. In any case, their similar background and many similar interests made for a happy and comfortable marriage.

While courting Jutta, Wolfram finished his Abitur course and passed his exams with marks high enough to win him a place to study mechanical engineering at the Technische Hochschule Hannover (Technical University of Hanover), to begin in 1920. The university was one of the top German engineering schools at a time when Germany probably had the best education system in the world. One advantage to the German engineering schools was the quality and experience of the faculty. It was normal for the engineering professors to spend much of their time working as consultants to engineering firms, which meant that the German engineering professors were on the cutting edge of developing new technologies. The German approach to engineering education appealed greatly to von Richthofen's practical, rather than scholarly, turn of mind.

Wolfram and Jutta were married in the Lutheran Church in Breslau on 18 September 1920. After a short honeymoon they moved into a comfortable apartment in Hanover, and Wolfram began his studies. The von Richthofen family had close connections with Hanover because, on his mother's side, Wolfram was related to the Welf family that had been the ruling dukes of Braunschweig and Lüneburg until Bismarck deposed them in 1866 and annexed the provinces into Prussia. Another branch of the Welfs had been monarchs of Hanover until the German revolution of 1918 swept away all the German ruling houses. The von Richthofens had cousins in Hanover, so Wolfram and his new wife had an immediate social entrée. In addition, Wolfram and Jutta often visited family at the Barzdorf estate in Silesia.

Wolfram and his wife developed habits early on that would stay with them throughout their married life. They apparently made no major overseas trips in the 1920s, although they would start taking skiing vacations in Switzerland in the 1930s. They took regular holidays and returned often to visit the family and relatives at the Barzdorf estate in Silesia. Given the economic troubles in Germany in the early 1920s, the couple could be counted as fairly well off. But in the tradition of the German nobility, they lived modestly while Wolfram was completing his studies.

Their first child, Wolfram (nicknamed Wolf), was born in Hanover on 25 May 1922. He was followed by Götz, born in Potsdam on 27 November 1925, and Ellen, born in Breslau on 15 February 1928. In 1922 Wolfram's father, who had been in poor health for some time, died. The family would sort out the inheritance in an interesting fashion. Although Wolfram was the eldest son, the family estate was passed to his younger brother Manfred. Their father's brother Manfred, the retired cavalry general, had no children and so would legally adopt Wolfram as his son and heir, leaving Wolfram his estate at Bersdorf upon his death. Bersdorf was a large estate near the home estate of Barzdorf. While it sounds strange to be adopted as an adult by one's uncle it was not considered so unusual among Germany's landed nobility, who worked to arrange that titles and land would remain within the family in the case that a noble family was childless. Because the adoption was arranged in 1926, Wolfram's two sons who had already been born (Wolfram and Götz) were not considered adoptive grandchildren under the law. Ellen, born after the official adoption of her father, was thus the sole adoptive grandchild.

Wolfram's older sister, Sophie-Therese, had married a Silesian noble and estate owner, Alfred von Wietersheim, in 1913. Wietersheim had survived the war, and he and his wife settled down on the Weitersheim estate in Upper Silesia. Wolfram's father was in poor health and needed Manfred, Wolfram's younger brother (nicknamed "Pet"), to stay at Barzdorf to manage the estate. The youngest sibling of Wolfram, his brother Gerhard, born in 1902 and known to the family as "Gerd," had been too young to serve in the war and was still in the Striegau Gymnasium when Wolfram returned home from the war. As the youngest of three sons he was not going to inherit an estate, so he would be expected to undertake university studies or enter a profession when he completed his high school courses. In an earlier era, the army would have been the perfect place to send a younger son of the nobility. But the tiny army of post–World War I Germany had few places for young men like Gerhard. Germany was beset by economic crisis and hyperinflation, so prospects for a business career looked bleak. When Gerhard completed school in 1920 he took the somewhat adventurous course of emigrating to the Portuguese colony of Angola in Africa. There he became owner of a large coffee plantation and remained there until he died in 1956.

At the Technical University of Hanover von Richthofen was required to complete a rigorous three-year program to be accredited as a certified engineer (Diplom Ingenieur) by the university. His final thesis required designing a piece of machinery, complete with blueprints; interestingly, he chose to design a farm harvesting machine. He was apparently engrossed in his studies and preparing himself for a career in Germany's growing aviation industry when fate intervened in the form of the German army's commander in chief, Col. General Hans von Seeckt. The commander was inspecting units of the Reichswehr and meeting with the army's senior commanders in Hanover in 1922 when he took the time to meet Wolfram von Richthofen.[1] It turned out that Wolfram had a family connection with Seeckt in the form of his uncle, Major Götz von Olenhusen, who was his mother's younger brother. Olenhusen was Seeckt's adjutant and served as a member of the personal staff of the army commander in chief. Seeckt, of course, knew much about the von Richthofens. Wolfram's uncle Manfred, who retired at the end of the war as a General der Kavallerie, had served as a corps commander with Seeckt from 1915 to 1917 on the eastern front. With two uncles speaking on his behalf, it was not hard to arrange for Wolfram to dine with Seeckt one evening.

Wolfram's first career choice had been the army, and now he wanted to sound out the chief of the army about the possibility of returning to serve as an officer once his engineering degree was completed. In fact, Wolfram was exactly the kind of officer that Seeckt wanted in the Reichswehr—one with technical knowledge. In fact, he had recently initiated a program to send promising officers to engineering school in lieu of the regular general staff course. Upon receiving their engineering degree, these officers would be posted directly to the general staff where, as part of the army's elite, they would receive preference in promotion and command opportunities. That Wolfram was a Prussian nobleman from families Seeckt knew certainly did not hurt his standing, either.[2]

And so it was arranged for Wolfram to return to the army as a general staff officer. The general staff status would entail much work and responsibility, but it was also a ticket to rapid advancement in the Reichswehr. It also provided an opportunity to be both an officer and an airman, and to use his engineering skills. When von Richthofen was awarded his engineering degree in 1923 he was quickly reinstated as a lieutenant in the Reichswehr with a relatively high position on the rank list so that he could expect to be promoted to first lieutenant quickly.

Germany Builds a Secret Air Force

The Versailles Treaty that Germany accepted under duress in June 1919 stipulated that the German Reich was allowed to have only a small army without modern equipment such as tanks. In addition, Germany was allowed no air force at all. This went against the desire of the army and government that Germany should possess modern and capable armed forces reflective of its major power status. At the Versailles Conference, Seeckt had argued forcefully that Germany should be allowed to have a strong and separate air force in the postwar period.[3] The Luftstreitkräfte had performed admirably during World War I and had demonstrated the potential to become a truly decisive military arm.

When Seeckt became commander in chief of the army in early 1920 he made it a high priority to lay the foundations for future aerial rearmament by establishing a secret air staff within the army headquarters and carefully selecting a cadre of future air force leaders by retaining over 150 of the Luftstreitkräfte's pilot officers in an army that was not allowed to have aircraft. By legal and illegal means, Seeckt worked to undermine the disarmament provisions of the Versailles Treaty. In the context of German politics and feeling, this was not a radical act. The whole of the army and the overwhelming majority of Germans despised the Versailles Treaty and usually referred to it as the "Versailles Diktat." Even though Germany was now a democracy, many of the liberal politicians—as well as some socialist ones—were willing to support Seeckt's program of treaty evasion. The Reichstag ensured that ample funds were made available to the army to secretly develop modern aircraft, tanks, and other weapons. On the civilian side, the German government generously subsidized German civil aviation, an act perfectly legal under the Versailles Treaty. With a modern aviation industry and civil aviation infrastructure, Germany would be prepared to develop an air force as soon as the Versailles Treaty was nullified. Few in the German government or military believed that the disarmament of Germany would be permanent, so throughout the 1920s the German army laid the foundation for the Luftwaffe.

Starting with a small cadre of officers and civilian aviation specialists placed throughout the army headquarters in 1920, Seeckt built a secret air arm within the army. If Germany were forced into a conflict with its current small army, he planned to be able to field at least a small air force out of his secret cadre and elements of German civil aviation. In the meantime, von Seeckt ordered his army without airplanes to be "air-minded" and train all personnel for modern warfare conditions—which included considering plans for employing a modern air force. From 1920 to 1927 the secret air staff was headed by Lt. Colonel Helmuth Wilberg, a general staff officer and one of Germany's first military aviators. Wilberg had won a reputation as an outstanding senior air force leader when he had commanded more than 500 aircraft of the Luftstreitkräfte defending the Flanders front in 1917. He was succeeded by other senior airmen with command experience and general staff training: Hugo Sperrle, Lt. Colonel Helmuth Felmy, and Wilhelm Wimmer. All were exceptionally capable officers who carefully built a solid doctrinal and personnel foundation for a Luftwaffe that would soon be officially reborn.

The air staff was initially spread throughout the general staff departments (the general staff was known as the Truppenamt) and the Weapons Office (known as the Waffenamt). In 1930 it was consolidated as one Air Office. Throughout the 1920s the shadow Luftwaffe wrote air doctrine, conducted training exercises, secretly developed aircraft prototypes in Russia, ran a secret program to train new pilots, and maintained a close liaison with the German aircraft industry and civil aviation authorities to systematically prepare for the day of rearmament and the creation of an independent air force as part of the German armed forces.[4]

Seeckt reorganized the army headquarters and general staff to provide clear lines of responsibility for technical development, which he believed was necessary for the army of the future. The Truppenamt consisted of the normal departments: Army Organization, Training, Intelligence, Operations, and Logistics. The Waffenamt, which had as its chief a general of equal rank to the chief of the Truppenamt, had approximately as many personnel as the Truppenamt. In the mid-1920s the Waffenamt employed sixty-four officers, including two major generals, two colonels, and twelve lieutenant colonels. An additional twenty-one officers worked at test sites for the Waffenamt.[5] The greater part of the secret air staff of the army was concentrated in the Waffenamt, where several offices were devoted to developing aircraft, aircraft weaponry, and radio equipment. The Waffenamt had some military officers, but most of the personnel were civilian engineers and experts.

The German army developed a new education ethic under General Seeckt. He was instrumental in developing a series of doctrine manuals that were the core of what would be called blitzkrieg operations in 1939—warfare that emphasized mobility and the employment of combined arms. The air force would play a pivotal role both as a strategic weapon and as a tactical support force.

The shadow air staff, like most other major air forces of the period, was busy developing doctrines that emphasized strategic bombing of the enemy homeland.[6] However, the shadow Luftwaffe also understood it would have two major missions: a strategic/operational campaign deep behind enemy lines, and a tactical mission of winning air superiority over the front lines and providing reconnaissance and strike support to the army. In the strategic/operational air campaign the Luftwaffe would fly deep into the enemy homeland and destroy factories and installations vital to the enemy war-making potential.[7] The shadow Luftwaffe developed the term "operational air war" to describe a campaign that emphasized crippling the enemy ground forces by attacks on the enemy transportation net and mobilization centers.[8] Starting with this doctrine, the shadow Luftwaffe would develop the kinds of aircraft suitable for the different missions. Like most air forces of the era, Germany's shadow Luftwaffe would emphasize the bomber as the main air weapon.

Another major reform of Seeckt's, and the one that would directly affect von Richthofen, was a new system of officer education. Seeckt and other general staff officers came out of World War I convinced that the general staff had failed to fully grasp the implications of modern technology in warfare.[9] Therefore a new track would be established for the education of general staff officers. Most general staff officers would still be selected by a rigorous examination and then put through an intensive three-year course that emphasized the operational level of warfare. However, a select few officers would instead be sent to engineering universities, ensuring that when rearmament came, the general staff would possess a corps of officers highly familiar with technical matters.[10] Other officers who later gained high rank in the Luftwaffe were, like von Richthofen, sent to engineering school instead of the Kriegsakademie course.[11] To ensure that the general staff contained officers who understood strategy and economics, some officers who completed the general staff course were enrolled at the University of Berlin in courses on politics and economics.[12]

Return to the Army

Wolfram von Richthofen received his degree in engineering in 1923 and was officially readmitted to the army as a lieutenant on 1 November 1923. On the army list he was officially assigned to the 11th Cavalry Regiment of the 2nd Cavalry Division. The 11th Cavalry Regiment carried the tradition of several cavalry regiments of the old Prussian army, and some of the squadrons of the regiment were stationed at Ohlau, which had been the prewar station of Wolfram's old regiment, the 4th Silesian Hussars. The 2nd Cavalry Division headquarters was in Breslau. With the family estate nearby, it would have been personally convenient if von Richthofen had actually served with the unit he was assigned to. However, it is likely that he never even visited the unit of his official assignment. His army records show that from the date of his assignment, he was detached for duty at the army headquarters in Berlin.

Such subterfuges were common in handling the flying officers of the Reichswehr. With more than 150 aviation officers in an army that was allowed no aviation branch, someplace had to be found to officially assign the officers so that the Allied inspectors, who remained in Germany until 1927, would not be suspicious. The Versailles Treaty had forced the Reichswehr to have a three-division cavalry force, a much larger cavalry corps than it wanted or needed. So the cavalry divisions became favored places to officially assign air officers, who, like von Richthofen, would be "detached" to carry out their actual aviation duties.

Developing German Aviation—in Open and in Secret

From 1923 to 1936 von Richthofen's career was centered on planning and developing the aircraft and aircraft technology that Germany would need to have when rearmament came. The Waffenamt, where von Richthofen was assigned, consisted mostly of civilian experts (usually former officers) and professional engineers and technicians.[13] The general staff developed ideas, doctrine, and training programs for new equipment and made requests for research for new weapons. The Waffenamt developed the new weapons and equipment for the army.[14] From 1923 until 1929 von Richthofen worked in the Reichswehr's Berlin headquarters as a key member of the shadow Luftwaffe's Waffenamt group.[15]

Wolfram and Jutta settled into married life and rented an apartment on Südende Oehlertstrasse in central Berlin. Their next child, Götz, was born in 1925 in nearby Potsdam. Their last child, Ellen, was born in 1928 in Breslau. As a certified engineer and experienced airman, von Richthofen was appropriately assigned to the Waffenamt's section dealing with aircraft development and testing. The records of the Reichswehr are very spotty for this period, but Wolfram's primary work can be deduced from his doctoral dissertation, written in 1928. During the period 1925–1929 von Richthofen and army officers from the secret air staff and the army Waffenamt worked closely with the Technical University of Berlin on a variety of open and secret projects concerning German rearmament. Many of the top faculty members of the university were employed by the Reichswehr in secret weapons development programs. Von Richthofen, already a trained engineer, was able to use the faculty and facilities of the university to facilitate a series of secret research projects for the development of Germany's secret air force while taking advanced courses for a doctorate in engineering.

From 1923 to 1928 von Richthofen served as a liaison between the Waffenamt and the major German aircraft manufacturers, keeping abreast of the latest developments in aircraft design and working with the aircraft designers to develop secret aircraft prototypes for Germany's future rearmament. By 1925 he was leader of a small staff group formed to study aircraft production and procurement. That year he wrote a report for the Waffenamt on the ability of the German aircraft industry to quickly produce aircraft. Von Richthofen examined the production methods of the Junkers, Dornier, Rohrbach, Focke Wulf, Arado, and Albatros aircraft companies—essentially a complete survey of the German aircraft industry. The production methods ranged from all-metal aircraft (Junkers, Dornier, and Rohrbach) to mixed wood and metal frame construction (Heinkel and Arado) to steel tube fuselage structure (Albatros). Von Richthofen's primary interest was in the ease of serial production of the various aircraft types. In his report von Richthofen set out some essential priorities for consideration of aircraft procurement for later German rearmament. Unlike purely civilian aircraft, which were likely to be produced in small numbers, the military's priority requirements were

Jutta talking to Wolfram as he sits warming up a light plane, circa 1932.

to acquire aircraft that were highly survivable, could be easily repaired, and could be produced quickly in large numbers. Von Richthofen rated each firm as to its suitability for wartime mass production of aircraft that could meet these requirements. Essentially, he provided the Waffenamt with a process to rate industrial efficiency.[16]

Von Richthofen's 1925 report was expanded into a much larger study on aircraft production methods and efficiency for the Waffenamt that formed his doctoral dissertation in engineering at the Technical University of Berlin. In 1926 Richthofen undertook an intensive study of the production of large aircraft made by the Junkers Aircraft Company in Dessau and the Dornier Company in Switzerland. That these two companies became the focus of his liaison work and doctoral dissertation made sense, as the German military airmen, like airmen of the other major powers, were primarily interested in developing heavy bomber aircraft. The Junkers and Dornier firms were Germany's primary manufacturers of large passenger and transport aircraft, and both companies were on the cutting edge of world aircraft design. Junkers pioneered rugged, all-metal transport aircraft and had made great advances in the use of metal and in the construction of wings in such aircraft as the Junkers F 13, W 33, and W 34. The Junkers trimotors, G 24 and Ju 52, were very popular outside of Germany.[17] A German-crewed Junkers W 33 aircraft

Von Richthofen as a major in Berlin with his daughter Ellen and the family dog, circa 1935.

crossed the Atlantic in 1928 and proved some of the capabilities of long-range passenger and cargo transport.[18] Dornier produced several models of passenger planes and was famed for building the largest aircraft of the era, the multiengine Dornier Wal ("whale"), which was a long-range flying boat. With the experience acquired by these companies, both could be expected to build modern bombers when Germany was allowed to rearm.

Von Richthofen's work was part of a comprehensive effort to build a secret air force in defiance of the Versailles Treaty. The civilian aircraft companies and the German civil aviation system were almost completely staffed with former pilots and officers of the wartime Luftstreitkräfte, who saw it as their patriotic duty to cooperate closely with their former wartime colleagues, like von Richthofen, who served in the Reichswehr. For its part, the German government and the Reichswehr provided generous subsidies to German civil aviation to ensure that German industry could produce military aircraft when the time came. Between 1926 and 1932, the German aviation industry

Dornier 11 bomber, one of the Luftwaffe's first generation of aircraft, which was secretly developed by the Reichswehr in the late 1920s and early 1930s. Because of the secret rearmament work done by the Reichswehr Weapons Office, where von Richthofen worked, this aircraft was ready for production when Hitler came to power. Von Richthofen specifically studied Dornier's capability to build large aircraft. (U.S. Air Force)

received 321 million reichsmarks in government subsidies, investment, research funds, and the like. According to the exchange rate of the time, this amounted to US$12.42 million per year. The civil aviation department used its money wisely to develop the necessary basic infrastructure for modern aviation.[19]

During this period von Richthofen came to know the small group of airmen in the Truppenamt and Waffenamt extremely well. Almost all of the air staff officers of the 1920s would become generals after the Luftwaffe was established. Von Richthofen worked closely with several men who would become his superior officers, including Hugo Sperrle, Helmuth Felmy, Wilhelm Wimmer, Albert Kesselring, and Hans Jeschonnek. Other officers who worked in the secret air staff included Martin Fiebig and Kurt Student.[20] Von Richthofen loved the technical side of his profession and greatly enjoyed working alongside aircraft engineers and designers. Although the Technical University of Berlin would have been where he spent most of his time, he also made numerous trips to the Junkers and Dornier factories. Von Richthofen developed some close friendships in this period.

During this period on the air staff von Richthofen became something of an older brother figure to Hans Jeschonnek, who had volunteered as a seventeen-year-old soldier in 1916 and had become a fighter pilot and saw action in 1918. Captain Jeschonnek had been accepted for the three-year general staff course and had graduated in 1925 at the top of his class. He was considered brilliant by his peers and superiors, who predicted that he would rise to the top of the air force. Another close friend was Colonel Wilhelm Wimmer, also a former airman of the Luftstreitkräfte, who was widely considered to have the best technical mind in the air staff. Von Richthofen greatly admired Wimmer, who took over as the chief of aircraft development in the Waffenamt in 1929.[21] He would be a central figure in Luftwaffe aircraft development until 1936 and was dedicated to building a German air force that would be technologically equal, or superior, to any air force in the world.

In 1932 army commander General Werner von Blomberg prepared and won approval for a plan to consolidate all the Reichswehr air activities into one department.[22] Under Wimmer's leadership of the Technical Office, each branch of the Luftwaffe (flak, communications, training, and weapons) submitted its requirements for new equipment. The general staff planning group developed general requirements from these lists and sent them to the Technical Office, which had six sections: airframes, engines, instruments, electrical equipment and radios, weapons, and ground service equipment. Requirements were then submitted to German industrial firms so they could develop prototypes.[23] The system to develop aircraft was similar to that used in World War I. Specifications for a new aircraft were sent to two or more aircraft firms, and each firm was given a contract to develop two or three prototype aircraft. Once the prototypes were delivered, they would undergo a testing process and finally a "fly-off," similar to the flying competition of January 1918 whereby the German Imperial Air Service decided to produce the Fokker D 7. The winning design would be selected for a production contract.

Throughout the 1920s the Reichswehr had various programs to secretly train new pilots and to build up a cadre for the secret Luftwaffe.[24] Von Richthofen was able to keep up his pilot skills by flying rented civilian aircraft at the Reichswehr's expense. In 1926, while practicing his flying, he had a landing accident in a light Albatros aircraft that broke the landing gear and cracked the propeller. Such mishaps were common in the early days of flying, and von Richthofen was apparently unbothered by the incident. He had himself photographed next to the damaged plane and had the cracked propeller turned into a chandelier for his personal study.

In 1929 von Richthofen published his dissertation and earned his doctorate degree at the Technical University of Berlin. For many years historians were unsure whether von Richthofen's doctorate was honorary or earned, as information concerning his dissertation was unknown—because it was top-secret work for the Reichswehr staff, and only a few officers involved in secret

Wolfram von Richthofen's landing accident with an Albatros airplane, 1926. During the interwar era, the Reichswehr made arrangements to rent civilian aircraft from civilian flight schools so that flying officers such as von Richthofen could keep up with their flying.

mobilization work were privy to it. Von Richthofen's dissertation, rediscovered in the 1990s, was titled, "The Influence of Aircraft Production Methods and Contrasting Model Types with Reference to Production of Military Aircraft."[25] With the Interallied Military Control Commission still active in Germany (until 1930) and still looking to uncover signs of illegal German rearmament programs—which this dissertation clearly alluded to—it would have been necessary to keep von Richthofen's research very closely held.

Von Richthofen's dissertation was an interesting mix of engineering and economics and shows that he had gained a comprehensive picture of the German aviation industry. In anticipating large-scale production for a reborn German air force, von Richthofen looked at the advantages and disadvantages of various materials in aircraft design as well as the industrial plant requirements for each type of production. The central thrust of von Richthofen's study was an analysis of the different production methods of Dornier and Junkers, two aircraft companies both involved in secret development work for the army. The comparison of the industrial methods included data and tables on worker productivity and per-hour requirements for airframe construction. This was correlated to the production cost of the aircraft.

Von Richthofen's database was relatively limited, as the Dornier and Junkers companies had relatively small production runs of their aircraft models (typical of all the aircraft producers of the 1920s). But based on a few year's worth of data, von Richthofen was able to determine that there was a measurable learning curve during the serial production of aircraft models, which led to a notable reduction in the working hours and costs per ton of aircraft over the life of a production run of a given model. Simply put, as workers and managers gained experience in manufacturing an airplane, the working time and effort to produce the airplane became less. Workers learned to cut metal more efficiently, and managers learned to maximize the efficiency of the assembly line. The improvements in production efficiency were most notable in the first year of a production run, but measurable improvements in efficiency and cost reduction were also noted in subsequent years. The learning curve model, which von Richthofen illustrated, was applicable to all the firms and aircraft models that von Richthofen analyzed.[26] Von Richthofen was among the first to develop a model for the measurement of "the learning curve," the rule that the direct amount of labor required to produce a given unit declines as the number of units is expanded.[27] Von Richthofen discovered that Junkers was able to reduce the number of man hours per ton of aircraft from 21,400 for the first aircraft of a production series to 3,600 for the fiftieth aircraft of the same series. Dornier was able to reduce the man hours per ton from 11,800 for the first aircraft of a series to 8,200 for the twelfth aircraft of the series.[28] Von Richthofen's dissertation provided some valuable insights into projecting aircraft production costs and manpower requirements for serial aircraft production. In the early 1930s, as rearmament became more open, von Richthofen study would form the basis of the Luftwaffe's early mobilization and aircraft production planning.

Von Richthofen was promoted to captain in 1929 and with his new rank and doctoral degree was selected by the army for an unusual assignment. He would be sent to Italy as an official Reichswehr representative to the Italian air force.

Von Richthofen to Italy

As the 1920s came to a close the Interallied Military Control Commission, which had overseen the disarmament of Germany and maintained the right to enforce the disarmament provisions of the Versailles Treaty, was shut down. Its final report noted that Germany had substantially complied with the Versailles Treaty. Although the commission had caught the Germans in numerous violations of the rules and suspected that there were still secret rearmament programs, an assumption in which it was entirely correct, the commission also noted the plain truth: that Germany had been substantially disarmed.

With the end of the commission's regime, Germany intensified its diplomatic efforts to end the system of reparations and to allow a limited degree of rearmament that would allow Germany some parity with other nations. Aside from France and Belgium, the European nations generally favored readmitting Germany to its status as an important power and renegotiating the issues of reparations and German rearmament. In this atmosphere, the shadow Luftwaffe saw the chance for some degree of open rearmament and the possibility that Germany would be openly allowed to have a small air force. The staff therefore developed a series of plans for limited rearmament with a small German air force.[29] One of the first steps of the semi-open rearmament program was to establish normal military relations with other powers under a military attaché system. Germany had been forbidden to have military attachés accredited to foreign nations after World War I, but the Reichswehr was eager to get the attaché system formally reestablished. Until the time that Germany could appoint formal attachés, the Reichswehr would move ahead by appointing informal ones. The Reichswehr air staff was especially interested in Italy. Although Italy was one of the parties of the Versailles Treaty, the Mussolini regime expressed no hostility toward Germany. In fact, the Italian view was that Italy had been treated badly in the post–World War I Allied negotiations when France had worked to strictly limit the expansion of Italian power in the Mediterranean. Because of this, and because Italy saw France, not Germany, as a threat and rival to its national ambitions, Germany was viewed as a natural ally. Italy sympathized with Germany's desire to revise the Versailles system, and a militarily stronger Germany would make an excellent counterweight to France.

Throughout the 1920s Italy looked to developing stronger trade and diplomatic links to Germany. Since both nations saw France as their primary threat, it also made sense to quietly establish military relations as well. Italy had one of the major European air forces at the time, and in the late 1920s it was considered to be a major power. It also had one of the world's largest aviation industries, and Italian pilots and aircraft had set a number of major records. By 1929 Italy was eager to allow German officers to be attached to its army and air force. The Italians admired Germany's military prowess and technological competence. After all, Italy had copied the German general staff system and training in the late nineteenth century for its own army. The Germans, for their part, desperately wanted to establish a closer contact with the nations that possessed modern air forces.

In 1929 von Richthofen was informed that he had been selected to serve for six months on attachment to the Italian air force. The Reichswehr air staff believed that much could be learned from the Italians, and this was Germany's first real opportunity to see how the air force of a major power operated. Von Richthofen was instructed by the Reichswehr air staff to report on the technology, training programs, and, most important, doctrine and tactics of Italy's air force.[30] He was specifically instructed by Major Felmy, chief of the Reichswehr air office, to study the airpower concepts of the Italians, and especially to report on the ideas of the famous Italian airpower theorist, General Giulio Douhet, whom Felmy described as "well-known and followed carefully in the magazines."[31] To prepare for the mission von Richthofen had to take an intensive course in Italian and become fluent enough to pass the translator test. The language training was a somewhat painful experience for him, as foreign languages were not his strength. He had received mediocre grades in English and Latin in school and, as his own family noted, "He had no gift for languages." However, he applied himself to the task and took pride in learning Italian to a good degree of fluency.

As von Richthofen began his attachment in late 1929, Germany's political relationship with Italy had improved to the point that when his attachment was completed, he would be stationed in Italy for two and one-half years to serve as the German air attaché to the Italian air force. In 1930 major power disarmament talks were underway, and the Germans and Italians guessed, correctly, that such Versailles Treaty provisions were not likely to last much longer. In fact, the final restrictions preventing Germany from having accredited military attachés to foreign countries were formally lifted in 1933. With von Richthofen in Italy, the Reichswehr had simply moved a bit faster than did the diplomats. Although he was not formally accredited as the attaché, he was recognized as such. He had a semi-official status with the German Embassy in Rome, but to maintain the proper form he always wore civilian clothes and worked out of an office in his home.

Despite the worldwide economic depression, the von Richthofens lived well in Italy. Berlin provided von Richthofen with a generous living allowance, and the family rented a comfortable house. They also had an automobile—their first. The work was not arduous, but one can surmise from von Richthofen's approach to all his work that he did a very thorough job in compiling detailed reports on the Italian air force and military equipment for the staff in Berlin. He and Jutta took vacations and outings with their three children—Wolfram and Götz were in elementary school, and Ellen was still a baby. The von Richthofens traveled around Italy, vacationed at the beautiful Lake Como (one of the most popular resort areas for the Italian upper classes), and returned to the family estate in Silesia for summer and winter holidays. Von Richthofen also had the opportunity to enjoy the hunting in Italy, especially the excellent duck hunting along the Po River.

Von Richthofen used his attachment and service as attaché to get to know the senior and midranking officers of the Italian air force. The Italians frankly admired the German military, and von Richthofen was warmly and readily accepted by the Italians. As a decorated World War I pilot and an expert in aviation technology he mixed freely with the Italian air force officers, who allowed him to visit their bases, fly their Italian planes, and tour Italy's aircraft factories. Von Richthofen got to know almost every officer of note in the Italian air force, including General Italo Balbo, a world-famous aviator and commander of Italy's air force. Von Richthofen and Balbo apparently became good friends, and Balbo's friendship guaranteed von Richthofen full access to the Italian air force.[32] In his diary entries written during the Spanish Civil War and during his command of the 2nd Air Fleet in Italy in 1943–1944, von Richthofen continually referred to Italian officers who he had first come to know between 1929 and 1932.

Immediately after his return from Italy in 1932 von Richthofen tested positive for tuberculosis, which he had apparently contracted on his tour of duty. It was not a severe case, but the Luftwaffe wanted one of its few qualified general staff officers to make a rapid recovery. Von Richthofen thus was sent to a sanitarium in the Swiss Alps for several weeks, where the mountain air would help him recover. He took Jutta with him and, true to his love of the outdoors, turned his sanitarium treatment into a skiing holiday. Although he recovered quickly, von Richthofen was physically weaker. He aged more quickly after that, and for the rest of his life he would have to contend with bouts of exhaustion that were probably aggravated by his tuberculosis.

Von Richthofen did not return to the air staff but was instead given command of a company of transport troops. The assignment was part of the regular progression for general staff officers, who needed command experience in order to be groomed for higher rank and responsibilities. It made sense to send someone as technologically gifted as von Richthofen to an army transport unit because the army transport corps was the primary force tasked to test motorized equipment and develop equipment, doctrine, and tactics for the mechanized army of the future.

This was an exciting period for the Reichswehr, for the maneuver war concepts developed under General Seeckt's tenure were finally bearing fruit. In 1932 the German army carried out a series of large-scale maneuvers with most of the army's ten divisions in order to test new concepts of organization and tactics for a motorized army. Von Richthofen, his health improved after

Von Richthofen and his wife, Jutta, skiing in Switzerland in 1938.

weeks in the sanitarium, took part in the fall maneuvers that year as an officer of the motorized troops. The exercises, held in eastern Germany, emphasized the employment of motorized infantry battalions, armored car units, and motorcycle battalions. In an attempt to test the combined arms and maneuver warfare doctrine developed in the 1920s, a fully motorized corps was created. These last major maneuvers of the Weimar Republic demonstrated how far the Reichswehr had come in a decade. Radio communications with the fast-moving forces were an important feature of the maneuvers. At the conclusion of the exercises, the Reichswehr was convinced that it was on the right track, and it made plans to accelerate the mechanization of the army.[33]

Rearmament Begins

On 30 January 1933, Adolf Hitler became chancellor of Germany. As was noted earlier, it was an event greatly favored by both the military and Germany's nobility. The social group that had produced von Richthofen had never been very comfortable with the Weimar Republic, and a disproportionate number of the nobles had become Nazi Party members even before Hitler came to power. The officer class, such as von Richthofen, saw Hitler as a man who would bring order to Germany, revoke the restrictions of the hated Versailles Treaty, and allow Germany to regain its place as a major power. From the beginning, von Richthofen, along with many of his fellow officers, fell under Hitler's spell.

With Hitler in power, an air ministry was established as a cabinet-level office. Germany's first air minister would be Hermann Goering, von Richthofen's former commanding officer from World War I. Goering would use the new Reichs Air Ministry, ostensibly a civilian organization, as an organizational vehicle to build a new air force. The Reichswehr's cadre of air officers, including von Richthofen, were officially "retired" from the army and brought over to the new air ministry en masse as civilian staff. In reality, the transferred officers retained their military ranks and wore new uniforms as Reichs Civil Aviation officers. In time, the "civilian" uniforms became the Luftwaffe uniforms when the existence of a German air force was officially announced on 1 March 1935. In reality, the Luftwaffe was established as an independent arm of the German military in 1933. Because there were only a handful (twenty-nine) of fully qualified general staff officers with aviation experience in the Reichswehr, the new war minister, General Werner von Blomberg, ordered the army staff to give up some of its most talented officers to help form a leadership cadre for what would become a large and modern air force. The army sent some outstanding officers to the new ministry, including Colonel Albert

Kesselring, Colonel Hans Jürgen Stumpf, and General Walter Wever. Giving Wever to the air ministry was hard on the army, as Blomberg and the army staff saw in Wever a prospective army chief of staff. Instead, he would serve as the Luftwaffe's chief of staff from 1933 to his death in 1936.[34]

Goering brought in Erhard Milch to be the state secretary for aviation, essentially the man who would lead the administrative, budgetary, and procurement side of the Luftwaffe. Milch had been a Luftstreitkräfte officer in World War I and ended the war as a captain and squadron commander. He went into civil aviation after the war and became the general manager of Lufthansa, Germany's national airline. He was a superbly competent manager, fully informed of German aviation developments, and was a good choice to serve as Goering's number-two man in the Luftwaffe. The senior Luftwaffe officers respected Milch greatly for his obvious management skills. But many, probably most, of the Luftwaffe's senior officers had no real liking for Milch because he clearly loved the politics of the job and was all too comfortable with the Nazi Party's leaders—who the professional officers generally disdained and somewhat rudely referred to as "Partei Bonzen" ("Party Big Wigs"). For all Milch's desire to be seen as an air commander, he was viewed by the professional soldiers as more of a businessman and politician—which was not an unfair judgment. Yet Milch played a vital role in building the Luftwaffe's infrastructure, and Germany's aerial rearmament would not have been as fast or effective without his managerial talent.

The Luftwaffe's commander, Hermann Goering, owed his position to his relationship with the Führer and his status as a hero of the First World War. Goering was corrupt and lazy and did not wish to be bothered by details, which Milch could attend to. Goering was useful for his influence with the Führer and the Nazi elites, and his status in Hitler's inner circle ensured that the Luftwaffe was given all the funds and resources it required. In short order, vast sums were made available to build the Luftwaffe. On the negative side, Goering was a dilettante who displayed no real knowledge or interest in modern aviation. Von Richthofen noted that outside of formal staff meetings, Goering never talked about modern aircraft or aviation during his work. On social occasions he would sit and drink with former fighter ace Ernst Udet, or his old wingman Bruno Loerzer, and talk about the good old days of Jagdgeschwader 1 in the Great War. Goering had not flown an airplane since 1923, and his view of aviation remained that of an open-cockpit biplane fighter ace. Von Richthofen found Goering's attitude appalling. Goering favored his cronies and would put some of them, like Udet, in top positions in the Luftwaffe with disastrous results. For all Goering's charm, none of the senior Luftwaffe officers trusted him or thought him competent.

General Walter Wever, first chief of the Luftwaffe general staff, 1935. (U.S. Air Force Historical Research Agency)

However, with Wever at the helm of the Luftwaffe, Goering's influence over the vital issues of doctrine and equipment were held in check. Wever quickly learned to fly and became an enthusiast for aviation. For three years he provided strong leadership and clear direction to the early stages of building the Luftwaffe. He was greatly respected by the Luftwaffe staff, and he ensured that only highly competent general staff officers headed each of the air ministry's branches and staff sections. Wever sensibly decided to keep

Wilhelm Wimmer as head of the Technical Office, charged with developing aircraft for the Luftwaffe. Von Richthofen, promoted to major in 1934, was appointed as branch chief of the aircraft development office to work under Wimmer. In 1934 the Technical Office consisted of four branches: research, aircraft development, production, and budget. The aircraft development branch that von Richthofen led had six divisions—airplanes, motors, aircraft instruments, radios, weapons, and production. Overseeing it was a very large responsibility for a major.[35]

The solid work done by the shadow Luftwaffe staff in the 1920s and early 1930s now paid off. The new air ministry inherited an excellent staff with a rational program for planning, training, and aircraft development, and brought in a large number of former Luftstreitkräfte officers who had gone into civil aviation and industry. Many of the most competent men in Germany's civil aviation industry were eager to put their uniforms back on. In addition, civilian specialists with backgrounds in civil aviation were enlisted into the special staffs of the new Luftwaffe, and many rose to high rank.[36]

With von Richthofen now at the air ministry, the family moved to Berlin to a house on Wittenbergerstrasse. Sons Wolfram and Götz were in primary school, and daughter Ellen would soon enter kindergarten. The family was only a few hours by train from the family home in Silesia, and they enjoyed regular holidays with their uncles and grandparents at the Barzdorf estate. Von Richthofen could indulge himself with the excellent hunting around Berlin, and he would often travel on business with one of his favorite shotguns in the plane or car so he could get in a few hours of hunting in the local forest after meeting with aircraft designers. As befitting a rising general staff officer, he had a regular social life. He and Jutta often had friends over for dinner and cocktail parties. In the evenings he would play cards or listen to the radio. In contrast to his very aloof manner as a general staff officer, he could unwind when he put on civilian clothes. He was no connoisseur, but he liked good food and wine.

In the late 1920s and early 1930s Wimmer's office, working with the German aviation industry, had developed several aircraft prototypes that were ready to be produced as soon as the ministry could provide contracts. These first-generation Luftwaffe aircraft included the Heinkel He 51 fighter, the Arado AR 65 fighter, the Heinkel He 45 light bomber and reconnaissance plane, and the Dornier Do 11 bomber. None of these planes would make any mark in aviation history. They were the products of an aviation era that was in transition from cloth-covered biplanes and fixed landing gear and small engines to all-metal monoplanes with engines over 1,000 horsepower. Even so, the first generation of the Luftwaffe's planes was roughly equal to its

General Wilhelm Wimmer, head of the Luftwaffe Technical Office, 1932–1936. Von Richthofen thought very highly of Wimmer, whom he described as the "best technical mind in the Luftwaffe." Wimmer was largely responsible for the success of the Luftwaffe's first two generations of aircraft.

counterpart aircraft flown by the air forces of the other major powers. Most important, they were ready to be quickly produced.

In August 1934 von Richthofen issued a statement of "development guidelines," making the case for putting relatively mediocre bombers, such as the Do 11 and its improved versions into full production, along with the Ju 52 transports that were being converted into bombers. The Do 11 was followed by an improved model, the Do 23, which had better engines and was somewhat faster.[37] Von Richthofen insisted that "a conditional, useful, operative piece of equipment is better than no equipment at all. Operational

Wolfram and Jutta at a family gathering in the mid-1930s.

equipment for every purpose must be developed in the shortest possible time even if it is an interim or emergency solution to a problem. The finest and most complete piece of equipment whose development is not finished is next to worthless. An air force must be ready for operations at all times. Only the equipment on hand will be used in the few hours given to achieve the desired, vital objectives."[38] The final sentence refers to the concept of the "risk air force," the air force that Germany would have to build immediately as a deterrent to any immediate response by France or its allies.

The program to get aircraft into production quickly in 1934 was a sound one, as the German aircraft companies, with assured orders, were able to rapidly expand their factories and design offices and develop experience in producing large numbers of aircraft. As German aircraft before 1934 had been produced on virtually a hand-work basis, the manufacturers were forced to learn to simplify production techniques and standardize their use of raw materials. Efficient production methods were von Richthofen's technical specialty, and the question of ease of production was central to his decision to recommend an aircraft for acceptance. With instructions to limit the import of foreign materials as a means to keep German foreign exchange in balance, the air ministry encouraged manufacturers to reduce the amount of specialty metals and resources imported from abroad and, whenever possible, to use materials readily available in Germany. By December 1934 the airframe plants had reduced the number of light metals used in production from eighteen to nine and the kinds of steel from twenty to fifteen.[39] The development of alloys in Germany made standardization possible, which was one of von Richthofen's top priorities in establishing Germany's aerial rearmament on a sound basis.[40]

Von Richthofen's 1934 guidelines also looked forward to the production of large serial runs of high-quality modern aircraft. While the German aviation industry was oriented to a mix of wood and metal fuselages in 1933–1934, von Richthofen pushed the industry to adapt to production of all-metal, stressed skin aircraft along the lines that the Americans had started producing. The all-metal, stressed skin Heinkel He 70, which was acquired by the Luftwaffe as a reconnaissance plane and light bomber at this time, was seen by von Richthofen as an important step in getting German companies to modernize their production techniques.[41]

Von Richthofen in the Technical Office

The long-term goal was to build a very modern Luftwaffe by 1937–1938. The first generation would be an interim force, which would serve to train the Luftwaffe and to build up the German aviation industry that had been badly battered by the worldwide depression. (German aircraft manufacturers had only 3,200 workers in 1932.)[42] The branch of the Technical Office that von Richthofen headed converted the general staff's requirements for aircraft into specific development guidelines and detailed specifications for the German aircraft industry. His office would issue the contracts, oversee the testing process, and send its recommendations for aircraft serial production to the Luftwaffe's commander and general staff chief. Essentially, his job was to shepherd along the next generation of Luftwaffe aircraft. Indeed, the aircraft programs that von Richthofen supervised from 1933 to 1936 were expected to surpass the aircraft of the other major powers in terms of speed, range, and capability.

In late 1933 Wever initiated a series of war games and exercises to train the air staff and to help identify requirements for new aircraft. They concluded that a small but very fast bomber armed with machine guns, cannon, and a small bomb load would be a good means of attacking point targets deep behind enemy lines. From this report came a Luftwaffe request to develop a "destroyer" aircraft, a multipurpose fighter bomber with heavy armament, high speed, and an all-weather capability. This became the genesis of the Me 110 twin-engine fighter.[43] Another lesson from the 1933 war games was the importance of dive bombers to attack targets such as bridges and rail lines. This led to a request for development of a dive bomber for the Luftwaffe. The report that was written at the conclusion of the war games suggested that an air corps commander should have two or three groups of Stukas as a reserve to be thrown into battle at the decisive point.[44] Heavy fighters, Stukas, long-range and high-speed reconnaissance planes, an all-metal fast interceptor, twin-engine medium bombers, and a heavy four-engine strategic bomber were requested in response to the war games—and it was von Richthofen's branch that translated these requests into specifications for industry. Out of these programs would come the Me 109 fighter, the Ju 87 Stuka, the He 111 and Do 17 medium bombers, and the Me 110 heavy fighter, as well as a host of lighter support aircraft such as the Henschel 126 reconnaissance plane and the Fiesler 156 light liaison plane.[45]

In December 1934 the Technical Office drew up specifications for a single-seat fighter that would be a major step beyond the biplane fighters common to the air forces of the major powers. The new fighter would be an all-metal, low-wing monoplane with retractable undercarriage. In February 1934 the aircraft manufacturers Arado, Heinkel, and Willi Messerschmitt's new firm, Bayerische Flugzeugwerke, were given contracts to produce prototypes.[46] Arado dropped out of the competition, but Heinkel and Messerschmitt carried on with the projects. In 1935 the Heinkel He 112 and the Bf 109 (later called the Me 109) prototypes made their first flights and were delivered to the Technical Office's flight testing center at Rechlin. Both aircraft were fast and maneuverable and represented an enormous advance in aircraft design. However, the elliptical wing of the He 112 was more difficult to build than the Me 109 wing, and the Me 109 was selected for series production as the Luftwaffe's main fighter plane.[47] Going from drawing-board concept to full production in under three years represented a remarkable accomplishment.

At this time von Richthofen strongly supported the development of a heavy two-engine fighter for the future needs of the Luftwaffe. In 1935 the brilliant Focke Wulf designer, Kurt Tank, who had a concept for a fast two-engine fighter, approached von Richthofen. Although the Luftwaffe general staff had not specifically requested such an aircraft, von Richthofen, on his own authority, in December 1935 awarded Tank a contract to develop such a plane. The resulting FW 187 was considerably faster than the Me 110 (in 1939 tests the FW 187 made the remarkable speed of 635 km/h at sea level — or 400 mph). However, Tank's design — which von Richthofen favored — was passed over for the Me 110 heavy fighter.[48]

There are some ironies to von Richthofen's work in developing the Luftwaffe aircraft in the early 1930s. In contrast to many in the Luftwaffe, von Richthofen was not enthusiastic about dive bombers. The problem with dive bombers, he argued, is that they were too slow and would be easy targets for antiaircraft guns and enemy fighters.[49] When the first prototypes of the Ju 87 Stuka were tested he recommended against acquiring the aircraft on account of its low speed. He was overruled, and the Ju 87 entered production. It would go on to win a place in history under von Richthofen's command. Another irony is von Richthofen's enthusiasm for the heavy strategic bomber. As a modern airman, he firmly believed that the top priority of an air force should be long-range strategic attacks against the enemy homeland. Along with Wimmer he pushed the development of two prototype heavy bomber models, Junker's Ju 89 and Dornier's Do 19. By 1936 prototypes of both four-engine planes had been produced and were in the process of testing. The initial performance evaluation was disappointing, for the best engines available could not give the bombers much speed. Rather than putting the mediocre aircraft into production as interim models while working on a better aircraft, the two projects were cancelled by General Wever in one of his last command decisions.[50] The Luftwaffe would try to jump a couple of generations of technology and build a heavy bomber that was faster and more advanced than those possessed by any other air force. It was a fundamentally wrong decision, as the next-generation heavy bomber, the Heinkel He 177, was a

108   Chapter 4

Dornier Do 19 prototype heavy bomber, 1936. Von Richthofen pushed the strategic bomber program as development branch chief in the Luftwaffe's Technical Office. (U.S. Air Force)

disastrously bad design. In the meantime, the Luftwaffe would be equipped with the excellent Do 17 and He 111 medium bombers, which were adequate for the immediate needs of the Luftwaffe. However, at the outbreak of the war in 1939 von Richthofen would remark, "We will regret going to war without a strategic bomber."[51]

The Luftwaffe Becomes a Modern Force

Wilhelm Wimmer and his deputy von Richthofen deserve a great deal of the credit for building the Luftwaffe into a major air force in the space of six years. Aircraft developed under Wimmer's tenure include the Me 109, Me 110, Do 17, He 111, and Ju 87. All were on the cutting edge of technology for the era. That these aircraft went from proposals to prototypes to production in an average time of three years is impressive. When the Luftwaffe went to war in 1939 it was with the second generation of aircraft developed before 1936. By October 1936 the first production program of the Luftwaffe began delivering modern planes, such as the He 111, Do 17, and Ju 86, to equip the Luftwaffe's front units. Because of the development program the German aviation industry had grown tenfold and was set for further expansion.[52]

Von Richthofen, promoted to lieutenant colonel in April 1936, had begun work on developing the third generation of Luftwaffe aircraft, which would replace the second generation just being fielded. In August 1935 the Reichs Air Ministry issued specifications for a high-speed bomber that would incorporate a large bomb load and high-altitude performance with a speed that exceeded that of most fighter airplanes. The Junkers Company responded with the Ju 88, which first flew on December 1936 and proved that it was everything that the Technical Office had called for.[53]

However, it was not just in the realm of airplanes that the Luftwaffe was forging ahead. Even before Hitler came to power, the Waffenamt, and Wimmer in particular, had expressed an interest in conducting research into rockets.[54] During the first phases of rearmament the air ministry had dismissed the possibility of developing rocket propulsion for high-speed airplanes. Since rockets had been the purview of the army artillery office since the 1920s, the air ministry decided to leave the issue with the army for the time being.[55] However, despite the air ministry's initial decision, von Richthofen saw potential for the Luftwaffe in rocket research and moved to reopen the issue. In early 1935 he visited the army's rocket development office (Section 1 of the Ordnance Office) and was briefed on its rocket projects.

Once informed about the scope of the army rocket programs, von Richthofen pushed for an Army-Luftwaffe alliance for rocket programs. In March 1935 a delegation of army scientists (including Werner von Braun), aeronautical designer Willi Messerschmitt, and a group of air ministry experts met in Munich to observe the experiments of engineer and inventor Paul Schmidt, who had been working on the idea of a pulse jet, an air-breathing reaction propulsion with intermittent combustion. The Luftwaffe was primarily interested in Schmidt's pulse jet as a means of powering an aircraft. Both the army and the Luftwaffe saw that the pulse jet idea held promise, and an agreement to fund further research by Schmidt was made in which the army would contribute half the funding while the Luftwaffe would contribute the other half and supervise the research program.[56] In its evolved form, Schmidt's pulse jet research would become the engine of the V-1 missile, the first practical cruise missile. The V-1 was better known as the "buzz bomb," and it was launched by the thousands against London, southern England, and Antwerp in late 1944.

It was an exciting time for von Richthofen as, finally, the German military had the money and resources to generously support cutting edge research programs that would provide the conditions for advances in aviation technology over the next decades. Von Richthofen and the leading aircraft designers in Germany understood that the piston-engine, propeller-driven airplane would probably reach the limits of its performance in the next decade. To go higher and faster would require a major jump in the technological evolution. At the time the most promising path for technological development seemed to be rocket-powered aircraft. In May 1935 von Richthofen met with Captain Leo Zansen of the army's Ordnance Office to discuss the possibility of an Army-Luftwaffe experimental rocket plane program. Junkers would be the primary company for development of the rocket aircraft.[57] Development of a rocket aircraft was not the case of military technocrats indulging their science fiction imaginations but rather pursuing a practical military line of research. In the near future it was expected that bombers could attack at high speed and from high altitude, over 30,000 feet, and that it would be difficult, if not impossible, for a slow-climbing piston-engine airplane to effectively intercept enemy bombers. On the other hand, a high-speed rocket plane, with a high rate of climb, might be able to get high enough and fast enough to successfully intercept high flying bombers. That June, von Richthofen met with the army to outline his concept for a rocket plane. It would be an interceptor aircraft that would be able to reach 50,000 feet after a forty-five-second boost. It would cruise or glide at high altitude for several minutes before gliding back to the ground. Eventually the rocket plane concept would emerge as the only operational rocket fighter of World War II, the Messerschmitt Me 163 Comet.[58] Von Richthofen had already cleared the program with a representative of the Junkers Company, and Junkers was ready to serve as the primary contractor.[59]

Due to secrecy concerns and the perceived need to keep the program under full military control—with companies serving only as subcontractors—the army objected to using Junkers as the primary contractor for the rocket plane. The army and Werner von Braun wanted their own rocket development center. This concept evolved into the research and production center at Peenemünde. In order to push research on rocket planes along, von Richthofen brought the Heinkel Company on board. Both Heinkel and Junkers began experiments with mounting rockets on to modified aircraft. Junkers eventually dropped out, leaving Heinkel to try a rocket with 1,000 kg of thrust mounted in the tail of a modified Heinkel He 112 fighter plane.[60] Looking for a better approach than the rocket idea, Heinkel also initiated a program to develop jet engines and jet aircraft. With only a small amount of government financing and a few engineers, Heinkel developed the first jet engine in Germany in the mid-1930s.[61] The culmination of Heinkel's efforts came in August 1939, when the Heinkel 178 became the first jet aircraft to fly.[62]

Wever's Death—Shakeup in the Luftwaffe's Leadership

It was a tragedy for the Luftwaffe when General Wever was killed in an air crash in June 1936. Wever's death offered Hermann Goering the opportunity to assert control over "his" Luftwaffe. Although Wever was replaced by the highly competent Albert Kesselring as the Luftwaffe chief of staff, Kesselring did not have the clout with Hitler's circle to overcome Goering's meddling. Kesselring, an extremely capable leader, lasted only one year in the job before he asked to leave. He was replaced by General Hans-Jürgen Stumpf, another very capable officer, who served as Luftwaffe chief of staff from 1937 to 1939. As with Kesselring, Stumpf did not have the clout to prevent Goering from carrying out a major reorganization of the Luftwaffe that had serious negative consequences for German airpower.

Instead of following Wever's rule of posting only experienced general staff officers to the branch and department chiefs, Goering decided to replace Wilhelm Wimmer with his old crony Ernst Udet. The knowledgeable and talented Wimmer, who never got along well with Goering, was relegated to minor commands for the rest of his career. The Luftwaffe Technical Office was turned over to a thoroughgoing incompetent with little management experience and no general staff background. Udet was completely unsuited to be chief of design and production. He was a highly skilled pilot who was famous as Germany's greatest living ace (sixty-eight kills in the war). He had made a living as a stunt pilot in the 1920s and was something of a playboy. He had even spent some time in Hollywood. He was also an alcoholic. Udet loved the fame and glamour of aviation but had no ability whatsoever as a leader or manager. Goering brought him into the Luftwaffe after an absence of seventeen years from the military with the rank of full colonel—passing over general staff officers such as von Richthofen, who had far more military experience and general staff training. Udet was originally made the inspector of fighter planes, which allowed him to be his own test pilot. It was the one job in the Luftwaffe that Udet was eminently suited for. But transferring Udet to head the Technical Office was a mistake of the first order. Udet had no experience in management or industrial production and had little interest in dealing with the large amount of paperwork and planning that went with the job.

From the time he took over the Technical Office in 1936 to his suicide in 1941, Udet made a series of decisions that crippled the Luftwaffe. Udet was a great believer in dive bombing as the only accurate means of putting bombs onto the target. He had tested dive bombers and was enthusiastic about their

General Ernst Udet, chief of the Technical Office, 1936–1941. Udet made a series of disastrous decisions for the Luftwaffe before his suicide in 1941. Von Richthofen, who worked only for a few months for Udet before he was able to transfer out of the Technical Office for service in Spain, considered him a thoroughgoing incompetent—a fair assessment of Udet's talents as a senior manager. (U.S. Air Force)

potential. In this view he was backed up by the Luftwaffe's chief of operations, Hans Jeschonnek, who would become the Luftwaffe's chief of staff in 1939. Udet directed the design teams to make *all* bombers capable of dive bombing—including two- and even four-engine bombers.[63] This pronouncement meant that highly promising advanced bomber designs, such as the Ju 88 fast bomber, were brought to a halt as the design teams worked feverishly to redesign the aircraft for the additional stresses of dive bombing. The Ju 88 medium bomber program was delayed for more than a year, as was

Hans Jeschonnek, colonel general and chief of staff of the Luftwaffe, 1939–1943. Jeschonnek and von Richthofen became close friends in the 1920s. Von Richthofen played the role of an older brother to the brilliant but emotionally unstable Jeschonnek. (U.S. Air Force)

the Do 217 bomber, which was designed to replace the Do 17.[64] The He 177 bomber, under development before the start of the war, was delayed by the requirement to redesign a heavy high-altitude bomber for low-level dive bombing. In contrast to the very efficient work done by Wimmer and von Richthofen in bringing the Luftwaffe's second generation of aircraft on line, under Udet most of the third generation of Luftwaffe aircraft were either delayed in development and production or were poor designs. Udet was generally unwilling to kill off bad projects, even after it became clear that some designs were hopelessly flawed. The He 177 heavy bomber concept was an example of the latter.[65]

A senior officer can be forgiven for one bad design project, but Udet had several. The Me 210, designed to replace the excellent Me 110 heavy fighter, was a mechanical nightmare, and the production line had to shut down soon after starting. The Henschel Hs 129, designed as a ground attack plane, was so underpowered it was almost impossible to fly with a full armament load. Poor cockpit layout made it difficult for the pilot to watch the instruments and fly the plane.[66] After a complete redesign it finally entered production and combat in 1943, where it earned the reputation of being a cranky aircraft with a low serviceability rate.[67] The only truly successful aircraft project under Udet's tenure was the FW 190 fighter, which is acknowledged as one of the best fighter bombers of the war.

In addition to a host of bad aircraft designs, the Army-Luftwaffe technical cooperation that von Richthofen had carefully forged fell apart under Udet. In 1936 the air ministry gave Austrian engineer Eugene Sänger lavish funding to set up a Luftwaffe rocket development center in Braunschweig. The institute even had a cover name, the "Aircraft Testing Center," in order to keep the program secret from the army. Sänger's program to develop rocket engines essentially duplicated the existing Army-Luftwaffe program at Peenemünde, and it was considered by Germany's top rocket experts to be a waste of effort and resources. Udet insisted, however, that the Luftwaffe had to have its own independent program, and Sänger's rocket center persisted until Udet's death. Shortly thereafter, the program was closed down after having consumed a great deal of money and resources without accomplishing much.[68]

Although von Richthofen had a special connection with Goering, having served under Goering's command in JG 1 during the First World War, the two clearly did not get along. By promoting Udet to chief of the Technical Office and bringing him into the Luftwaffe as a full colonel, Goering passed over the eminently more qualified von Richthofen—which certainly would have rankled von Richthofen. The poor relationship between the men was largely due to Goering's character. Although Goering and von Richthofen came from very similar aristocratic backgrounds and had both served as prewar regular officers, Goering's manner was virtually the opposite of von Richthofen's. Goering loved his life as a playboy, accumulated wealth as quickly as possible, and loved ostentation. His approach to work was essentially frivolous. He left the serious work of running the Luftwaffe to serious types like Milch, while he reveled in the trappings of power. In contrast, von Richthofen was the model of a proper general staff officer of the old school. He lived for his work and studied his profession diligently. Although well off financially, he lived fairly modestly and was a solid family man—exactly the kind of behavior that one expected from a proper general staff officer. Von Richthofen preferred the company of aircraft designers and engineers, and his interests were focused on aviation and its future. Unlike Goering, who talked incessantly about his glory days as a fighter pilot, no one can recall von Richthofen talking much about his World War I experiences. I suspect that this was because he found subjects like new aircraft designs and concepts for rocket planes to be far more interesting than telling stories about flying in fabric-covered biplanes.

Through the years of the Third Reich, Goering favored a few officers who were much like himself. Udet was a playboy, a hard drinker who lived ostentatiously and refused to take his job seriously—much like Goering. Bruno Loerzer, who had first flown with Goering in 1915, was a thoroughly mediocre officer and never would have made it through the rigorous general staff training that had been the pathway to advancement in the old army. But Loerzer was selected by Goering for rapid promotion due to their old friendship. Von Richthofen used to cynically remark (outside of Goering's hearing) that he hoped that Loerzer would be promoted because he could not move up until Goering had first taken care of his friend. Under General Wever, the Luftwaffe staff had been run along the lines of the traditional German general staff culture. With Wever's death, much of that was overturned as Goering took a more active role in managing the Luftwaffe.

Von Richthofen had enjoyed his years working with Wimmer. During that period he was able to put his mastery of technology to use and make a huge contribution to the Luftwaffe. He seems to have genuinely enjoyed the challenge of the work, with a major benefit being able to regularly meet and share ideas with some of the top engineers and designers in the world. One gets the impression that if he had not had his fateful meeting with Seeckt in 1922, and had remained a civilian, he would have forged ahead with an engineering career and entered the top ranks of the German aircraft industry. But with Udet as his boss, von Richthofen's job satisfaction waned quickly. Von Richthofen found himself at odds with most of Udet's ideas. After Udet took over the Technical Office he began promoting a concept of developing an airplane that combined the qualities and missions of a fighter, bomber, and dive bomber in one machine. Von Richthofen thought the idea absurd: "This is nonsense, you can't go against nature!"[69] Udet also ignored some of von Richthofen's fundamental principles for aircraft procurement—notably, that ease of serial production should be a primary requirement for acquiring specific aircraft models.

For Richthofen, working as the deputy for an incompetent alcoholic was bound to be a dead end. But the Luftwaffe was expanding rapidly, and certainly an opportunity for a major unit command would soon open up for a talented and highly respected general staff officer. Such an opportunity arose only a few weeks after General Wever's death—in the form of a war in Spain.

Chapter 5

The War in Spain, 1936–1939

By the fall of 1936 it was clear to von Richthofen that he should leave the Technical Office. He had no liking at all for Ernst Udet and believed that Udet's ideas about aircraft and airpower were hopelessly wrong. A command position away from Berlin would present the opportunity to prove himself as a commander of an air unit. That opportunity came in the form of a civil war in Spain.

The elections of the 1930s had divided the weak Spanish Republic between the hard right—Catholics, businessmen, landowners, and fascists—and the hard left, backed by industrial workers, tenant farmers, and agricultural laborers. The right wanted a return to an authoritarian Spain, and the left wanted drastic social reform. By 1936 there were few moderate forces in Spanish politics. The Spanish workers, in particular, tended to be some of the most radical in Europe, with many giving their allegiance to the anarchist parties. After a rise in violence that culminated in the murder of a leading rightist politician by government police, right-wing forces initiated a long-planned coup to topple the weak and fractious government. On 18 July 1936, Nationalist rebels seized power in cities throughout Spain, winning over many in the armed forces. But they failed to seize power in the key cities of Madrid and Barcelona. As the Nationalist cause faltered, General Francisco Franco, one of the Nationalist leaders, sent two German businessmen with Nazi connections to solicit aid from Germany. At the same time, the Nationalists also asked for aid from Italy.[1] The Nationalists saw Europe's two great fascist regimes as natural ideological allies. Events proved them right.

The Nationalist representatives met with Adolf Hitler on 25 July, and Hitler, seeing an opportunity to expand German influence in Europe and support a fascist government in sympathy with his own, ordered Hermann Goering to provide aid and equipment to Franco's forces. Goering passed the responsibility on to Lt. General Helmuth Wilberg, then commander of the Luftwaffe's war academy (advanced officers training course) in Berlin.[2] Within two days, Special Staff W (for Wilberg) was formed, and by 31 July,

German aircraft, aid, and personnel were on their way to Spanish Morocco.[3] Wilberg was appointed senior staff officer for Spanish matters, and he visited Spain in August 1936 to assess Nationalist needs. Three shiploads of warplanes, equipment, and Luftwaffe personnel were immediately dispatched.[4] The Nationalists had 25,000 first-rate troops of the African army in Spanish Morocco. Hardened veterans of the colonial wars, they were, by far, the most effective single military force in Spain. The problem was that most of the Spanish navy had remained loyal to the Republic and had cut off sea transport between the colony of Spanish Morocco and the Spanish mainland. The first mission of the Luftwaffe planes and pilots was to transport the African army and its equipment over the Straits of Gibraltar to mainland Spain so the Nationalists could begin their drive on Madrid and end the war. A handful of He 51 fighters accompanied the Ju 52s as protection, and the German pilots were ordered to avoid combat if possible. The Spanish Nationalists and the Germans believed that once the African army arrived on the mainland, the Republican forces, which were mostly militia, could be quickly crushed. However, when the Soviet Union threw its support to the Republic, and Italy sent air and ground forces to Spain, the conflict quickly became an international affair. By 28 August the prohibition against direct combat by German forces was lifted, and German aircraft could now bomb Republican targets.[5]

In September 1936, as the Luftwaffe's reinforcements arrived, Lt. Colonel Walther Warlimont was appointed German military representative to Franco's government.[6] Fearing that the war might drag on, Franco requested increased German aid, especially modern equipment and training for his forces and air units. Franco did not request, nor did he want, major German ground units.[7] Franco had a good sense of the international situation, and he did not wish to provide the nations that supported the Republic, namely France and the Soviet Union, with an excuse to increase their aid. The German high command approved this limited commitment to the Nationalists, and on 30 October 1936 decided to increase its force to an air corps of 5,000 men to be equipped with approximately 100 aircraft, complete with support, flak, and communications units. A small armored battalion would also be sent to gain combat experience and to help the Spanish build an armored force. Several hundred German officers and NCOs would be assigned to train the Nationalist forces. These German force levels in Spain were set early in the war and maintained throughout the conflict.[8]

The chief officer for managing the German force in Spain, General Wilberg was an exceptionally talented air force commander and general staff officer. He would have been a natural choice to become the first chief of staff of the Luftwaffe in 1933. He was a senior air commander in World War I, commanding 700 aircraft on the Flanders front in 1917, and he served as the chief of the shadow Luftwaffe from 1920–1927, where he laid the foundations for the later expansion of the Luftwaffe. He was highly respected by the general staff and the Luftwaffe officers and was the primary author for the Luftwaffe's operational doctrine. The only problem was that Wilberg's mother was Jewish, and it would have been impossible to appoint someone who was half-Jewish as one of the service chiefs of the Third Reich. However, Wilberg was so highly regarded by the Luftwaffe that Hitler personally issued a "decree of aryanization" that declared that Wilberg and his family were to be, under the laws of the Third Reich, considered fully Aryan and German. Wilberg's performance as a staff officer was phenomenal. Two days after he was given the order to support Franco, German planes and personnel were on the way. Wilberg would remain chief of the Spanish operation until his retirement in March 1938.[9]

Wilberg had the luxury of a free hand in selecting officers for service in Spain. When the decision was made in October 1936 to expand the newly named Condor Legion's presence in Spain, Wilberg called on Maj. General Hugo Sperrle to serve as commander in Spain.[10] Wolfram von Richthofen, now a lieutenant colonel, had known Wilberg since the early 1920s and was a well-known quantity in the Luftwaffe. The enlarged German force in Spain would contain a special air squadron, called the Test Squadron, which would be equipped with the latest German aircraft. The Luftwaffe saw the war in Spain as an ideal opportunity to test its aircraft, equipment, and doctrine, and von Richthofen was the best-qualified officer for such a command. So when von Richthofen offered to go to Spain, Wilberg was happy to offer him command of the Test Squadron. Von Richthofen, along with Sperrle and an advance party of the Condor Legion, departed for Spain in November 1936. Von Richthofen would not be a squadron commander for long. Sperrle needed a highly competent chief of staff with a proper general staff background, and there were very few such officers in the Luftwaffe of 1936.[11] Sperrle had known von Richthofen since the 1920s and, like most of the senior officers of the Luftwaffe, thought highly of him. So von Richthofen was appointed as Condor Legion chief of staff.

Sperrle and von Richthofen would make a good team in Spain. Sperrle, as commander in chief of the German forces in Spain, would deal with Franco and the Nationalist government at the strategic level. Von Richthofen would plan and oversee the daily combat operations of the Condor Legion. Von Richthofen's knowledge of Italian came in especially handy for his daily contact with the Spanish commanders. Since few Spaniards spoke German, and few Germans spoke Spanish, von Richthofen could speak to his Spanish colleagues in a kind of Italian-Spanish that the Spanish could understand.[12] In the old German general staff tradition, the elegance of the approach is much less important than whether it works. In time, von Richthofen would become fairly fluent in Spanish.

Both Sperrle and von Richthofen understood that the war in Spain was to be a limited commitment for Germany. Von Richthofen sized up the situation as soon as he arrived and recommended that Berlin not send too much aid: "The Spanish have to win this war for themselves,"[13] he wrote in a report. Both von Richthofen and Sperrle were convinced that Franco would never be seen as a legitimate ruler of Spain if the primary burden of the war was borne by foreign powers. Therefore, they set policies on keeping the German operations limited, and these remained in place for the entire war. Their most important contribution was in setting up an effective relationship with the Spanish. Although neither officer had what one could call a diplomatic personality or manner, both could deal with the Spanish as professional soldiers. Although the Germans and Spanish often disagreed, and the Spanish leadership found the Germans irritating, the Spanish also respected the Germans' professional competence and were ready to listen. The coalition worked well for the three years of the war.

Early Operations

The first German aircraft sent to Spain were of the Luftwaffe's first generation. The He 51 was its standard biplane fighter in 1936 and had been equal to most fighters of the early 1930s. But the Heinkel fighters, and most Luftwaffe aircraft, were clearly obsolescent by 1936. The Germans also deployed the Heinkel He 45, a two-seat biplane, as a light bomber and reconnaissance plane. The first bombers of the Condor Legion were the Ju 52 transports converted to drop a ton of bombs. Equipped with crude bombsights and armed with a couple of machine guns for protection, the Ju 52 was not much of a bomber. But it would have to do until the latest models could arrive. Italy had also sent a force to help Franco and, like the Germans, saw Spain as an opportunity to test its latest aircraft and weapons. But the most modern weapons would come later.

The first mission of the Luftwaffe force in Spain, the airlift of over 20,000 troops of the African army, had been a great success. Once this well-equipped and veteran fighting force arrived the Nationalists were able to advance quickly on Madrid. By November the Nationalists looked like they might take Madrid and end the war with one last push. With full approval of the Nationalist leadership, the German force carried out a series of bombing raids on the city with the hope that these would break the defenders' morale. The bombing was not, however, to be indiscriminate. Franco ordered a bomb safety zone established to limit civilian casualties as the attacks began. Between 14 and 23 November, several German raids, both by day and by night, caused 244 civilian dead and 875 wounded.[14] The bombing of Madrid had little effect on the populace, other than to strengthen their will to resist, and was called off because the tide of the war had changed. Military equipment and advisers from the Soviet Union had arrived to bolster the hard-pressed Republic. The Republicans could now arm their divisions with brand-new Soviet tanks and artillery. Soviet advisers were training and leading new forces being raised by the Republic, and that November the first of these were ready for a counterattack.

However, the Soviets, like the Germans, were also playing a cautious game in Spain. The Soviets wanted to support an ally and were willing to provide a considerable amount of equipment along with pilots, specialists, and advisers. But the Soviets refrained from sending ground forces as they also did not want to have an open confrontation with another great power on a Spanish battlefield. The Soviets and the Germans were bitter enemies in the international arena, but neither was prepared for open conflict. They would thus use the Spanish Civil War as a kind of proxy war.

The newly raised Republican divisions (armed with Soviet equipment) and Republican air units (armed with the latest Soviet fighter planes) mounted a series of large counterattacks on the Madrid front in November that gave the Nationalists their first defeat. In the air the German and Italian fighter units, all armed with biplane fighters, were completely outclassed by the new Soviet I-16 all-metal monoplane fighters. The quality of the Russian equipment came as a complete surprise to the Nationalists. The I-16 was one of the best fighters of its day, much faster and more heavily armed than the Italian Fiat and German Heinkel fighters. Facing a superior enemy in the air, the Nationalists called off the air attacks by the end of November. Madrid would be held for the Republic, and now that both sides had foreign partners and support, neither side could hope for a quick victory. The only way for either to win would be through a long attrition war.

During the winter of 1936–1937 the war settled into a stalemate, with long fixed fronts and trench systems reminiscent of World War I. Both sides built up their airpower as quickly as possible. Neither the Republic nor the Nationalists had modern air forces at the start of the war, so the Republic asked the Soviet Union to send planes and pilots and the Nationalists requested German and Italian aircraft and air units. The Condor Legion was relatively inactive that winter. Sperrle and von Richthofen spent their time organizing the Condor Legion, which would include a bomber group, a fighter group, and a reconnaissance squadron. Small numbers of prototype aircraft would be assigned to be used by the Test Squadron. In addition, a seaplane detachment capable of conducting reconnaissance, bombing, and torpedo operations arrived. The Condor Legion had a large signal element, which spent the winter setting up a proper communications net and installing modern radio landing and navigation systems at the German airfields. The most important event for the Germans was the arrival of a batch of Me 109 fighters. These were among the first production models of the Me 109 and were desperately needed by the Germans to contest the Republican I-16 fighters. The Condor Legion also received some fast He 70 monoplanes to use for long-distance reconnaissance. Firepower would be provided by the new He 111 and Do 17 bombers that began to arrive in early 1937. It would take some time for the Germans to absorb the new equipment and prepare it for combat. In the meantime they would continue to use the improvised Ju 52 bombers as their striking force.

German Strategy in Spain

Although Spain and the Mediterranean were not areas of major German interest, the Germans could nonetheless gain significant advantages by supporting the Nationalists. First, Germany's primary enemy, France, would be distracted and discomfited by a pro-German Spain on her southern border. With Italy already competing against France in the Mediterranean, France would have to face three unfriendly nations.[15] Second, with the Soviet Union providing equipment, pilots, and advisers to the Spanish Republic, a defeat for the Republicans would be a defeat for Soviet prestige and interests.[16] Third, Germany needed raw materials for its rearmament, and an allied Spanish Nationalist government could provide plentiful supplies of high-grade iron ore, mercury, wolfram, pyrites, and other necessities.[17] These reasons could not justify the risk of a major war, but they provided a strategic justification to send aid to the Nationalists.

At the war's start the Wehrmacht staff had just begun the massive rearmament program for the whole armed forces; thus there was concern that a major commitment to Spain would interfere with the program to equip the Wehrmacht units. In a meeting with Hitler on 22 December 1936, the high command argued for keeping German support to the Nationalists limited.[18] Generals Blomberg, Fritsch, and Beck pointed out that with Germany in the midst of rearmament, the shipment of thousands of ground troops to Spain would strip the military of the equipment and officers necessary to build a powerful new army. The high command was also concerned about provoking French intervention on the side of the Spanish loyalists and thereby starting a general European war—a war the Wehrmacht was not ready to fight in 1937 and 1938.[19] Hitler accepted these arguments, and throughout the conflict the general staff monitored the political situation.[20] Instructions were issued that no German aircraft were to fly within fifty kilometers of the French border. Although General Keitel, chief of the high command, thought the danger of French intervention was minimal, he nevertheless ordered that the policy of avoiding combat near the border remain in effect unless the Spanish requested otherwise.[21]

Sperrle and von Richthofen found themselves dealing with many strategic issues in Spain. It was not what their general staff training had prepared them for, but they managed it well. The reports and diaries of von Richthofen provide a good account of the German/Spanish and German/Italian strategic relationship. From the German side, the key to dealing with the Spaniards was to identify the most competent officers and work through them, regardless of rank, to establish plans and policies for the war. It was often very frustrating for Sperrle and von Richthofen to work with the Nationalist general staff, as the senior ranks of the Nationalists contained many officers with political influence but little knowledge of modern warfare. For example, von Richthofen found General Kindelan, chief of the Nationalist air force, to be an "old, used-up fellow."[22] On another occasion, he remarked that "Kindelan lies and has no understanding."[23] Given the weakness of the Spanish military leadership before 1936, these are fair assessments. Still, he and Sperrle found many of the mid ranking and senior Spanish staff officers to be competent and fully equal to their German counterparts. So, in order to get things done, the German leaders learned to find the most competent of the Spanish officers and route all their work through them to ensure that planning was properly done and operations properly executed. Major Sierra of Kindelan's staff was regarded as especially competent and useful, and he became a favorite of the German commanders.[24] Of Colonel Barosso, chief of Franco's operations section, von Richthofen remarked, "I'd trust him with my operational plans."[25] Colonel (later General) Juan Suero Diaz Vigón was their overall favorite Spanish officer. Vigón was intelligent, capable, and dynamic: a true general staff officer. He served as Franco's eyes and ears at the front and, when necessary, relieved incompetent commanders on the spot and assumed command himself. Vigón and the Germans served together for much of the war and developed a strong bond. Vigón served as General Mola's chief of staff for the northern campaign in 1937 and served thereafter on decisive fronts—usually with the Germans in support of his forces. In July 1938 Vigón was appointed as Franco's chief of staff, a move welcomed by the Germans. Von Richthofen commented on Vigón many times in his diaries and judged him to be "a thoroughly useful fellow."[26] For his part, Vigón was very friendly with the Germans and known as one of Spain's most pro-German officers.[27]

One advantage of the Condor Legion was its simple and direct command arrangements. When Sperrle arrived in Spain in October 1936 as Condor Legion commander he was also appointed commander in chief of all German forces in Spain. These included the military training teams sent to instruct in Spanish schools for officers, NCOs, and specialists, as well as the Condor Legion forces. Under the arrangements negotiated by the Wehrmacht high command with the Spanish, the Germans would serve under Spanish direction at the highest level, and Spanish requests and orders would be transmitted through the Condor Legion commander. These would be translated into operational plans and orders for the German units. The Condor Legion would remain a unified force under German command, but it would follow the strategic directions set by the Nationalist government. As part of the agreement to follow Franco's strategic direction, the Condor Legion commander and chief of staff were granted direct access to Franco and his war council. There the Germans had considerable influence over Spanish war policy and plans. For administrative and logistics support, the Condor Legion commander dealt directly with Special Staff W in Berlin.

Franco's relationship with the German military commanders was cordial and businesslike. Franco was a highly experienced combat commander who had served for many years fighting rebels in Spanish Morocco, and his exploits as commander of the Spanish Foreign Legion won him rapid promotion; he became the youngest general in the Spanish army. Franco had the credibility to speak with the German officers as one military professional to another. Although Franco does not seem to have liked the Germans—and he certainly distrusted Hitler—he accorded Sperrle, von Richthofen, and the German soldiers in Spain considerable respect. For their part, the surviving German records, including von Richthofen's diaries, show that the Germans had a great deal of respect for Franco as a leader.

The Opposing Air Forces

Since 1918 the only wars fought by the major powers had been colonial campaigns in which the fighting was usually carried out by native troops equipped with obsolete weapons. The British, French, and Italian air forces

General Juan Vigón, Franco's chief of staff, who was much admired by von Richthofen and other German officers. Vigón and von Richthofen struck up a strong friendship during the Spanish War.

had seen a lot of action, but the air forces in the colonies were usually organized into small detachments equipped with obsolete aircraft. No major air force had seen action against another modern air force, and no one really knew what modern aerial warfare might be like. The Spanish Civil War, which featured the involvement of three major powers with modern air forces, would be the first opportunity for the world to see how a modern air war might be fought. Both the Nationalist coalition and the Republicans possessed, for the era, relatively large and powerful air forces. In many respects, it was an equal match. The Republicans would use approximately 1,500 aircraft during the war, and the Nationalist coalition about 1,300 aircraft.[28] Neither side had a clear qualitative advantage, so success in the air would come down to the intangible factors of leadership, organization, and doctrine.

Both sides were also well-matched as to the quality of their pilots. The Soviets sent many of their best pilots to fly in Spain, and hundreds of the Republican pilots were trained by the Soviet air force.[29] The Republicans began the war with a clear advantage when most of the Spanish air force pilots sided with the Republic.[30] But the Germans and the Italians would select their best-trained pilots for deployment to Spain, and they set up a flight-training program for the Nationalists that would ensure that Franco would soon have a capable air force to match the Republic's.

The I-15 biplane Chato fighters, which the Soviets supplied to the Republicans, were superior to the German He 51s and equal to the Italian CR-32s. The Russian I-16 Mosca fighter, which the Republican air force used in large numbers, was one of the top fighters of its day. Only the Condor Legion's Me 109s could equal or surpass it. Both sides possessed some effective bombers. The Nationalist Savoia SM 79 (Italian) and Heinkel He 111 (German) bombers were two of the best bombers available in the late 1930s, and the SB-2 bombers that the Soviets supplied to the Republican air force were also among the fastest and best bombers of the era.[31]

Although the Italians maintained a considerably larger air corps in Spain than the Germans, an average of 140 aircraft to a German average of 100, the Regia Aeronautica was not as operationally effective as its German partner. For one thing, the Italians were slow to learn operational lessons. While the Germans worked to improve their bombing accuracy, the Italian bomber units made little progress. The Germans worked hard to develop a better fighter escort for their bombers. The Italians approached this problem in a haphazard manner.[32] Although the Italian air force had taken some steps toward improving its ground attack aviation in the years preceding the Spanish Civil War, it still entered the war without a comprehensive air doctrine or training in conducting operations with the other services.[33] This was in contrast to the Germans, who had put a good deal of effort into developing close air support doctrine. The failure of the Regia Aeronautica to develop tactical army/air coordination was dramatically exhibited at the Italian defeat at Guadalajara in 1937. At the operational level, Sperrle complained of the inability of the Italians to coordinate their plans with the Germans and Spanish.[34] In short, although the Italian air force pilots and lower-ranking personnel were brave and dedicated, the Italian leadership failed to respond to the requirements of modern aerial warfare. This was a theme that would carry on into World War II. From this point on the Germans saw the Italians as a weak and unreliable ally—and they sent many reports back to Berlin explaining just that.

Spring 1937—The Campaign in the North

The Italians began the first major operations of 1937 in February with an offensive mounted to overrun the city of Malaga in the south. Typical of the Italian behavior in the war, the Italian commander, General Mario Roatta, declined to fully brief the Spanish or German senior commanders on the Italian plans, which led to considerable irritation on the part of Italy's allies.[35] The Italian approach to the Spanish Civil War contrasted enormously with the limited war approach of the Germans. The Italians had grandiose ambitions in the Mediterranean and recognized few limits upon their military involvement. Large Italian ground forces arrived in Spain in December 1936 although Franco had not requested or wanted them. By mid-February 1937, almost 50,000 Italian soldiers were in Spain, organized into four divisions under Roatta's command—the Corpo Truppe Volontarie.[36]

The Italians won at Malaga, but their next major operation was a disaster. In March 1937 they launched an offensive at Guadalajara with four divisions. The Italian force advanced for a few days but was then struck by a strong Republican counterattack. They were forced back in a rout, and Italian casualties numbered in the thousands. The Republicans, who had air superiority over the front, used their air force to inflict heavy damage and many casualties among the retreating Italian troops packed on the roads leading away from the front.[37] The Guadalajara debacle colored the military relationships of the Nationalist coalition for the rest of the war. The Italians gained a reputation for military incompetence they were unable to shake. The Nationalists took some enjoyment in the defeat of the arrogant Italians—after all, the victors of Guadalajara were Spaniards, even if they were Reds. A popular song in the Nationalist army was entitled, "Guadalajara Is Not Abyssinia."[38]

Prior to Guadalajara, German and Italian air units had flown missions together on the Madrid front. After Guadalajara, the Germans and Spanish were reluctant to carry out operations with the Italians. Von Richthofen soon came to the conclusion that his former friends and associates were blithering incompetents.[39] There were still some signs of a combined air war after Guadalajara, and the Condor Legion occasionally flew in support of Italian troops and carried out joint missions.[40] But such operations were not common, and the attitude of the senior German officers toward the Italian senior officers was one of barely concealed contempt. Von Richthofen reported that he was infuriated by discussions with General Garda, the Italian air commander in Spain.[41] As the war progressed, the German and Italian air units normally flew on different sectors of the front. The Italians flew mostly in support of their own troops, while the Germans flew for elite Nationalist divisions—usually,

Navarese or Moroccan divisions that were considered the elite of the Nationalist army.

Since the Madrid front had developed into a stalemate by early 1937, the Nationalist high command looked to see where the limited resources of the Spanish Nationalists could be best employed. The answer was an offensive to overrun the weakest part of Republican Spain. During the stalemate, the Republic found itself divided into two large zones: Madrid and eastern Spain, including the cities of Valencia and Barcelona, were firmly in Republican hands; in the north, Asturias and the Basque region had been declared for the Republic but were cut off from the rest of Spain. The Basques had managed to raise and equip a large army but had little in the way of air support, and their isolated position meant that no reinforcements from the more populous zone of the Republic could be sent. If the Nationalists concentrated their available forces on the northern front, they would have a considerable advantage over the Basque and Asturian forces. With little in the way of Republican airpower in the northern sector, the Condor Legion could count on air superiority for its operations. In early 1937 General Mola, appointed as Nationalist commander in the north, began planning with the Germans for an offensive to destroy the Republic's northern enclave.

The Condor Legion commander approved of Mola's strategy and began planning to support the Nationalist attack. The Condor Legion moved its airfields and supply bases to Avila in northern Spain to be close to the action. The Condor Legion had to adapt to the conditions of the war in Spain, and one of those conditions was the weak state of the Nationalist artillery. Although some armaments shipments from Germany and Italy had arrived to equip the Nationalists, Mola's forces still lacked sufficient firepower to overcome the strong defenses that the Basques had built in the northern mountains. The Condor Legion had the firepower that the Nationalists lacked, and the Germans and Spanish leaders agreed that the primary mission of the German force would be to provide close support of the Spanish Nationalist forces.

To further bolster the Nationalists' firepower, von Richthofen decided to send part of his flak force to the front to be used as artillery. The Condor Legion had been provided with a reinforced flak battalion consisting of four batteries of heavy 88 mm guns and two batteries of 20 mm light flak guns. This force was deployed to protect the German airfields, but with little air opposition in the north, it made sense to use the excellent new flak guns to bolster the Nationalist artillery force. In fact, the flak guns proved to be superb weapons in the ground role. The 88 mm heavy flak gun, with its flat trajectory and high velocity, was an ideal weapon for destroying enemy bunkers and

Condor Legion He 111 bombers at Avila airfield, northern Spain, 1937.
(*Jahrbuch der deutschen Luftwaffe*, 1940)

defensive positions. When the Nationalist offensive began in late March, the flak guns soon proved their worth on the battlefield. The batteries used on the front lines were so successful that for the rest of the war it became normal procedure for the Condor Legion to deploy part of its light and heavy flak forces to the *Schwerpunkt* (point of main effort) of the Nationalist forces on the defense or offense. The importance of the flak gun support to the ground

The Luftwaffe's 88 mm antiaircraft gun in Spain. To the consternation of some on the air staff in Berlin, von Richthofen used the famed German gun to supplement the Spanish artillery on the front lines. As an artillery piece it was exceptionally effective in destroying enemy fortifications, tanks, and other targets. Based on the experience in Spain, the Germans made it standard doctrine to use the gun in the antitank and direct fire role; it was one of the most effective weapons of World War II. (*Jahrbuch der Luftwaffe*, 1940)

battle was noted in numerous detailed reports the Condor Legion sent back to Berlin, and the use of flak in the ground battle became part of the Luftwaffe's standard doctrine.[42] Von Richthofen was proud of his idea to deploy the flak guns in the ground role and remarked several times that this policy had caused consternation among the Luftwaffe flak theorists back in Berlin.

From the onset of the campaign the Condor Legion conducted large-scale close-support operations, and virtually the whole Condor Legion was deployed to support the Nationalist army offensive against the Basque state. From March to June 1937 the Nationalist army and the Condor Legion endured a hard campaign. The Basques were tough and capable fighters, and they occupied ideal defensive ground in their mountainous region. The Germans would have to mount a major effort to get the Nationalists through the Basque defenses. In the northern campaign, and usually through the whole war, the Condor Legion would operate from bases close to the front where it could generate a high sortie rate—sometimes three or more sorties per day. To gain this advantage, however, the Luftwaffe had to deploy a large force of ground personnel to set up and man the forward airfields. The Luftwaffe's logistics units had to be fully motorized and have enough vehicles to bring up fuel, ammunition, and spare parts. In Spain, the Luftwaffe's mobile logistics organization was tested under tough conditions.

The first problem was not conducting air operations per se but coordinating the air operations with the ground operations. The Nationalist army of 1937 was mostly a newly raised and poorly trained force. On several occasions in the early stages of the 1937 northern offensive, the Condor Legion would carry out air strikes on Basque positions on schedule, yet the effort was wasted because the follow-up ground attack by the Nationalist army was delayed due to poor staff work.[43] Von Richthofen expressed almost constant frustration over this problem in his diary.

Close support of ground troops is one of the most complicated missions for an air force. Although the Luftwaffe had begun a training program for air-ground liaison officers in 1935, by 1937 precise procedures for working out air-ground coordination had yet to be developed. Indeed, no one in the Luftwaffe had any clear idea just how difficult close air support could be. All of these issues came to light in northern Spain in the spring of 1937 when the first close support missions of the Condor Legion highlighted several problems. But German general staff officers were trained to solve problems. Von Richthofen, although he had no previous experience with coordinating army support before 1937, turned his full attention to the issue. A paucity of doctrine was, perhaps, an advantage. The air staff in Berlin was far away and not inclined to micromanage the effort in Spain, so Sperrle and von Richthofen had a free hand to work the best solutions.

Communications were the first major problem to overcome if the air strikes were to be effectively coordinated. Although most Condor Legion aircraft had radios, the planes could only communicate with each other and their home base, and there was no effective radio communication from the front lines to the aircraft. In response, von Richthofen and the Spanish staff quickly developed a system of ground signals. Sperrle and von Richthofen

Major General Hugo Sperrle, standing center in Spanish uniform, observing air strikes on Basque positions, spring 1937. Major Siebert, Condor Legion communications officer who would also serve as von Richthofen's communications officer in the Polish campaign, stands on left. In Spain von Richthofen and the Condor Legion staff worked out methods of directing airstrikes right on the front lines—a system that would have revolutionary consequences for operations in World War II.

would set up command posts on the front lines, usually on hilltops overlooking the point of a planned air strike and ground attack, and observe the battle directly. From their forward command posts the German commanders were linked by ground telephone to the aircraft home base, which could then relay messages from the ground commander to aircraft by radio. It was an awkward system designed to bypass the deficiencies of the Luftwaffe's radios—but it worked and soon became part of the Condor Legion's standard practice.

Despite the many teething problems, the Spanish learned quickly. Each operation had to be carefully planned between the German and Spanish staffs at the top level. At the lower levels of command, the Luftwaffe assigned special liaison and communications teams to the Nationalist army units to ensure effective coordination between the Luftwaffe and army.[44] With more attention paid to communications, the coordination of the air and ground forces improved markedly through the first half of 1937.[45] However, considerable friction still remained with the communications and signal system, and there were several instances of German and Italian aircraft accidentally bombing Nationalist infantry units in April 1937.[46]

Although the Luftwaffe doctrine of the period emphasized using airpower en masse to achieve maximum shock effect, one tactic that was found to be very successful in 1937 was the shuttle attack. The Condor Legion would send one flight of aircraft at a time to bomb enemy frontline positions. After the strike, the flight would return to base to rearm and refuel for a subsequent attack while the next flight in the squadron bombed the position. Because the Condor Legion air bases were close to the front lines, aircraft could fly three or more sorties a day against the same target. This tactic of shuttle bombing kept the enemy under continuous attack for hours on end and dramatically increased the psychological stress of the defenders. Sometimes Republican morale would break under air attack, allowing the Nationalist army to overrun strong positions with few casualties.[47]

Despite tough resistance from the Basques, through April and May 1937 the Nationalists systematically reduced the Basque defenses and slowly advanced on the major Basque city of Bilbao. The success of the Nationalist ground forces was largely due to the effectiveness of the air support provided by the Condor Legion. Von Richthofen was at the front daily, conferring with the Spanish commanders and personally ensuring that Spanish and German operations were tightly coordinated. The campaign culminated in June 1937 as the Nationalist army reached the final Basque defense line, a 35-kilometer-long line of well-sited concrete bunkers and trenches dug in on the hilltops and ridgelines before Bilbao. Between 12 and 14 June the Condor Legion made some of its heaviest attacks of the war, saturating sections of the "Iron Belt" defense line with high explosives. The accurate and devastating attacks by the Condor Legion enabled the Nationalist army to break the Basque defense line after several days of desperate fighting.[48]

Von Richthofen was especially proud of his work in personally planning and coordinating the air support that broke the enemy defense. With the Iron Belt taken, Basque morale collapsed. The Basque forces began surrendering as the Nationalists made their final advance. Bilbao fell on 19 June.[49] The northern campaign of 1937 marks a watershed in the use of air forces in supporting ground troops. From a doctrinal vacuum, von Richthofen and the Condor Legion staff had created effective procedures and tactics to provide highly effective air support to the Nationalist armies. Indeed, it had been decisive. The Basque forces were tough fighters and well dug in. Without the superb air support of the Condor Legion, the northern campaign could not have been won by the Nationalists. The loss of the Basque region was a huge blow to the Republic's morale.

The Attack on Guernica

The single most famous incident of the Spanish Civil War took place in the middle of the 1937 northern campaign—the air raid of the Condor Legion on the town of Guernica in the heart of Spain's Basque country. The Luftwaffe's bombing of Guernica on 26 April 1937 became one of the major news events of 1937, and a mythology developed around the attack that continues to this day.

The Condor Legion bombed Guernica as a routine tactical air operation. The attack leveled and burned about half of the town and killed approximately 300 people, mostly civilians.[50] The facts about the bombing of Guernica bear little resemblance to the myth. Guernica was a small town of 5,000–7,000 people, and not a "city" as described by the media of the day. In April 1937 it was located just behind the front lines of the Basque army. Its importance at the time was clear on the map. The Basque army was being pressed hard by the Nationalist forces, and Guernica had a bridge and an important road intersection that was vital for the withdrawal of twenty-three battalions of Basque army troops located east of Guernica. If the route through Guernica could be closed, the Basque forces would be hindered in their retreat to the heavily fortified defenses around Bilbao and could be cut off and destroyed. At least two Basque army battalions were stationed in Guernica, the 18th Loyala Battalion and the Saseta Battalion. The Nationalists were also rightly concerned that the Basques might turn Guernica into a fortified position. By all the rules of international warfare in 1937, Guernica was a legitimate target for aerial attack.[51]

Well before the German attack, Guernica had been singled out for special attention by von Richthofen because of its importance in the Basque road network. On 25 April von Richthofen ordered his fighters to attack all traffic on the important Guernica-Bilbao road. As the Nationalist forces approached the town, von Richthofen discussed the operation with Colonel Vigón, who agreed with von Richthofen that attacking Guernica and closing the roads through the town provided a good opportunity to cut off much of the Basque army's retreat toward Bilbao.[52] The bombing of Guernica was carried out with the full approval of General Mola and his staff.[53] On 26 April the Germans attacked the town with forty-three bombers and fighters and dropped approximately thirty-five tons of high-explosive bombs and incendiaries. In a raid lasting more than an hour, half the town was destroyed, and there were heavy civilian casualties.

There was nothing new about the attack on Guernica. Other villages on the Basque front lines, notably the town of Durango in late March, had been

Nationalist armor making the final advance on Bilbao in the summer of 1937. (von Richthofen's personal photo)

bombed in a similar fashion. Von Richthofen had carefully planned the attack and was generally pleased with the results. His major complaint was that the Nationalist ground commanders had failed to move quickly enough to take advantage of the shock and disruption caused by his bombers. Von Richthofen had wanted the Nationalist force to advance into Guernica, just six miles behind the front lines, within a day of the bombing in order to block the Basque retreat. But the usual caution of the Nationalist commanders came into play, and the town only fell four days after the bombing. The Basques were able to reopen the road and retreat through Guernica in good order. Interestingly, von Richthofen's complaints about the slowness of the army ground commanders would be repeated constantly in Poland, France, the Soviet Union, and other campaigns.

On 30 April, von Richthofen visited Guernica just after it fell to the Nationalist forces. In his diary he made a few laconic remarks, and none of them referred to any success in terrorizing the Basques. He noted that in most respects the attack had been a success. The town had been "leveled" and "the city was completely closed to traffic for twenty-four hours." This was, indeed, the effect he was trying to achieve. Von Richthofen also noted that the attack had been a real technical success in terms of the effectiveness of the Luftwaffe's new 250-kilogram bombs and the EC B 1 bomb fuse.[54]

Guernica was carpet bombed not because of any specific plan of the Germans to inflict terror, but because the German bombers of early 1937 had poor bombsights and were simply incapable of hitting precise targets. The German operational rationale for bombing towns like Guernica is outlined in a Condor Legion report to Berlin made on 11 February 1938: "We have notable results in hitting targets near the front, especially in bombing villages which hold enemy reserves and headquarters. We have had great success because these targets are easy to find and can be thoroughly destroyed by carpet bombing." In the report, it was noted that attacks on point targets, such as bridges, roads, and rail lines, were more difficult and generally less successful.[55] The Nationalists had no problem with this German tactic. Even the official Spanish histories of the Civil War written in the Franco era contain photographs of Spanish towns under aerial bombardment by the Nationalist air force.[56]

Despite the myths that arose around the bombing of Guernica, the Germans expressed little interest in bombing the Spanish Republic to induce terror. As a senior Condor Legion officer put it, "It would have been simple for the Nationalist Air Force to bomb Valencia, Barcelona or Madrid into ashes with incendiary bombs, but politically that was unacceptable.... What would be the purpose of destroying the valuable industries of Bilbao or the weapons factory in Reinosa if they would be occupied in a short time?... Fighting in one's own land is a two-edged sword."[57] The Condor Legion found it could put its aircraft to their best use by interdicting Republican supply lines, attacking shipping and port facilities, and flying in direct support of the Nationalist army as it did in northern Spain.

The bombing of Guernica was quickly turned into a major international cause célèbre. Foreign correspondents writing for the *Times* of London and for the *New York Times*, along with representatives of the Basque government, labeled the bombing of Guernica a "terror attack." One correspondent wrote, "The object of the bombardment was seemingly the demoralization of the civil population and the destruction of the cradle of the Basque race."[58] The attack was covered extensively by the press.[59] The *New York Post* printed a cartoon about Guernica showing mountains of civilian dead in "the Holy City of Guernica" as Hitler stood over the ruined city with a bloody sword, which was captioned "air raids."[60] The U.S. *Congressional Record* referred to poison gas used at Guernica—an event that never occurred.[61] In the British Parliament, speeches were made denouncing the attack and inaccurately describing Guernica as an "open city" that contained no military targets.[62] The Basque government's account of 1,654 dead and 889 wounded was accepted uncritically in the world press although the actual number of dead and wounded was less than a fifth of that number.[63]

Ironically, the attack on Guernica, which made for a brief flurry of pro–Spanish Republican propaganda, ultimately proved of great advantage to the Third Reich. Because the sensational press coverage gave the impression that Guernica was a city instead of a small town, the Luftwaffe was credited with the ability to wipe whole cities off the map—something far beyond the capability of the German air force at that time. The press had already been conditioned to expect the destruction of whole cities by air and believed that "terror bombing" would be a feature of a future war. In Spain, it appeared that the future had arrived.

The exaggerated reports of Guernica had the effect of confirming the predictions of the airpower theorists concerning civilian casualties. In the French cabinet during strategy sessions in 1938, extravagant estimates were made of the German ability to inflict casualties among French civilians by bombing.[64] General Dentz of the French air force predicted at the time of the Sudetenland crisis in 1938 that "French cities would be laid in ruins."[65] A French cabinet member said of possible German aerial bombardment, "Our towns will be wiped out, our women and children slaughtered."[66] During the Munich Crisis of 1938, fully one-third of the population of Paris evacuated the city to avoid possible German air bombardment.[67] The false belief that the German Luftwaffe could devastate European cities played a central role in pushing the major powers into the disastrous policy of appeasing Hitler in 1938.

The Battle Shifts

After the fall of Bilbao, the Nationalists turned their attention to the last Republican enclave in the north, the mountainous region of Asturias. Cut off by the Nationalist sea blockade and possessing few heavy weapons, the Asturians could be expected to put up a strong fight. But they had little chance of holding off Mola's victorious northern army supported by the Condor Legion. As the Nationalist army repositioned its forces and started the campaign against the final northern enclave, a major crisis arose that would test the leadership of Sperrle and von Richthofen.

While the Nationalists had been reducing the Basque region, the Republican army and air force had been preparing their forces for a grand counterattack that they hoped would turn the tide of the war. Soviet assistance to the

Republic had been generous, and the Republican army had raised a strong force of several new divisions that were supported by several hundred Russian tanks (complete with well-trained Soviet tank crews), artillery, and ample ammunition. The Republican air force had been equipped with the latest Soviet fighters, and it was ready to confront the Nationalists with a superior force.

On 6 July 1937, the Republicans began one of their biggest offensives of the war. The best Republican divisions, well-supported with tanks, artillery, and 400 Soviet aircraft, broke through the thinly held Nationalist lines at Brunete, a small town west of Madrid, with the objective of breaking the siege of Madrid and cutting off a large Nationalist force. It was one of the high points of the Republican army's operations in the war, and it represented the best chance that the Republic had of defeating Franco's forces. At the time, the Condor Legion and the best Nationalist divisions were far away in Asturias, beginning the campaign to reduce the last resistance in that enclave of the Republic.

The Nationalist lines at Brunete cracked under the Republican assault, and it initially seemed as if the whole Nationalist line would break. Sperrle and von Richthofen responded to Franco's call for help and immediately suspended operations in the north.

Doing some brilliant staff work, von Richthofen shifted the airfield and supply units of the Condor Legion south to airfields near Madrid. Because the Luftwaffe logistics and support units were fully motorized, they managed to move quickly. Two Condor Legion squadrons redeployed to airfields near Madrid and commenced operations against the advancing Republican forces on the second day of the battle. The rest of the squadrons followed within days. With a crisis at hand, the northern army was moved south and readied for a counterstroke. But in the meantime the Condor Legion headquarters was given command of all the Italian and Nationalist air units (more than 200 aircraft total) on the threatened front. The Italians were understandably unhappy with the arrangement, but Franco trusted the Germans to coordinate the air campaign against the Republican army. The Germans' highly mobile logistics system stood up well to the test and enabled the Condor Legion to get into action immediately.

The first task was to defeat the Republicans in the air and win air superiority. The Me 109 fighter was brought in for its first major combat operations, and it performed admirably. Until that point, no Nationalist fighter could hold its own against the Republic's I-16 Soviet fighters. The Me 109 was faster than the I-16, well-armed, and climbed, dove, and generally flew better. The Condor Legion's two squadrons of Me 109s could clear the skies of Republican fighter opposition. Escorted by Me 109s, the legion's bombers were able to put the Republican airfields under constant attack. By mid-July, the Nationalist coalition had won air superiority over the front.

Once the Nationalist air forces won control of the air, the next step was to use its bomber and fighter units to support the Nationalist defense and counterattack. The weak point of the Republican force was its logistics, so the Condor Legion and Nationalist air force put the Republican supply depots and transportation lines under constant attack. Von Richthofen shuttled between the front lines and his headquarters, first conferring with the Spanish commanders and then planning air attacks to support the most threatened sectors. The Condor Legion's ability to provide air support on the front lines, a skill recently learned in the northern campaign, was decisive in helping the Nationalist army to slow, then halt, the Republican attacks. Once the Republican fighters had been swept from the sky, the Republican soldiers were demoralized by the constant pressure of German, Nationalist, and Italian aircraft overhead. The Condor Legion bombers and fighters normally flew several sorties a day to interdict Republican reinforcements and provide close support for the Nationalist army.[68] During it all, the forward maintenance and supply units kept the Condor Legion at a high operational rate.

With the German and Nationalist air forces flying air support, the Nationalist ground forces mounted a counterattack that began on 24 July. The Republicans, having suffered heavy attrition and now short of supplies—thanks to the air interdiction campaign—were in poor shape. The Nationalist forces won a major victory in the next days.[69] The Republican forces were swept back beyond their starting point. By the end of the campaign in August, the best divisions of the Republican army had been badly mauled and would have to be rebuilt. Large quantities of equipment had also been lost, and Republican Spain would have to struggle to replace it. The Soviet aid did not come free of charge, and the whole Spanish gold reserve went to the Soviet Union to keep the armaments flowing. In many respects this was the greatest military defeat of the Republic. Never again would the Republican forces have an advantage in weapons, logistics, and air support. Without the air support and effective air leadership provided by the Condor Legion and its commander and chief of staff, Brunete would likely have been a disaster for the Nationalists.

After the successful counteroffensive at Brunete, the Condor Legion was again shifted north to mop up the last of the resistance in Asturias. From August through October the Condor Legion supported the Nationalist ground advance.[70] The Condor Legion bomber squadrons had been reequipped with new He 111 and Do 17 bombers. The He 51s had been replaced by Me 109s that swept the occasional Republican fighter sortie from the sky.[71] The He 51s had not been very good as fighter planes, but they performed well as ground attack planes. Through the Asturias campaign, the Condor Legion kept perfecting the techniques of close air support.

While overseeing the Republican forces in the north, Sperrle and von Richthofen also managed the activities of various German air detachments throughout Spain. As was noted earlier, when the Condor Legion was formed in late 1936 it included a seaplane squadron equipped with He 59 seaplanes capable of carrying bombs and torpedoes. The German unit operated out of Mallorca and combined its operations with the Italian and Spanish naval air units operating on the Mediterranean coast. The combined force carried out a very successful campaign against the Republican harbors and shipping, inflicting heavy damage to the Republican infrastructure.[72] During the war, the Republicans lost 554 ships, with 144 credited to German and Italian action. In addition, 106 foreign ships carrying supplies to the Republicans were sunk.[73] Air action sank a major proportion of these.[74]

During the campaigns in 1937 the Condor Legion officers, from Sperrle and von Richthofen to the squadron and flight commanders, set a Luftwaffe policy by regularly visiting the Spanish units at the front to observe close air support operations.[75] The junior officers of the Condor Legion also attempted to learn Spanish. Before and after missions, the pilots flying the missions tried to get to know the men they were supporting.[76] The German attitude was good for morale, and some of the Spanish units, especially the Moroccan and Navarese divisions, developed a close affinity for the Germans. Even while the war was progressing at the front, German officers and NCOs were training the personnel of the Nationalist air force. As the Condor Legion became equipped with modern aircraft from Germany, the He 51s, He 45s, and older planes were turned over to the Spanish. As German production increased, Spanish airmen would also be trained to fly the Me 109 and the He 111. The Nationalist and German air forces formed a close bond, and the two air forces commonly flew combined missions.[77] Captain José Larios, duke of Lerma and Nationalist fighter ace, regularly flew in conjunction with the Germans.[78]

In October 1937 Sperrle prepared to turn over the Condor Legion to a new commander, Maj. General Helmuth Volkmann. Having served for a year in Spain, most of the Condor Legion personnel would be replaced by others, who would also use the war as a training ground. After a short transition period to settle in the new commander, Sperrle could return home to take over a major command (what became the 3rd Air Fleet) having won some major battles and proven that modern airpower could have a decisive effect on the battlefield.

From mid-1936 to 1937 the Luftwaffe in Spain had led the way in developing modern air warfare doctrine. The transport operations of 1936 had shown that large forces could be efficiently moved long distances by air. On the battlefields in northern Spain and at Brunete, the Condor Legion had pioneered new concepts of close air support. Interdiction attacks had also proven an effective means to wear down and hamper a modern army. Von Richthofen's use of flak units in the artillery role prefigured the use of the 88 mm gun as a superb ground force support weapon in World War II. These doctrinal innovations would give the Luftwaffe a huge advantage in the coming European war. Perhaps most important, the commanders and staffs of the Condor Legion had learned how to handle modern air forces in combat against a modern enemy.

The Luftwaffe had also found Spain to be a superb testing ground for its equipment. The new bombers and the Me 109 fighter had proven their worth in battle, and tactical methods were constantly improving. Communications between ground and air units remained a problem, but the Luftwaffe had still managed to work with the equipment available and would speed up work on improved radios.

When Volkmann took command of the Condor Legion in November 1937, von Richthofen remained as the chief of staff. The new staff and personnel of the Condor Legion had little time to adjust before facing a new challenge. In November 1937 the Republic mounted a major offensive in Aragon, aimed at breaking the Nationalist defense lines at the town of Teruel. The Nationalist forces were forced to give up ground, and the Republic made some initial advances. The winter weather in the mountains of Aragon was atrocious, and soldiers and airmen on both sides had to deal with freezing temperatures and poor visibility. Even though the Teruel sector was not of great strategic importance, the Nationalist high command decided that it would have to make a major effort to throw back the Republican offensive. From a political standpoint, it was a sound move. A victory against the Nationalists would strengthen morale and demonstrate the viability of the Republic. If the Republicans won a round, they could expect to receive continued aid from the Soviet Union. The Condor Legion redeployed its forces to the Aragon front and carried out its usual program of interdiction and close support operations to hinder the Republican forces. As in the earlier battles, the Condor Legion won air superiority over the battlefield and readied itself to support a major Nationalist counteroffensive. Given the winter conditions, it was one of the toughest campaigns fought by the Germans in Spain.[79]

In the meantime, Volkmann and von Richthofen were not getting along. A large part of the problem lay in Volkmann's command style. Sperrle had tended to the strategic level of war and allowed von Richthofen free rein to handle the daily operations of the Condor Legion, and this had worked well. Volkmann, however, insisted on taking over the management of daily operations. At the same time, Volkmann's relationship with the Nationalist high command was not as amicable as the one that Sperrle and von Richthofen had established. With differing views of the strategic and operational situation, and very different styles of leadership, there was considerable friction in the command echelon of the Condor Legion. In January 1938 von Richthofen decided to ask for a transfer away from the Condor Legion, and it was readily approved by Volkmann. On 30 January 1938, just as the Nationalist counteroffensive was making progress at Teruel, von Richthofen left Spain and returned to Germany.[80]

Command of a Bomber Group

Von Richthofen was promoted to full colonel upon his return from Spain. Although the Germans were in Spain officially as "volunteers," and little was said openly about the Luftwaffe's role in the war until it was all over, everyone in the Luftwaffe knew that von Richthofen had been a senior officer in Spain and had performed brilliantly. As a general staff officer he would be expected to serve for a period in command of a unit in order to gain experience. He was informed that he would move to the large new Luftwaffe base at Lüneburg to take command of the 257th Bomber Wing.[81] Von Richthofen would be able to inform the young pilots and commanders of all that he had learned in Spain. As a wing commander, he rated a large and comfortable house near the air base, and his wife and children joined him. The Richthofens had cousins in nearby Hanover and knew the area well, and the whole family would settle in nicely. Von Richthofen's nine months in command of a bomber unit was a happy interlude for the family. He could spend time with his children, and the region afforded him ample opportunities for hunting. He also enjoyed skeet shooting with his officers. The Luftwaffe was expanding rapidly, and promotion opportunities would now come quickly for a man who had proven himself in combat.

Return to Spain

Although the Condor Legion continued to serve successfully in Spain and the Nationalists continued to make progress on the battlefield, relations

Von Richthofen (far left), then commander of Bomber Wing 257, at a skeet shooting tournament with his squadron commanders, circa 1938. If it was a shooting sport or hunting event, von Richthofen was usually there.

among the Condor Legion commander, the Nationalist government, and the Luftwaffe staff grew rocky. Whereas von Richthofen had understood the strategic need to limit German involvement in Spain, Volkmann bombarded the Luftwaffe staff in Berlin with demands for more personnel, support, and equipment. His reports to Berlin took on a very pessimistic tone, and in one report of June 1938 he frankly despaired of the Nationalist chances to make any progress.[82] In fact, his analysis was wrong. The 1938 Nationalist spring offensive had succeeded in driving to the sea and had cut the Republic into two parts, with Catalonia now separated from Madrid and the main sector of Republican Spain. If the Nationalists had bogged down, the Republic was in a strategically impossible position.

By the fall of 1938, both the Nationalists and the air staff in Berlin had lost patience with Volkmann. The Condor Legion's second commander was relieved in October 1938, and von Richthofen was tapped to take over as the new commander. The Nationalist high command was happy with this, as they respected von Richthofen and had worked well with him in 1936 and 1937. Some accounts have the Nationalist high command specifically requesting that von Richthofen return to Spain to command the Condor

Legion, and this is probably true. Von Richthofen assumed command of the German forces in Spain on 1 November 1938 with the rank of major general. The war was going well for the Nationalists and the Condor Legion, and when von Richthofen arrived in Spain for his second tour, the end of the war was in sight. In the late summer, the Republic had staged its last major offensive, driving down from Catalonia and pushing forces across the Ebro River in an attempt to reunite the two parts of the Republic. Largely due to the swift response of the Condor Legion and the much-improved Nationalist air force, the Republican offensive was halted after initial gains. In heavy fighting through October and November, the Republican army was pushed back to its starting point—having taken heavy troops losses as well as losing most of its heavy weapons.

In von Richthofen's absence, new aircraft had been sent to Spain, notably a flight of Ju 87 Stukas sent for testing in the field. Contrary to von Richthofen earlier beliefs, low-level operations and the use of Stukas in close support did not lead to heavy aircraft losses. Indeed, the Stuka became renowned as the most accurate weapon of the Spanish Civil War—the only aircraft that could routinely hit point targets such as bridges and bunkers. By this time the techniques of army support operations were well established and the ability of the Spanish to plan operations went much more smoothly than they had in early 1937. The next operation of the Nationalists was a drive to overrun all of Catalonia. Once Catalonia fell, Republican Spain would be boxed into the region of Madrid to Valencia and basically indefensible.

The final Nationalist offensive of the war began on 23 December 1938 with von Richthofen observing from the front as his aircraft provided close support to the Navarese and Moroccan divisions that spearheaded the advance. Behind the Republican lines, Condor Legion and Nationalist bomber squadrons pummeled the Republican transport system and logistics. The port of Barcelona was bombed to cut off shipments of arms to the Republic. The Nationalists, under cover of complete air superiority, advanced steadily, and on 26 January 1939 Barcelona fell. At this point the Nationalist offensive accelerated as the surviving Republican forces in Catalonia, accompanied by thousands of civilian refugees, streamed across the French border to be interned in France. On 10 February the Nationalist army reached the French border and ended the campaign in the north.

Characteristically, as Condor Legion commander, von Richthofen showed considerable understanding of the politics of the coalition. Indeed, he grasped the dynamics of the war better than did the German Foreign Ministry. In early 1939, with the end of the war in sight, von Richthofen recommended that a large part of his force be returned to Germany, as they were

Von Richthofen as major general and commander of the Condor Legion. Visiting Spanish troops on the Ebro front line, late 1938. (*Luftwelt*)

no longer necessary for operations. The Foreign Ministry disagreed with this suggestion, maintaining it "would send the wrong signal."[83] When Barcelona fell to the Nationalists, von Richthofen ordered the Condor Legion troops to stay out of the city and to give the Nationalists full credit for the victory. The Italians, blundering as usual, tried to claim the lion's share of the glory, demanding that Italian troops enter the city with the first Nationalist battalions.[84] Such behavior only alienated Franco and helped increase Spanish suspicion of Italy's motives in the Mediterranean.

With the fall of Catalonia the Republic began negotiations for the surrender of its last forces. In March the final surrenders took place and Franco entered Madrid as master of all Spain. During May 1939 the Condor Legion held its last reviews in Spain, and Franco showered medals on von Richthofen and his senior officers. Von Richthofen returned to Germany that month.

With the victory in Spain the full story of the Condor Legion and its role in the war could be told. Von Richthofen became a national figure and was much in demand as a speaker at Nazi rallies and events. Back home at Lüneburg, he accepted a request to give a speech at the 1939 Nazi "Party

Day" rally. It was a common practice in the Third Reich to hold local Nazi rallies and to celebrate the role of the party in the life of the people. As was noted earlier, military officers were not allowed to join any political party, even the Nazi Party, and were not expected to take part in party activities. Von Richthofen could have avoided Nazi activities, as did many senior officers. However, Hermann Goering wanted the Luftwaffe and its role in the Spanish War to receive as much attention as possible, so he pressured von Richthofen to speak at the Lüneburg Nazi rally and at other events as well. In 1939 von Richthofen was enamored of Hitler and enthusiastic about the rebirth of German nationalism under the Führer's leadership. He thus agreed to give some political speeches and make appearances at factory openings and other events. His speech at Lüneburg, of which there is a surviving recording, was straightforward. He told the audience that Adolf Hitler had led the German people to a new era and that the unity of Germany that Hitler and the Nazi Party had forged had made possible enormous progress. It was a theme of simple nationalism that went down well. It is interesting to note that von Richthofen never used the Nazi salute, even after the practice became common in the Wehrmacht later in the war. He always gave the standard military salute. It was one means to differentiate himself as a soldier from the civilians.

That summer there would be a last grand review of the Condor Legion in Berlin. Von Richthofen and his soldiers, sweltering in their heavy brown wool Spanish uniforms, were fêted as German heroes. On that day von Richthofen would receive the thanks of the Führer himself and be greeted and congratulated by Germany's top generals. Within three months, Germany would go to war, and von Richthofen's recent combat experience would make him an invaluable leader for the campaigns to come.

Lessons from the War in Spain

The Luftwaffe's Condor Legion deserves credit for the major share of the Nationalist success in the air, and for much of the success on the ground as well. German effectiveness on the battlefield was disproportionate to the German force's relatively small numbers of men and aircraft. The Germans entered the war in Spain with a military doctrine that was effective and adaptable. During the course of the war it was refined further. The Germans found that the key to victory on the battlefields in Spain lay in the effective joint operations system that the Nationalist army and the Luftwaffe had developed. Thanks to the Spanish experience, when World War II began, Germany, alone of the major powers, possessed a comprehensive military doctrine that made joint operations the focus of its operational planning and

Wolfram von Richthofen as major general and commander of the Condor Legion, spring 1939. He is wearing decorations given him by Franco.

Von Richthofen as a newly promoted major general and featured speaker at the Lüneburg Nazi Party Day Rally, summer 1939. After his return from Spain von Richthofen was a national hero and very much in demand as a speaker at Nazi events, factory meetings, and so on. Von Richthofen was personally asked by Goering to attend these events. As a military man, von Richthofen could have avoided these rallies, but he agreed to appear because of his strong belief in Hitler.

training. The doctrine factor alone magnified the battlefield impact of the Condor Legion.

During the war in Spain the Luftwaffe had consistently been good at learning lessons and adapting to the specific needs of the war—which was largely a function of the leadership of officers such as Sperrle, von Richthofen, and Volkmann. The Condor Legion had faced a strong enemy, and both sides had relatively equal air forces. The Republicans used approximately 1,500 aircraft during the war, and the Nationalist coalition about 1,300 aircraft.[85] And for much of the war neither side possessed any overwhelming advantage in equipment quality or quantity. The differences that had counted were in doctrine and leadership.

After the war in Spain, no major power could ignore the importance of airpower on the battlefield. Effective joint operations, under cover of air superiority, was the key to victory. In the campaigns in northern Spain in 1937 and in Aragon in 1938, the advance of the Nationalist ground forces depended upon the air force to open the way by reducing the enemy's fortifications. At first this was done by carpet bombing, but later the Ju 87 (Stuka) dive bombers proved that they could put 1,000-pound bombs with great accuracy upon enemy strong points and greatly improve the efficiency of the close support method. Interdiction had also proven to be a key to success in the operational campaigns. At Brunete in 1927 and on the Ebro in 1938 and 1939, the Condor Legion's interdiction campaign behind the Republican lines helped stop the enemy offensives by crippling the Republican transport and logistics.[86]

In terms of training the Luftwaffe's Spanish Civil War experience gave it a tremendous advantage at the start of World War II. Between 1936 and 1939 approximately 20,000 Luftwaffe personnel served in Spain on tours lasting between six and twelve months. The Condor Legion had conducted almost every type of major operation in Spain. On occasion, it carried out strategic strikes of vital Republican industrial targets. Interdiction of ports and rail and logistics lines were an important part of Condor Legion operations. The legion also carried out air superiority campaigns, attacking Republican airfields and engaging Republican aircraft over the front. This was a level of experience possessed by no other major European air force in 1939.

As Luftwaffe personnel returned from Spain they were posted to operational units, often as commanders or instructors, where they shared their combat experience. Many of Germany's leading fighter aces and bomber commanders of World War II, men such as Adolf Galland, Martin Harlinghausen, and Werner Mölders, got their first taste of aerial combat over Spain. Condor Legion commanders and staff officers had fought in numerous major operations employing large air forces. For example, during the Brunete campaign in 1937 the Condor Legion had command of over 200 Nationalist coalition aircraft. Moreover, the combat experience was gained under tough conditions against a very capable enemy. When the war began, the Luftwaffe had been a small force with a minimum of training. By the end of the war the Luftwaffe had vastly more experience in conducting a modern air war than any opponents it would be likely to face. In short, the Luftwaffe's participation in the Spanish Civil War was a central factor in the effectiveness of the force and provided the Luftwaffe with an advantage over its Polish, French, and British enemies in 1939–1940.

One of the most important tactical developments to come out of the Spanish War was the revolution in squadron fighter tactics. Up through the 1930s every major air force used a system of squadron battle formations that had been developed during World War I. The basic formation was a flight of three aircraft, usually flying in a "V." Three or four flights would constitute a squadron, which would fly into battle in a series of fairly complex large formations. In Spain the Condor Legion evolved a system of new squadron fighter tactics. Captain Werner Mölders, one of Germany's top fighter pilots, took command of the Me 109 squadron of the Condor Legion in January 1938 and is credited with instituting a new tactical system based on pairs of aircraft instead of threes.[87] Two aircraft made up the basic fighter formation (*Rotte*), with one pilot flying slightly behind and to the side of his wingman. Two Rottes would constitute a *Schwarm*, with four aircraft spread out in the "finger four" formation. Squadrons would fly as a group of Schwarms. It was a more open and more flexible formation than the tight squadron formations previously used and, by basing tactics on pairs, each pilot could concentrate on covering and supporting just one wingman rather than two.

The new tactical system proved its worth in Spain. With superior aircraft and tactics the Condor Legion won air superiority in early 1937 and never lost it. The Condor Legion shot down 327 Republican aircraft in air-to-air combat for seventy-two combat losses. After shooting down fourteen enemy aircraft in Spain, Mölders was brought back to Germany in late 1938 and set to work by the air staff writing a new fighter tactics manual and making the new tactics standard throughout the Luftwaffe.[88] These new fighter tactics gave the Germans a significant advantage in air-to-air combat against French and British fighters in 1940, because the Allied fighter units were still wedded to less effective squadron formations.[89] The Spanish experience also helped improve the effectiveness of the Luftwaffe's bomber force. The high accident rate for aircraft in Spain forced the Luftwaffe to put a strong emphasis on night flying and instrument training. One of General Sperrle's first orders to his Luftwaffe units upon his return from Spain was to increase the amount and intensity of instrument flying.[90] Because of this new emphasis on instrument flying and navigation, the Luftwaffe was better able to operate at night in 1940 than were its opponents.

Another valuable lesson learned in Spain was the importance of air transport and forward logistics. The success of the Luftwaffe's airlift of Franco's African army dramatically demonstrated a major new role for an air force, and in response the Luftwaffe built up a large air transport force. The war also illustrated the importance of highly mobile airfield companies and supply units that could deploy and support combat air units from frontline airfields. When World War II began, the Luftwaffe had a large force of mobile airfield units and supply columns that enabled the Luftwaffe fighter, bomber, and Stuka units to move close behind the army and provide close support for ground troops. The ability to quickly redeploy and operate close to the front was essential in giving the Luftwaffe a high sortie rate during the 1939 and 1940 campaigns. In Spain the Germans had tested the latest aircraft guns, bombs, fuses, antiaircraft guns, motor vehicles, and radios. The performance of specific items of equipment were detailed in most of the reports the Condor Legion sent to Berlin, and the Luftwaffe moved quickly to improve and modify equipment whenever deficiencies were found.[91]

As a direct result of the Spanish Civil War, in the summer of 1939 the Luftwaffe formed the "Special Purpose Division," an air division composed of four Stuka groups, one attack group, one reconnaissance squadron, and two fighter groups (for escort). This new force, which would be placed under von Richthofen's command, was organized and trained specifically for the close support for ground forces.[92] This is the force that von Richthofen would lead in the Polish campaign. There the importance of effective close-support operations would be proven even more dramatically than in Spain.

Chapter 6

The Polish Campaign, 1939

Germany formally annexed Czechoslovakia in the spring of 1939, thus violating the Munich agreement of 1938 that had granted Hitler the Sudetenland while guaranteeing the independence of the rest of Czechoslovakia. Britain and France, though shocked at the German aggression, took no action, and this lack of response convinced Hitler that his next round of territorial expansion would meet with no resistance by the major powers. While absorbing the Czech region and its valuable war industries into the German Reich, Hitler stepped up his diplomatic offensive to demand that Poland return the regions of the old German Reich that had been annexed by Poland in the aftermath of World War I.

Poland was militarily stronger than Czechoslovakia had been. The Czechs caved in when it became clear that Britain and France would not come to their aid. The Poles, in contrast, were far more likely to fight if confronted by German demands for their territory, and to be supported in their efforts by France and Britain. In the wake of Hitler's flagrant violation of the great power agreements over Czechoslovakia, Germany's massive military buildup, and the frankly aggressive tone of Hitler's rhetoric concerning Poland, the Western allies finally took action in the hope of deterring Hitler. In 1939 Britain joined with France in formalizing an alliance to guarantee Polish territory and sovereignty, and the major Western powers made arrangements to provide Poland with modern military equipment. However, despite these good intentions, both Britain and France were far behind Germany in the arms race and were desperately short modern equipment for their own forces; thus, they could spare little for Poland in the short term.

Although Hitler believed that the Western allies would again refuse to confront Germany, he understood that the Poles would resist Germany's aggression and that a major military campaign would be necessary to destroy Poland. In most respects, the Germans were well prepared for a war against Poland. After World War I the German Freikorps had fought and defeated the Poles in Silesia and the Weimar Republic had viewed Poland as a hostile nation. Throughout the 1920s Poland was at the top of the Reichswehr's list of probable war enemies, and the standard scenario of 1920s military exercises and war games was an attack upon Germany by a Polish-French alliance with a German counteroffensive against Poland. By the time Hitler came to power the German military had been thinking about how to fight a major war against the Poles for twenty years. Even in the 1920s German military thinking favored the employment of large mobile formations against the Poles, and encircling and destroying Polish armies in large envelopment operations. The secret Luftwaffe staff had put considerable thought into an air campaign designed to cripple and weaken the Polish forces. The "operational air war" concepts first developed in the 1920s were especially suitable for fighting Poland. In the air war doctrine that evolved through the 1920s and 1930s the first priority of the air force would be to gain air superiority by attacking and destroying the enemy air force on the ground. Once the Luftwaffe had operational freedom in the air, the next target priority would be the military infrastructure and national rail network.[1] With few good roads and motorized vehicles, Poland was almost completely dependent upon its railroads for mobilizing and moving its forces and supplying its army. If the rail network were crippled, the Polish army would be unable to mobilize forces and respond to a rapid German advance.[2] Those forces that managed to mobilize and attempted to maneuver against the Germans would be interdicted by the Luftwaffe, relentlessly attacked, and hopefully wrecked as a cohesive force long before they reached the front lines. A lower priority for the Luftwaffe was providing direct close support for German forces engaged in the ground battle.

Against Poland, and later against France and the Low Countries, this basic operational doctrine proved extremely effective in supporting a rapid war of maneuver. One of the many German advantages in planning for a war against Poland was good intelligence. Since Poland had long been the focus of German war planning, the military and civilian intelligence agencies had collected a large amount of information about Polish forces, war industries, and defenses.[3] The Germans thus had a clear understanding of Polish strengths and weaknesses. The Luftwaffe was poised to exploit the latter.

A quick victory in Poland was a strategic necessity. While Hitler did not expect Britain and France to fight to defend Poland, if they honored their commitments, Germany's western border would be highly vulnerable to attack as the Wehrmacht's most modern and effective forces would be committed to the war in the east. In 1939 German rearmament was in high gear and there were ample first-line army and Luftwaffe forces to defeat the Poles, but certainly not enough forces to fight a two-front war. The Polish campaign would require all of Germany's elite panzer and motorized divisions as well as its best trained and best-equipped infantry units. Most of the Luftwaffe would have to be deployed if the Polish air force were to be quickly destroyed and the Polish transportation net crippled. As long as the Wehrmacht was committed to Poland only a few dozen infantry divisions, mostly reserve units in a low state of training, would be available to defend Germany's western border. If the French and British decided to attack while Germany fought in Poland, they would have an enormous advantage in numbers, training, and tanks in artillery. In the air the Luftwaffe forces defending the western front would also face far superior Allied forces.[4]

Hitler gambled that if the British and French came to Poland's aid they would not have the nerve to move quickly against Germany. Still, for the weeks that the main German forces were in the east, Germany would be highly vulnerable. Thus the Polish campaign was planned with speed in mind to overrun Poland quickly and immediately redeploy German forces to the west if needed. However, the Germans had good reasons to believe that they could defeat Poland quickly. The Germans outnumbered the Poles in the air by a factor of seven to one, and the Germans had a huge advantage in terms of the quality and amount of their equipment on the ground and in the air. While the Poles had a large army, it possessed few tanks or even motorized vehicles. Its artillery was far inferior to the Wehrmacht's, and it was desperately short of essential equipment such as radios. Because the German military had long planned for a war with Poland it had a highly developed logistics infrastructure in place near the Polish border to support its forces. The Luftwaffe was especially well prepared for operations in the east. On Poland's southern flank the Luftwaffe's 4th Air Fleet had seventy-four airfields and nineteen airfield companies to support its operations. On the northern flank the 1st Air Fleet had twenty-nine airfields and twenty airfield companies in Pomerania and additional airfields and units available in East Prussia.[5]

The army and Luftwaffe plans for the campaign against Poland were developed and finalized in a major war game in May 1939, and the Luftwaffe staff issued detailed guidance to the 1st and 4th Air Fleets that were tasked to support the campaign.[6] The German plans for conquest followed thinking that had evolved since the 1920s; the Luftwaffe would first cripple the Polish air force on the ground, and then bomber and Stuka units would hinder the Polish mobilization and troop movement by shattering the rail network. Finally, the Luftwaffe would support a rapid advance by the army by air interdiction of Polish troop formations moving to the front. The army and Luftwaffe staffs planned to quickly crush Poland through two great simultaneous offensive thrusts from the north and south. The five armies of the northern and southern army groups would advance on Warsaw, in the center of Poland, using armored and motorized divisions in concentrated task forces to drive rapidly ahead and encircle the Polish armies concentrated on Poland's western and southern borders. The 1st Air Fleet, with 1,105 combat aircraft under the command of General Albert Kesselring, would be based in northeast Germany and East Prussia and was tasked to support the operations of the Northern Army Group (the Third and Fourth Armies, under the command of Col. General Fedor von Bock). The 4th Air Fleet was under the command of General Alexander Löhr, the former chief of the Austrian air force, who had joined the Luftwaffe as a senior officer upon the Anschluss of Austria with Germany in March 1938. Based in southeast Germany and Slovakia, the 4th Air Fleet would support the Southern Army Group (Eighth, Tenth, and Fourteenth Armies, under the command of General Gerd von Rundstedt). The 4th Air Fleet deployed 729 combat aircraft for the campaign. In addition to the combat aircraft of the two air fleets, the two army groups had 262 Luftwaffe reconnaissance aircraft, mostly light Henschel 126 planes, directly assigned to army command. One hundred fighters were posted along the Polish border for home air defense, and fifty-six aircraft were assigned to naval reconnaissance in the Baltic, for a German total of 2,152 aircraft for the eastern campaign.[7]

The primary German thrust would be made by Rundstedt's Southern Army Group, which was allocated four of the army's six panzer divisions. Rundstedt, in turn, determined that the main effort to break the Polish army would be made by Col. General Walter von Reichenau's Tenth Army, which was allocated two panzer divisions, two light divisions (motorized divisions with some tanks), and two motorized divisions—for 1939 an awesome concentration of mechanized and motorized might.[8] The Tenth Army's mission was to drive northeast to Warsaw from its base in Silesia. Its left flank would be covered by the Eighth Army, and its right flank by the Fourteenth Army, which would drive into central Poland from Slovakia. The Poles had positioned their armies along the border, with the bulk of the forces in western Poland, so a German drive to Warsaw would require overrunning some of the Polish forces while leaving most of them deployed on Poland's western border to be encircled and destroyed. Once the path to Warsaw was cleared, the capital was expected to fall quickly; with Warsaw taken, any serious Polish resistance was expected to collapse. At the time of the spring and summer war games Hitler did not inform the military leadership of his highly secret negotiations with Joseph Stalin that would ensure Poland's rapid destruction by inviting the Soviet Union to ally itself with Germany and invade Poland from the east. The German-Soviet Pact announced in August 1939 was a masterly stroke that ensured the swift defeat of Poland. With the Soviets joining the war, the Poles would be unable to retreat to the east.

Ju 52 transports were important to the Luftwaffe in moving men and matériel forward to captured airfields. (U.S. Air Force Historical Research Agency)

The Luftwaffe in 1939—Eve of the Polish Campaign

The Luftwaffe entered World War II with a large combat force of 4,333 aircraft.[9] If not the largest air force in the world (the Soviet air force had that distinction), the Luftwaffe was certainly the most modern. The German medium bombers—the He 111s, Ju 88s, and Do 17s—were equal or superior to the Allies' best bombers. The German fighter force, with over 1,000 Me 109s, was considerably more modern than the British and French fighter forces. Although British and French rearmament was picking up steam and the Allied air forces were reequipping with modern fighters, their frontline air units were still largely equipped with obsolescent planes. Of course, no other power had a strike force of dive bombers that could compare with Germany's Stukas. In addition to its modern and powerful combat forces, the Luftwaffe, with its 500 Ju 52 transports, had the largest and most capable air transport force in the world.

The Luftwaffe of 1939 possessed other significant advantages over its opponents, one of which was its superb training. Although other air forces had good pilot training programs that produced individual pilots equal to the Germans, the Luftwaffe had also emphasized training its large units and staffs and was mentally and doctrinally better prepared for war. From the official birth of the Luftwaffe in 1935 it had carried out an extensive program of large-scale maneuvers and had stressed training in cooperation with the army. Following the old general staff tradition, the higher Luftwaffe staffs also conducted a regular program of war games and communications exercises to familiarize the air corps and air fleet staffs with the complexities of major combat operations.[10] Air warfare doctrine and plans were tested as a means to expose flaws and identify requirements for new tactics, munitions, and equipment. The Luftwaffe's opponents, with a few exceptions such as the RAF Fighter Command, failed to conduct large-scale unit and staff training exercises and failed to test their own tactics and doctrine. Given the fairly slight numerical and technological advantages that the Luftwaffe had in 1939, the remarkable success of the Luftwaffe against its enemies from 1939 to 1941 can be largely attributed to the superior training program carried out before the war along with the Luftwaffe's experience of large-scale aerial combat in Spain.[11]

Richthofen's New Command—The Special Purpose Air Division

In May 1939, as the plans for the invasion of Poland were being finalized, von Richthofen was still in Spain, enjoying victory parades and arranging the return of the Condor Legion to Germany. With the end of the war in Spain, there was no more official nonsense about German "volunteers" aiding the Nationalists. With the war won, the role of the Luftwaffe in Spain was frankly acknowledged in the German press. Stories and photos about the war the Germans had fought in Spain soon appeared throughout the civilian and military press. Von Richthofen, as the last commander of the Condor Legion, received a great deal of press attention and was hailed as a national hero. On a more professional note, the Luftwaffe and Wehrmacht high command had been very impressed by von Richthofen's conduct of the air operations in support of the final Nationalist advances. Von Richthofen's next assignment was already set—the last air campaign in Spain had been centered on supporting the rapid advance of ground forces and was very much like the planned campaign for Poland. Moreover, the Condor Legion had proven highly successful in close support of ground forces, and von Richthofen was now the Luftwaffe's acknowledged master of this kind of operation. Indeed, there was no airman in any of the world's air forces in 1939 who could equal von Richthofen's experience in air support of ground forces.

Since von Richthofen had proven himself in commanding large air operations to support ground troops, the Luftwaffe selected him to play a major role in the campaign for Poland.[12] In the summer of 1939 the Luftwaffe created a special command whose specific mission was to support German ground forces, especially the armored and motorized forces that would bear the primary responsibility for the success of the campaign. Von Richthofen's "Special Purpose Division" was a provisional air division composed of four Stuka groups (160 aircraft), one He 123 group (40 aircraft), one Do 17 reconnaissance squadron, and one group of Me 109s from JG 76 (40 aircraft) to serve as escorts for the Stukas and attack planes. His division was allocated a Luftwaffe signals company and a battalion of flak guns to protect his airfields from attack by the Polish air force. In all, Von Richthofen's force amounted to about 250 planes.[13] This force would be used en masse and deployed to support the German forces at the "Schwerpunkt" of the campaign—the front of the German Tenth Army.

On 1 August 1939 the Luftwaffe's new chief of staff, and von Richthofen's close friend, Hans Jeschonnek, sent all the senior commanders guidelines for the employment of the Luftwaffe in support of ground forces.[14] The guidelines were based largely upon the Luftwaffe's experience in Spain and partly on the tradition of German operational thought. The first principle laid out was that the air commanders would decide where, when, and how to employ aerial forces against ground targets.[15] Commanders were enjoined to think in terms of the larger picture, that is, the objectives of the whole campaign, and not just in terms of their immediate mission. In this context the guidelines reminded commanders that attacks against enemy transportation targets, depots, and rear areas might have an even greater operational effect than attacks upon enemy forces in direct contact.[16] Indeed, the chief of staff's directives viewed air support for the army primarily as interdiction operations designed to cut off the forward elements of the enemy forces by destroying the roads and rail networks in the rear and attacking enemy columns on the roads. Such operations denied the enemy the ability to maneuver or retreat; in any case, it was far more efficient to destroy an enemy column on the road than one that was dispersed and deployed for battle. In the traditional German manner, the guidelines recommended that the Stuka groups not be broken into small groups for individual missions but used en masse, usually at group strength (thirty to forty aircraft), in order to achieve an operational effect and to be sure of destroying the target.[17] It was noted that aircraft were best employed outside the range of the army's artillery except on special occasions when aircraft-delivered bombs might be required to ensure destruction of an important target.[18] This latter advice made a great deal of sense because in 1939 the Luftwaffe, although possessing a highly sophisticated communications network for the time, did not have the capability of controlling or guiding aircraft attacks from the ground. The army practiced various ground signaling measures such as laying out panels on the ground, marking lines with colored smoke, and displaying swastika flags on the top of German tanks and armored cars as means of ensuring that Luftwaffe aircraft did not bomb German troops by mistake. German ground troops were also to be warned when the Luftwaffe was about to make attacks in their vicinity.[19] But the closer the Luftwaffe flew to German ground troops, the greater the chances for accidentally bombing one's own troops. At 12,000 to 15,000 feet, the usual height that Stukas started their diving attacks, German guns, troops, and vehicles on the ground looked much like Polish guns, troops, and vehicles. Therefore, the Luftwaffe and army commanders would determine a "bomb line" along the army front and forbid the Luftwaffe to bomb short of the line unless the circumstances were exceptional or in the case of a carefully planned attack upon a clearly identifiable enemy target.

To carry out his mission von Richthofen put together a first-rate staff, heavy on veterans with experience in Spain. His air division chief of staff was Lt. Colonel Hans Seidemann, who had served in Spain with von Richthofen. It was a happy partnership, and von Richthofen respected and worked well with him. Thanks to their Spanish experience the two knew much better than other German commanders just what kind of problems they could expect in Poland. Von Richthofen's chief of logistics was Major Paul Deichmann, another Spanish veteran. Seidemann and Deichmann would serve with von Richthofen in other campaigns, and in the course of the war both would be promoted to general and receive major commands of their own. To manage communications for his division von Richthofen had Major Siebert attached to the staff. Siebert had served as communications officer for the Condor Legion in 1936–1937, and von Richthofen gave him a great deal of credit for the success of their operations. In Spain, Poland, and other campaigns, von Richthofen exhibited one of the necessary traits of a good senior commander: he had a good eye for talent. When his subordinates performed well he worked to see that they were recognized and promoted. Those he found lacking were quickly dismissed from his staff or command positions, with von Richthofen's recommendation that they be assigned to some job where they couldn't do any harm.

The other major combat unit of the 4th Air Fleet was General Bruno Loerzer's 2nd Air Division. Before the campaign began von Richthofen was told that he would receive his guidance through Loerzer instead of directly through the air fleet. Richthofen was clearly unhappy with this or any arrangement that placed him under the command of Loerzer, who he thought of as a lightweight in terms of his abilities as a senior officer. Whereas von Richthofen had clearly earned his rank and command by virtue of his years on the general staff and recent experience as a combat commander in Spain, Loerzer owed his rapid promotion and high command to his close friendship with Hermann Goering. Loerzer had been a flier in 1914, and it was he who convinced Goering to transfer to the Luftstreitkräfte. From late 1914 to 1916 Loerzer flew as Goering's wingman, and the two became inseparable friends. After the war, Loerzer left the army and went into civil aviation, but when the Nazis came to power and Goering became Luftwaffe chief, Loerzer was brought back to active duty as Goering's personal adjutant with the rank of full colonel. Von Richthofen, and other officers who had stayed with the army and served on the elite general staff, were still majors when Loerzer was promoted straight to colonel, and the professional officers resented such favoritism. Von Richthofen cynically remarked to his closest officer friends that he was happy every time Loerzer was promoted because he knew that Goering would never advance him unless Loerzer was promoted first.

Taking command of the Special Purpose Division in August 1939, von Richthofen established his headquarters in a comfortable manor in Schönwald in Silesia. The main force of the Tenth Army would also advance from Silesia, and von Richthofen's headquarters lay near enough for rapid coordination. Next to his headquarters was a small landing field suitable for his personal aircraft, a Fiesler (Fi) 156 "Stork," as well as for Ju 52 transports. While organizing his units for the coming offensive von Richthofen carefully reviewed the plans and found a considerable number of faults. The most serious problem with the Luftwaffe and army plans was the thinness of the communications system; von Richthofen predicted that communications would be very difficult under the system that the air district headquarters had put in place for his command. As preparations for war with Poland were already far advanced, it was too late to start over, but von Richthofen assigned Major Siebert the task of adapting the communication nets in light of the Spanish experience. Von Richthofen was also concerned about the plan for the initial armored thrust into Poland during the first three or four days of the campaign. He felt it was vague in detailing the army's "Schwerpunkt," the main point of effort of the Tenth Army that the Special Purpose Division would be supporting.

Characteristically, during the week before the invasion of Poland, von Richthofen flew his Fiesler Stork around to his subordinate units and to the Tenth Army headquarters in order to personally confer with all the top commanders and ascertain their intents and requirements for the campaign. He met several times with General Reichenau, commander of the Tenth Army. Reichenau knew his business and seems to have gotten along well with von Richthofen. The army general was one of the German army's most knowledgeable and experienced armor commanders, and a major part of German panzer and motorized divisions were concentrated in his army. Along with von Richthofen, Reichenau hoped to demonstrate just what modern mechanized warfare was capable of. The Luftwaffe's full support of the Tenth Army was vital to the campaign as the Tenth Army was the main force expected to clear the path to Warsaw.[20] While meeting with General Reichenau, von Richthofen had the opportunity to visit with his brother-in-law Alfred Wietersheim, husband of von Richthofen's sister Sophie-Therese. Wietersheim was a reserve officer called to duty and then serving as the ordnance officer on Reichenau's Tenth Army staff. Characteristically, after a day of conferring with Reichenau and his staff, the three men went partridge shooting near the headquarters. After providing a few birds for the officers' mess, von Richthofen joined the staff for a game of bridge. In the week before the campaign began he also visited the Fourteenth Army headquarters, partly to discuss reconnaissance coordination with the army commander and partly to see his brother Manfred ("Pet"), who was serving with a reconnaissance unit of the Fourteenth Army on the Polish border. Manfred showed his brother one of the army's new Panzer IV medium tanks, which greatly interested von Richthofen.[21]

As was noted earlier, von Richthofen was an avid hunter, and even in the middle of a campaign he would look for good sites to hunt hare, partridge, pheasant, duck, deer, or wild boar. While making his unit visits and reconnaissance trips, he would note likely hunting spots on his personal map. After a long day of conferences and command responsibilities, he liked to spend an hour or two with his commanders, visiting officers, or personal staff, tramping the fields and bringing home some wild game to enliven the menu of the officers' mess. Von Richthofen's diaries repeatedly mention hunting and card games in the evening (he favored bridge and skat) with his staff and visiting officers. Throughout the war this was his means of getting away from the stress of command.

The success of the Special Purpose Division would depend on good communications and liaison between the army forces and the Luftwaffe. Much of the Luftwaffe's planning for the Polish campaign dealt with the details of establishing and maintaining good liaison so that the Stukas, medium bombers, and attack planes could be employed quickly and en masse to interdict and destroy major Polish troop concentrations and clear the way for the armored advance. In war games of late June the Luftwaffe staff worked on the details for establishing an effective liaison and command system for army support.[22] In planning for the Polish campaign the Luftwaffe was building on the army support system originally set up under General Wever's tenure as Luftwaffe chief of staff. Although Wever had made creation of a strategic bomber force the top priority of the Luftwaffe he did not ignore the importance of providing air support to the ground forces. In 1935 Wever placed a high priority in establishing and training a corps of air liaison officers who would be detailed to army headquarters with the mission of maintaining close coordination with the army commanders and the Luftwaffe air divisions and corps operating with them. In 1936, Wever directed that the air liaison officers be provided with communications teams to link army headquarters with supporting air units.[23] Luftwaffe officer training regulations also required that officers were to be "so familiar with the operations of the Army and Navy that they can effectively employ supporting air forces in cooperation with the other services."[24] This approach was in sharp contrast to the general lack of interest that the chiefs of the British and French air forces had on the subject of army/air cooperation. Those nations would pay a heavy price for this attitude in 1940.

By 1939 the Luftwaffe had developed two different and unconnected command organizations for supporting the army. The first was a Luftwaffe officer assigned to each army to command the short-range air reconnaissance units detailed to provide the army with tactical intelligence. The Koluft (Kommandeure der Luftwaffe—commander of the Luftwaffe) was directly under the command of the army. He could communicate with the major Luftwaffe field headquarters but had no authority to order attack missions in support of the army. His direct control was limited to the light reconnaissance units under his command, usually the light Henschel 126 open cockpit, two-seat airplane. The second means of army/Luftwaffe coordination were teams of air liaison officers (Flivos—Flieger Verbindingsoffiziere) that Wever had authorized. The Flivos were usually fairly junior officers with a communications team who were attached to army corps headquarters and at the divisional headquarters of the panzer and motorized divisions. The Flivos were tasked to keep the Luftwaffe air corps and air fleets informed of the situation on the ground. They remained under Luftwaffe command and could inform and advise but, like the Koluft, had no authority to call in strike missions or command aircraft. The authority to order strike missions rested with the Luftwaffe's air corps and air division commanders and their chiefs of staff. Ideally—and this would become the norm for the Luftwaffe in the 1940 campaign—the air corps and air divisions tasked with supporting the army would set up their headquarters next to, or as close as possible to, the army units they were supporting. As information flowed in, the senior commanders or their chiefs of staff would decide where and how the Luftwaffe forces could be best employed, and the air division or air corps headquarters would transmit mission orders to their subordinate groups. Later in the war the major combat formations, the air corps and some air divisions, established the position of "Close Battle Commander" (Nahkampfführer) responsible for tasking aircraft in close support of ground operations. However, the evolution of the German close support system had not progressed that far. Still, there was one doctrinal principle for support operations that was emphasized in the army and Luftwaffe plans. The Luftwaffe forces flying in support of the army would not be used in "penny packets" distributed throughout the army but would be prioritized with support concentrated and devoted to the army units at the Schwerpunkt of the campaign. The Luftwaffe and air fleet daily orders designated the Schwerpunkt for each day's operations.[25] In his guidance to his commanders, and in his meetings with superiors and army commanders, von Richthofen was adamant that his strike forces should only be used en masse, with at least an entire Stuka or attack group (thirty to forty airplanes) employed on a mission. Richthofen had learned in Spain that major operational effects could only be achieved by delivering major blows with many airplanes.

Luftwaffe Logistics in Blitzkrieg

When the war began, the Luftwaffe had a highly developed mobile logistics system geared to supporting short blitzkrieg campaigns. Whereas German bombers had the range to strike targets in Poland or France while flying from German bases, most of the Luftwaffe's fighters, Stukas, and reconnaissance planes had an effective range of only 100–200 miles. If the Luftwaffe was to support mobile army operations, it needed the capability to jump forward quickly, put captured airfields into operation, and keep its planes supplied with bombs and fuel. As armies advanced, short-ranged Luftwaffe aircraft could cover the front units, assure air superiority, and provide effective close air support. Moreover, operating from airfields near the front lines maximized sortie rates. During the Polish campaign von Richthofen's Stukas, Henschels, and Me 109 fighters were able to regularly fly four or more attack sorties per day.

In September 1939 the Luftwaffe possessed 117 airfield and engineering companies and motorized supply columns to support the air fleets and corps. As the army advanced, the airfield companies could move into a captured airfield, effect repairs, and open the field for operations within twenty-four hours. Motorized supply units advanced behind the armored spearheads, bringing fuel and munitions to the forward airfields.[26] In 1939 the Luftwaffe possessed the most effective forward logistics system of any air force in the world. Still, before the campaign began von Richthofen knew that his ability to provide effective air support after the opening days of the campaign would be completely dependent upon the Luftwaffe's supply units to quickly deploy forward. He worried that the mobile columns supporting his forces would not be enough to keep his attack units supplied with enough fuel, munitions, and spare parts to keep them combat effective. He assumed that he would need considerable support from the Ju 52 transport units that were allocated to air fleets for the operation. As the army's panzer divisions would also rely heavily upon air transport to move fuel forward, von Richthofen assumed that the logistics system would be strained to the fullest. Indeed, his predictions would prove correct.

The Polish Air Force

Nestled between Germany on one side and the Soviet Union on the other and lacking any natural defenses on its borders, Poland was in a poor strategic position, to say the least. Since 1919 the Poles had worked hard to create modern armed forces, but their primary obstacle was Poland's economic weakness. Poland had good soldiers and a highly competent officer corps but was also a relatively poor country and lagged far behind Western Europe in industrial development. As a mostly agricultural nation, Poland had difficulty earning enough foreign exchange to buy the modern weapons it needed to fight Germany or the Soviet Union. The Polish army consisted of a large force of infantry and cavalry divisions that were well-trained and well-led but lacked support arms, heavy artillery, communications equipment, and motor vehicles. The Polish military understood its weaknesses and desperately worked to modernize and mechanize its army in the 1930s. However, tanks and motor vehicles were expensive and had to be imported, and Polish funds were very limited. Still, on the eve of the war in 1939 the Polish army had managed to establish one tank brigade and was in the process of equipping and training another with tanks imported from France.

In terms of building a modern military the Poles were somewhat better off with their air force. In 1932 they established a national aircraft industry, and during the course of the decade they managed to produce several good aircraft designs. Poland's aircraft industry was small, but it was able to maintain itself by exporting military aircraft to several nations. Its greatest limitation was the lack of an aircraft engine industry. Engines had to be imported or licensed to be built from French designs. In the early part of the 1930s, when typical fighters were relatively light with small engines, the Polish PLZ

P 7 fighter, which began production in 1932, could be hailed as one of the best fighter planes of the era. But as the decade progressed, fighter planes got larger, heavier, and required much larger engines. The major powers began production of large in-line or air-cooled aircraft engines with more than 1,000 horsepower and with the potential to be developed into much more powerful engines. Poland, however, did not have access to the latest aircraft engines, so development of improved fighter planes lagged. By 1939 the Poles fielded a new fighter, the P 11, which was an improvement upon the successful P 7 design but enormously outclassed by the latest German fighters. The German Me 109s that the Polish P 7s and P 11s had to face were 100 mph faster and more heavily armed. Moreover, all the German aircraft had radios whereas in the Polish air force only squadron commanders had radios in the aircraft, and they had to pass instructions to the other pilots by hand signals—just as in 1918.[27]

In August 1939 on the eve of war the Polish air force had a frontline combat strength of 36 twin-engine Los medium bombers (an excellent bomber design), 118 P 23 Kara ground attack airplanes (a slow, underpowered, and clumsy design dating from the mid-1930s), and 159 P 7 and P 11 fighters.[28] The Poles fully understood their position and had ordered a host of modern fighters from Britain, France, and the United States. British Hurricanes and American Curtis Hawk fighters would have made the Polish campaign a much tougher one for the Luftwaffe, but none of these aircraft arrived before the outbreak of war. Without modern fighters the only real chance the Polish air force had of inflicting damage upon the Germans was for the obsolete Polish fighters to catch the Luftwaffe's lightly armed bombers or reconnaissance planes without their fighter escorts.

During August 1939 it was clear to the Poles that war was imminent; the Hitler-Stalin pact announced that month also made the war inevitable by assuring Germany of Soviet oil and raw materials in case the western Allies came to the aid of Poland and blockaded German ports. What the Poles and the world did not know were the secret provisions of the pact that divided Poland between the two great dictatorships and carved out all of Eastern Europe into German and Soviet zones of influence. Yet even if the Poles did not know the details of the treaty they guessed correctly that Poland was to be the next target of German aggression. As the diplomatic language heated up, the Poles quietly moved their combat air units to small auxiliary airfields in anticipation that their major air bases would be subject to immediate attack by the Germans upon the outbreak of the war. Thus, in the first days of the war when the Germans attacked the Polish airfields, the Luftwaffe failed to destroy the main strength of the Polish air force. Those attacks, however, still served to cripple the Polish air force. As a result of Poland's poverty its air force had a very limited infrastructure, and the aircraft workshops, fuel, parts, and reserve aircraft were concentrated at just a few major air bases. Although they had moved the airplanes out of immediate danger, the Poles had made little provision to store parts, munitions, and fuel at their temporary fields. When combat operations began and the Poles' supply and repair depots at Warsaw, Radom, and Cracow were destroyed by the Germans, the Polish combat units were left without the means to repair or maintain their aircraft. A Polish aircraft might survive a combat sortie with light damage, but the inability to make repairs put even lightly damaged planes out of action. The lack of fuel and munitions was also crippling. Within a few days of the start of the war the Polish air force was basically out of action.

Another serious deficiency of Poland's air force was the lack of a modern communications system. On several occasions the air force had planes available and could have intervened and done serious damage to German ground forces, but the weak Polish communications system had collapsed, and ground forces were rarely able to get requests to the air units in time for them to exploit their fleeting opportunities to attack the Germans. Within three days of the start of the German offensive, the Polish air force units were reduced to flying their own reconnaissance sorties and fighter sweeps to locate German targets. The Poles had no lack of courage and skill, and on several occasions Polish airmen were able to jump German bombers and even fighters and shoot down their adversaries. But such scattered attacks could not do much, and the lack of fuel and parts soon grounded those aircraft that had survived the extensive German flak defenses and combat with the superior German fighters. In all, the Polish air force lasted only two and one-half weeks in combat, flying its last combat mission on 17 September.[29]

The Campaign Begins—Supporting the Tenth Army

In most respects, the German air campaign against Poland went according to plan. The war began on 1 September with German ground forces advancing all along the frontier. The strikes against the Polish airfields were delayed for several hours by fog, but by the end of the first day of the campaign all the major Polish airfields had been heavily bombed. The next priority target was the Polish transportation system, and the two air fleets struck numerous major rail junctions and rail bridges throughout Poland to cripple the mobilization of Polish reserves and to limit the movement of the Polish ground forces. For the first three days of the campaign von Richthofen's division concentrated on the interdiction campaign, and it was particularly successful in attacking Polish columns on the main roads, allowing for the Tenth Army's rapid advancement. Von Richthofen's Stukas, fighters, and attack planes flew three or four sorties per day and, if necessary, as many as six sorties. The highly developed Luftwaffe ground and logistics infrastructure ensured that aircraft could be quickly fueled, loaded with munitions, and ready for the next mission in a matter of minutes.

Much to von Richthofen's relief, four days into the battle the Special Purpose Division was removed from General Loerzer's supervision and placed under the direct command of the 4th Air Fleet. Although Loerzer had not interfered with von Richthofen's operations, von Richthofen doubted Loerzer's competence and feared that Goering's old wingman might misuse his forces. In contrast, he believed that the 4th Air Fleet's General Löhr could be trusted to employ his air units competently.[30] Löhr had been a decorated pilot in World War I and had gone to the staff college and risen to command the Austrian air force before the Austrian armed forces were absorbed by the Wehrmacht in 1938. General Löhr had a reputation for solid competence among the Luftwaffe commanders. Throughout the campaign von Richthofen or his chief of staff coordinated daily operations with the Tenth Army, and most Stuka and Henschel strikes on any day were upon targets chosen by the Special Purpose Division after consultation with the army headquarters. Generally at least one Stuka or attack group with a squadron or two of Me 109s for escort would be kept fueled, armed, and ready to take off immediately to strike any target identified by the army or by the Special Purpose Division's own reconnaissance planes. Within minutes of receiving an attack order the Stuka or Henschel group would be on its way and protected by its escorts. This was a highly advanced system for its time. However, as the Tenth Army's tanks advanced rapidly through the Polish Cracow army, the main problem for both the army and the Luftwaffe was maintaining a "bomb line," a clear demarcation between German and Polish units in order to prevent the Luftwaffe from bombing German troops. The advance of the German armor forces was so rapid that neither the Tenth Army nor its corps or division headquarters were clear as to the location of the most advanced German forces. By the third day of the campaign von Richthofen's most common complaint was a lack of clear information as to the location of the Tenth Army's units. The Luftwaffe officers attached to the army with their own reconnaissance aircraft were no more helpful than the army in providing clear information on German or Polish troop dispositions. Von Richthofen deployed his own reconnaissance aircraft and his Flivos assigned to the Tenth Army and the corps headquarters to obtain information. He eventually took to flying around the battlefield himself in his Stork and personally coordinating almost daily with Reichenau and the Tenth Army headquarters.

In the first week of the campaign the Special Purpose Division interdiction operations focused on the Polish Lodz army group. The Polish transport system had been paralyzed by air strikes; bridges were destroyed, and several trains, including one of the Polish army's armored trains, were smashed by Stukas. On 3 September von Richthofen's airmen shattered an entire Polish cavalry brigade with repeated attacks.[31] Whenever a good target was identified, von Richthofen would order an attack—usually in group strength (thirty to forty Stukas or Henschel 123s). Facing little opposition in the air and only moderate antiaircraft fire from Polish forces, von Richthofen nonetheless continued to be troubled by the Luftwaffe's flawed communications and logistic support.[32] The lack of common radio frequencies between the army and the Luftwaffe posed a serious barrier to quickly passing vital information between the Luftwaffe and army and resulted in von Richthofen's headquarters often being in the dark as to the location of German army units and the conditions at the front.[33]

As the Tenth Army drove rapidly forward, the short-range Stuka and fighter units of the Special Purpose Division needed to deploy forward in order to provide timely support to the army and to maintain a high sortie rate. However, as the panzers and motorized combat units advanced, the supply columns were slow to catch up. A panzer unit could carry several days of food and enough ammunition for a couple of days of combat on its own vehicles, but it needed a great deal of fuel to keep moving—and fuel supplies became the factor that limited German operations. The 4th Air Fleet had allocated one Ju 52 transport group to support both General Reichenau and von Richthofen, and by 3 September the transports were already being used to fly fuel forward to keep up the momentum of the advance. The farther the panzers advanced into Poland, the more urgent became the need for air transport of fuel. On 3 September the Luftwaffe transports brought thirty tons of fuel forward for the Tenth Army's 1st Panzer Division, and on 5 September this requirement jumped to seventy-four tons. At the same time, von Richthofen began to move his Stuka and fighter units forward to former Polish airfields, and he needed all the air transport he could get to keep his planes supplied with fuel and bombs.

The jump forward initially went well, and the Luftwaffe airfield companies and engineers quickly repaired the formerly Polish airfields for occupation by von Richthofen's units. But the high sortie rate that the forward basing allowed also meant an exceptionally high level of supply, and by 8 September von Richthofen was complaining to his chief, General Löhr, that his supplies

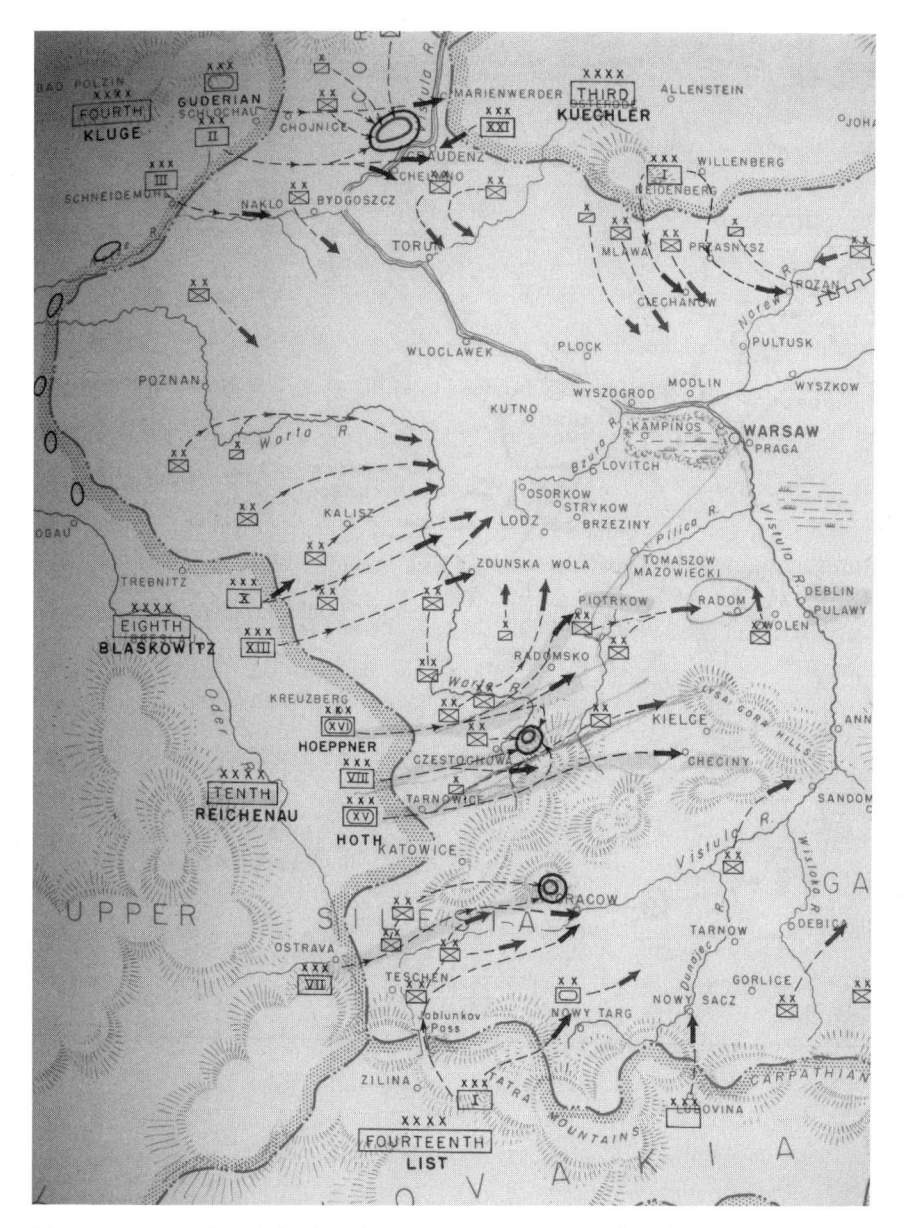

The German attack on Poland, 1–5 September 1939. Von Richthofen's Special Purpose Division served primarily in support of Reichenau's Tenth Army advance from the southwest. (*A Military History of World War II Atlas* [West Point: Department of Military History, 1953])

of fuel and munitions were so low that he would have to reduce his sorties. In fact, the shortages became so acute that on 11 September von Richthofen reduced the sortie rate for some of his Stuka and fighter groups to one sortie per day. The problem was eased on 13 September when the Luftwaffe allocated two additional Ju 52 squadrons to support the 4th Air Fleet. Von Richthofen's forward groups were immediately given transport priority, and the Stukas returned to their usual high tempo of four or more sorties per day.[34]

Proving Airpowers' Flexibility

The Germans were successful all across the front in the first days of the campaign. In the south, Rundstedt's army group took Cracow on 6 September. As the Tenth Army drove east toward Warsaw it literally overran the Polish Prusy army, which was still in the process of assembling. Polish troop units were torn apart by air attack while disembarking from their trains, and the units that had formed for battle were quickly overrun by German tanks. By 8 September the armored spearheads of the Tenth Army reached the outskirts of Warsaw; at this point came one of the crises in the campaign. The rapid drive to Warsaw had left the Polish Poznan army isolated in the west and threatened with encirclement. On 8 September the Poznan army pushed east to break out and reinforce the Warsaw defenders. Two German infantry divisions on the left flank of Rundstedt's advance were badly mauled by the Polish counteroffensive, and in response the Tenth Army halted its advance on Warsaw and turned ninety degrees to the west to block the Poznan army. The Poles were soon trapped on the Bzura River, where the Special Purpose Division Stukas, fighters, and Henschels kept the Polish forces under continuous attack. Blocked by panzers and under merciless air bombardment, the Poznan army surrendered with more than 100,000 men on 10 September.[35] After this brief but hectic interlude, the Tenth Army reversed course and continued its drive to Warsaw.

Warsaw had been targeted several times in the first week of the campaign with specific military targets, such as the airfields and rail yards, struck by medium bombers. With the Luftwaffe's short-range Stukas and attack aircraft stationed close enough, the Luftwaffe high command on 12 September ordered both air fleets to make large-scale attacks upon the capital. General Ulrich Grauert's 1st Air Division of the 1st Air Fleet struck the city from the north. Von Richthofen's Special Purpose Division, still heavily engaged in the ground battle, could muster only 183 sorties for the raid. When they arrived over the city von Richthofen's pilots found that many of the targets were obscured by smoke from Grauert's attack, so they could not bomb accurately.

Neither von Richthofen's nor Grauert's attack was coordinated, and none of the bomber units had attacked on schedule; thus, the attack had little effect on Warsaw's defenders.[36] Von Richthofen was furious that the attack had miscarried, and when he met with Goering at Radom the next day while Goering was making a tour of the front, von Richthofen insisted that a single air commander be appointed for the air assault upon Warsaw so that further attacks could be properly planned and coordinated. Von Richthofen made it clear that he would be the best choice to command the operation.[37]

Leadership under Fire

At the start of the campaign von Richthofen had stuck close to his headquarters, reading reports as they came in and issuing attack orders. However, by 4 September he was complaining of the inadequate information he was getting from the front. Although the army was supposed to provide him with constant updates, he noted in his diary that "army communications are worse than ours."[38] As in Spain, von Richthofen found it necessary to personally visit the front lines to find out what was really going on. Leaving his chief of staff, Lt. Colonel Seidemann, to manage ongoing battle operations, von Richthofen flew to General Reichenau's army headquarters to personally coordinate operations and flew over the front to conduct his own reconnaissance. On 6 September he flew over and then landed near the headquarters of the 1st Panzer Division, Reichenau's lead division on the drive toward Warsaw, in order to get a true frontline view of the situation. Von Richthofen landed at a small airstrip under Polish artillery fire in order to talk to the divisional commander. He learned that the lead units of the 1st Panzer Division had run into heavy Polish resistance and that the division's own artillery was stuck in a column to the rear and would take three to four hours to move up to provide effective fire support. Von Richthofen immediately proceeded to the army's communications net, which for once seemed to work, and contacted Seidemann, ordering his He 123 group to immediately fly up to attack the Polish units in front of the 1st Panzer Division. The Henschels soon arrived. They broke up the Polish counterattack and destroyed Polish strong points, thereby allowing the 1st Panzer Division to continue its advance.[39]

Von Richthofen personally did not favor using his Stukas as a substitute for the army's artillery as a normal practice, but in this case the 1st Panzer Division had the priority for support and needed air support to keep up the momentum of the advance. Such interventions by von Richthofen, coupled with his willingness to land a small plane under artillery fire, earned him and the

Luftwaffe a large amount of admiration among the army ranks. Throughout the battle von Richthofen thought in terms of organizing and reorganizing his forces as the situation changed and the army drove deeper into Poland. In the first week of the battle von Richthofen talked to the chief of staff of the 4th Air Fleet, General Günther Korten (later Luftwaffe chief of staff), and arranged to give up his Me 110 group to Loerzer's 2nd Air Division while getting all of KG 77, a medium bomber wing, to support his operations deeper into Poland.[40]

The Campaign Closes: The Bombing of Warsaw

Three weeks into the campaign, the Polish field armies had been mostly shattered. The last major concentration of Polish army forces was 150,000 soldiers now surrounded in Warsaw. As far as the Germans were concerned, capturing Warsaw would basically end the campaign. Von Richthofen sent a message to the Luftwaffe staff on 22 September to allow his units to strike a decisive blow. "Urgently request exploitation of last opportunity for large-scale experiment as devastation and terror raid . . . every effort will be made to eradicate Warsaw."[41] German forces from the north and south had surrounded Warsaw, and the suburbs of the city were already under German artillery fire. At this point, the situation for the Poles could only be described as hopeless. Britain and France had declined to attack Germany in the West, and there was no likelihood that any outside aid or Polish forces could break the German cordon. The Polish formations that had escaped German encirclement were flooding south to the Romanian border, where hundreds of thousands of Polish soldiers would cross the border to be interned. From there, most of the surviving Polish soldiers and airmen managed to travel to France and Britain, where they were reorganized and reequipped to fight the Germans again on other fronts.

If the Poles had wanted to, they could have forced the Germans to take Warsaw by storm and endure massive losses in a street-by-street battle. Germany's greatest fear was a protracted battle for Warsaw that would delay the end of the campaign and also delay the redeployment of German air and ground forces to the poorly defended western front. Therefore, forcing a quick surrender of Warsaw was viewed by the German high command as a strategic necessity. Von Richthofen firmly believed that massive air attacks upon the city would break Polish morale and force a quick surrender—so he planned for a massive aerial attack with all available forces for 25 September.

Von Richthofen's attack on Warsaw had many characteristics of an indiscriminate terror raid. Hundreds of sorties were flown, and by the end of the day his air units had dropped 632 tons of high-explosive and incendiary bombs on Warsaw, killing perhaps 7,000 Poles and wounding thousands more.[42] Since the Luftwaffe had already begun deploying some of its bomber formations to the western front, von Richthofen could only conduct a large attack by using his Ju 52 transports as bombers. The Ju 52s lumbered over the city as airmen literally shoveled thousands of small incendiary bombs out the cargo doors—not an act that one could describe as attacking only military targets or "avoiding unnecessary civilian casualties." However, the French air attaché in Warsaw also stated that the German attack had been in accordance with the laws of war and that civilian casualties had been located close to legitimate targets.[43]

In short order, huge clouds of smoke rose over Warsaw, and thousands of Poles died under the rain of fire and explosives. By all accounts, von Richthofen's terror attack was quite effective in lowering what little morale the Poles still possessed. However, it is doubtful that the massive air raid, the largest that had been seen to that time, was the actual cause of Warsaw's surrender. The Polish commander in chief, then interned in Romania, was already fully aware that the situation in Warsaw was hopeless and issued the order for Warsaw to capitulate on 26 September while also initiating negotiations to surrender the last major pockets of Polish forces. Essentially, the Polish government, already in exile, had not been terrorized into submission but simply saw that nothing could be gained by further resistance. By 29 September, the city of Warsaw and all the remaining organized Polish military forces had surrendered to the Germans.

Although von Richthofen's bombing of Warsaw had a small effect on the outcome of the Polish campaign and, at best, might have moved the Polish decision to capitulate forward by a day or so, it gave rise to part of the mythology of the blitzkrieg. The international press reported the numbers of casualties from the aerial attack on Warsaw as between 20,000 and 40,000 dead and that the one attack had destroyed more than 10 percent of the buildings in the city. Such figures remain in the history books over sixty years later.[44] In fact, sober analysis has to place the casualties and damage at a far lower level. Throughout World War II, Allied bombing raids on Germany and German bombing raids on Britain yielded an average of one fatality per ton of bombs dropped. The most lethal bombing raids in Europe for the entire war were the raids on Hamburg, Germany, in August 1943 and on Dresden, Germany, in February 1945. In those two raids the fatality level was 7.2–10.2 fatalities for each ton of bombs dropped—and both of these cities experienced huge fire storms caused by the incendiaries.[45] If the attack on Warsaw had matched the fatality rates of Dresden and Hamburg, between 6,000 and 7,000 casualties would have occurred. The 25 September attack inflicted considerable pain and damage, but to assess the Warsaw raid as three to six times more lethal than the Dresden or Hamburg raids is utterly improbable.

The sensational tone of the press coverage in the western nations served the German cause well. The international press presented the basically false image of the Luftwaffe as a force that could level whole cities and kill tens of thousands instantaneously—something beyond the Luftwaffe's powers at the height of its effectiveness. Press coverage made much of the ruthless German approach toward any people who might resist Germany. Ironically, this supported the message that the Nazi leaders wanted to send to the western allies. Shortly after the end of the campaign, Josef Goebbel's Propaganda Ministry produced a film titled *Feuerteufe (Baptism of Fire)* that was shown throughout Germany and abroad. This dramatic and highly effective film portrayed the German army in Poland as a mechanized force consisting of thousands of the most modern tanks and motor vehicles and gave a large role to the Stuka attacks. The reality was that only a small portion of the whole German army, less than a quarter in 1939, consisted of modern motorized and mechanized divisions and that the slow Stukas were highly vulnerable to antiaircraft fire. Most of the German army of 1939—and through 1945—consisted of infantry divisions that still relied upon huge numbers of horses to pull their wagons and artillery pieces. For most German soldiers Poland was a war of marching and infantry battles not too dissimilar from 1918, but the German Propaganda Ministry very cleverly put forward the largely false vision of ultramodern and, hence, unstoppable German forces. The images of the bombing of Warsaw and the dramatic films of German tanks rolling through Poland that were repeated by both the Western and German media had much to do with the rapid collapse of Holland and Belgium in May 1940 and the collapse of French morale the next month. Thus, the German cause had been wonderfully served by the magnification of the Luftwaffe's effectiveness by the international press and Germany's own propaganda chiefs.

As for complaints that bombing civilians was a crime under international law, the Luftwaffe could rightly maintain that Warsaw was a defended city under siege and that artillery and aerial bombardment were fully in accordance with the traditional rules of war. In this the Luftwaffe would be correct. The bombing of Warsaw was cruel and probably unnecessary, but under the laws of war in 1939 it was a perfectly legitimate act. From 1943 to 1945 the Americans and British would also target civilians and conduct a ruthless aerial bombing campaign against Germany's cities that would be equally cruel. And, as in Warsaw, the Allies could legitimately claim that Germany's cities contained military industries and military targets and could thus be targeted—despite the civilian losses that would occur.

Lessons from the Polish Campaign

The ashes of Warsaw were still cooling when the Luftwaffe and German army began a thorough process of analyzing their operational performance with the intent of learning lessons as quickly as possible and adapting their doctrine, force structure, equipment, and tactics in order to correct the deficiencies exposed by the actual fighting. For the Luftwaffe, it had not been an especially hard campaign. During the one month of heavy fighting the Luftwaffe had lost 285 planes from all causes (67 fighters, 78 bombers, and 31 Stukas) while a further 279 planes suffered more than 10 percent damage. This amounted to a loss rate of under 10 percent of the aircraft employed during the course of the campaign, with a total of 734 Luftwaffe personnel casualties.[46] These losses were quickly made good as new aircraft flowed from the factories and replacement personnel were sent from the training schools. The continued expansion of the Luftwaffe continued without a hitch.

The Polish army had been largely disabled in the first days of the campaign. Mainly because of the Luftwaffe's effective interdiction campaign, the Polish units were unable to maneuver or retreat without facing heavy air attacks. Polish units found that well-prepared defensive positions could be reduced by the Luftwaffe's heavy bombs. During a campaign that was over in one month's time, the Polish army recorded 65,000 killed, 144,000 wounded, and 587,000 taken prisoner. In contrast, the Germans recorded 11,000 dead and 30,000 wounded. For the German veterans of World War I, for whom their own losses represented the typical losses for a *single day* in a major battle of that war, the results of the panzer/Luftwaffe blitzkrieg tactics were impressive.[47]

But the army and Luftwaffe did not sit back on their laurels. The Luftwaffe headquarters knew that the campaign in Poland had exposed numerous flaws in doctrine, organization, and equipment. In early 1939 the Luftwaffe had established a special staff section dedicated to critically evaluating current operations and developing new tactics and equipment on the basis of lessons learned in operations. The Luftwaffe's operational research section quickly recommended numerous changes, and in October 1939 the Luftwaffe began publishing a series of tactical bulletins that were distributed to all major Luftwaffe commands and that provided updates of tactical and operational doctrine.[48] The army established a similar office and also moved to correct its deficiencies in equipment, organization, and tactics.

The first, and probably greatest, lesson learned in the Polish campaign by the Wehrmacht's senior leadership was the importance of full cooperation of army and Luftwaffe units. The willing desire for Luftwaffe and army commanders to plan and work together had produced decisive results. In the first assessment of the lessons learned from Poland made in October 1939 the Luftwaffe general staff argued for improved army/Luftwaffe communications links in order to further enhance the cooperation of both services.[49] This lesson very likely came directly from von Richthofen. Even though the Luftwaffe had set up an extensive communications system prior to the campaign, it had not proved sufficient under the rigors of active campaigning.[50] Von Richthofen had been vociferously critical about his communications problems both with higher and lower Luftwaffe headquarters and with the army units throughout the campaign. The communications sufficed if the Luftwaffe had a day to plan the operations, and in such cases the pre-planned attacks went very well. But under the pressure of highly mobile operations the liaison system had often broken down.

Von Richthofen and the Luftwaffe staff were not happy with the Koluft system. The Koluft officers and reconnaissance units that served the army could have been very useful to von Richthofen in identifying targets, but the Koluft was not in the same communications loop as the Luftwaffe air divisions and corps and consequently played a minor role in von Richthofen's operations. Under combat conditions the Luftwaffe found that it often took hours for the Koluft's reports, working their way through the army communications system, to reach the air fleet headquarters. The Flivos only operated at the higher army headquarters and, during the rapid ground advances of the Wehrmacht, were often unable to provide a current and accurate depiction of the ground situation. As a result, the Luftwaffe was often unsure of the location of the army's units, and there were several notorious cases of Luftwaffe bombers and Stukas attacking German columns.[51] In order to overcome some of the confusion, senior Luftwaffe commanders started imitating von Richthofen and flying around the battlefield and personally conducting reconnaissance and liaison with the senior army commands.

At the end of the campaign neither the army nor the Luftwaffe was happy with the liaison system. The army wanted better communications and more authority to the Koluft to direct operations. The Luftwaffe did not care much for the Koluft system, which divided liaison, information exchange, and coordination into two channels. The Luftwaffe's experience in Poland had rated the Flivos' performance as fairly effective and responded to the situation by creating more Flivo teams and giving the Flivos better communications and more mobility.[52] A top priority for von Richthofen and the Luftwaffe after the

Polish campaign was to improve the communications and reporting nets.[53] Eventually, in 1942, the Luftwaffe would dispense with the Koluft system and place all of the short-range reconnaissance aircraft directly under Luftwaffe operational command. In the short term, however, some improvements were made to Luftwaffe communications. During the Polish campaign the He 126 light reconnaissance planes could only transmit information to the artillery in Morse code. In the spring 1940 campaign they had voice radios installed for more effective artillery spotting.

The other major problem noted by von Richthofen was the difficulty of maintaining logistics in the middle of the campaign. This was the greatest limiting factor for an organization such as the Special Purpose Division, which employed mostly short-range aircraft and needed forward airfields to carry out its mission effectively. Despite the Luftwaffe's many motorized supply columns and airfield companies deployed for the campaign, the Special Purpose Division had still run desperately short of fuel and munitions in the middle of the campaign. The air transport assets allocated to support von Richthofen's logistics efforts had been grossly insufficient, and the supply situation was not sorted out until more transport aircraft were allocated to the 4th Air Fleet. For future operations the Luftwaffe would need more transport units to support a blitzkrieg-type campaign.

One lesson that the Luftwaffe failed to learn was the limitations of a logistics system designed only for short campaigns. While the Luftwaffe's airfield units could keep forward units supplied with fuel and bombs, the Luftwaffe groups and wings had only a minimal capability to repair and rebuild aircraft. If an aircraft needed major repairs, it had to be loaded onto a truck or rail car and shipped back to the factory in Germany. This lean repair and maintenance infrastructure saved the Luftwaffe money but also meant that damaged aircraft were out of action for a long time. The system worked in the short campaigns of 1939 and 1940, when the Luftwaffe could throw every available aircraft into the battle, win quickly, and rebuild the force after the battle. However, if the air war became an attrition war, the lack of forward maintenance and repair units guaranteed that the unit aircraft serviceability rates would drop precipitously. Starting with the Soviet campaign in 1941, this is precisely what happened.

Despite communications problems and numerous instances of "friendly fire" incidents, von Richthofen's operations in Poland greatly impressed the senior army commanders, and the army was quite willing to credit much of the success of the campaign to the tremendous effect of Luftwaffe interdiction attacks and attacks on Polish forces. Most of von Richthofen's and the Luftwaffe's efforts in support of the army had been interdiction attacks and not what one would describe today as close support operations, in which Stukas bombed targets close to friendly ground units. The interdiction attacks had worked well to cripple the Polish army's mobility, and in some cases large Polish units on the road were discovered by the Luftwaffe's tactical reconnaissance forces and cut to pieces by the Luftwaffe—features of the destruction of Polish forces in the Radom-Deblin area and on the Bzura River.[54]

Many of the German army after-action reports from the Polish campaign fail to mention support operations by the Luftwaffe due to the simple fact that most of the German army units in Poland got no close support from the Luftwaffe and had to rely on their own artillery for fire support. Von Richthofen and the army commanders followed a very traditional German approach to fighting in which the major combat power, in the army's case the panzer and motorized divisions, were concentrated at the decisive point; this is also where the Luftwaffe concentrated its efforts. There was little support for infantry divisions in the campaign, or for any divisions that were not considered to be part of the main effort for that day. One of the myths of the Polish campaign is the image of German troops advancing under the cover of the Stukas that would bring a rain of fire and steel on any forces blocking their way. In fact, German air assets were limited by numbers, range, weather, and logistics, and the only units that could call for help from the Stukas and expect to get support might be the panzer divisions at the tip of the effort. However, when the army got to see the Stukas and attack planes in action, it was suitably impressed.

The Stukas performed best in close air support operations when they could carry out carefully planned attacks. What was especially impressive is that even good troops in well-fortified positions, such as the Polish forces holding the fortress at Modlin, were unable to stand up to a systematic bombardment by the Stukas. In this case, von Richthofen's Stuka attacks caused the morale of a large defending force to collapse and surrender after a one-day bombardment.[55] The army was grateful for close actions such as these because they not only pushed the campaign to a speedy conclusion but also spared the lives of many thousands of German soldiers who would have died if defense lines had had to be taken by ground assault. Even the Luftwaffe leadership was surprised at the effectiveness of Stuka attacks on enemy ground forces. After the campaign the army generously gave full credit to the Luftwaffe: Reichenau declared that the attacks of the Luftwaffe's Special Purpose Division had "led to the decision of the battlefield."[56] By the end of the campaign, none of the Luftwaffe or army leaders could doubt that the Luftwaffe's role in the campaign had been decisive and that the Luftwaffe would be an equal partner in the campaign to follow in the West.

At the end of the Polish campaign, von Richthofen greets Hitler. General Walter von Reichenau is in the center, with monocle. Hitler took a great liking to von Richthofen, whom he considered one of his best generals. (U.S. Air Force)

The Luftwaffe began to modify its munitions and equipment in light of the Polish campaign. The Luftwaffe staff carefully studied the results of its air attacks against Polish targets and set to work to adapt its munitions to reflect the experience of the campaign. The Luftwaffe's standard 250 kg and 500 kg bombs had been quite effective against interdiction targets such as the Polish rail system, but against strong fortifications heavier bombs with delayed fuses and deep penetration capability were needed. Against ground troops in the open, the Luftwaffe learned that many small bombs were far more lethal than a few of the 50 and 100 kg bombs that were in the standard Luftwaffe inventory. Within a few months the first problem was solved, and when the Germans attacked France the Luftwaffe had available a 1,000 kg bomb with a delayed fuse and rocket assist for use against French fortifications.[57] The Polish campaign also highlighted the need for a more effective antipersonnel bomb, and Luftwaffe munitions experts went to work on the project. In early 1941 the Luftwaffe made a major advance in the development of effective munitions with the creation of the first modern cluster bomb—the SD-2. The SD-2 was a three-pound "bomblet" with an instantaneous contact fuse. Attached to the bomb was a small metal rod with two retractable metal "wings."

When the bomb was released the wings popped open and spun the bomb, thus arming it. A canister containing ninety-six of the small bomblets was developed so that when it was dropped from an airplane the canister would break open and scatter the SD-2s over a broad area. The bomblets had a devastating effect upon ground troops and unarmored vehicles. This weapon was ready by the Balkan and Soviet campaigns, where it would prove to be one of the most effective weapons in the Luftwaffe arsenal.[58] The SD-2 was such an effective design that the U.S. Air Force copied it after the war and used it as a U.S. munition throughout the 1960s.

Another important lesson of the Polish campaign had been the effectiveness of the flak units of the Luftwaffe. In contrast to the British and French doctrine, Luftwaffe and German army doctrine had long stressed the usefulness of flak on the battlefield. Flak had shot down large numbers of Allied aircraft in 1918, and the Condor Legion's flak units had been very successful in Spain in a variety of missions, to include the direct fire role against ground targets. By 1939 the flak corps was a large and valued part of the Luftwaffe, and Germany fielded a flak force of over 10,000 light and heavy guns—several times the flak arm of any Allied power. Luftwaffe airfields, even the forward temporary airfields, were well protected by flak guns, which freed up the Luftwaffe's fighter force from the mission of flying constant defensive patrols and allowed the fighters to fly offensive sweeps and effectively support the bombers and Stukas. During the Polish campaign a large part of the flak force was attached to the army for forward air defense. Such flak units belonged to the Luftwaffe but were under the army's operational control and were distributed throughout the army in battalions and regiments. In Poland the flak units served effectively in their primary mission of air defense and usually shot down or drove off the few attacks made by the Polish air force.[59] Another lesson from Spain that was reinforced by the Polish experience was the effectiveness of the flak units, especially the heavy 88 mm flak guns, in the ground battle. Thanks to the Spanish Civil War, the German flak force was trained and prepared for the ground support mission, and in Poland the highly accurate 88 mm guns proved ideal to take out Polish bunkers and fortifications.[60]

For the campaign in the West the Luftwaffe would increase the flak forces assigned to support the army. Two flak corps, each composed of three or four regiments and supporting troops, were created as permanent organizations for support of the army in the field. In light of the Polish experience flak doctrine was modified to ensure that flak units were not broadly dispersed but kept in concentrated formations to cover the primary troop movements at the points of decision and were also to serve as an operational reserve for the army.[61] In May 1940 flak would play a key role in the battle for air superiority, and the large German flak force would decimate attacking Allied aircraft at decisive points in both Belgium and France.

Immediately after the Polish campaign the Luftwaffe moved to reinforce the most successful aspects of its combat doctrine and organization in preparation for the campaign against France. On 3 October von Richthofen's Special Purpose Division, which had been a provisional organization, was renamed VIIIth Fliegerkorps and given a permanent status. The VIIIth Fliegerkorps would continue to specialize in close support operations in support of the army, as it had in Poland. The Stuka force, as with other branches of the Luftwaffe, was expanded as the Luftwaffe reorganized itself and began a phase of intensive preparations for the campaign in the West. As soon as Warsaw surrendered, the units of the VIIIth Fliegerkorps began deploying hundreds of miles west to bases in northwestern Germany. Von Richthofen instituted a program of intensive training to ready the units for the coming campaign. All of the aircraft and equipment of the VIIIth Air Corps were thoroughly overhauled. There were many lessons from the Polish campaign to absorb, and the VIIIth Fliegerkorps, as well as the Luftwaffe's other air corps and divisions, embarked on a series of war games, staff exercises, and air/ground maneuvers with the army units in order to prepare for the war in the West.

For von Richthofen the campaign in Poland reaffirmed the operational and tactical lessons he had learned in Spain. Of primary importance was a good command organization and effective communications. Airpower could only be used to its fullest potential if it was used en masse and used at the right time. Poland proved that aircraft could decisively affect the ground battle—but to do the same thing against the Western Allies he would need a far better communications network. He would use the coming months to solve these flaws and develop better training and doctrine in the units under his command.

In matters concerning aerial warfare von Richthofen was a perfectionist. In Poland Richthofen demonstrated his exceptional competence as a senior commander. In making decisions he never dithered. He showed an ability to accurately assess the highly confusing battlefield situation and to issue orders and commit his forces en masse and at the right place. In short, he demonstrated a mastery of the German approach to the operational level of war.

Von Richthofen was considered by superiors and subordinates to be a temperamental commander. He was never reticent in criticizing the campaign plan or command arrangements and in pushing his superiors for changes. When he needed additional resources or support to carry out his operations, as in his requests for more air transport in Poland, he did not hesitate to ask for them. If he believed that the doctrine or tactics were flawed he would say so—clearly and bluntly. No one could characterize him as a "yes man" or accuse him of being too diplomatic. Even so, his superiors knew that if von Richthofen were given a task he would do his best to fulfill the mission—and his best was very good indeed.

With subordinates he ruthlessly demanded superb competence and performance and had no time for anything less. His staff and subordinate commanders found him somewhat cold and aloof. He was a strict disciplinarian and stern taskmaster. In peacetime, or in between campaigns, he might take the time to train and develop his subordinates. But once the campaign was underway he had no patience for any staff member or unit commander who did not fully perform. He was perhaps too quick to relieve staff officers and commanders during operations, and it can be said that he relieved some officers who, under other commanders, proved very capable air commanders. At the same time he was quick to ensure that pilots and commanders who performed well in battle received decorations quickly and were recognized for promotion. In the middle of the Polish campaign von Richthofen would fly to his combat units and award Iron Cross medals to pilots and commanders who had distinguished themselves only days before. Despite his coldness von Richthofen was greatly respected by his staff and subordinate commanders, who admired his coolness under fire, his calm under periods of high stress, and his ability to size up a situation and make good decisions. By October 1939 he had proven to superiors and subordinates alike that he was eminently suited to high command and to serve at an even higher level.

Chapter 7

The Battle for France, 1940

The Luftwaffe faced an exceptionally tough mission in the campaign against France and the Low Countries in May 1940. The scope of the Luftwaffe's operations at the start of the campaign was enormous as the Luftwaffe had to simultaneously support major paratroop and air landing operations in Holland and provide close support for army units advancing upon northern France, Belgium, and Holland. The Luftwaffe would have to knock the British and French air forces out of the battle as quickly as possible if it was to successfully support the army's offensive operations. In contrast to the Polish campaign, the Luftwaffe in the West faced formidable opponents in the air and on the ground. While the Luftwaffe was generally superior to the Allied air forces in the number and quality of aircraft, the margin of superiority was not overwhelming. The Wehrmacht leadership understood that success in the campaign rested equally upon the ground and air forces. Failure of the Luftwaffe to win air superiority or support the ground forces would lead to the failure of the whole operation. Success in both required the Luftwaffe to outthink the enemy. Any decisive margin of superiority would have to come through better planning, tactics, and organization. Leadership and training would be the keys to ensuring a German aerial victory.

Transferred to the Western Front

At the conclusion of the Polish campaign, the VIIIth Air Corps was transferred to the 2nd Air Fleet, which covered northern Germany. The 2nd Air Fleet commander, General der Flieger Helmuth Felmy, was one of the "old Eagles" of the Luftwaffe and one of the most experienced senior commanders. Von Richthofen had worked with him closely in the 1920s and early 1930s and was glad to be under his command. The VIIIth Air Corps first moved its headquarters into a large hotel and then into a manor house, Schloss Dyck, at Grevenbroich near Münster. After the Polish campaign the air corps was reorganized into four large combat wings—each with 75–90 aircraft. KG 77 consisted of 3 Do 3 groups stationed in Düsseldorf; Stuka Wing 77 consisted of 3 Stuka groups stationed at Köln-Butzweilerdorf; Stuka Wing 2 consisted of 3 Stuka groups stationed at Köln-Ostheim; and JG 27, with 4 fighter groups, was stationed near Krefeld. A group of 40 He 123 attack planes stationed at Laufenberg rounded out the combat forces. Together, they comprised a formidable force of approximately 350 combat aircraft, supported by a transport squadron, a flak battalion for airfield protection, supply and airfield units, a signal battalion, and a motorized signals liaison detachment.[1] Once operations were under way other fighter or bomber wings would be attached as needed.

During the month of October the VIIIth Air Corps sorted itself out and von Richthofen wrote reports of his Poland experience, visited Berlin and briefed the Luftwaffe staff, and found time to visit his family. With his headquarters near Münster, von Richthofen could drive to Lüneburg to see his family in less than three hours. The ride was even shorter if he flew his Fiesler. Although his duties at the air corps came first, the winter of 1939–1940 would be one of the few times of the war when Richthofen could spend time with his family.

Von Richthofen and his staff made themselves comfortable in the manor at Dyck. The quarters were good and the headquarters mess had a reputation for good meals. Of course, the first priority for von Richthofen was always in establishing the best possible communications network. Luckily, the British and French showed no inclination to mount any offensive activity, so von Richthofen could allow his officers and men a few weeks of home leave during the fall and winter. As new units were assigned to the VIIIth Air Corps, von Richthofen took the time to visit them and to get to know their commanders and staffs. An important part of a senior commander's job was presenting medals in recognition of the Polish campaign, presenting unit flags and commendations, personally promoting officers, and taking part in the ceremonial side of the military. Von Richthofen made sure that he saw, and was seen, by as many of his troops as possible. Usually any promotion or decorations ceremony would require a brief speech to the assembled unit. A typical unit ceremony was the presentation of a battle flag to the 1st Group of JG 27 in the spring of 1940. Von Richthofen spoke to the assembled fighter wing, 100 pilots and several hundred ground and communications crew, about his experience as a fighter pilot in World War I. He advised the pilots that every fighter pilot had to have an aggressive approach to war and that there was no room in a fighter pilot's brain for thoughts of defense. Indeed, defensive thinking and tactics were characterized as "cowardice."[2] Von Richthofen encouraged fighter pilots with combat experience in Spain and Poland to pass on their tips on aerial combat to the newer pilots of JG 27—most of whom were well-trained but had seen little combat so far. One thing that von Richthofen did exceptionally well as a commander was to mentally prepare his aircrew and ground forces for the rigors of combat. He insisted that those who had considerable experience in combat operations pass on their tactical experience throughout the command.

Through the winter of 1939–1940, von Richthofen set his staff and air corps a busy schedule of exercises and staff war games. The lessons of Poland had to be absorbed quickly, and the VIIIth Air Corps would be facing a much more formidable enemy than the Poles. In Spain and Poland von Richthofen had earned a reputation as a strict disciplinarian and a hard taskmaster. His units trained constantly for the campaign to come. The air corps commander was not popular with the troops, and the men complained of the sometimes grueling regimen. But when the order to attack came, they would be ready.

Leave with the Family

At home in Lüneburg, Baroness (Freifrau) Jutta von Richthofen held the family together. The boys were both in high school, and Ellen, the youngest child, was ready to leave primary school and attend Gymnasium. Like any good father, Freiherr von Richthofen worried about his children's education. Young Wolfram ("Wolf" to the family) was preparing for the all-important Abitur examinations in the next year. His father arranged for special tutoring to prepare the young man for his exams. If he did well and passed the Abitur, Wolf could embark on a military career, like his father, and would be quickly accepted to the officer school. Wolf wanted to be a pilot. The children participated in school sports and activities, and membership in the Nazi youth organizations was mandatory for all German children, so Wolf and Götz were active in the Hitler Youth and Ellen in the Bund of German Girls.

On trips home von Richthofen could relax with friends and family, and he liked to entertain small groups. One recreation that he always found time for was hunting. If the weather was good and the season right, one might find him out on a brief afternoon expedition to shoot some pheasant or wild boar.

One anecdote explains something of life in the Third Reich and the military's attitude toward the official Nazi ideology. During winter 1939–1940, von Richthofen was able to spend some leave and weekends at home with his family. Thirteen-year-old Götz had acquired a copy of the American game Monopoly, which had become very popular in Germany in the 1930s. The Nazi Party condemned the game, describing it as a product of "Jewish monopoly capitalism." Yet this did little to hinder the game's popularity, even in

Nazi circles. Götz recalled that he and his father and his father's staff officers would often play Monopoly after dinner in the evening. For von Richthofen, it was one of the quietest times of the war.

He regularly went to Berlin for meetings with Goering and Jeschonnek, and it was an easy matter to stop off at his home on the way. During this time, he also had to take some leave to settle family business. Onkel Manfred, his adoptive father, had died just after the conclusion of the Polish campaign, and von Richthofen had become the legal owner of his uncle's estate at Bersdorf. However, his aunt, Luise, still lived on the estate and had full use of the property and its income until her death. She would outlive Wolfram von Richthofen and die in 1947.[3]

The Luftwaffe's Opponents

As the Luftwaffe developed its plans for the campaign in the West in late 1939 and early 1940 it faced a complex mission and a capable enemy. In terms of numbers the air forces of the Western Allies had close to numerical parity with the Luftwaffe forces in the West. In early May 1940 the French, British, Dutch, and Belgian air forces possessed a total of 4,469 frontline aircraft against a total of 3,578 German combat aircraft (fighters, bombers, attack aircraft, and Stukas) stationed in Western Germany. However, a great part of both the French and British air forces was stationed far to the rear. This would suffice for the medium bombers, which had a range of several hundred miles, but meant that most of the short-range fighter force would not be available at the start of the war. A count of the aircraft operational and ready for combat on the front lines of northwest France and Low Countries in early May 1940 totaled to just 1,453 (879 French, 384 British, 118 Belgian, 72 Dutch). In contrast, Germany had 2,589 combat aircraft ready for battle.[4] However, since hundreds of German aircraft were committed to the fighting in Norway, Germany had no combat reserves to fall back on whereas the Royal Air Force in France could draw upon a further 840 aircraft available in the United Kingdom. The French air force also had hundreds more aircraft in the interior of the country.[5] If the Luftwaffe had no significant advantage in terms of numbers it still had a significant advantage in terms of aircraft quality—especially when one compares the Luftwaffe to the French air force.

France had been on the cutting edge of aircraft design in the 1920s but had fallen behind the major powers in terms of aircraft design through most of the 1930s. By the late 1930s the French had designed some excellent aircraft—but getting them into large-scale production was another matter. The French production program lagged far behind expectations, and in the 1930s

A Stuka unit, 1940. The highly efficient Luftwaffe ground organization enabled the Stuka units to fly as many as six sorties a day—compared with less than a sortie a day for the French Air Force bomber. (*Signal*, September 1940)

it took the French two to four years longer to develop and deploy aircraft models than the Germans. The Dewoitine 520 fighter project, which was initiated at the same time as the Me 109, only entered production in 1940; the Me 109 had been mass produced since 1937.[6] At the start of the war, and still in the spring of 1940, most of the French fighter force was equipped with obsolescent craft. The French First Air Army defending northern France had only 312 single-seat fighters, and, of these, only the ninety-four Curtis Hawk H-75 fighters recently acquired from the United States could come close to matching the performance of the Me 109 in a fight.[7] Eight months later, the quality of French aircraft had only marginally improved.[8] When the campaign in the West began the French fighter force was equipped with fourteen groups of Morane-Saulnier 406s, ten groups of Bloch MB 152s, eight groups of Dewoitine 520s, four groups of Curtis Hawks, and one group of Arsenal VG 33s. Of these, only the Dewoitine 520s and Curtis Hawks could meet the Germans on anything like equal terms. All of the other aircraft were slower and less maneuverable than the Luftwaffe's Me 109s.[9] Whereas the Germans had tried to standardize aircraft models for production efficiency and ease of maintenance (the Germans built only one single-engine fighter in quantity before 1939—the Me 109), the French distributed aircraft production among the various aircraft companies and ordered small quantities of many different aircraft models. In 1939 the French were flying half a dozen different single-engine fighters to Germany's one. The same situation existed for bombers and reconnaissance aircraft.[10]

The French bomber force was in even much worse shape than the fighter arm. Its 800 planes looked impressive on paper, but the reality was that France was desperately short of modern bombers in 1940. Most squadrons were equipped with obsolescent designs from the early 1930s, such as the Amiot 143, and it was virtually suicidal for the French to fly such planes into the teeth of German fighter and flak defenses.[11] In the early stages of the campaign the French committed some of their bombers, and, as expected, they accomplished little while taking heavy losses.[12] France's large bomber force had almost no effect on the campaign.[13]

Yet another complication for the French air force was the large number of different aircraft models in the inventory. Air force supply and maintenance was a nightmare. A very high percentage of French aircraft remained grounded throughout the campaign only because they lacked some minor item of equipment, such as instruments or gunsights, which could have been quickly installed had they been available. More than anything, the French air force would be defeated because of its inefficient production and supply system. Even today, no one is sure of how many aircraft were grounded for lack of bombsights, radios, machine guns, or other basic equipment, but the official histories imply that the number was in the hundreds.[14] In some areas, the French simply declined to compete with the Germans. The most dramatic example of this is radar. In 1939 the French air force had no radar program—in contrast to the British and Germans, who had already deployed radar for homeland air defense.[15]

By the spring of 1940 the Royal Air Force was in considerably better shape than the French in terms of equipment. The Hurricanes that composed the RAF fighter force in France were reequipped with variable pitch propellers that improved their climbing and fighting ability. They also were installed with armor protection for the pilot and better radios. While slightly slower than the Me 109 and inferior to the Me 109 at high altitude, the Hurricane was still a dangerous opponent for the German fighters. Back in the U.K. the Spitfire, an aircraft fully equal to the Me 109, was now in full production, and squadrons of the RAF fighter command were being equipped with this

Allied fighters, destroyed in France 1940. (Heinz Guderian, *Mit den Panzern in Ost und West* [Berlin: Volk und Reich Verlag, 1940])

great fighter of World War II. The British medium bombers, the Blenheim and Wellington, were good aircraft and roughly equal to the German medium bombers in performance. However, some of the RAF's aircraft were best suited to providing target practice for German fighters and flak gunners. The Fairy Battle light bomber, which formed a large part of the RAF's striking force in northern France, was underpowered, slow, and carried only a small bomb load. The two-seater Boulton Paul Defiant was so inferior to the German fighters that it had to be pulled from the RAF inventory at the height of the Battle of Britain.

But in 1940 the greatest weaknesses of the Armeé de l'Air and RAF were not in their airplanes but in their ground organizations. The French air force had plenty of well-trained officer pilots and observers, but in dramatic contrast to the Germans the Armeé de l'Air had failed to recruit and train more than a fraction of the ground personnel it required to keep its aircraft flying. France had the necessary expertise and the industrial base to build a highly modern air force with a robust ground infrastructure. But the culture of the

French air force worked against its effectiveness in combat. Before the war the French air force was more of a pilots' club than a military organization. Senior commanders were interested in developing new aircraft but gave little thought to creating the infrastructure of an operational force, or in planning for industrial mobilization. As in Germany, France had many experienced veterans of World War I who had gone into civil aviation but still maintained their reserve commissions. Most of this group were now too old to serve as frontline pilots, but they still constituted a corps of men with aviation expertise who could have been called upon to serve as staff officers, logisticians, and air base commanders. But as rearmament accelerated in the 1930s the only interest that the regular air force had in their reserve officers was their flying proficiency.[16] It was a tremendous waste of human resources. In developing noncommissioned officers and enlisted support personnel, the French air force did even worse. When the war broke out, it was desperately short of enlisted specialist personnel, with the worst shortages in the NCO ranks. The French air force in 1939 had only 40 percent of the NCO radiomen it required and only 23 percent of the NCO mechanics who formed the backbone of the maintenance and repair crews that kept the fights and bombers in the air.[17]

The RAF was in far better shape in terms of ground personnel, but planning for deployment to France had been so poor that it was allocated poor landing fields and was short the specialized engineering units to set them in order. The whole of the army's Royal Engineers had only a few companies allocated to building airfields, and these units lacked the specialized equipment necessary for building runways and taxi strips. The RAF had learned in World War I that it required a large specialist engineer force to build and maintain airfields but had forgotten those lessons by 1939. The British contracted with civilian companies to build and maintain airfields, but the companies were inexperienced in such work, and projects that a Luftwaffe engineer battalion could accomplish in days or weeks took months for the RAF. Due to lack of engineers many of the RAF's forward airfields in France soon fell into disrepair, and some were barely useable by the time real combat began. At permanent stations on their home ground the RAF had a solid infrastructure, but moving a large force to France in 1939–1940 was marred by confusion and inefficiency.[18]

Absorbing the Lessons of Poland

From October 1939 to April 1940 the Germans used the lull in operations to absorb the lessons learned in the Polish campaign. While the basic equipment and operational methods of the Luftwaffe and army proved sound, the experience of combat exposed many flaws that needed correction. In the light of the Polish campaign the Luftwaffe paid particular attention to improving communications links through the Flivos and air force headquarters and also developing better communications nets with the army.[19] The whole array of army and Luftwaffe procedures was examined, and senior commanders and staffs found many things to improve. One of the major problems in coordinating air support between the army and Luftwaffe was that the two services used different maps with different scales. Thanks to the German policy of war games and planning exercises involving both the airmen and army staffs this discrepancy was discovered, and the army and Luftwaffe commanders decided that using a common map for the campaign in the West would improve coordination. In addition, in order to simplify reconnaissance and air support, the maps were marked off into a common numbered grid system. This would allow for easy plotting of enemy locations and marking of sites for Luftwaffe attack in the heat of battle.[20] Another important outcome for the army and Luftwaffe staff exercises was a discussion of the delivery of fuel and munitions to army panzer units by Luftwaffe transport. In a live exercise in early April 1940, the Luftwaffe practiced delivery of fuel and munitions by airdrop. Army and Luftwaffe supply units became practiced in the art of quickly loading and unloading transport aircraft and packaging supplies and rigging parachutes.[21]

During this time, the VIIIth Air Corps was especially active with staff war games and unit exercises, and von Richthofen made improving liaison and communications with the army and other Luftwaffe units a top priority. Major Wurm of the Luftwaffe signal troops was given the responsibility of organizing the close battle communications net, ensuring good communications with the Flivos and the Kolufts. On 7 November he received armored cars for his Flivos and modified them with appropriate radios so that they could effectively operate with the frontline panzer units.[22] In the spring von Richthofen experimented with controlling Stuka attacks from the ground using his Flivos in their armored cars. The exercises showed promise, but a standardized system could not be worked out on short notice and this experiment would have to wait for the Russian campaign to be realized.[23] In November 1939 the staff and headquarters of the VIIIth Air Corps received ten Fiesler "Storks" for use as liaison planes. These Fi 156s, with their astounding ability to take off and land on short fields, were a perfect airplane for liaison work, and with them von Richthofen's staff would be able to fly to forward units or back to rear headquarters for personal coordination. The ten Storks also provided the headquarters and staff of the air corps with the means to quickly move personnel to forward headquarters as they relocated during the battle.[24] Since von Richthofen was assigned to the 2nd Air Fleet, which would be supporting the northern zone of the German offensive, he would again be supporting the Sixth Army under General von Reichenau. Through November and December 1939 von Richthofen and his staff held talks with Reichenau's army staff and with General Otto Dessloch of the newly formed IInd Flak Corps, which would be supporting the ground forces and forward Luftwaffe units on the northern flank of the offensive into France.[25] From October through April the Luftwaffe and army held constant staff discussions to review the plans and arrange coordination.

The German army and air force used the lull in operations to train and improve unit equipment at all levels. For the Luftwaffe squadrons and groups this meant a round of practice at the gunnery ranges and flying mock dogfights against each other. Bomber units improved their ability to fly and navigate at night. Higher headquarters practiced command post operations and carried out staff war games. Large army and air force maneuvers were carried out with an emphasis on conducting joint operations. The contrast between the Wehrmacht and the Allied armed forces during this period, which came to be known as the "Phony War," is especially striking. The Germans trained and prepared with a sense of urgency for the campaign they knew was coming. The Allies carried out their normal battalion and regimental training exercises but very few large unit maneuvers or staff exercises. The French maintained an almost peacetime approach to training while the British Expeditionary Force (BEF) in France, ten divisions by the spring of 1940, generally ignored any large unit training. When General Bernard Montgomery, then 3rd Infantry Division commander with the BEF, conducted a series of division exercises, it was seen as a rare and revolutionary event. Indeed, Montgomery made some scathing comments about the lack of division and corps training in the British army of 1940. He pointed out that "in the years preceding the outbreak of war no large-scale exercises had been held in England for some time."[26] When the BEF was formed and shipped to France in the fall of 1939 there "was a total lack of any common policy or tactical doctrine throughout the BEF, when differences arose those differences remained and there was no firm grip at the top."[27]

The French air force and the RAF contingent sent to France were little better than the Allied armies in their attitude toward training. While von Richthofen's airmen and ground crews complained that they were being worn out by constant training exercises, a French air force officer recalled the "inactivity of the months before 10 May" on the part of the Allied air units.[28] While the Germans worked to absorb the lessons of Poland, the Allied powers seemed indifferent to learning from the most recent experience of modern war. It was not as if the British and French forces had no solid information about German tactics, doctrine, and weaponry. Several thousand Polish officers who had seen the German blitzkrieg managed to escape the final capitulation through Romania and made their way to France and Britain, where they were reformed as an exile army. But senior Allied commanders took little notice of their experience and remained confident that their doctrine, organization, and weapons were more than a match for anything the Wehrmacht could throw at them.

On the matter of organization and weaponry the Allied commanders had a point. Although the Luftwaffe could claim an edge over its opponents in terms of numbers and equipment, the German and Allied ground forces were very evenly matched, with several parts of the equation in the Allies' favor. The Germans had 136 army divisions facing 94 French divisions, 10 British divisions, 22 Belgian divisions, and 10 Dutch divisions—a total of 136 Allied divisions on the northeastern front.[29] The British and French armies had 22 armored and motorized divisions against the same number of German panzer and motorized divisions.[30] However, the Allies had a clear superiority in tanks, with approximately 3,000 tanks against 2,200–2,800 German tanks. In addition, the Allied tanks were heavier and better gunned and armored than their German enemies. The French army had 1,800 heavy and medium tanks, with the excellent Souma with its 47 mm gun and the Char B with its heavy armor, 75 mm hull gun, and 47 mm turret gun—possibly the best tank in the world in 1940.[31] In contrast, more than half of Germany's tanks were the light Mark I and Mark II tanks, and panzer divisions had only 627 of the Mark III and Mark IV medium tanks.[32] The French army also had a clear advantage in artillery, with 11,200 guns to Germany's 7,710. The one area where the Germans had a clear superiority was in the flak arm. France had only 1,500 flak guns of all types while the German army and Luftwaffe had 2,600 of the superb 88 mm heavy flak guns and 6,700 light flak guns.[33]

The failure of the French air staff to plan or organize for the broader requirements of technology was directly translated into extremely low readiness rates for French aircraft in May 1940. Exact figures for aircraft operational rates are not available (another sign of French disorganization) for May 1940, but a fair estimate from the numbers of aircraft that flew on missions is an average operational rate of about 50–60 percent for fighter units and no more than 40 percent for bomber units.[34] The French records of the campaign of 1940 are spotty, but some French squadrons probably had no more than 40 percent of their aircraft available for operations before May 1940, and French military historians estimate a very low operational rate for the French air force at the height of the battle in May 1940. The Armeé de l'Air consistently made group attacks with no more than 40–50 percent of the official group strength.[35]

The French army senior commanders had consistently underrated the importance of airpower on the battlefield before the war. The French military commander in chief, Marshal Maurice Gamelin, believed that the losses of aircraft in the first few weeks of the war would be so heavy that airpower would cease to be an important factor in the battle. In 1938, General Gamelin commented, "The role of aviation is apt to be exaggerated, and after the early days of war the wastage will be such that it will more and more be confined to acting as an accessory to the army."[36] Unlike the Germans the French leadership thought of airpower more in defensive than offensive terms. General Gamelin referred to the air force as "the Shield of the Army."[37] Air Minister Guy LeChambre believed that the priority of the Armeé de l'Air was to form a defensive line to protect army operations. In 1938 he commented that "In the initial phase of the war, however, what we'll need above all is to put our airspace under lock and key, as we've done for our frontiers."[38] Despite the lessons of Spain and now Poland that showed the effectiveness of airpower as an offensive weapon, the senior French leadership saw no need to modify their highly defensive doctrine or develop close army–air force links and planning on the German model.[39]

On the matter of learning lessons from Spain and Poland the RAF leadership was little better than the French. Even after the Polish campaign the RAF leadership ignored the concept of dive bombing and showed little interest in developing a specialist army support force.[40]

The German Plans

The lack of army/air force coordination and planning as well as outdated doctrine and little operational-level training largely doomed the Allied air forces to defeat even before the campaign began. In the spring of 1939 the Luftwaffe general staff carried out an analysis of the French and British air forces in case the Luftwaffe would have to fight a campaign in the West. The Luftwaffe's analysis of the French and British weaknesses and capabilities was highly accurate and tends to refute the common image of the Luftwaffe intelligence section and its chief, Colonel Josef "Beppo" Schmidt, as generally incompetent. In regards to planning the air campaign in France the Luftwaffe staff got it right. The intelligence staff noted the large number of French aircraft but also correctly concluded that a large part of the French air fleet was obsolescent and of limited worth. The Luftwaffe also remarked upon the poor French ground organization and weak logistics system and predicted serious supply and operational problems for the French. The RAF was expected to deploy forces to northern France in case of war, and intelligence reports concluded that a deployed RAF force would probably have a weak ground organization and consequent operational problems.[41] With the German and Allied ground forces being relatively equal in size and capability, the German military commanders planned on their superior Luftwaffe to provide a decisive margin of superiority in any campaign in the West.

The initial plan for the 1940 campaign was essentially a repeat of the 1914 Schlieffen Plan, with the major weight of the German forces to be put on the right flank and to advance into Holland and Belgium. The Germans hoped to defeat the British and French forces in northern Belgium, but the Germans had little expectation of making a major advance into France. Some within the general staff, in particular a brilliant general named Erich von Manstein, were dissatisfied with the plan that achieved only a "partial victory." When a plane carrying a copy of the original plan accidentally made a forced landing in Belgium in January 1940 and the plan was compromised, a group of general staff officers saw it as a perfect opportunity to push for a complete revision of the campaign plans along bolder lines. A new concept of operations was approved, and a new and much bolder plan took shape. The main point of German effort would be with Panzergruppe von Kleist (under the command of General Ewald von Kleist), which would have the concentrated striking power of three panzer/motorized corps, including seven of Germany's ten panzer divisions. Instead of coming on the German right flank, Kleist would break through the Allied center in the Ardennes forest. If opportunity arose, Kleist could advance either to Paris or straight across northern France to the English Channel, and cut off the British and French northern armies. It was a plan that offered a good chance for a decisive victory if executed properly.[42]

The VIIIth Fliegerkorps and the Battle for France and the Low Countries

On 10 May all the German preparations were in place and the great offensive in the West began. Von Richthofen's forces began the battle at dawn with strikes on the main Belgian airfields, destroying most of the obsolescent Belgian air force on the ground. To his north, German airborne troops seized key airfields in Holland, and the German Sixth Army, which he was assigned to support, crossed the Belgian frontier and advanced rapidly. The following day, the VIIIth Air Corps pounded the prepared Belgian defenses and helped the 3rd Panzer Division secure a crossing over the Albert Canal. The first main Belgian defense line was broken in two days. During the first four days of the campaign the two air fleets put a major effort into winning air superiority by attacking French and British airfields across northern France. The Germans had some success. A little more than half of the Allied airfields in northern France were attacked, and, in some cases, the Germans caught whole Allied squadrons on the ground and left them burning wrecks.[43] However, the blow was not crippling; the French and British had plenty of aircraft in reserve, and such losses could be replaced. Even so, the relentless German offensive in the air had a psychological effect far out of proportion to the physical damage inflicted. From the start of the battle the Allies were thrown onto the defensive and merely reacted to the German moves rather than initiating major strikes of their own. Rather than seeking the Germans, the French fighter units tended to fly patrols over their assigned defense sectors—largely a waste of time and effort. The strength and rapidity of the German ground advance also dislocated the Allied commanders. There was no coherent Allied plan or doctrine that ensured the air forces would support the British and French advance into Belgium. At the start of the campaign the Allies reacted slowly to the German attack. As the center of the German thrust poured through the Ardennes toward Sedan, German vehicle columns backed up on the roads and created a traffic jam all the way back to the Rhine. It was a magnificent target for a major strike by the British and French air forces, but instead the Allies carried out a series of small and uncoordinated attacks, usually using bombers with little or no fighter escort. For the advancing German flak and fighters the first days of the offensive were almost like target practice. The RAF's support force of light bombers assaulted the German panzer advance with incredible bravery. It was a futile gesture. With little damage inflicted on the Germans, the 135 serviceable bombers of the Advanced Air Striking Force (AASF) had dwindled to seventy-two serviceable planes by the evening of 12 May.[44]

Indeed, over Belgium the Allied air activity was so weak that von Richthofen noted in his diary on 12 May, "Where is the enemy air force?"[45] On 13 May the VIIIth Air Corps was told to divert its efforts to supporting the German attack across the Meuse at Sedan. Since von Richthofen's force was stationed in the center of the German offensive, it was simple to redirect efforts from Belgium to Dean, which lay just south of the German Sixth Army's area of operations. In the morning the Stukas flew in support of the Sixth Army in Belgium, and in the afternoon the whole air corps joined most of Sperrle's 3rd Air Fleet in repeated attacks upon French defenses and artillery positions

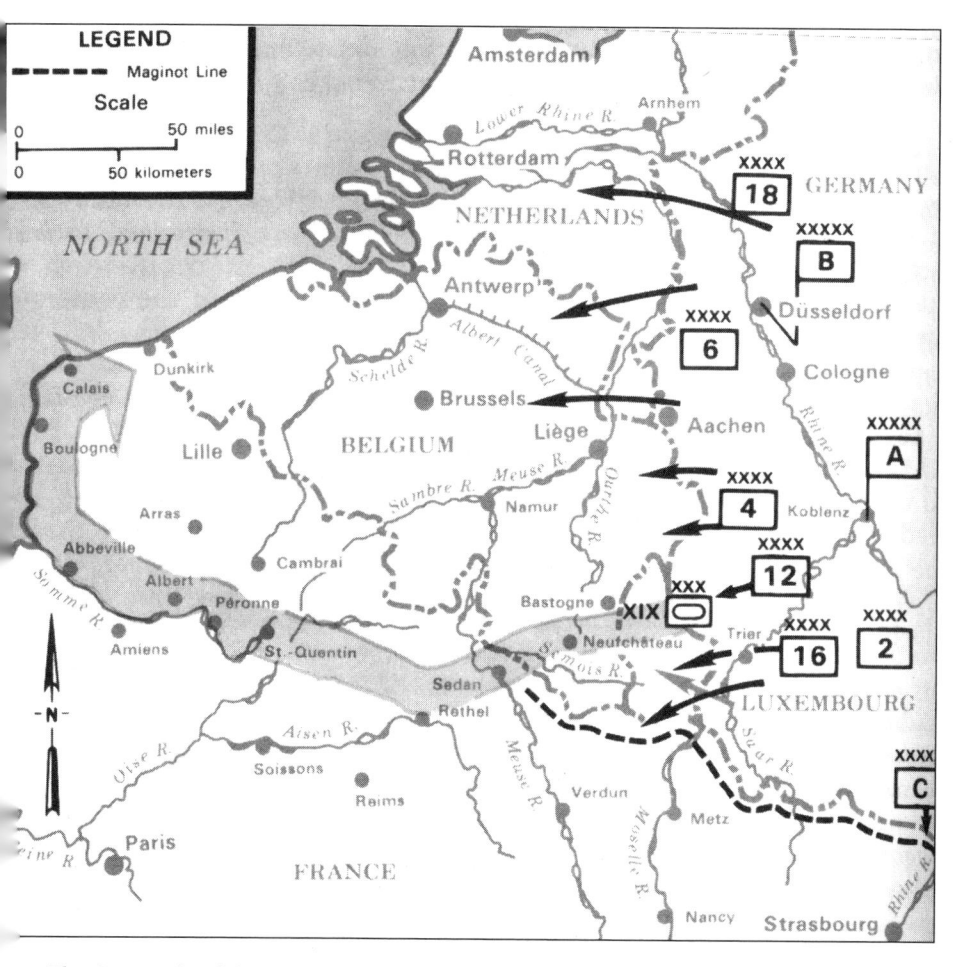

The German breakthrough and race to the English Channel, May 1940. Von Richthofen's VIIIth Air Corps supported Panzergruppe Kleist's offensive depicted here. (Roger Spiller, ed. *Combined Arms in Battle since 1939* [Ft. Leavenworth, KS: Combat Studies Institute, 1992])

around Sedan. The day before, the Luftwaffe had planned to concentrate its forces for one massive attack on the French with the intention of paralyzing the defenders with one great blast of firepower. But the 3rd Air Fleet staff had already planned to support the crossing of General Kleist's panzer divisions by a series of squadron and group attacks that would keep the French under constant pressure throughout the day, and it was too late to put together a new plan. In fact, this was fortunate for the Germans because the constant attacks that the VIIIth Air Corps participated in delivered just the effects that Panzergruppe von Kleist needed to establish a bridgehead across the river. The rain of bombs on the French defenders looked impressive but actually inflicted only moderate damage. However, the French defenders at Sedan were mostly poorly trained reservists with only a few antiaircraft guns to shoot back with, and any gun that fired would make itself an immediate target for German aircraft—so the relatively little fire was brought down upon the German attackers at their most vulnerable moment as they were crossing the river.[46]

With little support from their own artillery and air force the French defenders cracked. Whole units began to retreat away from the river simply to avoid the German bombs. By the end of the day several French divisions were in retreat and Panzergruppe von Kleist had succeeded in crossing the river at several points. The middle of the whole Allied defense line had been forced, and for the next three days Kleist would concentrate on getting his forces across the river barrier, pushing his reconnaissance out, and preparing for another major push. Von Richthofen met with Kleist on 14 May to coordinate plans and air support, and Kleist told the airman that he was delighted to have the VIIIth Air Corps in partnership. In the meantime, von Richthofen still had to support the Sixth Army advance into Belgium, and his Stukas, fighters, and attack planes flew at a high rate of tempo. On 15 May, von Richthofen sent his Stukas against some of the French Maginot Line forts near Lüttich. Despite being pounded by artillery and dive bombers using the new armor-piercing bombs developed since the Polish campaign, the massively constructed forts fought on, and one even fired some antiaircraft bursts near von Richthofen's Stork as he watched the attack from the air. Yet by evening the forts capitulated, and von Richthofen was convinced that his Stukas had done the trick by demoralizing the defenders.[47]

It took some time for the French and British high commands to realize that a huge gap had been blown in the middle of their front. When the Allies did understand that the Germans were across the Meuse in force, their counterattacks by land and air were poorly organized and slow in coming. The slowness of the Allied response was a godsend to the Luftwaffe, which gained time to prepare air defenses at the Meuse bridgehead. On 14 May, as the Germans were building up their bridgehead, the RAF light bomber force in France attacked the German positions at Sedan, and here the Luftwaffe's decision to deploy large, mobile flak forces to support the army's forward units paid off. The Luftwaffe stationed dozens of heavy and light flak guns around the Meuse bridgeheads from Dinant to Sedan and also put up a strong fighter cover. The RAF's attempts to destroy the German bridges met with disaster: the RAF lost thirty-five of sixty-three Battle bombers and five of eight Blenheim bombers dispatched—a loss rate of 56 percent of the attacking force. The RAF's attacks of 14 May amounted to an aerial Charge of the Light Brigade—but with even worse consequences. No air force can sustain such losses for any time, and after 14 May the morale of the RAF force in France was largely broken.[48]

Once the Germans had forced the Meuse barrier, their greatest vulnerability lay in the exposed masses of men and vehicles that were jammed up from the German spearpoint at Sedan all the way back to the Rhine River. The Germans provided a target that would have been hard for Allied aircraft to miss, but attempts to interdict the German columns behind the Meuse crossing were feeble. Instead of intervening in the ground battle or attempting an interdiction campaign, the RAF bomber command turned its attention to strategic attacks on Germany. Even if successful, such attacks offered no support for the hard-pressed French and British ground forces. On the night of 15 May, while fighting along the Meuse was still intense, the RAF bomber command sent ninety-nine medium bombers to bomb cities in the Ruhr. On 17 May, as the gap in the Allied front grew larger and a true crisis was at hand, the RAF bomber command responded to desperate appeals from the army for support by sending its bombers to attack Hamburg and Bremen. Neither attack inflicted any serious damage on the German war machine. In fact, the only major damage caused by the RAF in Bremen was the destruction of two large warehouses full of furniture confiscated from Jews.[49]

By 17 May, when the Germans were across the Meuse in force and advancing, they could see a noticeable slackening of the Allied air effort. A week into the campaign, the Luftwaffe's strategy to win air superiority had clearly succeeded. However, in contrast to Poland, the Luftwaffe had paid a heavy price to control the airspace of northern France and Belgium. In the first two days of the campaign the Luftwaffe had lost 126 aircraft (including 69 bombers, 35 fighters, and 8 Stukas), a higher daily loss rate than in the Battle of Britain.[50] For the next three weeks losses would remain high—but for the Allies it was worse.

Supporting Panzergruppe von Kleist to the Sea

Von Richthofen demonstrated his competence as a senior air commander and operational innovator during the events of the next week. The second week of the campaign (16–22 May) would also demonstrate the potential for properly applied airpower to decide a campaign. The rapid advance of the German armored forces across the Meuse caused consternation in the German high command as a large gap was opening between the fast-moving panzer formations leading the offensive and the slow-moving infantry divisions following behind. The infantry divisions, which relied mostly upon foot marching and horse transport, had the vital mission of protecting the flank of the German offensive. If the gap continued to widen, the French would have the opportunity to move forces in behind the armored advance and cut them off from their logistics support. General Rundstedt responded to the nervousness of the army high command and on 16 May ordered Kleist to slow his advance in order to allow the infantry divisions time to catch up.[51] For its part the army high command focused more on the danger of a French counterattack than on the tremendous opportunities that had now opened to them. If Panzergruppe von Kleist continued its advance, there was little to stop it between Sedan and the English Channel. Once the channel was reached, the fully motorized British Expeditionary Force, which contained the cream of the British army divisions and the British 1st Armoured Division, and the French northern army group, which included the best divisions of the French army as well as the bulk of the Allied motorized and armored forces, would be cut off in Belgium and pressed in by German forces from the north, east, and south. In the mind of Kleist and von Richthofen, the opportunity of a war-winning victory had presented itself.

Flying back to Berlin for a quick staff conference on 16 May, von Richthofen presented his case to Goering and Jeschonnek. He argued that his forces were well positioned to support Kleist's advance and that he should be given the mission of supporting the panzer group as it was now the decisive force in the Western campaign and deserved the concentrated support of his entire air corps. Von Richthofen believed that the VIIIth Fliegerkorps could effectively protect the flanks of General Kleist's panzer force and convinced his superiors it could be done. That day Goering directed the VIIIth Fliegerkorps to "follow Panzer Group von Kleist to the sea."[52] It was a tremendously bold gamble, but it was the only means by which Kleist's force could maintain its rapid advance. The Germans had the initiative, and any delay would allow the French and British the opportunity to assemble reserves and halt the Germans short of their goal. All the senior German commanders remembered World War I and just how formidable the British and French could be in war and their capability to counterattack if given time to prepare.

The army initially doubted that von Richthofen could make good on his promise to protect the panzer division's flanks. However, it soon became clear that the French would not mount another "miracle on the Marne" as they had in 1914. The high command calmed down and ordered the panzer advance to continue. Von Richthofen ordered his forces to screen and protect Panzergruppe von Kleist's open flanks as their primary mission and to execute attacks in front of the panzer advance as the secondary mission.[53] He quickly made good on his promise to protect the panzer group's flanks. Reconnaissance units of the VIIIth Fliegerkorps spotted French divisions moving to counterattack and relentlessly bombed troop columns as well as French tank units that appeared on the German flanks. Von Richthofen's Stukas helped repel attacks by General Charles de Gaulle's 4th Armored Division at Montcornet on 17 May and on 19 May at Crecy-sur-Serre.[54] The Luftwaffe attacks on enemy tanks were rarely successful as direct bomb hits on tanks were rarely achieved and the Ju 87s and Hs 123s of the VIIIth Fliegerkorps carried no heavy cannon.[55] However, the aircraft attacks separated the tanks from their supporting fuel and ammunition vehicles and inflicted heavy damage to the French infantry and artillery units. Most of the VIIIth Air Corps operations consisted of interdiction attacks that decimated and delayed French units moving on Kleist's line of advance. As Wellington said at Waterloo, "it was a close run thing," but the VIIIth Air Corps performed brilliantly by finding enemy units and quickly bringing major attacks upon them. The French and British forces that threatened the German advance were decimated or, at least, thrown into confusion. The infantry divisions were granted just enough time to move up and protect the Panzergruppe's flanks.

The Luftwaffe's reforms after the Polish campaign were a key factor in enabling von Richthofen to provide effective air support to Panzergruppe Kleist during his drive through the Allied center. The ground and logistics reorganization proved highly efficient in quickly putting captured Belgian, Dutch, and French airfields into operation as fighter and Stuka bases. The short-ranged Me 109s, Stukas, and Henschels were most effective if they could operate from forward airfields just behind the ground troops. Usually the Luftwaffe airfield companies could put a captured airfield into full use for the Luftwaffe within twenty-four hours. The Luftwaffe's motorized supply columns moved as quickly as they could, but deploying air units forward required a considerable number of the reliable Ju 52 transports to get fuel and bombs forward—at least for the first days of operation. As in Poland, von Richthofen demanded and got more transports from his air fleet commander, General Hugo Sperrle. With limited assets and with heavy demands for airpower, the Luftwaffe could only carry out its missions by maintaining a high sortie rate. In May 1940 in France the Stukas and fighters of the VIIIth Air Corps normally flew four sorties a day—and when necessary sometimes as many as six.[56]

More than anything else, the Luftwaffe's ability to generate a high sortie rate gave it a big margin of air superiority in 1940. Early in the campaign, French fighters flew an average of only one sortie per day, and bombers flew an average of only one sortie every four days.[57] This was largely due to the weak

Field Marshal Hugo Sperrle, commander of 3rd Air Fleet and von Richthofen's commander for most of the 1940 campaign.

infrastructure and the especially weak communications system of the French, which could not support getting planes into the air as often as the Germans. Thus, the Allies were overwhelmed in the air not by the number of German aircraft, but rather by a more effective ground organization.

But even with a superior ground organization and logistics infrastructure von Richthofen's forces felt the strain of serious supply problems. On 18 May von Richthofen expressed his concerns about logistics for his forces and the capability of 3rd Air Fleet's transports to get enough airfield units and fuel and munitions forward to keep his Stukas, Henschels, and fighters flying at a high sortie rate.[58] The problem was that the 300 Ju 52 transports available were heavily strained by the requirement to get fuel and ammunition forward to Kleist's panzer units as well as to supply von Richthofen's air units. This requirement was met with increasing difficulty as the panzers and aircraft advanced further from their supply columns.[59]

The Luftwaffe at Dunkirk

On the evening of 20 May, Panzergruppe von Kleist reached the sea west of Abbeville and effectively cut off the French northern army and the BEF from the rest of France. Almost half a million men of the BEF and French army, as well as the whole Belgian army, were encircled with their backs to the sea. The British and French forces cut off in Flanders consisted of the cream of the Allied armies, with most of the motorized forces and most modern equipment. At this moment, however, the German corridor from Sedan to the sea was a narrow one and quite vulnerable to attack on the flanks. Now that the German logistics lines were extended, von Richthofen's forces would be sorely stretched to maintain the same level of support as at the start of the campaign. Attaining air superiority and maintaining constant support of the German armies had been costly for the Luftwaffe. By 20 May the Luftwaffe recorded 527 aircraft either destroyed or with more than 60 percent damage. This amounted to 20 percent of the total starting force.[60] However, despite the army and Luftwaffe vulnerabilities von Richthofen doubted that the enemy still had the will to counterattack. On the day that Kleist's panzer group reached the sea and cut the Allied armies in half, Kleist's headquarters reported capturing the commander of a French army and fifty staff officers of another French army. Whatever the Allied capabilities still looked like on paper, they could not accurately reflect the state of an army whose senior officers were starting to surrender in large numbers. Von Richthofen was delighted by the report that the captured Frenchmen had commented on the demoralizing effect of German air superiority.[61] The next step would be to

Results of a Luftwaffe attack on Allied column, France, 1940. (U.S. Air Force Historical Research Agency)

push Stuka and fighter forces forward as quickly as possible in order to support further operations by Kleist's panzers.

On 22 May, von Richthofen told Sperrle of his plans to shift Stuka and fighter groups forward to the airbase at St. Pol in order to support the army's drive into Flanders. Sperrle was unsure whether he had the logistics to support such a move, but von Richthofen obtained the air fleet commander's approval when he pointed out that many of the logistics problems had been solved by the army's capture of a huge Allied supply depot near Arras. The Luftwaffe's greatest supply requirement, namely aviation fuel, was neatly solved by the use of Allied logistics.[62]

Although the Germans were vulnerable at this point, the Allied armies had little stomach for more counterattacks, and their window of opportunity to regain the situation had passed. The Allies were more interested in retreating and saving what forces they could, and the German commanders sensed this. Despite the worries of the high command back in Berlin, General Kleist was ready to now turn his forces north and clear the channel ports as quickly as possible.

Calais was the next objective of the army, and on 25 May von Richthofen flew forward to meet with General Heinz Guderian, commander of the XIXth Panzer Corps, at his headquarters 10 miles east of Boulogne in order to jointly plan the attack on Calais. This was probably the first meeting, or at least the first long conversation, between two German generals who were considered masters of the blitzkrieg. In the Polish campaign Guderian had commanded a panzer division in the northern army group and therefore had not worked with von Richthofen before. Von Richthofen's comments on his planning session with Guderian are interesting and even a bit amusing. In his diary von Richthofen noted that Guderian was, just like most army commanders, completely ignorant of the employment of airpower and that he had to brief the corps commander on the basics of air support "just like he had to do in Spain."[63] In any case, von Richthofen worked out a joint attack plan on the Allied garrison at Calais for the next day.

Flying over the scene of the recent German advance, von Richthofen could note the huge columns of British and French prisoners trudging east and southeast in such numbers that no one was even counting any more. The terrain was all very familiar to him as he noted flying over his old airfield from 1918 at St. Quentin. Most of the memoirs of the German generals that recount the 1940 campaign mention the familiarity of the terrain that they had spent years fighting over decades before. One can see a considerable level of astonishment in the minds of the older German officers who had quickly won towns and positions in 1940 that had taken them years to achieve in the First World War. Even more astonishing was the level of casualties in comparison with 1914–1918. The casualties seem severe enough—over 20,000 German soldiers and airmen in the Battle for France in 1940. But to officers who had served through World War I these were, in fact, relatively light losses in men and material considering the objectives that had been achieved.

Von Richthofen expected to support the advance of Guderian's XIXth Panzer Corps all the way to Dunkirk (Dunkerque), and he was clearly a bit nervous about the expected opposition. As the Germans moved up the coast toward Dunkirk they came within range of RAF units based in southern England, and the air battle, which had gone in von Richthofen's favor from the start of the campaign, began to turn against the Luftwaffe's advanced forces. At this point Guderian noted a lessening of Luftwaffe activity over his corps' front and fierce British air opposition.[64] The advance up the coast toward Dunkirk was one of the most difficult periods of the campaign for the VIIIth Air Corps; between 21 and 25 May von Richthofen's air corps suffered 25 percent of the total Luftwaffe losses for that period.[65] On 25 May, von Richthofen noted that the British had put up a strong fighter screen over Calais, and as the British withdrew toward Dunkirk, their fighter squadrons flying from England—including squadrons equipped with Spitfires—began to fly combat patrols over the Flanders coast and aggressively engaging the Luftwaffe's aircraft.

Salvation for the trapped BEF and French forces in Flanders came from a directive from Hitler on 24 May that stopped the advance of Guderian's corps into the final Allied defensive lines around Dunkirk. At this point Guderian's panzers had advanced to the River Aa, less than twenty-five miles from Dunkirk. Guderian was appalled at the order, which had been issued by Hitler on the advice of Hermann Goering. The Luftwaffe's commander in chief had promised Hitler that there was no need to commit his panzers, as his Luftwaffe would deliver the final coup de grace and destroy the Allied armies by air attack.[66] The destruction of the Allied armies at Dunkirk would be carried out primarily by Kesselring's 2nd Air Fleet, but von Richthofen's VIIIth Air Corps was also detailed to support the operation. Both Kesselring and von Richthofen protested Goering's order, which was made in the heat of the moment without any consultation with commanders at the front or any serious analysis. It was typical of Goering's style of command and one of the strategic decisions that ensured that Germany would eventually lose the war. Both Kesselring and von Richthofen told the Luftwaffe high command that their forces had taken heavy losses in two weeks of incessant combat and that the Stukas and their fighter escorts would be flying at the higher limits of their range. Moreover, neither general was confident that they could win clear air superiority over Dunkirk.[67]

In fact, the RAF fighter command made a supreme effort during the next week to cover the Allied withdrawal, and German bomber and fighter crews took heavy losses. On 27 May the IInd Air Corps lost twenty-three aircraft and sixty-four personnel over Dunkirk, heavier losses in one day than it had had for the previous ten.[68] On that day von Richthofen's air corps concentrated on attacking the columns of Allied troops retreating into the Dunkirk enclave. On the morning of 27 May, von Richthofen flew to the headquarters of the Luftwaffe's Ist Air Corps at Cambrai, commanded by General Grauert, to coordinate air attacks on the shipping at Dunkirk.[69] Later that day von Richthofen met with General Sperrle, who was concerned about reports that the Allies were mounting a major counterattack in Flanders. He reassured Sperrle that these were just "panic reports" that had likely originated from the Luftwaffe general headquarters in Berlin. It seems that the whole affair had been triggered by a local counterattack by British armor at Amiens, and von Richthofen replied by sending a Stuka group to assist the German panzers in repelling the attack.

The citadel at Boulogne after its surrender to German forces. Von Richthofen's Stukas pounded the fortifications at Boulogne in support of the panzer advance on Dunkirk. The ability of the Luftwaffe to destroy fortifications was one of the foundations for the success of the German panzer advances in 1940. (Heinz Guderain, *Mit den Panzern in Ost und West* [Berlin: Volk und Reich Verlag, 1942])

As far as von Richthofen was concerned, both the army and the Luftwaffe senior commanders were far too prone to overreact to garbled and partial information from the front and issue cautious orders to stop advances and go onto the defensive. He remarked in his diary, "This nervousness, worry about flanks and various fears seem to be the natural approach to operations present in the higher leadership." Throughout the French campaign he complained of the caution and tendency to overreact that was characteristic of Sperrle and the army and Luftwaffe staffs. With a bit of smugness he noted in his diary that he seemed personally immune from such fears and possessed much steadier nerves than other commanders.[70] Although this sounds egotistical—and von Richthofen was never shy in asserting his own talent for warfare and command—there is some truth in his self-assessment. By any standard von Richthofen possessed very steady nerves, and even in the heat of battle he tended to remain an island of calm and deliberation. He, quite sensibly, tended to discount initial reports from the front as exaggerations—which they usually were. When a genuine crisis did appear he possessed an unusual ability to perceive the problem and take immediate action to deal with the situation.

As the British initiated the operation to evacuate the Allied troops from Dunkirk on 27 May (Operation Dynamo), the weather intervened on their side to limit German operations. Poor weather made it impossible for Kesselring's forces to attack Dunkirk on the afternoon of 28 May and on the morning of 29 May. Attacks resumed as the weather cleared, with Kesselring and von Richthofen's units concentrating on Allied shipping. The aerial fighting from 27 May to 4 June was intense: the Luftwaffe lost 100 aircraft over Dunkirk while the RAF's fighter command lost 106 planes.[71] Yet, despite the loss of a large number of ships and the constant harassment of the troops massing on the beach to embark for England, the Allied evacuation was a success. By the time the rear guard at Dunkirk surrendered on 4 June, the boatlift had pulled 338,000 British and French troops out of the trap.[72]

Last Phase of the Campaign

As the German army reached the channel coast the Luftwaffe and army high commands began planning for the final phase of the battle for France. Once the BEF and French army in the northern pocket were eliminated, the full weight of the army and Luftwaffe would turn south and drive to Paris and beyond. General Bock's Army Group B, with forty-four divisions, would advance to the Seine River and break the left of the defense line the French had established across northern France. Panzergruppe von Kleist would redeploy to the left of Bock's army group and was given the mission of driving forward and isolating Paris. The left flank of the German advance would be Rundstedt's Army Group A, with forty-five divisions.[73] They would strike toward Rheims with Guderian's panzer force in the lead. Their mission was to break the French center and envelop the French forces on the right.[74] The VIIIth Air Corps would remain under the 3rd Air Fleet and fly in support of Panzergruppe von Kleist and the Sixth and Ninth Armies. While finishing up the battle at Dunkirk, von Richthofen had to redeploy his air units to recently captured airfields in north-central France. To ensure proper coordination and support of the army he had to reorganize his signals networks and supply services within a few days. With the major offensive into central France due to begin on 5 June, he did not feel that his forces were ready. His air units had been in constant battle since 10 May, and his Stuka units had taken heavy losses. On the eve of the new offensive only half of his losses had been replaced. Indeed, the Luftwaffe as a whole was feeling the effects of the battle across northern France. Even with replacements that had arrived from Germany, the Luftwaffe had no more than 2,500 total aircraft for the campaign, considerably fewer than what it had started with on 10 May.[75]

Despite the state of von Richthofen's forces, his Stukas, Henschels, and fighters provided very effective support to Panzergruppe von Kleist when the German offensive kicked off on the morning of 5 June. For close support work von Richthofen organized a battle group of two fighter groups, two Stuka groups, and two Henschel squadrons. For the next days the Luftwaffe's operations were largely a replay of opening battles in May. The VIIIth Air Corps and other Luftwaffe formations concentrated on attacking the French airfields in the first two days of the campaign. Nineteen French airfields were attacked, and although French losses on the ground were far less than the German estimates, they were enough to disorient the French air force. At the start of the final battle for France the Armeé de l'Air put up some serious opposition. The French had replaced their May losses and massively reinforced their air forces in central France and, at this point in the campaign, probably had more aircraft than the Germans. But the French air force supply and maintenance system, never very robust, was already breaking down, and this limited operations.[76] On 6 June the French air force flew a respectable 598 sorties and made a number of attacks upon the German panzer columns. Between 5 and 9 June the French lost 130 planes, and every day saw the French air force effort lessening. By 9 June the Armee de l'Air flew only 179 sorties against the Germans.[77] French bomber losses had been especially heavy, and the units that had been in heavy combat were largely ineffective.[78] Indeed, France's large bomber force ended up having almost no effect on the campaign—much as the Luftwaffe intelligence staff had predicted before the battle.[79] While France still had a large air force at the end of the battle, it was no longer in a state to fight effectively.[80]

The campaign in France and the Low Countries had been an exceptionally hard one for the Luftwaffe. In May and June 1940 the Luftwaffe lost more than a quarter of its total aircraft—more than 1,200 planes. Add to that the number of aircraft heavily damaged and requiring a rebuild in the German factories, and the total aircraft lost amounted to about one-third of the Luftwaffe's combat forces in the West. However, the Allies had suffered even heavier losses in the air. The French air force had lost 892 aircraft in combat, and the RAF 1,029. The British had made a maximum effort and retained only enough squadrons in Britain to provide the minimum necessary aircraft for home defense. In the battle of France the RAF committed 30 percent of its fighter command to the battle and had lost 446 aircraft in May and June 1940, proportionately heavier losses in pilots and aircraft than the Germans.

Yet, despite the proportionally high losses, much heavier losses for the Luftwaffe than for the army, the Luftwaffe had proven that airpower in the form of close air support and close interdiction could be a decisive factor in enabling victory on the ground. By effectively guarding the flanks of Kleist's panzer group in the race to the sea, von Richthofen had made a revolutionary advance in the conduct of modern warfare. Although the Germans had no decisive advantage on the ground in terms of numbers or tanks, the employment of well-coordinated airpower and mechanized forces proved a combination that the doctrinally backward Allies could not beat.

The campaign of 1940 highlighted other aspects of the Luftwaffe's way of war. The flak corps were highly effective in the campaign, and the army after-action reports noted the important contributions of the large flak units. Massed Luftwaffe flak forces, operating with the forward forces of the army, decimated whole Allied squadrons attacking the crucial bottlenecks at the Maastricht and Sedan bridgeheads in the first four days of the campaign. Throughout the campaign, the Flak Korps I and II shot down 586 allied aircraft and provided superb support in the direct fire mode as they helped destroy Allied fortifications and Allied tanks.[81] The Luftwaffe's 88 mm gun proved its worth as one of the premier antitank weapons of the war, and Luftwaffe flak forces were credited with destroying or disabling 326 Allied tanks.[82] After 1940 the Luftwaffe would create more flak corps; the organizations saw extensive service in Russia, where they excelled in both the antiaircraft and ground support roles.

The most dramatic changes demonstrated in the battle for France were new tactics for the close air support units of the Luftwaffe. General Wolfram von Richthofen proved himself to be the most innovative of the senior air leaders in this regard. Unhappy with the poor communication between Luftwaffe and army in the Polish campaign, he placed his own headquarters adjacent to the army headquarters that he was supporting. When situations arose that required Luftwaffe action, he or his chief of staff could confer with the army commander and chief of staff, make a decision, and send dispatch aircraft to the front lines.[83] In order to get a better picture of the ground situation, von Richthofen put additional Flivo teams into armored cars positioned close to the front lines. Throughout the campaign, the VIIIth Fliegerkorps kept one Stuka group and one Me 109 group for escort available at a forward airfield ready for immediate takeoff. Good reconnaissance, better communications, and close coordination with the army enabled von Richthofen to make quick decisions to employ his forces in close support operations. Once the decision was given, the Stukas, covered by the Me 109s, would be in the

Von Richthofen as General der Flieger, 1940. (U.S. Air Force)

attack within 45–75 minutes. By the standards of 1940, it was remarkably effective close air support.[84]

Because of superior communications, logistics, and ground services, the Luftwaffe fighter, attack, and Stuka units averaged an impressive four to six sorties per day throughout the campaign—and this at a time when French fighters were flying an average of only one sortie per day. The lesson was clear to von Richthofen and the other senior Luftwaffe commanders: good planning and superior logistics and support were the keys to maintaining effective air support in large-scale operations. Yet this operational-level understanding did not translate at the strategic level into any major restructuring of the Luftwaffe or to any significant increase in the Luftwaffe's transport and logistics force. In one sense the Luftwaffe and the Wehrmacht were victims of their success. In 1940 they had created a superb force capable of delivering victory in short, sharp campaigns. With the kind of success achieved in Poland and in France, the senior leadership of the Wehrmacht saw no urgent need to build up the support elements of the force to fight an extended campaign where attrition of aircraft and aircrew would become deciding factors in maintaining air superiority and the ability to deliver close air support. With final victory in sight, Hermann Goering and the Luftwaffe general staff failed to get aircraft production in high gear and failed to significantly increase the aircrew training program. The seeds for the future failure of the Luftwaffe had already been sown.

Von Richthofen, like the other senior officers of the Wehrmacht, remained focused on the operational level of war—on fighting battles and campaigns—and failed to see the structural problems in the Luftwaffe. In a short-sighted manner, no one at the top of the German leadership envisioned the ability of Britain to recover from its defeats and go on to produce an air force larger than Germany's. Nor did the German high command anticipate the enormous aircraft production capability of the Americans and how in the next two years it would play an increasingly larger role in maintaining the British in the air.

Other innovations made themselves felt in the 1940 campaign. In attacks against some of the outlying forts of the Maginot Line at Brisach, Stukas dropped the new 1,000 kg armor-piercing bombs on the French bunkers. These proved fairly effective against even the strongest fortifications. However, despite the major advances of the Luftwaffe there were still many sticky problems of air-ground coordination to be worked out. As in Poland, there were numerous instances of "friendly fire" attacks by Luftwaffe aircraft against German ground troops. One of the most notable instances of this occurred on 14 May, when Stukas of I and II Groups of Stuka Wing 77 attacked the 1st Panzer Division near Sedan in error and inflicted dozens of casualties.[85]

The campaign in France was one of von Richthofen's greatest triumphs. Although he had done some impressive things in the campaign in Poland, he was still a major general and believed that he had not gotten the credit he deserved for his role in the campaign. Hitler and Goering would make up for the lack of personal recognition in Poland with the presentation of the Knight's Cross to von Richthofen on 18 May 1940 for his work in Poland and the first week of the campaign in France. As soon as the campaign in France was finished, a delighted Hitler showered the military leaders with promotions and decorations. The Luftwaffe was given as much recognition as the army for its role in the campaign. Kesselring and Sperrle were both to be promoted to field marshal rank. Promotions flowed down the chain of command. On 19 July von Richthofen was promoted two steps, to the rank of General der Flieger—completely missing the rank of lieutenant general. Spain had made von Richthofen known in Germany, but Poland and France served to make him a leading Luftwaffe hero. There was much of the glory hound in von Richthofen's makeup, and he would soon have the opportunity to add to that glory.

Chapter 8

The Battle of Britain—The Luftwaffe's First Defeat

There was little pause for the Luftwaffe staffs after the surrender of France on 22 June 1940. When Britain rebuffed Hitler's initial offer to make peace on the basis of Britain retaining its empire while Germany controlled Europe, the Wehrmacht began planning for an invasion of Great Britain. Of course, any invasion of Britain would have to be preceded by an air campaign designed to win full control of the air over Britain. Without control of the air, any attack across the English Channel in the face of a Royal Navy that was far superior to Germany's Kriegsmarine would be suicidal for the Germans. But if the Luftwaffe controlled the air over the channel and southern England, the Royal Navy could be held at bay while the German army divisions could be ferried across the twenty miles of sea between the Pas de Calais and Kent. If the German army reached the shore of Britain, it would make quick work of any British forces in its way. During the campaign in France the British government had deployed almost every fully trained and equipped division. Although most of the British Expeditionary Force had escaped at Dunkirk and returned to the U.K., virtually all of the BEF's tanks, artillery pieces, trucks, armored cars, and other equipment had been destroyed or abandoned in France. If the Germans got across the channel, their armored forces could be counted on to make swift work of a disorganized enemy that not only lacked tanks and artillery but was also short of small arms and ammunition.

At that point, the most serious obstacle to the German invasion of Britain was the Royal Air Force, most specifically, the RAF's Fighter Command. This was the only force that could deny the Germans control of the air over southern England and thus make a German invasion impossible. The Luftwaffe had faced the RAF in the skies over France and had been victorious. Since the Luftwaffe had defeated the French, British, Belgian, and Dutch air forces in fairly rapid order in May 1940 and gained the air superiority necessary to carry out the blitzkrieg advance through France, the German leadership assumed that the Luftwaffe could dispose of the RAF in fairly short order.

The Campaign Plan against Britain

In 1938–1939 the Luftwaffe's 2nd Air Fleet, stationed in northern Germany under the command of General Helmuth Felmy, had carried out exercises and war games with a scenario of a strategic attack against England. At that point the Germans were thinking in terms of waging a long-distance campaign against Britain; they did not plan for a campaign with the Luftwaffe based in Belgium and France and able to employ its tactical aircraft. Felmy and his staff examined a number of scenarios, including attacking Britain's urban areas and even terror bombing London. They concluded that a strategic air campaign against Britain would be very difficult with the forces available to the Luftwaffe, that the Britons would not be likely to crack under terror attacks, and that decisive operations from the air would not be likely. Felmy strongly recommended that the Luftwaffe's best strategy would be to concentrate on attacking Britain's maritime traffic, with aerial mining of Britain's sea approaches and attacks on shipping out to sea.[1]

With the beginning of the war and the need to plan for the campaigns against Poland and France the Luftwaffe general staff was overburdened simply to deal with immediate operations and could spare no personnel to develop further plans against Britain. A few small operations against Britain were nonetheless mounted: the Luftwaffe's bomber force executed a surprise raid against the British fleet at Scapa Flow in the fall of 1939, and the naval air arm of the Luftwaffe dropped some mines in the English Channel. But at the moment of France's fall and in the aftermath of Germany's amazing victories in Poland, Norway, and Denmark, then France and the Low Countries, the German leadership in June 1940 suffered from a serious bout of "victory disease." Until the summer of 1940 every campaign had gone well for the Wehrmacht. From a purely logical viewpoint, it made no sense for the British to continue as a combatant power—especially since Hitler offered Britain generous peace terms after the fall of France. Hitler and the German leadership basically expected that Britain would soon accept German terms, which basically allowed Germany to dominate Europe while Britain and its empire remained untouched. The Wehrmacht did not expect another major campaign in 1940, and if one did come, it would certainly result in another resounding German victory.

This overconfidence affected German air force and army planning in the summer of 1940. Goering and most of the Luftwaffe's senior generals had not been impressed with the RAF's performance in France. The desperate and effective fight that the RAF put up to deny the Luftwaffe free use of the air over Dunkirk should have warned the Germans what the British were capable

Newly promoted Milch and von Richthofen in France, preparing for the campaign against Britain, 1940.

of when flying from their home airfields. The performance of the Spitfire fighter—first encountered by the Luftwaffe in the skies over Dunkirk—as well as the competence of the RAF Fighter Command pilots, ought to have alerted the Luftwaffe to the difficulty of the mission. However, the Luftwaffe's intelligence section was surprisingly uninformed about the RAF and blithely assumed that the RAF's fighters were inferior and that the Luftwaffe's battle-tested units could win control of the air over southeastern Britain in three days of solid battle.

More than a few historians have noted that the army planning for the invasion of the U.K. seems to have been especially haphazard. Simply put, the German leadership, both military and civilian, seems to have assumed that a real fight for Britain would not be necessary. As soon as the Luftwaffe drove the RAF from British skies and could guarantee the German army and navy the freedom to cross the English Channel, the British would immediately sue for peace and accept Hitler's offer. This assumption of an easy campaign against Britain would be one of Germany's major strategic mistakes of the war. While Hitler was reluctant to put the German economy on a full war footing, seeing as how unnecessary that would be, the British were mobilizing every resource within Britain and the considerable manpower and economic resources of the empire as well, with the first priority going to aircraft manufacture and flight personnel training. Indeed, in 1940 the British, with a far smaller economy than Germany's, would actually surpass the Third Reich in aircraft production.[2]

Moreover, having decided that air attack would be the only practical means of striking back against Germany for the foreseeable future, Britain and the Commonwealth nations had instituted a huge program (the Commonwealth Air Training Scheme) to train pilots, navigators, gunners, and every type of specialty required by a modern air force. Canada and Australia had schemes underway to produce large numbers of aircraft on their home soil. Moreover, the United States was rearming and would soon be able to supply large quantities of aircraft to Britain. While such measures, except for the expanded single-seat fighter production in the U.K., could do little for Britain's defense in the short term, in the long term Britain would be in a position to challenge the Germans for air superiority over Europe. However, in June 1940 few Germans were thinking about long-term strategy.

Von Richthofen Does Diplomatic Duty

With the fall of France, Hitler looked to Spain to become an active German ally. He assumed that extra pressure on Britain, such as a Spanish attack on Gibraltar, would help force Britain to the peace table and accept a peace that allowed Britain to retain its empire while Germany had a free hand in Europe. Hitler mounted a diplomatic offensive to help convince Spain to formally join the Axis cause. On 24 July, just as the channel battles were in swing, Hitler met with von Richthofen and briefed him on Spain. Hitler was well aware of von Richthofen's good relationship with Franco and the top Spanish generals and was ready to use every means to help convince Spain to enter the war. As a first step, Hitler wanted the British base at Gibraltar taken by Spain, an action that would help push Britain out of the Mediterranean and help Italy. Germany was prepared to offer Spain aid and supplies and perhaps even some of France's territory in North Africa. The exact negotiation points were unclear, but von Richthofen was instructed to travel to Biarritz on the French-Spanish border to meet with his old friend General Juan Vigón, now a member of Franco's cabinet, and sound him out on the possibility of Spain becoming a German ally. At the same time, Hitler was pursuing the Spanish alliance through his foreign ministry and through Italy.[3]

In the middle of an active campaign, von Richthofen left the front and traveled briefly to meet with Vigón on 15 August 1940. It was a cordial meeting. The two had formed a fast friendship during the Spanish Civil War and corresponded regularly (in Spanish). But Vigón, acting per Franco's instructions, was not willing to commit Spain to a major war that would likely prove ruinous. Vigón expressed admiration for Germany and for the recent German victories and expressed the hope that Germany would continue with its success. However, he pointed out that Spain was in an economically weak position after the civil war and would need a large amount of supplies and support. When Hitler met with Franco that summer it was much the same story: Franco expressed his hope for German victory and appeared willing to join the conflict as Germany's formal ally, then proceeded to demand a huge amount of aid and military support as necessary to come into the war—knowing well that the support demanded was more than Germany was willing or able to pay.[4] Von Richthofen met with Vigón again on 9 September 1940 to further discuss the aid that Germany might provide to Spain.[5] The Spanish were again unwilling to commit to a war that might prove ruinous for Spain. Von Richthofen's meetings with the Spaniards were only part of a larger diplomatic attempt to get Spain into the war. The German foreign ministry was working all out on the issue, and Hitler was even going through the Italians to put alliance proposals through to Spain.

The Opposing Forces

The RAF had been a tough opponent in the skies over France, but it had fought with many disadvantages and had been generally outclassed by the Luftwaffe. However, on its home turf the RAF—especially the RAF's Fighter Command, charged with the air defense of Great Britain—was better prepared for the coming campaign than was Goering's Luftwaffe. For one thing, the RAF in France had been far from its repair and logistics system and had suffered from continual maintenance and supply problems. In France the RAF fighters had operated from ill-prepared airfields, many of them so wet and poorly laid out that they were barely useable. RAF and Allied air communications in northern France had not functioned well, and the French and British air forces had lacked radar, which left Allied airfields open to surprise attacks by the Luftwaffe.

While the RAF in 1939–1940 had been poorly prepared for an expeditionary type of war in which it would have to send air forces abroad, on its home territory the RAF would be able to fight the kind of battle it had carefully prepared for since the end of World War I. Although the Fighter Command had officially been formed only in 1935, it had carefully built upon the excellent air defense organization that had been created to defend Britain from

German air attack during World War I. This system was maintained and developed throughout the 1920s and 1930s. In 1918 the RAF observer and communications system could identify German raids coming over the English Channel and put British fighters on an interception course within five minutes of a sighting. But the problem in 1918 was the lack of radios in the fighters. Once airborne, fighter aircraft were unable to receive any further information from the ground controllers. In contrast, in 1940 the RAF Fighter Command had not only radios but also a chain of radars that could identify approaching aircraft. Backing up the early warning system was an extensive communications network that was tied in ground-based antiaircraft artillery, and an observer corps of trained civilians that watched the skies and reported on all movements. Fighter units were organized into groups, wings, and sectors, and all were controlled by sector and group command centers. Once enemy aircraft were spotted, RAF fighters could again be dispatched in less than five minutes to intercept. Each aircraft had radio contact with its sector station and was given constant updates on enemy numbers, altitude, and course heading changes in order to effectively manage an intercept.

From the end of World War I to the mid-1930s the RAF conducted regular air defense exercises to test and improve the island's aerial defense system. By the mid-1930s the RAF had developed the most comprehensive and effective air defense system in the world. The addition of the radar system in 1938–1939 made a very good system even better. Although the radar system in place at the start of the war was fairly primitive, it could still give warning of German aircraft 50–70 miles distant and provide information on the speed and direction of the enemy aircraft. With this advance warning, RAF Fighter Command could send up squadrons to intercept attackers and order other squadrons to a higher state of readiness. Radar, coupled with a centralized command and control system, basically doubled the effectiveness of the RAF fighters.[6]

The Luftwaffe's greatest disadvantage was the lack of information about the RAF defenses it was about to attack. There were many weaknesses in the RAF defense system and tactics, but the Luftwaffe intelligence on the U.K. was so poor that the Germans were unable to exploit these weaknesses. One of the consequences of poor intelligence was an attitude of overconfidence on the Luftwaffe's part. The German intelligence picture was not due solely to incompetence on the part of the Luftwaffe's intelligence staff, but rather to Hitler's insistence through most of the 1930s that Germany would not have to fight the British in any war for the domination of Europe. In the summer of 1940 Hitler became a victim of his own strategic worldview. Partly on the grounds that the English shared the same racial heritage as Germans, and partly because of Hitler's admiration of the British Empire, Hitler believed that the natural destiny of Great Britain was to become an ally of a revitalized Germany. He ignored British protests against Nazi rearmament measures in the early 1930s and perceived Prime Minister Neville Chamberlain's attitude of appeasement as a sure indication that Britain intended to remain on the sidelines in case of any future conflict. Therefore, while Germany prepared intensely for war against Poland, Czechoslovakia, and France, the collection of information about Britain's military and war industries had a low priority for the Luftwaffe and other intelligence services.

Only in 1938, when Britain's hostility to German plans became obvious even to Hitler and Britain's rearmament program had entered high gear, did Hitler come to the belated recognition that he might have to fight Britain after all. In April 1938 Hitler directed the Wehrmacht high command to consider Britain a potential enemy, and to add the British to Germany's war-planning scenarios. However, developing a comprehensive intelligence collection program against a major power—an intelligence program that included espionage, signals intelligence, economic intelligence, and military information—takes even a first-rate intelligence organization a long time to organize. Even if Germany had possessed a well-organized intelligence system—and it did not—a year and a half was not enough time to develop anything more than the most superficial understanding of British capabilities and defenses.

France, Czechoslovakia, and Poland had always been considered probable enemies of Germany, so the Wehrmacht and Luftwaffe had developed a fairly accurate assessment of the armed forces of those nations. When Germany had attacked Poland and France it had a good picture of the enemy air force dispositions and their air defense systems. In contrast, with little more than a year to collect and analyze information on the RAF, the Luftwaffe had a very inaccurate picture of RAF capabilities and order of battle. It also had little understanding of the capability of British industry to manufacture aircraft.[7] Indeed, some of the intelligence omissions were glaring. In the spring of 1940, Luftwaffe intelligence estimates insisted that British Hurricane and Spitfire fighters were greatly inferior to the Luftwaffe's Me 109s and Me 110s. As late as mid-July 1940, the Luftwaffe's general staff published intelligence reports that did not mention British radar. An example of the Luftwaffe's intelligence weakness is its understanding of the RAF Fighter Command's deployment. The Luftwaffe knew the locations of the major British airfields but was unsure of which ones belonged to the Fighter Command and which ones to the coastal, training, and bomber commands. This lack of intelligence meant that the attacking force wasted a great deal of its effort on targets of little to no operational importance, such as Coastal Command airfields. Although such attacks inflicted losses upon the RAF, they also acted as a diversion from the real target—the RAF's Fighter Command.

The Germans could not help but notice the existence of a British radar system, as the main radar stations were mounted in tall aerial masts spaced regularly along the coast. However, Luftwaffe intelligence had little understanding of the capabilities of the British radar, or of its vulnerabilities that could be exploited. The Luftwaffe mistakenly believed that the very flexible British fighter control system was a rigid system that bound each squadron to defending the airspace over its own base. Nor did the Germans understand the aircraft control system, and the sector and group organization, all of which allowed the RAF to quickly shift fighter squadrons from one sector to another. In short, the Luftwaffe was about to engage the best air defense system in the world with little knowledge of how that system worked. Given this lack of intelligence, it is surprising that the Luftwaffe did as well against the RAF as it did.

Through June and July 1940 the RAF worked to rebuild its fighter squadrons that had been badly battered in France. In contrast to the poor support system the RAF had in the battle for France, on home turf the RAF had a superb repair and maintenance system that ensured a high aircraft serviceability rate. Throughout the Battle of Britain the serviceability rate for the RAF's fighters stayed in the 80–90 percent range while the Luftwaffe's serviceability rates were considerably lower, in the 65–80 percent range. The Luftwaffe did not have an extensive forward depot system that could carry out major repairs on aircraft; this would remain a major problem throughout the war. During the 1930s, Ernst Udet had proposed one of his few good ideas during his five-year tenure as chief of the Luftwaffe's Technical Office. He advocated that the Luftwaffe create a forward depot system that would give the air fleets the capability to conduct major repairs, engine rebuilds, and complete overhauls of aircraft close behind the front lines. Such a system would have served to keep the unit operational rates at a high level for an extended campaign. Unfortunately for the Luftwaffe, Hermann Goering and Erhard Milch rejected the proposal as too expensive. Hitler, Goering, and the Wehrmacht high command counted on fighting short, sharp campaigns so that any elaborate frontline repair capability would not be necessary. This meant that the Luftwaffe would go into all of its campaigns with just unit-level maintenance. If an aircraft were severely damaged, it would be sent by rail back to the factory in Germany to be rebuilt. Although this could be seen as a good cost-saving measure, the Luftwaffe repair process was a slow one. If a campaign lasted for any length of time, the Luftwaffe's frontline maintenance and repair organizations would quickly become overloaded, and units at the front would be short of aircraft.

The Luftwaffe's weak repair system was a serious operational weakness in the Battle of Britain, and throughout the campaign the Luftwaffe's operational rates were far lower than those of the RAF. In the summer of 1940 the RAF repair system and British aircraft factories could return aircraft that were virtually shot to pieces back to duty in a matter of days. Lord Beaverbrook, appointed minister for aircraft production by Prime Minister Winston Churchill on 14 May, also took emergency steps to increase the production of single-engine fighters. The manufacture of Hurricanes and Spitfires dramatically exceeded production goals in the summer of 1940—and considerably exceeded the production rate of Germany's Me 109 fighters. Throughout the campaign the RAF Fighter Command had more than 700 operational fighters to face the German threat. Its most serious problem thus was a shortage not of aircraft, but of trained pilots. A year or two was needed to train a fighter pilot to the point where he was effective in combat, and Britain had just begun a large-scale program to train fighter pilots. It would be a year before the RAF could count on having enough trained pilots available to replace heavy combat losses. The RAF carried out some expedients, such as sending pilots from the Coastal and Bomber commands through short fighter courses, but hastily trained fighter pilots were of marginal value in battle. The burden of Britain's defense rested on a small cadre of a few hundred experienced fighter pilots, a group that had just taken heavy losses in France. In short, the RAF's center of gravity lay not with its airplanes but with its pilots.

Going into the campaign the Luftwaffe had a larger reserve of airplanes and a larger number of pilots. However, a careful look at the figures shows that the German advantage was marginal. Germany had plenty of excellent medium and light bombers such as the He 111, Ju 88, and Do 17. But German bombers had very light defensive armament—usually three machine guns on the He 111—and they were easy prey for enemy fighters unless they were strongly escorted by German fighters. Thus, the ability of the German bombers to do their mission was limited to the effectiveness of the German fighter escort. The escort requirement for Stukas was even more pronounced. The Stukas, which were slow and had little defensive armament, were easy prey for any Allied fighter unless well protected by German fighters. The Luftwaffe air fleets attacking Britain (the 2nd, 3rd, and 5th) had an advantage in fighters—but not a decisive advantage. The Me 110, of which the Luftwaffe had 246 to employ in the battle, was a fine reconnaissance plane and a very effective fighter-bomber. It would later prove to be an excellent night fighter. But

An Me 110 over England, summer 1940. The Me 110 was a fine airplane in several roles, but it did not match up to the RAF's Spitfires or Hurricanes. Like the Stuka, the Me 110 was eventually pulled from operations over Britain. (*Signal*, October 1940)

the Luftwaffe would quickly learn that it could not hold its own in a dogfight with the more maneuverable Spitfires and Hurricanes.

The Luftwaffe would not only face a first-rate organization but for the first time in the war would be up against enemy air force commanders fully equal to the Luftwaffe's air fleet and air corps commanders. Commanding the RAF Fighter Command and the chief of Britain's air defenses in 1940 was Hugh Dowding. A pilot veteran of World War I, Dowding was fifty-eight years old and slated for retirement. He had headed the Fighter Command since its formation in July 1936 and was one of the most scientifically minded officers in the RAF. Dowding had overseen the introduction of radar into Britain's air defense system and had succeeded in developing the best air defense command and control system in the world. On the negative side, Dowding was somewhat worn out and was rigid in his approach to tactics, insisting that the RAF fighter squadrons adhere strictly to complicated squadron tactics based on groups of three airplanes even as the Germans in the Spanish Civil War had proven the superiority of flying in pairs and groups of pairs.

The man whose forces would bear the brunt of the battle over England was Air Chief Marshal Keith Parks, commander of 11 Group. He was an experienced airman who had served as a fighter pilot in World War I. He was a calm and knowledgeable commander and highly respected by his subordinates. Commander of 12 Group, Air Marshal Trafford Leigh-Mallory, was also an experienced commander. Mallory had a first-rate understanding of fighter tactics, and he pushed for changes in the RAF Fighter Command's operational method. His views and manner put him in conflict with Dowding, but his squadron commanders and pilots respected him. Although personality clashes existed, the RAF was lucky to have such competent leaders holding the Fighter Command senior posts.[8]

The campaign against Britain in 1940 illustrated the problem of having Hermann Goering as the Luftwaffe's supreme commander. Goering was usually absent from the front and preferred to remain at his grand estate, Karinhall, during the aerial battles of July and early August. He made little attempt to coordinate the efforts of the two air fleets. When he did get around to visiting his air fleets he offered no constructive advice, but instead directed a stream of abuse at the Luftwaffe commanders and pilots when things did not go according to plan. When the battle went against his pilots in September 1940, he again railed against them and accused them of cowardice. This was Goering's consistent behavior throughout the war during each crisis. In most respects, it would be hard to find a worse air force commander.

At the level of squadron and wing commander, both the RAF Fighter Command and the Luftwaffe had a cadre of experienced and capable leaders who had already proven themselves in combat. In both forces, there was a tradition that fighter unit commanders led by example and flew combat missions with their men. Fighter unit leaders who were not aggressive and tactically competent were soon relieved and replaced by pilots who had demonstrated skill in combat. It was also a highly individualistic form of fighting, in which aircraft would pair off in single combat dogfights and the pilot with the better skill, marksmanship, and nerves would emerge the victor. In the Battle of Britain, and in aerial combat in World War II, the majority of kills in air-to-air combat on both sides were made by a small number of aces who had special and indefinable qualities of piloting, marksmanship, and hunting skill. For example, Major Adolf Galland, commander of the top-scoring Luftwaffe Fighter Wing 26, shot down an astonishing 14 percent of the total kills of his unit of 120 pilots.

VIIIth Air Corps' Role in the Campaign

The primary German air forces arrayed against England were the 2nd Air Fleet, based at Pas de Calais, and the 3rd Air Fleet, based on the Cherbourg peninsula. In early July 1940 the two air fleets had a strike force of 1,131 medium bombers and 316 Ju 87 dive-bombers, supported by 150 reconnaissance aircraft. The 5th Air Fleet, based in Norway and Denmark, could employ 130 bombers and 35 long-range Me 110 fighters against targets in northern England. However, the primary focus of the German effort would be against southern England. Covering the bombers of the 2nd and 3rd Air Fleets were 246 Me 110 heavy fighters and 809 Me 109E single-engine fighters. To defend Britain, the RAF Fighter Command in July 1940 could field a force of 700 Hurricane and Spitfire fighters as well as some Defiant two-seat fighters. As the air campaign heated up in early July, Fighter Command had nineteen Spitfire squadrons and twenty-two Hurricane squadrons operational. Ten additional squadrons were in the process of forming or being rebuilt and could be deployed to relieve squadrons decimated in battle. The RAF Bomber Command's forces were held back out of easy range of German attacks and were ready to be employed in a last-ditch effort to attack German land and sea forces if the invasion came.

On 30 June, Goering issued the 2nd and 3rd Air Fleets' preparatory orders for the air campaign over Britain; on 2 July the air fleets and air corps issued detailed instructions to their subordinate units.[9] The Luftwaffe's 2nd and 3rd Air Fleets would be reorganized and relocated to conduct the campaign against Great Britain. Because of the short range of the fighters, most of the Luftwaffe's Me 109 wings were moved to the Pas de Calais area, where they were only a few minutes' flight time over the channel to southeast England. The Luftwaffe's bomber units, all of which had plenty of range to hit targets in southern England, were stationed in central France or in the Normandy region. The VIIIth Air Corps, assigned to the 3rd Air Fleet under Field Marshal Sperrle, was stationed on airfields in the area of Normandy. The fighters were located on airfields near Cherbourg, and the Stukas were in the vicinity of Le Havre. Von Richthofen placed his fighter headquarters at Deauville near Caen, and the air corps headquarters was located just outside of Le Havre. All the bombers were taken from VIIIth Air Corps; what remained was a specialist force consisting of about 180 Stukas supported by some fighters and some Do 17s and Ju 88s for long-range reconnaissance.

Late June and July was a hectic period for the officers and men of the VIIIth Air Corps. The two air fleets in France were in the process of reorganizing their forces. Aircraft were repaired, and replacement aircraft and pilots flowed from the depots and factories in Germany. The 2nd and 3rd Air Fleets had lost over 20 percent of their total force in the May and June fighting and needed several weeks to get their forces in order. Fuel and munitions had to be moved forward, and the captured French airfields had to be improved by the Luftwaffe's field engineer units. Logistics was simplified as the French rail network, damaged in the spring campaign, was put back in order.

Establishing air superiority over the English Channel and attacking British ports were the first steps in preparation for the sea invasion of Britain. The most important task of the Luftwaffe was to destroy the RAF Fighter Command and win air superiority over southern England. The Luftwaffe would break the RAF through a series of massive attacks to destroy Fighter Command aircraft on the ground and wreck its bases. With the Luftwaffe's superiority in numbers (although not nearly as much as the Luftwaffe imagined) and belief that its aircraft were superior (which was not true), the Luftwaffe high command expected the RAF to be broken in three days. After that, the Luftwaffe would concentrate on attacking British military installations across southern England and crippling the British transportation network as final preparations for landing the German army on England's southern coast.

In June and July 1940 there were several large staff meetings of the senior Luftwaffe commanders in Berlin, and meetings of the 3rd Air Fleet senior officers and staffs in Paris to finalize plans for the air campaign against Britain. Milch, state secretary for aviation and Goering's top deputy, and Jeschonnek, Luftwaffe chief of staff, were present to review the issues. At one of the staff meetings, von Richthofen opened the proceedings with a somewhat pedantic lecture about the need to establish air superiority over Britain, with the best means using von Richthofen's Stukas against the British airfields—the same methods that he had used against the Belgian and French air forces. The account that von Richthofen had a pedantic teaching style at staff meetings is entirely in character, especially if there were senior army generals at the meeting. Von Richthofen considered the army generals as a group to be hopelessly ignorant of airpower theory and practice, and he took every opportunity to educate them about the proper use of airpower.

Unlike the other campaigns in which von Richthofen had participated, the first part of the campaign against Great Britain would only include air forces. Indeed, if the campaign went as the Germans hoped, once the Luftwaffe had gained air superiority over Britain the British would likely sue for peace even before German ground troops invaded. In contrast with the previous campaigns, the air division and air corps commanders would have little to do. Instead, directives came from the Luftwaffe general staff in Berlin and from the air fleets that specified the targets and missions every day. The Luftwaffe high command coordinated the efforts of the air fleets attacking Britain, and unit attack orders and target lists flowed straight from the air fleets to the wings and groups. Air division and corps commanders such as von Richthofen could influence the course of the battle in commanders' conferences, but they had little to do with the day-to-day development of the campaign.

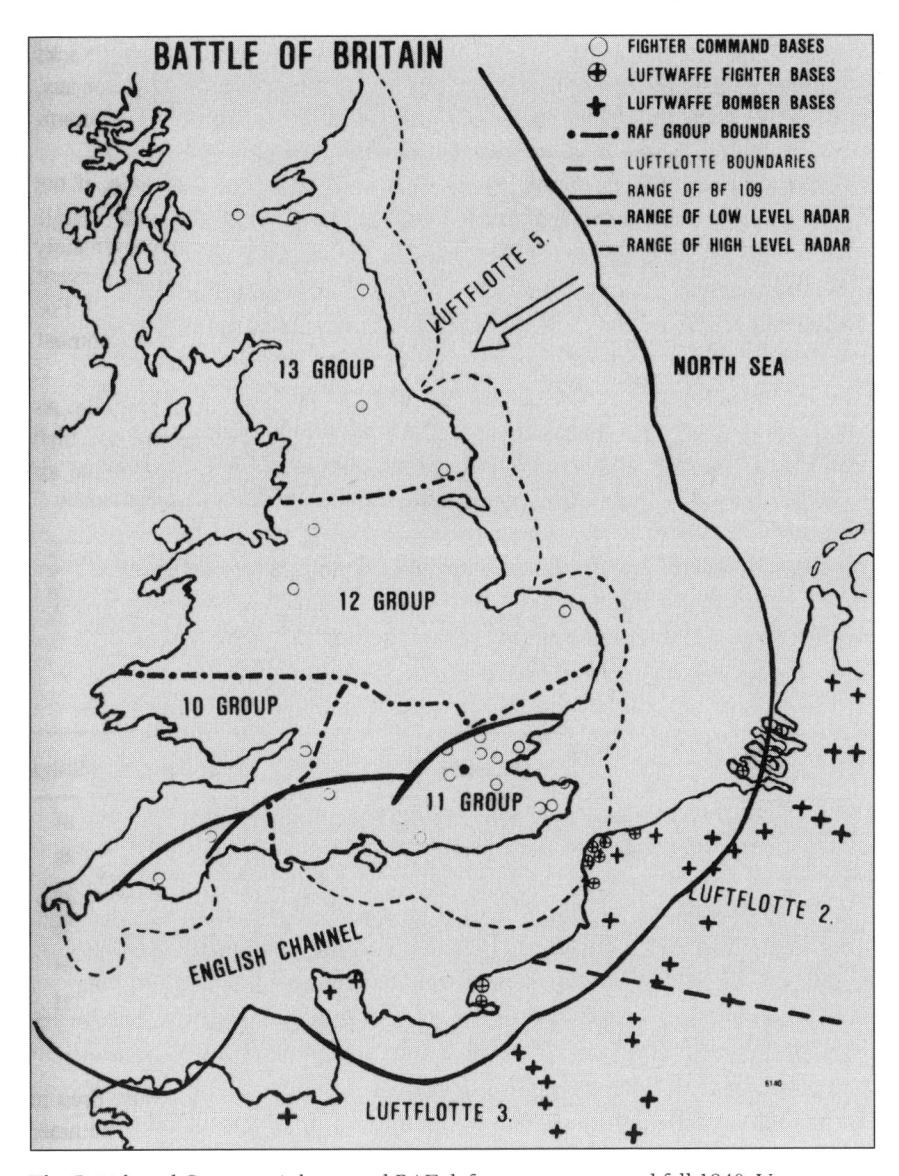

The British and German air bases and RAF defenses, summer and fall 1940. Von Richthofen's VIIIth Air Corps was stationed on the Normandy coast. (Williamson Murray, *Strategy for Defeat: The Luftwaffe 1933–1945* [Maxwell AFB: Air University Press, 1983])

With little decision-making or combat leadership required on his part, von Richthofen took some time out to rest and relax during the air campaign against Great Britain. In behavior that was typical of his love of the outdoors, he explored several golf courses that had been built in the Normandy region. It is unlikely that von Richthofen had more than a minimal acquaintance with the sport, as Germans in his era, even upper-class Germans, rarely played, and there were few golf courses in Germany. However, he apparently took up golf in the summer of 1940 (there is no mention of the sport in any earlier letters or diary entries), and his diary entries note that he played regularly on the Normandy courses when the weather cooperated. By his own admission, von Richthofen was "an awful player," but he seems to have enjoyed the sport nonetheless. While flying to commanders' conferences in the Pas de Calais he also had a habit of flying low over the French forests in order to check out the hunting possibilities, especially for deer and wild boar. He took note of specific locations for later hunting trips. In the evenings he watched films with his immediate staff, played cards, and caught up with his letter writing. Von Richthofen and his staff amused themselves by driving a captured new Hudson automobile, one of the first cars to be built with an automatic transmission. Not as visionary about automobile technology as with airplanes, von Richthofen thought the American transmission to be "a very strange arrangement."

The VIIIth Air Corps in the Channel Battles, 4 July–10 August

Because of their precision, the Stukas were the Luftwaffe's best antishipping weapon in 1940. To attack ships the Stukas could carry a 1,100-pound bomb; one direct hit would sink a merchant ship or a destroyer and was capable of inflicting severe damage on any larger armored warships. The VIIIth Air Corps' specific mission was to establish air superiority over the southern part of the English Channel and to clear British shipping in the area between Portsmouth and Portland.[10] In this phase of the campaign the RAF held few advantages. RAF radar could not pick up the German aircraft early enough to enable the RAF fighters to mount effective intercepts of the Germans. Both British and the German fighters would fly at the far limits of their range over the English Channel. With a limited number of planes and with limited range, the Fighter Command's 11 Group was unable to keep standing patrols over shipping convoys. Over the channel, it was the Luftwaffe that had the initiative as the Germans could concentrate their forces and pick their targets.

Historians mark the "official" beginning of the Battle of Britain as 10 July, when the Luftwaffe's 2nd and 3rd Air Fleets began a systematic campaign to gain air superiority over the channel and to drive shipping out of the British channel ports. In fact, von Richthofen's VIIIth Air Corps began its part of the battle with an attack by 33 Stukas on British convoy OA178 in the waters off Portland on 4 July.[11] As was characteristic throughout this stage of the battle, German pilots reported tremendous success and the virtual destruction of the whole convoy.[12] In fact, the Luftwaffe wildly overestimated the damage it inflicted upon British shipping. The British reported that some small coasting vessels had been sunk or damaged.[13] In the eyes of a Stuka pilot, a small coastal freighter of 2,000 tons became a large merchantman, destroyers were reported as cruisers, and damage that might leave a ship limping was reported as a definite sinking.

The attacks on British ports and shipping by the VIIIth Air Corps steadily increased throughout July. On 10 July, von Richthofen's air units bombed the Portsmouth harbor; on 13 July, convoys off Harwich and Portland were attacked; and on 16 July, convoys off the south coast of England were bombed. On 19 July the Stukas attacked targets at Plymouth and off the Isle of Wight.[14] On 20 July the Stukas, escorted by Me 109 fighters, attacked a convoy near Jersey; British fighters from No. 501 Squadron, based in Hampshire, rose to intercept and were roughly handled by the German fighters.[15]

The VIIIth Air Fleet used its Do 17 long-range reconnaissance aircraft to locate British convoys off the south coast, and when informed of the convoy composition and direction, von Richthofen's headquarters would dispatch Stukas with fighter escort to attack. Normally von Richthofen sent a full group of Stukas to attack a convoy and held other groups in reserve for repeat attacks. Throughout July the VIIIth Air Corps carried out its daily reconnaissance to spot ship convoys and set up attacks. The weather, however, was not very cooperative. Days of fog and rain over the channel and south coast kept the VIIIth Air Corps on the ground for much of the campaign. When weather permitted, German bombers, protected by strong fighter cover, flew over the channel to attack coastal convoys and ports. RAF fighters from 11 Group rose to meet the challenge, and numerous large-scale air battles took place. In one major battle on 25 July, 2nd Air Fleet units intercepted a British convoy and sank eight merchant ships and damaged several others, including two Royal Navy destroyers. In these battles, the Ju 87 dive bombers and Me 110s (acting as fighter bombers) proved effective in conducting accurate attacks on shipping, but they also proved to be vulnerable to any British fighters that could get past the Me 109 escorts.

By 24 July the Luftwaffe's 2nd Air Fleet was even attacking convoys in the Thames estuary. On that day the VIIIth Air Corps carried out attacks on shipping near the Isle of Wight and sank three merchant ships for the loss of two aircraft shot down near Portland. On 27 July the VIIIth Air Corps had an exceptionally busy day: a convoy off the south coast was attacked, and German bombers sank a Royal Navy destroyer. Von Richthofen's planes operated off of Wick and Plymouth and laid mines off the Portland channel.[16] In July and early August the IInd Air Corps battle group in Calais and the VIIIth Air Corps in the south attacked twenty-six convoys in the English Channel.[17] By the end of July, twenty-five merchant ships of 50,528 gross tons had been sunk in home waters. In reality, these figures were far less than the Luftwaffe believed them to be, but they were still a sharp blow to the British.[18] The channel attacks continued into early August as the Luftwaffe prepared for the great strike against the RAF's Fighter Command. On 8 August, Channel Convoy CW 9 was attacked by von Richthofen's Stukas, which damaged several ships and sank three merchant ships. The latter ships represented 3,581 gross tons lost to the British; von Richthofen's pilots, with their usual exuberance, reported 48,500 tons of shipping sent to the bottom.[19]

By early August, German air attacks had forced the Royal Navy to abandon Dover as an advance base, and the Luftwaffe began to attack Britain's major south-coast ports. The RAF Fighter Command responded with a major effort to protect Britain's shipping, and on 30 July the RAF flew 688 sorties over the channel. During July both sides had a taste of the intensity of the battle that was to come. That month, with most of the action in the last two weeks, the British lost 145 fighters and the Germans lost 270 planes of all types over the channel. British shipping had been hurt and four Royal Navy destroyers sunk as well.[20] Victory for the battle's first round can be given to the Luftwaffe, for on 11 August the Royal Navy temporarily suspended ship traffic in the English Channel.[21]

The fight over the channel exposed some weaknesses of the RAF. Although the radar system enabled the Fighter Command to intercept German attacks, the British response was usually too slow to effectively cover the convoys, and British fighters were forced to operate at the limit of their effective range. Another weakness was the Boulton Paul Defiant, the command's heavy fighter, which turned out to be hopelessly outclassed by the Me 109. This was dramatically demonstrated on 19 July when nine Defiants of 141 Squadron flew into battle, only to lose six of their number to Me 109s in a few minutes. RAF Fighter Command pulled the Defiants out of the battle. One advantage of the Luftwaffe's was its efficient air/sea rescue service. Specially equipped He 59 seaplanes were on hand to land in the channel to recover Luftwaffe crewmen who had to bail out or ditch their aircraft at sea. The British had no such rescue service for their pilots. This meant that Germans shot down over the English Channel had a high chance of surviving and fighting again, whereas RAF pilots in similar circumstances were not likely to survive.

Even so, Luftwaffe intelligence was still largely in the dark about British strength. Luftwaffe units consistently claimed three times the number of British planes shot down as were actually lost (the RAF claims were about two to one), so as Eagle Day approached, the Luftwaffe wrongly believed that the RAF had already been seriously weakened.

Von Richthofen was in an exuberant mood because on 17 July, General Korten, chief of staff of the 3rd Air Fleet, told him that he was to be promoted to General der Flieger. At the same time, Hitler would be promoting von Richthofen's boss, General Hugo Sperrle, to the rank of field marshal. Korten quoted Hitler as saying that "the Luftwaffe should also have their own field marshals."[22] For the senior Luftwaffe officers, 1940 was a heady moment, as they had now reached the point where they were seen as a service equal to the army.

The Attack on Fighter Command

On 2 August the Luftwaffe high command finalized its orders for a brief campaign to destroy the RAF Fighter Command with massive strikes directed at airfields across southern Britain.[23] On 6 August the senior Luftwaffe commanders—including Kesselring, Stumpf, and Sperrle—met with Goering at his rural retreat at Karinhall. The final discussions and briefings were made for "Adlertag" (Eagle Day), which the Germans saw as the decisive battle for air superiority that would make the land invasion of Britain possible. In any case, the Luftwaffe had to win control of the air over southern England by late September, when shorter days and worse weather would postpone any chance for an invasion for months. Weather permitting, Eagle Day was set for 10 August.[24] The Luftwaffe, having been victorious in earlier campaigns, was afflicted with overconfidence, and Goering boasted that the Luftwaffe would defeat the RAF in days. After defeating the RAF, the Luftwaffe would pulverize British military installations across southern England in preparation for the land invasion.

On 12 August the Luftwaffe switched its targeting from ports and sea traffic to the RAF Fighter Command. The Luftwaffe had observed the use of radar by the British throughout the July battles, and it set out to destroy every RAF radar station between Portland and the Thames estuary in order to open up RAF airfields and vital industrial targets to attack by Luftwaffe bombers.

Me 110s serving as fighter-bombers and the Stukas from the 2nd Air Corps battle group bombed the Dover, Pevensey, and Rye radar stations and inflicted heavy damage. VIIIth Air Corps Stukas attacked the Ventnor radar station later in the day and knocked it out completely. The Observer Corps and other radar stations were able to take up some of the coverage for the damaged stations, and the RAF worked frantically to repair radar sites and rush mobile stations to the coast. The Luftwaffe had struck the most vulnerable element of the British air defense. Although British efforts to get radar coverage back on line were successful, sustained attacks on the stations would have left the British warning system in shambles. The Fighter Command's effectiveness would have been about halved, as the Observer Corps could have only provided warning once German aircraft were actually over England. Because the RAF radar system still basically functioned at the end of the day, the Luftwaffe gave the radar system a lower priority in the attack plans. It was one of the great miscalculations of the battle.

That day also saw attacks on Fighter Command airfields. Manston, Lympne, and Hawkinge airfields were heavily damaged by Luftwaffe raids. By day's end the Luftwaffe had lost thirty-six aircraft with fifteen badly damaged, and the RAF lost twenty-seven fighters with sixteen badly damaged. Even worse than the aircraft losses for the RAF was the loss of twenty-six pilots, a loss rate that the command could not sustain for long. The opening of the battle for aerial superiority had generally gone favorably for the Luftwaffe.

Heavy fighting continued on 13 August with 1,485 sorties against Britain, but the Luftwaffe made a mistake in not maintaining its previous level of attacks on the RAF radar system. The main effort that day was against the RAF bases and the Royal Navy bases at Portland and Southampton, hit hard by von Richthofen's Stukas. But one Stuka unit lost several aircraft when the Spitfires of RAF No. 609 Squadron got past the escorts and sent several Stukas down in flames.[25] The most notable event of the day was the disastrous attack of the 5th Air Fleet bombers against northern England. Without inflicting any notable damage, the fleet lost 24 of 149 attacking planes. This unacceptable loss rate ended any further participation of the 5th Air Fleet in the Battle of Britain.

As intense as they were, the operations of 12 and 13 August were essentially seen by the Luftwaffe as preparations for Adlertag, now set for 15 August. It was the beginning of an all-out aerial offensive against the Fighter Command's airfields in 11 Group's sector; between 12 and 18 August, thirty-four RAF airfields would be attacked. On 15 August the Luftwaffe flew 2,199 sorties to the RAF Fighter Command's 974. In a series of attacks by Stukas and by bombers flying at low level, several Fighter Command airfields were badly damaged. But RAF resistance had been ferocious. The Luftwaffe lost 75 planes that day (the RAF claimed 182) while the British lost 34 planes (the Luftwaffe claimed 87 fighters and 14 other aircraft).[26]

The day after Adlertag, the Luftwaffe general staff issued its summary of the condition of the RAF. The Luftwaffe claimed that since 1 July it had destroyed 572 RAF fighter planes, including 372 Spitfires. At this point, Hans Jeschonnek believed that the RAF Fighter Command possessed only 300 serviceable aircraft.[27] In fact, despite its losses the command was still in good shape, with over 700 operational aircraft.[28] Indeed, despite wildly optimistic Luftwaffe intelligence reports, at no point in the battle did the RAF fighter strength fall below 700 aircraft. However, despite the successes of the Luftwaffe, some obvious problems were evident. The Me 110s and Ju 87s were seen as extremely vulnerable to enemy fighters on the occasions when RAF fighters had gotten through the Luftwaffe's fighter escorts. Stuka losses so alarmed the Luftwaffe high command that on 15 August, Goering issued a directive that future Stuka attacks should be carried out with a ratio of three escort fighters for every Stuka.[29] Another day of heavy combat occurred on 16 August, with 1,715 Luftwaffe sorties over Britain. It was also a day of heavy casualties for the Luftwaffe, with the loss of forty-five aircraft. That day the RAF lost twenty-two fighters.[30]

Due to inclement weather there was little activity on 17 August, but 18 August would see heavy aerial fighting and be the most fateful day for von Richthofen's Stukas over England. Along with Stuka Geschwader 77 and Group I of Stuka Geschwader 3, his Stukas were detailed to attack airfields and radar stations in southern England. In the afternoon, 111 Stukas, heavily escorted by Me 109s, targeted airfields at Ford, Thorney Island, and Gosport. Some of von Richthofen's attacks were quite successful. Gosport airfield was heavily damaged, and no Stukas were lost. Ford airfield was also torn up by von Richthofen's attackers before British fighters could intervene. At that field, thirteen planes were destroyed on the ground and a further twenty-six damaged and the hangars all wrecked. The destruction of an airfield and loss of thirty-nine aircraft would have been a notable triumph in most circumstances—but Ford airfield was an installation of the Royal Navy Fleet Air Arm, and no fighter planes were based there. Thanks to poor Luftwaffe intelligence that listed Ford airfield as a Fighter Command base, a major effort had been made upon a target that was irrelevant to the outcome of the battle.[31]

The worst damage inflicted by the VIIIth Air Corps that day was the attack on the Poling radar station, where the Stukas again proved their worth as a means of precision bombing. The radar installation was hit by ninety bombs and so completely destroyed that it was out of action until the end of August.[32]

But the VIIIth Air Corps' luck could not hold. At Thorney Island, Group I of Stuka Geschwader 77 met up with RAF No. 43 and 152 Squadrons just when the British fighters were in a perfect intercept position. In moments the group was cut to pieces—in von Richthofen's words the group was "virtually exterminated."[33] Of Group I's twenty-eight aircraft, twelve were shot down outright and six were so badly damaged that they had to be scrapped. Stuka units had also taken a beating elsewhere with a further twelve either shot down or so badly damaged as to be written off. Losing more than 10 percent of the available Stuka forces in one day was too much for the Luftwaffe and the air fleets, and the decision was made to pull the Ju 87s out of the battle.[34]

End of the Battle

In the battle on 18 August the Luftwaffe lost thirty-five bombers and twenty-seven fighters; the RAF had lost forty-five fighters that day (ten of those were destroyed on the ground). As usual the Luftwaffe overclaimed and reported 142 British fighters destroyed.[35] Despite the loss of the Stukas and the restrictions put on the employment of the Me 110—which had proved it could not win in a dogfight with the more nimble Hurricanes and Spitfires—it looked like the Luftwaffe's plan was working and that the RAF Fighter Command would soon be knocked out of the air. The campaign against the British airfields continued, and by early September both the Luftwaffe and RAF had taken heavy losses. From 26 August to 6 September, the Luftwaffe lost a total of 322 planes, mostly bombers, while the RAF lost 248 fighters.

In early September the Luftwaffe changed its strategy again. Luftwaffe intelligence incorrectly reported that the Fighter Command was down to 150–300 fighters, and Goering believed that if London were made the target for German bombers, it would force the command to send up its last reserves. Then the numerically superior Luftwaffe fighters would clear the RAF from the skies. The new German strategy was a disastrous mistake. In attacking London, the Me 109s would be flying at the extreme limit of their fuel endurance and would have fuel for only ten minutes of fighting over the city. Any plane that stayed too long in the battle area was likely to run out of fuel on the way home. By switching the target to London, the Luftwaffe unknowingly gave the badly battered 11 Group a chance to repair its airfields. Since the Luftwaffe was flying relatively deep, 12 Group squadrons had time to form up into wings and fly south to meet Luftwaffe attacks with relatively equal numbers.

The first great attack on London came on 7 September when the Luftwaffe sent 372 bombers covered by 642 fighters to bomb the London docks.

For the next week the Luftwaffe mounted large attacks on the British capital and continued to meet fierce opposition from a Fighter Command that was supposedly on its last legs. En masseive aerial battles on 15 September, the Luftwaffe discovered—to its dismay—that the RAF Fighter Command was by no means a broken organization. That day the Luftwaffe lost fifty-six aircraft to the RAF's twenty-six. For weeks the attrition battle had gone against the Luftwaffe, and now it was clear that the Luftwaffe could not gain air superiority before the fall weather set in. On 17 September, Hitler indefinitely postponed the invasion of Britain.

Last Actions for the VIIIth Air Corps

In October 1940 the British resumed normal ship traffic in the English Channel. The Germans were not going to let this pass, so in October and November von Richthofen's battered Stuka units resumed their antishipping campaign. About 100 sorties were flown in that period, a pale reflection of the more than 100 Stuka sorties a day flown in July. But by this time the RAF Fighter Command was confident and aggressive, and it put up a strong defense against the Stukas. With little hope for success, the Stuka operations of the VIIIth Air Corps were ended by December.[36] Von Richthofen would finally have time for a few weeks of leave and rest at home. The VIIIth Air Corps would replace its planes and pilots and undergo a thorough training program in order to be ready for a resumption of the campaign against Britain in the spring.

Chapter 9

The Balkans Campaign, 1941

By any measure the German-Italian alliance was not a happy partnership. Italy only declared war on the Western Allies on 10 June 1940, when Britain had withdrawn from the continent and the French armies had already suffered catastrophic defeat. Italy joined the war at the time the real fighting was over but just in time to put in a claim for some of France's Mediterranean possessions at the peace settlement. Germany, which would probably have benefited more with Italy as a friendly neutral than as an ally, soon found that an alliance with Italy had a great many disadvantages. While, on paper, Italy possessed a formidable armed forces, the reality was that Italy was financially weak, lacked basic military and industrial resources, and possessed armed forces that were largely obsolescent when compared to France or Britain.[1] Until 1940 Germany had little strategic interest in the Mediterranean and Balkans—but with Italy in the war Germany would be required to divert considerable forces and resources to bolster a weak ally.

The weakness of the Italian air force and armaments industry was well-known to the Luftwaffe leadership when Italy entered the war. A study by the Luftwaffe general staff in May 1939 assessed the Italian air force as "inferior to the British and French air forces by a wide margin."[2] Italian aerial rearmament was proceeding very slowly, advanced aircrew training was weak, most of the Regia Aeronautica's aircraft were obsolescent, and the Italian antiaircraft force was thoroughly obsolete. Essentially, the Luftwaffe viewed Italy as a weak nation that would likely retard the German war effort. Nevertheless, Italy served two strategic purposes: first, the Italians could disrupt British and French transport in the Mediterranean; and second, the Italians could help divert French and British sea power. But little more could be expected.[3] Perhaps because of Italy's weak position, the Luftwaffe general staff formulated no plan to work with the Italians if war broke out. Thus, when Italy joined the war there were no arrangements for liaison or cooperation between the two air forces. Three months after Italy became a German ally, the Luftwaffe sent General Ritter von Pohl to serve as liaison officer between the two air staffs.

The first instance of coalition air operations came in October 1940, when the Italians committed an air corps to the Battle of Britain. The Italian air corps flew only a few raids and suffered heavy losses when their bombers and fighters proved no match for British defenses.

It was typical of the mistrust in the Italian-German alliance that Italy's premier, Benito Mussolini, did not inform Hitler of his decision to invade Greece from the Italian protectorate of Albania until right before the act.[4] Mutual mistrust was apparently the foundation for Germany's military relations with its allies. Hitler tried to dissuade Mussolini, but the Italians had set their course and on 28 October declared war on Greece.[5] Italy had not gained much with France's surrender in June and was looking for an easy conquest that would expand Italy's strategic position in the Mediterranean. Prepared for an easy advance through the outnumbered Greek army, the Italians soon found themselves in terrible trouble. The mountainous Greek/Albanian border was ideal defensive terrain, and Greek troops stopped the Italian offensive and forced the Italian army to retreat. By December the Greek forces were advancing into Albania. It was a tremendous humiliation for Mussolini.

In December 1941 the situation for the Italians in North Africa fell to pieces. Whereas defeat in Albania was an embarrassment, the defeat of the Italian forces in Libya was catastrophic. During the fall of 1940 the British had reinforced their ground and air forces in Egypt, and by December the British were ready to go on the offensive. While the British forces were greatly outnumbered by the Italians on the African front, the British had all the advantages in training and leadership as well as possessing superior tanks and aircraft. On 12 December 1940 the British "Western Desert force" of 30,000 armored and motorized troops crossed the Libyan border and began a surprise offensive against the Italian Tenth Army at Sidi Barani. The Italian defensive position fell in two days, and with it the British took 38,000 prisoners, 273 guns, and 73 tanks. During the next week the British continued their pursuit and rolled up the Italian forces in eastern Libya while capturing the main Italian defensive positions at Sollum and Fort Capuzzo and taking 30,000 more Italian prisoners. They next advanced farther into Libya, where they won even greater victories over the Italians. With the Italian position collapsing, Mussolini requested German aid for his forces in Libya and agreed to commit further German forces to the Mediterranean.

Hitler, who had been watching the mess Mussolini was making in the Mediterranean, understood that his ally was now in such serious trouble that German assistance would be necessary simply to shore up the Italian position. In December 1940 Hitler made the decision to provide direct support to his Italian ally and immediately dispatched the Luftwaffe's Xth Air Corps, a large force that had been the Luftwaffe's main effort in the Norwegian campaign and that had considerable experience in antishipping operations. In January 1941, as the Italian position in North Africa collapsed further, Hitler and the general staff decided to commit a panzer corps commanded by General Erwin Rommel to reinforce the Italian army in North Africa. For the Germans, the Mediterranean was not a vital theater of war, and it had a low priority in the concept of German force commitments. While the British should be attacked if the opportunity arose, Hitler saw the mission of the Afrika Korps primarily to defend Tripolitania (the western province of Libya) and reassure his foundering Italian allies. As far as Hitler was concerned, the real war was going to be fought that summer against Russia.

The Xth Air Corps was to be based in Sicily and would assist the hard-pressed Regia Aeronautica in their attacks upon the British base at Malta and in driving British shipping out of the Mediterranean. The Luftwaffe's impressive ability to quickly transport men, aircraft, and matériel at this point in the war again proved its worth. Within days of the order to deploy the Xth Air Corps with 14,389 Luftwaffe personnel, 226 combat planes, and 31 transports had arrived in Italy. Soon Malta and the British shipping in the central Mediterranean were under heavy attack.[6]

The German army also moved swiftly to transport the elements of three panzer and motorized divisions to North Africa (15th and 21st Panzers and 90th Light Division) throughout February and March 1941. Rommel was instructed to prepare an offensive as soon as possible.[7] Although he did not plan for his advance against the British in Libya to coincide with the German offensive in the Balkans, the timing worked very well in Germany's favor. In the spring of 1941 the British would find themselves hard-pressed in the Mediterranean as they faced strong German forces in both Greece and North Africa with too few soldiers, planes, and ships to fight two battles at once.

Von Richthofen Is Transferred South

As Hitler issued his directive for the German invasion of Greece, von Richthofen was ordered to Berlin where the Wehrmacht high command informed him that he and his VIIIth Air Corps would be transferred to the Balkans to provide air support for the invasion of Greece. The air corps would be redeployed from France to Romania over the next several weeks, with later deployment of his force to Bulgaria once the final negotiations with that nation to join the Axis powers were settled. Von Richthofen had the time to take some Christmas leave with his family and ready his staff for the movement across Europe. That he was selected to be the air commander for Germany's next blitzkrieg operation was a sign of the high confidence that the Luftwaffe and army high command had in von Richthofen's competence. On 8 January 1941 he was personally briefed by the Führer on the operation.[8] Von Richthofen's VIIIth Air Corps would be strongly reinforced and would contain bomber and long-range fighter (Me 110) units as well as his Stukas, Henschels, and Me 109 fighters. The air corps would still have a strong ground attack capability, but the addition of medium-bomber and Me 110 units made it a well-rounded force suitable for long-range as well as short-range operations. The preparations for the attack on the Soviet Union were well under way by this time, and Hitler probably told von Richthofen of the need to defeat the Greeks as quickly as possible in order to redeploy his forces again for the great offensive against the USSR a few weeks later. On 2 March, Hitler directed that all preparations for the operation were to be completed by 15 May. Hitler would need von Richthofen's highly trained air units and Field Marshal Wilhelm List's four panzer divisions to be available for the Soviet campaign, so everything in the Balkans had to be settled quickly.[9]

Although nominally under the command of General Löhr and the 4th Air Fleet, based in Vienna, von Richthofen clearly would be the air commander for operations over Greece. After being briefed in Berlin he reported to General Löhr at the 4th Air Fleet headquarters in Vienna.

For the campaign in Greece the VIIIth Air Corps would be able to draw on support from the bomber groups of the 4th Air Fleet that were stationed in Austria, and then reequipping and preparing for the coming campaign against Russia. The Xth Air Corps units in Italy were also available to support von Richthofen. The preparations for the offensive were not without some comic overtones, as von Richthofen was expected to carry out some of his planning as a covert operation. He was to have a civilian passport made and would enter Bulgaria in February wearing civilian clothes and carrying that passport along with a tourist travel visa. At the time Bulgaria was in final alliance negotiations with Germany (the alliance with Germany would be announced on 1 March 1941). In the meantime, von Richthofen, looking strangely uncomfortable in his civilian suit, would have a chance to meet with Czar Boris of Bulgaria and the senior Bulgarian military staff and sort out the requirements for moving the VIIIth Air Corps onto Bulgarian territory. Along with von Richthofen more than 100 Luftwaffe signals specialists in civilian clothes entered Bulgaria, presumably on tourist visas such as von Richthofen's, and were detailed to help the Bulgarians set up an adequate signals network.[10] As usual, setting up effective communications was von Richthofen's first priority.

Moving by rail and air, the VIIIth Air Corps had quietly deployed to Romania throughout late January and early February 1941. Moving the ground forces, flak units, supplies, spare parts, and motor vehicles quickly into Bulgaria and deploying in battle order in case the Greeks or British should launch a preemptive attack required considerable planning on the part of the VIIIth Air Corps staff. Scheduling the trains, arranging the motor columns, and preparing a communications network were all highly complex operations, but the air corps staff put together an effective plan, and the movement of thousands of personnel and large quantities of equipment, supplies, and vehicles in winter transpired with very few problems.[11] On 1 March, when Bulgaria's entry into the Axis alliance was announced, the VIIIth Air Corps immediately moved 120 of its aircraft and fifteen flak batteries to Bulgarian airfields. Setting up an adequate support and logistics infrastructure in Bulgaria was a headache for von Richthofen and his staff, as the Bulgarian rail system and roads were underdeveloped and the airfield facilities were relatively primitive. Bulgaria was a poor nation and very much a reluctant ally of Germany. While making its territory available for the Germans it had little else to offer in the way of support. One of the first tasks of von Richthofen's signal and engineer units was to improve the Bulgarian and Romanian communications infrastructure—and to have it all ready by 1 April.[12]

Once Bulgaria was officially part of the Axis and the German forces were officially invited into the country, von Richthofen could put away his civilian suit and wear his uniform. As one of the two senior Wehrmacht officers in Bulgaria during March 1941, von Richthofen was expected to do a considerable amount of socializing with Czar Boris and his senior military officers. On 16 March, von Richthofen and Field Marshal List met with the czar and royal family for a formal lunch in the royal palace in Sofia. Von Richthofen was able to converse with the queen, partly in Italian and partly in German. He found the royal family to be friendly, informal, and intelligent. In describing the occasion in his diary von Richthofen allowed a bit of German aristocratic snobbery to surface. He remarked that the royal palace was fairly simple, really just a large villa, and that the czar's taste in furniture was "very middle class"—although "he did display a few precious things."[13] The next couple of days were the high point of von Richthofen's stay in Bulgaria; he and a Luftwaffe liaison officer were invited to use the czar's hunting lodge and grounds in the mountains. Accompanied by the president of the Bulgarian Hunt Society, they were driven to Belitza, where they were provided horses for a two-hour ride to the mountain lodge where they could hunt bear. Von Richthofen enjoyed the excursion immensely. He described the Bulgarian horses as simply "superb" and "some of the best horses [he] had ever seen." Often in his diary one sees a glimpse of the young cavalry officer that von Richthofen once was. He might have a Ph.D. in engineering and enjoy developing jets and rocket planes for the Luftwaffe, but he also clearly loved to ride a good horse.[14] The area abounded in wolves, bears, and wild boar—but the hunting party had little luck in shooting big game. In the evening the Bulgarians hosted an enjoyable dinner complete with caviar, three strong red wines, fish, steak, and dessert. Von Richthofen was impressed at the drinking abilities of his hosts, who apparently drank by the kilo rather than by the liter. The next day he hunted again and then in the evening returned to the "paper wars," feeling much refreshed by his outing.[15] On 19 March, von Richthofen returned Czar Boris's favor with a major review of the VIIIth Air Corps and a demonstration of Stuka dive-bombing techniques. Von Richthofen's good impression of Czar Boris was reinforced. He found the czar to be likeable, pleasant, and very interested about all the VIIIth Air Corps' aircraft—especially the new Ju 88 bombers.

The German army force for the invasion of Greece was Field Marshal List's Twelfth Army, which would include a strong panzer and motorized element, Panzergruppe 1, under General Ewald von Kleist. List's army was a powerful force of five corps with two elite mountain divisions, eleven infantry divisions, and von Kleist's powerful mechanized formation of four panzer divisions and one motorized division.[16] The poorly equipped Greek army, short of artillery and tanks and lacking antitank guns, would be completely outclassed. If the Germans could get through the strong Greek border defenses, there would be little chance of holding such a force back. During the weeks leading up to the attack, von Richthofen conferred with List and his staff and worked out the details of the offensive. Von Richthofen arranged for the Twelfth Army Koluft, a Lt. Colonel Krueger, to be under his administrative control—a means by which Richthofen could call him in and tell him exactly how he wanted the Twelfth Army's Luftwaffe reconnaissance squadron to cooperate with the VIIIth Air Corps reconnaissance units. After the experiences of Poland and France, von Richthofen wanted to ensure that his headquarters received timely information from all major commands.[17] He stood out in his attention to these kinds of details and his insistence upon carefully reviewing all the arrangements for communication and coordination before the start of a campaign. It was his ability to think through these issues and come up with good solutions that made von Richthofen's VIIIth Air Corps the premier close-support force in the world in 1941—far surpassing the best efforts of the Soviets and British in this regard.

Operation Marita was set to begin on 1 April 1941, but politics would intervene to change the scope of the campaign. One faction of the Yugoslav government favored an alliance with Germany, and on 25 March the Yugoslav government officially requested a formal alliance with Germany. This

Visit of Czar Boris (left) of Bulgaria to the VIIIth Air Corps just before opening the campaign against Greece. Czar Boris was a gracious host and von Richthofen found him a personable and intelligent man. Von Richthofen especially enjoyed a visit to the czar's hunting estate.

action so outraged the Yugoslavian king and Serbian members of the government that two days later a coup threw out the pro-German government and the new government promptly repudiated the alliance with Germany. Facing a now hostile Yugoslavia, Hitler postponed the attack on Greece by five days and ordered the German Second Army and the 4th Air Fleet stationed in Austria to prepare to invade Yugoslavia along with Greece.[18] To support the Yugoslavia operation the Luftwaffe quickly dispatched fifteen bomber groups from France and Germany to reinforce the 4th Air Fleet. It is again a testament to the Luftwaffe's ability to rapidly shift forces that within a few days the additional air units were ready to undertake a campaign that was literally

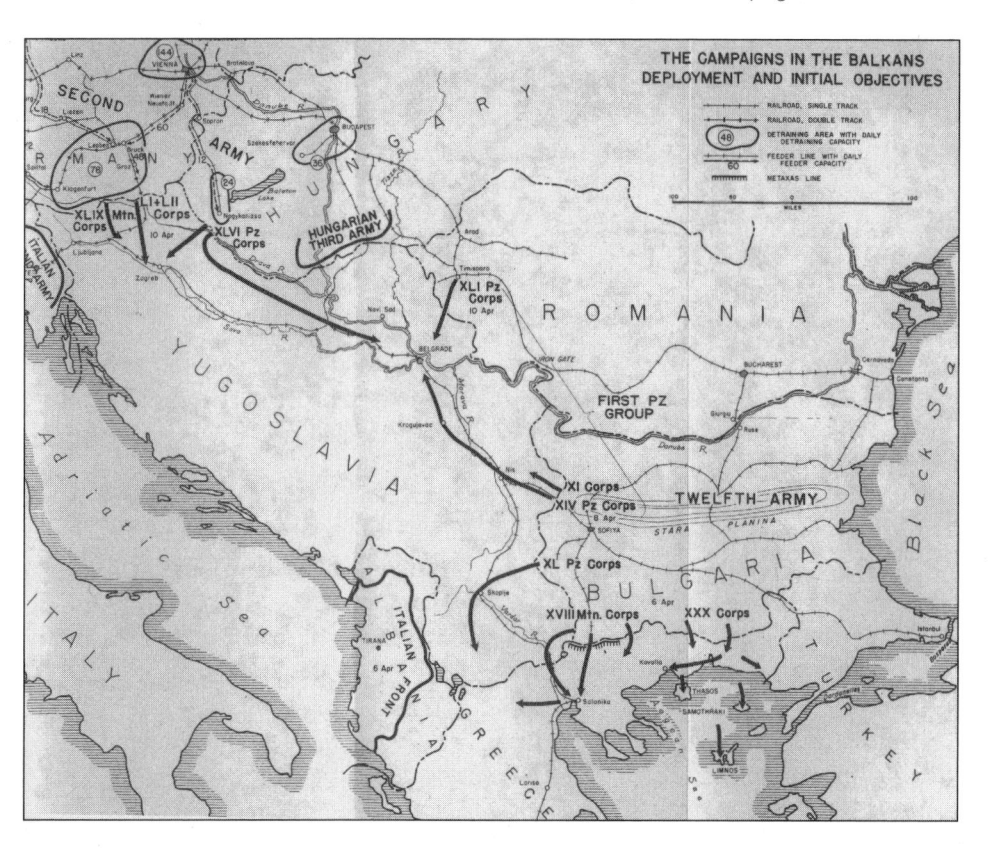

The German attack into Greece and Yugoslavia, April 1941. The VIIIth Air Corps, based in Bulgaria, provided support to the Twelfth Army offensive into Greece. (*The Campaign in the Balkans [Spring 1941]* [Washington, DC: U.S. Army Center for Military History, 1984])

planned on the fly. With the reinforcements added to von Richthofen's force in Bulgaria, the 4th Air Fleet would have a total of 946 combat aircraft backed up by hundreds of transports. In terms of both quantity and quality the Luftwaffe would outnumber the combined air forces of Greece and Yugoslavia and the RAF units that had been committed to Greece.[19]

On 31 March and 1 April 1941, von Richthofen and his staff revised the attack order to include attacks on the Yugoslavian air force and Yugoslav army in the southern part of that country at the start of the offensive. In fact, Yugoslavia's hostility to Germany and its inclusion as an official enemy made the Twelfth Army's and VIIIth Air Corps' mission much easier. Rather than attack the Greek defensive positions head on, they could now cross over the poorly defended border of southern Yugoslavia, swing around, and come upon Greece's army in Thrace from an unprotected flank. Taking out Greece's northern army was the key to the campaign. The army facing the Germans in Bulgaria included Greece's best-trained and -equipped divisions. If that force could be quickly knocked out of the battle, the rest of the Greek army would likely lose heart.

The British Commit to Greece

The RAF forces in the Mediterranean were stripped to provide squadrons to support the British expedition to Greece. In early 1941, General Archibald Wavell, commander in chief of the Mediterranean theater, committed an army corps with 58,000 army and RAF personnel to support the Greeks in what was to be a disastrous adventure.

Von Richthofen was very aware of the British units stationed in Greece as he moved into Bulgaria and understood that his main problem would be in defeating the British. By 5 April, British forces were flowing into Greece, and on that day General Thomas Blamey opened up the headquarters of the Ist Australian Corps. The British forces were far from prepared to fight, though. The New Zealand division was listed as being in position, but only forward elements of the 6th Australian Division had moved into the front lines. The Air Headquarters Middle East was trying to move units into Greece but was apparently unclear as to the location and status of its squadrons. No. 113 Squadron was presumed to be in Greece, and No. 45 Squadron was also supposed to have arrived, but in the daily report to the Air Ministry the Air Headquarters Middle East chief of staff crossed out that entry and noted that the squadron was "still in Cyrenaica." Clearly RAF communications were not working effectively. This was in contrast to von Richthofen, who made setting up an effective signals network the first priority of his air corps when it moved into Bulgaria. In any case, by 5 April the RAF had only ninety-nine aircraft in Greece, including nineteen Hurricanes and seventy-four Blenheim bombers. It was not much of a force to face von Richthofen's 500 aircraft.[20]

The Air Forces

When Italy declared war on Greece in October 1940 it looked as if the Greeks had little chance. The Greek army was essentially an infantry force with well-led and well-trained divisions but lacking in vehicles and heavy weapons. In the air there was a similar mismatch. The Italians had a large air force with over 2,000 combat aircraft and, although they were largely obsolescent, some bomber and fighter units equipped with airplanes that were roughly equal to any of the Allied aircraft of the day. To support its invasion of Greek Macedonia the Italians had 187 bombers and fighters based in Albania, which could be supported by 194 aircraft based in southern Italy.[21] In contrast, the small Royal Hellenic Air Force was a mishmash of obsolescent aircraft bought from Poland, Britain, France, and Germany. The Greek fighter force consisted of thirty-six PLZ P 24 Polish fighters, twelve Gloster Gladiator biplanes, and nine Bloch MB 151 fighters from France. The bomber force consisted of twelve Fairy Battles and twelve Bristol Blenheims. For reconnaissance the Greeks had sixteen short-range Henschel He 126s and twelve longer range Dornier Do 22 float planes. The mix of widely different models and engine types made maintenance and support of the air force a nightmare; under the best conditions, Greece could field about 150 operational aircraft.[22] In early 1941, the Curtis Hawk 75 fighters and Curtiss P-40s that had been ordered from the United States had not yet arrived.[23] It was a constant story of the early years of World War II—governments recognizing the need to rearm just a bit too late and paying a huge price for the delay.

The Yugoslavian air force was considerably larger and more modern than the Greek air force. However, it also consisted of a mishmash of aircraft acquired from several countries: the 468 combat aircraft it possessed on 6 April 1941 were eleven different models with twenty-two different engines. To make matters worse, only about half of its airplanes were flyable. In order to prevent being destroyed on the ground by a German surprise attack, the entire air force had been widely dispersed to small auxiliary airfields—much as the Poles had done in 1939. This broad dispersal resulted in maintenance and supply problems. With the Yugoslavian air force's weak communications system, it would be impossible to concentrate airpower for major attacks upon the Germans.[24]

Many of Yugoslavia's preparations for defense became moot when a Croatian staff officer of the Yugoslavian air force quietly provided the Luftwaffe with its order of battle and defensive plans. For once, the Luftwaffe would go to war with perfect intelligence of the enemy force and his deployments. It would make the German effort to establish air superiority far simpler.[25]

The Campaign Opens

Luftwaffe assessments of its enemies throughout the war were often very inaccurate, but in the invasion of the Balkans in 1941 the assessment of von Richthofen's staff turned out to be spot-on. Even with the commitment of British forces to Greece, the Allies would be outnumbered and outclassed in the air. The VIIIth Air Corps staff did not expect to have great difficulty in attaining air superiority at the opening of the campaign—and they were right. On 6 April 1941, the first day of the campaign, the 4th Air Fleet and VIIIth Air Corps concentrated their efforts on knocking out the Allied air forces. Von Richthofen's units targeted the Greek airfields and Yugoslavian air force units in the south, largely destroying the Yugoslavian air force on the ground the first day. For a loss of 37 planes, mostly to ground fire, the Luftwaffe could claim 145 planes destroyed, 60 percent of these on the ground. The attacks on the Yugoslav airfields continued into 7 April, and by the evening of that day the Yugoslavs had only 177 aircraft left of the more than 400 on the books the day before.[26]

On the ground it took only three days for List's Twelfth Army to break through the Greek defense lines along the northern border and cut off Greece's northern army. The frontal attack on the Metaxas Line proved to be a difficult task for the army and the Luftwaffe. The Stukas of the VIIIth Air Corps targeted the major positions of the Metaxas Line, which had already been carefully plotted by air reconnaissance flights, with 1,000 kg bombs (2,200 lbs.). Ordinarily the heavy bombs would have crippled the Greek defenses, but the Greeks had cleverly built many of their bunkers into the cliff sides. When the Stukas arrived, the soldiers could retreat into the caverns and then return to man the defenses as soon as the aircraft departed. If the Metaxas Line had been the only route into northern Greece, the Germans would have had a much tougher time. Ironically, Yugoslavia's hostility toward Germany and the last-minute addition of Yugoslavia to the invasion plans worked wonderfully in Germany's favor. The opportunity to swing through Yugoslavia and attack from the flank was a lucky break for the Germans. Yugoslavia had no equivalent of the Metaxas Line, and the lightly defended border offered the German motorized positions the perfect opportunity to swing through the southernmost region of Yugoslavia and emerge behind the main Greek defense lines. The Yugoslavs might have made a better defense and slowed down the Germans, but the Serbs broke easily under air attack and had proved to be ineffective soldiers. "Their heart wasn't really in it," noted the VIIIth Air Corps staff diary.[27] At the same time List's panzer forces were swinging around the Greek flank, the German army's two elite mountain divisions managed to break the Greek defenses by attacking over the highest mountains—which, of course, were very lightly defended. Once through the Greek lines, the German mountain troops could attack Greek strong points at the lower elevations from the rear.

On 9 April, List's forces broke through the Greek defenses and took Salonika. This act caused the Greek army in Thrace, which contained most of the best-equipped and trained Greek units, to be cut off from the rest of Greece with no hope to escape. Despite the relief of their commander and orders from Athens to hold to the last soldier, the Greek senior officers in Thrace saw the situation as hopeless and refused to sacrifice their army. Thus, they began negotiations with Field Marshal List for the surrender of their forces.[28] Once the northern Greek army fell, the only forces capable of fighting the Germans on anything like even terms were the British divisions committed to central Greece.

German ground forces made their first contact with the British, running into the New Zealand Cavalry Regiment, on 9 April. Information about the contact took twenty-three hours to reach General Henry Wilson, commander of the British forces in Greece, an indication of the poor communications and confusion that plagued the British forces through the Greek campaign. At this point the presence of the British did not greatly worry the German commanders. The British were greatly outnumbered and outgunned by List's forces, and von Richthofen's air corps had established air superiority over northern Greece and southern Yugoslavia in the first days of the battle. The RAF was under constant attack and was able to do little to support British ground forces. On 15 April the surviving RAF aircraft began a withdrawal from Greece.[29]

Advance into Greece

From 9 April until the fall of Athens and evacuation of the last British forces from mainland Greece on 30 April, the campaign, in the words of the VIIIth Air Corps staff war diary, became a grand "pursuit operation." Stukas and bombers hit the road and rail network and relentlessly attacked British and Greek columns. Stukas also provided close support for List's motorized and panzer troops when they encountered British and Greek defenses.[30] As the British and Greek forces retreated into central and southern Greece, logistics became the VIIIth Air Corps' major concern. The Me 109s, Henschels, and Stukas, still the "B" models, were all short-ranged aircraft, and, as the British retreated, the only way for the VIIIth Air Corps to continue the pursuit was to jump 150 miles to a new forward operating base. Allied shipping was the most lucrative target of the campaign, and as long as the Stukas operated out of Bulgaria and the newly captured airfield in Salonika they did not have the range to attack Piraeus or the southern Greek ports. Only the Ju 88s were able to reach that far, but they would have to fly without fighter escort to do so.

When the British evacuated the Larissa airfield in north-central Greece on 13 April, the Germans found it to be geographically well suited as a new base. From Larissa the Stukas and their Me 109 escorts could easily range south to Athens and southern Greece (Larissa is about 150 miles from Athens and Piraeus) and attack the Allied ships that were evacuating British forces and Greek army units.[31] Von Richthofen organized an air task force of about 100 of the VIIIth Air Corps aircraft to move forward to Larissa and to act as a close battle force. However, conditions made supplying the Larissa base almost impossible. It was still winter in the northern Greek mountains, and the roads, which at their best were pretty awful, were closed by mud and snow. Luftwaffe motor columns carrying the fuel and munitions for the task force at Larissa became hopelessly bogged on the mountain roads leading from the main supply depots in Bulgaria. So von Richthofen rounded up every transport aircraft in the Balkans as well as a few bombers and loaded them with ground crews, fuel, and munitions to maintain the Larissa base. Luckily, the Royal Air Force, which had based some squadrons at Larissa, left behind a large supply of aviation fuel. With transport aircraft and the maximum use of captured supplies, the VIIIth Air Corps was able to operate from its forward base and keep the pressure on the British.

In the middle of the campaign von Richthofen made his own personal reconnaissance of the front lines in his Fiesler Stork. On 15 April, while observing the German advance, he noted that a fuel depot near Lorina, which the British were still defending, lay untouched and unguarded. He quickly gave orders to one of his flak units serving with the army on the front lines to race to the depot and secure it before the retreating British could blow it up. Once the fuel was secured he sent up a Stuka and a fighter group to occupy the nearby airfield and support the attack southward.[32]

Although the British accounts of the campaign refer to constant air attack by the Germans, from 15 April until the final British evacuation on 30 April the Luftwaffe's main targets were the evacuation ports. With little antiaircraft or fighter protection, the merchant vessels cramming the Greek harbors made lucrative targets. The VIIIth Air Corps bombers and Stukas were assisted by Xth Air Corps bombers flying from Sicily. Luftwaffe staff estimated that between 15 April and 2 May, the two air corps sank sixty Allied ships, with a gross tonnage of 280,000 tons.[33] In contrast to the outrageously exaggerated shipping claims made by the VIIIth Air Corps flying against British shipping in the summer of 1940, these claims were approximately correct.

On 21 April it was clear to the British commanders in Greece that they could not hope to make an effective defense in central Greece. The next day, General Wilson ordered the evacuation of all British forces from Greece.[34] For the British it would be a race to the ports to try to evacuate as many men and as much equipment as possible.

Attack on Shipping

The Xth Air Corps based in Sicily, with long-range bombers that specialized in antishipping operations, and von Richthofen's Stukas and bombers flying out of Bulgaria and northern Greece, carried out a relentless attack on Allied shipping throughout the Balkans campaign. Indeed, the campaign would include some of the most successful Luftwaffe antishipping operations of World War II. After attacking the port of Salonika at the start of the battle, the air corps shifted their attention to the port of Piraeus near Athens, Greece's most important port, and also attacked a host of smaller ports that were used in the disembarkation of the British forces in Greece. By 26 April the last of the British forces in Greece had embarked. Of the 58,000 men committed to Greece, more than 16,000 had become casualties or prisoners.[35] Many of the losses occurred when the ships bearing the troops away from Greece were bombed and sunk by the Luftwaffe. Most of the prisoners had been taken in the last days of the campaign when evacuation by the Royal Navy became impossible due to German air attack.

Between 6 April and 30 April the Allies lost seventy merchant ships in Greek waters—almost all to air attack. Most of the vessels were Greek or British, but other Allies, including the Dutch, also lost ships. The Luftwaffe targeted both large and small vessels: from small 1,000-ton coastal boats to large merchantmen and 8,000-ton tankers. The climax of the antishipping battle came between 21 and 24 April, when the Germans sank forty-three merchant vessels, mostly in Piraeus and southern Greek ports, for a total of 63,975 tons lost. Taking the whole campaign into context, the battle for Greece and Crete from April to June 1941 struck a serious blow to Allied maritime and naval power in the Mediterranean. Total Allied shipping losses were recorded as 360,000 tons.[36]

Attack on Crete

Many of the British troops that had been evacuated from Greece were transported the short distance to Crete to build an Allied garrison there. In the long run, with the Germans holding a clear margin of air superiority, the island was probably untenable. However, the British, having been run out of Greece, decided to make a stand at Crete. The British were at least correct in assuming that the Germans would be likely to assault the island. On 20 April, General Kurt Student approached Goering and proposed an airborne assault on Crete with his paratroop force. Student longed for a grand opportunity to prove the decisive value of his paratroops, and an airborne operation made sense in the light of Germany's airpower and naval weakness in the Mediterranean. Student argued that Crete would serve as a springboard to the Suez Canal — and there was considerable sense in the argument, as holding Crete would give Germany effective control of most of the eastern Mediterranean. Hitler agreed to Student's plan on 25 April but, due to the upcoming invasion of the Soviet Union and the urgent requirement to shift forces from the Mediterranean to the Soviet Front, gave him a deadline of 16 May to begin the invasion.[37]

As soon as Greece fell, General Löhr would move the 4th Air Fleet to Romania in preparation for the Soviet invasion. Von Richthofen, with his VIIIth Air Corps reinforced by some units from the 4th Air Fleet, would serve as the air commander of the Crete operation while Student would command the paratroops, ground divisions, and air transport units. To support the Crete operation, von Richthofen would have command of 552 combat aircraft. A further fifty-one Italian aircraft would support the German attack. To bring the paratroops and glider troops and to carry reinforcements and supplies to Crete, the Luftwaffe assembled 504 Ju 52 transports, the greater part of the transport fleet of the whole Luftwaffe. One hundred DFS 230 gliders were also available to transport part of the initial assault force.[38]

Student argued that the operation should have one overall commander, but Löhr and von Richthofen were strongly opposed. In the end, the Crete operation would be conducted per the standard German command system of separate ground and air commanders. Student proposed a bold plan of landing his paratroops and glider troops at three widely separated points in order to seize both of Crete's main airfields in the first moments of the campaign. Both Löhr and von Richthofen thought Student's plan was highly risky and agued in favor of one major paratroop/glider landing at the airfield at Heraklion. Their idea was that once an airhead was established, it could be quickly reinforced; then the German force, which would be fully concentrated, would advance west under cover of strong air support from the VIIIth Air Corps. Goering rejected von Richthofen and Löhr's arguments and let Student's plan stand. Shortly before the attack, in a typically acerbic comment in his diary, von Richthofen expressed his misgivings about Student and his plan: "Student plans his operations based on pure suppositions and preconceived notions."[39] For the rest of the war, von Richthofen held a low opinion of Student as a senior commander. In fact, his judgment about Student and the Crete operation proved correct. The Luftwaffe and the German paratroops force were about to walk into a near disaster.

As usual during the war, the Wehrmacht intelligence was incredibly wrong about Crete and its defenses. German intelligence and General Student

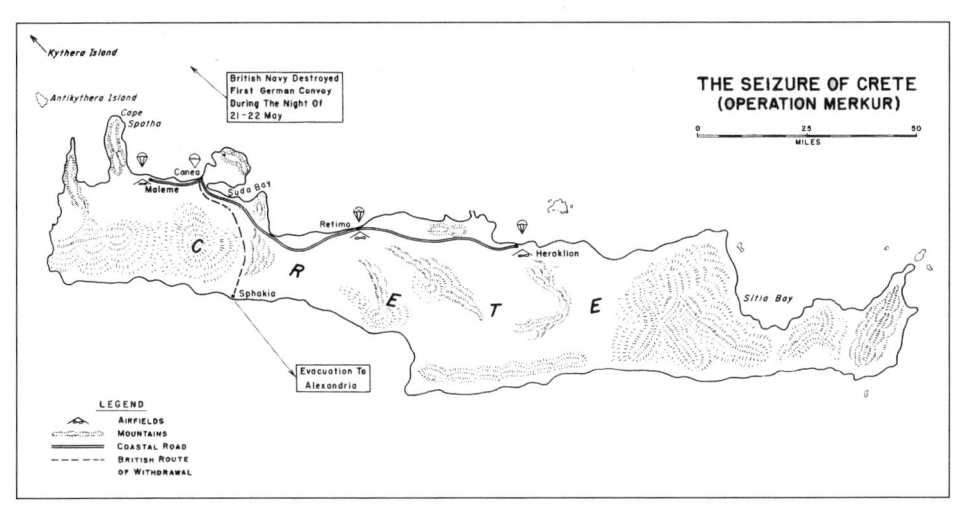

Crete during the German air assault of May 1941. (*The Campaign in the Balkans [Spring 1941]* [Washington, DC: U.S. Army Center for Military History, 1984])

believed that Crete was lightly defended and that the whole garrison consisted of 5,000 Allied soldiers. Such a force would be easily overwhelmed by Student's elite 7th Paratroop Division, supported by another infantry division (the 5th Mountain), which could be brought in by air after the airfields were secured. In fact, the Allies had 42,000 troops on Crete, mostly Australians and New Zealanders who had been evacuated from Greece. Although Crete's defenders were short of heavy weapons such as artillery and tanks—most of which had been destroyed or abandoned in Greece—the British and Greek forces (about 10,000 Greek troops were on the island) had their full complement of light weapons, including machine guns and mortars. The British forces had dug in around Crete and were prepared for a sea or air landing. They had carefully camouflaged their positions, and even under daily Luftwaffe reconnaissance, the size of the British force and the extent of their fighting positions had not been spotted.

The weak German logistics system again hampered the German planning. Despite having captured large quantities of British fuel in Greece, the Luftwaffe still had too little fuel to support the Crete operation. Hitler's deadline of 16 May had to be put off until 20 May to allow a tanker with 9,000 tons of fuel for the Luftwaffe to arrive.[40] Von Richthofen used the extra days to mass his air units, to build airstrips on the nearby Peloponnesian and Aegean islands, and to ready his aircraft for the campaign. He began the aerial preparation phase of the battle on 14 May, when his bombers started regularly pounding the two main airfields on Crete. The RAF had a small force to defend Crete—twenty-five fighters, supported by radar—but the RAF could not sustain its units under the constant German bombardment. By 19 May the RAF had withdrawn its last airplane from the island.[41]

The German assault began on the morning of 20 May and came close to complete disaster for Student's paratroops. Things went wrong from the start. For an hour before the airborne drop the bombers of KG 2 and KG 20 along with the Stukas of Wing 2 pounded the known British positions and the antiaircraft sites. The paratroop drops were planned to begin immediately after the air strikes, but the transport engines kicked up so much dust on the dirt-surfaced Greek airfields that the transports were slow to take off and assemble. So there was a time gap between the air strikes and the paratroop drops that allowed the British troops to organize themselves. Finally, the 493 Ju 52 transports began dropping the 7th Division's paratroops and glider-borne troops on landing sites near the two major airfields on Crete—Maleme and Heraklion. Then even more things went wrong. The 7th Division commander and his staff were killed in a takeoff accident when the rope towing their glider broke prematurely. Many of the paratroops landed in the midst of strong British troop concentrations and were immediately slaughtered by withering British fire. Some troops that had been badly scattered managed to assemble and mount an attack upon Maleme airfield. After heavy fighting in which the Germans got the worst of it, the British pulled back from Maleme. The next day, the paratroops had cleared enough of the runway for transports to fly in reinforcements and supplies. However, British fire on the airfield was intense, and many of the transports were shot down or crashed on landing. Still, enough German troops and supplies managed to arrive that the paratroops could go on the offensive and begin clearing and securing the airhead.

Von Richthofen's aircraft had little contact with the beleaguered paratroops the first day because almost all of the paratroops' radios were destroyed or damaged when the gliders carrying most of the heavy equipment crashed into the small and rock-strewn Cretan farm fields that were the only suitable landing sites. In the confusion of battle the VIIIth Air Corps tried to assess the situation and direct air support through light reconnaissance planes, usually the Henschel 126, that hovered over the battlefield trying to spot targets. When British heavy weapons or troop concentrations were spotted, the Stukas and bombers were called in to attack. These constant air attacks almost certainly saved the 7th Paratroop Division from total annihilation on 20 May. The German bombing and strafing, which was nearly constant, served to keep the British from moving, at least during the day. With the British keeping their heads down, the surviving paratroops had a chance to organize and begin fighting as coherent units.

It was a highly stressful time for von Richthofen, who was trying to direct the air operations from his headquarters in Piraeus with very little information about the fighting on the ground. Most of the 7th Paratroop Division's radios had been lost or destroyed in the landing operations, so for the first two days of the operation, von Richthofen and the VIIIth Air Corps were largely dependent upon air reconnaissance reports assessing a very confusing picture on the ground. Luckily for the Germans, the British forces were as much in the dark about the operational situation as were they. As a further complication, the Italians were also supposed to take part in the Crete operation and sent a naval force to support sea landings and intercept the British fleet steaming to Crete's relief. But von Richthofen had learned in Spain not to rely upon the Italians for support, and when the Italian naval force failed to appear it came as no surprise to von Richthofen and his fellow officers.

During high tempo operations such as this, von Richthofen liked to listen to classical music recordings to relieve the stress. He listened to a recording of Beethoven's Seventh Symphony so often during the difficult days of late May 1941 that he afterwards referred to it as "the Crete Symphony." He recalled that the operation in Crete caused him as much anxiety as any operation of the war, claiming that his first gray hairs appeared in May 1941.

The most important decisive effect of von Richthofen's air corps in the campaign was its success in driving the Royal Navy out of Cretan waters. The Royal Navy managed to stop German seaborne reinforcements in Crete on 22 May, but then its ships cruised within range of the VIIIth Air Corps airfields—and von Richthofen's Stukas and bombers attacked them. Ju 88s of Training Wing 1 sank the cruisers HMS *Gloucester* and HMS *Fiji* and seriously damaged the cruiser HMS *Naiad*. The cruiser HMS *Carlisle* and battleship HMS *Warspite* were damaged soon afterwards by air attack. The next day the destroyers HMS *Kashmir* and HMS *Kelly* (commanded by Lord Louis Mountbatten) were sunk by Stukas. Von Richthofen had definitely proven that ships could not operate if the enemy controlled the skies.[42]

By 23 May the crisis had passed and the German forces were well established on the island. The VIIIth Air Corps had driven the Royal Navy out of the waters off of northern Crete, and the Germans were able arrange for supplies and more reinforcements to be flown in. The Germans then began to systematically clear northern Crete of British forces. During the first three days—the crisis period—of the operation, Berlin was extremely nervous and had plagued von Richthofen in his headquarters in Pireaus with demands of updates of the situation. It was a trying time for von Richthofen in that he not only had to direct the air operations but also had to contend with continual telephone calls from Jeschonnek demanding information.[43] Von Richthofen received welcome reinforcement in the form of Stuka Wing 1, which had been sent to the Xth Air Corps in Sicily in February 1941 to attack the British base at Malta. With the Soviet campaign in the offing, Stuka Wing 1 was ordered to Germany to refit on 22 May but on the way was diverted to Greece to support operations on Crete. Staging out of the airfield at Argos, the Stukas attacked British shipping in Suda Bay. After quickly finishing off the damaged cruiser HMS *York*, the Stukas turned their attention to supporting the advance of the German paratroops and infantry. Close support could not be conducted because the army did not have the same air-to-ground communications that existed in the panzer units. So the Stukas were given sectors to patrol and carried out attacks on any targets of opportunity. Loitering overhead throughout the day, the Stukas' presence restricted any daytime movement by the British. All the British accounts of the battle note the demoralizing impact of the German airpower.[44]

After 23 May the campaign progressed in the Germans' favor. Under constant air attack, which had a strong psychological effect on Crete's defenders, the British were steadily pushed toward the southern part of the island. One Royal Navy attempt to strike a blow at the Germans went awry when the aircraft carrier HMS *Formidable*, which had sent out its planes to attack German airfields, was attacked by Stuka Wing 2. The *Formidable* was badly damaged by German bombs and had to be withdrawn for repairs.[45] On 27 May, London decided that the situation in Crete was untenable and that the island would have to be evacuated. As Royal Navy ships arrived off the southern coast to bring out the British forces they became prime targets for the VIIIth Air Corps bombers and Stukas. On 29 May two destroyers were sunk and two cruisers were badly damaged.[46] Between 27 May and 2 June the Royal Navy suffered more losses of cruisers and destroyers to add to the already heavy losses incurred in Greek waters in April.

Before the Allied troops left on Crete were forced to surrender on 1 June, the Royal Navy had been able to successfully evacuate a large portion of the army but, like Dunkirk, without any of its vehicles or heavy weapons. In the spring of 1941 the British had sent in a large force and a vast amount of equipment to Greece, but by the beginning of June virtually all the airplanes, tanks, guns, ammunition, radios, and vehicles had been lost—all in a cause that the British theater commander warned beforehand would probably fail. The British had taken heavy casualties, and the Germans had captured more than 10,000 Allied troops on Crete alone. Both British army and RAF units would have to be rebuilt and reequipped before they could fight again.

The massive losses to Allied merchant shipping have already been noted, yet the Luftwaffe inflicted equally significant damage upon the Royal Navy in the Greek and Crete campaigns and crippled its ability to conduct major operations at a time when the battle for North Africa and the Mediterranean was seriously in doubt. Between April and June the Royal Navy saw four cruisers and eight destroyers sunk, with 1,975 naval personnel killed in action and thousands more wounded. The Greek navy also lost five destroyers. In addition the Royal Navy and Greek navy lost a large number of small auxiliary vessels. The battles in Greek waters and especially the action around Crete resulted in a large number of Royal Navy warships damaged, many of them so seriously as to require months in the dockyard before they could be fit for duty. In the course of the campaign three battleships and one aircraft carrier were damaged as well as eight cruisers, nine destroyers, and two assault ships. The damaged ships suffered the loss of 290 naval personnel killed, with hundreds more wounded.[47]

The Greek and Crete campaigns were a strong blow against the British in the Mediterranean. Of the 58,000 British troops sent to Greece between February and April 1941, some 12,000 became casualties. In Greece the British army lost hundreds of tanks and 8,000 trucks, and the RAF lost 209 aircraft.[48] In the May 1941 Crete campaign the British forces recorded 5,357 killed, 1,920 wounded, and 11,835 taken prisoner. The RAF lost forty-three planes, and the Royal Navy recorded one carrier and three battleships damaged, three cruisers and six destroyers sunk, and six cruisers and seven destroyers damaged.[49]

For the victorious Germans it had been a hard campaign. The Crete operation cost the Luftwaffe 259 aircraft, including 121 transports (48 to accidents). The Luftwaffe lost 438 aircrew, including 311 dead or missing (185 from the VIIIth Air Corps). These were serious losses but not crippling. However, the 7th Paratroop Division had taken massive losses in the Crete campaign. Of the 10,000 personnel in the division, 4,500 were casualties, including 3,022 dead or missing. It would be a long time before the 7th Paratroop Division would again be capable of fighting.[50] Ironically, General Student's desire to prove the efficacy of paratroops had the opposite effect upon Berlin. Although, considering the much heavier British losses, the division certainly had not failed in its mission, it had nonetheless failed to show that paratroops could be truly decisive.

Despite its victory in the Mediterranean, the Wehrmacht was not in a position to take advantage of its success. The demands of the upcoming invasion of the USSR took precedence, and the Germans had to quickly move their forces out of the Mediterranean theater and prepare them for what would be the greatest campaign of the war. The Luftwaffe was already spread too thin among the fighting theaters and could not be effective simultaneously in the Mediterranean and in the Soviet Union—and the latter took precedence. So, instead of serving as a springboard to the Suez Canal, Crete became a base for a small force of Luftwaffe bombers and Me 110 fighters left behind to bomb Egypt and carry out raids against British bases in North Africa. For a time, the defeated British were left in peace to rebuild their forces.

Although the Balkans was a major victory for German arms it also served to delay the invasion of the Soviet Union by five weeks and likely gave the Soviets just enough time to organize their successful defense of Moscow in the winter of 1941. For von Richthofen, the campaigns in Yugoslavia, Greece, and Crete brought the air commander even more fame and won him the favorable attention of Adolf Hitler. Having commanded more than 500 aircraft in tough combat, he had proven himself the master of the tactical air war. His personal leadership had driven his forces to operate at a higher tempo than his enemies, and the air support provided by his forces had made a rapid campaign possible.

Some important lessons came out of the Balkans campaign that the Luftwaffe failed to learn. While von Richthofen and his staff proved they were far superior to their opponents in planning and executing an air campaign, the VIIIth Air Corps had barely scraped through in maintaining the supply lines that kept the aircraft flying. Only through the most rigorous improvisation did von Richthofen and his staff manage to jump their supply base forward 150 miles so they could continue the air campaign without pause. Neither von Richthofen nor his staff saw in the Balkans campaign a warning sign of what was to come in the USSR. If the Germans had found it hard to move 150 miles forward, what would it do when it had to advance 600 miles? They would soon have the answer—and it was not in the Luftwaffe's favor.

The Luftwaffe had again proven it had no equal in the world in conducting a short, sharp, and very successful campaign. But the weaknesses of the force were already showing. German aircraft production and its pilot training program were operating at just enough capacity to provide replacement aircraft and pilots, but little more. The Luftwaffe combat forces were not much larger than they had been in 1939. But von Richthofen and his airmen were so buoyed by the successful campaign in the Balkans that little thought was given to such things.

Chapter 10

The Soviet Campaign Opens, 1941–1942

The summer of 1941 would see the Luftwaffe at its high point in terms of conducting successful offensive campaigns against Germany's enemies. On the western front the bombers of the 3rd Air Fleet carried on a nighttime blitz of British cities, while its small but elite fighter force effectively held off RAF incursions into northern France and Belgium. In the Mediterranean, the Luftwaffe crushed the Greek and Yugoslav air forces and delivered a stinging defeat to the RAF and Royal Navy in the Greece and Crete campaigns. Luftwaffe units in North Africa supported Rommel's offensive that pushed the British army back hundreds of miles to the Egyptian border and put the port city of Tobruk under siege until November 1941.

Now the Wehrmacht was preparing for its greatest operation so far in the war—the invasion of the Soviet Union with the intention of destroying the huge Soviet military in a matter of weeks, occupying European Russia, crippling the Soviet state, and winning for Germany a vast territory for economic exploitation. Given the string of successes so far, with the one exception of failure over Britain in 1940, the Wehrmacht and Luftwaffe both had a strong case of victory disease. Luftwaffe units were confident, superbly trained, and battle tested—but the force was spread far too thin for what had become a three-front war. The Luftwaffe had to maintain a considerable bomber force in the West to carry on the war against Britain. It had to keep fighters in northern France and Belgium to defend against the RAF nighttime bomber attacks against Germany that were becoming more frequent. Although RAF attacks on the German homeland in 1941 were little more than a nuisance, meeting the defensive needs of the homeland required that fighters and flak guns be diverted to homeland defense in ever greater numbers. In the Mediterranean, the German army and Luftwaffe scored impressive victories in the first half of 1941. But the Luftwaffe was now heavily engaged in a theater where Hitler had never planned to fight. Supporting the Italians and Rommel's Afrika Korps required the diversion of several hundred aircraft. After taking Greece, General Löhr had to leave some bomber groups behind on Crete to carry out raids on British shipping in the eastern Mediterranean and in the Suez Canal.

If the German leadership had been thinking in grand strategic terms, which it rarely did, it might have been alarmed for the future of the Luftwaffe. For all its success in battle, the Luftwaffe was already losing the all-important war of production. While Britain, Canada, and the United States were dramatically increasing the production of every kind of aircraft, the German aircraft production had barely increased over its 1939 levels. In 1939 the Germans produced 8,295 aircraft; in 1940 this figure had risen to 10,247. In 1941, the German aircraft production was only 11,776 aircraft—not nearly close to the numbers required to replace the steady losses that the Germans were experiencing on all the war fronts.

In the meantime, British aircraft production surpassed Germany's by a wide margin. Even though the United States was not yet in the war, American aircraft were beginning to flow to Britain in large numbers. All of this meant that the Luftwaffe would go into the Soviet campaign in 1941 with considerably fewer aircraft than it had deployed against France in 1940. In March 1940 the Luftwaffe, fighting on one front, could field 3,692 combat aircraft. In June 1941 the Luftwaffe, now fighting on three fronts, had only 3,451 aircraft.[1] In the east in June 1941, the Luftwaffe would field 2,232 planes, supported by a further 570 aircraft assigned to the army's and navy's air arms. This was approximately 1,000 aircraft fewer than had been available for the 1940 campaign. Even more disturbing was the shortage of bombers. In the east in 1941, the Luftwaffe had 838 bombers—only half the number that had been available for the 1940 campaign in France.[2] These figures tell only part of the story. Where the Luftwaffe had had to support operations over a front of about 200 miles in 1940, it would now have to carry out the same mission over a front six times longer and far deeper—and with fewer airplanes.

The Luftwaffe would have some help in the form of its allied air forces. The armies and air forces of Finland, Romania, and Hungary would all participate in the invasion of the Soviet Union alongside the Germans. The three allied air forces in the east would be able to deploy over 1,000 aircraft for the battle—a considerable help to the Germans. Germany's allies, of which Finland was the most capable, had air forces equipped with a broad mix of obsolescent aircraft bought from many countries, as well as small numbers of light aircraft produced by small home industries. The limited industrial base of Germany's allies meant that their air force infrastructure was weak and allied operational rates would be low. Still, these allied air forces, though small and obsolescent, still fielded aircraft that were roughly equal to those of the Red Air Force of 1941.[3]

Henschel 123, a very rugged biplane designed for ground attack. From 1939 to 1941 the Hs 123 performed very well as a close support airplane, and von Richthofen had a group of them under his command in Poland in 1939, France in 1940, and Russia in 1941. (U.S. Air Force)

On the positive side, 1941 saw some important improvements in the Luftwaffe's force structure and equipment. The Focke Wulf FW 190, which would turn out to be one of the great fighter and attack planes of World War II, was entering full production and was fielded in the summer of 1941 on the western front, where it quickly proved superior to the latest model of the British Spitfire (the Mark V). The greatly improved Ju 87 D model, with twice the bomb load and twice the range of the B model, was replacing the earlier models (older aircraft were given to the Italians and other allies). Improvements had been made to the Me 109: the latest production model, the Me 109 F, was a superb dogfighter and could only be equaled by the British Spitfire on the Allied side. The Luftwaffe had improved and enlarged the Flivo system of liaison with the army. All armored and motorized divisions now had Flivos equipped with light armored vehicles and able to operate with the forward elements of those units and communicate effectively with the air wings and air corps headquarters. Von Richthofen's 1940 training experiments with putting forward air controllers in armored vehicles with radios able to talk with the aircraft above them and provide directions for close attacks were finally ready for operational use. On a limited basis, the VIIIth Air Corps would employ air liaison teams to control aircraft in close air support in 1941. It was the first such use of ground-based air controllers in warfare and a huge advance in the capability of the Luftwaffe to provide accurate air support right on the front lines.

Often, many of the major advantages in warfare are things that cannot be seen or easily measured, such as training, morale, leadership, and tactics. In 1941 the Luftwaffe held an enormous advantage over its enemies, especially when compared to the Soviets, in terms of command effectiveness, doctrine, and training. By 1941 the senior commanders of the Luftwaffe and of the army had worked together as a team for almost two years of intensive combat. From Poland to France to the Balkans, von Richthofen had worked closely with army generals Kleist, Guderian, Reichenau, and Leeb, and a host of other senior officers who would lead the German army into the USSR. The same can be said of the Luftwaffe's other top commanders. In June 1941 the German military had by far the most experienced and best trained operational military leadership in the world. Moreover, the Luftwaffe and the army were exceptionally effective in learning tactical and operation lessons. After every campaign both the Luftwaffe and the army had carefully analyzed their operations and modified their tactics and doctrine. Equipment was modified in light of ongoing experience. In terms of pure combat effectiveness, soldier for soldier and plane for plane, the Germans were far ahead of the Allied powers at this point in the war.

Although von Richthofen might continually complain that the army really did not understand the effective use of airpower or the capabilities of the Luftwaffe—and he was largely correct in this assessment—the German army and air force were still far ahead of the other major powers in planning joint operations and conducting campaigns as an effective air-ground team. In terms of conducting close air support and liaison with the army, the Luftwaffe of 1941 was about two years ahead of the British and Americans. Between the Germans' and the Soviets' ability to plan and conduct air campaigns and support their ground forces in 1941, there was simply no comparison. The Soviets had made few improvements since Spain, and until 1943, few of the Soviet aircraft even had radios. This meant that the Soviet air force (VVS) would fly and fight looking for hand signals from the commander—just as in World War I. In contrast, the Luftwaffe had an extensive ground and air communications network. Not only did all aircraft have radios, but air unit commanders could report the situation at the front and in the air, and higher headquarters could react within minutes to the changing conditions. This alone gave the Luftwaffe a huge advantage over the Soviet air force; it would not be until 1943 that the VVS finally developed a modern communications system.

One of the great steps forward in air war methods would be introduced by von Richthofen in the summer of 1941. Since 1939 he had experimented with a system of directing close air support from the ground, using Luftwaffe personnel in armored vehicles and appropriate radios to direct action from the front lines. He had finally perfected the system in 1941, and that summer he put Luftwaffe airmen in armored vehicles on the front line to direct Stuka attacks on fortified enemy positions. The special teams for close air support were allocated to the panzer divisions and proved enormously effective in reducing friendly-fire incidents and in identifying the most valuable ground targets to attack. Von Richthofen's 1941 innovations made the Luftwaffe much more effective in supporting the German ground forces. It would be two years before the British and Americans could field similar teams to coordinate their air support for the ground armies.

The Soviet Army and Air Force in 1941

The Soviet air force in 1941 was strong on paper—but only on paper. The Soviets had created a large aircraft industry from scratch in the 1920s and had expanded their air force in the 1930s and had built the largest air force in the world. Soviet design teams had proven in the 1930s that they could design and build fighters and bombers equal to, or better than, the aircraft of the other major powers. But despite the large numbers and the impressive infrastructure the Soviets had built, Joseph Stalin had crippled his armed forces with massive purges of the officer corps from 1936 to 1939. Most of the top generals of the army and air force, including brilliant figures such as army chief of staff Marshal Tuchaschewski, had been killed or sent to rot in the gulags. The army and air force general staffs had been especially targeted for destruction. The result of Stalin's almost insane paranoia was the appallingly bad performance of the Red Army and Soviet air force in the war against Finland from November 1939 to March 1940. Although the Soviets would bring overwhelming numerical superiority against the Finns as well as a qualitative advantage in tanks, aircraft, and artillery, the small and poorly equipped Finnish army and air force had been able to repulse all the early Soviet offensives and inflict massive losses on the Soviet forces. In the north and to center of the line, the Finns had enveloped and destroyed whole Soviet divisions. In the air the tiny Finnish air force was able to shoot down hundreds of Soviet aircraft with little loss to themselves. Finally, though, the Soviet manpower and material advantage turned the tide, and the Soviets were able to force the Finns to cede the Karelia province of southern Finland in a negotiated settlement. Although tiny Finland had lost territory, the Finnish War was seen as a huge moral defeat for the Soviets. It showed Stalin's armed forces to be a true hollow shell. If the Soviet army and air force could barely eke out a victory against tiny Finland, then how well could it be expected to perform against the well-equipped and superbly trained Wehrmacht? The results of the Finnish War emboldened Hitler to see the whole Soviet state as a rotten edifice that would collapse with one good push. Indeed, the German analysis of the weakness of the Soviet military as demonstrated in Finland was fairly accurate.

However, the Finnish War had come as a shock to Stalin, and he moved quickly to rebuild the army and air force from the damage that he had inflicted upon them. Experienced officers, technicians, and specialists who had survived the wave of liquidations in the 1930s and were consigned to labor camps were pulled out of the gulag and given their commands back. Generals and officers who had proven ineffective against Finland were relieved, and officers who had shown their competence were promoted. General Zhukov, who was not a general staff officer but was famous for delivering a sharp defeat to the Japanese in a short conflict with them along the Mongolian border in 1940, was recalled from the Far East and promoted to chief of staff of the army. After Finland, Soviet doctrine, tactics, and organization were reformed and training improved. But in June 1941 the Soviet armed forces were still in a state of flux and confusion. In the air force, 91 percent of the major unit commanders had held their posts for less than six months.[4] The situation was similar for the army. In 1941, the Red Army and VVS would pay a huge price in blood for Stalin's purges.

German Intelligence Failure

When Hitler in late 1940 had made known to the Wehrmacht his intention to go to war with the Soviet Union, the Luftwaffe mounted an extensive campaign of aerial reconnaissance and intelligence gathering against the Soviet forces. The Germans had correctly assessed that the Soviets had moved the main portion of their armed forces to their new western border, which consisted of the eastern half of Poland, seized in September 1939, and the Baltic countries, seized in June 1940. However, despite a major intelligence effort, Wehrmacht intelligence specialists grossly underestimated the size and capabilities of the Soviet forces. In August 1940 the Wehrmacht estimated that the Red Army had 221 divisions or mechanized brigades, with 143 of these stationed close to the USSR's western frontier. In May 1941, just before the campaign began, the Wehrmacht revised its estimates to assume that the Soviets had two million men under arms, with the vast majority of Soviet forces deployed far forward along the western frontiers. The final German estimate of Soviet army mechanized strength put the Soviet tank force at 10,000 tanks. In fact, the Soviets, frantically reforming their forces after the war with Finland, had put more than five million men under arms. The Soviets had more than twice as many tanks as the Germans expected, approximately 20,000–25,000 tanks. The most dangerous of the Wehrmacht's beliefs was that the vast majority of the Soviet forces had been placed on the western frontier and that there would be little to fight once those forces had been destroyed. In fact, the Germans had overestimated the size of the Soviet forces in the West; the Soviet high command had retained half of the army in reserve deep in the USSR or in the second line of defense hundreds of miles into Russia.[5] The Luftwaffe intelligence chief, General Beppo Schmidt, had also underestimated his opponents.

The Luftwaffe had estimated the Soviet air strength at twenty-three air divisions. Actually, the Soviets had seventy-nine air divisions, fifty-five of which were stationed in the western region of the Soviet Union. The Germans estimated that the Soviets had 7,300 aircraft in European Russia, with 3,000 in the interior and 2,000 in the Far East. Actually, the VVS had several thousand more aircraft than the Germans thought, with more than twice as many aircraft in the Far East (4,140) than the Germans had estimated and a further 1,500 home defense fighters and 1,445 navy aircraft that the Germans had not reckoned on. However, the German assessment that the Soviet aircraft were overwhelmingly obsolete and no match for the German airplanes was true. The main Soviet fighter of 1941, the I-16, had been a great aircraft in Spain in 1937, but was clearly now obsolete. Of the new Soviet fighters — the LaGG-1, the Mig 3, and the Yak 1 — only the Yak 1 was roughly equal to Germany's Me 109.[6] However, the new bombers and attack planes would prove very effective in the battles of 1942–1945. The most important of these was the IL-2 Sthurmovik ground attack plane, which entered service in 1940 and would prove to be one of the great airplanes of World War II. Designed solely as a close attack plane, it was equipped with heavy armor to protect the pilot, fuel, and engine and a thick screen of bulletproof glass to protect the pilot. The IL-2 carried heavy cannon and up to a ton of bombs. It was simple to fly and maintain and could be operated from forward airfields by pilots with just sixty hours of training.[7] The tactics of the Shturmovik were simple: simply fly a mass of them straight to the enemy position, strafe, and drop the bombs. The heavy armor and incredible ruggedness of the plane meant that it was impervious to all but a direct hit from an antiaircraft gun. German fighters found the IL-2s to be exceptionally difficult to shoot down.[8] The Yak 3, a superb fighter plane, was coming into production, and the Pe-2, a very capable light bomber/dive bomber, was just entering service in 1941. Essentially, by concentrating on just a few types of good airplanes the Soviet aircraft industry was able to manufacture very large numbers of aircraft during the war.

Yet, despite a solid program for the development of the Soviet air force, the main weaknesses of the force in 1941—and indeed through the first two years of the Soviet campaign—were in training and infrastructure. The VVS turned out a lot of pilots, but training was very basic and the pilots lacked the skills to fly at night or in bad weather. The air force had an exceptionally weak communications system that would limit its operational effectiveness until 1943, when large quantities of U.S. Lend-Lease aircraft and other equipment became available. For example, in 1941 the Soviets had a few radars, mostly sited around Moscow for air defense, but the Soviet radar system was fairly ineffective, and Moscow's air defenses were nothing as formidable as the Germans had faced in 1940 against Britain.

The German Plan

The Germans would deploy more than 3 million men and 148 divisions in the campaign in the east in 1941. The German army forces included nineteen panzer and fifteen motorized divisions, which, per standard practice, were organized into panzer groups or armies, each consisting of a force of six or more panzer and motorized divisions. The panzer groups would be the main strike forces of the campaign, designed to rush forward, outflank, and envelop the Soviet armies in huge encirclement operations. Supporting the panzer groups would be 114 infantry divisions, or 75 percent of the German army. The infantry divisions were scarcely blitzkrieg organizations. They possessed only a few transport trucks and some motor vehicles for their reconnaissance units, headquarters, and artillery. The main transport force for the 1941 German infantry division was the horse. The German army in the East would deploy 3,350 tanks, 7,184 artillery pieces, 600,000 motor vehicles, and 625,000 horses.

Assisting in the German invasion would be the Finnish and Romanian armies. The Finns, by far the most capable of Germany's allies, would deploy 500,000 men in fourteen divisions and three brigades. For the campaign the Romanians had 150,000 men in fourteen divisions and three brigades—all understrength.[9] The Hungarians agreed to support the German plans but would not commit any major forces until 1942. Germany's allies would fight in their own sectors with the objective of making limited territorial gains. The national air forces of Germany's allies would fly in support of their own forces, although there would be some cooperation between the Luftwaffe and the allied air forces later in the campaign. Yet, for the most part, Germany's allies fought parallel wars alongside Germany, and true strategic and operational cooperation was limited. On no front did the Germans develop a true coalition command system—and this would be one of the weaknesses of Germany's war-making methods in the East and in the Mediterranean.

The German forces were organized into three large army groups: North, Center, and South. The groups would control seven German armies, normally infantry forces, and four panzer groups. Three Romanian armies would fight independently but under general German strategic direction. The Luftwaffe deployed three air fleets for the campaign, each to support the operations of one of the army groups. The First Air Fleet, based in East Prussia and under the command of General Alfred Keller, was a small force with only 379 aircraft. It was assigned the mission of supporting Army Group North under Field Marshal Wilhelm von Leeb, whose objective was to advance along the Baltic coast and seize Leningrad. Army Group Center, based in Poland and under the command of Field Marshal Fedor von Bock, contained the largest proportion of the German army invading the USSR. Army Group Center was expected to destroy the main Soviet armies in western Russia and then drive on to Moscow. The 2nd Air Fleet, under the command of Field Marshal Albert Kesselring, had 1,223 aircraft assigned—more than half of all the Luftwaffe forces in the invasion. All of the available Stuka and ground attack groups were assigned to the 2nd Air Fleet. As part of this fleet, von Richthofen's VIIIth Air Corps was assigned the mission of supporting General Hermann Hoth's Panzergruppe 3 and the Ninth Army on the left flank of Army Group Center's advance. General Heinz Guderian's Panzergruppe 2 and German forces on the right flank of the army group would be supported by General Bruno Loerzer's IInd Air Corps. The 2nd Air Fleet also included Flak Corps I of the Luftwaffe, equipped with a large number of heavy and light flak guns. Army Group South, commanded by Field Marshal Gerd von Rundstedt, would be supported by General Alexander Löhr's 4th Air Fleet with 630 aircraft.[10] The Luftwaffe's Flak Corps II would also be deployed for the campaign.

The sheer scale of the operation was as much of a problem for the Wehrmacht as was fighting its way through the Soviet armies. Essentially, the low number of German aircraft for the vast front meant that only key areas and operations could count on getting air support. The relatively few German aircraft would have very little operational effect unless concentrated and used en masse at the decisive point. The first mission of the Luftwaffe would be to win air superiority by taking out the Soviet air force in the first days of the campaign, preferably by destroying air units on the ground. Once air superiority was won, the Luftwaffe would support the main German thrusts, primarily the advance of the panzer groups, with an interdiction campaign meant to paralyze the Soviet transportation network and troop movements. Finally, when major results could be achieved, the Luftwaffe would fly in close support of the army to destroy Soviet units and fortifications. Soviet strategic targets deep in the Soviet heartland would be struck when the opportunity arose. It was a classic version of what the Luftwaffe referred to as the "operational air war," a grand campaign that combined strategic bombing and deep and shallow interdiction to paralyze the enemy movement and operations. The war in the USSR was the kind of air war that the Luftwaffe leadership had long wanted to fight. When Hans Jeschonnek was informed of Hitler's plans to invade the Soviet Union, he exclaimed, "At last! A proper war!"[11] Hitler and the German military leadership expected a short campaign of only a few weeks, and they expressed few misgivings about the operation before it began. Yet the Wehrmacht's and Luftwaffe's major weakness, the lack of logistics infrastructure, would come to play a decisive role in the campaign and ensure that the Germans would not reach their primary objectives. The Luftwaffe, even more than the army, was a force designed for short, sharp campaigns. Now the Luftwaffe would be involved in a three-front attrition war that would cripple the force within two years.

The Balkans campaign ought to have been a warning signal to von Richthofen and other Luftwaffe commanders, but there had been little time to absorb the lessons from that engagement. In April, von Richthofen had had a very difficult time deploying one air task force forward from Bulgaria to the airfield at Larissa, a 150-mile jump. To maintain just one forward task force he had employed most of the available ground and air transport. Now the Luftwaffe was expected to jump units forward 600 miles in a country with a different rail gauge and few good roads. The heavy losses of transports in the Crete campaign, the heavy requirement for air transport to support the German army in North Africa, and the failure of the Luftwaffe staff to rapidly expand the air transport force meant that the Luftwaffe logistics system would quickly be stretched far beyond its capability to carry out the mission. Any sensible Wehrmacht planner could have foreseen the failure of German logistics to support so large an advance, but German overconfidence was so great in 1941 that such basic considerations were simply brushed away.[12] The Soviet Union had only 51,000 miles of railroads—all of a different gauge than the Western European one—and to be useful to the Germans, all the track would have to be relaid. It supposedly had 150,000 miles of all-weather roads—but the falsity of this description would be borne out when the rain and snow came. In fact, the Soviet Union in 1941 had a fairly primitive transportation system and only 40,000 miles of paved roads.[13] Yet none of the senior German commanders expressed any doubts whether the logistics system could support such a huge enterprise over such long distances. The attitude of Germany's commanders, including von Richthofen, was that somehow it would all work out. It was a trademark of the German military senior leadership in the war — operational and tactical brilliance combined with a failure to understand the basic requirements of strategy.

The Campaign Begins

Even as the Balkans campaign was winding down in late May 1941, von Richthofen was busy redeploying the VIIIth Air Corps out of the Balkans to southern Poland, where the force would prepare to support Army Group Center in the Soviet offensive. The air corps would be subordinate to Kesselring's 2nd Air Fleet. Since the VIIIth Air Corps had been part of the 2nd Air Fleet during a portion of the 1940 campaign in the West, the commanders and staffs knew each other well and understood the planning and staff procedures.

Von Richthofen complained in his diary that the VIIIth Air Corps had no time to rest and refit before being thrown into another major operation. By the eve of the offensive most of his air corps had arrived, but some units were still under way. Most of von Richthofen's units had lost aircraft and had not received a full complement of replacements before the Soviet campaign. So he would start the campaign with units at a 70 percent operational rate or even below. His ground support units were short spare parts as well. Prior to the start of the Soviet campaign von Richthofen had only a few days at home before flying to the front for a full round of briefings and planning conferences. Despite all the transport and logistics problems, the air corps was ready to carry out its mission on 22 June when Operation Barbarossa began. Before dawn that day, VIIIth Air Corps bomber and Stuka units pounded the Red Army airfields inside the Soviet frontier in the central sector of the front. The Soviets were taken completely by surprise and paid a high price for their unreadiness.

On 22 June the 2nd Air Fleet hit thirty-one Soviet airfields and destroyed an estimated 1,800 Soviet planes in the first wave of attacks — with only two German aircraft reported lost. The second wave of attacks later that morning destroyed 700 Soviet planes with thirty-three German aircraft lost. The initial strikes on the Soviet air force were more successful than von Richthofen or Kesselring had believed possible. Some Soviet units managed to get airborne and attempt to fly against the German army. Whole wings of unescorted bombers were quickly shot out of the sky by the Luftwaffe's fighters. Within three days Kesselring could declare the Soviet air force essentially broken and order that his forces concentrate on interdiction and close air support

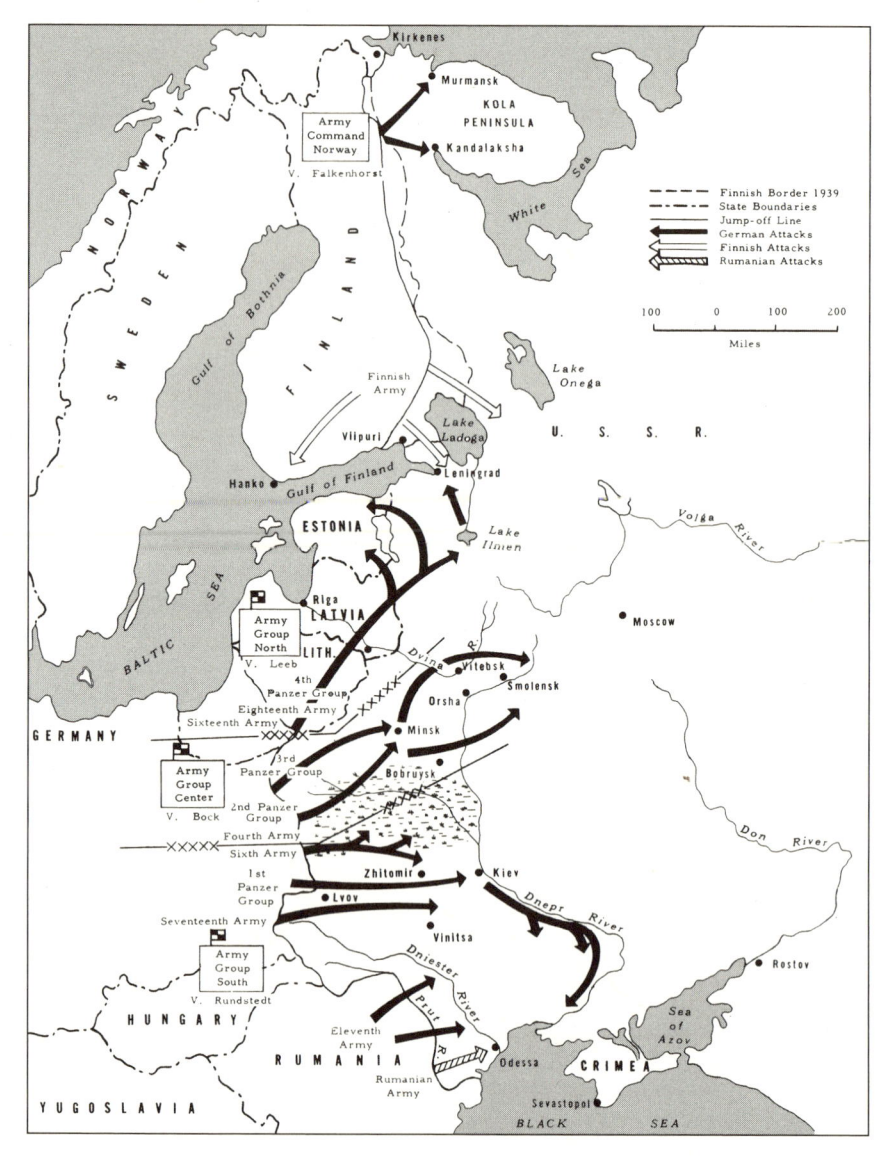

From June to August 1941 the VIIIth Air Corps supported Army Group Center's drive on Moscow. In August and September the VIIIth Air Corps was sent north to support Army Group North's drive on Leningrad. (Lt. Gen. Hermann Plocher, *The German Air Force versus Russia, 1941*, USAF historical Study No. 153, circa 1954)

missions to support the rapid advance of Army Group Center. Indeed, the Luftwaffe for once had not exaggerated the damage it had inflicted upon an enemy air force. Soviet sources indicate that the VVS lost 3,600 planes in the first three weeks of the campaign, but it was likely many more.[14] One estimate is that of the 10,000 Soviet aircraft in the western frontier area on 22 June, approximately 8,000 had been lost by October.[15] The initial German air superiority campaign was so successful and the Soviet air force had lost so many aircrew, ground personnel, aircraft, and infrastructure that it would not reappear to challenge German air superiority until late 1942.[16]

In the first days of the campaign the Luftwaffe bomber and fighter units flew up to six sorties per day, and the Stukas flew as many as eight sorties. Von Richthofen performed brilliantly, as usual. His Flivos, operating with the infantry corps and each of Panzer Group 3's divisions, were able to arrange effective Stuka support to reduce Soviet strong points. The response for requests for support to aircraft striking the target was about two hours—very impressive performance by 1941 standards.[17] The advance of Panzer Group 3 was so rapid that the previous system of bomb lines was abandoned and the army deployed signal panels, flares, and other signals to avoid friendly-fire incidents. Unfortunately, in the confusion of the rapid advance German units were often bombed by mistake by the Luftwaffe.

After the initial breakthrough battles of June, Bock's army group advanced deep into the Soviet Union in July. Though some Red Army units fought well, most of the force performed clumsily. Much of the Red Army was trapped in pockets and forced to surrender. In the first two weeks of the campaign the Germans captured 360,000 Soviet soldiers; by 5 August, 774,000 Red Army soldiers had entered the German POW cages. Early in the campaign Army Group Center, with the VIIIth Air Corps in support, enveloped a Soviet army at Minsk, capturing over 300,000 Red Army soldiers.[18] In late July Army Group Center enveloped a Soviet army group at Smolensk, and when the pocket was completely annihilated on 6 August the Germans could count over 300,000 Soviet prisoners and 3,000 Soviet tanks captured or destroyed. Again, von Richthofen's airmen had played a key role in the grand victory.[19] During these grand envelopment operations von Richthofen's units flew mostly interdiction operations, destroying Soviet columns on the road and preventing the escape of major Soviet forces from the thinly held German pockets. While many thousands of Soviets were able to break out of the pockets and live to fight again, they usually did so without their tanks, artillery, or trucks, which were the Luftwaffe's main target. In addition to destroying Soviet units on the roads, VIIIth Air Corps paid particular attention to the Soviet rail network, working to paralyze rail movement of troops and supplies in the forward area.

Destruction of a Russian airfield, June 1941. Thousands of Soviet aircraft were knocked out on the ground by Luftwaffe attacks in the first week of the war. It took the Soviets more than a year to recover from the initial devastating losses. (U.S. Air Force)

The Soviet army, with far more units than the Germans had ever expected, carried out a series of major counterattacks to try to halt the German advance. In July the Soviet Reserve Front launched a counteroffensive north of Smolensk against Guderian's Panzer Group 2, which was supported by von Richthofen's force. Von Richthofen responded quickly with medium bombers and Stukas that ruthlessly attacked the Soviet columns, destroying dozens of vehicles. Rail yards in the Soviet rear were also a prime target of von Richthofen's airmen.[20]

The SD-2 bomb, the first true cluster bomb, was first used in a large scale in the 1941 Soviet campaign and provided a huge increase in the Luftwaffe's effectiveness. The new bomb was far more lethal than the Luftwaffe's conventional bombs when attacking ground troops or vehicles in the open. Since each SD-2 was a container of ninety-six bombs that covered an area of a few hundred meters, one aircraft dropping two or three of the canisters could effectively wipe out an entire Soviet road column. The cluster bomb was so effective in the interdiction missions against the Red Army that it was accorded the top priority for German munitions production. The U.S. Air Force found the SD-2 such an effective weapon that it copied and produced the bomb after the war; the SD-2 remained in the U.S. inventory as a standard munition into the 1960s.

German Stukas break the Soviet rail lines on the central front in the summer of 1941. In the first weeks of the war the Luftwaffe enjoyed incredible success. Soviet transportation was paralyzed, whole columns of Soviet troops and tanks destroyed, and Soviet fortified positions knocked out by accurate bombing. (U.S. Air Force)

In the first weeks of the campaign von Richthofen constantly flew his Fiesler Stork, now his trademark aircraft, between the headquarters of the 2nd Air Fleet, Army Group Center, and the panzer armies that he was supporting. His diary notes frequent conferences with senior army and air commanders. In the meantime, his staff managed the moves forward—the VIIIth Air Corps headquarters moved more than a dozen times during the 1941 campaign— each time having to ensure that communications with the rapidly advancing army units was maintained without interruption. In as early as mid-July the logistics problem of operating over vast distances began to kick in. The VIIIth Air Corps units suffered a fairly low attrition rate, nothing that would cripple the force, but the large distances ensured that replacement aircraft and pilots were slow to arrive. A few weeks into the campaign the combat operational rates of the VIIIth Air Corps units were approaching 50–60 percent. It was much the same for the whole Luftwaffe in the East.[21]

Move to the North

One of the problems of the Soviet campaign was Hitler's capricious approach to strategy. While the army favored Moscow as the main objective of the campaign, Hitler also wanted to ensure that Leningrad was taken. As a result, he ordered that both operations be undertaken, with the first priority given to Leningrad. In early August, as the destruction of the Smolensk pocket was coming to an end and the way opening up for Army Group Center to advance on Moscow, Hitler ordered von Richthofen and the VIIIth Air Corps to be transferred north to support Leeb's Army Group North advance on Leningrad. Army Group Center would hold its position while Army Group South took Kiev and completed another grand encirclement operation.

Von Richthofen would move north with nine groups of his air corps (262 aircraft) and leave two of his Stuka groups behind to be transferred to Loerzer's IInd Air Corps. This left only 600 aircraft to support all of Army Group Center's operations. By August 1941 the insufficient Luftwaffe forces in the East, coupled with the steady attrition of the campaign, were starting to have a noticeable effect upon the ability of the Luftwaffe to carry out its missions. Although the Soviet air force was not much in evidence, Soviet ground fire and antiaircraft fire could be fierce and effective. Von Richthofen's Stukas, fighters, and ground attack planes suffered a steady attrition rate. Accidents from flying and landing on rough forward airfields and trying to maintain aircraft in primitive conditions were also common. From 22 June to 5 July the Luftwaffe in the USSR recorded 491 aircraft destroyed and 316 damaged. Between 6 and 19 July a further 283 aircraft were lost and 194 damaged.

Between 19 July and 31 August the Luftwaffe lost 725 aircraft.[22] While German aircraft production could make up the losses of destroyed aircraft, it took time to get replacement aircraft and aircrew forward. Of particular concern were the damaged planes. Luftwaffe units were not equipped to perform major overhauls and repair severely damaged planes, and it became more and more difficult to get damaged aircraft back to Germany to be rebuilt as the advance continued and the supply lines over the primitive transportation network grew longer and longer. With repair parts slow to arrive, even supreme efforts by the Luftwaffe's ground crews could not put damaged aircraft back in the air. So serviceability rates dropped, and by late summer the Luftwaffe's units, including the VIIIth Air Corps, were commonly operating at about 50–60 percent strength.

Arriving in the northern sector of the front, von Richthofen emphasized the principle of concentration when employing his Stukas and bombers. General Leeb, operating on a narrow front hemmed in by lakes and rivers, gave the Eighteenth Army and Panzer Group 4 the mission of advancing on Leningrad. The VIIIth Air Corps began operations in support of these units on 6 August.[23] In twelve days von Richthofen's air corps flew 4,742 sorties and dropped 3,351 tons of bombs. The results were dramatic: on 11 August, Panzer Group 4 broke through the Soviet fortified line; ten days later, Army Group North reached the northern tip of Lake Ilmen and the Gulf of Finland.[24] Desperate to defend the approaches to Leningrad, the Soviets put up an increasingly tough resistance, but with accurate and effective attacks against the Soviet front units and their rear transport, the Eighteenth Army was able to push all the way to the suburbs of Leningrad.[25] As an example of just how devastating the Luftwaffe attacks could be, on 10 August the VIIIth Air Corps attacked targets throughout the Lake Ilmen area and destroyed more than 200 Soviet vehicles, fifteen artillery batteries, five transport trains, and several major command posts and ammunition dumps. During the course of the day von Richthofen's airmen shot down fifty-four Soviet planes.[26] In late August accurate bombing by the Stukas of Stuka Wing 2 helped the German army breech the first of the major Soviet defense lines before Leningrad.[27] By early September the capture of Leningrad was in sight. On 8 September the land communications between Leningrad and the rest of the Soviet Union were cut; now the encircled city could only receive supplies and reinforcements by boat over Lake Ladoga. At this point the VIIIth Air Corps concentrated on attacking the last supply lines to Leningrad, and Stukas sank several supply ships on Lake Ladoga.[28] At the same time the Stukas and bombers of the VIIIth Air Corps carried out a series of attacks to cripple the Soviet Baltic fleet. Accurate German bombing badly damaged two Soviet battleships and two cruisers, essentially putting the main strike force of the Soviet fleet out of action.[29]

Yet, with the capture of Leningrad in sight, Hitler and the Wehrmacht high command changed direction again and on 6 September issued a directive that the destruction of the Soviet armies around Kiev and the resumption of the advance upon Moscow were the new priorities for the German forces. With orders to be transferred back to the 2nd Air Fleet and support Army Group Center, on 15 September von Richthofen redoubled his attacks on Leningrad itself and the Soviet forces in the north. Leeb desperately wanted to keep von Richthofen's air corps in support, but his request was turned down. With most of his air support gone he saw the chance of taking Leningrad fade away. However, Stuka Group 2 under the command of Colonel Oskar Dinort would stay with the 1st Air Fleet to support the final drive to encircle the city and put it under blockade.

In the north von Richthofen had been remarkably effective in getting the army to within final striking distance of Leningrad, but the operation had been expensive. In the August offensive the VIIIth Air Corps had lost twenty-seven aircraft, with a further 143 damaged.[30] Von Richthofen would return his tired and depleted forces to the 2nd Air Fleet in order to carry out Operation Taifun, the final drive to take Moscow by Army Group Center. Kesselring would have over 1,000 planes, at least on paper, as well as two flak corps for the final drive on Moscow.

The Drive on Moscow

Army Group Center's first task was to destroy the main Soviet armies defending the route to Moscow. Through September and early October, Army Group Center carried out the envelopment of two large Soviet armies, by now the routine method of German army operations in the East. With the destruction of the main Soviet armies the Germans assumed that the path to Moscow would be opened and the war would be over by Christmas. By 20 October a large Soviet force in the Bryansk pocket had been reduced and the atmosphere in the German high command and army group headquarters was optimistic that the end of Soviet resistance was near. In the south, Guderian and Kleist's panzer groups, operating under von Rundstedt's Army Group South, carried out a massive envelopment campaign at Kiev in September. The German forces won their greatest victory to date when 665,000 Russians were taken prisoner, and 3,018 artillery pieces, 884 tanks, and 418 antitank guns were captured. With the Soviet defeat at Kiev the way into southern Russia was opened, and on 24 October German forces took Kharkov and Kleist's panzer group was advancing upon Rostov.

In late October, Jeschonnek telephoned von Richthofen and told him that he expected that the VIIIth Air Corps would soon return to Germany and the units could expect to spend Christmas in Bavaria and Austria.[31] Von Richthofen was skeptical. When given the mission of supporting the left flank of Bock's offensive (Ninth Army and Panzer Group 3), von Richthofen was unsure whether he could effectively see it through with his depleted force. Von Richthofen was feeling somewhat depressed at this time as his very talented chief of staff, Colonel Rudolf Meister, had been shot down in his Fiesler Stork while visiting the 1st Panzer Division headquarters and had been wounded in the crash. Although Meister would recover and return to battle, and later be promoted to general, it was a hard blow to lose a man who had proved a superb staff planner through the Balkans campaign and the first four months of the Soviet campaign.

In late October, Guderian drove toward Orel on the southern flank of Moscow. Now the weak logistics system of the Wehrmacht was the Soviets' greatest advantage as they prepared the final defense of Moscow. By this time, due to combat losses, breakdowns, and lack of parts and fuel, German panzer forces before Moscow had no more than 20–30 percent of their normal vehicle complement available. Serviceability rates for Luftwaffe aircraft were similar to that of the army's equipment. Between 22 to 25 October, the entire 2nd Air Fleet was only able to generate between 614 and 662 sorties a day. This was a small fraction of what it had been able to do at the start of the campaign.[32]

In addition, nature would provide the Soviets considerable breathing space in the form of the "Rasputitsa," which was translated as "the time without roads." The fall rains and early snow turned the Soviet Union's primitive road system into deep mud, which made the roads impassable for the Wehrmacht's wheeled vehicles. Nor could the Germans count on the Soviet rail system to supply the forward units, as the switch to the narrower German rails was incomplete. Von Richthofen moved his headquarters to Kalinin, and his units were now largely dependent upon air supply provided by the Luftwaffe's small transport force. Fuel, always the most important supply item for the Luftwaffe, was in short supply because the air transports could only bring in limited amounts. Unlike the campaigns in France and Greece, when the Luftwaffe could maintain its advance by capturing large quantities of fuel from the enemy, the Soviet campaign saw fuel and supplies destroyed as the Red Army retreated toward Moscow. The weather also reduced air operations by turning many of the captured Soviet airfields into bogs. The Luftwaffe's airfield engineers had their hands full trying to keep a few airfields operating in the bad weather.

As November progressed the Soviet resistance before Moscow stiffened. With army and Luftwaffe logistics in disarray, and the weather steadily deteriorating, operations by the 2nd Air Fleet and VIIIth Air Corps significantly decreased. The fuel shortage at the front was a major factor in limiting German operations at this point. Furthermore, von Richthofen's planes were largely worn out, and many planes that needed parts and overhaul were grounded. His air units were now deep inside the Soviet Union at the end of a tenuous supply line. Since June, von Richthofen had moved his headquarters seven times, and his fighter and Stuka units were now operating from rough and poorly constructed captured Soviet airfields. Combat and operational losses had not been made good by the Luftwaffe, and as the final drive on Moscow was readied it was not the force that it had been at the start of the campaign. A further blow to the German plans to take Moscow came in November when Kesselring was directed to transfer his 2nd Air Fleet to the Mediterranean theater. He would leave von Richthofen and the VIIIth Air Corps behind to support Army Group Center while he took Loerzer's air corps and thirteen air groups with him to the Mediterranean.[33]

The initiative to transfer forces out of the theater just before the final battle for Moscow is an indication of how unrealistic the view from Berlin was. While Hitler was preparing to celebrate victory, army chief of staff General Franz Halder noted in his diary on 22 November that the German army had reached its limits of endurance. By 1 December he was convinced that the German army in the USSR was no longer fit for operations. He noted that Hitler and his immediate circle "have no idea of the condition of the troops."[34] Expecting imminent victory at Moscow, Kesselring departed for Dresden for the south on 29 November and von Richthofen took over command of the Luftwaffe on the Moscow front.

An indication of the poor condition of the VIIIth Air Corps is its low sortie rate in November and December. Bad weather, fuel shortages, and low serviceability rates ensured that the VIIIth Air Corps flew only 269 sorties on the Moscow front on 30 November, 227 on 1 December, and 423 on 2 December—a very low rate of operations compared to the first two months of the campaign. However, most days in late November and early December the weather was so bad that the Luftwaffe hardly flew at all. By early December it was clear to the Wehrmacht and Luftwaffe high commands that Moscow would not fall to Operation Taifun before the end of the year. However, the Germans would use the time to rebuild and resupply their forces for the final drive. Essentially, the Germans believed that the Soviet armed forces had largely been finished off in the summer and fall campaign and that only the last reserves stood before them and complete victory. On 18 November 1941, General Halder noted that he and Field Marshal Bock were convinced that the Russians were "throwing in the last ounce of strength" on the Moscow front. The Germans, tired as they were, needed only to push on, and the Soviets would soon collapse as they had "nothing left in their rear."[35] The Germans had good reason to believe that the Soviets could not hold out much longer. In the first six months of the campaign the Soviet army had recorded 2.5 million men dead or missing, 20,000 tanks destroyed, and over 10,000 aircraft lost (one estimate has this as more than 17,000). Per the German intelligence estimates, the back of the Soviet armed forces had been broken and, although the Soviets were trying to rebuild their forces, they would not be able to mount any offensive operations until March 1942.[36] In fact, despite the enormous losses, the Soviets were far stronger than the Germans realized. In mid-October 1941 German intelligence estimated that the Red Army had 160 divisions and forty separate brigades—with most formations at below 50 percent strength. In fact, on 1 November 1941 the army had 269 divisions and sixty-five brigades with a total of over four million men under arms. The Germans would soon find out how wrong their intelligence estimates had been.

The Soviet Winter Offensive

With the Japanese decision to go to war against the Western Allies in the Pacific, a fact that the efficient Soviet spy ring in Tokyo had picked up, the large and well-equipped Soviet army force of more than fifty divisions could be freed from the mission of defending Siberia against the Japanese and transported to the Moscow front to form the core of a counteroffensive against the Germans. Marshalling their reserves of men, tanks, artillery, and aircraft at key points, the Soviets were able to establish local superiority over the exhausted German forces, which, like many of the Soviet forces, were fighting at far below strength. In the Moscow region, where the VIIIth Air Corps was operating, the VVS had amassed 1,376 aircraft (859 serviceable) and had the advantage of being able to use the good all-weather airfields in Moscow.[37] Von Richthofen and the other Luftwaffe commands now paid the price for having gone to war with far too few aircraft to complete their mission. With only a handful of reconnaissance aircraft, von Richthofen's ability to collect intelligence was noticeably impaired. With reconnaissance efforts further restricted by bad weather throughout November, the Luftwaffe had failed to spot the large Soviet troop movements and preparations behind the front. In great secrecy, General Georgy Zhukov, commander of the Soviet forces on the western front, had assembled three new tank armies to spearhead a major offensive in the Moscow area. Between 24 November and 5 December he was able to move his forces into assembly areas without alarming the Germans.[38]

On 5 December, when the Soviet winter offensive began, the Germans were taken by surprise. The Soviet air force, though not especially effective, surprised the Germans further by putting up a strong showing throughout December. With an average of 480 sorties a day, the VVS for the first time in the campaign was more in evidence than the Luftwaffe. Using far better tactics than in the summer battles, and advancing under the cover of massed artillery, the Soviets broke through the German lines at several points as whole divisions reeled back from the onslaught. Zhukov's forces struck with a massive blow with four powerful armies north of Moscow on Army Group Center's left flank. Simultaneously, two armies struck major blows south of Moscow. Further to the north another Soviet army attacked in the vicinity of Kalinen.[39]

The Soviets timed their attack well. The German advance had culminated at the end of October as the Germans had far outrun their supply lines. The panzer units were down to a small fraction of their normal strength in heavy weapons, and Luftwaffe units were in a similar state, with only a quarter of their assigned aircraft available for operations.[40] German factories were turning out aircraft and tanks enough to replace the losses, but getting the replacement equipment the vast distance to the front was another matter. Fuel had been a major concern of von Richthofen's since October. Even with maximum use of the Luftwaffe's air transport fleet to bring fuel to the front, the daily requirements far exceeded the ability of the Luftwaffe and army to get supplies forward. Added to these problems was the Soviet winter. By December 1941 the cold was so severe that vehicle engines would freeze up if not kept running continuously. There were no permanent shelters for Luftwaffe aircraft at the front, so aircraft mechanics had to build tents over the aircraft engines at night and keep small fires burning to keep the oil from freezing solid. Another method was to empty the oil out of the engine at night into a drum and to keep the drum heated during the night. The engine might start the next day after the warm oil was poured back in.

Finally the steady attrition of personnel started to affect the Wehrmacht's fighting ability. By midsummer the Wehrmacht high command noted that the German army would soon be unable to replace its losses in the Soviet Union. On 3 August, General Halder of the army staff noted that the Germans had already suffered 179,500 casualties in the USSR in the first six weeks of the campaign and that the home forces in Germany had only 300,000 trained replacements available. By October the German manpower losses in the Soviet Union, while not massive at the time, had already outstripped the Wehrmacht's ability to meet the replacement requirements. By December, many infantry divisions were well below strength, exhausted, and losing troops daily to illness and frostbite. In contrast, the Soviets had fifty fresh divisions from the Far East to throw into the fray and had far more experience with operating tanks, trucks, automobiles, and aircraft in the winter than did the Germans.

The German divisions on the Moscow front, especially the infantry divisions, reeled back after the surprise Soviet onslaught. After the debacles of the summer and fall, the Soviet military leaders were finally improving their operational competence. In great secrecy they had massed a large force, spearheaded by three fresh armies, and threw them at the German forces before Moscow.[41] German panzer divisions made some local counterattacks to stem the Soviet advance with some local successes. However, the Soviets soon broke through the German front at several points and threatened von Richthofen's forward airfields. Always calm at moments of crisis, von Richthofen dealt with the situation with his own ruthless brand of leadership. His inclination was to doubt initial reports as being the products of panic; he usually felt that the situation was not as bad as the staff and other commanders made out. In contrast to the army officers, who wanted a large-scale withdrawal to the rear to more defensible lines, von Richthofen opposed any retreat. Apparently he underestimated the Soviet effort as a kind of last gasp of the Soviet state.

Von Richthofen countered the threats to his airfields by pushing Luftwaffe flak units forward to plug gaps in the line. This made sense, as the Luftwaffe had two flak divisions assigned to Army Group Center's front, and the 88 mm heavy flak gun crews were all trained and equipped to use their guns against tanks. Even the largest Soviet tanks in 1941 could be stopped at long range by an 88 mm shell. Luftwaffe airfield units, engineers, and other ground personnel who had at least some basic infantry training were also sent in to plug gaps in the line. Whenever the weather cleared, von Richthofen's airmen made a maximum effort to get their planes into the air and to attack the advancing Soviet columns and the Soviet supply lines. Beset at all sides with support requests from army division and corps commanders, von Richthofen maintained his policy of only employing his aircraft en masse—usually in attacks of one or two groups—and with the limited Luftwaffe forces available only the most dangerous Soviet concentrations were selected for attack. Most of the army divisions had to get along on their own and do without air support—a hard but necessary decision if the VIIIth Air Corps was to stem the Soviet advance.

On 16 December Hitler, furious at the demands to retreat made by the senior army commanders, issued a "hold fast" order for all the army and corps commanders on the Soviet front: not another inch of territory would be yielded without the express approval of the Führer himself. Most of the senior army commanders were appalled at Hitler's order, which they believed would cause unnecessary losses for German troops. Von Richthofen, in contrast, heartily approved of Hitler's order and issued his own stirring order to the air, flak, and ground troops on the Moscow front to not give into the temptation to retreat.[42] But von Richthofen also needed reinforcements in order to hold the line at Moscow. He flew his Stork in bad weather to East Prussia to meet with General Jeschonnek for a personal briefing. Jeschonnek told von Richthofen that Hitler was adamant about his order and that the top army generals, including army chief of staff Walter von Brauchitsch and army commander Heinz Guderian, were strongly opposed to Hitler's order. Jeschonnek also reassured von Richthofen that reinforcements to the VIIIth Air Corps were on the way.

The crisis in the USSR in December 1941 led to a wholesale shakeup in the command structure of the German army. General Brauchitsch resigned on 19 December as commander in chief of the army, and Hitler personally assumed that post. The next week saw Bock relieved as army group commander and replaced by Gunther von Kluge (Bock was sent to the "leaders' reserve"). Guderian, commander of the Second Panzer Army, met the same fate. Field Marshal Rundstedt was fired as commander of Army Group South. General Alfred Jodl, a staunch sycophant of Hitler, would replace General Halder as army chief of staff. Brauchitsch was in poor health and would remain retired, but the other generals would be recalled later for high commands.

General of Engineers Otto Förster, in command of the VIth Army Corps in the Central Army Group, was one of several generals whose units were forced to retreat under Soviet pressure despite Hitler's "stand fast" order. Hitler ordered Förster relieved of command on 30 December 1941 and gave von Richthofen command of the infantry corps with the order to hold the front.[43] The VIth Army Corps consisted of four infantry divisions (161st, 110th, 6th, and 26th), all of which were tired and understrength. Until another army general was found, von Richthofen found himself in command of both an air corps and an army corps.[44] He took command of the battle in a characteristic way. Through the 1939 and 1940 campaigns one of his most common refrains in his diaries was the judgment that army generals tended to lose their nerve during the campaign and to exaggerate the effects of even small reverses. He saw the same attitude in the Soviet Union. Early in December he complained that Bock and the senior army commanders lacked "decisiveness and clear thinking."[45] Von Richthofen believed that the Soviets would not break through as long as the Germans kept their nerve, fought carefully, and counterattacked quickly. He issued each division of the VIth Army Corps a strict "no retreat" order. He had issued similar orders to his air units two days previously and had told his commanders to keep up their hope and their spirits, and to keep up the spirit of their men: "You can accomplish this! Just make your fullest effort!"[46] He gave the VIth Army Corps priority for whatever air support could be provided from the few operational aircraft of his air corps. At this point the initial Soviet attack was running out of steam, and von Richthofen's line held. About a week later a replacement corps commander arrived and von Richthofen relinquished command.

Despite a tenacious defense by the Germans the Soviet December offensive pushed the German front back more than a hundred miles from Moscow. Von Richthofen's forces bore the main burden of the air battle against the Soviet onslaught and were reinforced by four bomber groups. The Luftwaffe's transport chief provided five transport groups to help move Luftwaffe fuel and supplies forward and, on Hitler's orders, von Richthofen was sent another four transport groups.[47] Because of his refusal to retreat and his willingness to serve as a ground as well as an air commander, von Richthofen had reinforced his position as a special favorite of Hitler's. From this point on von Richthofen would use this position to secure additional forces and supplies for his command.

Just when the Germans figured that the Soviet offensive had exhausted itself, the Soviets kicked off another grand offensive all along the front in January. They had again completely surprised the Germans by massing fresh reserves and secretly gathering a large force to unleash on Army Group Center north of Moscow. The Red Army hoped to break through to Smolensk and break the German logistics lines. It failed in this objective, although it was able to expand on the success of the December attacks and push the Germans back farther.[48]

The beginning of 1942 saw both air forces in the East exhausted. The Luftwaffe had declined noticeably in strength and effectiveness; at the start of the new year the Luftwaffe had 1,700 aircraft for the 2,000 miles of front between Murmansk and the Red Sea. Yet the Soviet air force was in worse shape. Aside from the Moscow front, where the Soviets had massed their last reserves of airplanes, Soviet air strength was weak along the major fighting fronts. The Fourth Air Army of the northwestern front had only fifty-three battle-worthy planes, and these included eighteen obsolete Po-2 biplanes.[49] Marshal Novikov, the new commander of the VVS, pushed major changes in

Soviet air organization in the winter of 1941 and 1942 and worked to create a reserve of aircraft that could be deployed to support Red Army counteroffensives in the 1942 campaign.

In early January, just as the Germans thought that the Soviet offensive had petered out, Stalin ordered a general offensive by Soviet forces across the whole front. This attack was less concentrated and focused than the December offensive, and the Germans found the line easier to hold than during the previous attacks. January saw some heavy fighting and some gains by the Soviets, but nothing like the December offensive. By the end of February, the winter battles had largely run their course. When the front line finally stabilized after the Soviet winter offensive, the Wehrmacht could expect a pause in operations. With spring coming, the roads would be so muddy that neither side would be able to conduct major attacks. The Luftwaffe finally had time to replenish supplies, repair aircraft, and receive replacement aircraft and personnel for the exhausted units. Von Richthofen would finally have the chance for a few weeks' leave at home.

With the crisis at the front over, Hitler and the army and Luftwaffe staff could now contemplate a new campaign for 1942. On 26 February von Richthofen received an order to report to Hitler's headquarters in East Prussia. He flew to the "Wolfschanze" in a Ju 52 transport the next day and was promoted to the rank of colonel general and cited by Hitler for his performance in the winter campaign. Walter Model of the army was also promoted to colonel general on the same day. The promotion was a singular honor for a general not yet in command of an air fleet. It was clear that von Richthofen was now one of Hitler's favorites among the senior Luftwaffe officers.

After the promotion ceremony von Richthofen was invited to lunch with the Führer and was given the seat of honor next to Hitler. Although von Richthofen had briefed Hitler on several occasions, this was an opportunity for Hitler to turn on the charm. The two talked during lunch, and von Richthofen came away highly impressed. He described Hitler as "very vigorous, clear in his thinking, and well informed."[50] Upon his return to VIIIth Air Corps headquarters, von Richthofen was met by a military band and a parade in his honor; that evening he was feted in a formal dinner put on by the air corps staff. Von Richthofen was deeply touched by his promotion and recognition and issued an order to the VIIIth Air Corps commending the whole force, from the lowest privates to the top officers, for their brilliant performance in the winter campaign. He then looked over the situation reports from the Central Army Group sectors and noted that the Soviets were still maintaining the offensive, though their attacks were now weak and without a clear plan.⁵¹ Under such circumstances, the Germans could hold the line and prepare for better weather and a return to the offensive.

The year 1941 had been perhaps the worst in the history of the Soviet state. A great part of European Russia had been lost, Leningrad was under a siege with a blockade that would kill over a million of its population before the winter was over, and the Soviet army and air force had taken horrendous losses. Still, Moscow had been saved and the Soviets had shown that they could conduct a successful offense against the Germans. The winter offensive proved that the Wehrmacht was not invincible. Along with the military success of the Soviet winter offensive, the Soviets had been successful in evacuating ten million workers east to safety behind the Ural Mountains. Just as important, during their retreat the Soviets had managed to dismantle many of their factories and transport the machines and tools to land beyond the Urals, far out of range of German bombers. Weapons production was started again in improvised industrial complexes. Although production of aircraft, tanks, trucks, and heavy weapons was interrupted by the German invasion, the Soviets made an incredible comeback during 1942. They would build 25,436 aircraft in 1942—in contrast to the German aircraft production of 15,409 for that year.⁵² Just as important, the Soviets were able to put new aircraft into production that would equal the Luftwaffe's planes. The excellent Yak 9, which served as a fighter and fighter-bomber, and the La-5 fighter made their appearance in 1942. The IL-2 and the Pe-2 light bomber, both planes that had proven their effectiveness, were agaen masse-produced in the new factories.⁵³ Although the Soviet bomber arm would remain weak during the war, the fighter and ground attack arms would continue to improve in effectiveness and capability. The Soviet air force needed time to build a strong offensive force and was in no condition to seriously contest German air superiority early in 1942, but by the end of the year at Stalingrad it would reappear as a force that could directly challenge the Luftwaffe for control of the skies.

Chapter 11

The Campaign in the Soviet Union, 1942–1943

After the resurgence of Soviet power in December 1941, and the retreat and then stabilization of their front, the Germans could no longer look to short-term strategy to defeat the Soviet Union. It was now clear that the war would last much longer than Hitler and the Wehrmacht had hoped. Germany would now have to assure itself that it had the necessary resources to maintain its economic growth and rearmament programs. Modern mechanized warfare and modern economies require large amounts of oil. And oil was a strategic commodity that Germany had in relatively limited supply.

Romania, a major oil-producing nation in 1941, provided its German ally with a large part of the fuel necessary for the Wehrmacht. But that nation was already producing and refining oil at maximum capacity. Germany met some of its fuel requirements by producing synthetic fuel from coal—a resource that Germany had ample quantities of. However, it was an expensive process. Even though Germany had built more than thirty plants to transform coal into liquid fuel in the 1930s, it could not hope to meet the rapidly expanding fuel requirements of the Wehrmacht by this means. Germany had a few small oil fields, and Hungary some larger ones, but these reserves were much too small to meet Germany's growing needs. General Georg Thomas, the chief of the Wehrmacht Economic Planning Office, warned Hitler and the high command in 1941 that Germany would soon run short of oil. He pointed out that unless Germany seized the huge Soviet oil resources in the Baku region (now Azerbaijan) it could not prosecute the war. In 1941 Baku and the area around the Caspian Sea was one of the great oil-producing centers of the world; acquiring Baku's oil would solve Germany's fuel problems in a stroke.[1] At the same time, an advance into Baku would deprive the Soviet Union of one of its most important economic resources. Without Baku's oil the Red Army and Soviet air force—and the Soviet economy—would be crippled.

Briefed on the oil situation, Hitler turned his attention south for the 1942 campaign. During that year, the Germans would concentrate the army and

Luftwaffe forces in the south of the USSR and hold the front in the north and center, although it was hoped that another push might cause the fall of Leningrad. However, an offensive from the Ukraine, which had fallen to the Germans in 1941, to Baku was a drive of more than 800 miles—a greater advance than the Germans had made in 1941. Whether it was possible at all was very debatable, but Hitler saw it as the logical strategy, and he ordered Baku to be made the main objective. First, though, the Soviet forces in the Crimea would have to be neutralized.

During 1941 German and Romanian forces had cleared most of the Crimea, with the exception of the Soviet fortress city of Sebastopol. The Soviet counterattack that December had left a large force in the eastern end of the Crimea, inside the Kerch Peninsula. There the Soviets had seventeen rifle divisions, three rifle brigades, two cavalry divisions, and four tank brigades for a total of 210,000 well-equipped troops. These were dug in on a narrow front with successive defense lines. Sebastopol also had a formidable defense, with seven rifle divisions, one cavalry division, two naval brigades, and a rifle brigade. Sheltering behind massive modern fortresses, these forces were in a position to maintain a Soviet foothold in the Crimea indefinitely.[2]

General Bock, now commander of Army Group South, and General Manstein, in command of the Eleventh Army, which was also now assigned to Army Group South, both agreed that the Crimea would have to be cleared before undertaking any grand offensive toward Baku.[3] In fact, during the 1942 campaign the Crimea acted as a strategic diversion for the Germans as the Soviet forces inside the peninsula could have easily been sealed in by a few German and Romanian divisions while the main German force advanced east. Instead, the Crimea became something of a fixation for both the Soviets and Germans in 1942.

Since the Crimea operation was to be the opening move of the Germans that year, Hitler took a deep personal interest to see that it would succeed. He decided to give the responsibility for the campaign to two of his favorite commanders, General Erich von Manstein and Wolfram von Richthofen. Hitler would reinforce Manstein's Eleventh Army for the Crimea campaign. Against the wishes of the German army and the Luftwaffe high command, the VIIIth Air Corps was to be pulled out of Army Group Center's sector of the front and sent down to support the Eleventh Army offensive in the Crimea, which was slated to begin in May. Special command arrangements were set up for the Crimea campaign. Although the VIIIth Air Corps would be operating in the sector of General Löhr's 4th Air Fleet, von Richthofen's air corps would not come under Löhr's command. Von Richthofen would receive orders directly from the Luftwaffe high command.

Manstein's staff went to work, and on 31 March he issued a directive for Operation Trappenjagd, or "Bustard Hunt" (the bustard was a large game bird common to southern Russia and the Crimea). Manstein, von Richthofen, and their staffs enjoyed hunting whenever they found a bit of time, and the bustard was a favorite game bird. The name of the operation seemed appropriate.

By March there was little action to report from the front, and orders were issued to deploy the VIIIth Air Corps back to Germany for several weeks to rest and refit for the Soviet summer campaign. On 12 April, von Richthofen arrived home in Lüneburg for a few weeks of much-needed leave. But only six days later, as he was entertaining guests at his home, he received a telephone call from General Jeschonnek at Luftwaffe headquarters telling him that he and his air corps would be deployed to southern Russia to provide the air support for the Crimea campaign. The next day von Richthofen flew to Berlin, where he met with Jeschonnek and received a briefing from Hitler over the telephone. Hitler praised von Richthofen and told him that the operation was of special concern to him, and that von Richthofen was "the only person who could do the job."[4]

The VIIIth Air Corps needed a large number of new aircraft to replace lost and worn out planes. Personnel replacements were also needed. Since Hitler took a highly personal interest in the success of the Crimea operation, von Richthofen could ask for additional forces and support and, within reason, expect to get them. The VIIIth Air Corps units could expect to start the campaign close to full strength and, for once, with generous logistics support. In fact, von Richthofen used his personal access to the Führer to ensure additional units and supplies were made available for his units. By using his influence so openly, von Richthofen raised the ire of army and Luftwaffe generals in the East who resented his favored position, and resented as well the special priority that Berlin gave to the units under von Richthofen's command.

In most respects the logistics for the 1942 campaign would be better than they were in 1941. Using labor from prisoners of war (POWs) as well as German labor and engineer units, a large part of the Soviet rail network had been rebuilt to the German rail gauge, and German units at the front could now be supplied by rail. The Soviets had established guerrilla forces behind the German lines, but at this point in the war the partisan forces were relatively ineffective and were not in a position to interfere with German supplies. In the Crimea, the VIIIth Air Corps would fly from airfields in the center of the peninsula. In preparation for the summer campaign the Luftwaffe made a major effort to improve its airfields and logistics, not just in the Crimea but across southern Russia. In early May 1942, some 12,000 Reichs Labor Service construction

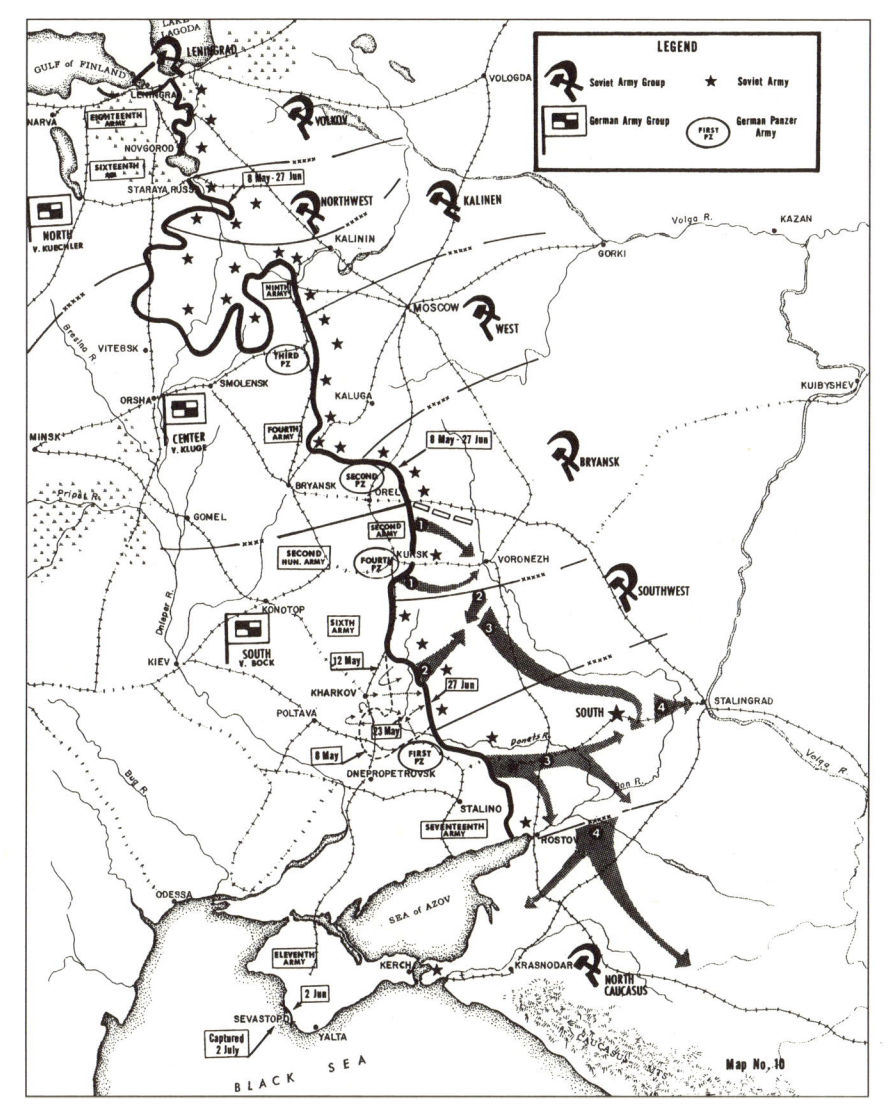

Von Richthofen's VIIIth Air Corps first supported the German Eleventh Army offensive that overran the last Soviet resistance in the Crimea. Taking over the 4th Air Fleet on 4 July 1942, von Richthofen was responsible for supporting Army Group South's offensive drives toward Stalingrad in the east and into the Kuban to the south. (Earl Ziemke, *Moscow to Stalingrad: Decision in the East* [Washington, DC: US Army Center for Military History, 1987])

troops were deployed to the Kiev Air District, which was responsible for Luftwaffe logistics and support throughout southern Russia. Along with thousands of Soviet POWs, the Labor Service would improve airfields throughout southern Russia. Some of the fields would be turned into all-weather fields. On most airfields the Germans improved the maintenance facilities and build revetments for the protection of aircraft from enemy air attack.[5] The Germans had learned a few lessons from the 1941 campaign and worked hard during the spring of 1942 to prepare their logistics for the next campaign.

On 21 April, von Richthofen flew to the 4th Air Fleet headquarters at Nilolayev in southern Russia to meet with Jeschonnek and be briefed on the upcoming Crimea operation. Under an unusual command situation, von Richthofen's VIIIth Air Corps would work in coordination with the 4th Air Fleet, which was responsible for the whole sector of southern Russia. But the corps would not be subordinate to the air fleet, and von Richthofen would answer only to Hermann Goering and the air staff in Berlin. The 4th Air Fleet commander and staff were considerably offended by this unusual command arrangement—as well they should have been. The 4th Air Fleet chief of staff, Günther Korten (later Luftwaffe chief of staff), demanded that the VIIIth Air Corps be placed under the 4th Air Fleet's command—but he was firmly rebuffed by Jeschonnek. In his diary, von Richthofen noted that the 4th Air Fleet staff were "deeply peeved and viewed my arrival with considerable mistrust."[6] After staff discussions with the fleet, von Richthofen made some acerbic comments about General Löhr and his staff in his diary. Von Richthofen believed that the 4th Air Fleet staff had done a poor job of preparing for the upcoming offensive—criticism that may have been justified.[7]

The Soviet air force, slowly rebuilding itself and trying to create a large reserve force to employ in future offensive operations, was in no position to attack German logistics lines. As the Germans entered the 1942 campaign season, the Luftwaffe held air superiority over the whole Soviet front. Indeed, the Luftwaffe's easy victories over the air force in 1941 had caused the Luftwaffe leaders and intelligence officers to underestimate the capability of the Soviets to restore aircraft production, produce modern aircraft, and build up enough forces to challenge the Germans. Yet, even as 1942 began, the Soviets, having transported whole factories from western Russia during the summer of 1941, had reestablished aircraft production on the other side of the Ural Mountains, out of range of German bombers. By the spring of 1942 the Soviet aircraft industry was making an impressive recovery—and would be able to play a major role in supporting the Red Army as the tide turned at Stalingrad later that year. However, for the time being, the Luftwaffe saw little threat from the Soviet air force.

Von Richthofen and Germany's Allies

In southern Russia von Richthofen would be fighting alongside Germany's allies, notably the Romanians and Hungarians. Both of those countries had small air forces, with Romania being the larger and most capable of the two, and the VIIIth Air Corps and 4th Air Fleet would have to coordinate operations with their allies. As was noted earlier, German strategic coordination with its allies during the war was generally poor.[8] German allies, such as Romania and Hungary, generally distrusted the Germans—which showed some strategic sense on their part. Romania and Hungary fought as German allies for very specific and limited goals. For example, Romania went to war with the Soviet Union primarily to take back the Moldavian territory the Soviets had annexed from Romania in 1940. The primary limitation of Germany's allies was the poor state of their military equipment, which tended to be obsolete. The poor state of allied equipment was largely Germany's fault. Both Hungary and Romania had aviation industries and had long requested the right to build modern German aircraft under license. The Reich Air Ministry had consistently refused Germany's allies, which left the allied air forces and the Luftwaffe on the front in an awkward state.[9]

The dilemma for the Germans in 1942 was the shortage of German forces on the eastern front. This, in turn, required Germany's allied armies to hold large stretches of the front. But the obsolete equipment, and lack of firepower and motor vehicles of Germany's allied forces, ensured that their sectors always remained more vulnerable should the Soviets attack in strength. With allied forces serving as an obvious weak link in the German strategy, the Wehrmacht's senior officers had to pay attention to the state of the allied forces. Although the allied armies had been supported by their own air forces during the 1941 campaign, the 1942 campaign promised to be tougher and require greater allied support and German/allied cooperation. So arrangements would have to be made to coordinate the air units along the whole front. Germany's allied air forces, just like their armies, were generally equipped with obsolete aircraft and lacked effective communications. If the allies were to function effectively the Luftwaffe would likely have to fill in many needs, and also be prepared to provide additional air support on the allied sectors of the front.

When Romania entered the war against the Soviet Union in 1941, it fielded an air force of over 400 aircraft. It was an eclectic mix of modern and obsolete aircraft, including not only Romanian-built and -designed aircraft but also Italian, British, German, and French aircraft. The combat force included IAR 80s (Romanian-designed and -built fighters), twelve British Hurricanes, thirty-eight British Bristol Blenheim bombers, and twenty-one French Potez 63 bombers.[10] The Romanian air force suffered from deficiencies in training, aircraft armament, communications equipment, and ground infrastructure. The same was true for the smaller Hungarian air corps serving at the front. However, in a huge theater of war where there were far too few aircraft to adequately support operations, even the largely obsolete 400-plus Romanian planes, and the 150 planes of the Hungarian air corps, were important additions to Axis air strength in the theater.

Although relations between the German and Romanian governments were generally strained, the two air forces had worked fairly well together since the start of the war. The Luftwaffe mission to Romania came under the command of the 4th Air Fleet, and General Löhr worked well with the Romanians. The two Romanian army corps in the Soviet Union were provided with Luftwaffe liaison officers, who passed information gained from Romanian reconnaissance and battle reports to 4th Air Fleet, and passed Luftwaffe intelligence to the Romanians.[11] The Romanian army and air force came under the strategic direction of the German army, although Romanian air force squadrons normally flew in support of their own forces. The Romanian air force, however, required some fuel and support services from the 4th Air Fleet.[12] As the campaign in the USSR progressed, Romanians flew more often in combined operations with the Germans, at times supporting German troops.

Operating on a front with large Romanian forces supported by Romanian air units, von Richthofen tried to assess the needs of his allies in establishing a more effective system of cooperation. Indeed, von Richthofen was fairly unusual among the senior Luftwaffe leaders in his attempts to improve German relations with allied forces. On 6 June 1942, just as the battle for Sebastopol was beginning, von Richthofen met with the Romanian dictator Marshal Ion Antonescu and noted that the marshal had made a very favorable impression on him. Per von Richthofen's view, Antonescu had considerable strategic and operational sense, and he was deeply committed to supporting the fight against the Soviet Union. Richard DiNardo, a historian of Axis coalition operations, notes that the Romanian leader impressed "the not easily impressed Richthofen."[13]

The Crimea Campaign

Tactically and operationally, the Crimea campaign of May and June 1942 was something of a minor masterpiece of German warfare. A German ground force that was greatly outnumbered by the enemy would attack a series of well-defended prepared positions. The Crimea offered little room for the

Von Richthofen (left) with Romanian dictator Ion Antonescu, summer 1943.

characteristic blitzkrieg attacks around the flank. It would be a series of frontal assaults against prepared positions.

The Crimea campaign began what became a very effective partnership between army commander Erich von Manstein and Luftwaffe commander Wolfram von Richthofen. In the words of historian Joel Hayward, who has written extensively on the air campaign in the East, the two great generals got along "famously."[14] Von Richthofen met with Manstein on 22 April 1942, and the two had a lengthy conference about the upcoming campaign. Von Richthofen found Manstein to be one of those rare army generals who understood the capabilities of airpower and accepted that airpower would play a central role in the campaign. Unlike many other army generals, Manstein was not eager to micromanage the air effort; he was, in fact, happy to let von Richthofen handle all air matters. What mattered was that he and von Richthofen coordinate their efforts. For this reason, Manstein brought the Luftwaffe into his planning process and worked closely with the 4th Air Fleet staff. The Crimean campaign plan took into account the logistical and operational requirements of the Luftwaffe, such as airfield locations and command and control units. The Eleventh Army tried to conform its objectives and combat phases so that the Luftwaffe could provide the best support possible. Like von Richthofen, Manstein did not believe in dispersing his combat strength but in concentrating the available forces at the decisive point. This shared approach explains a good deal about the harmonious partnership that the two developed. Following the 22 April conference, von Richthofen noted in his diary that "Manstein was surprisingly mellow and accommodating. He understood everything. It was completely uplifting."[15] This was quite a contrast with his feeling about the army before Moscow in 1941, when he had faced continual requests from army generals to employ his air units in penny packets that would have little operational effect.

At Operation Trappenjagd's start, von Richthofen had a strong air force of eleven bomber groups, three dive bomber groups, and seven fighter groups. Because of Hitler's special interest in the Crimea campaign, von Richthofen had the top priority for fuel, parts, and munitions for the whole eastern front. In addition to the reinforcement of his air units, von Richthofen was provided a flak division to protect his airfields. Operations in the whole southern sector of the Soviet Union would have to wait until the Crimea campaign was concluded. General Manstein looked forward to the support the Luftwaffe would bring. In developing his operational plans he said that the Crimea operation would have "concentrated air support the like of which has never existed."[16]

With limited ground forces under his command, Manstein would have to rely heavily upon air support to defeat the Soviets. Manstein told his senior commanders on 2 May that "Trappenjagd is a ground operation, but its main effort is in the air." Given the nature of the terrain and the strong Soviet defense positions to be overcome, Manstein noted that the Luftwaffe would have to "pull the infantry forward."[17] Field Marshal Bock, commander of Army Group South, inspected the Eleventh Army and VIIIth Air Corps in late April and was impressed by their "careful preparations" for the operation. Still, he was uneasy about the campaign. The Soviets had a lot of firepower and were holding well-prepared defensive positions. As the battles around Leningrad and Moscow had proven, Soviet fighters could be exceptionally tenacious on the defense, and the Crimea held the most extensive fortifications system that the Germans had seen on the Soviet front. Despite the optimism of Manstein and von Richthofen that the operation could be carried off successfully, Bock, with good reason, feared that the campaign would be exceptionally bloody for the Germans.[18]

Von Richthofen made the creation of an effective air/ground liaison system a top priority. In 1942 the coordination between the army and Luftwaffe

Ju 87 of VIIIth Air Corps over Crimea, spring 1942. (USAF Historical Research Agency)

was simplified with the abolition of the Koluft system, in which the army had Luftwaffe air reconnaissance units under its own command. All reconnaissance assets were now centralized under the Luftwaffe's direction, and army requests for support went straight to the Luftwaffe supporting command rather than wading through two command systems as before. In preparation for the campaign, extensive aerial reconnaissance was done of the Soviet lines. The Flivos, the Luftwaffe air liaison teams able to report on the ground situation, were now deployed down to the regimental level. The additional Luftwaffe communications on the front would help the senior commanders stay informed of the battle situation. Through 1942 von Richthofen issued a series of instructions to the VIIIth Air Corps specifying the methods and signals to be used for Luftwaffe units providing close air support for the army. Signal flares and ground panels were to be used to mark the army's forward positions in order to avoid attack by Luftwaffe forces. In readying the Luftwaffe for the Crimea campaign, von Richthofen worked to ensure that any barrier to close cooperation was removed. He ordered the VIIIth Air Corps to communicate directly to the army corps without a requirement to coordinate with the intervening army and air fleet headquarters.[19]

For the attack against the Soviet positions on the Kerch Peninsula at the eastern end of the Crimea, Manstein's Eleventh Army had available five infantry divisions, one panzer division, two Romanian infantry divisions, and one Romanian cavalry division. Manstein could not use his army's full strength because he had to deploy three German infantry divisions and two Romanian divisions to contain the large Soviet force inside Sebastopol. In their defenses in the Kerch Peninsula the Soviets were weak in air support, but they had considerably more artillery and mortars than did the attacking Germans. They also outnumbered the Germans 387 to 100 in tanks.[20] Given these numbers, the only possible way for the Germans to defeat the Soviets was to use their superiority in airpower to maximum advantage. It was a highly risky operation, and one can see why Bock had serious misgivings.

Trappenjagd began on 8 May. The weather was excellent for air operations, and the VIIIth Air Corps made a maximum effort of over 2,000 sorties that day. Manstein and von Richthofen stayed in constant contact. Under cover of von Richthofen's air umbrella, the Germans broke through the Soviet defenses at several points and advanced six miles by the end of the day. The next day, after a powerful preattack air bombardment, the German ground advance continued. Despite all the work at planning for close coordination, the system occasionally broke down. On 9 May one of the German panzer units advanced so rapidly that it crossed the "bomb line" and fell victim to Luftwaffe aircraft that mistook them for Soviet tanks. During the next days von Richthofen spent a good deal of time in the air in his Stork, monitoring the progress of the battle and looking for targets for his airmen. He personally sent a stream of reports on the ground battle back to his headquarters. The relatively narrow space of the ground battle also offered von Richthofen the chance to personally observe the progress of the German forces from close up. He set up forward tactical command posts on hills and ridgelines, where he could see the operations and personally coordinate some of the air strikes. Part of this behavior was simply giving in to the temptation of micromanaging the battle. The other part was a need to inspire his airmen, and the soldiers of the Eleventh Army, and to let them know that senior officers went to the front and were willing to share their dangers.

Four days after the start of the offensive the Soviet headquarters had lost control of their units, and the fighting turned into mopping up isolated pockets of Soviet resistance. The Soviets managed to evacuate a few thousand of their soldiers by ship, but the vast majority of the Soviet forces on the Kerch Peninsula were compelled to surrender. By 19 May, Manstein could declare the operation on the Kerch Peninsula over. His forces had taken 170,000 Red Army soldiers prisoner.[21] After a brief rest and some hard work to count up the large numbers of Soviet prisoners and impressive quantities of captured equipment, Manstein began to redeploy the Eleventh Army to the Sebastopol

Soviet column in the Crimea destroyed by von Richthofen's VIIIth Air Corps. The Luftwaffe played a central role in this campaign, pulverizing the Soviet forces and strongpoints and "pulling" the German ground forces forward. (U.S. Army)

area to mount a final attack that would finish off the Soviet fortress. In the environs and city itself, the Soviets had massed 188,000 soldiers. They were well equipped with 600 artillery pieces, and dug into defensive positions far more formidable than those at Kerch. The attack on Sebastopol would be a siege operation, essentially a series of limited attacks. The Germans would have to move against the Soviet defenses under the cover of massive firepower and systematically reduce each Soviet strongpoint. It was the most grueling kind of warfare, and von Richthofen's VIIIth Air Corps would provide most of the heavy firepower for the operation.

In the meantime, the Soviets had put together a strong armored force to the north of the Crimea and on 12 May launched an offensive to retake the city of Kharkov. Von Richthofen immediately sent several of his bomber groups north to support the IVth Air Corps in its fight against the Soviet offensive. The Soviet attack was badly planned and poorly coordinated. After an initial advance, the Soviet forces were stopped, and then the forward armor elements were cut off and destroyed. The Luftwaffe played a major role in defeating the Soviets through an interdiction campaign that pummeled the Soviet rear and destroyed much of the Soviet force even before it got to the front lines. Whole Soviet vehicle columns were left burning by Luftwaffe bombers and fighters. By 28 May the battle was over, and General Kleist's army group and the Sixth Army had captured 240,000 prisoners, 1,200 tanks, and 2,600 guns.[22] Although the Soviet war industries were recovering, and excellent new equipment was being produced in ever increasing amounts, the Red Army was still learning how to effectively coordinate large operations. In fact, the premature offensive by the Soviets at Kharkov in 1942 was of great benefit to the Germans. The Soviets' poor planning and execution had managed to destroy their main tank and reserve forces on the southern sector of the front. This opened the way for the Germans to go on the offensive later in the summer.

Von Richthofen's next major operation was to support the Eleventh Army's attack to reduce the fortress of Sebastopol. Beginning on 7 June the battle consisted of a systematic campaign of massive air strikes on a series of pinpoint targets. There were sixteen massive forts on the outskirts of the city itself, and each had to be pounded into submission. Operating from nearby airfields in the central Crimea, the Stukas and bombers could fly several sorties a day. During June the 390 bombers and Stukas of the VIIIth Air Corps (some of von Richthofen's forces had been deployed north to the IVth Air Corps) flew a total of 23,751 sorties against Sebastopol and dropped more than 20,000 tons of bombs. The Soviet air defense was ineffective, and during the Sebastopol operation the Luftwaffe lost only thirty-one aircraft—a very small loss for the number of sorties flown. For the most part, the Luftwaffe's air support was accurate and devastating. Von Richthofen set up his tactical command post at the front and personally directed some of the strike missions. On one occasion, von Richthofen's enthusiasm caused a friendly-fire incident. On 29 June, he ordered an attack on what he believed to be Soviet armored forces east of the Tim River. It turned out to be part of the Grossdeutschland Division—which took losses of sixteen dead and many wounded. Von Richthofen had not been informed that German forces were in the area. In his diary he noted, "It was my own fault because I ordered it and did not expect such a rapid (German) advance."[23] However, such incidents were common in the fog and friction of warfare, and neither von Richthofen nor Manstein agonized over such mistakes.

Von Richthofen and Manstein continued to work well together, but some disagreements arose. The VIIIth Air Corps's flak division had batteries of 88 mm antiaircraft guns that were also some of the best guns in the world against tanks and fortifications. Indeed, the Luftwaffe flak units in the Soviet Union spent as much time in the front lines fighting Soviet tanks as they did shooting down Soviet aircraft. A flak division contained enormous firepower, and

Von Richthofen with binoculars observing air attacks at the front, probably Crimea. (USAF Historical Research Agency)

General Manstein requested that the Luftwaffe flak units be detached to his Eleventh Army to destroy the Soviet strong points. Von Richthofen, who had pioneered the use of the 88 mm gun in Spain in just such a role, did not disagree with using his 88 mm batteries in such a manner. He insisted, though, that if the 88s were sent to the front the Luftwaffe would retain command of them. Yet von Richthofen also assured Manstein that he would see that flak guns would be "deployed in great concentrations at Schwerpunkte against ground targets. The army wants formally to control them and spread them throughout divisions and . . . fritter them away. . . . I remain stubborn and let the army commands continue to rage."[24]

Von Richthofen also carried out his usual habit and flew above the battlefield in his Stork to observe operations. While he did this he was a regular target for Soviet antiaircraft guns and, sometimes, from German flak as well. On 25 June as von Richthofen was flying over the front, the German 387th Infantry Division mistook his Fiesler Stork for a Soviet plane and fired at him, puncturing a fuel tank and wounding his copilot. Von Richthofen was forced to make an immediate emergency landing just inside the German lines. Luckily, unlike most planes, the sturdy little Fiesler could land wherever there was a small field clear of obstructions. The next day the German division headquarters received a sarcastic letter from von Richthofen. The Luftwaffe colonel general pointed out that it had been a clear day and that his plane was clearly marked with German insignia. He advised them to fire at the Soviets next time. In his diary he was furious, calling the army unit "damned dogs."[25]

Air Fleet Commander—From the Crimea to Stalingrad

On 4 July the last resistance at Sebastopol collapsed, giving the Germans over 90,000 prisoners.[26] On that day von Richthofen assumed command of the 4th Air Fleet and General Löhr was transferred to be the German commander in Yugoslavia. Von Richthofen was now commander of more than half of the Luftwaffe forces on the eastern front. But he had little time to celebrate this promotion to a top command position. With the Soviets defeated in the Crimea, and their Kharkov attack a disaster, the way was finally open for a major German offensive, and there was much to do to prepare for the campaign. The first stage of the German offensive that would drive to the Caucasus kicked off on 28 June with three major thrusts by Axis forces. In the Kursk region the Fourth Panzer Army and Second Army drove west toward Voronezh, and the Sixth Army drove on a parallel course to their south toward the Don River. In the southern sector of the front the First Panzer Army and the Seventeenth Army drove west to open the gateway to the Caucasus. In two weeks the Germans advanced more than 100 miles facing only weak Soviet resistance.

The summer 1942 campaign was much different that the campaign of the previous summer. For one thing, the shortage of German troops meant that the Wehrmacht had to rely heavily upon its allies to hold large stretches

Von Richthofen in Russia, 1942. (Bundesarchiv/Militaerarchiv Freiburg)

of the line as they guarded the flanks of the advancing German forces. Of the forty-one new divisions made available for the 1942 campaign, twenty-one came from Germany's allies (six Italian, ten Hungarian, five Romanian). None of the allied divisions were as well equipped as corresponding German divisions. The main difference in the 1942 campaign was the failure of the German army to encircle and destroy the Soviet armies. The premature offensive at Kharkov had taught the Soviets a hard lesson. The Germans were still the masters of maneuver warfare, and standing and fighting on terrain that offered the Germans a chance to maneuver and bypass resistance meant sacrificing large forces to huge envelopment operations—such as those that had come close to seeing the destruction of the Red Army the summer before. As the Germans advanced and drove to the Don River, they were punching mostly empty air. The Soviets fought brief delaying actions and then retreated to conserve their strength and wait for an opportunity to strike back. Thus, even as the Germans occupied a vast amount of Soviet land, the tally in Soviet prisoners and destroyed equipment was not high. Only at Stalingrad did the Soviets decide to make a serious stand.[27]

Von Richthofen now had to deal with supporting several large operations over an immense region with about 500 operational combat aircraft (fighters, bombers, reconnaissance, and Stukas).[28] On 18 July he moved the 4th Air Fleet headquarters forward to Mariupol on the Sea of Azov. The 4th Air Fleet had already been separated into several air commands in order to simplify the support provided to the ground forces. The main forces of the air fleet were concentrated in the VIIIth and IVth Air Corps—with the IVth Air Corps concentrated on the southern flank of the German offensive and the VIIIth Air Corps in the center and north to cover the thrust on Stalingrad. A small air task force of a few squadrons was left behind in the Black Sea to carry out naval air operations with Romanian support.[29] As the logistics and communications lines lengthened with the German offensive, von Richthofen would have to further dilute his limited forces and create more air task forces for specific support missions. At this point in the war the German airmen were superbly trained and were easily able to win air superiority whenever they could be massed. But massing forces in the way that von Richthofen preferred became increasingly difficult.

The Germans had an advantage over their enemies in the quality of their leadership and staffs. Von Richthofen was lucky to have some superb staff officers through most of 1942. Martin Fiebig served brilliantly as chief of staff of the VIIIth Air Corps before taking over that command upon von Richthofen promotion. Already serving as 4th Air Fleet chief of staff was Lt. General Günther Korten, an exceptionally capable officer. But von Richthofen

Von Richthofen at command post, Russia 1942. (USAF Historical Research Agency)

would not have Korten's services for long, as Korten was transferred and given command of his own air corps in August. Von Richthofen's luck with good staff officers ran out when Colonel Hans-Detlef Herhudt von Rohden was appointed chief of staff of the 4th Air Fleet. In many cases the negative comments that von Richthofen made in his diary about fellow Luftwaffe officers tended to be unfairly harsh. But von Richthofen's negative assessment of Herhudt von Rohden as a second-rate officer seems to have been justified. After the Stalingrad airlift, von Richthofen would have him transferred.

Having quickly reached the Don River, the Germans would now drive forward with two major axes of advance, one toward the Caucasus and the other toward Stalingrad.

As German and Axis forces advanced over a broad front, the amount of airpower available to the troops at the front was stretched further. In August von Richthofen met with the Romanian commanders at his headquarters to improve coordination between the allies. Romania's air force would be tasked primarily to support the Romanian Third and Fourth armies. But as the Germans were spread thin, the Romanians agreed to help by detaching some of their squadrons to fly under command of the VIIIth Air Corps.[30] In August the German Seventeenth Army and First Panzer Army had moved fast and far and had reached the Kuban, the region before the foothills of the Caucasus. Von Richthofen's theater of operations kept getting larger, but he had few aircraft to cover all the missions. He therefore turned to the Romanians for extra air support. He created a special Luftwaffe Group Caucasus for support of the Seventeenth and First Panzer armies, and the Romanians agreed to send the 20th Romanian Reconnaissance Squadron and the 43rd Romanian Fighter Squadron forward as part of that task force.[31] On other sectors of the front the Germans and Romanians worked out procedures to support each other. On the Black Sea, Romanian naval air units routinely supported German naval air operations under Colonel Wolfgang von Wild's command.[32]

Although distance and logistics problems made it more difficult, von Richthofen could still concentrate airpower for major operations. He still flew around the battlefield in his Fiesler, and he met constantly with the army commanders to discuss their plans and arrange for the best air support possible. In July and August he met several times with General List, the commander of Army Group B. As General Friedrich von Paulus's Sixth Army approached Stalingrad, one of Hitler's major objectives for the campaign, von Richthofen wanted to ensure a decisive blow, and so he threw the VIIIth Air Corps into a full-scale assault on the city on 23 August. The corps flew 1,600 sorties and dropped 1,000 tons of bombs on Stalingrad, cutting off the utilities and paralyzing the city. But General von Paulus did not use the opportunity to take Stalingrad in a quick thrust. He held back for a few days—just enough time for the Soviets to reinforce the city and prepare final defensive lines.[33] Von Richthofen was furious with the weak performance of the Sixth Army's commander. This was not the kind of bold action that had won victories in Poland, France, and Greece.

Even as the German armies advanced, Soviet resistance seemed to be stiffening. The long supply lines also worked to slow the German pace of advance. In early August the Germans advanced further into the Kuban region and overran the Maikop oil fields.[34] Then the German armies began their advance into the Caucasus, but started to slow down. To help the First Panzer and Seventeenth armies move forward, von Richthofen briefly diverted almost all of his bombers to the IVth Air Corps to support the advance into the Caucasus. But applying concentrated forces was now exceptionally difficult. By 10 October the whole 4th Air Fleet had no more than 129 serviceable bombers. This was only a 55 percent operational rate. The inability to repair and maintain aircraft was another sign that the Luftwaffe's logistics were breaking down in the vast theater of war. When the campaign had begun in late June, von Richthofen had deployed 323 operational bombers.[35]

By late October the whole German offensive had simply bogged down. The VIIIth Air Corps, operating with a very low strength, did its best to provide close air support for the Sixth Army in the ruins of Stalingrad. Hans-Ulrich Rudel, the famed "Stuka ace" of the eastern front, commanded a squadron of Stuka Wing 2, flying support for the Sixth Army as it fought its way through the streets of Stalingrad. He noted how his unit marked their targets on aerial photos and dropped bombs with great care, as German troops were often just meters away. Von Richthofen complained that his Stukas were now dropping bombs within grenade-throwing range of the enemy.[36] In his view, this was the wrong way to use airpower. Since the Stalingrad campaign began in August, von Richthofen had been upset with the Sixth Army and its commander, General von Paulus, in particular. He greatly resented General von Paulus's insistence on using the Luftwaffe as flying artillery when the army's own direct fire weapons would have been more appropriate.

The Soviets Rebuild

Throughout 1942 the Soviets showed an impressive ability to create new armies and, furthermore, were able to successfully keep this secret until they were thrown at the Germans. With Soviet armaments production recovering from the debacle of 1941 the Soviets created fifteen new tanks corps and five new tank armies in the spring and summer of 1942. Two of the new tank corps were wasted in the misconceived Soviet offensive at Kharkov in May 1942. However, throughout the late summer and early fall, as the Germans advanced deep into Russia, the Soviet high command, the Stavka, managed to assemble a large force of tanks, artillery, and aircraft and readied them for a grand blow against the German Sixth Army at Stalingrad. In 1942, as in 1941, German intelligence had grossly underestimated the Soviet capability to produce new weapons and to build new divisions.[37] Careful Soviet planning, good operational security, and camouflage and deception measures kept the Germans from spotting the full extent of the massive buildup of forces north and south of Stalingrad. For the offensive designed to trap the German forces in the Stalingrad region, the Soviets massed over one million men, 1,115 planes, and 900 tanks. The Soviet force did not greatly outnumber the Germans in the theater, but the German and Romanian armies were spread very thin and the Soviet force was concentrated into two large armies to the north and south of Stalingrad.[38] For three months the Stavka carefully massed these forces to strike the kind of blow against the Germans that the Germans had struck against the Soviets in the summer of 1941. In addition, the Soviets stockpiled enough fuel and ammunitions to sustain the offensive for weeks. It was one of the turning points in the war. From this point on the Soviets would have a clear logistical advantage over the Germans. Part of the Soviet strength came from American Lend-Lease aircraft, vehicles, locomotives, and other supplies that were beginning to flow into the Soviet theater of war in large quantities. The Lend-Lease equipment, coupled with the resurgence in Soviet war production, was tipping the scales strongly in favor of the Soviets.

The Soviets had another stroke of luck in the form of the Allied landings in North Africa on 8 November. Hitler had to reinforce Africa immediately, and von Richthofen was called on to volunteer some of his air units for immediate redeployment to the Mediterranean. He loyally offered the Führer three bomber groups of the 4th Air Fleet—an offer that would further dilute the strength of his already weak force. On 11 November the German Sixth Army made what it hoped would be its last great assault on Stalingrad. But by this time, there was very little Luftwaffe air support available to help the Sixth Army.[39] In fact, there were a number of indications that something was up along the Soviet side of the Volga. Early in November, VIIIth Air Corps reconnaissance noted extensive Soviet bridge building activity on the Don River, and considerable Soviet troop movement and other activity behind the lines north of Stalingrad.[40] But the picture remained unclear. The weather was generally too poor for reconnaissance, and the 4th Air Fleet had too much area and too few airplanes to keep a proper watch on the Soviets. Von Richthofen was still uneasy about the situation, so on 17 November he dispatched a small air support force to the Romanian army front north of Stalingrad, where he thought the Soviets might attack.[41]

The Soviets Attack

On 19 November the Soviets opened their offensive, called Operation Uranus, with a massive attack by the Soviet Fifth Tank Army and Twenty-first Army on the Third Romanian Army front north of Stalingrad. Hit with the full power of hundreds of the superb Soviet T-34 tanks, which were supported by masses of heavy guns and strong air support, the poorly equipped Romanians broke immediately.[42] Hitler, on vacation at Berchtesgarten, was informed of the developments in the Soviet Union. At first he and his general staff believed the attack could be quickly contained. Col. General Maximilian von Weichs, commander of Army Group B, was ordered to stop the attack on the Soviet forces within Stalingrad and to transfer whatever reserves

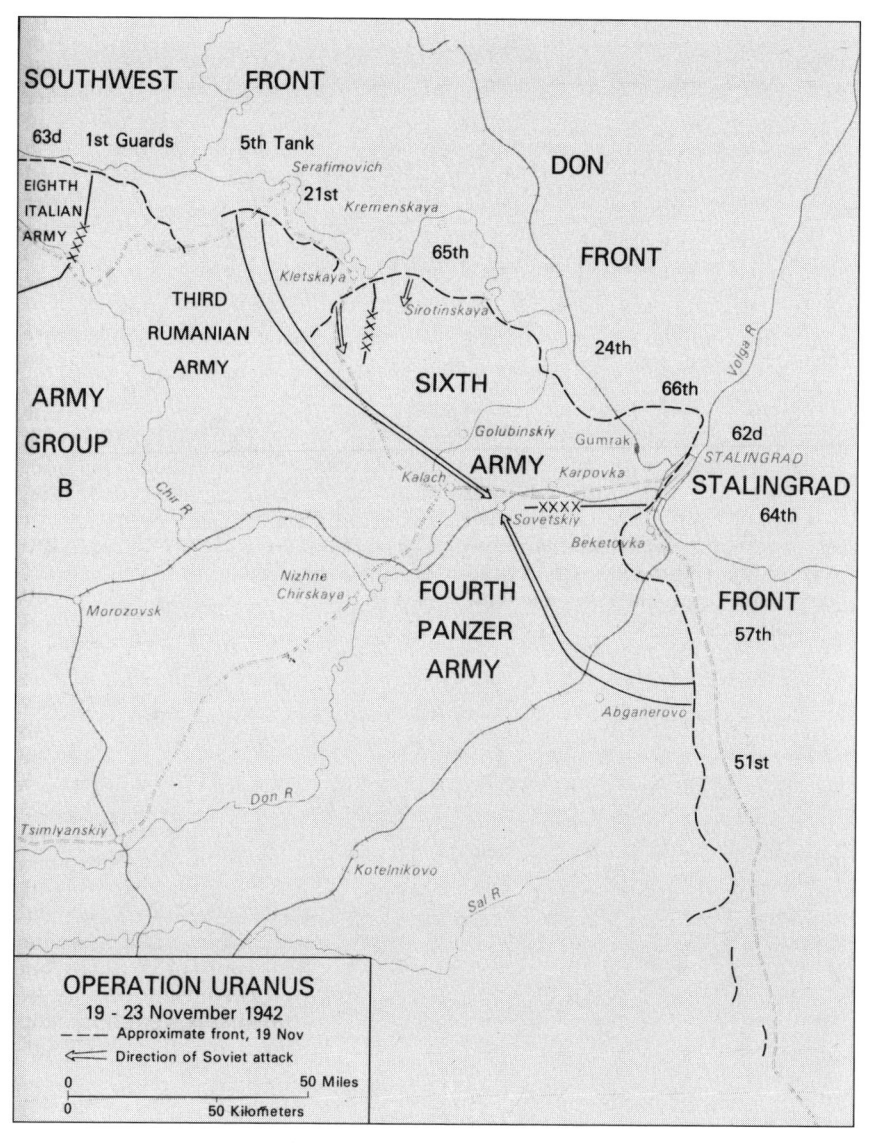

The Soviet offensive of November 1942 that encircled Stalingrad. As the Soviet noose around the doomed German Sixth Army grew tighter, von Richthofen's transport aircraft had to fly ever-longer distances in their attempt to supply the army. (Earl Ziemke, *Moscow to Stalingrad: Decision in the East* [Washington, DC: US Army Center for Military History, 1987])

he had to his northern flank. But the situation was much worse than anyone in Berlin or Berchtesgarten could imagine, and the few local reserves could not handle an attack of this scale. The Soviets managed to quickly exploit the huge hole they had made in the Axis front and drove their armored forces deep behind the German lines. They then began to turn south to begin the encirclement of the German Sixth Army.

This operation was not like the previous Soviet attacks that had gained some initial success but then had always been stopped and contained. The day after the attack in the north, Soviet armored forces to the south of Stalingrad, supported by massive artillery fire, broke a hole through the thinly held German lines and also sent their armored spearheads deep behind the German lines with the intent of closing the pincers and trapping the Sixth Army and part of the Fourth Panzer Army.[43] With a major crisis brewing, Hitler called on Manstein, who had been sent north to take Leningrad after the Crimea campaign. Manstein was ordered to take over the German forces in southwest Russia in a new command to be called Army Group Don. If anyone could defeat the Soviets, it was General Manstein.

However, Manstein quickly discovered that his forces were in serious trouble. The Third Romanian Army was broken and unable to offer any defense. The Sixth Army was isolated inside Stalingrad, and much of the Fourth Panzer Army was in danger of being cut off as well. Throughout southern Russia, the German forces were worn down and understrength, and the general staff could offer only two infantry divisions as immediate reinforcements. Hitler promised Manstein a further six infantry and four panzer divisions, but these units would not be available until early December. For the next two to three weeks, Army Group Don would be largely on its own.[44]

Hitler made the fateful decision to hold the Sixth Army inside Stalingrad and to supply it by air on 20 November after briefly discussing the situation with Jeschonnek and Goering. Jeschonnek was always eager to please Hitler, and he had what seemed a reasonable answer. The year before, a German corps surrounded by the Soviets in central Russia had been successfully supplied by airlift. But the situation in Stalingrad was much different. The Luftwaffe leadership in Berlin had grossly underestimated the situation in southern Russia and had made promises to Hitler before consulting von Richthofen or General Martin Fiebig, the senior air commander in the Stalingrad sector. Jeschonnek and Goering had advised Hitler that supplying the Sixth Army by airlift was possible until the front could be restored and the Soviet offensive driven back. Hitler's decision of 20 November 1942 would doom the German Sixth Army to destruction, and turned what would have

A briefing in Hitler's East Prussian headquarters, 1942. Von Richthofen is in the rear, second from the right.

been an operational setback into a major disaster for the Third Reich. Indeed, Stalingrad is seen as one of the great turning points of World War II.

Jeschonnek assumed that the army would be able to counterattack quickly and relieve the Sixth Army, so that the airlift would be a temporary expedient—lasting only days or a couple of weeks. In the previous winter the Luftwaffe had supplied 100,000 troops in the Demyansk pocket for several months. However, the comparison was a spurious one. The corps trapped in that pocket in central Russia in 1941–1942 had only required 300 tons of supplies per day, and Soviet air activity had been minimal. This had allowed the Luftwaffe to operate in a relatively benign environment. Still, the operation had required almost 500 Ju 52 transport aircraft (each carrying about a two-ton cargo load) to do the job in tough winter conditions—conditions that guaranteed a low operational rate.[45] It had been a huge strain for the Luftwaffe to support one corps by air. Supporting a large army was simply beyond the capacity of the entire transport force of the Luftwaffe.

The Stalingrad airlift required supporting almost three times as many men as the Demyansk operation—an absolute minimum of 750 tons. Furthermore, the Luftwaffe was facing heavy opposition by a revived VVS (Soviet air force) that was capable of inflicting heavy losses on the slow transports. To keep losses to an acceptable rate, the Luftwaffe would have to find a strong fighter escort for each transport flight. After a more thorough study of the situation, Jeschonnek and the air staff came to the conclusion that the Luftwaffe had nowhere near the number of transports available. And even if a bare number of transports could be found, one would also have to reckon with heavy attrition.

But for Hitler, Stalingrad had an emotional significance. Earlier in the month he had prematurely proclaimed to the German people that his forces had taken Stalingrad. Retreat from the city now would be an enormous embarrassment. So, on the afternoon of 21 November, Hitler sent orders to General Paulus to hold his position "despite the danger of temporary encirclement." Paulus was assured that he would be supplied by air, and the army commander and his staff developed a plan to deploy the Sixth Army in an all-round defense of Stalingrad.[46] That afternoon General Fiebig, commander of the VIIIth Air Corps and the Luftwaffe officer responsible for the Stalingrad sector, called Paulus to tell him that aerial supply of Stalingrad was simply impossible. The 4th Air Fleet did not have enough transport aircraft, and the weather was bad and likely to get worse, which would work against the Luftwaffe's efforts. Still, during the crucial days of 22–23 November, Paulus failed to demand from Berlin the authority to break out of the pocket. At this time, when his forces were strong and had a supply reserve sufficient for several days, it could have been done. The Soviet noose was not yet tight, nor were the encircling Soviet forces strong enough to prevent a concentrated thrust against one sector from breaking through their new front lines. Hitler might have relented if Paulus, Manstein, and all his senior officers had demanded a breakout operation at that time.[47] But, in this case, Hitler deferred to the commander on the spot. Indeed, General Paulus's dithering had as much to do with the Stalingrad debacle as did Hitler's hold order.

Von Richthofen was horrified by the order to supply the Sixth Army by air. He got on the telephone and called Jeschonnek at Berchtesgarten, General Kurt Zeitzler at Army Headquarters in East Prussia, and even Reichsmarschall Goering in Berlin to try to convince them that the 4th Air Fleet lacked an adequate number of transport and bomber aircraft to sustain the Sixth Army. He made repeated attempts to talk to Hitler on the phone, but no one in Hitler's entourage would put his calls through. Von Richthofen believed that the only workable strategy was for the Sixth Army to immediately mount a breakout operation through the Soviet forces that were just closing the net around Stalingrad.

On 27 November, von Richthofen flew to Manstein's headquarters to confer about the Stalingrad crisis. Manstein's adjutant, Major Alexander Stahlberg, was sent to the airfield to pick up von Richthofen in a headquarters staff car. Stahlberg recalled that von Richthofen was palpably upset. As the major drove von Richthofen to headquarters he heard him muttering, "impossible . . . even to imagine such a thing."[48] From the time of the airlift decision, von Richthofen's staff and the senior officers of the 4th Air Fleet described him as both upset and somewhat in a state of shock. For once he could not keep up his outward expression of calm in a crisis. After conferring with von Richthofen, Manstein crafted a carefully worded request to the Führer recommending that his forces force a gap in the Soviet lines in order to allow the Sixth Army an escape route from the Stalingrad pocket. Manstein admitted that a retreat from Stalingrad would cause a drop in the army's morale, but if the Sixth Army were preserved the Germans could soon regain the initiative and win back the ground.[49] By this time the German intelligence noted that the Soviets had assembled seven armies with seventy-one divisions and brigades in the Stalingrad area, and had a further twenty-six divisions and brigades ready for follow-on operations. Even though most of the Soviet formations were smaller than the equivalent German units, the sheer number of Soviet forces convinced Manstein and von Richthofen that holding Stalingrad was impossible.[50] At a conference the next day, Maj. General Wolfgang Pickert, commander of the 9th Flak Division and the senior Luftwaffe officer in the Stalingrad sector, told General Paulus and his staff of the impossibility of counting on the Luftwaffe.

The Luftwaffe and 4th Air Fleet strained every resource to bring enough transport aircraft to southern Russia to supply Stalingrad. By 5 December the 4th Air Fleet had eleven transport groups, two groups of obsolete Ju 86 bombers, and four He 111 groups available to fly supplies.[51] But weather and lack of fuel and parts meant that the operational rates for the bomber and transport units remained low. The weather refused to cooperate, and on many days no airlift missions at all could be flown. On most days there were fewer than 100 transports available. Despite every effort, including Field Marshal Milch moving to the Soviet front and making the Stalingrad mission the top priority of the Luftwaffe, there was no chance of success. The best airlift day was 7 December when 363.6 tons of supplies were flown in.[52]

As the Soviets strengthened their forces around Stalingrad, one of the primary German airfields for the transport operation, the Tatsinkaya airfield, fell to Soviet troops on 24 December.[53] Now the closest German airfield to Stalingrad was over 150 miles away. At least 70 transports were lost when the

Plowing snow at a Luftwaffe airfield in southern Russia, winter 1942. Freezing temperatures and snow combined to frustrate German attempts to supply the trapped Sixth Army in Stalingrad by air. (U.S. Army)

Soviets occupied Tatsinkaya airfield. It was a needless loss due to the strict hold orders from Berlin that limited any German retreat in the Stalingrad sector of the front. Compounded by the loss of aircraft on the ground, the German transport losses mounted quickly. As soon as airlift reinforcements arrived, more transports would be quickly lost to Soviet fighters and antiaircraft fire. Between November and the surrender of the Sixth Army on 31 January 1943, the Luftwaffe lost 488 transports and bombers and more than 1,000 aircrew in the futile operation to supply Stalingrad.[54] It was a hard blow to the Luftwaffe. At Stalingrad a German army of more than 200,000 men was destroyed. Approximately 90,000 men of the Sixth Army became prisoners when the army surrendered. Of these, only 5,000 survived to return to Germany after the war.

With the fall of Stalingrad, Army Group Don and the 4th Air Fleet had to face a series of new Soviet attacks that aimed for similar encirclement operations. To face a strong Soviet ground and air force, the Luftwaffe had fewer planes on the eastern front than it had when the Soviet campaign began in June 1941. Only 989 Luftwaffe aircraft of all types were operational at the time Stalingrad fell.[55] The 4th Air Fleet units were spread all over southern

Russia and divided into seven air commands to cover the widely separated German forces. Far to the southeast of Stalingrad, the Seventeenth Army and First Panzer Army had to pull back from the Caucasus, and the Soviets mounted a major offensive to take Rostov and cut off the two German armies. In the middle of the fight around Stalingrad, Manstein had to divert some of his strongest forces to Army Group A, which was to the south, and help cover their retreat to the Ukraine.

Even as the Stalingrad operation was being concluded, von Richthofen's battered transport force flew supplies to the far-flung units and evacuated the wounded soldiers of Army Group A. Shocked by the Stalingrad debacle, Hitler was finally willing to listen to reason, and he allowed the German army to yield some ground for tactical reasons. Although the Germans were in a weak position after Stalingrad, the Soviets had also dissipated their efforts and were in a poor position to continue the offensive. By February 1943, both the Soviet and German forces were spread out, exhausted, and understrength. However, General Manstein now believed he had the measure of the Soviets, and he was ready to deliver some sharp counterblows. Von Richthofen began to concentrate what combat forces he could in the center part of his sector so he could support Manstein's plan for a counteroffensive to retake Kharkov.

Discussions with the Führer

After the debacle at Stalingrad, Hitler understood that he would have to do a considerable amount of fence mending with his top generals, who, quite rightly, would blame decisions made in Berlin for the greatest defeat that Germany had so far experienced during the war. On 3 February, Hitler sent for Field Marshal Milch to discuss the Stalingrad operations. Hitler apologized to Milch for his decision not to pull the Sixth Army out of Stalingrad and praised Milch's efforts to manage the airlift. On 6 February, Manstein was called to Hitler's headquarters for a day of discussions. Hitler told Manstein that the Stalingrad decisions had been his mistake, then calmly listened to Manstein's ideas for the conduct of further operations in the Soviet Union. Manstein was convinced that the Germans might have to temporarily cede more ground in the USSR, but that was in preparation for a counterattack that would inflict maximum damage upon the Soviet forces and throw them back. Hitler essentially agreed with Manstein and, most important, indicated that he would allow Manstein more operational freedom.[56]

On 11 February it was von Richthofen's turn to visit the Führer. Von Richthofen first met with Goering, who was very concerned that von Richthofen would blame him for the disastrous promise to supply Stalingrad by airlift.

Von Richthofen argued strenuously with Goering, not so much about the Stalingrad defeat but about Goering's unwillingness to disagree with Hitler and his allowing Hitler to accept bad advice. After this confrontation, von Richthofen met with Hitler for a long discussion. Certainly to Goering's relief, von Richthofen did not use his meeting with Hitler to criticize Goering. Instead, he reviewed the mistakes of the recent campaign and frankly told Hitler that he had been wrong on several counts. Von Richthofen pointed out that Hitler had been let down by his close advisers, and that Hitler's operational micromanagement of the campaign was a mistake. Hitler took all this very calmly and admitted that he bore the ultimate responsibility for the campaign. Von Richthofen pressed the point and argued that the commanders at the front "must be given tactical freedom to act as their own local experience dictates."[57] In this instance, Hitler was willing to accept criticism of his leadership from a senior commander. It helped that Hitler genuinely liked von Richthofen and knew that he was personally loyal.

Hitler's response to von Richthofen's criticism was to praise the air fleet commander for his efforts at Stalingrad and to assure him that he would receive additional resources to restore the situation in the Soviet Union. Hitler then took another tack, and alluded to criticism of Manstein that officers in his circle had leveled. Von Richthofen stoutly defended his friend and colleague and argued that "Manstein is the best tactical and operational commander we have."[58] Von Richthofen left the meeting assured that he still held the confidence of the Führer and that Hitler was open to the operational ideas of his front generals. The meeting, and von Richthofen's readiness to frankly disagree with Hitler, worked to the air fleet commander's advantage. Hitler must have been impressed with von Richthofen because four days later he announced that von Richthofen would be immediately promoted to the rank of field marshal.

In the wake of Stalingrad, and the heavy blow to German civilian and military morale that it represented, Hitler felt it necessary to do something dramatic to raise the morale of the army at the front. So, on 17 February, Hitler and part of his entourage flew to Manstein's army group headquarters at Saporoshie, only 100 kilometers from the front lines. At the time Manstein and von Richthofen were dealing with a new Soviet offensive on the northern flank of Army Group South, and the Germans were about to launch a major counteroffensive on their own southern flank. Manstein was confident that his plan would succeed, and he had already outlined his concept to Hitler only ten days before. On 18 February Hitler conferred briefly with Manstein, von Richthofen, and Kleist (commander of Army Group A, which had withdrawn from the Caucasus in January). He was briefed by his senior

Wolfram and Jutta von Richthofen, early 1943, after von Richthofen was promoted to field marshal.

commanders but seemed uninterested in making strategic decisions, and it became obvious that Hitler's visit to the front was more for publicity than for serious strategic discussions. Some of Manstein's staff officers believed that Hitler wanted to visit Manstein at this moment so that he could later claim that the German counterattack was his inspiration.[59]

Hitler's promotion of von Richthofen just before his visit to the front was neatly timed. Hitler used the promotion as a means to signal his confidence in his senior military leadership on the Soviet front. Although von Richthofen felt a good deal of frustration toward the Führer after Stalingrad, Hitler had again won over his favorite airman with this signal honor. Von Richthofen tried to seem offhand about the promotion, but this is one time he was ecstatic. Not yet fifty years old, he would be the youngest officer promoted to field marshal in German history. He would now be part of a very select group of German generals. Although he would not openly admit it (it was, after all, not part of the Prussian military tradition to openly flaunt one's ambition), von Richthofen hungered for fame. And this was fame indeed.

After Hitler left, Manstein unleashed his counteroffensive. It was a brilliant stroke, well supported by the 4th Air Fleet. Recovering from his earlier losses, von Richthofen's airmen managed to fly 1,145 sorties on 22 February, and 1,486 sorties on 23 February. When German forces could concentrate, they were still able to drive the Soviets out of the skies and create havoc among the Soviet road columns and rear areas.[60] Kharkov was recaptured on 15 March, and the Soviets suffered heavy losses: over 23,000 Soviet soldiers were killed and 9,000 captured. More than 600 Soviet tanks and 350 artillery pieces were also captured. The argument of Manstein and von Richthofen that the senior army and air commanders at the front be allowed a wider operational freedom had borne fruit. But Hitler's demonstration of operational common sense in early 1943 would not last long. Convinced of his own genius and surrounded by sycophants at his headquarters, Hitler would relapse into his preference to micromanage the operations at the front in 1944. He would again issue a series of disastrous "no retreat" orders that would doom the German armies to destruction. Hitler would eventually fire Manstein and other top commanders for disagreeing with his disastrous orders.

Preparing for Citadel

Much of the ground and air fighting in the spring of 1943 was centered in the Kuban, as the German forces that had fought all the way to the Caucasus conducted a fighting retreat to avoid being cut off by the Soviets. The campaign in the Kuban is notable as the first time the Soviet air force would fight

Hitler visiting General Erich von Manstein (center) and von Richthofen at Manstein's headquarters in southern Russia, February 1943.

the Germans for control of the air and come out on top. The American Lend-Lease aircraft were flowing into the Soviet Union. Soviet factories beyond the Urals were producing new Mig and Yak fighters and ground attack planes for the VVS. All of this meant that the Germans could no longer count on having an edge in aircraft quality at the front. Unlike the 1941 and 1942 campaigns, by early 1943 the Soviet planes now had radios and radars deployed to the front. If Soviet training was not quite equal to the Germans, it was getting a lot better as German training declined. In fact, the new equipment gave the Soviet air force an air command and control network that was fully equal to the Germans.[61] In addition to better equipment, Soviet pilots employed new, and very effective, tactics. To support the ground forces, the VVS had learned to mass the superb IL-2 ground attack planes in attacks against German panzer formations and rear areas. The IL-2s were also used to spray smoke before the Soviet forces to mask their advance against German antitank guns. The Soviets also formed special fighter groups with veteran pilots who were given the mission of aggressively seeking out and destroying the Luftwaffe's fighters.[62]

As the 1943 spring season turned roads to mud, which restricted all movement of armies along the front, both they and the air forces could take a breather. The Soviets were getting stronger, and the Stalingrad victory and the operations in the Kuban had given them a new confidence. The Germans had taken a beating and were exhausted. But the front had held after

Stalingrad, and Manstein and von Richthofen believed that the German forces could deliver a major defeat to the Soviets in the summer of 1943. The plan was to destroy Soviet forces in the great salient around Kursk; the operation would be called Citadel.

After numerous reforms in 1942, German aircraft production was on the rise. This meant that the Luftwaffe aircraft losses could be replaced and the air fleets rebuilt. Von Richthofen could finally take some well-deserved leave, and many of his units could pull back from the front and replace aircraft and pilots. The 4th Air Fleet would also be equipped with new model aircraft to support the summer offensive at Kursk.

Von Richthofen's ground attack units would receive an undated model of the Henschel Hs 129B, a properly designed tank killer. The main armament was a 30 mm cannon, which, when firing armor-piercing shells against the poorly armored top and rear of Soviet tanks, was exceptionally lethal.[63] Although the Stukas were still in service and had become superb tank killers thanks to the addition of an automatic 30 mm cannon like that on the Hs 129B, the problem of Stuka vulnerability to ground fire was an issue. Even when the Germans held complete air superiority, attrition of Stukas from ground fire was fairly heavy. With the numbers and lethality of Soviet forward antiaircraft units increasing, the Luftwaffe needed a more survivable aircraft. The Hs 129B was the answer to the survivability problem in that the pilot and engine were encased in heavy armor—much like the IL-2 Sthurmovik. Unfortunately for the Luftwaffe, the Hs 129B never lived up to its promise. It was a very difficult aircraft to build and maintain, so production numbers were always low. Because of their cranky engines, Henschel units had a below-average serviceability rate, around 40–50 percent of aircraft available for combat. However, when it did get into the air, it was an impressive killing machine indeed.

In other theaters serious crises had developed. German forces were collapsing in North Africa, and many in Berlin doubted that Italy could remain in the war. Germany itself was coming under siege by Allied bombers that attacked targets by day and night. Unlike the small and inaccurate raids characteristic of the early days of the war, the 1943 attacks were capable of inflicting massive damage to German cities. The Soviet Union had been the center of the war in German eyes from 1941 to 1943, but now the center of air operations would shift. The main threat to Germany was now coming from the western Allies. In the midst of all of this, there was talk of the need to change much of the Luftwaffe's senior leadership. With von Richthofen now a noted field marshal, this might be his chance to become the Luftwaffe's chief of staff. The campaign of 1942 had included some notable successes for von

Richthofen, namely Crimea and the holding of the line after Stalingrad. Of course, Stalingrad had been a terrific failure, but von Richthofen had argued strongly against the operations and could not be held responsible. Indeed, few could have done better in such an impossible situation. In any case, despite the disappointments of the previous year, von Richthofen was still regarded as the Luftwaffe's premier field commander.

Chapter 12

Von Richthofen's Last Campaign — Italy, 1943–1944

In May 1943 von Richthofen was busy preparing the 4th Air Fleet to support Manstein's planned summer offensive at Kursk. At the same time, he was also in contact with Berlin and angling for the post of Luftwaffe chief of staff. Although his diary only hints at his ambition, the top officers of the Luftwaffe apparently all knew that von Richthofen was quietly putting himself forward for the job. Hans Jeschonnek had clearly failed as the Luftwaffe's chief of staff. From his insistence at the start of the war on making all bombers into dive bombers, to his failure in 1940 and 1942 to build up the Luftwaffe's training and support structure to meet the demands of war, Jeschonnek had made one bad decision after another.

By mid-1943 Germany was under increasingly heavy Allied air attack, and the home defense was hard-pressed to meet the threat. On the fighting fronts, the Luftwaffe was being overwhelmed in the Mediterranean and was gradually losing its superiority on the eastern front. Jeschonnek, facing constant abuse by Goering for the Luftwaffe's failings, was in such a state of constant depression that all the senior officers of the Luftwaffe had noted it. Jeschonnek was clearly exhausted by the demands of the job and wanted to leave. Hopefully he could get away to command one of the air fleets in the field, a job for which he was eminently qualified. Appointing him as chief of the Luftwaffe's general staff had been one of Goering's major mistakes. Von Richthofen corresponded and talked with Jeschonnek regularly, and he knew that his old friend was overwhelmed and on the point of a nervous breakdown. Von Richthofen believed that Jeschonnek would be far better off as a field commander. He also sounded out his old colleague about being his replacement.[1]

Other major command issues arose. Having been defeated in North Africa and recalled to southern Germany, Field Marshal Rommel was put in charge of a new army group to defend northern Italy should the Allies land. Italy would clearly be the next major theater of war, and Rommel was lobbying hard to be appointed as its commander in chief. He was strongly opposed in his ambition by Field Marshal Albert Kesselring, who had served as commander in chief

"South" and also commander of the 2nd Air Fleet since late 1941. Kesselring admired Rommel's tactical skills but believed that he was unsuited to theater command. Kesselring and Rommel had feuded constantly since Rommel had come into the Mediterranean theater. In 1942 Rommel had gone around Kesselring and used his status as one of Hitler's favorites to scuttle Kesselring's carefully planned strategy of taking Malta and securing the German logistics lines before advancing on Cairo. Rommel had the attack cancelled and charged on toward Egypt. As Kesselring predicted, Rommel ran out of supplies and was eventually defeated. Kesselring's assessment that he was more suited to theater command than Rommel was undoubtedly true. Rommel was a great tactician, but had little strategic sense. But if Kesselring were to remain in Italy and be responsible for that country's defense, he could not be expected to serve as both ground and air commander. The Mediterranean front was in a crisis situation, and if the Germans were to have any chance of holding Italy, the front needed the best tactical airman of the Luftwaffe.

Von Richthofen traveled to Berlin in early June 1943 for several days of briefings and meetings with Goering and Jeschonnek. The Wehrmacht staff expected an Allied invasion of Italy soon and wanted von Richthofen to take over the 2nd Air Fleet stationed in Italy. Von Richthofen's hope was that he would only take over air operations in Italy for four to eight weeks in order to meet the expected Allied attack. Goering expressed optimism that the Luftwaffe and the German army reinforcements then pouring into Italy could repel a major Allied landing attempt. Even at this late date, Hitler was confident that Italy could be held by the Axis. Von Richthofen was not so sure. Taking part in a large staff conference on 11 June, von Richthofen believed that most of the advice that Hitler was getting from his staff was "empty straw."[2] Von Richthofen was still hoping that he could soon be appointed as the Luftwaffe's chief of staff and wanted to stay an extra day in Berlin for a personal discussion with Hitler. But Goering barred von Richthofen's access to Hitler and insisted that von Richthofen depart immediately for Italy. Goering had every reason to want von Richthofen far away because he knew the Führer's mind, and knew how favorably disposed Hitler was toward von Richthofen. Goering would never have stood for an officer of von Richthofen's strong temperament and popular stature to hold the office because, as Luftwaffe chief of staff, von Richthofen would have been a direct threat to Goering's status. There was no doubt that von Richthofen would have asked for a much freer hand than Jeschonnek had been allowed and, because he was a favorite of Hitler's, it is likely that Hitler would have granted this.

Goering and von Richthofen had never gotten along well, and it is likely that the two had seen each other as rivals ever since World War I, when von

Richthofen had flown under Goering's command in late 1918. Von Richthofen had always viewed Goering as a shallow and corrupt man who was essentially ignorant about modern airpower. In contrast, von Richthofen's prestige was very high at this point. Only four months earlier he had been promoted to field marshal, and no one could deny that he was an outstanding field commander and a very logical choice as chief of staff. So, from this point on, Goering worked hard to limit von Richthofen's access to Hitler, and especially to prevent von Richthofen from having a personal discussion with Hitler in which he might criticize the leadership of Germany's Reichsmarschall. Publicly, von Richthofen was respectful to Goering, but his personal feelings about the man, expressed in his diary, became increasingly sour. From 1943 to his last entries in 1944, von Richthofen's personal record of his meetings and discussions with Goering were highly critical, with Goering's ideas and plans usually labeled as "nonsense."

Still, with an imminent crisis on the Italian front, von Richthofen was the obvious choice to command the Luftwaffe in that theater. Other talented generals on the eastern front understood the conditions there, but von Richthofen had lived in Italy and knew Italian, and if anyone could help bolster a faltering ally and improve coordination between the Italian and German air forces, it was von Richthofen. Moreover, he had repeatedly proven that he could do a great deal with limited resources. In the anticipated tactical battles, he would be stretched to the limits of his ability.

German Strategic Situation in May 1943

In May 1943 it was not yet clear to the German high command that the war had turned irrevocably against the Axis, but German forces had clearly lost the initiative. Rommel, posted to command the German forces in northern Italy after the Africa debacle, told his chief of staff, Lt. General Fritz Bayerlein, "We have lost the initiative, of that there is no doubt. . . . There can be no question of taking the offensive for the next few years, either in the West or the East, and so we must try to make the most of the advantages which normally accrue to the defense. . . . Our main effort must be directed toward beating off any attempt of the western Allies to create a second front. . . . If we can once make their efforts fail, then things will be brighter for us."[3] Though the words were not von Richthofen's, the sentiment was. In the West the war had turned completely defensive as the Allies had the initiative and greatly outnumbered the Germans. Von Richthofen would have to make the best of a bad situation.

The Tunisia campaign of November 1942 to May 1943 had been another disaster for the Wehrmacht. After winning a few operational victories early in the campaign, the German and Italian forces had been overwhelmed by Allied ground and airpower and forced to surrender. It was a disaster not quite on the scale of Stalingrad, but the loss of over 200,000 Axis troops, and over 100,000 German soldiers, was a severe blow. Italy's will to remain in the war was highly questionable, and Kesselring and his staff in Rome were quietly preparing plans for continuing the fight in Italy if the Italians capitulated. In the homeland the German cities were taking a beating from the increasing RAF night raids, but German air defenses were formidable and the Luftwaffe was confident that it could win the aerial attrition battle. In any case, fighting on two major fronts and with the skies over Germany now a third front, the Luftwaffe was simply stretched too far. Von Richthofen would have inadequate resources for the mission. Probably for that reason, he had been reluctant to take on the job.

Although the strategic situation in the Mediterranean looked bleak, with Italy clearly the next target of any Allied offensive, the Wehrmacht high command was feverishly working on plans to reinforce Italy in the hope that the expected Allied landings could be thrown back into the sea. If that failed, then at least Allied losses might be so heavy as to produce a stalemate. The Luftwaffe was expected to have a major role in repelling any landing attempts. However, the air war in the Mediterranean in 1943–1944 was a sideshow for both the Luftwaffe and the Allied air forces, overshadowed by the great air battles on the eastern front and over the skies of Germany. It was nonetheless a very important campaign and one the Luftwaffe fought with considerable effort and ingenuity.

In mid-1943 the Luftwaffe's greatest problem was not its supply of airplanes but of trained aircrew. Luftwaffe chief of staff Jeschonnek, along with Goering and his deputy, Field Marshal Milch, had ignored the most fundamental infrastructure of the Luftwaffe: at the start of the war the Luftwaffe's pilots were usually better trained than their opponents. By 1942 the situation was reversed. The need to conserve limited aviation fuel resulted in a pilot training regimen that drastically cut the flying hours for trainee pilots and aircrew. By 1943 the Luftwaffe's new bomber pilots were sent into combat with a little over 100 hours' total flying time. This was a fraction of the flying time possessed by Allied pilots.[4]

By the spring of 1943 the Allied air forces were able to use their superiority in numbers, equipment, and training to drive the Luftwaffe from the skies of North Africa, interdict Axis shipping, and render the Axis airfields in Africa inoperable. Just before the end of the collapse in Africa, the Germans and Italians pulled their battered air formations out of Tunisia to Sicily and the Italian mainland, leaving behind hundreds of wrecked and damaged aircraft. Many of the planes were in good condition but unflyable due to a lack of spare parts that never arrived.

After the loss of Tunisia, the German high command assessed the Italian armed forces as incapable of offering serious resistance to an Allied invasion of Italy. The fighting worth of the Italian army was low due to lack of equipment, obsolete equipment, poor training, poor morale, and weak officer leadership. The Italian air force was rated as largely ineffective. While there were a relatively large number of planes on hand, only a few of the latest fighters were capable of taking on Allied aircraft on an equal basis. The Italian bomber force of several hundred planes was regarded by the Germans as so hopelessly obsolete that it was rated as having no value for the defense of Italy. The Italian aircraft industry and air force logistics system, never very capable in the first place, were close to a breakdown. Operational rates for the Regia Aeronautica were about 30–40 percent due to a lack of parts and spare engines. In 1942 and 1943 Italy could put planes in the air only by cannibalizing its existing machines.[5]

The only really useful units of the Regia Aeronautica were the fighter units that had recently been reequipped with the Fiat G 55s and Macchi 202s and 205s. In those fast, maneuverable, and well-armed aircraft the Italians had planes that were roughly equal to the American P-40s and British Spitfires. Italy's most modern and effective force was its navy, but the Germans doubted that the Italians could stand up to the U.S. or British navies in battle.[6] On 2 March 1943 the Italian *commando supremo*—Mussolini—sent Hitler a message outlining Italy's precarious strategic situation and demanding large quantities of modern equipment from the Germans. The next day, after conferring with his staff about the crisis on the southern front, Hitler replied to Mussolini. To reassure his ally, Hitler promised large quantities of German matériel and assistance to include tanks and artillery for the Italian army, and to reequip the Italian bomber fleet with German Ju 88 medium bombers. A large number of flak guns and radar units were also promised, and Hitler said that the German equipment was to flow immediately.[7] In the meantime, German army and air reinforcements were ordered to Italy.

Hitler's grandiose promises meant little. In the six months before the Italian surrender, the Luftwaffe managed to provide only forty Ju 88s to reequip one Italian bomber group. Italian-German cooperation was hampered by other factors. For instance, since German and Italian radios were incompatible, Italian aircraft flying missions with the Luftwaffe could not communicate

Italian Reggianne 2005 fighter, summer 1943. By 1943 the Italian aircraft industry had produced some superb fighter planes such as this Reggianne and the Macchi 205 and Fiat G 55. These machines were equal to the best Allied fighters of the time, but a badly managed aircraft industry and a poor logistics and repair system ensured that only a handful of these excellent planes were available to oppose the Allied invasion in 1943. (U.S. Army)

with their partners.[8] In addition, the Luftwaffe only began providing the Italians with radar in early 1943.[9] The Germans were short of equipment themselves and had little to spare for an ally they saw as weak and incompetent. If Italy were to be held, then the Germans would have to carry the main effort.

In addition to von Richthofen the Luftwaffe sent several other proven commanders to meet the expected Allied attack on Italy. Colonel Dietrich Pelz was pulled from his post as inspector of Luftwaffe bombers and Stukas and sent to command the German bomber force in Italy. Pelz had won recognition as an outstanding bomber commander and tactician early in the war, and he was given the task of developing bomber tactics against the expected Allied invasion forces. The next year he would become the Luftwaffe's youngest major general, at age thirty-two.

The high command reorganized the command structure of the army and Luftwaffe in Italy. Throughout the North African campaign Field Marshal

Kesselring had worn two hats as commander of German army units and commander of the 2nd Air Fleet. When von Richthofen was pulled from the Soviet front to take over the 2nd Air Fleet, Kesselring relinquished command of Luftwaffe forces and became, in effect, commander of German ground forces in Italy. Although he still kept the title "Commander in Chief–South," his authority extended only to German army units and Luftwaffe flak units placed under army command. As in the Soviet Union, senior army and Luftwaffe commanders were expected to coordinate their plans and operations.

Von Richthofen had served under Kesselring's command in 1940 in the western campaign, and in the Soviet campaign in 1941. The two had worked closely together since their service on the Reichswehr staff in the 1920s. They were never close friends, and their relationship was something more like a rivalry. Von Richthofen, for example, believed that he had a far better understanding of air warfare than did Kesselring—and he was almost certainly right. But as a ground commander Kesselring was probably the equal of General Manstein. Whatever personal friction arose, both von Richthofen and Kesselring were consummate professionals in the old general staff tradition. They would work together effectively as a command team.

The Luftwaffe Prepares to Meet the Allies

When von Richthofen arrived in Italy on 12 June 1943, he was briefed by the 2nd Air Fleet staff, who presented him with a far more pessimistic view of the strategic and operational situation than he had just heard in Berlin. Goering's grandiose plans for the Luftwaffe to defeat an Allied invasion were pure nonsense. The Allies had "total air superiority" that allowed them "to attack any target in Italy at will."[10] Von Richthofen found out that the Italians were in even worse shape than he imagined. His first job was to assess his own resources and then develop his plans.

The 2nd Air Fleet was headquartered at Frascati, a small town near Rome, which also contained Kesselring's headquarters. The air fleet's IInd Air Corps had its headquarters in Sicily at Tavromina airfield. However, a more secure headquarters had also been prepared near Naples in case the Germans were forced to retreat.[11] Assigned to support the IInd Air Corps was Air Training Division 2, based in the south of France. The IInd Air Corps' main force consisted of a fighter command based at Tapani airfield in Sicily, with fighters and fighter-bombers at Vibo Valentia and Monte Corvine airfields. Light bomber and attack (fighter-bomber and Stuka) units were based in Sicily and southern Italy. There were also several aircraft groups based in Sardinia. Air Training Division 2 was a headquarters for bomber units that been badly

Von Richthofen meeting Mussolini. After the poor performance of the Italian forces in Spain von Richthofen had little regard for the Italian military leadership. When he got to Italy as Luftwaffe commander in June 1943 he was under no illusions that the Italians would be able or willing to put up much of a fight to defend their country from invasion.

mauled on other fronts and had been sent to a restful sector to be rebuilt, re-equipped, and retrained. It commanded Bomber Wing 100 (KG 100), which was being equipped and trained to employ the new radio-controlled bombs that were the first true precision-guided munitions. In addition to these flying commands, the Luftwaffe's representative to the Italian air force staff (Superaeria), General Ritter von Pohl, had a staff to conduct liaison with the Italians. As a flak specialist, he also commanded the Luftwaffe's ground forces and flak units in Italy.[12]

On the eve of the Allied attack, in early July 1943, the Luftwaffe had an official strength of 667 combat aircraft available for the defense of Italy. These included six Ju 88 bomber groups, each with forty aircraft, two understrength He 111 torpedo bomber groups, three "fast bomber" groups (one group of Me 210s and two groups of Me 110s), several attack groups in the process of transitioning from the Ju 87 Stuka to the FW 190 fighter-bomber, four groups of Me 109 day fighters, and one group of Ju 88 night fighters. For reconnaissance, the 2nd Air Fleet had one group of Ju 88 long-range reconnaissance planes, one group of He 111 bombers equipped with radar to track shipping, and one squadron of Me 109s equipped with cameras and drop tanks for extra range.[13] However, the official numbers are misleading. Most of the units of the 2nd Air Fleet were understrength. In most combat groups Luftwaffe units were at two-thirds strength or less. The Me 210 "fast bomber" group had only eighteen aircraft, and of these only twelve were operable. In fact, the Luftwaffe had only 443 operational combat aircraft in Italy and southern France in early July.[14] The Luftwaffe estimated that it and the combat units of the Regia Aeronautica were outnumbered by a factor of approximately five to one in the air. As Von Richthofen was soon to learn, it was an accurate assessment.

The Regia Aeronautica was in far worse shape than the Luftwaffe. Although Hitler had blithely promised substantial German assistance, by July the only reinforcements that had arrived were forty Ju 88s to equip an Italian bomber group—and this unit was not yet operational. The Italian bomber force of 400 aircraft was so obsolete that it was written out of German planning. The Italian aircraft production and maintenance program, the weak link in the Italian air force, was getting worse by the day. The Italian fighter arm had a strength of 530 planes, but of these only the Macchi 200s, 202s, 205s, and Re 2001s were considered modern enough to take on Allied planes, and only 130 of these latter craft were operational. The SM 79 and SM 84 torpedo bombers would be useful in attacking an Allied invasion fleet, but the Regia Aeronautica had only twenty-two of these able to fly. In the final reckoning before the Allies landed, the Italian air force paper strength of 1,042 aircraft translated into an operational strength of 164 relatively modern aircraft

A Savoia Marchetti 79 trimotor bomber in 1943. This obsolete plane from the mid-1930s was the mainstay of the Axis bomber force for the defense of Italy in 1943—a symbol of the Axis weakness in the air at this point in the war. (U.S. Army)

that could meet Allied aircraft on roughly equal terms.[15] By Italy's surrender in September 1943, the Regia Aeronautica possessed only 1,306 combat aircraft, less than half the number with which it had started the war.[16]

Von Richthofen arrived on 12 June 1943 to take over a battered and demoralized force. On his way to Italy, von Richthofen had been personally briefed by Goering in his vast Karinhall estate. Goering was convinced that the Luftwaffe's failure in North Africa had been due to poor leadership and lack of will. As he had done in the Battle of Britain, Goering blamed his pilots' lack of courage and aggressiveness for the failure against the Allies. Goering even drew up an order stating that any Luftwaffe pilot—up to wing commander—who showed any lack of aggressiveness would be demoted to private and sent to fight as a soldier on the Soviet front.[17] But Von Richthofen had little faith in Goering's strategic analysis, and he would make his own assessment when he got to Italy. In fact, von Richthofen's private assessment of the Luftwaffe's capabilities versus the Allies led to some pessimistic conclusions. Von Richthofen realized that if the British and Americans got ashore in force, neither the Italian army nor the small number of German ground units could hope to defeat them. He believed that the only way to defend Sicily or Sardinia was to catch the invasion fleet at sea, or at the moment of landing, and to sink enough transports and supply ships to cause an Allied logistics breakdown. He noted that "we can put every effort into attacking enemy shipping. . . . If we are successful in disrupting the supply over the beaches we can make his ground units ineffective and vulnerable to counterattack by our forces."[18] Luftwaffe intelligence estimated that the Allies had 1.5 million tons of cargo shipping in the Mediterranean to support landing operations. If the Luftwaffe and Regia Aeronautica could sink or disable 100,000 tons per day, any Allied assault would soon be crippled. As von Richthofen noted, "We can't predict a success with this strategy . . . but it's the only strategy that offers a possibility of success."[19]

After the fall of Tunisia the British and Americans intensified their air attacks designed to cripple the Luftwaffe and ensure Allied air superiority for the invasion of Italy. From May to July, the Allied heavy and medium bombers pounded German and Italian airfields in Sicily, southern Italy, and Sardinia. Luftwaffe bomber bases in southern France were also attacked. The American four-engine B-17 and B-24 bombers had the range and payload to hit every Axis airfield in the theater, including those in northern Italy and southern France. The large British and American twin-engine bomber force had the range and payload to hit targets in Sicily, southern Italy, and Sardinia. Through June the American and British bombers ranged all across Italy to bomb Axis airfields, rail centers, shipping, and munitions factories. The scale of Allied attacks made it impossible to maintain bomber units in Sicily, so von Richthofen began withdrawing his forces to well-defended fields in the Foggia area of southern Italy. Some fighters were pulled out of Sicily and based at airfields around Naples, Foggia, and Calabria. The few fighter groups that remained on the front lines in Sicily suffered from continual Allied attacks.

There are conflicting accounts of the Luftwaffe's relations with the Regia Aeronautica before the Sicily battle. Some Luftwaffe officers describe the Italians as being very cooperative and loyal allies at this point in the war. Other Luftwaffe officers complained that the Italians were deliberately dragging their feet and inhibiting full cooperation with the Germans. The lack of Italian engineers supporting the Luftwaffe delayed the process of rebuilding, repairing, and enlarging the airfields that the Germans urgently needed if they were to stage their units south and mount an air defense of Sicily.[20] I support the view that the Italians were still loyal allies of the Germans in mid-1943. Whatever the relations between the German and Italian army had been, and they were often marred by distrust and acrimony, the Regia Aeronautica had always done its best to support the Luftwaffe in North Africa. As for the slow pace of airfield building and repair, the Italian regime's incompetence is the most plausible explanation.

The Defense Plan

From May to June the Luftwaffe feverishly tried to set up an effective air defense system for Sicily, southern Italy, and Sardinia. As part of Hitler's aid package to bolster Mussolini, 100 German flak batteries arrived in northern Italy to defend the heartland of Italy's war industry. Many of the flak crews were, in fact, Italian soldiers, and German personnel manned the radars and gun control systems. Luftwaffe flak reinforcements were also deployed to southern Italy and Sicily, along with German ground troops. The 5th Flak Division was deployed to southern Italy to help repel the expected Allied landings. The Germans positioned long-range Freya radar in western Sicily and in Sardinia, and short-range radars were deployed to cover German bases.[21] One of the major problems the Luftwaffe faced was a shortage of trained technical specialists. The Luftwaffe had lost its most experienced fighter operations (radar) controllers in the Tunisian surrender in May, and trained men were hard to replace.[22]

In spite of Goering's admonition to simply fight harder, von Richthofen formulated detailed plans. In the short time before the Allied invasion, he and Pelz developed antishipping tactics against the expected Allied invasion that would hopefully inflict maximum damage on the Anglo-American fleet with minimal German casualties. Given the massive Allied superiority in fighters, they decided that the Luftwaffe's best chance would be to attack at night, at dawn, or at dusk, when Allied air cover would be at its weakest. Pelz directed that the bombers were to fly carefully planned courses out to sea and then drop to fifty meters (165 feet) altitude and change course to confuse Allied radar. As the planes approached the target they were to climb to 2,500 meters (8,250 feet) and attack the target in a 30- to 50-degree dive. The group commander would drop illumination flares and would use colored flares to mark the target for his bombers.[23] Due to the fuel shortage, each mission would be carefully calculated, with the most experienced pilots and navigators carrying larger bomb loads and less fuel, and the inexperienced crews smaller bomb loads and more fuel.[24] It was a very different kind of war than the one they had experienced at the eastern front. In Italy the Germans faced an enemy with better planes and equipment. The Allied air forces could put the Luftwaffe infrastructure under constant attack, whereas in the East the Soviet air force had rarely ventured more than thirty kilometers (about nineteen miles) beyond the front lines and only rarely attacked the Luftwaffe's airfields.

The plan called for German and Italian air reconnaissance to find the Allied invasion convoys well out to sea and give the air units plenty of warning.

With ample warning, the Axis airmen could hit the enemy hard and early. Pelz hoped that he could strike Allied shipping with large, coordinated attacks of fifty to eighty planes at once. The highly trained German bomber force of 1940 might have been able to carry out such complex plans, but after Russia and North Africa the Luftwaffe bomber force was a shadow of its former self. Despite a desperate shortage of trained bomber aircrew, Pelz hoped to quickly retrain his units to carry out antiship strikes. Since the Luftwaffe faced an enormous margin of Allied air superiority, von Richthofen and Pelz determined that the only chance the Luftwaffe had to strike a major blow against the Allies would be to attack their shipping in the vulnerable first days of an invasion. If the Allied logistics buildup were slowed down, German ground forces could be given the time to mass and organize an effective counterattack.[25]

From 1939–1942 the Ju 87 Stuka had been the most effective airplane for attacking ships. But by 1943, the Stuka had little chance to survive in combat against the Allies, who could be expected to put up strong fighter cover. Von Richthofen could certainly recall how his Stukas had been massacred by RAF fighters in the summer of 1940. In Italy, the enemy fighter cover would be even heavier. But there were other alternatives to reliance upon the Stukas. In 1942 the Luftwaffe had finally created a small force of He 111 torpedo bombers, and these planes had proven their worth in the antishipping role when they had inflicted heavy damage on Allied convoys to northern Russia that summer. Seeing the value of torpedo units, the Luftwaffe set up a torpedo bomber school in Italy at Grosseto. In the spring of 1943 the Germans were in the process of training and equipping two torpedo bomber groups to be ready to oppose the expected Allied landings. However, the German plan was set back when a massive Allied raid devastated the torpedo plane base. Von Richthofen withdrew the small torpedo plane force to relative safety in southern France.[26]

Von Richthofen placed considerable hope in his small, fast bomber and fighter-bomber force, which consisted of Me 210s, Me 110s, and FW 190s. These aircraft were expected to roar in at full speed at 50 meters altitude in order to evade Allied radar. At about a kilometer (0.62 mile) from the target they would climb slightly and then skip their bomb into the enemy ships while also strafing them.[27] The greatest problem with using these light attack planes was their limited range with heavy bomb loads, especially the FW 190. Some attack units would have to be held in central or southern Italy and then stage forward into Sardinia or Sicily if these islands were attacked. The problem was always the Allied air superiority and the Allied program of keeping the Axis airfields under constant attack. The closer a German airfield was to

Allied bases in North Africa, the more intense the Allied bomber attacks, and the heavier the daily attrition. To spare its limited aircraft force, the 2nd Air Fleet would have to pick just the right moment to stage the aircraft forward to the vulnerable Sicilian or Sardinian bases.

Commanding the German fighter force in Sicily was Maj. General Adolf Galland. Like Pelz, he was very young—his most recent promotion had been awarded the previous year, when he was thirty years old. Galland had been the inspector of fighters when the Berlin air staff sent him to take command in Sicily in the aftermath of the Tunisia surrender. He was initially shocked at the state of his command. The Luftwaffe fighter units that had evacuated Tunisia for Sicily were exhausted. They were short of spare parts and personnel, and the frequent attacks by Allied bombers against the Luftwaffe's supply lines made it impossible to rebuild the units to their former strength.[28] Throughout June the Axis airfields on Sicily took an especially hard pounding, with the 130 Me 109s stationed on the island the primary target. With few replacement pilots, and flying in the teeth of overwhelming Allied air superiority, the Luftwaffe fighters were able to do little against the Allied attacks. Goering was furious at the failure of his fighter units, who were flying in the face of far superior enemy numbers. When the fighters failed to intercept an Allied bombing raid, Goering lost his temper and ordered that one pilot from every group be court-martialed for cowardice.[29] As the situation worsened for the German fighters, Goering blamed the unit commanders for failing in the face of overwhelming Allied airpower. After the Allies landed in Sicily, Goering again lost his temper and sent a message on 12 July that his pilots in France, Norway, and Russia regarded the German fighter pilots in Sicily with contempt. He railed that if improvements were not made in the attitude of the pilots, then personnel from commanders on down were to be sent as infantry to the eastern front. Von Richthofen and the other senior Luftwaffe commanders, knowing the true situation, ignored Goering's demands to punish their pilots.[30]

The Intelligence Picture—Anticipating the Allied Assault

German intelligence left Kesselring and von Richthofen largely in the dark about Allied plans and forces. German signals intelligence was usually a very good source of intelligence on the Allies, but after Tunisia fell, the Allies maintained a pretty thorough radio silence in the Mediterranean. The Luftwaffe's only long-range reconnaissance asset capable of monitoring Allied shipping and port activity was a squadron of Ju 88 reconnaissance planes.

A train full of replacement Me 109s destroyed at the railyard near the Luftwaffe airfield at Trapani, Sicily, summer 1943. In preparation for the Allied invasion of Sicily in July, and of the Italian mainland in September 1943, Allied medium and heavy bombers relentlessly attacked Axis airfields and transportation throughout Italy. As fast as the Luftwaffe could rush replacement aircraft to the theater, they were likely to be destroyed on the ground by Allied air attacks. (U.S. Army)

Try as they might, it was hard to get past the Allied fighter cover to photograph the North African ports where Allied invasion forces were assembling. A few aerial reconnaissance reports came in during May and June, but there was nothing like a comprehensive coverage of Allied naval activity.[31] A handful of Italian and German flying boats and seaplanes patrolled the open sea to try to spot Allied convoys and ships. But they dared not get too close to the well-patrolled North African coast.

From all sources of intelligence, including agent reports, Wehrmacht intelligence in Italy estimated that the Allied powers had fifty to fifty-five divisions of ground troops in the Mediterranean, including the U.S. and British armies and the Free French forces. German intelligence even reported that the Americans had a force of three paratroop divisions based near Oran, and these were being readied for the invasion of Italy. Of this vast Allied force, which included the former Vichy French forces in North Africa, the Germans estimated that twenty-five divisions were fully equipped and trained and available for the coming campaign. Moreover, the Germans estimated that the Allies had the ships and landing craft to land 120,000 men and 4,000 tanks and vehicles in one lift.³² In fact, the German estimates were wildly inaccurate—almost double the true Allied strength figures. The Allies would use most of their ready combat forces in the theater, twelve divisions, in the Sicilian operation. Indeed, at their peak strength in 1944, the Allies would never have more than twenty divisions in Italy. As for airborne divisions, the Americans had only one in the theater, the 82nd Airborne. Only the estimate of Allied shipping capacity was fairly close to the mark. The British and Americans had the capability to land a force of 100,000 men on Axis shores.

From the scanty information available, von Richthofen believed that there were two obvious targets for an Allied invasion: Sicily and Sardinia. Of these, Sicily was the most probable site for an attack as it lay within fighter range of the British airfields on Malta. Sardinia was out of range of single-engine fighters but was within easy range of Allied light and medium bombers, and the British had carriers in the Mediterranean that could provide fighter cover. As an obvious target, Sardinia was reinforced by Italian and German ground forces, and a strong German and Italian air contingent was sent there. If the Allies took Sicily, they could base large numbers of aircraft there to support an assault on southern Italy. If the Allies took Sardinia, its airfields could cover more Allied landings in central Italy. As far as von Richthofen was concerned, the worst possible scenario was a simultaneous Allied attack on both islands. German and Italian ground and air strength was simply too thin to make an effective fight for both locations. Per the 2nd Air Fleet's assessment, the Allies "would do the Germans a favor" if they only attacked at one location, as the Luftwaffe and Regia Aeronautica only had enough airplanes to make a good fight on one front.³³

The Allies telegraphed their intention to move on Sicily when they seized the island of Pantelleria south of Sicily in early June. Pantelleria was a large, well-garrisoned island with a major airdrome and a radar station. The Allied air forces subjected the island to a massive two-week bombardment that broke the morale of the Italian defenders. The garrison surrendered as the first boats of the amphibious landing force touched shore. Pantelleria was vital to any Allied action against Sicily because its radar provided early warning of Allied raids. Its large airfields were within fighter range of Sicily and could serve as a base for the short-ranged Allied fighters to cover the landings in Sicily until Axis airfields could be captured.³⁴ The Germans correctly figured that the British and Americans would not make such a great effort to seize Pantelleria if Sicily were not the primary target. After Pantelleria, U.S. and RAF bombers ranged all over Sicily and southern Italy, striking logistics centers, rail centers, and, most important, German and Italian airfields. Von Richthofen noted that "the competition between us and the Allies is to see if we can repair our airfields as fast as the Allies could bomb them."[35] By 20 June, von Richthofen noted that the German airfields in Sicily had been so heavily damaged that the Luftwaffe's attack units "couldn't get off the ground in less than 45 minutes."[36] As air attacks on airfields across southern Italy increased in early July, the Germans and Italians placed their forces in Sicily and Sardinia in the highest state of alert.

As happened on more than a few occasions during the war, the Wehrmacht and Luftwaffe staffs in Italy were largely on their own in developing an accurate intelligence picture for their theater. Despite a lack of signals information and aerial reconnaissance, Kesselring and von Richthofen used their experience and common sense to predict the Allied moves with considerable accuracy. In June the increased tempo of Allied attacks on the German airfields in southern Italy and of vital rail lines in the peninsula clearly indicated that an attack was coming. The army and Luftwaffe intelligence staffs in Italy believed that the Allies had enough ships to land twelve ground divisions in Sicily—a fairly accurate assessment.

The British concocted an elaborate deception operation to plant false plans on a dead man with the fictional identity of a British Marine major that indicated an Allied attack in the Balkans rather than on Sicily. The dead "courier officer" had supposedly died in an air accident off the coast of Spain, and the British made sure the body washed ashore where it would be found by Franco's police, who would be sure to turn over the false documents to the local German agent.[37] This information was regarded as credible by German intelligence in Berlin but was disregarded by the intelligence staffs in the theater.[38] The few air reconnaissance missions that the Luftwaffe could fly confirmed there was little Allied activity in the eastern Mediterranean, while the ports in western North Africa were crammed with ships. This indicated an attack was coming soon on either Sicily or Sardinia—possibly both. In the first week of July, Kesselring and von Richthofen judged that an attack on Sicily was imminent; German and Italian forces there were put on the highest state of alert, and continual reconnaissance was flown over the sea to try to spot the approaching Allied invasion convoy.

Battle for Sicily

Early on the morning of 9 July an Italian reconnaissance plane spotted an Allied invasion convoy south of Pantelleria. Late that afternoon another Italian plane spotted five convoys steering north from Malta. The Italian and German forces on Sicily were all alerted. Within an hour a German reconnaissance plane reported a convoy thirty-three miles northwest of Malta. Axis

Field Marshal Albert Kesselring, commander of the German ground forces in Italy, 1943–1945. Kesselring was von Richthofen's commander for part of the French campaign in 1940 and in Russia in 1941. In Italy, von Richthofen would serve alongside Kesselring as the air commander for the theater. Although the two field marshals viewed each other as rivals, Kesselring had a high regard for von Richthofen's talents as an air commander.

reconnaissance units shadowed the Allied convoy movements until nightfall, and shortly thereafter the Italian air staff ordered its torpedo bombers based in Sardinia to attack.[39] The Axis forces were about to face the largest amphibious operation in history (to that time). The time and place of the attack was expected, and the Luftwaffe had prepared air attack plans.

On the morning of 10 July the Allies began landing six divisions at eight landing points along a 100-mile stretch of the southern Sicilian coast. With an

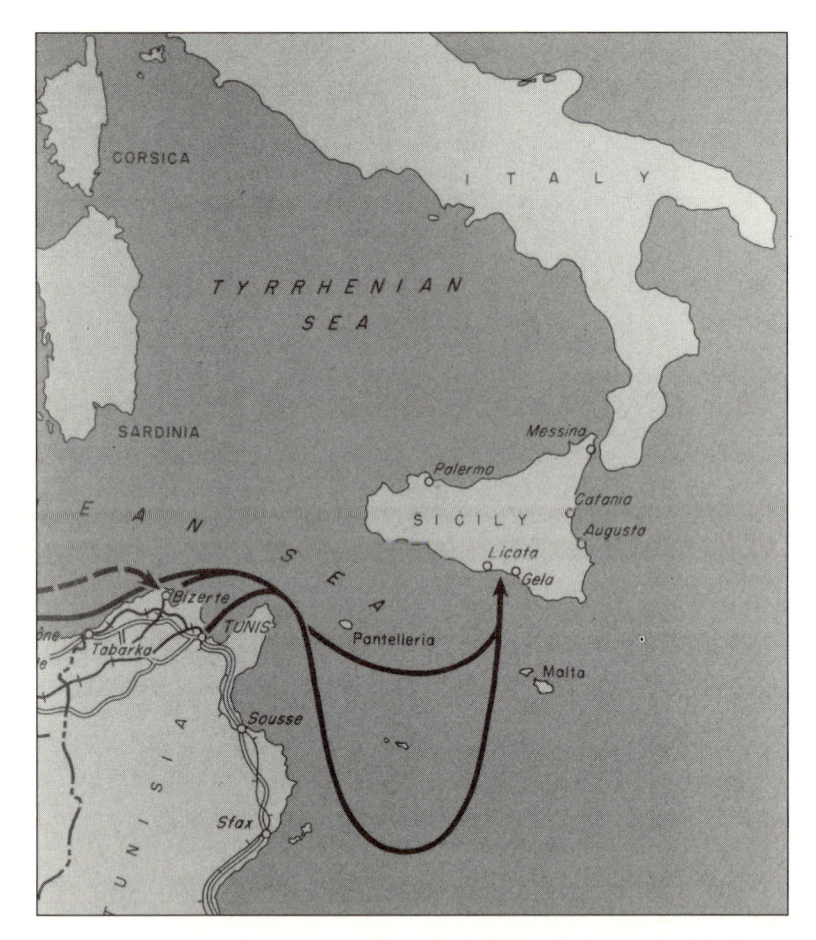

Allied invasion of Sicily, July 1943. The island of Pantelleria, south of Sicily, provided a vital base for Allied fighter aircraft protecting the invasion fleet. (Robert Coakley, ed., *U.S. Army in World War II: Global Logistics and Strategy, 1943–1945* [Washington, DC: U.S. Army Center for Military History, 1968])

invasion fleet of 1,365 warships, transports, and supply ships, as well as 1,225 smaller landing craft, it was, as one might say today, a "target-rich environment" for the Luftwaffe and Regia Aeronautica.[40] The Axis air forces began hitting the Allied armada before dawn.[41] At 0510 hours the U.S. minesweeper *Sentinel* was sunk by a direct hit from a Stuka, with ten sailors killed and fifty-one wounded. Several air attacks occurred on the Licata landing site, but no U.S. ships were hit.[42] At the Gela landing site, just before 0500 hours, a Stuka made a direct hit on the destroyer USS *Maddox*. The ship sank immediately, with heavy loss of life. Italian and German bombers flying from Sardinia attacked the Gela beachhead in the afternoon and inflicted minor damage to the destroyer USS *Murphy*. In addition, a Luftwaffe fighter-bomber sank USS *LST 313* off Gela, though a high-level bomber attack that night failed to hit any ships.[43]

In the British landing sector near Catania the invasion fleet came under heavy attack, mainly from the Luftwaffe bombers based in southern Italy. Four Liberty (cargo) ships and a Dutch auxiliary were hit by bombs, and two were sunk. Two British hospital ships, the *Dorsetshire* and *Talamba* were bombed, and the *Talamba* subsequently sank.[44]

The Luftwaffe had to fight through the Allied fighter cover over the invasion beaches. The British and American air forces had several hundred fighters based on Malta and Pantelleria, but the long flying distances limited the time the Allied fighters could patrol over the landing beaches. On 10 and 11 July the British and Americans put more than 1,000 fighter sorties over the beaches to protect the Allied ships.[45] With eight landings and over 100 miles of coast to cover, the Allied air forces could keep no more than a few planes patrolling over each sector, even with a maximum effort. So even though the Allies had plenty of aircraft, the numbers covering the beaches at any time were limited.

The German and Italian planes, which had orders to avoid combat with Allied fighters, managed to slip in to attack the Allied ships. The American 307th Fighter Squadron that covered the landing reported the German tactics of the first part of the invasion as "2–5 Me 109s or Fw 190s trying to sneak in and dive bomb the ships."[46] The U.S. unit claimed only two German aircraft in the campaign for the island.[47] The main resistance to the Axis air attacks was the shipboard antiaircraft fire, which managed to bring down several Axis aircraft during the first day. During the first two days of the campaign the Germans and Italians lost at least twenty-seven aircraft while attacking Allied ships—losses under the 5–10 percent rate that von Richthofen deemed acceptable attrition.[48]

On 11 July the German and Italian air forces attacked Allied ships throughout the entire landing area. In the American sector, ships' logs reported several large and well-coordinated attacks by German bombers. At 1540 hours a force of twenty-four to thirty-six Ju 88s roared in over the U.S. fleet. A direct hit was made on the SS *Robert Rowan*, an ammunition ship, and it began to burn. The crew was removed with no casualties, and the *Robert Rowan* blew up at 1700 hours in one of the most dramatic moments of the campaign.[49] The ammunition ship sent a column of smoke thousands of feet into the sky as debris and unexploded shells rained down over several square miles.

The event was captured on film—a U.S. military photographer at Gela was taking a photo of the beachhead just as the *Robert Rowan* exploded. That night the Italian and Luftwaffe bombers attacked for more than an hour using parachute flares for illumination, and the destroyer USS *Tilman* was slightly damaged by a near miss. In the British sector, the destroyer HMS *Eskimo* was badly damaged by a German bomb.[50]

After the first days of the invasion the Axis attacks tapered off as the Allied air forces put several captured airfields near Catania into operation and shifted fighter units to Sicily. Once RAF and Army Air Force (AAF) fighters were based in Sicily they quickly won air superiority over the whole island and made it far too dangerous for the Luftwaffe or Regia Aeronautica to operate in daylight. But until Allied air units were established ashore, the Luftwaffe kept up the attacks. On 13 July the Liberty ship *Timothy Pickering* was sunk, and on 17 July the Liberty ship *William Coleman* and HMS *Queen Emma* were badly damaged.[51]

The first days of the Allied landing at Sicily were to be the last time the Axis air forces would have any opportunity in the air due to the thin Allied air cover. It was also the last opportunity for the Germans to use their most lethal antiship weapon, the now-obsolete Ju 87 Stuka, in daylight operations. However, even in an all-out campaign against Allied shipping, the Luftwaffe and Regia Aeronautica accomplished relatively little. The Allied loss of twelve ships to Axis air attacks failed to hinder the landing of over 100,000 troops with their vehicles and supplies on the shores of Sicily.[52] The massive Allied air campaign against Axis airfields in June had also cost the Germans and Italians over 200 aircraft destroyed and more than 100 damaged.[53] The Allied air campaign against Axis airfields had minimized Axis airpower over Sicily. Once the Allies were ashore and could use the captured Italian airfields, they were able to put up such a strong fighter screen that Luftwaffe daylight operations became a hopeless proposition. Indeed, the amount of enemy airpower that von Richthofen faced in Italy was staggering by the standards of the eastern front. In the first week of the Sicily operation the British and American air forces flew 12,000 sorties and dropped 4,500 tons of bombs, with von Richthofen's airfields as a primary target.[54] In the face of such enemy forces, that the German and Italian airmen inflicted as much damage as they did was an impressive accomplishment.

The air battle over Sicily was the last gasp of the rapidly expiring Italian air force. As the Germans expected, the Italian bomber force proved worthless and Italian bomber raids sank no ships. The Italian torpedo bombers did somewhat better, sinking one ship and damaging the British carrier HMS

Indomitable on 16 July. The Italians indeed did their best as loyal German allies. The Regia Aeronautica coordinated operations with the Germans and pressed its attacks aggressively. But the Italians had little to fight with. The Italian 4th Fighter Wing that flew in the Sicilian campaign had a strength of 133 Mc 205 and Mc 202 fighters on the books, but only 49 operational planes. Italian air operations included escorting the Luftwaffe's Stukas to the target, and from 11–14 July the Italian fighters tangled with the AAF's P-38s and the RAF's Spitfires over the invasion beaches.[55] But after a few days the Italian air force was literally fought out, suffering from attrition and constant attacks on its airfields. By mid-July 1943 the Regia Aeronautica disappeared from the war as a cohesive force.

The lack of accurate intelligence remained a problem for the German commander and staffs. The reports on Allied losses sent to von Richthofen by the air units were wildly inaccurate. Apparently every near hit was counted as a sinking. With many of the attacks at night, air units simply estimated the damage inflicted on the Allied fleet. On 10 July, von Richthofen estimated that 100,000 tons of shipping had been sunk as well as a "large number of landing boats."[56] On 11 July, Luftwaffe units reported 5–6 large ships sunk along with many landing boats. By the end of the second day of the operation the Axis estimated that it had sunk or disabled 350,000 tons of Allied ships.[57] On 12 July another 100,000 tons were reported as sunk or heavily damaged.[58] Although von Richthofen believed his strategy of attrition against the Allies was working, reality in the form of growing Allied air superiority affected the German campaign plans. At dawn on 13 July a strike by Ju 88s suffered heavy losses when six were shot down. At the same time, a group of Me 110s shipped in from Germany to replace combat losses was destroyed on the ground by an Allied air attack. By 14 July, von Richthofen, still receiving reports of heavy Allied shipping losses, forbade large air attacks. Luftwaffe units were ordered to try to slip by Allied air cover in small groups to attack the invasion fleet.[59] By 15 July, five days after the landing, Kesselring and von Richthofen realized that the invasion was not going to be defeated, and the 2nd Air Fleet started to evacuate Luftwaffe personnel, equipment, and aircraft in Sicily.[60]

During the campaign for Sicily the 2nd Air Fleet employed Ju 52 transports to fly German paratroops into Sicily to reinforce the German ground effort.[61] The German army in Sicily fought a brilliant delaying action for five weeks and then successfully evacuated the German and Italian units on the island, with their supplies and heavy equipment, to the Italian mainland across the straits of Messina. The Luftwaffe's role in supporting this was essential. Under direction of General Ritter von Pohl, one of the Luftwaffe's best flak specialists, the Germans and Italians emplaced fifty-two flak batteries around Messina to protect the Axis evacuation. Although the Allied air forces made numerous attacks to cut off the Axis retreat, the flak protection was so intense that it pushed the Allied bombers to fly at high altitudes—where accuracy against the small targets, such as ferries, was poor.

The Luftwaffe continued small attacks through July and August and reported another few hundred thousand tons of Allied shipping lost. However, from mid-July on, the Luftwaffe's priority was to rebuild its force and prepare for the next stage of the war, the expected Allied invasion of southern Italy. In contrast to the massive Allied losses claimed by the Luftwaffe (over 500,000 tons) in the month of July, in fact, the Allies lost only fourteen merchant ships (80,000 tons) in the Mediterranean along with two warships (USS *Sentinel* and USS *Maddox*).[62]

The loss of Sicily forced the Wehrmacht staff in Berlin to reconsider the strategic situation in Italy. As it was clear that Sicily would be lost to the Axis, a meeting of the Fascist Grand Council on 24 July deposed Mussolini as prime minister and ordered his arrest. Field Marshal Pietro Badoglio took over as the head of the Italian government and immediately proclaimed, "Italy will continue the war at the side of our Germanic ally." Von Richthofen was called to Berlin to brief Hitler and the Wehrmacht staff on the conditions in Italy and the state of relations between the Wehrmacht and the new government. No one in Berlin was very sure of Badoglio's real position on the German alliance, and the most common view was that he was likely to betray the Axis alliance and take Italy out of the war. That view was, in fact, accurate. Even then Badoglio had begun secret negotiations with the Allies for the surrender of Italy.[63]

While briefing Hitler, Von Richthofen was somewhat more optimistic about Badoglio's sincerity as an ally, but he also pointed out that the sentiment in Italy had strongly turned against fascism, and that Badoglio might not be able to keep Italy in the war even if he wanted to. Preparations to deal with Italy's defection from the Axis alliance were stepped up. With Italy's forces in almost total disarray, even the most optimistic analysis predicted that German forces would now have to bear the main burden of defending Italy.

On an interesting note, at the 27 July staff meeting General Kurt Student first mentioned his ideas for an airborne operation to rescue Mussolini. Von Richthofen thought that Student's proposals bordered on lunacy. Yet two months later, a raid by German commandos would successfully carry out Student's plan and rescue Mussolini from a mountaintop prison in a daring operation that combined gliders and airplanes.[64]

The Salerno Campaign

The Sicily campaign ended on 17 August 1943 when the Allies marched into Messina. On that day Kesselring was busy rushing reinforcements to southern Italy and von Richthofen was working frantically to rebuild the Luftwaffe units that had been badly battered in Sicily. The Allied failure to follow up the victory in Sicily with an immediate jump across the straits to the Italian mainland was viewed as a godsend by the German commanders. British General Bernard Montgomery, with characteristic caution, waited more than two weeks to land the Eighth Army in Calabria on 3 September, and the Germans used the time to prepare strong defenses. The Bay of Salerno, with the great port of Naples, was the obvious target for an Allied landing on the Italian coast, although the Germans were still concerned about the possibility of an Allied landing on Sardinia and kept a strong air detachment there. At this time the 2nd Air Fleet had seven bomber groups based in the Foggia area and two at the southern Italian base at Viterbo. Three bomber groups (I KG 26, III KG 26, and III KG 100) were stationed in southern France, ready to stage south to support operations against an Allied landing. Although each bomber group was supposed to contain forty aircraft, some groups, especially KG 26 and KG 100, had taken heavy losses in Sicily. The attacks on the Foggia and Viterbo airfields cost the Germans more aircraft destroyed on the ground. In early September 1943 most of the bomber groups were at half strength or less, giving the Luftwaffe fewer than 200 bombers for the whole theater. As the Allies prepared to attack Salerno, the Luftwaffe prepared to withdraw its bombers to airfields in the far north of Italy, in Piedmont, Bergamo, and Piacenza, in order to make them less vulnerable to Allied attack.[65] The German fighter, light bomber, and fighter-bomber units were dispersed to airfields in Calabria and Apuleia within range of any probable Allied landing sites. After the losses in Sicily, the fighters and attack units were also weak, operating at half strength or less.

For the Luftwaffe, Salerno would be a tougher air campaign than Sicily. The British and Americans had captured and repaired the numerous airfields in Sicily. Although the Allies would again fly at long range, they were in a better position to keep a strong air presence over the beachhead than in the first days of the Sicily landing. To have any chance of seriously damaging the Allied fleet, the Luftwaffe needed new tactics and weapons. In fact, the Luftwaffe had just deployed a revolutionary new weapon to the theater that gave it the hope of turning back the expected Allied invasion of southern Italy. The new weapon was the radio-guided bomb, which could be dropped from high

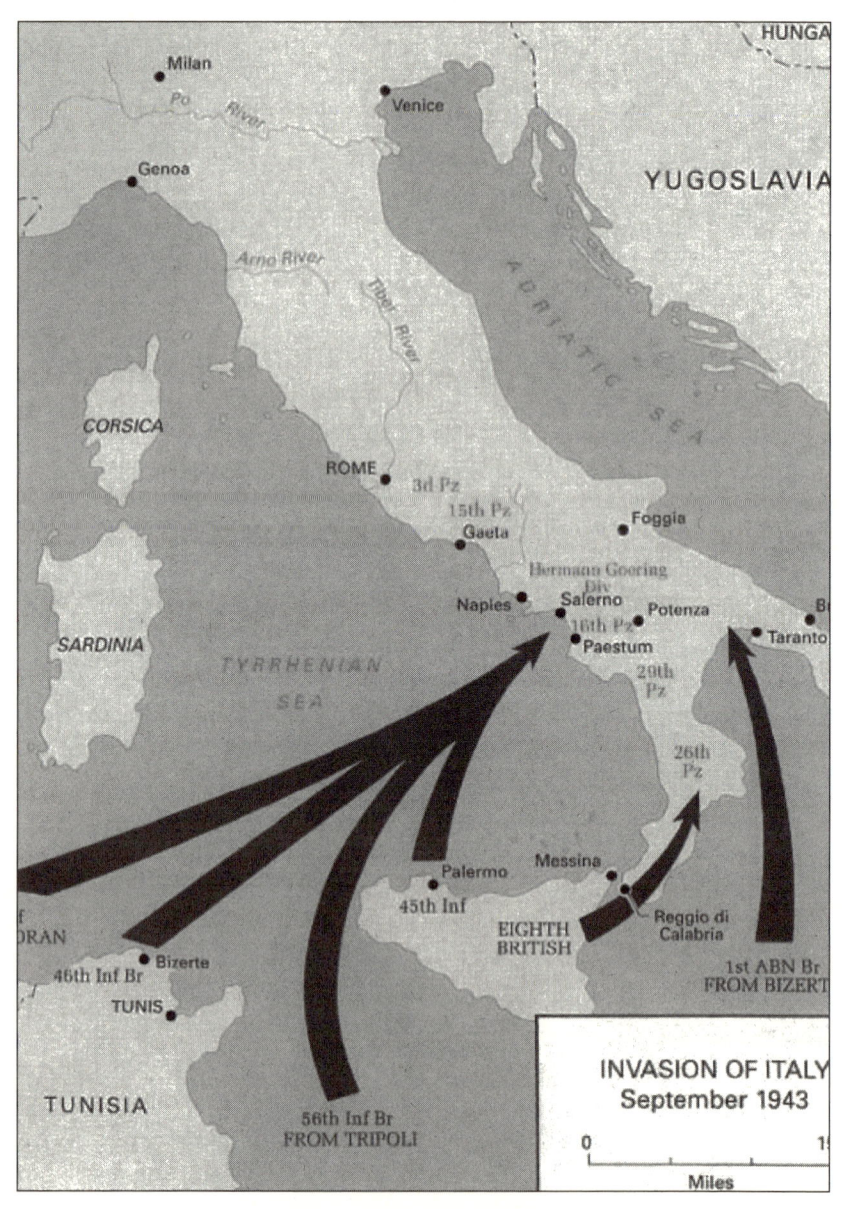

The situation in Italy before the Anzio landings of January 1944. By this time the 2nd Air Fleet had retreated to northern Italian bases and was on the defensive. However, the Luftwaffe could still mount enough combat power in the theater to carry out a strong offensive against the Allied landing at Anzio, near Rome. ("The German Operation at Anzio," Report of Mediterranean Theater Combined Staff, April 1946)

altitude, steered in flight by a bombardier with radio control, and able to hit a precise target, such as an Allied ship, with devastating effect. During testing the new bombs proved to be ten times more accurate than conventional bombs dropped at high altitude. The campaign at Salerno would be the first major test of the precision bomb in warfare.

The Luftwaffe developed two different models of radio-guided bombs. The first was the Fritz X, a 3,000-pound armor-piercing bomb designed with a large tail with controllable surfaces. The Fritz X was dropped at approximately 22,000 feet in a trajectory that would bring it close to the target. A flare in the bomb's tail gave the position to the bombardier, who used a joystick to manipulate the radio-controlled tail surfaces to steer the bomb to the target. The armor-piercing Fritz X was intended for use against Allied warships. The second bomb, the Henschel Hs 293, resembled a powered glider. The Hs 293 could be dropped from high or medium altitudes, and the bombardier could track it by a flare in the tail, as with the Fritz X. The Hs 293 would actually glide toward the target with the bombardier steering with radio guidance for the control surfaces. Once a target was sighted, the bombardier ignited a rocket engine to propel the bomb and its 700-pound warhead into a ship at almost 500 miles per hour. The Hs 293 was intended primarily to destroy softskinned merchant vessels and transports.

In September 1943 two bomber groups of Bomber Wing 100 (KG 100), each with twenty planes, had been trained and equipped to drop the Fritz X and Hs 293. Both groups employed Dornier Do 217 bombers. KG 100 had long been an elite bomber unit and was used by the Luftwaffe to develop new equipment and techniques. In 1940 KG 100 was employed as the Luftwaffe's elite "pathfinder" unit tasked to lead the way for the main bomber forces because of its mastery of aerial navigation. From that point it served essentially as the Luftwaffe's "special mission" bomber force. Because of the complex nature of the radio-guided bombs, the aircrew of KG 100 were a carefully selected and trained group. In dropping the Fritz X, for example, the pilot had to pull up and fly as slowly as possible after dropping the bomb so the bombardier could acquire the target. Moreover, the pilot had to fly straight and release the bomb within a 5-degree cone. Using radio-guided bombs required precise flying far above the standard coming out of the German pilot schools in 1943. The Hs 293 was considerably easier to use than the Fritz X, without the same requirements for staying on a direct course.[66]

On 8–9 September 1943 it must have seemed to the Wehrmacht in Italy as if everything was happening at once. In the late afternoon of 8 September a German reconnaissance plane spotted a vast Allied convoy north of Malta heading east for Salerno. A landing was expected within twelve hours, and the German forces were alerted.[67] That day the surrender of Italy to the Allies, which had been secretly negotiated the week before, was announced. So the Germans had to repel an Allied invasion and seize control of all Italy and disarm the Italian armed forces at the same time. In fact, the Germans had long been planning for this eventuality and had quietly put their forces in position to execute Operation Axis—the plan to secure Italy for the German Reich. The selection of the code name for the operation suggests that Kesselring had a humorous streak in his nature.

Of course, things can always get worse, and they did. That night the AAF launched a raid of 120 heavy bombers on the German army and Luftwaffe headquarters at Frascati. The outside buildings were leveled, and Kesselring was almost killed. About 80 of the 1,000 personnel at the headquarters were killed, and many more were wounded. The German headquarters' communications were shut down. However, the Germans had been lucky: most of the headquarters was located in deep tunnels and caves and was unscathed by the attack. In a brilliant performance, the Luftwaffe signal engineers restored full communications in only six hours.[68] On the morning of 9 September, von Richthofen was able to put the Luftwaffe's portion of Operation Axis into effect.

The first mission of the German bomber force was to see that the Italian navy did not end up in Allied hands. Part of the Italian fleet had sailed for Allied ports in North Africa during the night and was spotted off the coast of Corsica. Aircraft of KG 100 attacked their former allies and made two direct hits with Fritz X bombs on the Battleship *Roma*, the pride of the Italian fleet. The *Roma* sank almost immediately, taking almost all the officers and crew with her. It was an impressive debut for the guided bombs in warfare.[69] Several smaller Italian ships were sunk or damaged by German air attacks that day as the Italian fleet raced to safe Allied havens.[70]

At dawn on 9 September a force of 55,000 American and British ground troops, supported by 586 Allied warships, transports, and landing ships, landed in the Bay of Salerno.[71] With German bombers busy attacking the Italian fleet, the first Luftwaffe attacks were made by the IInd Air Corps Me 109 fighters and the FW 190 fighter-bombers of the attack groups. The Me 109s employed a new weapon in the form of 21 cm rocket launchers mounted on the wings. The FW 190s carried 500-kilogram bombs (1,100 pounds). With strong Allied fighter cover from Sicilian airfields and additional air cover provided by five British carriers, the only effective tactic for the Germans was to slip in at high speed, fire rockets and drop the bombs at likely targets, and run away at high speed. As in Sicily, the damage reported by the Luftwaffe was wildly exaggerated. Von Richthofen was told that two Allied cruisers had been sunk, and 150,000 tons of Allied ships taken out of action. In fact, fighter-bombers had only crippled one LST (landing ship, tank) and sunk another.[72] Some small landing craft were sunk or badly damaged as well, and the 21 cm rockets proved effective against small vessels.

That day was certainly the busiest for the Luftwaffe in Italy as it survived Allied air attacks, seized control of all the Italian air force installations and flak units, bombed the fleeing Italian navy, and attacked the Allied landing. As was characteristic during other crisis moments during the war, von Richthofen had expected these things, and he coolly directed the air side of the battle and the takeover of the Regia Aeronautica installations. His diary hardly mentions the Allied attack at Salerno but gives a detailed account of all the measures that had to be taken to secure the German lines of communication in Italy. It is a testament to the Luftwaffe's competence, and to von Richthofen's exceptionally capable leadership, that he and his staff could handle so many simultaneous crises.

It would be three days before the 2nd Air Fleet was ready to conduct major strikes against the Allied beachheads. In the meantime, fighters and fighter-bombers made low level raids, which mostly damaged Allied light craft. Most German bombers were relegated to night raids on the Allied fleet because of the lack of Luftwaffe fighters to escort them. The three battered Luftwaffe fighter groups still in southern Italy could only mass enough planes to escort the Do 217s of KG 100 on daylight raids. One of the Luftwaffe's most effective antishipping forces, the small group of torpedo bombers, could not be used in daylight due to the paucity of escort.[73]

On the evening of 11 September, the thing the Allies had most feared came to pass as Dorniers carrying Fritz X bombs arrived over the invasion fleet. The cruiser USS *Savannah* was badly damaged by a glide bomb. Two days later the cruiser USS *Philadelphia* had a narrow escape as it maneuvered frantically to avoid two guided bombs. The cruiser HMS *Uganda* was not so lucky. It was hit by a guided bomb and crippled on 13 September, and attacked again while being towed away the next day.[74] On 13 September the British hospital ship *Newfoundland* took a direct hit and sank. On 14 September the merchant ship SS *Bushrod Washington* was hit by a guided bomb, probably an Hs 293, and sunk. The next day KG 100 Dorniers struck the SS *James Marshall* with a guided bomb. The ship was wrecked but later salvaged. On 16 September, a week after the landing, KG 100 got its biggest prize of the campaign. The battleship HMS *Warspite*, which provided vital gunfire support for the Allied units engaged in desperate fighting ashore, was hit by two guided bombs and damaged further by two near misses. The *Warspite*

A U.S. transport, blowing up off Salerno, Sicily, September 1943, after being hit by Luftwaffe bombs. (U.S. Army Center for Military History)

was towed to Malta, repaired, and eventually returned to service, but would be out of action for several months.[75]

It was an auspicious beginning for the guided bomb in warfare. The small Luftwaffe force equipped with the new weapons had, in a week, disabled a battleship and two cruisers and had sunk or wrecked three other vessels. Still, it was not enough to seriously hinder the Allied landing and buildup. The Allies had vast naval power at their disposal and had planned to absorb far heavier losses. The Luftwaffe had a different picture of Allied losses and believed that it had sunk or disabled dozens of Allied warships and merchant vessels at Salerno—an estimated 400,000 tons by 18 September. The reality was far different. In September 1943 the Allies only lost 52,000 tons of merchant shipping in the Mediterranean.[76] Whatever the Luftwaffe's estimates, it was clear by mid-September that the Allies were successfully ashore and ready to advance up the Italian peninsula.

Luftwaffe combat losses during the Salerno battle were reported as "low." But there was still steady attrition from combat and Allied attacks on German airfields. By mid-September the Luftwaffe bomber force was described simply as being "fought out."[77] The southern Italian bases were in the path of the Allied ground advance, so these were evacuated on 20 September. Bomber units were sent to northern Italy, and the fighter and attack groups that had borne the brunt of the battle at Salerno were sent to the relative safety of central Italy. The Luftwaffe needed to reorganize, retrain, and rebuild its units after the Sicily and Salerno battles. Von Richthofen, who had been under heavy strain for months, was exhausted. He was beginning to show signs of poor health, and the past two years of the war had considerably aged him. Kesselring, who valued von Richthofen's competence, told Berlin to keep von Richthofen in the theater despite his health problems. Kesselring argued that he needed the Luftwaffe commander to rebuild his force for the battles expected in the spring.

By the fall of 1943 the German commanders in Italy could look at their campaign against the Allies as something of a success. They had fought a successful delaying action in Sicily that allowed them to bring their forces and equipment out to fight again. After the Allied landing at Salerno and the defection of Italy from the Axis, the Germans had taken control of the country and held off the Allied armies well south of Rome and forced a stalemate. For two years the Allies would be forced to fight their way up the Italian peninsula, taking heavy losses all the way. During the battles of 1943 the Luftwaffe had made a significant contribution, employing a new means of bombing and inflicting moderate damage on Allied shipping. Luftwaffe transports had played an important role in moving reinforcements and in successfully evacuating German forces from Sardinia and Corsica. Luftwaffe flak forces had performed brilliantly in protecting the evacuation of Axis forces from Sicily. As the war in Italy progressed, the Luftwaffe's air units would play a progressively decreasing role, and the flak units would become the Luftwaffe's main effort. However, the Luftwaffe was not yet finished as a strike force, and in the months to come von Richthofen would again prove his talent as an air tactician.

The Luftwaffe Reorganizes

Hitler's promise of massive reinforcements to von Richthofen made in the summer proved false. After the failure to stop the British and American landings at Salerno, the Luftwaffe in Italy was reorganized and reduced to a fraction of its former strength. The situation in Italy was seen as stable, and the demand of air units for the defense of Germany was pressing. The IInd Air Corps was detached and sent to France. The 2nd Air Fleet's bomber command was disbanded. KG 1 was sent to Germany to be reequipped with the He 177s. One bomber group (II KG 77), was sent to Germany to be trained as a torpedo unit. Another group (II/LG 1) was sent to Greece. However, it would still be able to support operations in Italy. Only three Ju 88 bomber groups, about 100 planes, were retained in Italy (I and II KG 76 were stationed at Aviano). Other bomber groups were sent to France to take part in the planned bomber offensive against England. Sardinia was evacuated and its air detachment brought to northern Italy. Three fighter groups (I JG 53, I JG 77, and I JG 4), a fighter-bomber wing of two groups (I SG 4, II SG 4), and some reconnaissance squadrons were retained and stationed in northern and central Italy.[78] By late fall 1943 the 2nd Air Fleet had fewer than 300 operational combat planes available.

However, even this reduced force was still capable of inflicting serious damage on the Allies. During November 1943 the Germans noted the weakness of the Allied air defenses at the port of Bari in southern Italy, one of the Allies' most important supply bases. Using reconnaissance planes flying from Albania, the 2nd Air Fleet kept Bari and its shipping under careful observation for two weeks.[79] In a raid meticulously planned by von Richthofen and his staff, a force of 105 Ju 88s—virtually every bomber in the Italian theater—attacked Bari harbor the night of 2 December. The Luftwaffe's tactics were superb. Most bombers first flew out to sea and dropped to low altitude to avoid Allied radar observation. Pathfinder bombers dropped "window" (aluminum foil strips) to jam the Allied air defense radars while the bombers systematically worked the port over by the light of parachute flares. The small port was crammed with ships. The Ju 88s hit an ammunition ship and a tanker; the former blew up and rained explosives on other vessels as the fire from the tanker's burning oil spread. In a short time sixteen Allied merchant vessels were destroyed and eight others damaged. The port facilities were heavily damaged and knocked out of operation for three weeks. Naval historian Samuel Morison described it as "the most destructive air attack since Pearl Harbor."[80] Yet the Bari raid was not to be repeated; Allied antiaircraft and night fighter defenses at the major ports, such as Naples, were simply too strong for the Luftwaffe's small bomber force.

Anzio

The Luftwaffe settled into a routine of small night harassment raids against Allied logistics during the winter of 1943–1944. By January 1944 things were so quiet that von Richthofen took a trip to the Po Valley to hunt ducks with some of his staff. While he was reducing the bird population of northern Italy an Allied invasion fleet of 370 ships and landing craft made the 150-mile jump from Naples to Anzio on 22 January 1944 and landed a corps of 50,000 American and British troops on the coast near Rome with virtually no opposition. In contrast to Sicily and Salerno, the landing came as a complete surprise to the Germans. The Luftwaffe's air reconnaissance force was, by this time, unable to provide more than the sketchiest picture of Allied shipping movements and convoys. However, the Germans had noted Anzio as a possible landing site and had enough reserves near Rome to throw against the invaders and slow the Allied advance.

Bad weather over northern Italy prevented von Richthofen from flying immediately south to direct operations against the landing from his headquarters near Rome.[81] Many German aircraft in northern Italy were grounded by bad weather for the first days of the battle, and the Luftwaffe's premier antishipping force, the guided bomb groups of KG 100, were dispersed around small airfields in southern France to evade the Allied bomber campaign against the larger German airfields. It took days to assemble the units and stage them south to airfields in Italy closer to the action. The Luftwaffe's fighter and attack groups in Italy had been badly weakened by constant attacks on their airfields in the three days before the Anzio landing and needed time to sort themselves out and move to airfields close to the landing site. When he arrived at his headquarters late on the evening of 22 January, von Richthofen gave the orders to deploy available air units to oppose the landing as well as ordering forty Luftwaffe flak batteries to the front lines to engage the Allied ground troops. Virtually all the Luftwaffe forces in Italy were ordered into the Anzio battle. In von Richthofen's words, "We couldn't have done more."[82]

In the meantime, the 2nd Air Fleet's only response to the Anzio landing was a few fighters stationed near Rome that evaded the Allied air cover and strafed the beach. Some fighter-bombers also attacked ships. For the next two days, poor weather hindered the Luftwaffe's deployment of forces to meet the Allied landing.[83] On the night of 23 January the Luftwaffe drew its first blood when the destroyer HMS *Janus* was hit by a German air-dropped torpedo and sunk and the destroyer HMS *Jervis* was damaged by a bomb.[84] The first large attacks came the next day. Fifteen fighter-bombers of Schlachtgeschwader 4 attacked the Allied fleet in the afternoon, forty-three aircraft attacked at dusk, and fifty-three bombers attacked at night. A 500-kilogram bomb from a fighter-bomber hit the destroyer USS *Plunkett* and caused heavy damage and casualties. That night the hospital ship *St. David* took a hit from a guided bomb and sank. The destroyer USS *Mayo* hit a mine and was badly damaged.[85] Throughout the campaign, the German bombers also dropped mines in the shipping lanes at night; between January and April 1944 more than 600 mines were dropped by the Luftwaffe near Anzio.[86]

As the fighting intensified, von Richthofen was often at the front to observe the air attacks of his unit from an observation post overlooking the bay.

General Pohl, commander of all the flak units in Italy, was appointed as the "close battle commander" of the 2nd Air Fleet with the responsibility of commanding all the flak and air units in the Anzio sector.[87] Within a few days, the German air campaign assumed a pattern. Groups of thirty to fifty fighters and fighter-bombers would attack ships and the beachhead once or twice a day, and the bombers, especially the KG 100 units with the guided bombs, would attack at night. The Allied commanders noted that Anzio saw the toughest German air opposition of the whole Mediterranean campaign. A dusk raid of FW 190s on 26 January damaged one LST, seven light craft, two merchant ships, and a tug.[88] On the night of 29 January, KG 100 had its best night of the campaign when its guided bombs sank the cruiser HMS *Spartan* and the Liberty ship SS *Samuel Huntington*.[89] One factor that made the German night attacks so effective was the Luftwaffe's large radar installation at Cape Circe that overlooked the Anzio beachhead. Despite many attempts by the Allies to destroy the site, the radar kept operating throughout the campaign and gave the Luftwaffe a clear picture of Allied air activity over the sector. In addition, the "window" used by the bombers proved effective in jamming Allied air defense radars.

Any air attack can be terrifying, but it is especially tough on sailors because there is no place to hide on a ship. The sailors that faced the nightly Ju 88 raids with conventional bombs took them fairly calmly. While the conventional bombers made a lot of noise, they rarely hit anything. This was not so in the case of the attacks with the Fritz X and Hs 293. Because the tail flare in the bombs and the rocket engine of the Hs 293 were highly visible at night, anyone under attack could see the bomb heading straight for the target. This leant a surreal quality to the raids by KG 100 on the Allied fleets at Anzio and Salerno. An American army sergeant at Anzio watched the attack that sank the cruiser HMS *Spartan* (probably an Hs 293) and described the "bright red spot [the flare] that seemed to hang in the sky for several seconds. . . . When the target was located it came down like a comet in a wide sweeping arc." The explosion was described as "tremendous."[90] After the initial landing, supplies were brought in by LSTs and Liberty ships that unloaded as quickly as possible and sailed away. Such ships might be unlucky enough to experience one such attack. However, the sailors manning warships like the HMS *Spartan* that stayed on station to provide gunfire support to the troops onshore had to suffer through several such attacks.

The guided bombs of 1943–1944 were not as accurate as their modern descendents, but like the kamikaze attacks in the Pacific, they had a demoralizing effect on those on the receiving end. The guided bombs were fairly effective at Salerno, but in the next months the Allies analyzed the attacks and developed countermeasures. The Allies occupied Sardinia and Corsica in the fall of 1943 after the Germans had quietly, and very successfully, evacuated their forces from those islands. Afterwards, the Luftwaffe carried out some guided bomb attacks on Allied ships in Corsican harbors, and after one attack the Allies recovered parts of an Hs 293 guided bomb. Allied technical intelligence analysts began to understand the bomb's effectiveness and limitations. When the Allies next attacked by sea, they would have destroyers specifically tasked with jamming the radio frequencies that they thought the Germans might use. The British and Americans also improved their night fighter capability in the theater and sent new night fighters with improved radar to Italy. The night fighters made it much more dangerous for KG 100 to make its night attacks. When the Allies landed at Anzio in late January 1944, the Luftwaffe predictably attacked with the Henschel and Fritz X guided bombs. The Allied night fighters could now intercept the German missions more frequently. When German bombers were intercepted by Allied night fighters, the normal procedure was to drop the bomb and run for safety. Even though KG 100 made many guided bomb attacks on Allied ships at Anzio, the Allied countermeasures were generally effective: only one cruiser and one destroyer were sunk, as well as some cargo vessels. On the other hand, to inflict these small losses caused the German bomber unit a steady rate of attrition. By early 1944 the guided bombs were no longer a major threat to the Allies.[91]

The German campaign against the beachhead reached a crescendo in mid-February when Kesselring mounted a major ground offensive to try to destroy the Allied beachhead. Massed Luftwaffe fighter-bombers provided close air support for the German panzer units advancing on the Allies, and 2nd Air Fleet bombers struck Allied depots and logistics. The Germans flew more than 150 sorties on 16, 17, and 19 February in a desperate attempt to break the Allied defense.[92] The all-out effort failed. The AAF and RAF were able to fly hundreds of sorties against the German attackers on the Anzio front as well as against the Luftwaffe bases in northern Italy. Between 16 and 19 February the Allies claimed twenty-six German aircraft shot down at Anzio.[93] By late February it was clear to Kesselring that his forces were not going to overrun the Allied beachhead. By this point it was also clear to von Richthofen that his units were exhausted and understrength due to the steady attrition imposed by the Allies. From mid-February to late May, when the Allies finally broke through on the Cassino and Anzio fronts and advanced on Rome, von Richthofen's forces were reduced to attacks designed to whittle away at Allied shipping and damage Allied logistics. Night attacks by von Richthofen's bombers continued, and an American Liberty ship and a landing craft, tank (LCT) at Anzio were struck by guided bombs and sunk on 15 February. The destroyer

HMS *Inglefield* was sunk by a guided bomb on 25 February and recorded heavy losses.[94] After this time the Luftwaffe effort lessened, turning instead to minor harassment raids.

The Luftwaffe's campaign in Italy in 1943–1944 is a snapshot of a force in rapid decline. Given the enormous Allied air superiority over the Germans, it is surprising that the 2nd Air Fleet did as well as it did. Von Richthofen and his gifted subordinates developed fairly effective tactics against the Allied invasion fleets and inflicted moderate damage on the Allies against great odds. From the perspective of Goering and the Luftwaffe staff in Berlin, the Luftwaffe's top field commanders and their airmen were at fault for Germany's defeats on the Mediterranean and Italian fronts. In Italy, von Richthofen's star declined rapidly. It was much the same for the other senior Luftwaffe field commanders.

The British and American commanders had chosen an effective strategy to deal with the Luftwaffe threat to the invasion fleets at Sicily, Salerno, and Anzio. German airfields throughout the Italian theater were attacked so frequently and effectively (with a lot of help from Ultra intelligence) that Luftwaffe units never recovered from their losses. Attrition was constant, and it was far worse than on the eastern front. No sooner would replacement aircraft arrive from Germany, sometimes in batches of thirty or more, then it would be blown to bits in an Allied bomber raid.[95] Allied attacks on forward German airfields forced the Luftwaffe to pull units away from the front and to fly at extreme range for much of the campaign, which forced the Luftwaffe to fight inefficiently.

The Luftwaffe's training command failed to meet the needs of the battle in Italy in several ways. The Fritz X and Hs 293 guided bombs dropped by the two groups of KG 100 were cranky weapons, and, as with any new and complex weapon, there were a lot of bugs to work out. The foremost was the shortage of trained aircrew. Considerable training was needed to learn to use the bombs effectively, but the training system in 1943 could not provide enough trained bomber crews—there were never more than forty airplane crews that were fully qualified to employ the guided bombs. That alone was a godsend for the Allied forces that faced the German attacks. The bombs were not hard to manufacture, nor was there a shortage of Do 217 bombers. The whole program was limited by the lack of well-trained aircrew.

Another issue that limited the effectiveness of the Luftwaffe's precision bomb attacks was the failure to provide enough battle-experienced pilots and commanders to KG 100. While the pilots and bombardiers of the precision bomber groups were the top graduates of the Luftwaffe training program, only a few of the squadron and flight leaders in KG 100 had considerable battle experience. Even a well-trained pilot or flight leader can become unnerved and confused in his first experience in combat. Several of the attacks made by KG 100 at Salerno and Anzio went off course and executed poor attack runs due to the inexperience of the flight and aircraft commanders. If the Luftwaffe had assigned some more "old hares" (combat-experienced bomber pilots) to KG 100 the attacks against Allied ships would likely have been pressed much more aggressively through the relatively ineffective Allied night air defenses. Instead, more than a fifth of all the Fritz and Henschel bombs dropped in combat were released as the bombers broke off combat. Many other bombs were dropped in such a haphazard fashion that the crew was unable to track the fall of the bomb.[96]

Still, the guided bombs represented a major evolution in bombing accuracy and also in making the aircraft more survivable. Pilot and bombardier crew notwithstanding, the bombs themselves were rife with problems. Of the 500 guided bombs dropped by KG 100 in 1943 and 1944, 28 percent malfunctioned, usually due to electronic or guidance malfunctions, and 20 percent were dropped in the emergency release mode, often out of fear that Allied night fighters were nearby. Even so, of the over 300 bombs dropped in actual combat, about a quarter of them either hit the target directly or landed close enough to inflict damage. Indeed, the damage inflicted by a few guided bomb raids on the Allied fleet in the Italian theater was impressive. The Luftwaffe's two small guided bomb units sank or disabled two battleships, sank one cruiser and disabled two, sank or crippled two destroyers, and sank seven merchant ships and transports and damaged at least seventeen more. A 25 percent hit rate for bombs seems poor by modern standards, but it represented a quantum leap in the capability of airpower in 1943–1944.[97]

Von Richthofen was reluctant to part with his bomber forces. In early April 1944 he called his old subordinate, General Korten, who had taken over as chief of the Luftwaffe general staff after the suicide of Hans Jeschonnek in August 1943. Von Richthofen wanted to retain his bombers for another major night attack on an Allied port in Italy in the hope that he could recreate the success at Bari and inhibit the Allied logistics buildup.[98] Korten reluctantly turned down von Richthofen's request. The Luftwaffe simply had no bombers to spare for operations that were becoming increasingly risky. From spring 1944 to the end of the war, the air war in Italy for the Germans would become essentially a flak operation. Yet von Richthofen, now on a secondary front of the war, would still try to use the Luftwaffe to inflict as much damage as possible on the Allies.

Chapter 13

Final Act—Von Richthofen's Last Days

After the failure of the German ground and air offensive against Anzio in April 1944 there was no opportunity left in the Italian theater for either the German army or the Luftwaffe to carry out any strong offensive blows against the Allies. With the great Allied invasion expected on the French coast in the next few weeks, the attention of Hitler and the general staff was turned to the western front. The greater part of von Richthofen's 2nd Air Fleet fighter arm—what remained of it after months of heavy attrition—was transferred to France to stand in readiness against the Allied invasion. Italy was now a secondary theater of war. The Wehrmacht would maintain about twenty divisions in Italy with the mission of holding the defensive lines as best they could while tying down as many Allied divisions as possible.

Unlike their experience in Russia, German forces in Italy were not issued "hold at all cost" orders. Hitler allowed Kesselring operational freedom and accepted the necessity of conducting a fighting retreat to trade space for time. Hitler also approved of Kesselring's order to prepare successive defensive lines across the Italian peninsula. If unable to hold the line south of Rome, the Germans could retreat back to the next line in an orderly fashion. In 1944, for the Germans, Italy had become no more than a strategic delaying action while the decisive operations were carried out on the eastern and western fronts.

The first half of 1944 was a period of general strategic confusion for the Luftwaffe high command. General Korten, as Luftwaffe chief of staff, made his first priority the defense of the Reich, which was coming under increasingly heavier attacks by Allied bombers. From the time he became Luftwaffe chief of staff in the summer of 1943, Korten worked unceasingly to increase fighter production. A surge in German fighter production in 1944 increased aircraft production to 39,800 for the year. The Luftwaffe again had plenty of airplanes—what it now lacked were trained pilots.[1] In order to bolster the Reich air defenses, the secondary theaters of war, such as Italy and the Balkans, were almost stripped bare of fighter defenses. Italy and the other secondary theaters also lost their bomber forces. For Germany to have any hope to counterattack and regain the initiative it would need an offensive air arm, and this was now the weak point of the Luftwaffe. Starting in late 1943, Korten pulled bomber units away from Italy, the Balkans, and the eastern front in an effort to organize a strong bomber force under the direction of the Luftwaffe high command that would be capable of being deployed as a decisive force should the Allies land in Normandy, or the Soviet armies break through in the East. Despite Korten's efforts, only 500 bombers could be assembled. This force was placed under the command of Maj. General Pelz, who, in turn, reported directly to Hermann Goering. In early 1944 Goering decided that the best means of employing the Luftwaffe's last bomber reserves was in a campaign against Britain designed to break the British morale. Of all the possible missions for the Luftwaffe's last bomber force, the one against the British cities would be the most difficult to execute and have the least likelihood of succeeding. It was yet another example of the dearth of strategic thinking in the Luftwaffe's top ranks.[2]

The bombing campaign against England that was ordered by Goering was a disaster for the Luftwaffe. The Luftwaffe could not fly unopposed at night over England as it had in 1940. British radar systems had improved, British antiaircraft defenses were far larger, and the RAF's night fighter units had developed into a very deadly arm of British defense. In contrast, Luftwaffe bombers were largely obsolete, and crew training was poor due to the cutback in training time and flight hours required by the aviation fuel shortage. Despite these glaring disadvantages, Pelz's bomber force carried out a series of large night raids on English cities between January and May 1944.[3] For very little damage inflicted, the Luftwaffe's losses were enormous. Some units still flew throughout the 1944 campaign in the West, but as losses occurred the Luftwaffe was unable to replace the loss of experienced aircrew with pilots of even minimal competence.[4]

In the skies over Germany the Luftwaffe's fighter force had held its own and inflicted heavy losses on American bombers in the fall of 1943. But the situation changed dramatically in early 1944. Before 1944, due to the range limitations of the American fighters, American bombers of the 8th and 15th air forces had fighter escort for only a portion of their fights over Germany. But the arrival of large numbers of the superb long-range P-51 fighter in early 1944—an aircraft that outclassed the Me 109 and FW 190—and the introduction of better drop tanks, which extended the range of the deadly P-47 fighter, meant that American daylight raids could be fully covered all the way to Berlin. The superior American fighters, flown by well-trained pilots, aggressively sought out combat with the Luftwaffe's fighter force, which was now receiving pilot replacements with fewer than 100 hours total flying time—about a quarter of what the newest American and British fighter pilots had.[5] Supported by long-range escort fighters, the Allied bomber offensive decimated the ranks of German pilots. In February, the Luftwaffe lost more trained pilots than it could replace. By March, losses had reached 22 percent of Reich air defense pilots. In April, losses rose to 38 percent of Reich air defense pilots and 24 percent of the 2nd Air Fleet's pilots. That month alone, the Luftwaffe lost 489 fighter pilots and trained only 396.[6]

When the Allies landed on the French coast in June 1944 they did so under the umbrella of overwhelming air superiority. The Luftwaffe scraped up its last reserves of fighters and bombers and threw them at the Allies in a last effort. It was a futile gesture. In every theater the Allies were vastly superior in aircraft quality, numbers, pilot training, and intelligence. Luftwaffe efforts to attack Allied shipping off the coast of France accomplished far less than the 2nd Air Fleet's attacks at Salerno and Anzio. During the whole course of the summer of 1944—in a "target rich environment," as airmen would say today—attacking Luftwaffe aircraft were rarely able to fight their way through the Allied antiaircraft and night fighter cover. The most successful part of the Luftwaffe's operation was the aerial mine-laying campaign off the Normandy coast, but fewer than thirty ships were sunk. The largest Allied warship to be lost was a destroyer.

Before the bomber units were pulled out of Italy that spring, von Richthofen's units carried out some small night raids on major Allied-held ports in Italy. But he could not repeat the success of Bari. The Allies deployed night fighter units and improved radars to defend the major ports, and the improved defenses made it impossible for the Luftwaffe to do anything more than small harassment raids.[7] The Allies noted that the Luftwaffe attacks were weak and that the German bombers dropped their bombs almost at random.[8]

German/Italian Production Cooperation

One of von Richthofen's major problems as air commander in Italy had been the weakness of the Italian air force. Italy had entered the war with a relatively large aircraft industry and a corps of highly talented aircraft designers and builders, but the industry was undercapitalized and production levels were low. Between 1939 and 1943, Italy manufactured only 10,000 aircraft, a smaller production number than Canada, which had entered the war with basically no aircraft industry.[9] The Reich Air Ministry, supremely confident of victory from 1940 to 1942, had little interest in helping to fund an Italian aircraft industry that might become a competitor for German aircraft after the war. The Italian aircraft industry, and the Italian air force, thus remained largely obsolescent despite Italian engineers' ability to design fighter aircraft equal to the latest Allied models. In 1940 designer Mario Castoldi of Macchi Aircraft mated the Italian MC 200 fighter airframe to a German Daimler Benz DB 601A-1 engine and produced an aircraft, designated the Macchi Mc 202 *Folgore* fighter, that performed equal to the Me 109.[10] But Italy was able to produce only a handful of the DB 601 engines, and the Reichs Air Ministry would only deliver a few engines surplus to the Luftwaffe's needs and had little interest in helping the Italians establish an efficient production system.[11] Between 1941 and 1943 the Italian aircraft industry only managed to produce 1,100 units of the excellent fighter.[12] In 1942 Castoldi mated an Mc 202 fuselage with a 1,475-horsepower German DB 605 engine and created the Macchi Mc 205 Veltro—a maneuverable fighter with a top speed of more than 360 mph.[13] Again, the weakness of the Italian production system meant that only a handful of this first-rate aircraft was ever produced.

Although von Richthofen had little confidence in the fascist leadership of Italy or the senior officers of the Regia Aeronautica, his personal views of the Italian leadership did not blind him to the fact that Italy had, with German assistance, a great potential to produce high-quality aircraft at a time when the sheer mass of Allied aircraft was overwhelming the Luftwaffe on several fronts. When he assumed command of the 2nd Air Fleet, he reported to the Reichs Air Ministry that the Italian aviation industry was underutilized. He strongly recommended that the Luftwaffe obtain Italian-designed and -produced aircraft for its units. One aircraft he had in mind was the Fiat G 55, another Italian airframe married to a German engine, which had a performance equal to the American P-51 fighter. In early 1944, von Richthofen wrote to the Air Ministry of the possibility for Italian production of spare parts, attack aircraft, and trainers for the Luftwaffe.[14] Von Richthofen's sensible recommendations met with a remarkable lack of interest. The Luftwaffe's response was to send an officer to Italy to serve as a contact point between von Richthofen and the Luftwaffe staff on issues of Italian aircraft production—but little came of this minimal effort.[15]

The idea of manufacturing aircraft for the Luftwaffe in Italy led to a few small initiatives. In 1943 the Luftwaffe ordered eighty-five Caproni Ca 313s, a variation of the Caproni Ca 310 light bomber designed in the late 1930s.[16] The Luftwaffe envisioned the Ca 313 as a multiengine trainer and light transport aircraft, and it was very suitable for both roles. Production arrangements broke down, however, and of the 905 Ca 313s ordered by the Luftwaffe, the Italian factories were only able to produce 271 planes.[17] Even the obsolescent bombers of the Italian air force could have been of tremendous help to the

Luftwaffe if they were converted into transport aircraft, of which Germany had a desperate shortage. In the fall of 1943, after Italy's surrender to the Allies, the Luftwaffe in Italy seized some Savoia Marchetti SM 81 bombers and Fiat G 12s to be employed as transport aircraft. By May 1944 the XIVth Air Corps had four transport groups equipped with 143 Italian aircraft.[18] By all accounts, the Italian aircraft served very effectively in the transport role. Yet again, there was little interest in converting existing Italian production lines to mass produce less complex aircraft for Germany. Von Richthofen's common sense in regards to advocacy of an aircraft production program in Italy stands in contrast to Goering, Milch, and Jeschonnek, who disregarded the Italian potential because their racial prejudice had convinced them that Italians were inferior and not capable of using German technology.[19]

In November 1943, after the crisis at Salerno had passed and the front had stabilized south of Rome, von Richthofen put forward a set of ambitious plans to help the new Italian fascist government that Mussolini had created, known as the Social Republic, to build large armed forces. He asked for personnel and aircraft from the Reichs Air Ministry to set up a fighter school and a torpedo bomber school for a new Italian air force. Richthofen wanted to recruit as many of the trained pilots and personnel of the old regime and quickly build a force, starting with fighter, transport, and torpedo bomber groups. He proposed that the Germans treat the Italians not as subordinates but as equal coalition partners. General Korten saw merit in von Richthofen's ideas and got Goering's approval. But when Hitler received the proposals he summarily turned them down with the comment that he did not want to hear about rearming the Italians.[20]

Although a large part of the Regia Aeronautica personnel had stood by the Badoglio government when it surrendered to the Allies, many of its pilots made their way to German-occupied northern Italy rather than the Allied-occupied south. When Mussolini established his new fascist state in late 1943, a cadre of officers and pilots from the old air force was ready to form a new one. Through the winter of 1943–1944, Mussolini's republic created a small air force: four fighter squadrons, two transport squadrons, and a bomber flight from the remnants of the old air force. This air force would not be truly independent but would serve under German command for the rest of the war.[21] Its four fighter squadrons were initially equipped with Italian-made G 55 and Re 2005 fighters, but because of the difficulty of supplying parts the Germans reequipped them with Me 109G fighters. By March 1944 the new air force had 8,644 volunteers.[22] Throughout 1944 and 1945, the Salo Republic Air Force, as it was commonly called, would make only a small contribution to the air defense of northern Italy.[23]

Although attempts to have the Italians build aircraft for the Luftwaffe failed, there were other more successful programs to contract Italian firms to build German equipment. Italian companies manufactured ammunition for the German army and Luftwaffe, and the Ducati Company made fuses for the 88 mm flak gun shells. Firms in Genoa were contracted to build 88 mm gun barrels, and Wehrmacht armaments experts rated their quality as "excellent." Italian companies also manufactured a large number of motor vehicles for the Wehrmacht. But most proposals to utilize Italian industry, such as a plan for the Italian production of the German Würzburg radar, fell through.[24] After Mussolini was deposed and the Italian government surrendered to the Allies, Germany's primary interest in Italy was not in its war industries. Instead, the Germans saw the Italians not as allies but as a pool of forced laborers who could be rounded up and transported to man the German factories. Over 100,000 Italian soldiers who surrendered to the Germans in September 1943 found themselves shipped to Germany as forced laborers. More were to follow in 1944, and eventually over half a million Italian forced laborers were working in German factories.

The Defense of Italy in 1944

After the Allies had established a firm beachhead at Anzio in early 1943 the primary duty of the Luftwaffe was to defend the vital rail connections between Germany and Italy. The rail system, which ran through the Alps, consisted of three lines, the most important of which was the line through Brenner Pass. In May 1944 the 2nd Air Fleet had an official force of fewer than 200 combat aircraft, with about 100 fighter planes and fighter-bombers operational.[25] The Luftwaffe's force in Italy consisted of a few German fighter units, a reconnaissance detachment, a small collection of transports, and a ground attack unit equipped with Ju 87s and some CR 42 biplane fighters seized from the Italian air force in 1943. This handful of planes faced overwhelming Allied air superiority in the form of hundreds of medium bombers and more than 1,500 fighters and fighter bombers.

The aviation force that von Richthofen now commanded was smaller than the air division he had commanded as a major general in Poland in 1939. In June the 2nd Air Fleet was officially abolished, and the Luftwaffe force in Italy was downgraded to the status of a special command, the Deutsche Luftwaffe in Italien (German Air Force in Italy). For the rest of the war, the major Luftwaffe opposition to the Allies in Italy would be its flak brigades. Von Richthofen, a field marshal, remained in command of a force more suitable for a major general. Perhaps it was Hitler and Goering's way of punishing him for the Wehrmacht's failure to hold the Allies in Italy. In any case, relegating a brilliant commander and tactician like von Richthofen to a minor command on what had become a backwater front when there were major air battles to come over Germany and on the western front is typical of the petty manner in which the Third Reich treated its top soldiers in the last two years of the war.

Fighting in a theater of war where the enemy held total superiority in the air required some improvisation on the German part to carry out any air missions. In December 1943 the Luftwaffe formed Night Attack Wing 9, which was equipped with a mix of Italian CR 42 fighters, Caproni Ca 314 light bombers, and a few Ju 87s.[26] The small unit had no more than forty aircraft at its peak, with usually about twenty-five aircraft available for operations. Throughout the Anzio campaign, Wing 9 conducted small night attacks against the Allied artillery positions at Anzio, as well as attacks against Allied depots and logistics. The attacks inflicted little damage upon the Allies and mostly served to harass British and American support troops.[27]

By the summer of 1944 Night Attack Wing 9 was employed mostly in supporting the armed forces of Mussolini's Social Republic and German security units in their operations against the partisan bands that had sprung up all over northern Italy in 1944.[28] The Germans had foreseen the potential for the large Italian partisan movement to disrupt the German supply lines and set up plans for a major antipartisan campaign. As the weather worsened in the fall of 1944, and the Allied drive to break through the mountain barrier and into the northern Italian plains was halted, the fascist and German forces were able to carry out large antipartisan operations that swept whole areas clear. The Axis operations in September and October 1944 killed an estimated 7,000 partisans and captured 3,800.[29] The pressure was kept on partisan operations throughout the winter, mostly carried out by units of Mussolini's new fascist republic set up in the small resort town of Salo.[30]

Some army and Luftwaffe rear security units were also involved in antipartisan operations. The Luftwaffe security units operating behind the front proved themselves to be every bit as willing to commit atrocities as the SS and units of the army. Mass execution of civilian hostages in reprisal for partisan activity was the norm throughout German-occupied Europe and in Italy; an estimated 10,000 civilian hostages were killed by the Wehrmacht.[31] Luftwaffe field divisions and security units in the rear areas were full participants in these brutal operations. For example, Luftwaffe Felddivision 19 massacred civilian hostages in Guardistallo, Italy, in the summer of 1944.[32] Von Richthofen almost certainly would have approved of ruthless action against partisans and their sympathizers. But Luftwaffe units involved in such operations came completely under the army's command, and not von Richthofen, so he cannot be connected to the war crimes of the Italian theater. Field Marshal Kesselring, in contrast, was convicted and imprisoned after the war for murderous actions carried out by forces under his command in 1944.

After the fall of Rome in early June 1944, the German army in Italy slowly retreated in good order to prepared defense lines in the northern Apennine Mountains. By late summer, the Allied armies had reached the main German defenses, called the Gothic Line. It might have been a repeat of the war in Spain, this time with the Allies pushing forward under massive air support from their air forces. However, the Allied invasion of southern France in August 1944 saved the German position in Italy. A great part of the force for that invasion was drawn from the Allied armies in Italy, and the divisions that remained were short of personnel and starved of replacements. At the crucial moment of the Allied offensive, a large part of the U.S. 12th Air Force, which provided the close support for the American army in Italy, was detached and sent to support the Allied landing in France. Greatly diminished in the air, and with steadily weakening ground forces, the Allied armies still made progress against the formidable Gothic Line defenses, but came just short of breaking into the northern Italian Plain before the winter set in and halted the offensive in the mountains.

The Flak Force in Italy

With few aircraft at its disposal, the Luftwaffe in Italy became a primarily flak organization by early 1944. The Luftwaffe had three large flak organizations in Italy by 1944: the 3rd Flak Brigade, with four flak regiments; the 22nd Flak Brigade, also with four regiments; and the recently organized 25th Flak Division, charged with the defense of northern Italy. The units all came under the command of Luftwaffe General Ritter von Pohl, who had served as the Luftwaffe's representative to the Italian general staff from 1941 to 1943. As a flak specialist, Pohl was the right man in the right job.

Kesselring and the army continually demanded Luftwaffe flak units to reinforce the front lines. The flak units were in great demand because the superb 88 mm flak gun was also one of the most effective antitank guns of the war. The gun could also be used very effectively as conventional artillery. Von Richthofen and Pohl had to help the army hold its lines while also deploying enough forces to defend the Italian transportation network. Although it led to constant arguments with the army, the two Luftwaffe generals were determined that defending the rail system had priority.

By the time of the Anzio campaign, the Luftwaffe had to strip flak defense away from the Italian cities in order to meet the needs of the front and to defend the rail lines. The Luftwaffe set up control sectors and radar units to help the flak detachments cover the most important rail junctions on the lines to Germany. Since the Allies had bombed the Po River bridges, the ferries across the Po were also allocated flak protection. The small Luftwaffe fighter force remaining in Italy could do little more than harass the Allied bomber attacks. However, the flak units continued to inflict losses on the Allies. Throughout 1944 and 1945, most of the Allied aircraft lost in the Italian theater were shot down by German flak.[33] Large concentrations of flak helped push the Allied bombers to higher and safer altitudes. But high-altitude bombing also reduced accuracy. From November 1944 to April 1945, the U.S. Army Air Force dropped more than 15,000 tons of bombs on the Brenner Pass rail lines.[34] Despite their efforts, the main rail lines continued to function until the end of the war.

It was something of a victory for the Germans to keep the rail lines open under heavy Allied attacks.[35] Von Richthofen was no flak specialist, and he gave Pohl the credit for the effective flak defense of Italy. To deal with Allied fighter bombers, the Luftwaffe used a number of innovative techniques, including building dummy installations that were carefully surrounded by hidden flak guns. The decoy installations were designed as "flak traps" to destroy the Allied aircraft.[36] In October 1944 the Luftwaffe in Italy claimed 100 Allied planes, virtually all from flak.[37] Although the Luftwaffe still mounted some fighter sorties against the Allied bombers attacking the Brenner Pass, it was a minor effort in comparison with the effectiveness of the flak force.[38]

One important fact about the German flak force in Italy was that it was only partly German. Starting in late 1943 all of the German armed forces eagerly recruited Italian soldiers who had remained loyal to Mussolini. More than 150,000 soldiers, sailors, and airmen had volunteered to serve in the armed forces of Mussolini's fascist state. Of the Italians that the Germans had interned, thousands volunteered to join the Wehrmacht—probably a better alternative than serving as a slave laborer in a German factory. The flak forces in Italy contained a large number of Italian soldiers, given the status of "Italian members of the Wehrmacht." Some of the flak units of the 25th Flak Division and 3rd and 22nd Flak Brigades were "mixed," manned with both German and Italian personnel. Many more of the flak units of the Luftwaffe in Italy were manned completely by Italian personnel. The flak brigades and divisions were large organizations, with probably more than 50,000 total personnel in the flak force in Italy. By late 1944 the flak units contained not only thousands of Italian enlisted soldiers but also 208 Italians serving as officers.

The Luftwaffe Signal Corps units that manned the radar systems contained a further 123 Italian officers. Including the Italian pilot officers flying with the Luftwaffe, by November 1944 the Luftwaffe in Italy had 623 Italian officers and officer cadets serving in its units.[39]

Family Tragedies

In late 1943 von Richthofen's oldest son, Wolfram (nicknamed "Wolf"), had completed his two-year course of officer and pilot training and had been commissioned a lieutenant in the Luftwaffe. He requested, and was granted, an assignment to a ground attack unit, and in 1944, after more training at the attack school, was sent to one of the Luftwaffe's most famous attack units—Schlachtgeschwader 2, "the Immelmann Wing"—the same Stuka unit that had served so brilliantly in von Richthofen's VIIIth Air Corps through France and Russia, now renamed the 2nd Attack Wing. In 1943–1944 the unit was reequipped with Focke Wulf FW 190s, an excellent fighter-bomber with bomb racks and cannon. It may not have had the pinpoint accuracy of a Ju 87, but it was a tough and fast airplane. It was also much more survivable than the Stuka, which required either a benign air environment or strong fighter escort. If the FW 190 encountered enemy fighters, it had the option of running away at high speed or engaging them on equal terms.

In 1944 the 2nd Attack Wing was with the Ist Air Corps, which was assigned to the 4th Air Fleet on the southern portion of the eastern front. In the early summer the Ist Air Corps was based in northern Romania and was flying in support of Wehrmacht forces desperately trying to slow down the 1944 Russian summer offensive that was threatening to knock Romania completely out of the war. From April to July 1944 the 1st and 3rd Groups of the wing were stationed at Husi, and the 2nd Group at Bacan. At the beginning of June, all three groups of the wing had been reduced by attrition to less than half strength and only fifty FW 190s remained in the whole wing.[40] By this point in the war, only the group commanders and some squadron leaders were likely to be experienced pilots. Most of the attack pilots were like Wolf, young men who had just completed a pilot's course that included about half the flying hours that their predecessors of 1939–1941 had flown.

The famed Stuka pilot Hans-Ulrich Rudel flew with the 2nd Attack Wing in June 1944, and his memoirs describe the kind of situation that young Wolf faced. The Soviets were reinforcing their divisions north of Husi, where part of the 2nd Attack Wing was based. Rudel was still flying the old Ju 87 Stuka, but most other pilots flew the FW 190. The unit flew as often as it could to support the German army units that were then locked in a desperate battle to hold off the Soviet advance in the area of Pruth. Due to fuel shortages, missions were often limited to a few aircraft at a time. In contrast to the 1941 and 1942 campaigns on the eastern front, the Germans no longer had air superiority, although if they massed their aircraft for an operation they might gain the advantage over a small sector of the front for a short time. The Soviets now vastly outnumbered the Germans, and Rudel recalled that they would throw masses of fast high-quality fighters, such as the Lagg 5, at the Luftwaffe. Soviet training and tactics were far better than they had been two years before, and now it was usually the German pilot at a disadvantage.[41] Average life expectancy for Luftwaffe attack pilots in 1944 was not long.

There is not much information about Wolf von Richthofen's final mission. What is known is that he went on a combat mission on 5 June 1944 over northern Romania and went missing. After a few days, he was presumed dead. At the time, most of the attack wing's combat missions were small flights of four to six planes. If the German fighter-bombers ran into Soviet fighters the small flights might easily break up and become separated. This was even more likely if the missions were flown by relatively inexperienced pilots like Wolf. In any case, Wolf never returned and his aircraft was never found. Most likely he was attacked by Soviet fighters and shot down over the rugged and heavily forested area. That the aircraft was never found is not unusual. Thousands of planes went missing during World War II, and even today the remains of planes lost over sixty years ago are sometimes found buried deep in an obscure field.

Von Richthofen apparently did not hear of his son's status as missing for three days. Fighter and Stuka pilots often had damage or engine trouble, and in such cases they might nurse their plane to a landing at the nearest available airfield. Then they might have to find an army unit to help them get back. Another common occurrence was for a pilot to bail out of his damaged plane and have to find a way back. There was also the possibility that he might have been shot down over Soviet lines. In any case, when a pilot went missing his unit would send out messages asking for his whereabouts. In the middle of a battle, communication might be difficult. It would not have been unusual for Wolf's unit to take several days before confirming that he was missing. Then it might take another day or so before the report would pass through the Luftwaffe's administration system in order to get to his father. All we know is that just after Wolf was shot down his father's diary entries abruptly stop. One can imagine that the field marshal simply could not put his emotions on paper. Perhaps he held out hope that his son might have been captured by the Soviets. It was obviously a traumatic moment for the family.

Von Richthofen, already depressed by the loss of his son, experienced another tragic blow in early August when he received news that his younger brother Manfred ("Pet"), who was serving as an army officer in France, was killed in Normandy. The von Richthofen clan had paid a heavy price in blood in World War I with several cousins lost. Now it was the field marshal's immediate family that was paying the price of war. Von Richthofen had always been close to his brother, and he would now have to see that Pet's wife and three children were looked after. As well as the losses in his immediate family, many von Richthofen cousins died during World War II.

On his own Italian front he was now reduced to holding a relatively insignificant command in a secondary theater. General von Pohl managed the flak force, which was now the most important part of the Luftwaffe in Italy. The few air units of the Luftwaffe in Italy flew only a few sorties a month. There was no chance to carry out another brilliant stroke such as the one at Bari simply because there were no Luftwaffe bombers left. Von Richthofen must have felt that the order that downgraded his command from an air fleet to a special command was a final insult from Hermann Goering, and that is a very likely explanation. In August 1944 Goering disbanded the 3rd Air Fleet, which had been shot to pieces in the battle for France, and sent Field Marshal Sperrle to the Leaders' Reserve—essentially a form of retirement. Certainly it was characteristic of Goering to find a way to blame his generals for his own years of bad decisions and mismanagement at the top of the Luftwaffe. In 1943 Goering blamed the weakness of the Luftwaffe in Italy on pilot cowardice, not because they were outnumbered at five to one. In 1944 he seems to have transferred blame for the Luftwaffe's failures from the pilots to the field commanders.

20 July Plot

On 20 July 1944, an extensive plot that involved a large number of military officers and distinguished German civilians made an attempt on Adolf Hitler's life that nearly succeeded. A bomb was planted in the conference room at Hitler's command post in East Prussia. Although the bomb went off close to Hitler and killed several people in the room—including Günther Korten, who was briefing Hitler at the time—the Führer was only dazed by the explosion. The aftermath of the 20 July plot was a huge blow to the German armed forces leadership—especially the army's leadership. Hitler and his SS henchmen put down the attempted coup in the most ruthless manner. As many as 5,000 officers and civilians were arrested. At least 200 were summarily executed. Others were paraded before show trials where they were abused and humiliated—and then executed by hanging. Former chief of staff General Ludwig Beck and Field Marshal Gunther von Kluge had been connected to the plot, and they committed suicide rather than face torture and trial. Field Marshal Erwin Rommel, who had agreed to support the coup attempt, was forced to commit suicide to spare his family any acts of revenge by Hitler's regime. General Franz Halder and retired general Friedrich von Rabenau were sent to concentration camps for their connections to the plotters.[42]

One wonders what von Richthofen felt about the attempt on Hitler's life. A number of officers whom he had known for years were involved in the plot. One of the notable aspects of the movement against Hitler was the large number of nobles involved. As a class, the nobles had never been comfortable with the Weimar Republic, and many welcomed Hitler's rise to power in 1933. A disproportionate percentage of nobles became Nazi Party members in the early days of the Third Reich. Von Richthofen's enthusiasm for Hitler and for Hitler's version of nationalism was a common attitude among the nobility. However, the barbarities of the war, and the fact that Germany was obviously losing, turned many of the more intellectual members of the nobility against the Nazi regime. Hundreds of members of von Richthofen's class offered their support for a new German government should Hitler be overthrown.

One of the 20 July plotters would have been very well known to von Richthofen. One of the figures involved in the plot was Count Michael von Matuschka, a Silesian nobleman and lawyer who had held a variety of offices in the Prussian state administration. Matuschka, five years older than von Richthofen, had been a reserve officer of the 4th Silesian Hussars, von Richthofen's regiment, during World War I. A German cavalry regiment was a small world indeed, and from August 1914 until he left for flight training in 1917, von Richthofen would have seen Matuschka daily, been in battle with him, and shared billets and meals.[43] Count Matuschka was arrested and executed in September 1944.

The July plot was an attempt by a very conservative class of people to end the Hitler regime and the war. It is most probable that von Richthofen, as a staunch admirer of Hitler, saw the 20 July plotters as traitors to the Reich. That was indeed the most common attitude on the German officer corps. Yet von Richthofen was also a man of strict reason. Certainly he understood by July 1944 that Germany had lost the war, and that Hitler was an impediment to cutting a peace deal that might save millions of German lives. Even so, the fact that so many members of his own class, as well as generals he had known for years, had joined in the movement against Hitler would have certainly come as a shock.

Failing Health

Von Richthofen's staff could see that their commander was in poor health in the summer of 1944. He suffered from headaches and exhaustion. Finally his staff convinced him to call for the staff surgeon, who diagnosed the field marshal as having a brain tumor. Von Richthofen was sent on medical leave to the Luftwaffe's premier hospital for neurological injuries, at Bad Ischl, Austria. The hospital had originally been the prestigious Neurological Clinic of Berlin, but Allied bombing raids and the constant disruption of life in the capital made Berlin a poor location to treat badly injured men recovering from brain injuries. In late 1943 the clinic was moved to the very quiet and scenic resort town of Bad Ischl, certainly a far better atmosphere for the treatment and recovery of patients. The clinic's chief brain surgeon, one of the most noted specialists in Germany, was Professor Dr. Wilhelm Tonnis. Before the war Tonnis had been a professor at the University of Würzburg and chief doctor of the neurosurgery clinic in that city. He was assisted by a young surgeon, Dr. Friedrich Loew, who had served as a field surgeon on the Soviet front in 1941 and 1942. Having learned the art of neurosurgery from the Luftwaffe's top surgeon, Loew would go on to a distinguished career in neurosurgery after the war.[44] Von Richthofen did not lack for medical care; the medical team that would treat him was one of the best in the world.

Professor Tonnis and von Richthofen got along well. While von Richthofen was preparing for his operation the two would play cards together in the officers' mess. On 27 October 1944, Tonnis operated on von Richthofen to remove the tumor.[45] At first it was thought that the operation was a success; von Richthofen seemed to recover some of his old verve. He was certainly in good spirits, and he contacted Berlin to argue that he ought to be allowed to return to his command in the field. But the tumor had only been slowed, not eliminated. That November, von Richthofen was relieved as commander of the Luftwaffe in Italy and officially transferred to the Leaders' Reserve.

The von Richthofens Become Refugees

One of von Richthofen's last acts as a field marshal was to arrange for the Wehrmacht to evacuate his family from Silesia in February 1945 in the face of the Soviet advance. On 2 February the Soviet armies reached Breslau and the Oder River. The Oder line was thinly held by the Germans, and despite the optimistic broadcasts coming out of Berlin, von Richthofen knew that the military situation was lost and that he would have to take action to see that his family and relations in Silesia were protected. Even a field marshal on the

The last known photograph of von Richthofen, taken in late 1944. One of von Richthofen's primary means of relaxing in the evenings was card playing with his staff. Here he is playing cards with the Luftwaffe staff doctor and renowned German neurologist Dr. Wilhelm Tönnis (right), who treated him for his brain tumor. He was operated on for the brain tumor just after this photograph was taken.

Leaders' Reserve list had considerable pull in the Third Reich, so von Richthofen mounted what was virtually a military campaign from his hospital bed. He called the local Luftwaffe district commanders, the officers in charge of the Luftwaffe ground and support services, and arranged for vehicles and Luftwaffe personnel to evacuate his relatives. He had the family home of Barzdorf evacuated and his mother sent to his home in Lüneburg. She had relatives in Hanover, so she soon moved in with them as the von Richthofen house filled up with family refugees from Silesia. The family of his dead brother Manfred was also sent on to Lüneburg, as were his wife Jutta's parents.

The only member of the family to refuse evacuation was von Richthofen's aunt Luise, the widow of General of Cavalry Manfred von Richthofen, the field marshal's adoptive father. She was an old woman, seventy-nine years old, and did not want to become a refugee at her age. She was well known in the region and had a reputation for charitable work among not only the German families but also the Polish ones. She insisted that her neighbors would not allow any harm to come to her, so she stayed. In fact, she was right. The

Soviets occupied the estate and, after the war, the Polish communist government collectivized the land. But the grand old lady Luise was allowed to live on in the old manor house at Bersdorf, the estate that von Richthofen had inherited, and her neighbors saw that she was cared for.

Von Richthofen's Death

In the spring of 1945, von Richthofen's condition declined steadily. The disruption of transportation in Germany at this point in the war made it impossible for his wife or daughter to visit. However, one of his Silesian cousins was working as a nurse in Bad Ischl, so he at least had the comfort of one family member during his last months. It is likely that Professor Tonnis conducted a second operation on von Richthofen, but the tumor had progressed too far for any hope of recovery. On 8 May 1945, Germany surrendered, and the Luftwaffe's hospital at Bad Ischl was taken over by the U.S. Third Army. The hospital continued to function under American command, only von Richthofen and his doctors were now officially prisoners of war. At this point the field marshal was heavily sedated, so he may have been barely aware that Germany had fallen, and the hospital had a flood of new patients from the slave labor camps in the area, the worst of the sick being treated at the Bad Ischl hospital complex. On 12 July 1945, Wolfram von Richthofen quietly died.

In some respects, von Richthofen was lucky to die in Bad Ischl, which was located in the occupation zone of the U.S. Third Army, commanded by General George Patton. The American commander was a brilliant modern soldier, but also a romantic at heart, and he would ensure that a German field marshal dying under his jurisdiction would receive full burial honors. For Patton it would be a matter of chivalry to a fallen opponent. Many of the other Allied generals, and certainly the Soviets, would not have been so generous to a dead field marshal.

Three days after his death von Richthofen was buried in the scenic Protestant cemetery of Bad Ischl in a section reserved for soldiers who had died in the military hospital. The funeral was a fairly large local event. Photos taken by von Richthofen's cousin indicate that the clergy and German military were out in full force. There were plenty of German military prisoners in the area, so the personnel for a proper military burial were present. Wehrmacht soldiers in uniform, with only the swastikas removed from the uniforms, served as pallbearers. A Wehrmacht chaplain, also in uniform, presided over the ceremony. Prayers were read by the local minister, and von Richthofen's simple wooden coffin was draped with a World War I German flag bearing the

Von Richthofen's funeral, July 1945, Bad Ischl.

Maltese Cross, a fitting symbol as that insignia had been used by the Prussian army for centuries. Several officers presented last salutes as the coffin was lowered into the grave. In the 1970s von Richthofen's coffin was moved to another part of the cemetery, with a fitting memorial with a large wooden cross erected over it.

The Family's Story

Von Richthofen's second son, Götz, completed his Abitur in 1943 at age eighteen and joined the Luftwaffe as an officer cadet. He was sent to basic training in Berlin and then accepted for pilot training. After completing basic flight training in 1944, with about forty flying hours in biplane trainers, he was sent on to advanced fighter training. But by this time, the fall of 1944, fuel was so scarce that the already shortened training course was further reduced. So Götz's pilot training was cut short, and in March 1945 he was sent with a group of officer cadets to serve as infantry to defend Thuringia against the advancing Soviet armies. In April 1945, as the Oder front collapsed, Götz and the other cadets were sent on to Berlin to serve in an antitank unit. His unit stopped along the way at the Gatow airfield, a large Luftwaffe base on the outskirts of Berlin. It turned out that the Luftwaffe unit there needed pilots who could fly aircraft on the field away from the advancing Soviet forces. Götz had a few hours of flight training in advanced fighters, so he was given the job of flying an FW 190 to Rechlin airfield north of Berlin, out of the path of the Soviet armies.

For the last three weeks of the war, Götz served with Fighter Wing 11 as it made an odyssey from airfield to airfield to avoid the advancing Soviet and Allied ground forces. JG 11 eventually surrendered to the British forces at Leck airfield on the Danish border. Götz became a British POW for a few months and served in a labor unit as a motorcycle driver. At nineteen years old he was quickly processed for release and was then immediately hired as a civilian employee of the British forces, driving trucks. The pay was low, but as an employee of the British he was entitled to free meals that were "off" the food ration book—and in 1945 and 1946 when the civilian food ration fell to little more than 1,000 calories a day, this was a major advantage. Götz's truck detachment was stationed in the north German city of Münster and later in Bielefeld. Both cities were nearby his mother's home in Lüneburg, so he could help look after his family and relations.

The end of the war was a hard time for Baroness Jutta von Richthofen and her daughter, Ellen, then only seventeen and still in school. When the war ended, the baroness lived in a large house in Lüneburg that the Luftwaffe had provided. In the early months of 1945 she had taken in her parents and the widow and family of the field marshal's brother Manfred. At the start of the occupation, British forces that occupied the region commandeered half the house for their own use. They eventually took over the whole house, forcing the von Richthofen family to move to an apartment that friends found for them. Conditions became even more crowded when other relatives from Silesia, now all refugees, sought out the baroness for shelter. Money was tight, and the family lived a bare existence for a time. Von Richthofen's considerable bank account was confiscated by the British, and a pension for the widow of the field marshal was only arranged months later as the German civil administration was established. In the meantime, the family received assistance in the form of money and packages from von Richthofen's brother Gerhardt, known to the family as Gerd. He had left Germany twenty years before and now owned a prosperous coffee plantation in Angola.

One of the problems of living under the occupation was how to hide some of the family heirlooms so that they would not be confiscated or vandalized. The British generally behaved quite properly as occupation forces, but even they were not above a bit of looting. A portrait of von Richthofen was vandalized, and a British officer made off with the field marshal's golf clubs (after some letters to the British commander, the golf clubs were returned). Several other family portraits were hidden and preserved, and other family mementoes saved.

Von Richthofen's mother lived on with her relations in Hanover until 1948, when she died. After the end of the occupation the family would end up living in Lüneburg. As Germany recovered from the war and the economy improved, Götz left his job with the British in 1949 and went to work for an import/export firm in Hamburg. He lived in nearby Lüneburg with his mother until 1955. That year he married and moved to Hamburg and made a career in the import/export business. Ellen also married and began a family in the 1950s. Baron Götz von Richthofen is retired and lives today in a middle-class home in Aumühle, a pleasant suburb of Hamburg that, coincidentally, was the last home of Reichschancellor Otto von Bismarck. The Baroness Jutta von Richthofen, wife of the field marshal, died at the age of ninety-five in May 1991 in Aining, a town on the Austrian border near Salzburg. In the decade after the war this strong-willed woman worked to take care of her family and relations, almost all of whom were part of the huge wave of refugees that were driven out of German lands occupied by the Russians, Poles, and Czechs.

EPILOGUE

Wolfram von Richthofen left an important legacy of thought and practice to modern military operations. The German military campaigns of 1939 and 1940 shocked the world with their speed, ruthlessness, and efficiency. It is hard to imagine today just how great the impact of those events were to the people who had lived through World War I and thought of an advance of one mile at the cost of thousands of lives as a signal success. Just over two decades later, the world witnessed a true revolution in warfare. In 1939 almost all the public, and even most of the senior military officers of the major powers, still thought of future wars as something that would look like the operations of 1918: heavy casualties, slow progress of ground troops, tanks and airplanes present as support weapons—but still a war dominated by trenches and defensive positions. When the Germans overran Poland in 1939 in three weeks—with total casualties for the campaign that would have been normal for the first day of a major offensive in World War I—even the Germans were astounded by their success. The panzer forces, of course, received star billing for the amazing victory of 1939. But the Luftwaffe also won for itself a costarring role. What the world saw as revolutionary was the effective coordination of tank and motorized forces and airpower.

More than anyone else, Wolfram von Richthofen had made the Luftwaffe a co-star in the operational method known as blitzkrieg. Throughout the campaign of 1940, airpower played an even more decisive role in assuring German arms of success. The German victory of 1940 cannot be explained by any superiority of German forces or matériel. The Germans were equal in ground forces to the western Allies and had significantly fewer tanks and artillery pieces. The Luftwaffe had a slight superiority over the Allies in terms of available aircraft and airplane quality. But it was not enough of a margin of superiority to account for the rapid advance of the Germans, the collapse of the Allied forces, and another astounding victory at a low cost in blood. In 1940 the German margin of superiority lay in its senior leadership and in superior tactics. One of the decisive elements of the campaign was the effective use of airpower in support of the German ground forces. The greatest superiority of the Germans lay in an operational method that enabled the air force to work closely with the army. In this respect, the Germans were years ahead of the Allies. Again, Wolfram von Richthofen was a major reason for this German superiority in technique. Indeed, without von Richthofen's air units protecting their flank, General Ewald von Kleist's panzer group could not have advanced so quickly across France and isolated the Allied Northern Army Group.

Von Richthofen certainly was not the first to think of using airpower in support of ground troops. It had been done in World War I and showed some promise. Between the world wars, a few generals and air commanders of the major powers developed theories that argued that the cooperation of air and ground forces would be an important factor in future warfare. It was not in the idea that von Richthofen was instrumental, but in putting the idea into practice. In the period from 1936 to 1942 no other airman put as much effort into developing air-ground tactics as von Richthofen. Nor did any other air commander achieve such a degree of success. From Spain to Poland and from the Balkans to the Soviet Union, he continually refined the techniques of air cooperation with ground forces. He pioneered many aspects of modern air-ground coordination, including being the first commander to put airmen on the ground in armored vehicles to direct air strikes from the front lines. Yet his methods were not entirely revolutionary. He combined modern aviation technology and communications with some of the traditional principles of war to produce decisive effects on the battlefield. The principles achieving the greatest effects by employing forces en masse, and at the decisive point, go back hundreds of years. Von Richthofen simply provided an airpower twist to this. If for nothing else, Wolfram von Richthofen deserves to be remembered as one of the masters of tactical air warfare.

Finally, von Richthofen deserves a place in history as one of airpower's visionaries. From the 1920s to his death he understood far better than most of his contemporaries the revolutionary changes that airpower had brought to warfare, and he worked to make that vision a reality. In the early 1930s, when most of the air force leaders of the major powers were thinking in terms of slightly larger and faster piston-engine airplanes, von Richthofen was looking a decade ahead to an era of large rockets, rocket planes, and jet propulsion. More important, he gave substance to this vision by encouraging and supporting the research and development of these technologies when he headed the Technical Office's Aircraft Development branch from 1933 to 1936. Von Richthofen issued the contracts that made possible the development of the jet engine, the V-1 rocket (the first practical cruise missile), and the larger V-2 rockets. His work of that period was an important part of the foundation for the airpower technology of the later twentieth century.

NOTES

Chapter 1. Introduction

1. Erich von Manstein, *Verlorene Siege* (Bonn: Athenäum, 1955), 258.

2. Among the biographies of Goering is David Irving, *Goering: A Biography* (New York: William Morrow, 1989). On Milch, see David Irving, *The Rise and Fall of the Luftwaffe: The Life of Luftwaffe Marshal Erhard Milch* (London: Weidenfeld and Nicolson, 1973).

3. Kenneth Macksey, *Kesselring* (St. Paul: Zenith, 2006).

4. For army memoirs, one can start with Manstein's *Verlorene Siege*; there are also Heinz Guderian, *Panzer Leader* (New York: Ballantine, 1957); and General F. W. von Mellentin, *Panzer Battles* (Norman: University of Oklahoma Press, 1956).

5. Edward Homze, "Wolfram Freiherr von Richthofen—Hitler's Schlachtfliegergeneral," in *Die Militärelite des Dritten Reichs*, Ronald Smelser and Enrico Syring, eds. (Frankfurt am Main: Verlag Ullstein, 1995), 446–459.

6. Of especial value on von Richthofen's operations and personality are the U.S. Air Force Historical Studies—monographs known as the Karlsruhe Collection—found in the U.S. Air Force Historical Research Agency, Maxwell Air Force Base, Alabama. See especially General Wilhelm Speidel, *The German Air Force in the Polish Campaign* (Study No. 151); *The German Air Force in France and the Low Countries, 1939–1940* (Study No. 152); Hermann Plocher, *The German Air Force Versus Russia, 1941* (Study No. 153); Hermann Plocher, *The German Air Force Versus Russia, 1942* (Study No. 154); and General Paul Deichmann, *German Air Force Operations in Support of the Army* (Study No. 163). Other special monographs that provide considerable background information about the senior commanders of the Luftwaffe are General Andreas Nielsen, *The German Air Force General Staff* (Study No. 173); and Dr. Richard Suchenwirth, *Command and Leadership in the German Air Force* (Study No. 174).

7. Horst Boog, *Die deutsche Luftwaffenführung, 1935–1945* (Stuttgart: Deutsche Verlags-Anstalt, 1982).

8. Edward Homze, *Arming the Luftwaffe: The Reich Air Ministry and the German Aircraft Industry, 1919–39* (Lincoln: University of Nebraska Press, 1976).

9. Joel Hayward, *Stopped at Stalingrad: The Luftwaffe and Hitler's Defeat in the East, 1942–1943* (Lawrence: University Press of Kansas, 1998).

10. Richard Muller, *The German Air War in Russia* (Baltimore: Nautical and Aviation Press, 1992).

11. Carl von Clausewitz, *On War*, Michael Howard and Peter Paret, eds. (Princeton, NJ: Princeton University Press, 1976), 100–112.

12. Joel Hayward, "A Case Study in Early Joint Warfare: An Analysis of the Wehrmacht's Crimean Campaign of 1941," *Journal of Strategic Studies* 22 (December 1999): 103–130. See 116.

13. Gotthard Breit, *Das Staats- und Gesellschaftsbild deutscher Generale beider Weltkriege im Spiegel ihrer Memoiren* (Boppard am Rhein: Harald Boldt Verlag, 1973), 159–160.

14. For a detailed study of Hitler's gifts to his generals see Gerd Ueberschär and Winfried Voge, *Dienen und Verdienen: Hitlers Geschenke an seine Eliten* (Frankfurt am Main: S. Fischer Verlag, 1999). On the various gifts to generals, see 221–222.

15. Ibid., 222–223, 238.

16. Ibid., 245, 110.

17. On Hitler's payments to his senior officers, see Norman Goda, "Black Marks: Hitler's Bribery of His Senior Officers during World War II," *Journal of Modern History* 72 (2000): 413–452.

18. "Wir werden sie ausradieren," *Der Spiegel*, no. 3, 13 January 2003.

19. Guernica was a major news item in the international press with "sensational" coverage provided by the *New York Times*, London *Times*, *New York Post*, and others. See James S. Corum, *The Luftwaffe: Creating the Operational Air War, 1918–1940* (Lawrence: University Press of Kansas, 1997), 196–200. In 1997, on the sixtieth anniversary of the attack, the German president officially apologized for the action. Germany's largest newsmagazine, *Der Spiegel*, described Guernica as "practicing for the terror to come."

20. "Wir werden sie ausradieren," 119.

21. See James Stokesbury, *A Short History of Air Power* (New York: William Morrow, 1986), 146; Alan Stephens, "The True Believers: Air Power between the War," in *The War in the Air, 1914–1994*, Alan Stephens, ed. (Fairbairn, Australia: RAAF Air Power Studies Centre, 1994), 60–61; Alan Cross, *The Bombers* (New York: Macmillan, 1987), 85; and William Shirer, *The Rise and Fall of the Third Reich* (New York: Simon and Schuster, 1960), 297.

22. For an examination of the Guernica mythology, see Corum, *The Luftwaffe*, 196–200.

23. Maj. General Wolfram von Richthofen, commander of an air division, sent a message to the Luftwaffe staff on 22 September to allow his units to strike a decisive blow. "Urgently request exploitation of last opportunity for large-scale experiment as devastation and terror raid. . . . Every effort will be made to eradicate Warsaw." See E. R. Hooten, *Phoenix Triumphant: The Rise and Rise of the Luftwaffe* (London: Arms and Armour, 1994), 187.

24. Ibid., 188.

25. For the 20,000 dead figure, see "Wir werden sie ausradieren," 119. For the 40,000 dead figure, see Hooten, *Phoenix Triumphant*, 188–189.

26. On the failure to set specific rules for aerial warfare in the interwar period, see L. H. Brune, "An Effort to Regulate Aerial Bombing: The Hague Commission of Jurists, 1922–1923," *Aerospace Historian* 29 (1982): 183–195.

27. "Wir warden sie ausradieren," 123. William Craig, *Enemy at the Gates: The Battle for Stalingrad* (London: Penguin, 1973), 61, gives the figure of dead from the 23 August 1942 bombing of Stalingrad at "nearly 40,000."

28. In three great raids on Hamburg between 24 and 30 July 1943, the RAF Bomber Command dropped 6,928 tons of bombs on Hamburg. This produced an estimated 35,000–40,000 German fatalities. See Martin Middlebrook and Chris Everitt, *The Bomber Command War Diaries* (London: Penguin, 1985), 411–415.

29. Anthony Read, *The Devil's Disciples: Hitler's Inner Circle* (New York: W. W. Norton,

2003), 681. Read also claims that 1,000 tons of bombs killed 40,000 at Stalingrad in 1942. That would make von Richthofen's attack four times more lethal in terms of casualties per ton of bombs than the Allied air raid on Dresden in 1945 or Hamburg in 1943. See 766.

30. Othmar Tuider, *Die Luftwaffe in Österreich, 1938–1945* (Vienna: Österreichischer Bundesverlag, 1985), 127.

31. For the period 1939–1945, there were in place the Hague Convention Respecting the Laws and Customs of War on Land of 18 October 1907, and the Geneva Convention Relative to the Treatment of Prisoners of War of 27 July 1929. There were no conventions regulating the conduct of aerial warfare.

32. Manfred Messerschmidt, "Strategischer Luftkrieg und Völkerrecht," *Luftkriegführung im Zweiten Weltkrieg*, Horst Boog, ed. (Herford, Germany: E. S. Mittler, 1993), 351–352.

33. Ibid. See also W. Hays Parks, "Luftkrieg und Kriegvölkerrecht," in *Luftkriegführung im Zweiten Weltkrieg*, 389–391.

34. Messerschmidt, "Strategischer Luftkrieg und Völkerrecht," 351.

35. Oberbefehlshaber der Luftwaffe, *Luftwaffe Dienstvorschrift 16, Luftkriegführung*, 1936, para. 143.

36. See Phillip Meilinger, "Trenchard, Slessor, and Royal Air Force Doctrine before World War II," 41–78; and Peter Faber, "Interwar U.S. Army Aviation and the Air Corps Tactical School: Incubators of American Airpower," 183–238, in *The Paths of Heaven: The Evolution of Airpower Theory*, Phillip Meilinger, ed. (Maxwell Air Force Base, AL: Air University Press, 1997).

37. Williamson Murray, *Strategy for Defeat: The Luftwaffe, 1933–1945* (Maxwell Air Force Base, AL: Air University Press, 1983), 129.

38. Larry Bidinian, *The Combined Allied Bombing Offensive against the German Civilians, 1942–1945* (Lawrence, KS: Colorado Press, 1976), 1.

39. *The United States Strategic Bombing Survey, Summary Edition* (Maxwell Air Force Base, AL: Air University Press, reprint 1987), 84, 92–102.

40. Ibid., 132.

41. For an overview of Hitler's war aims and discussion of Germany's goals, see Norman Rich, *Hitler's War Aims* (New York: W. W. Norton, 1973), 1–16, 208–223.

42. Bundesarchiv/Militärarchiv Freiburg (henceforth BA/MA) RW 4/578, OKW/WFSt LIV, Chefsachen "Barbarossa," *Richtlinien für die Behandlung politischer Kommissare*, 41–44.

43. Elizabeth Wagner, ed., *Der Generalquartiermeister: Briefe und Tagebuch Aufzeichnungen des Generalquartiermeister des Heeres, General der Artillerie Eduard Wagner* (Munich: Günter Olzog 1963), 210.

44. Theo Schulte, *The German Army and Nazi Policies in Occupied Russia* (Oxford: Berg, 1989), 181.

45. The photo collection of the United States Air Force Historical Research Agency, Karlsruhe Collection, includes many photographs of Soviet POWs repairing and maintaining airfields in the USSR.

46. Schulte, *The German Army*, 197.

47. For a thorough examination of the Soviet POW issue, see Schulte, *The German Army*, 180–181. Over two million Soviet POWs were taken in the first four months of the war in the East. It is estimated that between 33 percent and 60 percent of Soviet POWs died under German captivity. For Allied POWs from 1939 to 1945 the corresponding figure is 3.5 percent. From 1914 to 1918, when the Germans had millions of Soviet POWs, the death

rate for POWs was 5.4 percent. According to the surviving records, huge numbers of Soviet prisoners in 1941–1942 were simply worked to death. See Schulte, *The German Army*, 187–209. See also Christian Streit, *Keine Kamaraden: Die Wehrmacht und die sowjetischen Kriegsgefangenen, 1941–1945*, 2d ed. (Bonn: Dietz, 1997).

Chapter 2.
Wolfram von Richthofen's Early Life (1895–1914)

1. Striegau is now the city of Strzegom in Poland. The city maintains a website in German and honors its Czech and German foundation and history. Details of the German heritage and history of Striegau is found on the city website: http://www.strzegom.pl/2004/de/strony/index.htm.

2. The estate at Bersdorf was south of the Jauer River, held a large stone manor house, and was 550 hectares, 450 hectares being used for agricultural production and the other 100 hectares in woodland. The widow of General Manfred von Richthofen, Freifrau von Richthofen (born von Gerlach), lived in the house after Manfred's death and was the last owner of the property. She died shortly after the end of World War II.

3. Information on the family from Götz Freiherr von Richthofen, 15 June 2006.

4. See the Institut Deutsche Adelsforschung website, http://home.foni.net/~adelsforschung/, under "Verluste des preussischen Adels 1870/71." It contains a list of all the German nobles killed and wounded in the Franco-Prussian War.

5. For a good overview of Wilhelm II and his relationship with his nobles, see Isabel Hull, *The Entourage of Kaiser Wilhelm II, 1888–1918* (Cambridge: Cambridge University Press, 1982).

6. On the cadet schools, see Manfred Messerschmitt, "Militaer und Schule in der Wilhelmischen Zeit," *Militärgeschichtlichen Mitteilungen* 23, 1 (1978): 51–76.

7. In the period immediately before World War I in sixteen cavalry regiments and forty-nine infantry regiments of the Prussian army the noble officers were in the majority. There were a few regiments that took no bourgeois officers at all—only nobles. In four regiments even all the reserve officers were nobles. See Karl Demeter, *Das Deutsche Offizierkorps in Gesellschaft und Staat, 1650–1945*, 3d ed. (Frankfurt am Main: Berhard und Graefe Verlag, 1964), 27.

8. In Prussia in 1908 there were only four bourgeois officers in the Guards regiments; in 1913 there were fifty-nine. See Martin Kitchen, *The German Officer Corps, 1890–1914* (Oxford: Clarendon, 1968), 24. There is a large literature on the sociology of the German army before World War I. See Wilhelm Deist, "Die Armee in Staat und Gesellschaft, 1890–1914," in *Das kaiserliche Deutschland: Politik und Gesellschaft, 1870–1918*, Michael Stürmer, ed. (Dusseldorf: Droste Verlag, 1970), 312–339; Wiegang Schmid-Richberg, *Die Regierungszeit Wilhelms II: Handbuch zur deutschen Militärgeschichte, 1648–1933*, 3d ed. (Munich: Militärgeschichtliches Forschungsamt, 1979), 9–156; and Hans Hubert Hoffman, *Das Deutsche Offizierkorps, 1860–1960* (Boppard am Rhein: Bernard und Graefe Verlag, 1980).

9. Demeter, *Das Deutsche Offizierkorps*, 89.

10. See Messerschmitt, "Militär und Schule in der Wilhelmischen Zeit," 51–76.

11. Kitchen, *The German Officer Corps*, 119–124.

12. Information on German garrisons can be found in the *1898 Rang und Quartierliste der Königlich Preussischen Armee* (Berlin: E. S. Mittler, 1898).

13. The tunic was called an "Attila"; they also wore a fur hat, called a "Colback."
14. The "Song of the Braune und Schwarze Husaren" goes like this:

> Heiß ist die Liebe (Hot is the love)
> Kalt ist der Schnee, der Schnee; (And cold is the snow)
> Scheiden und Meiden (I have to leave you)
> Und das tut weh. (And that hurts so)
>   (Chorus:)
> Braune Husaren die reiten, (Brown Hussars they gallop)
> Die reiten niemals, niemals Schritt; (They never, never walk)
> Herzliebes Mädchen (Sweetheart girl)
> Du kannst nicht mit. (You can't come along)
> Weiß ist die Feder (White is the feather)
> An meinem braunen, braunen Hut; (On my brown, brown hat)
> Schwarz ist das Pulver, (Black is the gunpowder)
> Rot ist das Blut. (Red is the blood)
> Das grüne Gläslein (The goblet)
> Zersprang mir in der, in der Hand; (I raise in my hand)
> Brüder, ich sterbe (Brothers I die)
> Fürs Vaterland. (For the Fatherland.)
> Auf meinem Grabe, (On my grave)
> Solln rote, rote Rosen stehn. (Place a red, red rose)
> Die roten Rosen (The red roses are beautiful)
> Und die sind schön. (Just like you)

15. Edgar Graf von Matuschka, *Organisationsgeschichte des Heeres, 1890–1918* (Munich: Militärgeschichtlichen Forschungsamt, 1983).
16. Kitchen, *The German Officer Corps*, 13–14.
17. For a general background on the Prussian army during this period, see Gordon Craig, *The Politics of the Prussian Army, 1640–1945* (London: Oxford University Press, 1955). See also Manfred Messerschmitt, *Die politische Geschichte der preussisch-deutschen Armee—Handbuch zur Deutschen Militärgeschichte, 1648–1939*, vol. 4, 1 (Munich: Militärgeschichtliches Forschungsamt, 1975).
18. On German army regimental libraries of the pre–World War I era, see Heiger Ostertag, "Bibliotheksbestände und literarische Interessen: Indikatoren für das Bildungsniveau im Offizierskorps im Kaiserreich, 1871–1918," *Militärgeschichtlichen Mitteilungern* 47 (1990): 57–72.

Chapter 3. The Great War

1. The order of battle of the German units in World War I is found in Edgar Graf von Matuschka, *Organizationsgeschichte des Heeres, 1890–1918, Deutsche Militärgeschichte, 1648–1939* (Munich: Militärgeschichtlichen Forschungsamt, band 6, 1983). In 1914 a German cavalry regiment had 36 officers, 688 men, 769 horses, and 19 wagons. A cavalry brigade consisted of two regiments. A cavalry division consisted of three cavalry brigades, an artillery battalion of twelve light guns, a machine gun company with six machine guns, an engineer platoon, a signals platoon, and a supply column. Total strength of a cavalry division was about 5,000 men. An infantry division consisted of four infantry regiments organized into two

brigades. Each infantry regiment had a strength of 3,390 men. Divisions had artillery brigades with seventy-two guns as well as supporting engineer, signal, and supply units.

2. The 5th Cavalry Division consisted of the Ninth Cavalry Brigade (1st Silesian Dragoon Reg., 10th Uhland Reg.), Eleventh Cavalry Brigade (1 Silesian Life Cuirassier Rat., 2nd Silesian Dragoon Reg.), and Twelfth Cavalry Brigade (4th Silesian Hussar Reg., 6th Silesian Hussar Reg.). The division troops included a truck detachment, an engineer detachment, a machine gun detachment, a signals company, and the 3rd Mounted Battalion of the Niederschlesisches Field Artillery Regiment.

3. On the early cavalry campaigns of the war in the West, see Lt. General M. von Poseck, *Deutsche Kavallerie in Belgien und Frankreich, 1914* (Berlin: E. S. Mittler und Sohn, 1923).

4. General der Kavallerie M. von Poseck, *Der Aufklärunsdienst der Kavallerie* (Berlin: E. S. Mittler und Sohn, 1927), 11–12.

5. Ibid., 13–14. A good overview of German cavalry operations in World War I is found in Erich-Günther Blau, *Die Operative Verwendung Der Deutschen Kavallerie im Weltkrieg, 1914–18* (Munich: C. H. Beck'sche Verlagsbuchhandlung, 1934).

6. On the German cavalry arm in World War I, see H. F. Schulz, *Die Preussischen Kavallerie-Regimenter, 1913/1914* (Friedberg: Podzun-Pallas-Verlag, 1985). See also Major a.D. Jen von Egan-Krieger, *Die deutsche Kavallerie in Krieg und Frieden* (Karlsruhe: Schille, 1928).

7. Lt. General Maximilian von Poseck, "The German Cavalry in Poland," 254–258, The Cavalry School, *Cavalry Combat* (Harrisburg, PA: U.S. Cavalry Association, 1937). Information on 5th Cavalry Division operations in late 1914 can be found in Bundesarchiv/Militärarchiv Freiburg (henceforth BA/MA) PH/8/V 43—KTB Kavallerie Korps 1914.

8. Poseck, "The German Cavalry in Poland," 258.

9. A detailed account of 5th Cavalry Division operations in 1915 is found in the Kriegstagebuch of Kavallerie Korps Heydebreck in BA/MA Doc. PH 8/V/40 KTB 18.7—31.8 1915.

10. Kavallerie Korps order of 18.7. 1915 in BA/MA 8/V/40(a). On the cavalry operation on the Bug River battle, see BA/MA PH 8/V/41, KTB 5th Kavallerie Division and Kavallerie Korps Heydebreck.

11. By August 1915 the 5th Cavalry Division had a strength of 2,669 mounted troops, seven machine guns, and twelve artillery pieces. By any reckoning, this was a relatively small force, suitable only for supporting operations. See *Reports of Kavallerie Korps Heydebreck*, 9 August 1915, in BA/MA PH 8/V/42.

12. A brief account of the war record of the 4th Hussars is found in E. Fiebig, *Husaren heraus!* (Berlin: Kyffhäuser Verlag, 1933), 100–101. In 1917 the 4th Hussars conducted occupation duties behind the lines, and in 1918 the regiment was assigned to police duties in the occupied Ukraine.

13. For a list of divisions and their battle and campaign records, see Grosser Generalstab, *Die Schlachten und Gefechte des Grossen Krieges, 1914–1918* (Berlin: Hermann Sack, 1919).

14. Peter Supf, *Die Geschichte des deutschen Flugwesens*, vol. 2 (Berlin: Verlagsanstalt Hermann Klemm, 1935), 262.

15. On Manfred von Richthofen's career from the cavalry to command of a fighter squadron, see Peter Kilduff, *Richthofen: Beyond the Legend of the Red Baron* (New York: John Wiley and Sons, 1993), 11–70.

16. Ibid., 65–66.

17. See Major A. D. Freiherr von Bülow, *Geschichte der Luftwaffe* (Frankfurt am Main: Verlag Moritz Diesterweg, 1934), 88–135, for a complete account of the Luftstreitkräfte organization in World War I.

18. Kommandierende General der Luftstreitkräfte, *Weisungen für die Einsatz und die Verwendung von Fliegerverbänden innerhalb einer Armee* (*Directives on the Mission and Utilization of Flying Units within an Army*), May 1917.

19. Doctrine for reconnaissance and artillery spotting was outlined in Kommandierende General der Luftstreitkräfte, *Utilization and Role of Artillery Aviators in Trench Warfare*, 1917. U.S. Army War College translation, July 1917. Doctrine for direct support of ground troops was outlined in Kommandierende General der Luftstreitkräfte, *The Infantry Aircraft and the Infantry Balloon*, September 1917. U.S. Army War College translation, February 1918.

20. H. A. Jones, *The War in the Air*, vol. 4 (Oxford: Clarendon, 1934), 116–118.

21. Edward Westermann, *Flak: German Anti-Aircraft Defenses, 1914–1945* (Lawrence: University Press of Kansas, 2001), 24.

22. Ibid., 27.

23. Georg Neumann, *Die deutschen Luftstreitkräfte im Weltkriege* (Berlin: E. S. Mittler, 1920), 268–269.

24. Harald Potempa, *Die Königlich-Bayerische Fliegertruppe, 1914–1918* (Frankfurt am Main: Peter Lang, 1997).

25. Dennis Winter, *The First of the Few: Fighter Pilots of the First World War* (Athens: University of Georgia Press, 1983), 36. John Slessor, later marshal of the Royal Air Force, recalled that he flew his first combat mission in late 1915 straight out of pilot training and with a total of thirty-five hours flying experience. See John Slessor, *The Central Blue: The Autobiography of Sir John Slessor, Marshal of the RAF* (New York: Praeger, 1957), 7–10.

26. Richard Hallion, *Rise of the Fighter Aircraft, 1914–1918* (Annapolis, MD: Nautical and Aviation Publishing, 1984), 72–73, 160–161.

27. On British training losses, see John Morrow, *The Great War in the Air* (Washington, DC: Smithsonian Institution Press, 1993), 318.

28. H. A. Jones, *The War in the Air: Appendices* (Oxford: Clarendon, 1917), app. 37. British aircrew killed or missing in operations over the western front in 1917 were 2,090. Losses between June 1917 and October 1917 were 928 (almost all over Flanders). Total German operational aircrew losses for 1917 were 296 dead—with the vast majority lost over Flanders. Winter, *The First of the Few*, 76–77. Germans losses separate dead and missing in action (MIA), of which half were killed and half taken prisoner, but German MIA rates would add approximately 140 dead to the 296 confirmed dead figure. See Neumann, *Die deutschen Luftstreitkräfte im Weltkriege*, 587–588.

29. For a very detailed description of the German flight training program, see Potempa, *Die Königlich-Bayerische Fliegertruppe*, 118–150.

30. Norman Franks and Greg Van Wyngarden, *Fokker Dr 1 Aces of World War I* (Oxford: Osprey, 2001), 23.

31. Ibid., 23–24.

32. On the design and development of the Fokker Dr 1, see Hans Redemann, *Innovations in Aircraft Construction* (West Chester, PA: Schiffer Military History, 1991), 16–19. On the role of the Fokker Dr 1 in combat, see Franks and Van Wyngarden, *Fokker Dr 1 Aces of World War I*.

33. Peter Kilduff, *Richthofen: Beyond the Legend of the Red Baron* (New York: John Wiley and Sons, 1993), 172.

34. The Fokker D 7 with the BMW engine could climb to 5,000 meters in sixteen minutes, an astounding climb rate for the time. See Morrow, *The Great War in the Air*, 301.

35. Kenneth Munson, *Aircraft of World War I* (Garden City, NJ: Arco, 1977), 93–94; Richard Hallion, *Rise of the Fighter Aircraft, 1914–1918* (Annapolis, MD: Nautical and Aviation Press, 1984), 306.

36. Brig. General William Mitchell, *Memoirs of World War I* (New York: Random House, 1960, reprint of the 1926 edition), 306.

37. Manfred von Richthofen's fighter commander manual is translated and reproduced in full in Kilduff, *Richthofen: Beyond the Legend of the Red Baron*, 231–240.

38. John Morrow, *German Air Power in World War I* (Lincoln: University of Nebraska Press, 1982), 95–96.

39. Ibid., 119.

40. Ibid., 297.

41. Ibid., 298.

42. *Weisungen für die Einsatz und die Verwendung von Fliegerverbänden innerhalb einer Armee*, May 1917, para. 38.

43. Ibid., paras. 39–55.

44. For an excellent overview of the German air units of World War I, see Norman Franks, Frank Bailey, and Russell Guest, *Above the Lines* (London: Grub Street, 1993). On Jasta 11, see 33–34.

45. Cecil Lewis, *Sagittarius Rising* (London: Greenhill, 1993), 176–177. Originally published in 1936.

46. The triplanes were not fast but were prized for their maneuverability—an essential element in the dogfights of 1917. Of the fighter aircraft of the war, only the Sopwith Camel and the German Fokker D 7 equaled the triplanes in maneuverability. Cecil Lewis described flying the British Sopwith triplane: "It was so beautifully balanced, so well-mannered, so feather light on the stick . . . in its instantaneous response to the lightest touch, it remains my favorite." Lewis, *Sagittarius Rising*, 159–160.

47. Redemann, *Innovations in Aircraft Construction*, 16–23.

48. Gerhard Friedrich Dose, *Das Infanterie Regiment 187 in Flandern, bei Arras und Cambrai 1917/18*. http://www.lib.byu.edu/~rhd/wwi/memoir.html.

49. Franks and Van Wyngarden, *Fokker Dr 1 Aces of World War I*, 29–30.

50. Ibid., 31.

51. Kilduff, *Richthofen: Beyond the Legend of the Red Baron*, 197.

52. H. J. Nowarra and Kimbough Brown, *Von Richthofen and the Flying Circus* (Letchworth, UK: Harleyford, 1958), 105. For a detailed account of the aerial fight on 21 April, see 104–115.

53. For a thorough account of Manfred von Richthofen's death, see Norman Franks, Hal Giblin and Nigel McCrery, *Under the Guns of the Red Baron* (New York: Barnes and Noble, 1999), 204–208.

54. Kilduff, *Richthofen: Beyond the Legend of the Red Baron*, 210–212.

55. On the German offensives in the West in 1918, see Rod Paschall, *The Defeat of Imperial Germany, 1917–1918* (Chapel Hill, NC: Algonquin, 1989); and Randal Gray, *Kaiserschlacht, 1918* (Oxford: Osprey, 1991).

56. The British brought their fatal accident rate in training down from 0.37 fatalities per 1,000 flying hours in 1916 to 0.25 in 1918. See Lee Kennett, *The First Air War, 1914–1918* (New York: Free Press, 1991), 128.

57. Ibid., 120.
58. Ibid., 123–124.
59. Morrow, *The Great War in the Air*, 297.
60. Franks and Van Wyngarden, *Fokker Dr 1 Aces of World War I*, 46–48.
61. Ibid., 48–50.
62. Neumann, *Die deutschen Luftstreitkräfte*, 218–227.
63. Brig. Mitchell, *Memoirs of World War I*, 268.
64. Kilduff, *Richthofen: Beyond the Legend of the Red Baron*, 214; Terry Treadwell and Alan Wood, *The First Air War: A Pictorial History* (New York: Barnes and Noble, 1996), 143–145.
65. Treadwell and Wood, *The First Air War*, 103–105.
66. Morrow, *The Great War in the Air*, 316.
67. Treadwell and Wood, *The First Air War*, 137.
68. Bericht, Kommandeur der Flieger, 18 Armee, Abteilung Ia. 8–14 August 1918. In the U.S. National Archives, National Archives and Records Administration (hereafter, NARA), Record Group 165, Box 79, Folder 2.
69. Treadwell and Wood, *The First Air War*, 46. First Lieutenant Erich-Rüdinger von Wedel (thirteen aerial victories) took over as Jasta 11 commander on 8 September 1918 and led the squadron until the armistice.
70. Specific information on Wolfram von Richthofen's combat record is found at http://www.theareodrome.com/aces/germany/richthofen3.php.
71. The plaque presented to him for his second aerial kill, a French Spad, is inscribed "Second Aerial Victory: To Lt. Freiherr von Richthofen, Ludewig."
72. Potempa, *Die Königlich-Bayerische Fliegertruppe*, 300.
73. Kennett, *The First Air War*, 146.
74. Morrow, *German Air Power in World War I*, 138.
75. Ibid.
76. Morrow, *The Great War in the Air*, 317.
77. Treadwell and Wood, *The First Air War*, 136.
78. Nowarra and Brown, *Von Richthofen and the Flying Circus*, 132.
79. Morrow, *The Great War in the Air*, 316–317.
80. Franks and Van Wyngarden, *Fokker Dr 1 Aces of World War I*, 29–30.
81. Morrow, *German Airpower in World War I*, 120.
82. In a 1922 report on air operations in 1918, Major Helmuth Wilberg, commander of the Fourth Army's air units, stated that his air units received plenty of high-quality aircraft and equipment right to the end of the war but that Allied numerical superiority was becoming unbearable. He pointed out that the fuel shortages in late 1918 were severe and becoming worse. Wilberg's report was meant as a resounding refutation of the "stab in the back" argument that the German fighting men at the front had been let down by the failure of the workers in the homeland to produce enough material. See Major Helmuth Wilberg, Report to Col. Thomsen and Major Förster, 22 February 1922, in BA/MA RH 2/2275.
83. Morrow, *The Great War in the Air*, 310.
84. *Revue De L'Aeronautique Militaire*, July/August 1925.
85. Treadwell and Wood, *The First Air War*, 34.
86. Kilduff, *Richthofen: Beyond the Legend of the Red Baron*, 219–220.
87. James S. Corum, *The Roots of Blitzkrieg: Hans von Seeckt and German Military Reform* (Lawrence: University Press of Kansas, 1992), 29–31, 147–148.

88. Mathew Cooper, *The German Air Force, 1922–1945* (London: Jane's, 1981), 379. Seeckt also favored the creation of the air force as a separate branch of service, equal to the army. See Friedrich von Rabenau, *Seeckt: Aus seinem Leben* (Leipzig: Hase-Koehler Verlag, 1941), 529.

89. Morrow, *The Great War in the Air*, 352–354.

90. Morrow, *German Air Power in World War I*, 159–162.

Chapter 4. From Reichswehr to the Wehrmacht, 1919–1936

1. The best biography of Seeckt is Hans Meier-Welcker, *Seeckt* (Frankfurt am Main: Bernard und Graefe Verlag, 1967). Meier-Welcker details Seeckt's extensive travels during this period; see pages 327–332 for 1922.

2. As with his father's side of the family, the family of Wolfram's mother also had some very strong military connections. At the start of World War II General Leo Götz von Olenhusen, a relation of Wolfram's mother, was commander of the German Army's 40th Infantry Division. He ended the war as a General der Infanterie and retired.

3. Mathew Cooper, *The German Air Force, 1922–1945* (London: Jane's, 1981), 379. In 1919 Seeckt proposed that Germany be allowed a peacetime air force of 1,800 aircraft and 10,000 men. He also favored the creation of the air force as a separate branch of service, equal to the army. See Freiderich von Rabenau, *Seeckt: Aus seinem Leben* (Leipzig: Hase-Koehler Verlag, 1941), 529.

4. The best book on this period is Karl-Heinz Völker, *Die Entwicklung der Militärischen Luftfahrt in Deutschland, 1920–1933* (Stuttgart: Deutsche Verlags-Anstalt, 1962).

5. See Wehrministerium, *Rangliste des Deutschen Reichsheeres* (Berlin, 1925).

6. See James S. Corum, "The Development of Strategic Air War Concepts in Interwar Germany, 1919–1939," *Air Power History* 14, 4 (Winter 1997): 18–35.

7. The 1926 shadow Luftwaffe doctrine, *Directives for the Execution of the Operational Air War*, discussed in detail a doctrine for bombers attacking "the sources of enemy power" to include enemy cities, ports, rail yards, and vital industries. For a translation of the entire document, see James Corum and Richard Muller, *The Luftwaffe's Way of War* (Baltimore: Nautical and Aviation Press, 1987), 91–112.

8. Hans von Seeckt, *Gedanken eines Soldaten* (Berlin: Verlag für Kulturpolitik, 1929), 93–95.

9. Colonel Kurt Thorbeck, "Die Technische und Taktische Lehre des Krieges," April 12, 1920, in Bundesarchiv/Militärarchiv Freiburg (henceforth BA/MA) RH 12-2/94. Colonel Thorbeck's Denkschrift was very influential among the postwar general staff. Thorbeck ruthlessly criticized the general staff for not having officers conversant with the technical and material demands of war. He called the general staff's lack of technological familiarity "the basic mistake of the war."

10. On Seeckt's initial program to send Reichswehr officers to technical colleges, see Hans von Seeckt, Letter to General Groener, 17 February 1919, National Archives, von Seeckt Papers, File M-132, Roll 25, Item 126. For an overview of Seeckt's education reforms in the army, see James S. Corum, *The Roots of Blitzkrieg* (Lawrence: University Press of Kansas, 1992), 25–50.

11. Among the German senior officers who were sent to receive engineering degrees in the interwar period were Maj. General Robert Fuchs, commander, 1st Air Division; Gen. der Flieger Johannes Fink, commander, IInd Air Corps; Maj. General Friedrich Deutsch, com-

mander, 16th Flak Division; Lt. General Gerhard Conrad, air commander, XIth Air Corps; and Lt. General Richard Schimpf, commander, 3rd Paratroop Division.

12. Martin van Creveld, *The Training of Officers* (New York: Free Press, 1990), 32.

13. In the mid-1920s the Waffenamt employed sixty-four officers, including two major generals, two colonels, and twelve lieutenant colonels. An additional twenty-one officers worked at test sites for the Waffenamt. See Wehrministerium, *Rangliste des Deutschen Reichsheeres* (Berlin, 1925).

14. A good overview of the Waffenamt operations can be found in Erich Schneider's "Waffenentwicklung: Ehrfahrungen im deutschen Heereswaffenamt," in *Wehrwissenschaftliche Rundschau* 3 (1953): 24–35.

15. Von Richthofen was presented with a silver tablet from the Waffenamt that read, "1 November 1923 to 31 March 1928 from Waffenamt Section Wa B6." The name of Captain Volkmann is on the tablet as the presenter. Volkmann was later Condor Legion commander after von Richthofen.

16. On von Richthofen's work in the Waffenamt in the mid-1920s, see Lutz Budrass, *Flugzeugindustrie und Luftrüstung in Deutschland, 1918–1945* (Düsseldorf: Droste Verlag, 1998), 150, 218–222.

17. See Peter Brooks, *The Modern Airline: Its Origins and Development* (London: Putnam, 1961), 52–57 and 88–93.

18. See L. Hirschaier, ed., *l'Anneé Aéronautique, 1928–1929* (Paris: Dunoud, 1929), 98–100, 167, and 245. In 1929–1930 the Germans developed the four-motor Junkers G 38 aircraft, the largest commercial aircraft of the time, with 3,200 horsepower and thirty-eight-passenger capacity. See Peter Supf, *Das Buch der deutschen Fluggeschichte*, 2 (Berlin: Klemm, 1935), 613.

19. See Ralf Schabel, *Die Illusion der Wunderwaffen* (Munich: Oldenbourg Verlag, 1994), 103.

20. See BA/MA RH 8/v 3667WA. Prw. 6 F Personnel List 25, 10, 28, Reichswehr Waffenamt files. This file lists personnel involved in air equipment development and testing in 1928–1929. There are thirty-five persons, and sections are named for aircraft development, air photos, bombs, weapons, engines, aircraft instruments, and radios. The group leader was Captain Student, and Captain Jeschonnek was attached. Captain Lorenz was involved in the aircraft equipment section. The total personnel included fifteen civilian engineers, nine retired officers, and nine civilian employees.

21. For some of the aircraft requirements developed from Wever's war games, see National Archives and Records Administration (hereafter, NARA), T 177, Roll 9 "Ergebnis der Besprechung A-Amt und C-Amt 11 Mai 1934 Waffenamt Dept. 8." For evaluation of operational lessons learned from war games, see NARA T 177, Roll 9, "Auszug aus der Denkschrift zum Winterkriegsspiel 1933/34." These documents specified Stuka, fighter, bomber, and reconnaissance plane requirements.

22. Cooper, *The German Air Force*, 2–3.

23. Edward L. Homze, *Arming the Luftwaffe: The Reich Air Ministry and the German Aircraft Industry, 1919–39* (Lincoln: University of Nebraska Press, 1976), 76.

24. See BA/MA Doc RH 12–1/15 from TA Luft 30 Aug. 1926. This outlines a program to secretly train forty officers per year in civilian flight schools as they entered the army. In the document is also a list of refresher flight training for pilots in the Reichswehr.

25. Wolfram von Richthofen, 1929 Technische Hochschule Berlin-Charlottenburg, Ph.D. Eng. dissertation, "Der Einfluss der Flugzeugbauarten auf die Beschaffung unter besonderer Berücksichtigung militärischer Gesichtspunke."

26. For an analysis of von Richthofen's doctoral research, see Lutz Budrass, Jonas Scherner, and Jochen Streb, "Demystifying the German 'Armament Miracle' during World War II: New Insights from the Annual Audits of German Aircraft Producers," Yale University Economic Growth Center, Center Discussion Paper No. 905, January 2005. See esp. 16–18 and table 5 on 37.

27. Ibid., 16.

28. Von Richthofen, dissertation, table 19.

29. BA MA RH 8/v 9910 WA PRW 8, 8 Feb. 1931, page 3. Summary of weapons programs: disposition of development and testing of military and civil aircraft: Bomber: Ju G 24 as bomber, Rohrbach Ro VIII, BFW M 20, BFW M 28, Ju 52, FW A 38, FW A 36, Albatros L 83, Do K. Development priorities: 1. fighters, 2. Long distance recon, 3. close distance recon. See Fols. 159B 1931: Estimated industrial capability for future aircraft production: army 385 planes per year, navy 155; by 1933: 828 army, navy 302.

30. BA/MA DDR R 06 10/04.

31. BA/MA DDR R 06 10/04, p. 305.

32. Italo Balbo was commander in chief of the North African theater of war at the start of World War II. Only a few weeks later, Balbo was accidentally shot down by Italian antiaircraft gunners who mistook his aircraft coming into Benghazi as a British bomber. Balbo's untimely death was a severe blow to the Italians as he was regarded as one of their most competent senior officers.

33. On the 1932 maneuvers and mechanization experiments, see Robert Citino, *The Evolution of Blitzkrieg Tactics* (Westport, CT: Greenwood, 1987), 184–192.

34. The most detailed history of the Luftwaffe and its organization in this period is Karl-Heinz Völker, *Die Deutsche Luftwaffe, 1933–1939* (Stuttgart: Deutsche Verlags-Anstalt, 1967).

35. Budrass, Scherner, and Streb, "Demystifying the German 'Armament Miracle' during World War II," 339.

36. Of the more than 600 generals of the Luftwaffe serving between 1935 and 1945, approximately 150 had been involved with civil aviation between 1920 and 1934. Karl Friedrich Hildebrand, *Die Generale der deutschen Luftwaffe, 1935–1945*, Vols. I–III (Osnabrück: Biblio Verlag, 1990). Hildebrand has published the official service records of all 688 men who reached the rank of general in the Luftwaffe. Among those who came from civil aviation to the Luftwaffe are Erhard Milch, state secretary for aviation and field marshal, who served as a director of Lufthansa before rejoining the military; General der Flieger Robert Knauss, later to be commander of the Luftwaffe General Staff College, who came from the Lufthansa board of directors; Colonel General Alfred Keller, commander of the 1st Air Fleet from 1940–1943, who worked for Junkers and ran a flight school before 1934; Lt. General Werner Junck, wartime commander of Jagdkorps II, who worked for Heinkel before joining the Luftwaffe; and Lt. General Theo Osterkamp, a World War I Pour le Merité holder, who managed a seaplane station prior to returning to the Luftwaffe. Osterkamp would become the air commander for North Africa in 1941–1942.

37. William Green, *Warplanes of the Third Reich* (New York: Galahad Books, 1990), 110–112. Although its performance was not impressive, the Do 11 was roughly equal to the bomber aircraft of the major powers at the time. In 1933 the Reichs Air Ministry ordered some Do Fs, renamed the Do 11, as bombers. In 1934 the first of 372 Do 11s were delivered to the Luftwaffe to equip the Luftwaffe's first bomber units.

38. Homze, *Arming the Luftwaffe*, 86–87.

39. Ibid., 87.
40. Budrass, Scherner, and Streb, "Demystifying the German 'Armament Miracle' during World War II," 487, 693.
41. Ibid., 339–342, 354–355, 386–387.
42. Homze, *Arming the Luftwaffe*, 73.
43. Ibid., 127–128.
44. NARA File T-177 Roll 9, *Auszug aus der Denkschrift zum Winterkriegsspiel 1933/34*, para. 4.
45. On the programs to develop the He 111 bomber and the Do 17 bomber, see Joachim Dressel and Manfred Griehl, *Bombers of the Luftwaffe* (London: Arms and Armour, 1994), 25–32. The He 111 went from contract to prototype in two and a half years. It went into production in 1936. The Do 17 took a little over three years in development.
46. Joachim Dressel and Manfred Griehl, *Fighters of the Luftwaffe* (London: Arms and Armour, 1993), 11–12.
47. Ibid., 14–17.
48. Ibid., 30–31.
49. In 1934, as von Richthofen took over the Development Office, he declared that "diving below 2,000 meters is complete nonsense." See Paul Deichman, *Spearhead for Blitzkrieg: Luftwaffe Operations in Support of the Army, 1939–1945* (New York: Ivy Books, 1996), 43.
50. On the Luftwaffe's heavy bomber project, see James S. Corum, *The Luftwaffe: Creating the Operational Air War, 1918–1940* (Lawrence: University Press of Kansas, 1997), 164–166, 171–172.
51. Richard Suchenwirth, *Historical Turning Points in the German Air Force War Effort* (New York: Arno Press, 1968), 39–45.
52. Homze, *Arming the Luftwaffe*, 107.
53. Dressel and Griehl, *Bombers of the Luftwaffe*, 71–73.
54. BA/MA Doc. RH 8/v 9916, Conference of Feb. 1932, Waffenprüfungsamt Abt. 8. Wimmer chaired this conference in which heavy bomber development and rocket research were discussed.
55. Michael Neufeld, *The Rocket and the Reich* (New York: Free Press, 1995), 43, 46.
56. Ibid., 44.
57. Ibid., 45.
58. Ibid.
59. Ibid.
60. Ibid., 48.
61. Walter Boyne, *Messerschmitt Me 262* (Washington, DC: Smithsonian Institution Press, 1980). A small research team led by Hans von Ohain began developing a jet engine, the He S-3B, in April 1936, and completed and ran the engine in March 1937. The total cost was approximately $20,000.
62. Hans Redemann, *Innovations in Aircraft Construction* (West Chester, PA: Schiffer Military History, 1991), 106–109.
63. Horst Boog, *Die deutsche Luftwaffenführung, 1935–1945* (Stuttgart: Deutsche Verlags-Anstalt, 1982), 187.
64. Ibid., 50–51.
65. Green, *Warplanes of the Third Reich*, 359–361.
66. Ibid., 390–397.
67. Heft Henschel, Archives, Deutsches Museum, Munich.

68. Neufeld, *The Rocket and the Reich*, 62–63.
69. Boog, *Die deutsche Luftwaffenführung*, 48.

Chapter 5. The War in Spain, 1936–1939

1. Raymond Proctor, *Hitler's Luftwaffe in the Spanish Civil War* (Westport, CT: Greenwood Press, 1983), 16–20.
2. Wilberg held Imperial Pilot's License number 26. A general staff officer, he commanded over 700 aircraft in 1917 as Fourth Army Air commander. From 1919–1927 he served as chief of the shadow air force. In 1933–1934 he edited the primary operational manual of the Luftwaffe, *Luftkriegführung*. Since 1935 he had commanded the forerunner of the Luftwaffe's General Staff Academy. See Bundesarchiv/Militärarchiv Freiburg (henceforth BA/MA) MSG 109/2959, and interview by J. Corum with Hans-Joachim Wilberg, son of Helmuth Wilberg, 19 June 1992.
3. Proctor, *Hitler's Luftwaffe*, 21.
4. See Manfred Merkes, *Die deutsche Politik gegenüber dem spanischen Bürgerkrieg: 1936–1939* (Bonn: Ludwig Röhrscheid Verlag, 1961), 30.
5. Proctor, *Hitler's Luftwaffe*, 36.
6. Ibid., 30–32.
7. Ibid., 40–42.
8. For a table of organization of the Condor Legion, see Karl Ries and Hans Ring, *The Legion Condor* (West Chester, PA: Schiffer Military History, 1992), 38–40.
9. *Personnel File Wilberg*, BA/MA MSG 109/2959.
10. Sperrle was a pre–World War I flier who commanded aviation of the Seventh Army during World War I and served on the general staff after World War I. From 1927–1929, Sperrle served as the shadow Luftwaffe commander. He was commander of Air District (Luftgau) V when called upon to serve in Spain. See Sperrle Personnel Record, BA/MA MSG 1/1249, and interview of J. S. Corum with Hans-Joachim Wilberg, 19 June 1992.
11. Interview with Götz Freiherr von Richthofen by J. S. Corum, 21 June 1992.
12. Ibid.
13. See von Richthofen Report of 4 December 1936, in BA/MA N/71/1.
14. Proctor, *Hitler's Luftwaffe*, 66–67.
15. General der Flieger Karl Drum, "Die deutsche Luftwaffe im spanischen Bürgerkrieg," United States Air Force Historical Research Agency (henceforth USAF HRA), Karlsruhe Collection, Doc. K113.106–150, pp. 6–16.
16. Merkes, *Die deutsche Politik gegenüber dem spanischen Bürgerkrieg*, 25–26.
17. Ibid. On the economic advantages of German intervention, see also Robert Wheatley, *Hitler and Spain: The Nazi Role in the Spanish Civil War: 1936–1939* (Bowling Green: University Press of Kentucky, 1989), 74–87.
18. Ibid., 54.
19. See Chief of the Wehrmacht High Command, General Keitel's Message to the Foreign Minister of 22 March 1938, Document Number 549, in *Akten zur Deutschen Auswärtigen Politik, 1918–1945*, Serie D, Band III, 529–530. In later notes, this source is referred to as Akt.
20. Ibid.
21. Akt 549. On Franco's wish to prevent combat near France, see Akt 552.
22. Von Richthofen's diary, 20 January 1937.
23. Von Richthofen's diary, 2 March 1937.

24. Von Richthofen's diary, 5 February 1937.
25. Von Richthofen's diary, 22 January 1937.
26. von Richthofen's diary, 24 March 1937. On Vigón, see James Cortada, ed., *Historical Dictionary of the Spanish Civil War* (Westport, CT: Greenwood Press, 1982), 473–474.
27. Interview with Götz Freiherr von Richthofen, 21 June 1992.
28. See Cortada, *Historical Dictionary of the Spanish Civil War*, 11–13.
29. Ibid., 12–13.
30. Of 240 military pilots in July 1936, 150 went to the Republic and 90 joined the Nationalists. See Cortada, *Historical Dictionary of the Spanish Civil War*, 12.
31. See Gerald Howson, *Aircraft of the Spanish Civil War, 1936–1939* (Washington, DC: Smithsonian Institute Press, 1990), for a very detailed account of all of the aircraft used in the war, and their capabilities.
32. Brian Sullivan, "The Italian Armed Forces, 1918–40," in *Military Effectiveness*, vol. 2, Allan Millett and Williamson Murray, eds. (Boston: Unwin Hyman, 1988), 169–217. See especially 198.
33. Ibid., 199.
34. Report of General Sperrle, May 1937, cited in Proctor, *Hitler's Luftwaffe*, 136.
35. As von Richthofen complained in his report of 3 February 1937, "No one knows what the Italian plans are. Even Franco doesn't know." See BA/MA N/71/1.
36. Cortada, *Historical Dictionary of the Spanish Civil War*, 272.
37. For a contemporary account of the Guadalajara campaign, see Gen. der Infanterie Otto Wiesinger, "Der Bürgerkrieg in Spanien," in *Militärwissenschaftliche Mitteilungen* (1937), 386–387. Also see Jose Luis Nassaes Alcofar, *C.T.V.: Los Legionarios italianos en la Guerra Civil Española, 1936–1939* (Barcelona: Dopesa, 1972), 80–103.
38. Stanley Payne, *The Franco Regime, 1936–1975* (Madison: University of Wisconsin Press, 1987), 387.
39. Von Richthofen reported on 13 March 1937, "Abyssinia was a bluff. No fighting spirit . . . sensitive to panic," referring to an Italian division fleeing in panic. See also his report of 14 March 1937; both, BA/MA N 71/1. Lt. Colonel Paul Deichman, later General der Flieger, briefed Hitler on Spain in the spring of 1937. He regaled Hitler with stories of the Italian rout at Guadalajara, and accounts of Italian officers confronted with light enemy patrolling, who fell to their knees and started praying to the Virgin Mary. Gen. Karl Drum, "Die deutsche Luftwaffe im spanischen Bürgerkrieg," 83–84. The stories of the Italian officers, though possibly apocryphal, were common among the Condor Legion.
40. See *Lagebericht der Legion Condor*, 14 July 1938, "Germans Fly Support for Italian Ground Troops"; and 18 July 1938, "Germans Carry out Interdiction Attacks for Italian Troops," in BA/MA RL 35/4. Also see *Nachlass von Richthofen*, 9 April 1937, "Italian and German Bombers Carry out a Combined Attack on a Republican Explosives Factory," in BA/MA N 71/1.
41. Von Richthofen's report of 11 December 1937, in BA/MA N/671/2.
42. Von Richthofen's reports repeatedly noted the usefulness of the flak in supporting the ground forces. See his report of 1 April 1937 in BA/MA N/671/2.
43. Report of von Richthofen 1 April 1937 in BA/MA N/671/2.
44. Drum, "Die deutsche Luftwaffe im spanischen Bürgerkrieg," 199.
45. Proctor, *Hitler's Luftwaffe*, 122–123.
46. Ibid., 126.
47. Von Richthofen's diary 3 April 1937. See also Proctor, *Hitler's Luftwaffe*, 156.

48. Drum, "Die deutsche Luftwaffe im spanischen Bürgerkrieg," 183–184; see also Proctor, *Hitler's Luftwaffe*, 138–141.

49. Proctor, *Hitler's Luftwaffe*, 136–142.

50. For detailed information on the Guernica attack, see Gordon Thomas and Max Witts, *Guernica: The Crucible of World War II* (New York: Stein and Day, 1975); and Hans-Henning Abendroth, "Guernica: Ein fragwürdiges Symbol," in *Militärgeschichtliche Mitteilungen* 1 (1987): 111–126.

51. Ibid. See also James Corum, *The Luftwaffe: Creating the Operational Air War, 1918–1940* (Lawrence: University Press of Kansas, 1997), 198–200.

52. Von Richthofen's diary, 25 April 1937. Von Richthofen noted, "Guernica has to be destroyed if we are to strike a blow against enemy personnel and matériel." He cites Colonel Vigón of Franco's staff saying that if his Nationalist troops advanced and cut the roads south of Guernica, and the German aircraft closed the road in the town, "We have the enemy in Marquina in the sack."

53. See Nachlass von Richthofen in BA/MA N 671/2. Condor Legion Chief of Staff Lt. Colonel von Richthofen reported on 26 April 1937 that the Guernica attack was discussed and approved by Col. Vigón, Mola's chief of staff. See also Thomas and Witts, *Guernica*, 118–123.

54. Von Richthofen's diary, 30 April 1937.

55. BA/MA Daily Reports of Condor Legion, 11 February 1938.

56. Manuel Aznar, *Historia Militar de la Guerra de España*, vol. 1 (Madrid: Editoria Nacional, 1958), 302 (bombing of Brunete), 304 (bombing of Azuara). Also see Estado Mayor del Ejército, *Historia Militar de la Guerra de España* (Madrid: Tomo Tercero Altimira S.A., 1963), 82 (photo of Alcubierre).

57. Oberst Jaenecke, "Lehren des Spanischen Bürgerkrieges," in *Jahrbuch des deutschen Heeren* (Leipzig: Verlag von Breitkopf und Hörtel, 1940), 143.

58. Account of George Steer of the *London Times*, cited in Peter Wyden, *The Passionate War: The Narrative History of the Spanish Civil War* (NY: Simon and Schuster, 1983), 357–358.

59. The *London Times* covered the accounts of the Guernica attack in detail, every day, for more than ten days after the attack.

60. Cited in Allen Guttman, *The Wound in the Heart: America and the Spanish Civil War* (New York: Free Press, 1962), 106.

61. Ibid., 108.

62. Report of Parliamentary Debates, *London Times* (27 April 1937), 7.

63. After the Spanish Civil War, the Franco regime allowed no discussion or research about the Guernica bombing. Rather than suppress the incident, this approach acted to keep the mythology alive. A 2003 Canadian History Channel documentary, "Turning Points of History: Guernica," examined the raid and interviewed survivors of the attack. Historians at the museum in Guernica gave the figure of dead from the attack as "about 300"—considerably less than the over 1,600 figure that is still found in the history books. The official Guernica casualty figures warrant a much closer examination. If these figures are correct, then the Condor Legion's bombing of Guernica resulted in approximately 41 fatalities per ton of bombs (1,654 dead for approximately 40 tons of bombs). This is an astounding figure when one compares Guernica with the most devastating aerial raids carried out in Europe in World War II. In the Hamburg raid of July 1943, the RAF dropped 4,644 tons of bombs to produce approximately 7.5 fatalities per ton of bombs. In the American and British bombing against

Dresden in February 1945, Allied forces dropped 3,431 tons of bombs, producing approximately 7.2–10.2 fatalities per ton of bombs. See Martin Middlebrook and Chris Everitt, *The Bomber Command War Diaries* (London: Penguin, 1990), 413–414, 663–664.

64. George Quester, *Deterrence before Hiroshima* (Oxford: Transaction, 1986), 96.

65. Ibid., 97.

66. Ibid.

67. Ibid., 98.

68. Von Richthofen Report of 18 July 1937, in BA/MA N/671/2.

69. Ries and Ring, *The Legion Condor*, 68–72; Howson, *Aircraft of the Spanish Civil War*, 19, 22.

70. Proctor, *Hitler's Luftwaffe*, 157–169.

71. Ibid., 166

72. R. Dan Richardson, "The Development of Airpower Concepts and Air Combat Techniques in the Spanish Civil War," in *Air Power History* (Spring 1993): 13–21, especially 18–19.

73. Payne, *The Franco Regime*, 154.

74. See Drum, "Die deutsche Luftwaffe im spanischen Bürgerkrieg," 221–226, on the sea interdiction campaign carried out by the Luftwaffe.

75. A photograph from the von Richthofen family album, taken by von Richthofen in the summer of 1937, shows Sperrle, Major Siebert (the Condor Legion communications officer), and several German and Nationalist officers watching a village being blown off the map. The scene is reminiscent of a picnic, with officers relaxing and lying on their jackets; the only object missing is the checkered tablecloth.

76. Ernst Obermaier and Werner Held, *Jagdflieger Oberst Werner Mölders* (Stuttgart: Motorbuch Verlag, 1986), 79.

77. Ibid., 79.

78. José Larios Lerma, *Combat over Spain* (London: Neville Spearman, 1965), 141, 238.

79. On the Teruel campaign, see Ries and Ring, *The Legion Condor*, 111–126.

80. Ibid., 117.

81. As the Luftwaffe was being rapidly expanded, the bomber groups were being turned into wings.

82. Proctor, *Hitler's Luftwaffe*, 211–212, 237–238.

83. Akt 709, Message, Commander of Condor Legion, with Foreign Office comment, 6 January 1939.

84. Ries and Ring, *The Legion Condor*, 210.

85. See Cortada, *Historical Dictionary of the Spanish Civil War*, 11–13.

86. For a comprehensive account of the air war in Spain, see Jesus Salas Larrazabal, *Air War over Spain* (London: Ian Allen, 1969; English ed. 1974).

87. Mölders very probably formalized a tactical system that had already been used for some time in Spain. Supposedly, when the first BF 109s became available, only six were available for bomber escort. Normally bombers would be escorted by three groups of three fighters covering the bomber formation from three sides. With only six fighters available, the bombers could only be escorted by three flights of two aircraft. This expedient soon proved to be superior and was adopted as normal tactics.

88. Obermaier and Held, *Jagdflieger Oberst Werner Mölders*, 14.

89. Richard Bickers, *The Battle of Britain: The Greatest Battle in the History of Air Warfare* (London: Salamander, 1999), 127–128.

90. Headquarters, Luftwaffenkommando 5, Directive 8, 8 October 1937, in BA/MA RL 4/15.

91. Von Richthofen's major comment on the bombing of Guernica was "complete technical success of the 250 kg EC.B.1 bomb." See report of 30 April 1937 in BA/MA N/671/2.

92. Hans Detlef Herhudt von Rohden, ed., *Luftkrieg: Heft 5: Die Planung und Vorbereitung des Luftkriegs gegen Polen 1939*, ms. in Air University Library, November 1946.

Chapter 6. The Polish Campaign, 1939

1. On the major doctrine documents of the operational air war, see James Corum and Richard Muller, *The Luftwaffe's Way of War* (Baltimore: Nautical and Aviation Press, 1998). See especially the 1926 Operational Air Doctrine, 86–112, and Luftwaffe Regulation 16, which was the main operational doctrine for the Luftwaffe, 118–157.

2. In 1934 the Luftwaffe staff carried out a study on how to paralyze the Polish forces in case of war and concluded that the Polish rail system was especially vulnerable to German Stukas and bombers and would be the center of gravity for a German attack. See National Archives and Records Administration (henceforth NARA) T-78, Roll 128, Reichswehr Ministerium, "Die Zukünftige Kriegführung in der Luft und ihre Auswirkung auf die Bewegungen des Heeres."

3. Some German intelligence documents from the 1920s on Poland still exist. In January 1927 the Luftwaffe Section of the Reichswehr's Intelligence Office produced a detailed analysis of the Polish air force—its organization, equipment, and major bases. See NARA T-177, Roll 9, Memo: T. A. (Luft) *Polnische Luftstreitkräfte*. Berlin, 25 January 1927.

4. During the Polish campaign the Luftwaffe forces on the western front consisted of the 2nd Air Fleet, with 557 planes, and the 3rd Air Fleet, with 579 planes, for a total of 1,136 combat aircraft—a force far inferior to what the Western Allies could deploy. See E. R. Hooten, *Phoenix Triumphant: The Rise and Rise of the Luftwaffe* (London: Arms and Armour Press, 1994), 189.

5. Hans Detlef Herhudt von Rohden, *Luftkrieg Heft 5: Die Planung und Vorbereitung des Luftkrieges gegen Polen*, Ms. in Air University Library, 1946. Anlage 6.

6. Oberbefehlshaber der Luftwaffe, *Planstudie 1939*, 1 May 1939, NARA T-321, Roll 172.

7. Hooton, *Phoenix Triumphant*, 177.

8. Robert Citino, *The German Way of War* (Lawrence: University Press of Kansas, 2005), 257–262.

9. On 1 September 1939 the Luftwaffe had 1,180 bombers, 771 fighters, 408 Me 110 destroyers, 40 He 123 attack planes, 721 reconnaissance planes, 240 naval aircraft, and 552 transports. See Hans Detlef Herhudt von Rohden, *Die Deutsche Luftruestung, 1935–1945*. *Luftkrieg Heft 6*. Ms., Air University Library, circa 1950.

10. See James S. Corum, "Preparing the Thunderbolt: Luftwaffe Training Exercises before World War II," in *1998 National Aerospace Conference: The Meaning of Flight in the Twentieth Century*, ed. John Fleischaer (Dayton, OH: Wright State University, 1999), 294–302.

11. James S. Corum, "The Luftwaffe and Lessons Learned in the Spanish Civil War," in *Air Power History: Turning Points from Kitty Hawk to Kosovo*, Sebastian Cox and Peter Gray, eds. (London: Frank Cass, 2003), 66–92.

12. Wilhelm Speidel, *Die Luftwaffe im Polenfeldzug 1939*, United States Air Force Historical Research Agency (henceforth USAF HRA), Karlsruhe Collection, Doc. K 113.106–151, 18.

13. Hans Detlef Herhudt von Rohden, ed., *Luftkrieg Heft 5: Die Planung und Vorbereirung des Luftkriegs gegen Polen 1939*. Ms., Air University Library, November 1946, II. This document provides a good overview of the Luftwaffe's plans and preparations for the Polish campaign.

14. Oberbefehlshaber der Luftwaffe (signed Jeschonnek), *Richtlinien für den Einsatz der Fliegertruppe zur unmittelbaren Unterstützung des Heeres*, 1 August 1939. In NARA T-321, Roll 76.

15. Ibid., para. 1.

16. Ibid., para. 15–16.

17. Ibid., para. 12.

18. Ibid., para. 14.

19. Ibid., para. 22.

20. The Luftwaffe plans for the Polish campaign are set out in Oberbefehlshaber der Luftwaffe, *Planstudie 1939: Weisungen für den Einsatz gegen Osten*, May 1939, in NARA T-821, Roll 176.

21. Von Richthofen's diary, 27 August 1939.

22. Further discussions of the Luftwaffe plan and details concerning the employment of the Special Purpose Division are found in Bundesarchiv/Militärarchiv Freiburg (henceforth BA/MA) RL 7/160, *Generalstabsresise 1939*, Anlage 1, "Besprechung des 1. Speiltages der Generalstabsresise," 29 June 1939.

23. Reichminister der Luftfahrt und Oberbefehlshaber der Luftwaffe, "Bemerkungen des Oberbefehlshabers der Luftwaffe zur Ausbildung und zu den Übungen im Jahre 1935," in NARA T-177, Roll 1, 4 January 1936, 6.

24. Luftwaffe Dienstvorschrift 7, *Richtlinien für die Ausbildung in der Luftwaffe*, part 6, Berlin (1937), paragraph 17.

25. The Luftwaffe close air support doctrine was outlined in Oberbefehlshaber der Luftwaffe, *Richtlinien für den Einsatz der Fliegertruppe zur unmittelbaren Unterstützung des Heeres*, Air Staff, Berlin, 1 August 1939.

26. The Luftwaffe's primary forward logistics doctrine is set out in Luftwaffe Dienstvorschrift G 90, *Die Versorgung der Luftwaffe im Kriege* (1938), translated in Corum and Muller, *The Luftwaffe's Way of War*, 186–191.

27. For an excellent overview of the Polish air force in the 1930s and in the 1939 campaign, see Michael Peszke, "The Forgotten Campaign: Poland's Military Aviation in September 1939," *Polish Review* 39, 1 (1994): 51–72. See also Michael Alfred Peszke, "Poland's Military Aviation, September 1939: It Never Had a Chance," in *Why Air Forces Fail*, Robin Higham and Stephen Harris, eds. (Lexington: University of Kentucky Press, 2006), 13–40.

28. Norman Franks, *Aircraft versus Aircraft* (London: Grub Street, 1999), 70.

29. For a useful account of the Polish campaign from Polish sources, see Adam Zamoyski, *The Forgotten Few: The Polish Air Force in the Second World War* (New York: Hippocrene, 1995), 17–33.

30. Von Richthofen's diary, 4 September 1939.

31. Hooten, *Phoenix Triumphant*, 181–182.

32. On 2 September von Richthofen noted that the Polish air force was scarcely to be seen. Von Richthofen's diary, 2 September 1939.

33. Hooten, *Phoenix Triumphant*, 183–184.

34. Ibid., 184.

35. Citino, *The German Way of War*, 262–264.

36. Hooten, *Phoenix Triumphant*, 186.

37. Ibid.
38. Von Richthofen's diary, 4 September 1939.
39. Von Richthofen's diary, 6 September 1939.
40. Von Richthofen's diary, 4 September 1939.
41. Hooten, *Phoenix Triumphant*, 187.
42. In the 25 September attack on Warsaw the Luftwaffe dropped 560 tons of high explosive and 72 tons of incendiary bombs. Only two Ju 52s were lost in the attack. See Hooten, *Phoenix Triumphant*, 188.
43. Ibid. On the French air attaché's comments, see Mike Spick, *Luftwaffe Bomber Aces* (London: Greenhill, 2001), 40.
44. For the 20,000 figure, see "Wir warden sie ausradieren," *Der Spiegel* 3, 13 (13 January 2003): 123. Hooten gives the figure of 40,000 Poles killed. See Hooten, *Phoenix Triumphant*, 188.
45. James S. Corum, *Inflated by Air: Common Perceptions of Civilian Casualties by Bombing*. Air War College thesis (Maxwell Air Force Base, AL: Air University, April 1998), 14–15.
46. Adolf Galland and Karl Ries, *Die Deutsche Luftwaffe, 1939–1945* (Dornheim: Podzun Verlag, 2000), 19.
47. For a good overview of the Polish campaign and the Luftwaffe's doctrine and role, see Klaus Maier, "Totaler Krieg und Operativer Luftkrieg," and Horst Rohde, "Hitler's Erster Blitzkrieg und seine Auswirkung auf Nordosteuropa," in *Das Deutsche Reich und der Zweite Weltkrieg, Band 2*, Klaus Maier, Horst Rohde, Bernd Stegemann, and Hans Umbriet, eds. (Stuttgart: Deutsche Verlags-Anstalt, 1979).
48. Examples of the tactical directives outlining lessons from the Polish campaign sent by Luftwaffe headquarters to the air fleets are found in Luftwaffe General Staff, Operations Branch, Richtlinien (Directives) to Luftflotte 2 (October 1939–January 1939). See NARA T-321, Roll 172.
49. "Taktik Luftwaffe: Taktische Erfahrungen Nr. 2. Ausfertigung für Führungsstellen," circa October 1939, in BA/MA RL 2 II/280, 15.
50. For a good analysis of the Luftwaffe's communications system in the Polish campaign, see Karl Klee, "Die Luftnachrichtentruppe im Feldzug gegen Polen," *Wehrwissenschaftliche Rundschau* 4 (1954): 71–123. The Luftwaffe deployed 70,000 signal troops for the campaign with five Luftwaffe signals regiments deployed as well as parts of two others.
51. Speidel, *Die Luftwaffe im Polenfeldzug*, K113.106–151, 157–158.
52. Ibid., 149.
53. Williamson Murray, "The Luftwaffe Experience, 1939–1941," in *Case Studies in the Development of Close Air Support*, Benjamin Franklin Cooling, ed. (Washington, DC: Office of USAF History, 1990), 78–79.
54. Ibid., 81.
55. Herhudt von Rohden, *Luftkrieg Heft 5*, II.
56. Speidel, *Die Luftwaffe im Polenfeldzug*, 9–11.
57. Speidel, *The Campaign for Western Europe, Part 1*, 144.
58. Green, *The Warplanes of the Third Reich*, 382.
59. On German flak in Poland, see Horst-Adalbert Koch, *Die Geschichte der Deutschen Flakartillerie, 1933–1945* (Bad Nauheim: Verlag Hans-Henning, 1955), 35–36.
60. Ibid.
61. Ibid., 38.

Chapter 7. The Battle for France, 1940

1. Bundesarchiv/Militärarchiv Freiburg (henceforth BA/MA) RL 8/43 Kriegstagebuch VIII Fliegerkorps Mai 1940. Anlage 1.
2. Hans Ring and Werner Girbig, *Jagdgeschwader 27* (Stuttgart: Motorbuch Verlag, 1991), 19.
3. In February 1945 she refused to flee from her estate as the Russian army advanced through Poland toward Silesia. Luise was seventy-eight years old and had no desire to be a refugee. She had always been active in the community and had a reputation for charitable work among both the German and ethnic Polish population of Silesia, and she believed that the Silesians would allow no harm to come to her. She was right. Although the estate was collectivized after the Soviets occupied the region, she was allowed to live on in the manor house and the neighbors who had not fled from the Russians made sure she was cared for.
4. Karl-Heinz Frieser, *Blitzkrieg-Legende: Der Westfeldzug, 1940* (Munich: Oldenbourg Verlag, 1995), 57.
5. Ibid.
6. Enzo Angelucci, *The Rand McNally Encyclopedia of Military Aircraft* (New York: Gallery, 1990), 222.
7. Charles Christienne and Pierre Lissarague, *A History of French Military Aviation* (Washington, DC: Smithsonian Institution Press, 1986), 326.
8. The Bloch 152 fighter, a mainstay of the Armeé de l'Air in 1940, had a maximum speed of 316 mph and an armament of two 20mm cannon and two machine guns. It was slower than even the German Me 110 heavy fighter. See Kenneth Munson, *Fighters, 1939–45* (London: Blandford, 1969), 39.
9. Christienne and Lissarague, *History of French Military Aviation*, 329.
10. According to Emmanuel Chadeau, *De Blériot à Dassault: Histoire de l'Industrie Aéronautique en France, 1900–1950* (Paris: Fayard, 1987), 343, "In May 1940... the French forces employed 23 aircraft types, 38 models in 42 versions."
11. The Amiot 143 bomber, used by the French in 1940, was designed in the late 1920s and had a maximum speed of 193 mph and a bomb load of 1,300 kg. The Bloch 210 was designed in 1932 and had a maximum speed of 200 mph and a bomb load of 1,600 kg. The primary German bombers of 1940 were the Heinkel He 111 and the Dornier Do 17. The He 111 had a maximum speed of 252 mph and a bomb load of 2,500 kg. The Do 17 was faster, at 255 mph. Both clearly outclassed most of the French. The only French bomber relatively equal to its German counterparts in 1940 was the Loire 45, roughly equivalent to the German He 111, Do 17, and Junkers 88 bombers. The LO 45 (also known as the Leo 451) was a good medium bomber with a maximum speed of 250 mph and a bomb load of 1,500 kg. Although it compared well with German aircraft in 1940, only five were operational as of September 1939, and perhaps only 110 were operational by June 1940. See Angelucci, *Rand McNally Encyclopedia of Military Aircraft*, 281–282.
12. Ibid., 328–333. On 14 May 1940 the French would throw the Amiot 143 bombers at the German bridgehead across the Meuse at Sedan. The Amiots suffered heavy losses. Of nineteen bombers in the 14 May attack, seven were lost. See Christienne and Lissarague, *History of French Military Aviation*, 348.
13. David Griffin, "The Battle of France 1940," *Aerospace Historian* (Fall 1974): 144–153. See especially 147.
14. See Christienne and Lissarague, *History of French Military Aviation*, 336–370.

15. Although the French air force had no radar program, the French navy had one for shipboard use. By 1939 the French had developed seaborne radar for the Liner Normandie. See Kenneth Macksey, *Technology in War* (New York: Prentice-Hall, 1986), 120.

16. See Thierry Vivier, "Les Réservistes de l'Air (1919–1939)," *Revue Historique des Armeés* 174 (March 1989): 63–76.

17. Christienne and Lissarague, *History of French Military Aviation*, 335.

18. On the problems of the RAF airfields and poor infrastructure in France in 1940, see Robin Higham, *Bases of Air Strategy: Building Airfields for the RAF, 1939–1945* (Shrewsbury, UK: Airlife, 1998), 107–112.

19. Michael Forget, "Die Zusammenarbeit zwischen Luftwaffe und Heer bei den Französischen und deutschen Luftstreitkräften im Zweiten Weltkrieg," in *Luftkriegführung im Zweiten Weltkrieg*, Horst Boog, ed. (Herford, Germany: E. S. Mittler, 1993), 497–525; see especially 511–512.

20. Florian Rothbrust, *Guderian's XIXth Panzer Corps and the Battle for France* (Westport, CT: Praeger, 1990), 40–42.

21. Ibid., 42–43.

22. BA/MA N 671/5, Nachlass von Richthofen, Kriegstagebuch der VIII Fliegerkorps 5.10.39–9.5.40, 8.

23. Williamson Murray, "The Luftwaffe Experience, 1939–1941," in *Case Studies in the Development of Close Air Support*, Benjamin Franklin Cooling, ed. (Washington, DC: Office of Air Force History, 1990), 89.

24. BA/MA N 671/5, Nachlass von Richthofen, Kriegstagebuch der VIII Fliegerkorps 5.10.39–9.5.40, 6.

25. Ibid., 9–10.

26. Bernard Montgomery, *The Memoirs of Field Marshal Montgomery* (New York: Signet, 1958), 43.

27. Ibid., 43, 49.

28. Anthony Cain, *The Forgotten Air Force: French Air Doctrine in the 1930s* (Washington, DC: Smithsonian Institution Press, 2002), 124.

29. Alistair Horne, *To Lose a Battle: France 1940* (New York: Penguin, 1969), 217.

30. Ferdinand Otto Miksche, *Vom Kriegsbild* (Stuttgart: Seewald, 1976), 149.

31. Horne, *To Lose a Battle*, 218.

32. Ibid.

33. Ibid., 219–220. On the French antiaircraft arm, see Robert Frankenstein, *Le Prix du Réarmament Français, 1935–1939* (Paris: Publications de la Sorbonne, 1982). The French lagged behind in the development of antiaircraft guns. In the 14-billion-franc rearmament program of September 1936, only 4.3 percent of the equipment funds were devoted to antiaircraft defense. Up to 1940, the mainstay of the French antiaircraft force was a slightly improved 75 mm gun from World War I. The armament programs of 1937–1939 funded only 356 new 75 mm antiaircraft guns. See also Ministère de la Defense, *Les Programmes d'Armament* (Chateua de Vincennes, 1982), 182–183.

34. See Christienne and Lissarrague, *History of French Military Aviation*, 335.

35. Williamson Murray, *Strategy for Defeat* (Maxwell Air Force Base, AL: Air University Press, 1988), 43. See also Pierre Paquier, *l'Aviation de Bombardement Française en 1939–1940* (Paris: Berger-Levrault, 1948). See 8–9 and 208–235 for a log of French air activity between 10–20 May 1940.

36. Cited in Anthony Adamthwaite, *France and the Coming of the Second World War* (London: Frank Cass, 1977), 162.

37. Martin Alexander, *The Republic in Danger: General Maurice Gamelin and the Politics of French Defense, 1933–1940* (Cambridge, UK: Cambridge University Press, 1992), 150.

38. Ibid., 163.

39. On the weakness of French air doctrine see Anthony Cain, "L'Armeé de l'Air, 1933–1940: Drifting toward Defeat," in *Why Air Forces Fail*, Robin Higham and Stephen Harris, eds. (Lexington: University Press of Kentucky, 2006).

40. See R. J. Overy, "Air Power, Armies, and the War in the West, 1940," in *The Harmon Memorial Lectures* (Colorado Springs: United States Air Force Academy, 1989), 1–24. See especially 8–10.

41. BA/MA RL 2 II/3 Luftwaffe General Staff, *Planstudie 1939 Heft II*, 1–6.

42. See Erich von Manstein, *Lost Victories* (Novato: Presidio, 1982). On the original plan, see 95–98. On the development of the 1940 campaign plan, see 105–126. See also Robert Citino, *The German Way of War* (Lawrence: University Press of Kansas, 2005), 273–279.

43. On 10 May, forty-seven airfields in France, fifteen in Belgium, and ten in Holland were attacked. Von Richthofen's units concentrated on airfields in Belgium, where they had considerable success. In Holland, seventy-five Dutch aircraft were destroyed on the ground. See Mike Spick, *Luftwaffe Bomber Aces* (London: Greenhill, 2001), 55–57.

44. Horne, *To Lose a Battle*, 338.

45. Von Richthofen's diary, 12 May 1940.

46. The most detailed account of the Sedan battle of 1940 is Robert Doughty, *The Breaking Point* (Hamden, CT: Archon, 1990).

47. Von Richthofen's diary, 15 May 1940.

48. Williamson Murray, "The Luftwaffe against Poland and the West," in Cooling, *Case Studies in the Achievement of Air Superiority*, 65–114. See 83.

49. Martin Middlebrook and Chris Everitt, *The Bomber Command War Diaries* (London: Penguin, 1985), 43.

50. Murray, "The Luftwaffe against Poland and the West," 83.

51. Horne, *To Lose a Battle*, 474–475.

52. W. Speidel, *The Campaign for Western Europe, Part 1*, United States Air Force Historical Research Agency, Karlsruhe Collection, Doc. K 113.107-152, 171.

53. Ibid., 185–186.

54. Horne, *To Lose a Battle*, 481–482, 527–528.

55. Spick, *Luftwaffe Bomber Aces*, 62–63.

56. Speidel, *The Campaign for Western Europe*, 156.

57. In May 1940 the French fighter force flew an average of 0.9 sorties per day and the bombers only 0.25 sorties per day. See Overy, "Air Power, Armies, and the War in the West," 1–24. See especially 13.

58. E. R. Hooton, *Phoenix Triumphant: The Rise and Rise of the Luftwaffe* (London: Arms and Armour Press, 1994), 258.

59. Ibid., 256. On 12 May the Luftwaffe began flying supplies to Guderian's XIX Corps armored spearhead. On that day Luftwaffe aircraft delivered twenty-seven tons of fuel to keep Guderian's forward units moving.

60. Ibid., 256–257.

61. Von Richthofen's diary, 20 May 1940.

62. Von Richthofen's diary, 24 May 1940.
63. Von Richthofen's diary, 25 May 1940.
64. Heinz Guderian, *Panzer Leader* (New York: Ballantine, 1987), 94.
65. Hooten, *Phoenix Triumphant*, 257.
66. Herbert Mason, *The Rise of the Luftwaffe* (New York: Signet, 1973), 353.
67. Ibid., 353–357. See also Karl-Heinz Frieser, *Blitzkrieg-Legende* (Munich: Oldenbourg Verlag, 1995), 386–388.
68. Mason, *The Rise of the Luftwaffe*, 354. On 27 May the Luftwaffe lost 24 of 225 bombers sent against Dunkirk. It was one of the most costly days of the campaign for the Luftwaffe. See Ernst Bombek, *Jagdwaffe: Attack in the West, May 1940* (Crowborough, East Sussex, UK: Classic, 2000), 36–37.
69. Von Richthofen's diary, 27 May 1940.
70. Ibid.
71. Hooten, *Phoenix Triumphant*, 261.
72. Mason, *The Rise of the Luftwaffe*, 356.
73. For a good summary of the last phase of the battle for France, see Horne, *To Lose a Battle*, 621–645.
74. Hooten, *Phoenix Triumphant*, 261.
75. Ibid., 261–265.
76. Cain, "L'Armeé de l'Air, 1933–1940," 126.
77. Hooten, *Phoenix Triumphant*, 263–265.
78. Cain, "L'Armeé de l'Air, 1933–1940," 126.
79. Griffin, "The Battle of France 1940," 143–153. See especially 147.
80. French Air Minister Pierre Cot reported that the strength of the air force at the start of the war was approximately 2,100 planes and that after 22 June the French had 4,238 planes on the continent and a further 1,800 in North Africa—*after* losses of 2,000 aircraft in combat. See Cain, "L'Armeé de l'Air, 1933–1940," 132.
81. Koch, *Die Geschichte der Deutschen Flakartillerie*, 42–43.
82. Ibid.
83. In his monograph *The Campaign for Western Europe*, Speidel provides a thorough description of von Richthofen's command and operations in the May and June battles.
84. Speidel, *The Campaign for Western Europe*, 181.
85. Spick, *Luftwaffe Bomber Aces*, 61.

Chapter 8. The Battle of Britain—The Luftwaffe's First Defeat

1. Luftwaffe Kommando 2, "Schlussbesprechung des Planspiels 1939," signed General Felmy, 13 May 1939, in Bundesarchiv/Militärarchiv Freiburg (henceforth BA/MA) RL 7/43.
2. In 1940 Germany produced 10,247 aircraft. The U.K. produced 15,049 aircraft. See Richard J. Overy, *The Air War, 1939–1945* (Chelsea: Scarborough House, 1980), 77.
3. On the German policy toward Spain in 1940, see Norman Goda, *Tomorrow the World: Hitler, Northwest Africa, and the Path toward America* (College Station: Texas A&M Press, 1998), 62–64.
4. Ibid. On Germany and the Spanish strategy, see Andreas Hillgruber, *Hitlers Strategie: Politik und Kriegführung, 1940–1941* (Munich: Bernard und Graefe Verlag, 1982), 184–185.
5. Von Richthofen's diary, 15 August and 9 September 1940.

6. For a description of the Chain Home radar system and RAF Fighter Command communications, see Alfred Price, *Blitz on Britain, 1939–1945* (Stroud, UK: Sutton, 2000), 5–6. Several books provide excellent description and analysis of the RAF defense system and tactics in the Battle of Britain: see especially Derek Wood and Derek Dempster, *The Narrow Margin: Battle of Britain, 1940* (Washington, DC: Smithsonian Institution Press, 1990); Richard Overy, *The Battle of Britain: The Myth and the Reality* (New York: W. W. Norton, 2000); Len Deighton, *Fighter: The True Story of the Battle of Britain* (London: Harper Collins, 1977); and John Ray, *The Battle of Britain* (London: Cassells, 1994).

7. Wood and Dempster, *The Narrow Margin*. On Luftwaffe intelligence on Britain, see 64–71.

8. For a good overview of the RAF leaders in the Battle of Britain, see Ray, *The Battle of Britain*.

9. Wood and Dempster, *The Narrow Margin*, 170.

10. Ibid.

11. E. R. Hooton, *Eagle in Flames: The Fall of the Luftwaffe* (London: Arms and Armour Press, 1997), 42.

12. Von Richthofen noted in his diary that his units had sunk eight large ships and hit ten others, with one loss due to flak. "A really fine initial effort!" Von Richthofen's diary, 4 July 1940.

13. Richard Townsend Bickers, *The Battle of Britain* (London: Salamander, 1997), 209.

14. Ibid., 209–212.

15. Ibid., 212–213.

16. Wood and Dempster, *The Narrow Margin*, 182–184.

17. Hooton, *Eagle in Flames*, 43–44.

18. Ibid., 43.

19. Ibid.

20. Wood and Dempster, *The Narrow Margin*, 184–185.

21. Hooton, *Eagle in Flames*, 44.

22. Von Richthofen's diary, 17 July 1940.

23. Price, *Blitz on Britain*, 50.

24. Wood and Dempster, *The Narrow Margin*, 164.

25. Ibid., 201–203.

26. Ibid.

27. Ibid., 209–211.

28. Olaf Groehler, *Geschichte des Luftkrieges* (Berlin: Militärverlag der DDR, 1981), 267. Summaries of Fighter Command operational aircraft in summer 1940: 3 August, 708; 10 August, 749; 17 August, 704; 24 August, 758; 31 August, 764; 7 September, 746; 14 September, 725; and 21 September, 715.

29. Wood and Dempster, *The Narrow Margin*, 209.

30. Ibid., 209–211.

31. Price, *Blitz on Britain*, 69.

32. Richard Hough and Denis Richards, *The Battle of Britain* (New York: W. W. Norton, 1990), 214–216.

33. Von Richthofen's diary, 18 August 1940. Von Richthofen noted that Stuka Geschwader 77 "had its feathers well and truly plucked."

34. Hough and Richards, *The Battle of Britain*, 216–217.

35. Price, *Blitz on Britain*, 72.

36. E. R. Hooten, *Phoenix Triumphant: The Rise and Rise of the Luftwaffe* (London: Arms and Armour Press, 1994), 44.

Chapter 9. The Balkans Campaign, 1941

1. For the best analysis of the Italian armed forces in 1940, see Brian Sullivan, "The Italian Armed Forces, 1918–40," in *Military Effectiveness*, vol. 2, *The Interwar Period*, Allan Millett and Williamson Murray, eds. (Boston: Unwin Hyman, 1988), 169–217. For a general overview of the Italian forces from 1940–1943, see MacGregor Knox, "The Italian Armed Forces, 1940–3," in *Military Effectiveness*, vol. 3, *World War II*, Allan Millett and Williamson Murray, eds. (Boston: Unwin Hyman, 1988), 136–179.

2. Chef des Generalstab der Luftwaffe, *Gedanken zur Luftlage in Europe* (early 1939), in United States Air Force Historical Research Agency (henceforth USAF HRA), Karlsruhe Collection, Doc. K 113.3111, vol. 2, 34.

3. Ibid.

4. Maj. Gen Burkhart Mueller-Hillebrand, *Germany and Her Allies in World War II*, U.S. Army History Study, circa 1946. Part I, 114.

5. Richard DiNardo, *Germany and the Axis Powers: From Coalition to Collapse* (Lawrence: University Press of Kansas, 2005), 72–76. DiNardo offers a detailed analysis of German-Italian relations in the Mediterranean strategy of World War II.

6. E. R. Hooten, *Eagle in Flames: The Fall of the Luftwaffe* (London: Arms and Armour Press, 1997), 78.

7. For an excellent strategic overview of the campaign, see Bernd Stegemann, "Die Rückeroberung der Cyrenaica und das Scheitern der Angriff auf Tobruk," in *Das Deutsche Reich und der Zweite Weltkrieg*, band 3, Gerhard Schreiber and Bernd Stegemann, eds. (Stuttgart: Deutsche Verlags-Anstalt, 1984), 615–630.

8. Hooten, *Eagle in Flames*, 80.

9. Christopher Shores and Brian Cull with Nicola Malizia, *Air War for Yugoslavia, Greece, and Crete, 1940–41* (London: Grub House, 1987), 171. This book is the best general overview of the air campaign in the Balkans in 1941.

10. Hooton, *Eagle in Flames*, 80.

11. Kriegstagebuch VIIIth Fliegerkorps 1941, Bundesarchiv/Militärarchiv Freiburg (henceforth BA/MA) RL 8/237, 10–14.

12. Hooton, *Eagle in Flames*, 80.

13. Von Richthofen's diary, 16 March 1941.

14. Von Richthofen's diary, 17 March 1941. Von Richthofen also remarked on the high quality of the French horses when he was stationed in Normandy in the summer of 1940.

15. Von Richthofen's diary, 18 March 1941.

16. Shores, Cull, and Malizia, *Air War for Yugoslavia*, 170.

17. Von Richthofen's diary, 23 March 1941.

18. A good strategic overview of the Balkans campaign is Klaus Olshausen, *Zwischenspiel Auf Dem Balkan* (Stuttgart: Deutsche Verlags-Anstalt, 1973).

19. Hooten, *Eagle in Flames*, 80–83.

20. Robin Higham, *Diary of a Disaster: British Aid to Greece, 1940–1941* (Lexington: University Press of Kentucky, 1986), 209.

21. See Shores, Cull and Malizia, *Air War for Yugoslavia*, 22–25. In Albania the Regia Aeronautica had fifty-five Savoia S 81 and S 79 bombers and sixty Fiat Cr 32 and Cr 42

fighters. The Italian fighters were obsolescent but a rough match for Greece's fighter force. In southern Italy the Regia Aeronautica had more modern Cant 2100 bombers, Fiat Br 20 bombers and twelve Macchi C 200 and thirty-three Fiat G 33 fighters—the most modern fighters in the Italian inventory. These fighters were far superior to anything the Greeks had and equal to the RAF's Hurricanes. The Italians also had a force of twenty Ju 87 B Stukas acquired from the Germans. As with the Germans, the Italians had trained their Stuka crews as an elite force to specialize in antishipping strikes.

22. Shores, Cull, Malizia, *Air War for Yugoslavia*, provides a detailed order of battle information for all the air forces involved in the Balkans campaign of 1941. On the Greek air force, see 8–9.
23. Hooten, *Eagle in Flames*, 81.
24. Ibid.
25. Ibid.
26. Ibid.
27. Kriegstagebuch VIIIth Fliegerkorps 1941, BA/MA RL 8/46, 32.
28. Klaus Olshausen, *Zwischenspiel auf dem Balkan*, 98–99.
29. Higham, *Diary of a Disaster*, 222.
30. Kriegstagebuch VIIIth Fliegerkorps 1941, BA/MA RL 8/237, 63–64.
31. Ibid., RL 8/46, 39.
32. Ibid., RL 8/46, 42.
33. Ibid., RL 8/237, 64–65.
34. Higham, *Diary of a Disaster*, 228–229.
35. Ibid., 231.
36. For a list of Allied ships lost in the Greek and Crete campaigns, see Shores, Cull and Malizia, *Air War for Yugoslavia*, 405–407.
37. Hooten, *Luftwaffe in Flames*, 84.
38. Ibid., 84.
39. Ibid., 85.
40. Ibid., 84.
41. Ibid.
42. Mike Spick, *Luftwaffe Bomber Aces* (London: Greenhill, 2001), 124–125.
43. Hooten, *Luftwaffe in Flames*, 86.
44. Brig. General Hans-Joachim Rath, Report, *The 1st Stuka Wing in the Mediterranean Theater, Feb.-May 1941*, Study D-064 EUCOM Headquarters, Chief Historian European Command. Circa 1946.
45. Hooten, *Luftwaffe in Flames*, 86.
46. Spick, *Luftwaffe Bomber Aces*, 126.
47. Shores, Cull, and Malizia, *Air War for Yugoslavia*, 402, 408–409.
48. See Maj. General S. O. Playfair, *History of the Second World War: The Mediterranean and Middle East*, vol. 2 (London: HMSO, 1956), 2, 104.
49. Ibid., 121–151.
50. Hooten, *Luftwaffe in Flames*, 86.

Chapter 10. The Soviet Campaign Opens, 1941–1942

1. On aircraft numbers, the failure of German production, and the Allied aircraft production, see R. J. Overy, *The Air War, 1939–1945* (Chelsea: Scarborough House, 1991), 50, 71.

2. E. R. Hooten, *Eagle in Flames: The Fall of the Luftwaffe* (London: Brockhampton, 1999), 92–93.

3. In 1941 the Romanian air force fielded approximately 500 aircraft, with its main strength being 104 bombers (including twenty-one He 111s, fourteen Savioa 79s, nine Pzl-37s, fourteen Potez 63s, and fourteen Bristol Blenheims) and 170 fighters (including twenty He 112s, thirty Me 109s, fifty-four Pzl-11s, twenty Pzl-24s, and ten Hurricanes). The Finnish air force had 559 aircraft with Bristol Blenheim bombers and a fighter force consisting of Hurricanes, Gladiators, Curtiss Hawk 75s, Brewster Buffalos, Fiat G-50s, and Morane-Saulnier 406s. Hungary could field 326 combat aircraft with a small bomber force equipped with Italian Caproni 101, 135, and 310 bombers and a fighter force equipped with Fiat Cr 32s, Cr 42s, and Reggiane Re 2000s. Slovakia also had a small air force of 171 aircraft, with one group of biplane fighters equipped with Avia B 534s and a reconnaissance group equipped with Letov S-328s. This common mix of small numbers of British, German, Italian, Polish, French, Czech, and U.S. aircraft—not to mention Romania's aircraft designed and built by its indigenous aircraft industry—meant that maintenance was a constant struggle and that aircraft serviceability rates were consequently very low. For a detailed overview of Germany's allied air forces and their effectiveness in the Soviet campaign, see James S. Corum, "The Luftwaffe and Its Allied Air Forces in World War II: Parallel War and the Failure of Strategic and Economic Cooperation," *Air Power History* 51, 2 (summer 2004): 4–19.

4. Hooten, *Eagle in Flames*, 94.

5. For a general overview of German strategy and intelligence in 1941, see Geoffrey Megargee, *War of Annihilation: Combat and Genocide on the Eastern Front, 1941* (Lawrence: University Press of Kansas, 2006).

6. For a general overview of the Soviet air force in 1941, see Kenneth Whiting, "The Soviet Air Force against Germany and Japan," in *Case Studies in the Achievement of Air Superiority*, Benjamin Franklin Cooling, eds. (Washington: Office for Air Force History, 1994), 179–222.

7. Whiting, "The Soviet Air Force against Germany and Japan," 200.

8. One German fighter pilot told me that to shoot down an IL-2 you had to aim directly for the small radiator intake—the only vulnerable point on the aircraft. A hit there would hit the fuel or damage the engine. One had to be an exceptional marksman with a fighter to hit the IL-2's vulnerable spot. The German pilot, who had shot down a large number of Soviet planes, commented on the Shturmovik, "I only got two of them."

9. Earl Ziemke and Magna Bauer, *Moscow to Stalingrad: Decision in the East* (Washington, DC: Center of Military History, United States Army, 1987), 7.

10. Hooten, *Eagle in Flames*, 92–93.

11. Richard Muller, *The German Air War in Russia* (Baltimore: Nautical and Aviation Press, 1992).

12. For a good overview of the German logistics for the 1941 USSR campaign, see Martin van Creveld, *Supplying War* (Cambridge: Cambridge University Press, 1977), 142–180.

13. Ziemke and Bauer, *Moscow to Stalingrad*, 14.

14. Hooten, *Eagle in Flames*, 95–96.

15. Whiting, "The Soviet Air Force against Germany and Japan," 188–189.

16. Hooten, *Eagle in Flames*, 96.

17. Ibid.

18. Ziemke and Bauer, *Moscow to Stalingrad*, 27–28.

19. Hooten, *Eagle in Flames*, 97. See also Ziemke and Bauer, *Moscow to Stalingrad*, 32.
20. Christopher Bergström and Andrey Mikhailov, *Black Cross, Red Star. Air War over the Eastern Front*, vol. 1 (Pacifica, CA: Pacifica Military History, 2000), 116, 129.
21. Bergström and Mikhailov, *Black Cross, Red Star*, 84.
22. Ibid., 95.
23. On the German advance to Leningrad in 1941, see David Glantz, *The Battle for Leningrad, 1941–1944* (Lawrence: University Press of Kansas, 2002).
24. Lt. General Hermann Plocher, *The German Air Force versus Russia, 1941 – USAF Historical Study No. 153* (USAF Historical Division, Air University, New York: Arno, 1965), 147.
25. Glantz, *The Battle for Leningrad*, 98.
26. Plocher, *German Air Force versus Russia*, 147.
27. Bergström and Mikhailov, *Black Cross, Red Star*, 186.
28. Ibid.
29. Ibid., 186–187.
30. Hooten, *Eagle in Flames*, 98.
31. Ibid., 101.
32. Ibid., 102.
33. Ibid., 103.
34. Plocher, *German Air Force versus Russia*, 240.
35. David Glantz, *Soviet Military Deception in the Second World War* (London: Frank Cass, 1989). For a good description of the Soviet plans and buildup for the winter offensive, see 47–57.
36. Hooten, *Eagle in Flames*, 103.
37. Ibid.
38. Glantz, *Soviet Military Deception in the Second World War*, 47.
39. Ibid., 50–52.
40. General Guderian had begun the campaign with 1,000 tanks in his panzer group in June. By mid-November 1941 he reported that he had no more than 150 serviceable vehicles.
41. Glantz, *Soviet Military Deception in the Second World War*, 22–23.
42. Fliegerkorps VIII Tagebuch Russland-Mittelabschnitt, Bundesarchiv/Militärarchiv Freiburg (henceforth BA/MA) RL 8/49.
43. Helmut Heiber and David Glantz, *Hitler and His Generals: Military Conferences, 1942–1945* (New York: Enigma, 2002); published in German as *Hitler's Lagebesprechungen* (Stuttgart: Deutsche Verlags-Anstalt, 1964), 803. General Förster was cleared by an honor court of ordering a withdrawal and was given other duties.
44. Fliegerkorps VIII Tagebuch Russland-Mittelabschnitt, BA/MA RL 8/49, entry for 28 December 1941.
45. Ibid., entry for 2 December 1941.
46. Ibid., entry for December 1941.
47. Hooten, *Eagle in Flames*, 104.
48. Glantz, *Soviet Military Deception in the Second World War*, 23–24.
49. Von Hardesty, *Red Phoenix: The Rise of Soviet Air Power, 1941–1945* (Washington, DC: Smithsonian Institution Press, 1982), 82, 89.
50. Fliegerkorps VIII Tagebuch Russland-Mittelabschnitt, BA/MA RL 8/49, entry for 28 February 1942.
51. Ibid., RL 8/49, entry for 1 March 1942.

52. Overy, *The Air War*, 77.
53. Whiting, "The Soviet Air Force against Germany and Japan," 198–199.

Chapter 11. The Campaign in the Soviet Union, 1942–1943

1. Joel Hayward, *Stopped at Stalingrad: The Luftwaffe and Hitler's Defeat in the East, 1942–1943* (Lawrence: University Press of Kansas, 1998), 6–7.
2. Ibid., 65–66.
3. Ibid., 64.
4. Ibid., 70–71.
5. U.S. Army Historical Study, Document D 256, EUCOM Historian, Reichs Labor Service on the Eastern Front, 1942. Circa 1947. 1–3.
6. Hayward, *Stopped at Stalingrad*, 72–73.
7. Ibid.
8. For the best general overview of the Luftwaffe's relations with its allies, see R. J. Overy, "The Luftwaffe and the European Economy, 1939–1945," *Militärgeschichtliches Mitteilungen* 21 (1979): 55–78. This article provides information about the aircraft production of Germany's allies. However, the main thrust of the article is about the Luftwaffe's use of captured industrial assets. Another useful article on this subject is Richard DiNardo, "The Dysfunctional Coalition: The Axis Powers and the Eastern Front in World War II," *Journal of Military History* (October 1996): 711–730. DiNardo discusses the German coalition command relationships in detail, but his emphasis is on ground operations.
9. A Romanian request to buy 50 Ju 87Bs was turned down by the air ministry in 1940. Between 1934 and 1940 several Hungarian missions to buy German aircraft resulted in the purchase of some older aircraft considered surplus to the Luftwaffe's needs. In 1939 Romanian overtures to license-build the Me 109 fighter and Junkers Jumo 211 aircraft engine were rebuffed. See Mark Axworthy, "On Three Fronts: Rumania's Aircraft Industry during World War II," *Air Enthusiast* 56 (Winter 1994): 15.
10. Martin Thomas, "To Arm an Ally: French Arms Sales to Rumania, 1926–1940," *Journal of Strategic Studies* (June 1996): 252.
11. Ibid., 164.
12. Hayward, *Stopped at Stalingrad*, 248.
13. Richard L. DiNardo, *Germany and the Axis Powers: From Coalition to Collapse* (Lawrence: University Press of Kansas, 2005), 106.
14. Joel Hayward, "A Case Study in Early Joint Warfare: An Analysis of the Wehrmacht's Crimean Campaign of 1941," *Journal of Strategic Studies* 22 (December 1999): 103–130. See 118.
15. Von Richthofen's diary, 22 April 1942.
16. Earl Ziemke and Magna Bauer, *Moscow to Stalingrad: Decision in the East* (Washington, DC: U.S. Army Center for Military History, 1987), 264.
17. Hayward, "A Case Study in Early Joint Warfare," 118; Ziemke and Bauer, *Moscow to Stalingrad*, 264.
18. Ziemke and Bauer, *Moscow to Stalingrad*, 264.
19. See the full text of "VIIIth Air Corps Directive: Instructions for the Cooperation of Ground Troops with Units of the VIIIth Fliegerkorps, 24 May 1942," and "VIIIth Air Corps Directive: Employment of Reconnaissance Units, 29 July 1942," in James Corum and Richard Muller, *The Luftwaffe's Way of War* (Baltimore: Nautical and Aviation Press, 1997), 217–227.
20. Ziemke and Bauer, *Moscow to Stalingrad*, 262.

21. Ibid., 269.
22. Ibid., 273–282.
23. Hayward, "A Case Study in Early Joint Warfare," 121–122.
24. Ibid.
25. Ibid., 119.
26. On the Sebastopol battle, see Ziemke and Bauer, *Moscow to Stalingrad*, 312–321.
27. An excellent overview of the summer 1942 campaign is found in Robert Citino, *Death of the Wehrmacht: The German Campaigns of 1942* (Lawrence: University Press of Kansas, 2007), 156–181.
28. Richard Muller, *The German Air War in Russia* (Baltimore: Nautical and Aviation Press, 1992), 89.
29. Hayward, *Stopped at Stalingrad*, 153.
30. DiNardo, *Germany and the Axis Powers*, 142.
31. See Bezw. Kuban, Erfolge der Luftwaffengruppe Kaukasus (25 November 1942 to 6 February 1943), in Bundesarchiv/Militärarchiv Freiburg RL 8/59.
32. For a history of this subject, see J. L. Roba and C. Craciunoiu, *Seaplanes over the Black Sea: German-Romanian Operations 1941–1944* (Bucharest: Editura Modelism, 1995).
33. Ziemke and Bauer, *Moscow to Stalingrad*, 382–397.
34. Ibid., 373–375.
35. Hayward, *Stopped at Stalingrad*, 175–179.
36. Mike Spick, *Luftwaffe Bomber Aces* (London: Greenhill, 2001), 142.
37. Citino, *Death of the Wehrmacht*, 153.
38. Hayward, *Stopped at Stalingrad*, 224.
39. Ibid., 219.
40. Lt. General Hermann Plocher, *The German Air Force versus Russia, 1942*. United States Air Force Historical Study 154 (New York: Arno, 1966), 246–248.
41. Muller, *The German Air War in Russia*, 91–92.
42. Erich von Manstein, *Verlorene Siege* (Bonn: Athenaum, 1955), 326.
43. For a summary of the Stalingrad campaign, see Ziemke and Bauer, *Moscow to Stalingrad*, 468–501.
44. An excellent analysis of the decision to supply Stalingrad by airlift is Joel Hayward, "Stalingrad: An Examination of Hitler's Decision to Airlift," *Airpower Journal* 11, 1 (Spring 1997): 21–37.
45. Fritz Morzik, *German Air Force Airlift Operations*. United States Air Force Historical Study 167 (Maxwell Air Force Base, AL: USAF Historical Division, Air University, 1961), 145–160.
46. Manfred Kehrig, *Stalingrad, Analyse und Documentation einer Schlacht: Beiträge zur militär und Kriegsgeschichte*, band 15 (Stuttgart: Deutsche Verlags-Anstalt, 1974), 163.
47. Hayward, *Stopped at Stalingrad*, 238.
48. Alexander Stahlberg, *Bounden Duty: The Memoirs of a German Officer, 1932–45* (London: Brassey's, 1990), 221–222.
49. Ibid., 222.
50. Ibid., 223.
51. Muller, *The German Air War in Russia*, 92–93.
52. Ibid., 96–98.
53. Von Hardesty, *Red Phoenix: The Rise of Soviet Air Power, 1941–1945* (Washington, DC: Smithsonian Institution Press, 1982), 108, 111.

54. Ibid., 110. Germans acknowledge the loss of 266 Ju 52s, 42 Ju 86s, 165 He 111s, 9 FW 200s, 5 He 177s, and 1 Ju 290.
55. Muller, *The German Air War in Russia*, 106.
56. Hayward, *Stopped at Stalingrad*, 318–319.
57. Ibid., 320–321.
58. Ibid.
59. Ibid.
60. Muller, *The German Air War in Russia*, 106–109.
61. Kenneth Whiting, "The Soviet Air Force against Germany and Japan," in *Case Studies in the Achievement of Air Superiority* (Washington, DC: Office of Air Force History, 1994), 204. On the improvements in Soviet tactics and equipment in 1943, see Lt. General Walter Schwabedissen, *The Russian Air Force in the Eyes of German Commanders*. USAF Historical Study 175 (Maxwell Air Force Base, AL: USAF Historical Division, Air University, 1960), 253–261.
62. Hardesty, *Red Phoenix*, 136–137. See also Muller, *The German Air War in Russia*, 109–110.
63. Spick, *Luftwaffe Bomber Aces*, 143–144.

Chapter 12. Von Richthofen's Last Campaign—Italy, 1943–1944

1. For a good overview of the tensions and relationships within the Luftwaffe general staff, see Horst Boog, *Die deutsche Luftwaffenführung, 1935–1945* (Stuttgart: Deutsche Verlags-Anstalt, 1982). On Jeschonnek and his career, see Richard Suchenwirth, *Command and Leadership in the German Air Force*, USAF Historical Study No. 174 (New York: Arno, 1969), 213–291.
2. Von Richthofen's diary, 11 June 1943.
3. Cited in Joseph Balkoski, *D-Day: June 6, 1944* (Mechanicsburg, PA: Stackpole, 2004), 34.
4. At the start of the war the German pilots went into combat with more than 250 hours total flight time, more than their RAF opponents. By 1943 German pilot training had been cut to 100–150 total flight hours while Allied pilots had 325–400 hours of flight time before they entered combat. James S. Corum, "Defeat of the Luftwaffe, 1935–1945," in *Why Air Forces Fail: The Anatomy of Defeat*, eds. Robin Higham and Stephen Harris, pp. 203–226 (Lexington: University Press of Kentucky, 2006), 219–220.
5. Interrogation report, "History of Italian Air Force." Intelligence Branch, Supreme Allied Headquarters, 1944–1945, in United States Air Force Historical Research Agency (henceforth USAF HRA) Doc. K 113.60–506.63/4–9. See 22.
6. General Paul Deichmann, ed., *Die deutsche Luftwaffe in Italien*. Monograph, April 1956. USAF HRA Doc. K113.310–8 1943–1945, part 1, 18–22.
7. Ibid., 25.
8. Burkhart Mueller-Hillebrand, *Germany and Its Allies in World War II: A Record of Axis Collaboration Problems* (Frederick, MD: University Publications of America, 1980), Part II, 35.
9. Ibid., 35–36.
10. Von Richthofen's diary, 12 July 1943.
11. Deichmann, *Die deutsche Luftwaffe in Italien*, part 2, 3.
12. Ibid.
13. Ibid., 5.

14. Ibid.
15. Ibid., 7.
16. Jonathan Thompson, *Italian Civil and Military Aircraft, 1930–1945* (Los Angeles: Aero Publishers, 1963, 299. For detailed statistics on the strength of the Italian air force in 1943, see Chris Dunning, *Courage Alone: The Italian Air Force, 1940–1943* (Aldershot, UK: Hikoki, 1998).
17. Deichmann, *Die deutsche Luftwaffe in Italien*, 36.
18. Von Richthofen's diary, 12 July 1943.
19. Ibid.
20. In his diary von Richthofen expresses continual distrust of the Italian high command and its intentions. General Paul Deichmann in his monograph on the Italian campaign, *Die deutsche Luftwaffe in Italien*, often describes the Italians as doing their best.
21. Deichmann, *Die deutsche Luftwaffe in Italien*, 37–40.
22. Ibid., 40–41.
23. Ibid., 53.
24. Ibid.
25. Von Richthofen's diary, 12 July 1943.
26. Deichmann, *Die deutsche Luftwaffe in Italien*, part 2, 13.
27. Ibid., 26.
28. On the German fighters in Sicily, see Adolf Galland, *The First and the Last* (New York: Henry Holt, 1954), 186–188.
29. Johannes Steinhoff, *Messerschmitts over Sicily* (Baltimore, MD: Nautical and Aviation Publishing, 1987), 43–46, 56.
30. Ibid., 189.
31. See Bundesarchiv/Militaerarchiv (henceforth BA/MA) Doc RL/2/II/305, "Lageberichte Air Fleet II," for the surviving reconnaissance reports of April–June 1943. The Germans only occasionally got reconnaissance planes over the major Allied ports in North Africa, such as Algiers, Oran, Bizerte, and Bone.
32. Deichmann, *Die deutsche Luftwaffe in Italien*, chapter 2, 1–3, and part 3, 45–47.
33. Von Richthofen's diary, 9 July 1943.
34. Ibid.
35. Ibid.
36. Von Richthofen's diary, 20 June 1943.
37. See Ewan Montagu, *The Man Who Never Was* (Philadelphia: Lippincott, 1954).
38. Lt. General Andreas Nielsen, "The German Air Force General Staff" (USAF Historical Study No. 173, 1959), 178–179.
39. Samuel Eliot Morison, *History of United States Naval Operations in World War II: Sicily, Salerno, Anzio, January 1943–June 1944* (New York: Little Brown, 1954), 69.
40. http://www.naval-history.net/WW2194306.htm, World War II, 1943, Sicily, Salerno, Italy, 4.
41. Morison, *History of United States Naval Operations*, 85.
42. Ibid., 88.
43. Ibid., 107–108.
44. Ibid., 164.
45. Harry L. Coles, "Participation of the Ninth and Twelfth Air Forces in the Sicilian Campaign, July–August 1943" (USAF Historical Study 37, 1945), 99.
46. USAF HRA Doc. SQ FI 307-HI, *307th Fighter Squadron Outline History* to 31 December 1943.

47. Ibid.
48. Brig. General C. J. Molony, *The Mediterranean and Middle East*, vol. 5 (London: HMSO, 1973), 66.
49. Morison, *History of United States Naval Operations*, 120.
50. Ibid., 158.
51. Ibid., 164–165.
52. Richard G. Davis, *Carl A. Spaatz and the Air War in Europe* (Washington, DC: Center for Air Force History, 1993), 241. The Allied planners had expected to lose as many as 300 ships to air attack.
53. Molony, *The Mediterranean and Middle East*, 48.
54. On the Allied air operations in the Sicily campaign, see Wesley Frank Craven and James Lea Cate, eds., *The Army Air Forces in World War II*, vol. 2, *Europe: Torch to Pointblank, August 1942 to December 1943* (1949; New imprint, Washington, DC: Office of Air Force History, 1983), 434–260.
55. Antonio Duma, *Quelli Del Cavallino Rampante: Storia Del 4 Stormo Caccia* (Rome: Edizioni Dell'Ateneo, 1980), 347–349.
56. Von Richthofen's diary, 10 July 1943.
57. Von Richthofen's diary, 11 July 1943.
58. Von Richthofen's diary, 12 July 1943.
59. Von Richthofen's diary, 13 and 14 July 1943.
60. Von Richthofen's diary, 15 July 1943.
61. See USAF HRA Doc. K 113.60, "Allied Supreme HQ Intelligence Report on German Air Force Air Transport." Circa 1946. The Germans used seven transport groups to reinforce Sicily. Air transports were also used to successfully evacuate German forces from Sardinia and Corsica.
62. See http://www.naval-history.net and David Brown, *Warship Losses of World War II* (Annapolis, MD: Naval Institute Press, 1990), 87–88.
63. Von Richthofen's diary, 27 July 1943.
64. Ibid.
65. Deichmann, *Die deutsche Luftwaffe in Italien*, part 3, 71–72.
66. Ibid., part 2, 46. On the difficulties in using the Fritz X and He 293, see A.I. 2 G Report 1813, "German Difficulties in Guiding the Remote-Controlled Glider Bomb," October 1945, in USAF HRA Doc. 170.2278B.
67. Deichmann, *Die deutsche Luftwaffe in Italien*, part 3, 80.
68. Ibid., 85.
69. The Luftwaffe employed a few Fritz X and Henschel PGMs against Allied merchant shipping in the Bay of Biscay on 25 August and in the Mediterranean on 29 August. The first use of the weapons against armored warships was on 9 September. See William Green, *Warplanes of the Third Reich* (New York; Galahad, 1970), 154.
70. Morison, *History of United States Naval Operations*, 244; see also Deichmann, *Die deutsche Luftwaffe in Italien*, part 3, 86.
71. http://www.naval-history.net, Salerno.
72. Von Richthofen's diary, 9 September 1943.
73. Deichmann, *Die deutsche Luftwaffe in Italien*, part 3, 83.
74. Morison, *History of United States Naval Operations*, 290–292.
75. Ibid., 296–300.
76. http://www.naval-history.net, Salerno.

77. Deichmann, *Die deutsche Luftwaffe in Italien*, part 3, 88–89.
78. Ibid., 89–93.
79. See BA/MA RL/2/II 304, Intelligence Reports Air Fleet 2 November–December 1943 and BA/MA/2/II/369 Air Fleet 2 Lageberichte November–December 1943.
80. Morison, *History of United States Naval Operations*, 319, 322.
81. Von Richthofen's diary, 22 January 1944.
82. Ibid.
83. Ibid.
84. Morison, *History of United States Naval Operations*, 344.
85. Ibid., 345–346.
86. Deichmann, *Die deutsche Luftwaffe in Italien*, part 4, 110.
87. Ibid., 105.
88. Morison, *History of United States Naval Operations*, 349.
89. Ibid., 355.
90. "History of the 3rd AAA Air Support Control Squadron," in USAF HRA Doc. SQ-A-Sup-Cont-3-HI, February 1944–February 1946, 3.
91. Mike Spick, *Luftwaffe Bomber Aces* (London: Greenhill, 2001), 168–172.
92. USAF HRA Doc. 650.430-3, HQ 12th AF, A–2 Section, "Enemy Air Activity over Anzio Beachhead," January–April 1944.
93. Ibid.
94. Morison, *History of United States Naval Operations*, 363–364.
95. Attrition in the Mediterranean was far worse than on the eastern front. With a fighter force of 296 planes in the Med in September–December 1943, the Luftwaffe lost almost 400 planes. In the Soviet Union during the same period, the Luftwaffe had almost 500 fighters but lost fewer airplanes. Most of the attrition, about 70 percent, was due to aircraft lost on the ground to Allied raids. At each stage of the Allied advance, the Luftwaffe abandoned dozens of aircraft, sometimes only slightly damaged, on airfields in Sicily, southern Italy, and Sardinia. The weak Luftwaffe forward maintenance structure could not cope with the number of aircraft repairs required.
96. Interview with Herr Ulf Balke, historian at the Bundesarchiv/Militärarchiv Freiburg, 14 May 2003. Herr Balke's father served in KG 100, and he is writing a book on that unit.
97. In 1945, KG 100 did a careful study of its experience in using the guided bombs. See translation of Air Force Research Station Karlshagen, "Considerations on the Employment of New Technical Special Weapons," 18 February 1945 in USAF HRA Doc. 170.2278B.
98. Helmut Heiber and David Glantz, eds., *Hitler and His Generals: Military Conferences, 1942–1945* (New York: Enigma, 2002), 429 (conference of 6 April 1944).

Chapter 13. Final Act—Von Richthofen's Last Days

1. Richard Overy, *The Air War, 1939–1945* (Chelsea: Scarborough House, 1991), 77.
2. In late 1943 and early 1944 the Luftwaffe commanders on the eastern front proposed to use German bombers against Soviet industry. On the Italian front, von Richthofen wanted bombers to carry out more attacks on Allied ports, such as the highly successful raid on Bari. In France, Field Marshal Sperrle wanted a strong Luftwaffe bomber force to be in readiness for the expected Allied landings. All of these proposals for employing the Luftwaffe's last bomber reserves made more sense than the actual decision to attack Britain.

3. Rolf Schabel, *Die Illusion der Wunderwaffen* (Munich: Oldenburg Verlag, 1994), 141. Also see Basil Collier, *The Defense of the United Kingdom* (London: HMSO, 1957), 512.

4. Interview with Hansgeorg Wilberg, September 1993. Wilberg received his pilot training in multiengine aircraft in 1943. He entered combat as a Ju 188 pilot in late 1943, with a little over 100 hours' total flight time. He maintains the only reason he survived as a pilot is that he was deployed as a reconnaissance pilot to the eastern front, where the air opposition was not nearly as effective as on the western front.

5. For a good account of the Luftwaffe's losing battle in the air over Germany, see Steven McFarland and Wesley Newton, *To Command the Sky* (Washington, DC: Smithsonian Institution Press, 1991); and Donald Caldwell, *JG 26: Top Guns of the Luftwaffe* (New York: Orion, 1991).

6. Caldwell, *JG 26*, 231, 241.

7. United States Air Force Historical Research Agency (henceforth USAF HRA) Doc. 248: 532–596, "Mediterranean Air Forces Special Report, AAA in Mediterranean Air Defense," May 1944.

8. Ibid.

9. Overy, *The Air War*, 150.

10. William Green, *Famous Fighters of the Second World War*, vol. 2 (Garden City, NJ: Doubleday, 1962), 54.

11. Ibid., 57.

12. Enzo Angelucci and Paolo Matricardi, *Combat Aircraft of World War II, 1940–1941*, vol. 4, 56. By Italy's surrender in 1943, only 122 Folgores were on the books of the Regia Aeronautica, and of these, only 53 were operational. See Green, *Famous Fighters*, 59.

13. Green, *Famous Fighters*, 58.

14. Generalluftzeugmeister, *Amtsbesprechung* (18 January 1944), in USAF HRA Doc. K113.82, vol. 3, 3.

15. Ibid.

16. Generalluftzeugmeister, *Amtschefsbesprechung* (13 April 1943), in USAF HRA Doc. K 113.82, vol. 3, 4. On the Caproni Ca 310, see David Donald, ed., *The Complete Encyclopedia of World Aircraft* (New York: Barnes and Noble, 1997), 231–232.

17. Donald, *Complete Encyclopedia of World Aircraft*, 231–232.

18. Alfred Price, *The Luftwaffe Data Book* (London: Greenhill, 1997), 127–128.

19. Ibid., 187–190.

20. Karl Gundelach, *Die deutsche Luftwaffe im Mittelmeer, 1940–1945*, band 2 (Frankfurt am Main: Peter Lang, 1981), 738–743.

21. Ibid., 830. From July 1944 to April 1945 the Italian fighter force had between seventy-four and thirty-four aircraft, with about 60 percent operational at any time.

22. Lutz Klinkhammer, *Zwischen Bündnis und Besatzung* (Tübingen: Max Niemeyer Verlag, 1993), 382.

23. Surviving Luftwaffe reports mention the Italian air units. In November 1944 the 2nd Italian Fighter Group lost three planes but claimed eight Allied planes. See Bundesarchiv/Militärarchiv Freiburg (henceforth BA/MA) RL 9/4 Fiche 1. Kommandierende General der Luftwaffe in Italien, *Lagebericht*, November 1944. In January 1945 the Italian fighter unit lost five planes but claimed eight Allied planes. See *Lagebericht*, January 1945.

24. U.S. Army Historical Study, EUCOM Historian, German Study D 029, Dr. Ing. Ernst von Horstig, *Aufgaben und Taetigkeit des Deutschen Wehrwirstschaft-Offiziers italien und Sonderbeauftragten des OKH Waffenamtes in Italien* (April 1947), 15–17, 25–28.

25. On 31 May 1944 the 2nd Air Fleet had eighty-one fighters, forty-eight bombers, fifteen ground attack planes, twenty-one night ground attack planes, seven long-range reconnaissance planes, eight tactical reconnaissance planes, and thirty-five transports, for a total of 215 operational planes. See Alfred Price, *The Last Year of the Luftwaffe, May 1944–May 1945* (London: Wren's Park, 1991), 22.

26. See Nick Beale, *Ghost Bombers: The Moonlight War of NSG 9* (Crowborough, UK: Classic Publications, 2001), 200.

27. Ibid., 22, 34.

28. Ibid., 62–65. On the Italian partisan movement, see F. Parri and F. Venturi, "The Italian Resistance and the Allies," in *European Resistance Movements, 1939–1945* (New York: Macmillan, 1964), xiii–xliii.

29. BA/MA RL 9/4 Fiche 1. Kommandierende General der Luftwaffe in Italien, *Lagebericht*, October 1944.

30. Richard Bosworth, *Mussolini's Italy: Life under the Dictatorship* (New York: Penguin, 2006), 521–522. There were an estimated 60,000 partisans in Italy in December 1944. From 1943 to 1945 the Italian partisan losses are estimated at 44,720 killed in action and 9,980 killed in reprisals. On the German antipartisan offensive in October and November 1944, see Parri and Venturi, "The Italian Resistance and the Allies." The German/fascist campaign broke the back of the major resistance forces.

31. Lutz Klinkhammer, "Der Partisanenkrieg der Wehrmacht, 1941–1944," in *Die Wehrmacht: Mythos und Realität*, Rolf-Dieter Müller and Hans-Erich Volkmann, eds. (Munich: Oldenbourg, 1999), 822.

32. Ibid., 832

33. Between May 1944 and December 1944 the U.S. Army Air Forces in the Mediterranean (operating mostly over Italy) lost 627 aircraft to German and Axis aircraft. During the same period, the Americans lost 1,367 aircraft to German flak—mostly over Italy. See USAF HRA, USAAF Staff, *The USAAF Statistical Summary of Wartime Operations*, 1946, Table 160, "Airplane Losses on Combat Missions in the Mediterranean Theater of Operations."

34. *The United States Strategic Bombing Survey, Rail Operations over the Brenner Pass*, January 1947.

35. U.S. Army History Study, EUCOM History Office, German Army Study, MS D 191, Ritter von Pohl, "Commitment of Flak and Fighters to Protect the German Routes of Supply in Italy (1944–1945)." Study circa 1946.

36. Ibid., 4–7.

37. The German figures seem to be accurate. The *USAAF Statistical Summary* for airplane losses in the Mediterranean in October 1944 lists only six losses to enemy airplanes and seventy-four to flak. Counting in RAF and other Allied air forces, the figure of 100 claimed losses is plausible.

38. BA/MA RL 9/4 Fiche 1. Kommandierende General der Luftwaffe in Italien, *Lagebericht*, October 1944.

39. BA/MA RL 9/10. Kommandierende General der Luftwaffe in Italien, "Übersicht über Technische Verbände," 25 November 1944.

40. At the start of June 1944, Schlachtgeschwader 2 was equipped with two FW 190As, twenty-nine FW 190F-8s, two FW 190F-3s, four FW 190G-3s, and thirteen FW 190F-8s.

41. Hans-Ulrich Rudel, *Stuka Pilot* (New York: Bantam, 1979), 163–170.

42. For a general history of the July 20 plot, see Joachim Fest, *Plotting Hitler's Death* (London: Weidenfeld and Nicolson, 1996).

43. Count Michael von Matuschka (29 September 1888–14 September 1944) studied law and graduated from the University of Breslau in 1910. He served for a year as an officer cadet in the 4th Silesian Hussar Regiment and then was a civil servant in the Provincial Government of Westphalia in Münster until 1914. At the beginning of World War I he was called back to serve with the 4th Hussars as a reserve officer and participated in all the regiment's campaigns on the eastern front. After the war he was admitted to the bar, and from 1919 on he held several government positions in the Province of Upper Silesia. In May 1923 he was appointed county commissioner of Oppeln. Matuschka married Countess Pia von Stillfried und Rattonitz, with whom he had three sons and a daughter. He campaigned successfully for the Center Party in the Prussian Landtag elections of 1932 but was removed from Parliament and office for political reasons in 1933 as the representatives of democratic parties were purged from elected office. In the following years he was employed by the Prussian state administration in Berlin and in the Province of Silesia in Breslau, where he maintained close contacts with the Silesian deputy regional commissioner, Count Fritz-Dietlof von der Schulenburg. Schulenburg was involved in the 20 July planning and persuaded Matuschka to accept the office of regional commissioner in Silesia in the event of a successful coup. In 1942 Graf Matuschka was appointed economic adviser to the administration in annexed Katowice. After the unsuccessful assassination attempt of 20 July 1944, Matuschka's involvement with Count von der Schulenberg was uncovered and he was arrested by the Gestapo. He was sentenced to death by the People's Court on 14 September 1944, and executed the same day in Berlin-Plötzensee.

44. Constanze Hasselmann, "*Prof. Dr. med. Friedrich Loew: Vita eines deutschen Neurochirurgen*," diss., der Universität zu Lübeck–Aus der Medizinischen Fakultät–Aus der Klinik für Neurochirurgie Universitätsklinikum Schleswig-Holstein Campus, Lübeck, 2005.

45. Edward Homze, "Wolfram Freiherr von Richthofen—Hitler's Schlachtfliegergeneral," in *Die Militärelite des Dritten Reichs*, Ronald Smelser and Enrico Syring, eds. (Frankfurt am Main: Verlag Ullstein, 1995), 455.

INDEX

Albania, 237, 245, 348
Albatros Aircraft Co., 53, 66, 88, 92, 93
Allied armies (1940), 9, 192–193, 195, 198, 200, 204–206, 208
Allied air forces (1940), 183, 193–194, 196, 199, 210, 218, 222
Amiens, France, 72, 206
Antonescu, Marshal Ion, 290–291
Anzio, Italy, 342, 348–354, 356, 359–360, 362
Arado Aircraft Co., 88, 102, 106
Arado Ar 65 fighter, 102
Ardennes, 48, 195–196
Aschaffenburg, 76
Asturias, Spain, 128, 138, 140
Athens, 247–249
Australian army, 65, 66, 244
Austria, 155, 239, 242, 275, 367
Austrian air force, 155, 167
Austrian army, 49, 52, 167

Bad Ischl, Austria, 367, 369–370
Badoglio, Field Marshal Pietro, 340, 358
Baku, 284–285
Balbo, General Italo, 97
Balkans, 236–256, 260, 266–267, 275, 334, 374
Barcelona, 117, 128, 136, 145
Bari, Italy, 348, 353, 356, 365
Barzdorf Estate, Silesia, 28, 31, 82–82, 102, 369
Basque army, 131–138
Basque Region, 21, 131–138
Bavaria, 38–39, 40, 76, 275
Bayerische Flugzeugwerke, 106
Bayerlein, Lt. General Fritz, 320
Beck, General Ludwig, 122, 366
Belgium, 48, 95, 174, 181, 183, 195–196, 198–200, 215, 257
Belgian air force, 195

Belgrade, 22
Berchtesgarten, 304, 306, 308
Berlin, Technische Hochschule Berlin (Technical University of Berlin), 88–89, 91–92
Berlin, von Richthofen home, 88, 90, 102
Berlin University, 87–89
Bersdorf Estate, Silesia, 31–32, 82, 186, 369
Biarritz, France, 217
Bilbao, Spain, 133–137
Black Sea, 300, 302
Blamey, General Thomas, 244
Blomberg, General Werner von, 17–18, 92, 99, 100, 122
Bock, Col. General Fedor von, 26, 155, 265, 277, 280–281, 285, 292, 294
Bohemia, 29–30
Boris, Czar of Bulgaria, 239–242
Boulogne, 205, 207
Brauchitsch, General Walter von, 280
Braun, Werner von, 13, 80, 109–110
Brenner Pass, 359, 362
Breslau, 30–33, 36, 41, 50, 81–82, 87–88, 367
Bristol Blenheim bomber, 189, 199, 244–245, 290
Britain, 19–20, 26, 40, 152–153, 156, 165, 172–173, 193, 236, 257–258, 355
Britain, aircraft industry, 211, 222, 258, 289
Britain, air force. See Royal Air Force (RAF)
Britain, Battle of, 189, 199, 209, 214–235, 237, 257, 264, 327
Britain, navy. See Royal Navy
Britain, Parliament, 136
British Army, 10, 40, 48, 51, 66–67, 72–73, 192, 200, 214, 237–238, 244–255, 257, 332–333, 341, 344, 348–349
British Expeditionary Force (BEF), 192–195, 199–201, 205, 208, 214

413

Brown, Captain Roy, 66
Brunete, Spain, 9, 138–139, 141, 149
Bryansk, Russia, 274
Bukovina, 52
Bulgaria, 22, 238–240, 242–244, 247–249, 266
Bzura River, Poland, 170, 178

Calabria, 328, 341
Calais, 205, 214, 224–225, 228, 230
Canada, 217, 258, 356
Cappy, France, 64, 65
Caproni Aircraft, 357, 360
Castoldi, Mario, 357
Catalonia, 143–145
Catania, 337–338
Caucasus, 298, 301–302, 311–312, 314
Chamberlain, Neville, 220
Cherbourg Peninsula, 224–225
Clausewitz, General Carl von, 8 10
Commonwealth Air Training Scheme, 217
Condor Legion, 1, 3, 5, 9, 11, 26–27, 119–151, 157, 159, 180
Corpo Truppe Volontarie, 127
Corsica, 344, 347, 351
Cracow, Poland, 166–167, 170
Crecy-sur-Serre, France, 201
Crete, 3, 249–257, 266
Crimea, 7, 285–298, 306, 317
Curtis Hawk H-75 fighter, 165, 187–188, 222–223, 225, 234, 245
Czechoslovakia, 152, 220

Deauville, France, 225
De Gaulle, General Charles, 201
Deichmann, General Paul, 7, 159
Demyansk, Russia, 307
Denmark, 215, 225
Dessloch, General Otto, 192
Dewoitine 520 fighter, 187
Dinant, France, 48, 198
DiNardo, Richard, 290
Dinort, Colonel Oskar, 274
Dnjester River, 52
Don River, 298, 300–301, 304
Dornier Aircraft Co., 68, 88–91, 93–94, 102
Dornier Do 11 bomber, 1, 102–103
Dornier Do 17 bomber, 106, 108–109, 113, 122, 156, 158, 183, 222, 225, 229
Dornier Do 19 bomber, 107
Dornier Do 23 bomber, 103

Dornier Do 217 bomber, 113, 343, 345
Douhet, General Giulio, 96
Dover, England, 230, 232
Dowding, Air Marshal Hugh, 223–224
Ducati Company, 399
Dunkirk, 9, 203, 205–208, 214–216, 254
Durango, Spain, 134
Düsseldorf, 33, 184

East Prussia, 49, 154–155, 265, 280, 282, 307–308, 365
Ebro River, 144–145, 149
Egypt, 237, 256–257, 319
English Channel, 3, 9, 195, 197, 200, 214–216, 219, 226, 228, 230–231, 235

Fairy Battle light bomber, 189, 245
Felmy, General der Flieger Helmuth, 85, 91, 96, 183, 215
Fiat Aircraft Company, 121, 257
Fiat G 12 bomber, 35
Fiat G 55 fighter, 357
Fiebig, General Martin, 91, 300, 306, 308
Fiesler Fi 156 "Stork," 106, 160–161, 184, 191, 248, 272, 275, 298, 302
Finland, 258, 261–263, 273
Finnish air force, 258, 261
Finnish army, 258, 261
Flanders, 55, 58–59, 63, 85, 203–204, 206
Flivos (Flieger Verbindingsoffiziere), 162, 167–168, 176–177, 191, 210, 259, 269, 293
Focke Wulf Aircraft Co., 88, 107
Focke Wulf FW 187 fighter, 107
Focke Wulf FW 190 fighter, 114, 259, 326, 330, 337, 344, 350, 355, 363, 371
Foggia, Italy, 328, 341
Fokker, Anthony, 59–60, 63
Fokker Dr 1, 59–60, 63–65, 68
Fokker D 7, 60, 68–69, 72, 78, 92
Förster, General of Engineers Otto, 280
France, 2–3, 9, 37, 40, 48–49, 55, 57, 67, 95, 105, 118, 122, 135, 144, 152, 163–165, 172, 179, 181, 214–218, 220–221, 225, 236–238, 241–242, 245, 257–260, 276, 302, 324, 326, 328, 331, 341, 347–349, 354, 356, 361, 363, 365, 374
France, air force (Armeé de l'Air), 137, 162, 183, 186–193, 196, 209, 226, 236
France, army, 49, 70, 72, 193–208
  1940 Campaign, 183–213

France, Vichy forces, 332
Franco, General Francisco, 117–121, 123–127, 136, 138, 145, 147, 150, 217–218, 334
Franco-Prussian War, 34, 41
Frascati, Italy, 324, 344
Frederick the Great, 28–30, 41
Fritz X guided bomb, 334–345, 350–352

Galicia, 52
Galland, General Adolf, 2, 149, 224, 331
Gamelin, Marshal Maurice, 194
Geneva Conventions, 25–26
Genoa, 359
German army general staff, 18–19, 24, 34, 38–40, 55, 77, 84–86, 88, 120, 131, 160, 195, 238, 261, 304, 306, 354
German army General Staff Academy, 40, 46–47, 84, 86, 87, 92, 115
German Army Units, World War II
  Army Groups
    Army Group A, 208, 311–312
    Army Group B, 208, 302, 304
    Army Group Center, 265–269, 272, 276, 278–281, 285
    Army Group Don, 306, 310
    Army Group North, 265, 268, 272–273
    Army Group South, 265, 272, 275, 280, 285, 287, 292, 312
  Armies
    Afrika Korps, 238, 257
    First Panzer Army, 298, 302, 311
    Fourth Panzer Army, 298, 306
    Sixth Army, 3, 10, 41, 192, 195–196, 198, 296, 298, 302–304, 306–311
    Ninth Army, 265, 275
    Eighth Army, 155
    Tenth Army, 168
    Eleventh Army, 265, 285, 292–294, 296, 297
    Twelfth Army, 241, 243, 246
    Fourteenth Army, 155, 161
    Seventeenth Army, 298, 302, 311
    Eighteenth Army, 272
    Panzergruppe von Kleist, 3, 9, 195, 197–204, 208–209, 275, 319, 374
    Panzergruppe 1, 241
    Panzergruppe 2, 265
    Panzergruppe 3, 265
  Corps
    VIth Corps, 280
    XIXth Panzer Corps, 205

Divisions
  1st Panzer Division, 168, 171–172, 213, 275
  3rd Panzer Division, 196
  5th Mountain Division, 251
  15th Panzer Division, 238
  21st Panzer Division, 238
  90th Light Division, 238
  387th Infantry Division, 298
German Foreign Ministry, 144–145, 217–218
Gibraltar, 118, 217
Goebbels, Josef, 174
Goering, Reichsmarschall Hermann, 2, 10, 12, 18, 37, 68, 75–76, 78, 99–101, 111, 114–115, 117, 146, 148, 160, 167, 186, 200, 206, 212–213, 215, 218, 221, 224–225, 231, 233–234, 249–250, 288, 306, 308, 311–312, 319–321, 324, 327, 329, 331, 352, 355, 358–359, 365
Gotha, 78
Gothic Line, 361
Grauert, General Ulrich, 171, 206
Greece, 4, 236–256
Greek air force, 245, 246, 257
Greek army, 3, 237, 241, 243–244, 246–248
Greek navy, 255
Grosseto, Italy, 330
Guadalajara, Spain, 126–127
Guderian, General Heinz, 2, 18, 20, 26, 205–208, 260, 265, 270, 274–275, 280
Guernica, 21–23, 26, 134–137
Gutschdorf Sugar Company, 34

Hague Convention of 1907, 23, 25
Halder, General Franz, 28, 276–277, 278, 366
Hamburg, 78, 372
Hamburg air raids, 22, 173–174, 199
Hanover, 82–83, 142, 368, 372
Hanover, Technische Hochschule Hannover (Technical University of Hanover), 82–83
Hawker Hurricane fighter, 165, 188–189, 220, 222–223, 225, 234, 244, 289
Hayward, Joel, 7, 10, 291
Hehrhudt von Rohden, General Hans-Detlef, 7, 301
Heinkel Aircraft Co., 88, 106–107, 110, 120
Heinkel He 45 bomber, 102, 120
Heinkel He 51 fighter, 102, 121
Heinkel He 59 seaplane, 140, 230

416 Index

Heinkel He 70 recon, 102, 105
Heinkel He 111 bomber, 106, 108–109, 122, 126, 129, 139–140, 156, 222, 309, 326, 330
Heinkel He 112 fighter, 107, 110
Heinkel He 177 bomber, 107
Henschel Hs 123 attack plane, 163, 167–168, 170–171, 201, 203, 209, 239, 247, 259
Henschel Hs 126 recon, 106, 155, 162, 245, 252
Henschel Hs 129B attack plane, 114, 316
Henschel Hs 293 guided bomb, 343, 345, 350–352
Heraklion, Crete, 250, 252
Hindenburg, Field Marshal Paul von, 16–17, 19, 40, 50, 52
Hitler, Adolf, 5, 10, 12, 16–21, 24–27, 78, 91, 99–100, 111, 117, 119, 122–124, 136–137, 146, 148, 152–154, 165, 179, 206, 213–221, 231, 235–239, 242, 250–251, 256–257, 262, 266, 272, 274, 276, 280–282, 284–286, 292, 302, 304, 306–308, 311–312, 314–315, 319–320, 322, 324, 326, 340, 347, 354, 358–359, 365–366
Hoeppner, General of Cavalry Ernst von, 55, 77
Homze, Edward, 2, 7
Hoth, General Hermann, 265
Hungary, 52, 258, 284, 289
Hungarian air corps, 289–290

Ilsemann, Lt. General Karl von, 48
Interallied Military Control Commission, 93–94
"Iron Belt" defense line, 133
Irving, David, 2
Italy, 3, 94–95, 97, 117–118, 120, 122, 146, 217, 239, 316, 318–353, 359–365
Italy, aircraft industry, 95, 97, 236, 322–323, 356–359
Italy, air force (Regia Aeronautica), 94–97, 118, 236, 238–239, 244–245, 322–323, 326–329, 333, 340, 345, 358
Italy, Allied landings, 328, 333–353
Italy, army, 118, 244, 321–322
Italy, Salo Republic, 358–359

Japan, 24, 262, 277
Jauer, Silesia, 31
Jeschonnek, Colonel General Hans, 12, 24, 91–92, 112–113, 158, 186, 200, 226, 233, 254, 266, 275, 280, 286, 288, 306–308, 318–319, 321, 353, 358
Jodl, General Alfred, 12, 18, 280
Jünger, Ernst, 56
Junkers Aircraft Co., 88–94, 108–110
Junkers Ju 52 transport, 21, 89, 103, 118, 120, 122, 156, 160, 164, 168, 170, 173, 203, 210, 250, 252, 282, 307, 339
Junkers Ju 87 Stuka, 3–4, 22, 106–108, 144, 149, 151, 154, 156, 158–159, 161–163, 167–168, 170, 171, 174–178, 180–181, 183–184, 186–187, 191, 196, 198–201, 203–204, 206–210, 212–213, 221–223, 225–226, 228–230, 232–235, 239, 241, 246–249, 252–254, 259, 261, 265, 267, 269–276, 292, 296, 300, 303, 316, 323–324, 326, 330, 336, 338–339, 359–360, 363–364
Junkers Ju 88 bomber, 109, 112, 156, 222, 225, 241, 247, 253, 322, 326, 331, 337, 339, 348, 350
Junkers Ju 89 bomber, 107–108

Kalinin, Russia, 275
Karinhall, 224, 231, 327
Karlsruhe Collection, 7
Keitel, Field Marshal Wilhelm, 12, 18, 20, 123
Keller, General Alfred, 265
Kerch Peninsula, 285, 293–295
Kesselring, Field Marshal Albert, 2, 11, 26, 91, 100, 111, 155, 206, 208, 213, 231, 265, 267, 269, 274, 276, 318–319, 321, 324, 331, 334–335, 339, 341, 344, 347
Kharkov, Russia, 275, 295–296, 298, 300, 303, 311, 314
Kiev, Russia, 272, 274–275, 288
Kindelan, General Alfredo, 123
Kleist, General Ewald von, 3, 19–20, 26, 195, 197–201, 203–204, 208–210, 241, 260, 275, 296, 312, 374
Kluge, General Gunther von, 280, 366
Köln-Butzweilerdorf, 184
Köln-Ostheim, 184
Koluft (Kommandeure der Luftwaffe), 162, 176–177, 191, 241, 293
Korten, General Günther, 2, 172, 231, 288, 300–301, 353–355, 358, 365
Kriegsakademie, 39, 87
Kuban region, 287, 302, 314–315
Kursk, Russia, 298, 316, 318

Lake Ilmen, 273
Lake Ladoga, 273
Larissa, Greece, 247–248, 266
Lawrence, D. H., 34
LeChambre, Air Minister Guy, 194
Leeb, Field Marshal Wilhelm von, 26, 260, 265, 272–274
Le Havre, 225
Leigh-Mallory, Air Marshal Trafford, 224
LeMay, General Curtis, 11
Lend-Lease, 264, 304, 315
Leningrad, 265, 268, 272–274, 283, 285, 292, 306
Lewis, Cecil, 62–63
Libya, 237–238
Lieth-Thomsen, Colonel Hermann, 77
List, Field Marshal Wilhelm, 239–241, 246–247
Loerzer, General Bruno, 106, 115, 159–160, 167, 172, 265, 272, 276
Loew, Dr. Friedrich, 367
Löhr, General Alexander, 2, 155, 167, 170, 239, 250, 257, 265, 285, 288, 290, 298
Luftkriegführung, Regulation 16, 24
Luftstreitkräfte, Imperial Air Corps, 53–80, 84–85, 90, 92, 100, 102, 160
Luftstreitkräfte units
    Jagdgeschwader (JG) 1, 1, 4, 58–59, 62–73, 75–76, 78, 114
    Jasta 4, 62
    Jasta 6, 62
    Jasta 10, 62
    Jasta 11, 53, 59, 62–64, 66–68, 70
Luftwaffe branches
    Luftwaffe general staff, 3, 4, 92, 97, 99, 101, 106, 107, 111, 115, 119, 157, 176, 194, 212, 215, 220, 226, 233, 236, 261, 277, 318, 334, 353
    Luftwaffe Intelligence, 194–195, 209, 216, 219–221, 231, 233–234, 245, 288, 290, 328, 334
    Luftwaffe Signal Corps, 158, 191, 239, 344, 363
    Luftwaffe Technical Office, 3, 92, 102–109, 111–112, 114–115, 117, 221, 374
Luftwaffe units
    Air fleets
        First Air Fleet, 154–155, 168, 171, 274
        Second Air Fleet, 97, 183, 192, 206, 215, 222–225, 229–230, 265, 267, 272–276, 319, 324, 326, 333, 339–351, 354, 356–359
        Third Air Fleet, 140, 196–197, 202, 208, 222, 224–226, 229, 231, 257, 365
        Fourth Air Fleet, 7, 22, 154–155, 160, 167–168, 170, 172, 177, 201, 234, 239, 242–243, 246, 250, 265, 285, 287–291, 298, 300–304, 308–310, 314, 316, 318, 363
        Fifth Air Fleet, 222, 225, 232
    Attack wings
        Night Attack Wing 9, 360
        Schlachtgeschwader (Attack Wing) SG 2, 363
        Schlachtgeschwader SG 4, 348–349
    Bomber wings
        Kampfgeschwader KG 1, 347
        Kampfgeschwader KG 2, 252
        Kampfgeschwader KG 20, 252
        Kampfgeschwader KG 26, 341
        Kampfgeschwader KG 76, 348
        Kampfgeschwader KG 77, 172, 173, 347
        Kampfgeschwader KG 100, 326, 341, 343–345, 349–353
        Training Wing 1, 253
        257th Bomber Wing, 142–143
    Corps
        Ist Air Corps, 192, 363
        Ist Flak Corps, 192, 210, 265
        IInd Air Corps, 265, 272, 324, 347
        VIIIth Air Corps, 3, 7–9, 22, 25, 181, 183–185, 191, 196–198, 201, 205–206, 208–209, 224–225, 227–230, 232–235, 238–256, 259, 265, 267–276, 279, 282, 285–289, 292–296, 300, 302–304, 308, 363
        Xth Air Corps, 238–239, 248, 254
        IXth Air Corps, 358
    Divisions
        Special Air Division, 3, 151, 157–158, 160–161, 167–171, 177–178, 181
        1st Air Division, 171
        2nd Air Division, 160, 172
        2nd Air Training Division, 324
        5th Flak Division, 329
        7th Paratroop Division, 251–253, 255
        9th Flak Division, 309
        25th Flak Division, 361–362
    Fighter wings
        Jagdgeschwader JG 4, 348

Luftwaffe units
    Fighter wings, *continued*
        Jagdgeschwader JG 11, 371
        Jagdgeschwader JG 27, 184
        Jagdgeschwader JG 53, 348
        Jagdgeschwader JG 76, 158
        Jagdgeschwader JG 77, 172, 183, 348
    Flak brigades
        3rd Flak Brigade, 361–362
        22nd Flak Brigade, 361–362
    Special commands
        Deutsche Luftwaffe in Italien, 359
        Luftwaffe Group Caucasus, 302
    Stuka wings
        Stuka Wing 1, 254
        Stuka Wing 2, 184, 213, 252, 254, 273–274, 303
        Stuka Wing 3, 233
        Stuka Wing 77, 183, 213, 233–234
Lüneburg, 16–17, 23, 82, 142, 146, 148, 184–185, 286, 368, 371–372

Macchi Aircraft Company, 322
Macchi Mc 202 fighter, 322, 326, 357
Macchi Mc 205 fighter, 322, 326, 357
Madrid, 117–118, 120–121, 127–128, 136, 138–139, 144, 146
Maginot Line, 198, 212
Maleme, Crete, 252
Malta, 238, 254, 319, 333–334, 337, 343, 346
Manstein, Field Marshal Erich von, 1–3, 10, 13, 20, 26, 195, 285–286, 291–297, 306, 308–309, 311–316, 318, 324
Matuschka, Count Michael von, 366
Mediterranean, 127, 140, 146, 217, 236–238, 244, 249–250, 255–258, 265, 276, 304, 318–319, 321, 328, 331–334, 340, 342, 346, 350, 352
Meister, Colonel Rudolf, 275
Messerschmitt, Willi, 106, 109
Messerschmitt Me 109 fighter, 106–108, 122, 126, 138–141, 150, 156, 158, 163, 165, 167, 187–188, 201, 210, 220, 222, 225, 229–230, 233–234, 239, 247–249, 259, 263, 326, 331–332, 337, 344, 355, 357–358
Messerschmitt Me 110 heavy fighter, 106–108, 114, 172, 220, 222–223, 225, 229, 232–234, 239, 256, 326, 330, 339

Messerschmitt Me 210 heavy fighter, 114, 326, 330
Messina, Italy, 339–341
Meuse-Argonne, 72–73
Meuse River, 48–49, 96–99
Milch, Erhard, 2, 18, 24, 100, 114, 216, 221, 226, 309, 311, 321, 358
Minsk, Russia, 269
Model, Field Marshal Walther, 2, 282
Mola, General Emilio, 123, 128, 134, 137
Mölders, Werner, 2, 149–150
Montcornet, France, 201
Montgomery, General Bernard, 19, 192, 341
Morison, Samuel, 348
Moscow, 3, 256, 264–265, 268, 272, 274–283, 287, 292, 305
Mountbatten, Lord Louis, 253
Mussolini, Benito, 95, 237, 322, 325, 329, 340, 358–360, 362

Nahkampfführer (Close Battle Commander), 163, 350
Netherlands, 174, 183, 195, 214
Netherlands air force, 186, 201
Netherlands army, 193
Netherlands navy, 249, 337
New Zealand army, 244, 247, 251
Normandy, 225, 227–228, 355–356, 365
North Africa, 217, 237–238, 255–257, 266, 304, 316, 318, 321, 323, 327–328, 330–332, 334, 344
Norway, 186, 215, 225, 331
Novikov, Marshal Alexander, 281–282

Ohain, Hans von, 80
Ohlau, Silesia, 41, 43, 87
Olenhusen, Major Götz von, 83

Pantelleria, Italy, 333–337
Parks, Air Chief Marshal Keith, 223
Pas de Calais, 214, 224–225, 228
Patton, General George, 369
Paulus, Field Marshal Friedrich von, 302, 303, 308–309
Peenemünde, 110, 114
Pelz, Maj. General Dietrich, 2, 323, 329–331, 335
Pickert, Maj. General Wolfgang, 309
Pinsk, Poland, 52

Piraeus, Greece, 254
Plocher, General Hermann, 7, 268
Pohl, General Ritter von, 236, 326, 339–350, 361–362, 365
Poland, 49, 220, 262, 265, 267
Poland in World War I, 49–52
Poland 1939 campaign, 3, 32, 135, 152–182, 184–185, 190, 192, 194, 199, 201, 212–213, 241, 259–260, 302, 359, 373–374
Polish air force, 154, 158, 164–166, 180
Polish army, 153, 155, 164, 167–168, 170–175, 178–179
Pomerania, 154
Portland, UK, 228–232
Prussia, 4–5, 11, 13, 19, 28–38, 82, 366
Prussia, army, 4–5, 31, 34–47, 88, 370
Prussian/ German army units (World War I)
 Second Army, 69
 Third Army, 48–49
 Eighth Army, 49–50
 Ninth Army, 49–50
 Frommel's Cavalry Corps, 49–50
 Guards Cavalry Division, 48
 Ist Cavalry Corps, 48–49
 5th Cavalry Division, 48–52
 Twelfth Cavalry Brigade, 48, 52–53
 Prussian Guards Cavalry, 31
 4th Silesian Dragoon Regiment, 48
 4th Silesian Hussars, 41–43, 48, 50–53, 58, 79, 366
Pruth, Romania, 52, 364

Rabenau, General Friedrich von, 366
Radom, Poland, 166, 171, 178
Rechlin, 107, 371
Reichenau, Col. General Walter von, 18, 155, 161, 168–169, 171, 178–179, 192, 260
Reich Propaganda Ministry, 174
Reichs Air Ministry, 99–102, 105, 109, 114, 244, 289, 356–358
Reichstag, 73, 85
Reichswehr, 5, 17, 32, 40, 79–99, 153, 324
Reinhard, Captain Wilhelm, 68
Rhine River, 196, 199
Richthofen, Baroness Jutta von (wife, born von Selchow), 6, 15–16, 81–82, 88–89, 96–98, 102, 104, 185, 313, 368, 371–372
Richthofen, Bernhard Freiherr von, 32
Richthofen, Dieprand Freiherr von, 32

Richthofen, Ellen von (daughter), 82–83, 88, 96, 102, 185, 371–372
Richthofen, Freiherr (Baron) Wolfram von (father), 28, 31, 82–83
Richthofen, Baroness Frieda von, 33
Richthofen, General of Cavalry Manfred Freiherr von, 31–33, 48, 82–83, 186, 368
Richthofen, Gerhard von (brother), 28, 35, 83, 371
Richthofen, Götz Freiherr von (son), 82–83, 88, 96, 102, 185–186, 370–372
Richthofen, Götz von (brother), 35
Richthofen, Heinz Freiherr von, 32
Richthofen, Hugo Freiherr von, 32
Richthofen, Lieutenant Lothar von, 37, 48, 53, 59, 67, 78
Richthofen, Ludwig Freiherr von, 33
Richthofen, Manfred Freiherr von (brother), 28, 31, 35, 76, 82–83, 161, 365, 368, 371
Richthofen, Oswald von, 32
Richthofen, Professor Doktor Ferdinand Freiherr von, 32
Richthofen, Professor Doktor Karl Freiherr von, 33
Richthofen, Rittmeister Baron Manfred von, 1, 26, 37, 48, 53–54, 58–68, 71, 76
Richthofen, Sophie-Therese Freifrau von (married Wietersheim), 28, 83, 161
Richthofen, Therese Götz Baroness von (born von Olenhausen), 28
Richthofen, Ulrich Freiherr von, 34
Richthofen, Walter Freiherr von, 33
Richthofen, Wolfram von (son), 6, 16, 82–83, 102, 363–365
Rickenbacker, Captain Eddie, 72
Roatta, General Mario, 127
Rohrbach Aircraft Co., 88
Romania, 172–173, 193, 238–240, 250, 284, 289, 363–364
Romanian air force, 258, 265, 289–290, 300–302
Romanian army, 258, 264–265, 284–285, 290, 294, 300–304
Rome, 96, 321, 324, 342, 347–349, 351, 354, 358, 361
Rommel, Field Marshal Erwin, 2, 238, 257, 318–320, 366

Rostov, Russia, 275, 311
Royal Air Force (RAF), 23–24, 67–68, 72, 124, 150, 156, 162, 165, 183–184, 186, 188–190, 194, 196, 205–209, 214, 216, 218–226, 235, 236, 254, 260, 328, 332–333, 337
   Advanced Air Striking Force (AASF), 196
   RAF Bomber Command, 149, 199, 220, 222, 225
   RAF Coastal Command, 220–221
   RAF Fighter Command, 157, 214–235
Royal Flying Corps, 53, 55, 57–64, 66
Royal Naval Air Service, 59
Royal Navy, 215, 255, 337–339, 344
Rudel, Hans-Ulrich, 2, 303, 363–364
Rundstedt, Field Marshal Gerd von, 2, 26, 155, 170, 200, 208, 265, 274, 280
Russia, army, World War I, 49–53

Salerno, 341–347, 349–350, 352–353, 356, 358
Salonika, Greece, 246–247, 249
Sandhurst, 40
Sänger, Eugene, 114
Sardinia, 324, 327–331, 333–335, 341, 347–348, 351
Savoia Marchetti SM 79 bomber, 326
Savoia Marchetti SM 81 bomber, 126, 358
Saxon Army, 38, 40
Saxony, 38, 40
Scapa Flow, 215
Schloss Dyck, 183
Sebastopol, 285, 290, 294–299
Sedan, 3, 198–200, 203, 210, 213
Selchow, Günther von, 81
Sicily, 238, 248–249, 254, 322–341, 344, 346–347, 349, 352
Silesia, 13, 28–32, 41, 78, 81–83, 87, 97, 102, 152, 153, 160, 366–369, 371
Slovakia, 155
Smolensk, 269–272, 281
Soviet air force, 126, 156, 261–270, 278, 281, 283–284, 288, 314–315, 329
Soviet aviation industry, 264, 283, 288, 315
Soviet Union, 3, 7, 25, 121, 126, 191, 210, 238–239, 257, 354, 363
Soviet Union, Campaign of 1941, 257–283
Soviet Union, Campaign of 1942–1943, 284–317
Spanish Civil War, 117–151
Spanish Morocco, 117–118, 124

Spanish Nationalist Air Force, 121, 123, 125–126, 136, 138–140, 148–149
Spanish Nationalist Army, 118, 120–137, 139, 141–142, 144–146, 148
Spanish Navy, 118
Spanish Republican Air Force, 121, 125–126, 128, 138–140, 148
Spanish Republican Army, 121, 127–128, 133, 138–140, 144
Speidel, General Wilhelm, 6
Sperrle, Field Marshall Hugo, 2, 26, 85, 91, 119–121, 123–124, 126, 131–132, 137–138, 140, 142, 148, 150, 196, 201–202, 204, 206–207, 213, 225, 231, 365
Stahlberg, Major Alexander, 309
Stalin, Joseph, 155, 165, 261–262, 282
Stalingrad, 10, 22, 26, 287–288, 300–317, 321
Steinhoff, Johannes, 2
St. Quentin, France, 49, 70, 205
Striegau, 28, 30, 35–36, 41, 83
Student, General Kurt, 91, 249–252, 255, 340
Stumpf, General Hans-Jürgen, 2, 100, 111, 231
Sudetenland, 152
Suez Canal, 250, 256, 258
Supermarine Spitfire fighter, 188, 220, 222–223, 225, 234
Switzerland, 81–82, 89, 98

Tank, Kurt, 107
Tannenberg, 49–52
Teruel, Spain, 141–142
Thrace, 244, 246, 247
Thirty Years' War, 29–30
Truppenamt (Troops Office), 85–86, 91

Udet, General Ernst, 59, 67, 100, 111–117, 137, 221
Unger, Lt. General Fritz von, 48
United States, 19, 33, 40, 187, 217
U.S. Air Force, 180, 270, 272
U.S. Air Force archives, 7
U.S. Army, 6, 40, 67, 73, 75, 332–333, 341, 344, 347–350, 360–361, 369–370
U.S. Army Air Forces (USAAF), 1, 23–24, 175, 322, 328–329, 333, 337–338, 351, 355–357, 361–362
U.S. Army Air Service, 57–58, 67–74, 78
U.S. aviation industry, 105, 165, 212, 217, 258, 264
U.S. Navy, 322, 336–340, 344–346, 348–351

V-1 Missile, 109, 374
V-2 Missile, 374
Vienna, 239
Vigón, General Juan Suero Diaz, 123–125, 135, 217–218
Volkman, Maj. General Helmuth, 140–143, 148

Waffenamt (Weapons Office), 85–89, 91–92, 109
Warlimont, Colonel Walther, 118
Wavell, General Archibald, 244
Wehrmacht 9, 18, 23–25, 27, 80, 123, 146, 153–154, 167, 176, 191–193, 212, 215, 255, 257, 262, 265–266, 278, 283–284, 298, 319, 321, 362–363, 367, 369
Wehrmacht Economic Planning Office, 284, 359
Wehrmacht High Command, 25, 122, 124, 157, 183, 212, 214, 220–221, 238, 244, 274, 277–278, 321, 334, 340
Wehrmacht Intelligence Staff, 153, 250, 262–263, 277–278, 303, 309, 331–332, 334

Weichs, Col. General Maximilian von, 304
Weimar Republic, 5, 16, 19–20, 78, 99, 152, 266
Wenzl, Lieutenant Richard, 64
Wever, General Walther, 100–101, 106–107, 111, 115–116, 162
Wilberg, General Helmuth, 77, 85, 117–119
Wilhelm II, Kaiser, 16, 33–34, 36, 41, 43–44, 46, 73
Wilson, General Henry, 247–248
Wimmer, General Wilhelm, 85, 91–92, 102–103, 107, 109, 111, 113, 115
Württemberg, Württemberg Army, 38–40, 46

Yugoslavia, 242–243, 245–247, 256, 298
Yugoslavian Air Force, 245–247

Zeitzler, General Kurt, 308
Zhukov, General Georgy, 262, 278